SCRIPTURE
CANNOT BE BROKEN

Six Objections to Verbal Inspiration

Examined in the Light of Scripture

St. Louis, Mo.

CONCORDIA PUBLISHING HOUSE

1944

PREFACE

When several years ago the *Concordia Theological Monthly* in the issues extending from April, 1941, to December, 1942, brought a series of articles by Dr. Theodore Engelder on the subject "Verbal Inspiration — a Stumbling-Block to the Jews and Foolishness to the Greeks," it was soon recognized that here there were submitted to the Church discussions of peculiar merit which might render important service in the controversy now in progress — on the full inspiration and the inerrancy of the Scriptures. Lutherans in other synods took notice of these articles. A paper published outside the Synodical Conference circles expressed the opinion that material of this kind should be available to every pastor. A District president of the American Lutheran Church whom the undersigned happened to meet stated that he regarded these articles as truly outstanding and hoped they would be given to the Church in book form. In our own ranks one again and again heard the wish uttered that the series might be rescued from the comparative retirement into which every article appearing in a journal is forced through the ephemeral nature of this class of publication and be given the status of a work that can be conveniently re-read and consulted at any time. This view was entertained especially by the men who were more intimately associated than anybody else with the esteemed author as these articles made their appearance month after month — his fellow-members of the editorial committee of the *Concordia Theological Monthly.* As they with delight and profit perused the proof sheets and witnessed the learning, the industry, and the consecrated skill of their revered colleague, the wish that this material might be given a more permanent form and be made easily accessible to a large number of readers grew in them. The Literature Board of the Missouri Synod and the Board of Directors of Concordia Publishing House both gave their *placet,* and the work now is placed before the reader as a neat volume, ready to serve in its new livery.

The title of the book is different from that of the series of articles. It was thought the old title was somewhat cum-

[3]

bersome and that a shorter one was desirable. Hence the well-known words of the Savior in John 10:35 were chosen to give the treatise a distinctive name. An apt designation it is. The book contends for the truth expressed in the words of Christ: "The Scripture cannot be broken." The Bible student knows that Jesus here speaks of the use of the term "gods" with respect to the judges of Israel. It is a strange usage, but it must stand as correct and proper, says Jesus, because the Scriptures have it, and they cannot be broken, that is, be declared false or erring. The truth is implied that whatever the Scriptures say is inviolable, that nothing of what they utter, let it appear ever so insignificant, may be regarded as erroneous. As in the treatise *The Foundations Must Stand*, by Dr. P. E. Kretzmann, published by Concordia Publishing House several years ago, so in this study the full inspiration and inerrancy of the Scriptures are set forth.

The Lutheran Church in America has evidently in its development reached definite crossroads. It must decide whether it will adhere to the time-honored teaching of verbal inspiration and the inerrancy of the Scriptures or join the so-called progressive group, which without hesitation avows its belief that the Bible contains errors. May the author's aim to do his part so that the flood of unbelief will not engulf the Church be realized, and may to the end of time our dear Lutheran Church defiantly say to all prophets trying to rob our sacred Book of its authority and reliability, "The Scripture cannot be broken."

Besides an index the reader will find in the rear of the book a table of contents and a list of the Bible passages referred to.   W. ARNDT

PROLOG

Verbal Inspiration — a Stumbling-Block to the Jews and Foolishness to the Greeks

The moderns look upon Verbal Inspiration as an evil, unclean thing. They call it a foul spook. The Lutheran Zaenker, Landesbischof of Silesia, used the term "Das Gepenst der Verbalinspiration" and asked the preachers of the Gospel to make it their business to lay this ghost. (See *Conc. Theol. Monthly*, VIII, p. 149.) Karl Barth feels the same way. "Er straeubt sich gegen den Vorwurf, er fuehre das Gespenst der Verbalinspiration wieder herauf." (*Allg. Ev.-Luth. Kirchenz.*, 1935, p. 987.) The moderns look upon Verbal Inspiration as a dangerous thing. "The pitfalls of a possible theory of literal, verbal inspiration" was the term used at a meeting of Episcopalian churchmen and theologians of the Lutheran Augustana Synod held in the interest of church union. (See *Lutheran Companion*, Jan. 11, 1936.) Verbal Inspiration is "a handicap," declares H. E. Fosdick. More than that: "I reached the shocking conviction that such traditional Bibliolatry is false in fact and perilous in result" (*The Modern Use of the Bible*, pp. 181, 273). These men look upon Verbal Inspiration as a disreputable thing. No self-respecting theologian can afford to deal with it. "It is the way of obscurantism," says J. S. Whale (*The Christian Answer to the Problem of Evil*, p. 78), and *Folkebladet*, the organ of the Norwegian Free Church, stated in 1926 (Nov. 17): "Now, however, there are very few theologians, and assuredly no eminently learned ones, even of the conservative school, who hold the old doctrine of verbal inspiration." These few theologians, says Dr. E. H. Delk, "think in the forms and categories of an age long past for the modern mind. Their position is outmoded" (*Luth. Ch. Quart.*, 1936, p. 334). These men do not feel at ease in the company of theologians who teach Verbal Inspiration — and they would not feel at home in a church-body that believes in it. Writing in the *Lutheran Church Quarterly*, 1935, p. 417, Prof. E. E. Flack, of the Hamma Divinity School in Springfield, Ohio, asks: "Is not the inspiration of Scripture too high and holy a reality to be defined in terms of stenography? Does one exalt the Word of God by dehumanizing it?" and then states: "It may be confidently asserted that the achievement of closer unity among Lutherans in this country, and indeed throughout the world, will require, for one essential, a higher view of Scripture than is represented by the theory of inspiration by dictation." [1]   Men who feel like Dr. Flack do not like to associate with those who harbor the idea of Verbal Inspiration. [2]   Wilhelm Moeller describes the situation correctly when he says: " 'Verbalinspiration!' Jeder Theologe schaudert bei dem Wort ordentlich zusammen; es wirkt wie das rote Tuch auf den Stier; und wenn man sonst nicht sehr einig ist in der Theologie, links und rechts, darin ist man einig: nur keine Verbal-inspiration!" (*Um die Inspiration der Bibel*, p. 63.)   The moderns in the Reformed and in the Lutheran churches, liberals and con-servatives alike, fear and hate this thing and deplore with Emil Brunner that the churches "are still suffering from the incubus of the old mechanical theory of inspiration" (*The Mediator*, p. 181).

The moderns abhor and detest Verbal Inspiration, and they are not at all backward about telling us why they cannot accept it with a good conscience.   They offer a great variety of reasons why the Church should get rid of it as soon as possible.   Let us examine six of these objections.   Are they well founded?   Or are the objectors making a fatal mistake?

---

1) When the moderns denounce "the theory of inspiration by dicta-tion," "the mechanical theory," they have in mind, as will be shown later on, the doctrine of verbal inspiration.

2) Negotiations in the interest of church-fellowship between the United Lutheran Church and the Missouri Synod came to an end be-cause the representatives of the U. L. C. found themselves unable to accept the doctrine of verbal inspiration. "A point of serious difference concerned the definition of inspiration, particularly the presentation of verbal inspiration as given in the *Brief Statement* of the Missouri Synod. . . . Our commission was unable to accept the statement of the Missouri Synod that the Scriptures are the infallible truth 'also in those parts which treat of historical, geographical, and other secular matters.'" (*Minutes of the 1938 Convention of the U. L. C. A.*, p. 468.) The report of the convention appearing in *The Lutheran* of Nov. 2, 1938, states: "The doctrine known technically as 'The Verbal Inspiration of the Bible' was deemed out of accord with the Lutheran Confession." These men feel, as Dr. Flack expresses it, that there can be no close unity with bodies that hold the low view of Scripture which the doctrine of verbal inspira-tion implies. On the other hand, we of the Synodical Conference find ourselves unable to give the hand of fellowship to those who hold such a low view of Scripture as the denial of Verbal Inspiration implies. "Dr. E. Ryden overlooks that he can entertain no hope of fellowship with 'Missouri' as long as the official organ of the Swedish synod (Augustana) prints attacks on the doctrine of verbal inspiration." (*Lutheran Witness*, Nov. 26, 1940.) The denial of Verbal Inspiration is one of the chief obstacles in the way of Lutheran union. For that reason a discussion of this matter is always in order. For that reason the present essay is being written. Its purpose is to show, once again, that those who view Verbal Inspiration with horror are laboring under a hallucination.

CHAPTER I

Does the Bible Contain Errors?

They tell us, in the first place, that they cannot accept the doctrine of verbal, plenary inspiration of the Bible because of the errors, the many, the countless errors, in the Bible.

"Wir sind Wirklichkeitsmenschen," said Theodor Kaftan. We are men who deal with realities, with facts. When we examine the Bible, we find certain facts which forbid us to believe that everything in the Bible is inspired. So say the liberals. H. E. Fosdick declares: "So we used to think of inspiration as a procedure which produced a book guaranteed in all its parts against error and containing from beginning to end a unanimous system of truth. No well-instructed mind, I think, can hold that now. Our ideas of the method of inspiration have changed; verbal dictation, . . . uniformity of doctrine between 1000 B. C. and 70 A. D. — all such ideas have become incredible in the face of the facts." (*Op. cit.,* p. 30.) H. L. Willett: "This is one of the chief reasons why the doctrine of verbal inspiration has been discarded as incapable of proof and incompatible with the evident facts." (*The Bible through the Centuries,* p. 284.) Some of these men would perhaps like to retain the old teaching of the Christian Church on this point, but they cannot do it in the face of these undeniable facts. That appears from the statement of J. De Witt: "Must this beautiful conception, which anchors the soul fast to permanent and unchangeable truth and excludes every blemish from the Scriptures, be abandoned or even modified? We answer, however reluctantly, that it must surely be put aside, unless it corresponds with the observed facts and is confirmed by other than *a-priori* reasoning. . . . Indeed, we distinctly claim that facts have already been discovered that discredit the exactness of statement so earnestly affirmed." (*What Is Inspiration?* P. 12 f.) And here the conservatives are in full accord with the liberals. James Orr stoutly maintains that, "if there is inspiration at all, it must penetrate words as well as thought, must mold the expression," but on the very next page he declares: "In the result 'Verbal Inspiration' may be held to imply a *literality* in narratives, quotations, or reports of discourses which the facts as we know them do not warrant." (*Revelation and Inspiration,* pp. 209, 210.) E. A. Garvie is another "Wirklichkeitsmensch." In *Hastings' Dictionary of the Bible* he writes, *s. v.* Inspiration: "The theory of verbal inspiration affirms that each human author was but the mouthpiece of God and that in every word, therefore, God speaks. But the actual features of the Bible, as studied by reverent and believing scholarship, contradict the theory." So is Friedrich Buechsel, professor at Rostock. "Selbstverstaendlich kam die alte Inspirationslehre — die Lehre von der Verbalinspiration, die Behauptung: die Schrift stammt nicht nur ihrem Gehalte, sondern auch, und gerade ihrem Wortlaute nach, aus dem Geiste Gottes — damit in Widerspruch zu den einfachsten Tatsachen in den Schriften der Bibel." (*Die Offenbarung Gottes*, p. 112 f.; ed. 1938.) Dr. J. A. W. Haas is another Wirklichkeitsmensch: "In the problem of inspiration the facts of course refute any mechanical theory of inspiration in minute detail." (*The Lutheran*, Jan. 23, 1936.) "The irresistible logic of facts" has compelled the moderns to discard Verbal Inspiration. Strahan tells us that he and the "Protestant scholars of the present day, imbued with the scientific spirit, have no *a-priori* theory of the inspiration of the Bible. . . . They do not open any book of the Old or New Testament with the feeling that they are bound to regard its teaching as sacred and authoritative. They yield to nothing but what they regard as the irresistible logic of facts." (Hastings, *Encyclopedia*, VII, p. 346.) In the light of the facts Verbal Inspiration is a fiction.

THE ALLEGED ERRORS IN THE BIBLE; SCIENTIFIC AND HISTORICAL ERRORS

Now, what are the facts on account of which the doctrine of verbal, plenary inspiration, the doctrine of the absolute infallibility of the Bible, cannot be true? They are, first, the errors in the Bible, the mistakes and blunders committed by the writers of Scripture. The list which enumerates these alleged errors is a long one, and the compilers of this list warn us that, as human knowledge increases, the list will grow in length. The various sections of this long list are labeled: Scientific errors (blunders in natural history, historical errors, etc., etc.); statements in conflict with the findings of higher criticism; contradictions in the Bible (inexact, false quotations; unfulfilled prophecies; and just plain contradictions). And every single one of these "facts" disproves Verbal Inspiration.

Georgia Harkness feels that she must repudiate Verbal Inspiration because of the facts established by science. "The revolt against Fundamentalism has centered upon the other great pitfall of reliance on the authority of the Bible, namely, the disregard of historical and scientific fact that ensues from belief in its literal inspiration. The battle is not yet won. Like the poor, literalism is always with us." (*The Faith by which the Church Lives*, p. 57.) In order to win the battle they remind us that Moses, or whoever wrote this part of the Bible, was weak, for instance, in natural history. See Lev. 11: 5, 6! Everybody knows that the "hare" and the "coney" do not chew the cud! "This presents," says Robert Tuck, "a striking illustration of the unscientific character of the Scriptures. They record popular fallacies in matters of science. Moses repeats the common opinion of his day in all such things as natural history." (*Bible Difficulties,* p. 343.) And see Prov. 6:8! Contrary to the popular opinion that Solomon was wiser than all men, well posted in zoology, including entomology and the other branches of natural history (1 Kings 4:31-33), he did not know much about ants. "The scientific skeptic affirms that the ant, being a carnivorous insect, could not gather her food in the harvest and that the very nature of that food would prevent it from being laid up in store; and that Solomon committed the blunder of many amateurs, in mistaking the white cocoon of the ant-pupae, properly known as ant-eggs, for grains housed for future use." A. T. Pierson, from whose book *Many Infallible Proofs* this is quoted (p. 133), hears the scientific skeptic ask: "What, then, becomes of Solomon's inspiration? If he blunders in science, he may have blundered in theology." (The question of who is committing all these blunders will be answered in a later section.) Our list contains numerous examples from the other branches of science. Studying them, H. L. Willett concludes: "Nor were the writers of the Bible safeguarded supernaturally or in any other manner from the usual historical and scientific errors to which men of their age were liable. Their work is not a text-book of either of these subjects." (*Op. cit.,* p. 284.) Joseph Stump, of the U. L. C., comes to the same conclusion: "The holy writers were inspired with a supernatural knowledge of God and of His will, and on these subjects their words are final and infallible. On scientific matters they neither knew nor professed to know more than other men of their day." (*The Christian Faith,* p. 319.) The scientific information they give is unreliable. "Wer etwas ueber naturwissenschaftliche Dinge wissen will," says Prof. Fr. Baumgaertel of Rostock, "gehe zum Naturwissenschaftler." (W. Moeller, *op. cit.,* p. 31.) And when the professor of natural philosophy is not in accord with Scripture, you will have to say that the professor is right and Scripture is wrong. "Does not modern science contradict the Scriptures?" asks Dr. A. J. Traver in the "Young People Column" of *The Lutheran* of Feb. 22, 1939. Yes, indeed, he answers, but that is to be expected, for the "Bible-writers wrote with the background of their age and its scientific beliefs." "The Bible is true in all matters that pertain to religion," he writes in the issue of May 10, 1939, but "it is not a text for biology or chemistry." Just admit that the Bible abounds in scientific blunders. "Is Scripture inerrant?" asks Prof. J. Aberly in the *Luth. Church Quarterly,* April, 1935, p. 124, and tells us that "the question must be faced whether there may be factual errors in the sacred records," and goes on to point to the errors "in matters of psychology" which the Biblical writers committed and their errors "in cosmology." These errors are so glaring that the Christian youth must be warned against accepting them as truth. Writing in the *Luth. Church Quarterly* of July, 1939,

p. 299, Prof. O. F. Nolde says: "Pupils may later discard the scientific import of the story" (the creation story). "They ought forever to accept the story itself because of literary and religious merit." And so the commissioners of the U. L. C. are unable to teach Verbal Inspiration, to teach that "the Scriptures are the infallible truth 'also in those parts which treat of historical, geographical, and other secular matters.'"

Historical errors are here mentioned by the U. L. C. theologians. Georgia Harkness, too, speaks of the disregard of *historical* and scientific fact that ensues from belief in the literal inspiration of the Bible. The list of historical blunders found in the Bible is a long one. They used to say that writing was unknown at the time of Moses, so that Moses was not the author of the Pentateuch. (Thus von Bohlen; see *Conc. Theol. Monthly,* IV, p. 178.) It was written centuries later. The battle of the four kings against the five kings, related Gen. 14, is pure fiction or, at best, wild exaggeration. Wellhausen wrote in 1889: "That four kings from the Persian Gulf should, 'in the time of Abraham,' have made an excursion into the Sinaitic Peninsula, that they should on this occasion have attacked five kinglets on the Dead Sea littoral and have carried them off prisoners, and finally that Abraham should have set out in pursuit of the retreating victors, accompanied by 318 men servants, and have forced them to disgorge their prey — all these incidents are sheer impossibilities, which gain nothing in credibility from the fact that they are placed in a world which has passed away." (See *Fundamentals,* II, p. 26. Also *Lehre und Wehre,* 59, p. 259.) — The Hittites occupy much space on the black-list we are studying. "Many regarded the Biblical statements regarding this mysterious people as mythical and an indication of the general untrustworthiness of Biblical history. A prominent English Biblical critic declared not many years ago that an alliance between Egypt and the Hittites was as improbable as would be one at the present time between England and the Choctaws." "In 1904 one of the foremost archeologists of Europe said to me: 'I do not believe there ever were such people as the Hittites.'" (*Fundamentals,* II, pp. 15, 31.) — Daniel, or whoever wrote the Book of Daniel, blundered badly in his reference to Belshazzar. "The scientific skeptics laughed at the credulity of the simple souls who take the Bible as their guide though it asserts that Belshazzar was king when Babylon fell and on the night of its capture was slain." (A. T. Pierson, *op. cit.,* p. 140.) Does not history tell us that the king of Babylon at that time was Nabonidus? As late as 1937 this item was kept on the black-list. The expert on the *American Weekly* declared that Nebuchadnezzar never had a son by the name of Belshazzar and that Babylon fell to Cyrus and not to Darius the Mede. (See *Conc. Theol. Monthly,* VIII, p. 397.) "Darius the

Mede is not a historical figure," says J. De Witt, on the authority of an "accomplished scholar" (*op. cit.*, p. 48), and N. R. Best finds that "the lordly manner in which Darius at the end of the chapter wrote to call the peoples, nations, and languages that dwell in all the earth sounds very little as if he were aware of having the mighty Cyrus or any other potentate as overlord" (*Inspiration*, p. 92). Baumgaertel-Rostock: "Einen 'Meder' Darius hat es nicht gegeben." (*Allg. Ev.-Luth. Kirchenz.*, 1926, No. 45.)

The New Testament writers, too, are guilty of many blunders. Even St. Luke, who claims that he had "had perfect understanding of all things from the very first," "having accurately traced every-thing from the start" (Luke 1:3), garbled the story of Christ from the very start. "It has been maintained by many scholars in modern times that the census is either a fiction or a blunder. . . . It is affirmed that Quirinius never governed Syria during the life of Herod." (See Kretzmann, *Pop. Commentary*, New Testament, I, p. 278.) And this same Luke did not know the difference between a proconsul and a propraetor. "It has been only a few years since the destructive critics had nothing but scorn for any one who accepted Luke's statement (Acts 13:7) that the island of Cyprus was ruled by a 'proconsul.' " (L. Boettner, *The Inspiration of the Scriptures*, p. 53.)

The chronology, too, of the Bible is in bad shape. Prof. H. C. Alleman's *The Old Testament — a Study* declares: "It is impos-sible to be dogmatic about Bible dates. The chronology of the Bible is not a matter of divine revelation." (P. 21.) Nor were the genealogical lists written by inspiration. Not even the genealogy of Jesus is reliable. Dr. P. E. Scherer said over the radio: "The genealogies [of Jesus] are not to be regarded as inspired docu-ments; they are included as 'honest attempts to ascertain the truth.' " (*The Lutheran*, Feb. 20, 1936.) And so the moderns, Reformed and Lutheran, liberal and conservative, cannot believe that the Scriptures are the infallible truth "also in those parts which treat of historical, geographical, and other secular matters."

The Miracle-Myths

These men charge the Bible with many errors on the authority of science, of common, lower science. And with many, many more errors on the authority of higher science. When men deal with facts, observe the phenomena of nature, etc., they are engaged in what we shall call lower science. But when they depart from the realm of observed facts and go into the realm of speculation, assume the right to pass judgment on things that lie beyond the area of observation, we shall call that higher science. *They* call it, in effect, "higher" science; they pride themselves on the progress which the modern mind, trained in scientific methods, has made beyond the childlike age of man, when man was ready to believe almost anything. The modern "scientific" mind can no longer do that.

And so the Modernist is compelled to charge the Bible with a lot of additional errors. His scientific mind cannot accept the miracles recorded in the Bible as facts. And therefore he can no longer believe in Verbal Inspiration. Let H. E. Fosdick speak in the name of higher science. He "used to think of inspiration as a procedure which produced a book guaranteed in all its parts against error." "But all such ideas have become incredible in the face of the facts." Here are the facts: "The modern mind finds itself in a cosmic system which is regular with a vengeance. . . . What happened to the idea of miracle when this onrush of *inductive science* overtook it is clear. . . . An ax-head might usually sink in water, but there was no reason why God should not make it float if He wished to do an extraordinary thing. It was surprising when He did it, but it presented *no intellectual problem whatever.* No laws were broken, because *no laws were known.* No Hebrew ever dreamed of such a thing as a mathematical formula of specific gravity in accordance with which an ax-head in water ought invariably to sink. . . . Without the slightest idea of laws to be suspended or broken, the writers of the Bible described the unusual activities of God and indiscriminately treated as miracles such things as the Red Sea held back by a wind and God's restoration of sinners to His favor, resurrection from the dead, and God's sending rain upon the soil, a fish swallowing a man, and the exaltation to safety of those who mourn. . . . When, then, one has said all that needs to be said about the new views of the Bible, about *critical processes of study,* how empty is the issue of it all if it does not liberate our minds free from handicaps, etc. . . . To be a Bible Christian, must we think, as some seem to suppose, that a fish swallowed a man, or that the sun and moon stood still at Joshua's command, or that God sent she-bears to eat up children who were rude to a prophet, or that saints long dead arose and appeared in Jerusalem when our Lord was crucified?" (*Op. cit.,* pp. 30, 136 f., 141, 181.) [3]

A. Harnack agrees with Fosdick and declares: "Miracles, of

---

3) One more quotation from Fosdick, to show what he is unable to believe and what he is able to believe: "There are some narratives of miracles in the Bible which I do not believe. . . . Joshua making the sun stand still *may be poetry,* and the story of Jonah and the great fish *may be a parable.* . . . Certainly, I find some of the miracle-narratives of Scripture *historically incredible.*" (*Op. cit.,* p. 163 f. Italics here and above our own.) Fosdick is able to believe that when the writer of Josh. 10:12 wrote: "Then spake Joshua," etc., he did not mean to say that Joshua actually spoke or that the sun actually stood still, but that he was writing a poem and hoping that in the last days a man would arise who would be able to interpret the mysterious words "And the sun stood still."

course, do not occur. That the earth once stood still in its course, that an ass spoke, that the tempest was stilled with one word, we do not believe that and never again shall believe it." (See *Lehre und Wehre*, 49, p. 4.) The archbishop of York, W. Temple, agrees with Harnack and Fosdick: "Some have attached the divine guarantee to the actual statements contained in the Bible when literally understood. Because they accept the Bible as the Word of God, they regarded themselves as pledged to believe and to teach that the world was created out of nothing in a week or that strange astronomical occurrences took place in connection with the battle of Bethhoron." (*Revelation* [1937], p. 102.)

Dr. Delk agrees, in principle, with Dr. Fosdick. He says, in the *Lutheran Quarterly:* "The theologian must not only indicate the content and significance of any science and discipline as related to theology; he must know *the processes and technique* of such sciences in order to properly value and schematize the whole religious problem. . . . He must know the few *large conclusions* of modern thought and so relate them to the fundamental and permanent elements of religion that his preaching shall be vital and addressed to his contemporaries in education and culture." And applying the "scientific technique," he must and will accept evolution, as Dr. Delk does, and reject the Bible account and cast away Verbal Inspiration, as Dr. Delk does. (See *Lehre und Wehre*, 59, 146 ff.) Dr. T. A. Kantonen follows Dr. Delk in agreeing with Dr. Fosdick with respect to the functions of higher science. In his "Canned Theology" article (*The Lutheran*, Dec. 12, 1935, to Jan. 2, 1936) he calls for "the application of *scientific and historical methods* to the study of the Bible," for "a change in the *methodology* of Lutheran scholarship," and warns the Church against "holding to an erroneous *pre-Kantian conception* of truth as a static quantum." "The Church needs to interpret the eternal verities in *the terms of the age*." Drs. Kantonen and Delk and Fosdick, whose minds are trained in scientific methods, cannot possibly accept Verbal Inspiration.

Errors Discovered by Higher Criticism

The Bible is in conflict with science, say the moderns, and, what is worse in their estimation, in conflict with higher criticism. True, the Bible is decidedly in conflict with higher criticism. And the devotees of higher criticism consider that the unpardonable error. How can those portions of the Bible be true which do not agree with the sacred pronouncements of higher criticism? And how can any man who honestly believes in higher criticism believe in Verbal Inspiration? *Christendom* says: "Modern historical and literary criticism, not to mention modern 'science' generally, has rendered it (the Protestant dogma of the plenary verbal inspiration of holy scripture) increasingly untenable." (I, No. 2, p. 242.) And Dr. Delk agrees. "Higher criticism has set theology free from that tyrannous literalism and false idea of inspiration which made all attempts at the adjustment of theology with modern thought in history, science, and philosophy either impious or revolutionary. . . . No theory of verbal inspiration is any longer tenable." (*Lutheran Quarterly*, 1912, p. 568.) Now, what do the higher critics and their disciples believe, teach, and confess? First, that many portions of Scripture were not written by the men whom Scripture names as the authors, but by men who, for purposes of their own, for good purposes, palmed them off upon the unsuspecting Church under the name of some great prophet. In plain language, some of the Biblical documents are forgeries. "Source-criticism" has established that. Moses wrote very little of what goes by the name of "the books of Moses." For instance: "The functions of the Levites are recorded, in a late hymn of the tribes of Northern Israel, put by the authors of Deuteronomy into the mouth of Moses." (H. L. Willett, *op. cit.*, p. 63.) The prophet Daniel did not write the book of the prophecy of Daniel. This book was not written at the time of the Babylonian Captivity. Prof. R. T. Stamm is incensed at those who "tear the book of Daniel out of its origin in the revolt of Judas the Maccabee against King Antiochus Epiphanes in 168 B. C." (*The Lutheran*, July 3, 1940.)[4] H. L. Willett: "The Book of Daniel is often classed with the prophetic books by uncritical readers. . . . At the time of the Maccabean uprising the Book of Daniel seems to have appeared, whose purpose was to inspire the loyal with courage to persevere in their constancy until the dark days of persecution should cease and the tyrant should fall. This it was confidently expected would take place within an interval not too long to be endured. This measure of time, as in other apocalyptic works, was usually described as three years and a half." (*Op. cit.*, pp. 114, 119.) Willett has a chapter on "the Making and Remaking of the Old Testament." Nor did St. Paul write all of the Pauline epistles. He did not write the Pastoral Letters. Prof. W. C. Berkemeyer writes in the *New Testament Commentary*, p. 581 f.: "We must conclude that behind the Pastoral Epistles and in them there is a genuine Pauline tradition. . . . They are sub-Pauline but based on genuine Pauline tradition. . . . It seemed legitimate in that age to put words on the lips of a man whose mind was being interpreted," to practice a mild *fraus pia*. And did St. Mark write all of his gospel? Read the story of the making and remaking of this gospel in the *Lutheran Church Quarterly*, April, 1936, on "The 'Cursing' of the Fig-tree." Jesus really did not curse the tree but simply "said in effect: Your

---

4) To be exact, an unidentified Jew took up his pen in *January*, 164 B. C., to write this book. Kautzsch says so.

usefulness is over, — the tree was dying. . . . Those who got *these* original words of Jesus from the Twelve would repeat them to others, and so on down the years *until* some day some brother with the gift of insight, as he would probably put it, would sense a far more intimate connection between the words of Jesus and the. death of the tree than had previously been thought of. For the first time it would seem to this person that the tree must have died not merely *as* Jesus saw and said that it *would,* but *because* He said it *should,* in short, because He cursed it. . . . This person must have left the resulting chaos just as he made it, without a thought of editing out the incongruities just as Mark would have done — and did."

Now, any one who accepts these theories of higher criticism as gospel-truth (Wellhausen's documentary-historical-evolutionary theory or any later similar theories, also those covering the New Testament) cannot in good conscience accept Verbal Inspiration. He cannot have the Holy Ghost engage in forgeries.

In the second place, the higher critics get their disciples to believe, teach, and confess that Holy Writ contains, both in its spurious and in its authentic sections, much that is fiction. Believing that, they cannot believe Verbal Inspiration. They certainly cannot let the Holy Ghost present fiction to men as truth. And so the Rostock professor F. Buechsel, who tells us, "Der historisch Geschulte wird . . . legendaere Stuecke [in der Heiligen Schrift] feststellen," cannot but conclude: "Der Gedanke der Inspiration von Worten muss aufgegeben werden." (*Op. cit.,* pp. 77, 115.)

Name some of these legendary stories! (You need not mention the "miracle-myths." We had plenty of that above.) Well, Abraham is a legendary figure. Adam and Eve, too. M. Jastrow, a Jewish critic, declares that the Biblical tradition is nothing more than an adapted form of specifically Babylonian folk-lore, that the episodes of Gen. 3 "all are pictures that belong to the naivest folk-lore period of primitive culture," and Prof. H. C. Alleman, in *The Old Testament — a Study,* asks: "What is meant by 'the Hebrew Tradition'?" and answers: "Consult M. Jastrow, Jr., *Hebrew and Babylonian Tradition."* [5] J. M. Gibson: "The first form which is found in the history of the world's literature is that of myth and legend. . . . If we would only think ourselves back to the conditions of the olden time, so far from finding fault or suggesting difficulty, we should recognize the marvelous grace of God in so lifting up the best legendary literature of the world, such as the story of the Garden of Eden or of the Fall, as to make

---

5) Read the article of Dr. W. A. Maier "The Old Testament at Gettysburg," in CONC. THEOL. MONTHLY, VI, p. 267 ff.

it the vehicle of high and pure revelation." (*The Inspiration and Authority of Holy Scripture*, p. 157.) [6]

Georgia Harkness states that "the majestic creation myth with which the Old Testament opens was written late in the priestly post-exilic era" (*op. cit.*, p. 140, and *Christendom* I, p. 492) and finds the account of the creation in Genesis to be the poetic expression of some profounder or larger truth.

Prof. T. A. Kantonen agrees with them. "Relying upon the theory of the verbal inspiration of the Bible, rejecting *a priori* the results of constructive historical criticism, the adherents of this approach have regarded the stories of the Temptation and the Fall as mere historical narratives rather than profound prophetic philosophy of history." (*The Luth. Church Quart.*, July, 1935, p. 211.) [7]

Then, there are books in the Bible which are pure "fiction" — fiction in the sense of novels and romances. "Historical novels" is the term employed by Best (*op. cit.*, p. 91). Willett calls them "Biblical romances," "works of fiction written with a definite bearing on current thought and intended to be tracts for the times." "They are Ruth, Jonah, Esther." "The Book of Jonah . . . is given the mold of a novel. The Jonah of this book can hardly be called the hero of the narrative. Nor can he be described as the villain of the plot. . . . Perhaps it would be more accurate to say that he is the fool of the story, for his character appears as a foil for the real lesson of the book. . . . The incidents of the storm, Jonah's deliverance by the great fish, are perhaps intended as a symbol of Israel's engulfment and restoration." (*Op. cit.*, pp. 59, 107, 110.)

These findings of higher criticism being true, how can one still retain the doctrine of verbal inspiration? Even if the Holy Ghost would want to write historical romances, He could not attempt to palm them off as history. And so the modern man, as J. S. Whale

---

6) In the introduction to this book Principal Forsyth says: "Dr. Gibson began in the old theory of inspiration, in which he would have remained had his been a metallic, inert, or mechanical mind," had he not taken a course with the higher critics.

7) Professor Kantonen discards the story of the Fall as unhistorical. Professor Nolde wants the pupil later to discard the scientific import of the creation story. They are still in the lowest grade of the school of higher criticism. The higher grades have learned to discard still more Bible-stories. *Christendom* is in the highest grade. It says: "The account of the creation in Genesis, the Christmas-story of the Incarnation, the resurrection of the body of Christ, . . . the doctrine of the resurrection of the body, the doctrine of the Virgin Birth and the divinity of Christ, — all these conceptions, intended at first quite literally, have for many devout Christians today only a symbolic function. . . . Hence they are still scrupulously retained, lovingly cherished, but considered as poetic expressions of some profounder or larger truth than that which their formulators realized." (I, No. 3, p. 492.)

puts it, has been freed from the prison-house of verbal infallibility. "It is no use shilly-shallying here; loyalty to truth in the shape of literary and historical criticism forbids it." (*The Christian Answer*, etc., p. 77.)

Unfulfilled Prophecies

The next section of the black-list enumerates the unfulfilled prophecies. Willett: "The hopes of the Book of Daniel were not realized in the manner anticipated. But they kept the faith of the people alive through days of peril and distress. And in that fact they proved their worth." (*Op. cit.*, p. 125.) Baumgaertel-Rostock lists an even more serious case: "Die zentrale Weissagung, die messianische, hat sich nicht so erfuellt, wie die Propheten sie dachten. Die nationalen ueberspannten Erwartungen mancher prophetischer Worte, die als Gottesworte ausgegeben sind, traten nicht in Erfuellung." (See W. Moeller, *op. cit.*, p. 26.) G. Adam Smith: "Isaiah's forecast of Judah's fate was therefore falsified by events," "discredited by contemporary history." Isaiah was a "visionary" (*Modern Criticism and the Preaching of the Old Testament*, pp. 25, 140, 141).

In some cases the prophets themselves recognized that they had been mistaken in their prophecies and revised and corrected them. Baumgaertel: "Hesekiel 26: Der Koenig von Babel wird Tyrus einnehmen. In Kap. 29 ist der Prophet zu einer Selbstkorrektur gezwungen: da die Einnahme nicht erfolgt ist, wird dem Nebukadnezar Aegypten als Ersatz in Aussicht gestellt." (*Op. cit.*, p. 25.) C. H. Dodd (Oxford) repeats Baumgaertel's charge concerning Ezekiel: "Ezekiel withdrew his forecast of the fall of Tyre (Ezek. 26-28, 586 B. C.; 29:18, 568 B. C.). Ezekiel's dirge over Tyrus was indeed somewhat 'previous,' for Tyre was a flourishing city and continued to flourish for centuries after the prophet had predicted its doom." "Jeremiah found his expectations in several points falsified." Isaiah, too. This proves, says Dodd, that some of its (the Bible's) greatest writers contemplate the possibility that they may be mistaken or even confess that in some points they have been mistaken." And, believe it or not, Dodd even offers this as proof: "Jeremiah at one time wondered if he had really been deceived. Jer. 20:7: 'Thou hast deceived me, and I was deceived.'" (*The Authority of the Bible*, pp. 15, 65.)

All of which proves, says Dodd (p. 9) and Willett and Baumgaertel and all the rest, that "no balanced mind" can hold the doctrine of verbal inspiration, the teaching that "every statement of Scripture, whether concerning the mysteries of the divine Being, the processes of nature, or the facts of history, past or future, is exactly and literally true." Can the Holy Ghost utter unfulfilled prophecies? Would He raise false hopes in the hearts of the persecuted Jews, just to tide them over their present afflictions? The anonymous writer of the so-called prophecy of Daniel might have had such an idea, but those who teach that the Book of Daniel was given by inspiration are charging the Holy Ghost with the commission of a *fraus pia*.

Misquotations and Contradictions

Next we have the alleged misquotations. This black-list starts out with Matt. 27:9: "spoken by Jeremy the prophet." That is an error, the critics say. The reference should have been to Zechariah (11:12, 13). Indeed, it is an error, says De Witt, due to a "lapse of memory." "A simple lapse of memory, utterly unimportant," but an error nevertheless (*op. cit.*, p. 38). Heb. 10:5 ("A body hast Thou prepared for Me") and Ps. 40:6 ("Mine ears hast Thou opened") are next put on the list and many other "inexact" quotations. It is charged that the writers were careless in these instances, or if they were careful, they suffered a *lapsus memoriae.*

A variety of the case of misquotation is found in those instances where the writer wilfully misquoted. H. L. Willett: "In the text cited (1 Tim. 5:18: "Thou shalt not muzzle the ox," Deut. 25:4) Paul appears so anxious to enforce his teaching about the rights of Christian presbyters and evangelists, including himself, to share in the temporal blessings of their disciples that he treats the Old Testament text as though it had no application to the domestic creatures for whose benefit it was obviously intended and related only to the ministry of the Gospel." (*Christian Century*, March 16, 1938.)

De Witt says this matter is unimportant, that is, for his theory of inspiration, but tells us plainly that it gives the death-blow to Verbal Inspiration. Introducing his chapter of misquotations and other inaccuracies, he says: "We have now reached the most ungracious part of our task — that of mentioning inaccuracies in the Bible which make it necessary to reconstruct the theory of inspiration as generally accepted. . . . The definition referred to" (Verbal Inspiration) "as untenable claims absolute inerrancy for the whole." (*Loc. cit.*)[8] K. F. A. Kahnis, one of the instigators of

---

8) Even James Orr, who is for plenary inspiration, is ready to give up Verbal Inspiration, because " 'Verbal Inspiration' in the result may be held to imply a *literality* in narratives, quotations, or reports of discourses which the facts, as we know them, do not warrant." (*Op. cit.*, p. 210.) When he goes on to tell "the advocates of verbal inspiration" that "the end is gained if the *meaning* of the saying is preserved, though the precise form of words varies," the warning cannot be meant for us. We hold with him that the precise form of words may vary.

the revolt, within the Lutheran Church, against Verbal Inspiration, puts it this way: "Is not that conception of inspiration which ascribes to the Holy Ghost . . . all these inaccurate quotations . . . derogatory of the Holy Ghost?" (See F. Pieper, *Christliche Dogmatik*, I, p. 297.)

To be sure, if the premise of Kahnis and De Witt and Willett is correct, the conclusion is inevitable. If a man is convinced that the writers of the New Testament were careless in quoting from the Old Testament or let their memory play them tricks or took liberties with the statements of the prophets, they could not have written by inspiration of God. The moderns believe that they are fighting for the honor of God in repudiating Verbal Inspiration. They say: You must not saddle the Holy Ghost with these glaring mistakes.

The *index errorum,* finally, contains a list of alleged contradictions in the Bible. It is a long list. Ancient heathen writers, Celsus and Porphyry, worked on it. The infidels Voltaire and Paine and Ingersoll worked on it. The rationalist Lessing worked on it. And now the moderns have taken up the work. They are engaged in "a furious search for discrepancies." [9] The more discrepancies they find, the better. For these discrepancies, *Unstimmigkeiten,* contradictions, are the heavy artillery in the assault on Verbal Inspiration, the *Panzerdivision,* against which Verbal Inspiration cannot stand. "The Bible contains contradictions — this has been ever considered the weightiest and most serviceable objection against Verbal Inspiration. They say there are contradictions and there could be no contradictions if the Holy Ghost were the real author of the sacred books and had dictated every single word; the infallible Holy Ghost cannot contradict Himself, can He?" (A. Hoenecke, *Ev.-Luth. Dogmatik*, I, . 367.) The moderns, by convincing themselves that the Bible contains contradictions, have convinced themselves that they cannot with a good conscience retain the old teaching of the Church on inspiration.

To cite a few instances, Baumgaertel proves his thesis "Die Inspirationslehre der alten Dogmatik ist unhaltbar" thus: "Die Sintflut dauert nach 1 Mos. 7:4 und 17 vierzig Tage, nach 7:24 betraegt sie hundert und fuenfzig Tage." (He adduces a lot of other proofs, but this will do for Baumgaertel.) H. L. Willett proves his statement that "the Bible is not an inerrant record" thus: "The

---

9) That is Philippi's phrase: "Die moderne Differenzjagd." (See Pieper, *op. cit.,* p. 291.) And it is Luther's phrase. "Wiewohl die Historie denen, die *sich befleissigen, dass sie allzugenau die widerwaertigen Sprueche in der Schrift klauben,* deucht ganz verworren zu sein, werden sich doch christliche Leser leichtlich darein finden." (II, p. 1024.)

Hebrew records waver between the statement that Moses wrote the words of the Law, Ex. 24: 4; 34: 28; Deut. 31: 24, and insistence upon the fact that Jahve Himself wrote them, Ex. 31: 18." (*Op. cit.,* pp. 67, 318.) In his elaboration of the theme "The Mirage of Inerrancy" N. R. Best says that "the Bible-reader needs only to compare the twentieth chapter of Exodus with the fifth chapter of Deuteronomy and note the differences between the recital of the Ten Commandments in these two passages." (*Op. cit.,* p. 72.) Later on he offers this: "An instance of the tireless zeal with which these rationalistic efforts [10] are carried on is the labor that has been spent to explain how it happened that King Saul did not recognize the youth who fought Goliath if that youth, according to the letter of the history, had already been Saul's favorite harper in his own court. The higher critic says: 'Two traditions' — and lets it go at that." (*Op. cit.,* p. 121.)

Dr. G. A. Buttrick, President of the Federal Council for 1940, contributes this: "The second besetment was the discovery of contradictions in the Bible. These need not be pursued from Dan to Beersheba. If only one self-refutation is found, the doctrine of literal infallibility is slain and pursuit is needless." Name one or two of these contradictions! "There are two accounts of creation, and they do not agree. There are two accounts of David's census-taking: in the Book of Samuel we are told that God instructed him to number the people, and in the Chronicles, that Satan 'moved' him. . . , In retrospect it seems incredible that the theory of literal inspiration could ever have been held." (*The Christian Fact and Modern Doubt.*)

De Witt has this: "Such, too, is the discrepancy between Matt. 20: 29, 30 and Luke 18: 35. In the former we have two blind men crying after Jesus as He *went out from* Jericho, in the latter, of one blind man as He *drew nigh* to that city. This makes it necessary to reconstruct the theory of inspiration as generally accepted." "The difference between the gospels about the hour of crucifixion" also makes it necessary. Once more: "If error were impossible under the divine afflatus, we should not find the martyr Stephen, when 'full of the Holy Ghost,' making unconsciously at least two statements that contradict the Old Testament." (*Op. cit.,* pp. 37, 38, 73.) — Kahnis points out the difference in the records of the institution of the Lord's Supper and declares that it would be derogatory to the Holy Ghost to make Him the author of these records.

---

10) Best is charging the verbal-inspirationists with rationalism. "It may seem a jesting '*tu quoque*' to say of the literally orthodox in Bible-studies that they are more inveterate rationalists than the higher critics, whom they so unanimously condemn." We shall study this curious phenomenon in a later section, p. 200.

The moderns make much of the difference in the wording of the inscription on the cross. One of them puts it thus: "The Fundamentalist asserts the verbal inspiration of the Scriptures. Permit me to remind the Fundamentalist that, while each of the four gospels cites the inscription on the cross, no two give it the same words. What, then, of verbal inspiration?" — The "contradiction" between Acts 9:7 and Acts 22:9 also figures prominently in the list of errors. Saul's companions heard the voice, and they did not hear the voice! (See L. Boettner, *op. cit.*, p. 55.) And then there are the contradictions in the story of the resurrection! St. John, for instance, mentions only one woman going to the tomb. Matthew two, Mark three, Luke still more. Matthew and Mark speak of one angel, Luke and John two angels. Etc., etc. Lessing used to make much of these glaring contradictions. (See *Lehre und Wehre*, 32, p. 321.)

The latest manifesto against Verbal Inspiration was issued by Dr. H. C. Alleman: "By the theory of verbal inspiration we are justified in expecting that we shall find no errors or contradictions or even any imperfections in what the Bible has to say concerning Christ and His ministry. . . . There should be no discrepancies in the statements concerning the Savior. If He can be quoted as saying in John 10:35 (as the verbal inspirationists hold) that 'Scripture cannot be broken,' and if that means that it is without error or contradiction, how are we to square this statement with those instances, particularly in the Sermon on the Mount, in which He deliberately breaks Scripture? For example, does not Matt. 5:39 abrogate Ex. 21:24, and does not Mark 7:19 repeal Lev. 11? . . . It would seem that there should be no uncertainty as to when the Last Supper was celebrated, whether in connection with the Passover (the Synoptists) or at the weekly social-religious meal Kiddush (the fourth gospel). Matt. 21:7 says the disciples placed their garments upon *them* (the ass and the colt) and He sat on *them*. Does that mean that Jesus sat upon both animals? In Mark 2:26 Jesus says that David got the showbread from *Abiathar;* according to 1 Sam. 21:1-6 it was from *Abimelech.* Matthew and Luke both correct Mark at this point by omitting the name. Neither of them thought that Mark was 'errorless.'" (*Luth. Church Quart.,* Oct., 1940, p. 356.) [11]

The Biblical writers are even charged with holding opposing principles and teaching contradictory doctrines. H. L. Willett, for instance, finds "Jonah" in opposition to Ezekiel. "The book of

---

11) A somewhat complete list of these "contradictions" is given in *Lehre und Wehre*, 39, pp. 33—273; *Proceedings, Synodical Conference,* 1902, pp. 5—56; and in Dr. W. Arndt's books *Does the Bible Contradict Itself?* and *Bible Difficulties.* See also J. W. Haley, *An Examination of the Alleged Discrepancies of the Bible.*

Jonah is a prophetic answer to the narrower nationalism of Ezekiel, Joel, and Esther. . . . Ezekiel was a nationalist of pronounced views." (*Op. cit.*, pp. 59, 108.) And H. E. Fosdick contributes this: "For one thing, we are saved by it" (by discarding Verbal Inspiration and using the new approach to the Bible) "from the old and impossible attempt to harmonize the Bible with itself, to make it speak with unanimous voice, to resolve its conflicts and contradictions into a strained and artificial unity. . . . Listen to Ecclesiastes: 'That which befalleth the sons of men befalleth beasts. . . . Man hath no preeminence above the beasts,' Eccl. 9:4-6 and 3:19. And here is a passage from First Corinthians: 'This mortal must put on immortality,' etc., 1 Cor. 15:53-55. No ingenuity of exegesis ever can make those two agree. The fact is that at the beginning Hebrew religion had no hope of immortality." (*Op. cit.*, p. 24 f.)

Things are in a bad shape in the Bible. It takes the "new approach," higher criticism, to bring order into the confusion. "Higher criticism has explained the seeming contradictions and conflicts of Biblical statements which were in former periods the targets of captious and often successful attack." (H. L. Willett, *op. cit.*, p. 264.) Higher criticism explains for instance, as N. H. Best has told us, the baffling fact of Saul's not recognizing David by the simple expedient of assuming "two traditions." The baffling fact is not, of course, explained. The difficulty remains, but the *fact of the contradiction* is explained by assuming two sources and a high degree of inefficiency in the compiler. And the Holy Ghost is cleared of the charge of having made an incredible statement, which charge must stand, as long as Verbal Inspiration stands.

Verbal Inspiration Denounced as Wicked and Harmful

And so, because of these mistakes and contradictions in the Bible, Verbal Inspiration must be cast out. Paine and Lessing and Alleman say with C. H. Dodd: "The theory of 'verbal inspiration' maintains that the entire corpus of Scripture consists of writings every word of which was directly 'dictated' by the Deity. . . . Any attempt to confront this theory of inspiration with the actual facts which meet us in the study of the Biblical documents leads at once to such patent confusions and contradictions that it is unprofitable to discuss it." (*Op. cit.*, p. 35.) These men *cannot* believe in it, cannot teach it. Granted that the Bible contains many mistakes or even one mistake, verbal, plenary inspiration cannot be maintained. We are here in full accord with them. "It is, of course, useless to contend that the sacred writers were infallible if in point of fact they err." (C. Hodge, *Systematic Theology*, p. 169.) "So God once breathed through human lips upon a series of parchments which are called the Scriptures. . . . Wherefore it must have been inerrant truth, since it is unthinkable that God should breathe a lie." (D. J. Burrell, *Why I Believe the Bible*, p. 18.) The thesis that, if the Bible contains mistakes, God cannot have inspired these portions of the Bible is absolutely true. And since Paine and Lessing and Alleman are convinced that the Bible is full of errors, they must reject Verbal Inspiration. James Brooks, in an address before theological students in 1880, declared: "The theory now so popular that the words of Scripture are not inspired has been *invented to account for the supposed errors* in the Bible. If you come to anything that does not agree with your ideas, you fall to this theory to the dishonor of God's Word." (See *Lehre und Wehre*, 57, p. 129; 32, p. 303.) Hugh M'Intosh raises the same charge: "The truth is, the reasons that led to the adoption of this theory" (which denies Verbal Inspiration) "were not originally derived from Scripture at all. They do not even profess to found it on direct, explicit passages. They were first used by the foes of the Christian faith — by the Rationalists and infidels — who, in their hostility to Christianity, seized eagerly upon the difficulties and discrepancies of Scripture. . . . Our new apologists, not seeing their way to meet these objections, and thinking by mistake that, if they maintained the truthfulness, trustworthiness, and divine authority of Scripture, they were logically bound to solve all these difficulties; and fancying that they could without loss and with much advantage yield this ground to the enemy, . . . therefore they abandoned the true Bible claim and surrendered to the foe the position that had for centuries been held so well." (*Is Christ Infallible and the Bible True?* P. 597.) And this serious charge is readily admitted by the foes of Verbal Inspiration. De Witt plainly told us: "The inaccuracies in the Bible make it necessary to reconstruct the theory of inspiration as generally accepted." Marcus Dods says: "The fact that those who record the sayings of our Lord greatly differ in their reports appears to be incompatible with the idea of verbal inspiration" (see *Theol. Monthly*, 7, p. 257) — the theory of verbal inspiration must be reconstructed. Hans Rust insists: "Eine falsch beratene Theologie versuchte im 17. Jahrhundert dem fehlbaren Menschenwort der Bibel durch die Lehre von der woertlichen, ja buchstaeblichen Inspiration der Heiligen Schrift das Fragwuerdige zu nehmen und damit das Aergernis des fehlbaren Menschenwortes aus dem Wege zu raeumen. Man erklaerte kurzerhand, die Bibel koenne keine Irrtuemer enthalten" (*Vom Aergernis des Menschenwortes in der Heiligen Schrift*, p. 30) — that was ill-advised; we must get rid of this mistaken notion. H. E. Fosdick: "*We used to think* of inspiration as a procedure which produced a book guaranteed in all its parts against error." But when one who "knows modern biology hears that, when a dead body touched the skeleton of Elisha and sprang to life again, or that after our Lord's resurrection many of the saints long deceased arose"; when one who "knows modern physics reads that light was created three days before the sun and that an ax-head floated when Elisha threw a stick into the water" (*op. cit.*, pp. 30, 34), he feels the need of constructing a new theory of inspiration. Prof. J. Aberly, too, calls for a reconstruction of the old doctrine. "I found that I could not meet these" (modern men) "by falling back on the claim that this Bible was the literal Word of God. . . . It compels one to do what Dr. E. Stanley Jones found himself compelled to do, to shorten his lines of defense. He states that, when he went to India, he felt called on to defend the Bible from Genesis to Revelation, but he soon found it necessary to retire into the citadel and limit himself to Jesus Christ, and Him crucified. . . . One may well ask the question whether men have not been repelled at times by a mishandling of the scriptures. . . ." (*The Luth. Church Quart.*, April, 1935, p. 116 f.)

When, therefore, E. Brunner feels that "we have to chisel off the incrustations of the past from the Bible" (*The Word and the World*, p. 102) and D. F. Forrester, that "the wheat must be sifted from the chaff and what is warped and ill balanced must be corrected" (*The Living Church*, Feb. 11, 1933), and H. C. Alleman, that "the pure Scriptures must be separated from their dregs and filth" (*The Lutheran*, Jan. 14, 1937), it is but natural that they call for a theory of inspiration which permits them to go ahead. And when they go ahead and chisel off the incrustations and junk one part of the Bible after the other, Dr. Willett commends "those devout and scholarly men who have labored nobly to disengage the Bible from the cerements of traditional views" (*op. cit.*, p. 262).

They feel that they are doing a good work and feel that it would be immoral if they retained Verbal Inspiration. Yes, *immoral.* E. Brunner says it would not be honest. "The orthodox doctrine of verbal inspiration has been finally destroyed. It is clear that there is no connection between it and scientific research and *honesty.*" (*The Mediator*, p. 105.) And J. A. W. Haas uses stronger terms. "The claims of a mechanically infallible Bible, verbally perfect, do not hold in the light of the facts. But facts cannot be set aside without injury to truth and *damage to moral sincerity* when they are clearly recognized." (*What Ought I to Believe*, p. 29.) J. S. Whale uses similarly strong language: "It is no use shilly-shallying here; *loyalty to truth* in the shape of literary and historical criticism forbids it. A Christian knows that he has to serve God with the mind as well as with heart and will and that the obligation to be intelligent is itself a *moral obligation.*" (*Op. cit.*, p. 77.) These men are so thoroughly convinced that the Bible is full of errors that they doubt the honesty of those who refuse to find them. Kahnis charges them with lacking the sense of truth. "Dass sich in der Schrift Widersprueche finden, kann nur Mangel an Wahrheitssinn bestreiten." (See W. Rohnert, *Die Inspiration der Heiligen Schrift und ihre Bestreiter*, p. 259.) Since, therefore, these men are honestly convinced that there are mistakes in the Bible, they are in conscience bound to fight the teaching of the verbal, plenary inspiration of the Bible. It would be immoral, on their part, to accept it. De Witt demands "if it be fairly proven that the inspiration of the Bible is a delusion," that we face that fact "like honest men. There may be infinite peril in refusing to strengthen our position" (by discarding Verbal Inspiration) "if we find that which we have hitherto occupied to be no longer tenable" (*op. cit.*, p. 13). V. Ferm is of the same mind. "The doctrine of the complete inerrancy of the Bible, upon which historic Lutheranism has built up a system of orthodoxy, can hardly, without a *loss of intellectual integrity* and vitality, be today maintained in the light of the historical method of understanding the Scriptures." (*What Is Lutheranism?* p. 293.) And Johannes Haenel declares: "Den Vaetern war die Autoritaet der Schrift gestuetzt durch die Ueberzeugung, dass jedes Wort der Schrift den Verfassern von Gott diktiert sei. Bei *gewissenhafter* Wertung des Tatbestandes kann das *nicht mehr gehalten werden.*" (*Das Wort Gottes und das Alte Testament*, p. 9.)

The moderns refuse to teach Verbal Inspiration for the additional reason that it works great harm. On the last page of his book Fosdick asseverates: "From naive acceptance of the Bible as of equal credibility in all its parts because mechanically inerrant, I passed years ago to the shocking conviction that such traditional bibliolatry is false in fact and *perilous in result.*" Willett is equally emphatic: "No error has ever resulted in greater discredit to the Scriptures or *injury to Christianity* than that of attributing to the Bible such a miraculous origin and nature as to make it an infallible standard of morals and religion." (*Op. cit.*, p. 289.)

In the first place, "let it be said in all seriousness that Lutheran *exegesis will be seriously handicapped* unless it abandons once and for all the unpsychological and mechanical theories of inspiration and unhistorical views of verbal inerrancy which the application of scientific and historical methods to the study of the Bible has rendered obsolete." Prof. T. A. Kantonen said this in his "Canned Theology" articles. He and *The Lutheran* (which published these articles) want more leeway in their exegesis. The Church would suffer great loss if science, etc., were deprived of the right to improve on Scripture.

Again, Verbal Inspiration has forced many to turn their backs on Christianity. The complaint is that when men are told that these "erroneous" statements of the Bible (including the "false" ethical standards of the Bible — which will be treated later) are God's truth, they will inevitably become skeptical of *all* the teachings of the Bible. In connection with Verbal Inspiration and "theological obscurantism" Fosdick complains of "the intellectual stumbling-blocks over which many young people are falling when they read the Bible. . . . We are paying for it in the loss of our more intelligent young people." And he tells us of "educated laymen" who complain: "We open the church-door on a land of topsyturvy where axes float, dry sticks change into serpents, and bedeviled swine run violently into the sea." (*Op. cit.*, pp. 53, 59, 61.) J. M. Gibson: "Take the utterances which trench on the domain of science," insist that these utterances speak the truth, "and men like Tyndall and Huxley are forced into skepticism." "A man is suddenly confronted with an array of Bible difficulties to which he cannot find any satisfactory answer. . . . Because there are some things in the Bible he cannot be quite sure of, he gives it all up." "There are tens of thousands of people" in this case; they finally "reject the Bible as if it were waste paper and give up the Church of God as a discredited relic of the past." (*Op. cit.*, pp. 121, 169, 195.) Baumgaertel, too, would rather sacrifice Verbal Inspiration than call upon the men of learning to bring the required sacrifice. We heard him say: "It will not do to make allowance only for those who are deficient in intellectual training and to exact from the learned classes a *sacrificium intellectus* which they simply cannot bring. That bars them from the Church." (See W. Moeller, *op. cit.*, p. 36.) We must "shorten our line of defense," J. Aberly told us, give up the teaching that "the very words of Scripture are the Word of God," if we would gain men whose "Weltanschauung, or philosophical outlook, is different" (*Luth. Church Quart.*, April, 1935, p. 116 f.). When these men hear a sermon on the absolute inerrancy of Scripture, they are filled with alarm and fear for the welfare of the Church. Dr. E. H. Delk: "This idea of a verbal inspiration of Holy Scripture is more likely to close the ears of informed students of the Bible to Dr. Maier's message than to win them to its revelation of God in the face of Jesus Christ." (*The Luth. Church Quart.*, 1936, p. 426.) E. Brunner sounds the alarm in these words: "The destruction of the dogma of Verbal Inspiration with its emphasis on an Infallible Book, by the modern process of research in natural and historical science inevitably carried away with it *the whole Christian faith* in revelation." (*The Mediator*, p. 34.) Dr. S. P. Cadman sounded the alarm in the *Herald Tribune* of New York thus: "The claim that the Scriptures are a perfect whole has wrought more mental distress and created more skepticism *than any other dogma* of Christian or Jewish theology known to me." (See *The Presbyterian*, July 12, 1928.) He makes the same statement in *Answers to Every-day Questions,* p. 253. De Witt implores us to cease and desist from such preaching: under such preaching "poor souls pass off into the outer darkness" (*op. cit.,* p. 15).

Such preaching is also harmful to ethics. C. E. Montague cites the very bad physics of the Bible bound on the modern mind by tradition and so vitiating the effect of its very good ethics. The disbeliefs generated by the physics have brought on skepticism as to the authoritative nature of the ethics. "I believe that it is not open to doubt that a large part of the immoralisms and confused egoisms of the day are due to the inevitable aftermath of a morality based on a divine power, faith in whose existence has been lost." (See M. H. Krumbine, *Ways of Believing,* p. 42.)

And still greater disaster is wrought. In the article "Ein oeffentliches Bekenntnis zur Inspiration der Heiligen Schrift in Deutschland" (*Lehre und Wehre*, 69, p. 297 ff.) Dr. Pieper writes: "The charge is made that those who still believe that Scripture is the infallible Word of God, and accordingly make Scripture the sole source and norm of the Christian doctrine, exert an evil influence on the Church. . . . This clinging to the *words* of Scripture, or, as it is usually put, to 'the letter of Scripture,' engenders 'intellectualism,' a mere head-Christianity, and hinders 'living,' 'warm-blooded,' Christianity." (See also *Chr. Dogmatik*, I, p. 317.) Yes, indeed, says O. L. Joseph in *Ringing Realities* (pp. 91 and 217), "if we are to escape the pitfall of barren intellectualism," we must not "imprison the reason within a Chinese wall of traditionalism," demanding a Bible which "is historically correct," free from "errors," and does not deal in "folk-lore" and relying upon "proof-texts" to establish doctrine. — What evils hath this dogma of Verbal Inspiration wrought! The moderns cannot help loathing and abhorring it. As W. Moeller puts it: " 'Verbal Inspiration'! The bare word sets our theologians a-trembling."

One more reason why the moderns abhor the doctrine of verbal inspiration, of the inerrancy of Scripture: they are convinced that Scripture does not teach this doctrine, and they will not have it foisted upon the Church. The *Auburn Affirmation* declares: "There is no assertion in Scripture that their writers were kept 'from error.' " [12)]   It is surprising that Christian theologians should make such a statement, in the face of the many Scriptural statements to the contrary (2 Tim. 3:16; John 10:35; etc.); it is still more surprising that so many can agree with the Auburn Affirmation. Men have been able to convince themselves that the Scriptures do not claim inerrancy.[13)] N. R. Best is able to say: "The demand for an inerrant Bible is an artificial stipulation which men would impose on the Spirit who has inspired the Scriptures, but which *gets no recognition whatever within the Scriptures* themselves." (*Op. cit.*, p. 96.)   S. P. Cadman has found it possible to answer the question "Why do you think it incredible that God was not able to protect the inspiration of His chosen witnesses against mistakes?" thus: "Nowhere does the Book itself claim for the entire content of its literature what you assert in its behalf. . . . It is a baseless assumption that every word of Holy Scripture must be regarded as practically infallible." (*Answers to Everyday Questions*, p. 253.)   C. H. Dodd can actually pen these words: "The Bible itself does not make any claim to infallible authority for all its parts." (*The Authority of the Bible*, p. 14.) And when the United Lutheran Church of America found itself unable to accept "the doctrine known technically as 'The Verbal Inspiration of the Bible' " and "its commission was unable to accept the statement . . . that the Scriptures are the infallible truth 'also in those parts which treat of historical, geographical, and other secular matters' " (see above), it asserted in effect that the Bible does not teach it.   That was asserted in so many words, for instance, by the *Lutheran World*, Nov. 19, 1903.   Commenting on a statement of *Lehre und Wehre*: "Die Schrift lehrt klar, dass jedes Wort der Heiligen Schrift vom Heiligen Geiste eingegeben und darum untruegliche Wahrheit ist," it said: "This strikes us as a case of orthodoxy overdone. The writer fails to cite passages in proof of the amazing statement that the Scriptures themselves teach that 'every word' contained in them is inspired by the Holy Ghost." (See *Lehre und Wehre*, 50, p. 39.)

Men who honestly believe that Scripture does not teach verbal, plenary inspiration are conscience-bound to protest against this

---

12) The statement following this sentence comes under the heading: Harmfulness of Verbal Inspiration. "The doctrine of inerrancy, intended to enhance the authority of the Scriptures, in fact impairs their authority for faith and life and weakens the testimony of the Church."

13) Recall the statement of M'Intosh: "The truth is, the reasons that led to the adoption of this theory were not *originally* derived from Scripture at all. They do not even profess to found it on direct, explicit passages." But *convinced* that the Scriptures contain errors, they are driven to divest 2 Tim. 3:16 and John 10:35 of their real meaning.

teaching. And they couch their protest in strong language. Dr. J. H. Cotton, the president of the Presbyterian Theological Seminary of Chicago, declares that "the Bible is not 'letter' and that the Church's doctrine of the infallible Bible is a *heresy.*" (See *Conc. Theol. Monthly,* XI, p. 631.) The name for this heresy is "verbalism." Let no man plague the Church with Verbal Inspiration!

This, then, is the situation: men are thanking God that He has delivered the Church from a fearful incubus. They are glad that they have been freed from "the naive acceptance of the Bible as inerrant" (Fosdick, see above) and thank God for the great progress theology has made: "When I came to the seminary years ago, I fully believed in the verbal inspiration of every book in the Bible. . . . I fancy I had plenty of company in my jejune conception and belief that the Bible in all its statements was inerrant. . . . What a change has been wrought in the sphere of New Testament scholarship during the last fifty years!" (E. H. Delk. See *Theol. Monthly,* VII, p. 172.) Now they can again look the world in the face! The world no longer looks upon them as obscurantists. And they are grateful to "those devout and scholarly men who have labored nobly to disengage the Bible from the cerements of traditional views. . . . The higher criticism has forever disposed of the fetish of a level Bible; it has destroyed the doctrine of verbal inspiration." (Willet, *op. cit.,* pp. 264, 262.) It has demonstrated that many a Scripture must be broken.

W. Gussmann is thankful that the Lutheran Church in Germany, at least its leaders, no longer worships this fetish and only wishes that the Lutheran Church in America could enjoy the same good fortune. "The day of Verbal Inspiration has passed, and we shall have to tell our American brethren: We cannot turn the course of history backwards." (*Luth. Zeitblatt,* Jan., 1924.) Voices from America assure him: We are with you! Dr. C. E. Wendell (Augustana Synod): "A stilted veneration for the Word betrays an inward weakness rather than a virile faith, and out of it proceeds a nervous anxiety to prove the 'complete inerrancy' of the Bible 'from cover to cover.' This may be *good Fundamentalism,* but hardly *good Lutheranism.*" (*What Is Lutheranism?* P. 236.) Dr. P. E. Scherer has been warning the students at Gettysburg against this un-Lutheran Fundamentalism. He spoke to them of "the panic which resorts to such ineffective devices as Fundamentalism with its untenable theory of verbal inspiration." And the professor (R. T. Stamm) commended him for this timely warning. (See *The Lutheran,* June 9, 1937.)

The revolt against Verbal Inspiration is gaining in force. Must we join it?

THE CHRISTIAN ATTITUDE

We are asked to give up the doctrine of verbal inspiration because of the alleged erroneousness of the Bible. The moderns are asking us to do that. And our own flesh is suggesting it.[14] We find it impossible to do so. One reason for that is that the arguments advanced by the rationalists against the infallibility of Scripture are in conflict with sound reason. We shall demonstrate this in a later section, and that demonstration will serve a good purpose. But that is a matter of minor importance. The chief reason, the real reason, why we cannot give up Verbal Inspiration is that our Christian conscience, formed and guided by God's Word, forbids it. By doing it we should be violating the Christian faith and putting the Church and the individual believer in grave danger. To those who would entice us away from an inerrant Bible we give this answer: No Christian can declare, in his sober mind, that God's Word contains errors. And when the Christian realizes that Scripture *is* God's Word, he cannot, absolutely he cannot, declare that the Holy Scriptures contain errors. Nor will he ever be ready to place the Bible in the hands of his fellow-men with the warning that it is not reliable in all its statements.

Faith Refuses to Criticize and Censure Scripture

No Christian will, in his sober mind, say that Scripture, the Word of God, contains a single error. Dr. Pieper says: "All objections to the divine inspiration and the inerrancy of the Bible are unworthy of a Christian." (*What Is Christianity?* p. 257.) Having quoted Luther: "When you hear people who are so blinded and hardened that they deny that what Christ and the apostles spoke and wrote is the Word of God, . . . just keep silence, do not say one word to them; say only this: I shall give you sufficient ground from Scripture; if you believe, well; if not, just go your way" (IX:1238), Dr. Pieper comments: "It is, according to Luther, utterly unworthy of a Christian to refuse to accept that which Christ and the apostles spoke and wrote as God's Word and

---

14) Dr. G. Stoeckhardt: "It is true that, through the grace of God, no tendency to sympathize with the wisdom of modern theology has as yet manifested itself in our church-body. However, we should never forget that the seed of doubt, of unbelief, is implanted in all of us by nature. And this doubting, continually arising in the natural heart, has in all ages questioned particularly the truth of Scripture, the fountain of all divine truth." (*Lehre und Wehre*, 32, p. 164. On p. 313 ff. Dr. Stoeckhardt deals with the "errors" and "contradictions" in the Bible on which our doubt feeds. See also *Proceedings of Ev. Luth. Synodical Conference*, 1902, p. 21, on the doubts aroused in the hearts of the Christians by these "contradictions.") The following lines are not addressed to the moderns, who will cast them aside as representing the outmoded theology of obscurantism. They are addressed to the disturbed Christian who needs to be shown the wickedness of his doubtings.

inerrant." (*Christliche Dogmatik,* I, p. 293.) The thought that the Bible is a mixture of truth and error cannot find permanent lodgment in the Christian heart.

The Christian thinks too much of his Bible for that. We look upon the Bible, and God wants us to look upon the Bible, as a most holy thing. "Halte von dieser Schrift als von dem allerhoechsten, edelsten Heiligtum." (Luther, XIV: 4.) It is clothed with divine majesty. It is the *Word of God.* What is written in the Scriptures was spoken of the Lord by the prophets and apostles (Matt. 1: 22). What Moses wrote is "the Word of God" (Mark 7: 10, 13), and what Paul wrote "are the commandments of the Lord," 1 Cor. 14: 37. The Scriptures are "the oracles of God," Rom. 3: 2. And we stand in holy awe of these words, the very words of our God and Lord. Every single word and letter of Scripture is to us sacred and inviolable. "The Holy Scriptures," 2 Tim. 3: 15. (See *Proceedings, Iowa Dist.,* 1897, p. 28.)

Holy Scripture is to us the most holy thing in the world. That is the attitude which God requires of the Christian. "To this man will I look that trembleth at My Word," Is. 66: 2. We cannot treat it as a human book, subject to criticism and censorship. What we read in this Book we receive not as the word of men but, as it is in truth, the Word of God. 1 Thess. 2: 13. When the Christian preacher proclaims the contents of this Book, he knows that he is speaking the oracles of God, 1 Pet. 4: 11. With awe and reverence St. Peter read his Bible, for here "holy men of God spake as they were moved by the Holy Ghost," 2 Pet. 1: 21. So Luther looked upon the Bible. "To me God's Word is above all, and the majesty of God is on my side." (XIX: 337.) "You must follow straight after Scripture and receive it and utter not one syllable against it, for it is God's mouth." Even when this Book speaks of mere temporal matters, "you are so to deal with it that you think that God Himself is saying this" (III: 21). Every single passage of Scripture is clothed with the majesty of God. "As for me, every single Bible-text makes the world too narrow for me." (XX: 788.) John Wesley, too, "saw God at the beginning of every section of Holy Scripture. . . . To Wesley, there were two great realities — the visible Book and its invisible but ever-present Author." (See J. A. Cottam, *Know the Truth,* p. 28.) The holy awe that dominates the Christian's study of the Bible makes it utterly impossible for him to utter such a prayer as this: Dear Lord, enlighten my mind that I may separate the errors in Thy Word from the truth it contains. Whatever evil thoughts arise in the Christian's head, his heart will not permit him thus to dishonor God's Word.

Again, the Christian loves the Bible. He loves it because he owes to it everything he prizes. Searching the Scripture, he has found therein eternal life (John 5:39), certainty in doubt, comfort in affliction, strength in weakness, and all spiritual blessings. And loving this Book above all things, he will not permit any man to cast aspersions upon it and dishonor it. Do the moderns really believe that, when they besmirch and befoul the Bible, they have the approbation of the Christian?

The Christian's attitude is this: "I have rejoiced in the ways of Thy testimonies as much as in all riches. I will delight myself in Thy statutes. Open Thou mine eyes that I may behold wondrous things out of Thy Law," Ps. 119:14 ff. Stop the mouth of those who are disfiguring its lovely beauty! — "O precious Book, a book above all books! Thou art a peaceful pool here on earth, which reflects the light of all the stars of the invisible heaven; thou art the letter sent from our eternal home to comfort us in the strange land; thou art the key of heaven for the faint-hearted pilgrim, wandering through this world filled with error, doubt, fear, and trouble; thou art the Word of our God, of our heavenly Father." (Walther, *Kasualpredigten*, p. 297.)

Moreover, this Book which all Christians love and revere, solemnly warns us against ascribing errors to it and demands instant acceptance by us of all of its statements. "All Scripture is given by inspiration of God," 2 Tim. 3:16. This little Bible-text makes the world too narrow for us. If we should deny that every word of Scripture is true, we could nowhere in the wide world find escape from the judgment this text would pronounce against us. "The Scripture cannot be broken," John 10:35. Nowhere does Scripture make a misstatement. If any man dares to eliminate the least statement of Scripture as untrustworthy, he is condemned by this Scripture, and the world has become too narrow for him. It is unworthy of a Christian to refuse to accept any portion of Scripture as the inerrant Word of God. Again: "Thy Word is truth," John 17:17. And: "These sayings," the sayings of Revelation and of the entire Bible, "are faithful and true," Rev. 22:6. Will men still speak of mistakes, discrepancies, contradictions, found in certain sayings of the Bible and demand that these sayings be eliminated from the "Word of God"? If they will do so, let them ponder the awful saying of Rev. 22:19: "If any man shall take away from the words of the book of this prophecy, God shall take away his part out of the book of life," etc. No; one who takes the Bible for his guide will not sit down with those who occupy themselves with making lists of "errors in the Bible."

St. Augustine would not do so. He wrote to Jerome: "This I have learned to do: to hold only those books which are called the Holy Scriptures in such honor that I finally believe that not one of the holy writers ever erred." Quoting this statement,

Luther endorses it and declares: "The Scriptures have never erred." (XV: 1481.) Yes, and "the Scriptures *cannot* err" (XIX: 1073). "It is certain that Scripture cannot disagree with itself." (XX: 798.) "It is impossible that Scripture should contradict itself, only that it so appears to the senseless and obstinate hypocrites." (IX: 356.) Luther was so filled with awe of the sacredness of Scripture that he would not and could not admit the possibility of errors and contradictions in Scripture, could not permit any portion of it to be violated and broken. "One little point of doctrine means more than heaven and earth, and therefore we cannot suffer to have the least jot thereof violated." (IX: 650.)[15]

Listen to the host of Christian theologians who up to the present time bear witness to the inviolability of Scripture, of all of Scripture. D. J. Burrell speaks thus: "The Book claims to be inspired, 'breathed of God.' . . . Wherefore it must have been inerrant truth; since it is unthinkable that God should breathe a lie." (*Why I Believe the Bible*, p. 18.) L. Boettner: "We believe that the Bible is without an error from Genesis to Revelation. . . . This has been the historic Protestant position concerning the authority of Scripture. It was held by Luther and Calvin. In more recent times it has been reasserted by Hodge, Warfield, and Kuyper. . . . They have held that the Bible does not merely *contain* the Word of God, as a pile of chaff contains some wheat, but that the Bible in all its parts *is* the Word of God." (The *Inspiration of the Scriptures*, p. 17.) Without an error from Genesis to Revelation — let Quenstedt enlarge on that. He wrote — and the moderns quote his words again and again as a *dictum horribile*, while we find our heartfelt conviction expressed in them —: "In the canonical Scriptures there is found no falsehood, no misstatement, no error, not even the least, neither in the subject-matter nor in the words, but whatever they present, the whole of it and every part of it, is completely true, whether this pertain to the doctrines of faith or of morals, history or chronology, geography or nomenclature; no want of information, no thoughtlessness or forgetfulness, no lapse of memory, can or dare be ascribed to the penmen of the Holy Ghost as they wrote the sacred writings." (*Systema*, I, p. 112.)

And let Dr. Walther tell us who it is that wants us to find errors in the Bible. "The moderns charge this up against us as an error that we refuse to find errors in the Bible. . . . They ask us to deny with them the divine origin of the divine Word and to say, when we read any passage of the Bible: Yea, hath God really

---

15) "The context shows that Luther here has in mind every tittle of doctrine as expressed in the definite inviolable *words* of Scripture." (Pieper, *op. cit.*, I, p. 268. Look up this passage in Pieper.)

said this? But we refuse to make these words of *the fallen angel* our own. Nay; as often as we open our Bible, and wherever we open it, there comes to us a voice charging us: 'Hear, O heavens, and give ear, O earth, for the Lord hath spoken,' Is. 7:2." (*Lutherstunde.* See *Proceedings, Iowa Dist.,* 9, p. 53.) Many today refuse to see God at the beginning of every section of the Bible. The more reason that we should say with Walther: "As Peter at the time when many fell away was the more ready to confess Christ: 'We believe and are sure that Thou art that Christ, the Son of the living God' (John 6:69), so we should, now that so many are becoming ashamed of the holy Book, proclaim the louder to the world: We believe and are sure that this despised Book is the truth, the Word of the living God." (*Kasualpredigten,* p. 304.)

And what Walther and Luther and Augustine said St. Paul said before them: "I worship the God of my fathers, believing all things which are written in the Law and in the Prophets," Acts 24:14. Can you conceive of Paul saying that it is not incumbent on him or any other Christian to receive as true all that is written in the Old Testament and in the New Testament? Can you conceive of such a situation that the Holy Spirit, who spoke 2 Tim. 3:16, would at the same time permit His Christians to reject portions of Scripture as not inspired, as erroneous? Can you understand the psychology of a Christian who honestly believes in the Bible and yet feels at liberty to break Scripture here and there? It is utterly unworthy of the Christian to speak of mistakes in the Bible. Hugh M'Intosh takes the same position as Dr. Pieper. "In regard to the greater and supreme question as to the infallibility and divine authority of the teaching of the Lord on everything on which He clearly uttered His mind, and especially on the prime root question of the truthfulness, trustworthiness, divine origin, authority and inviolability of all Scripture, I hold firmly that my great teacher" (Prof. W. Robertson Smith) "took up *the only true, safe, and tenable position on which a Christian can take his stand.* This position . . . steadfastly rejects and precludes every theory of inspiration that questions or impugns, far more that disowns or denies, the infallibility and divine authority of the teaching of the Lord on anything He ever taught, or any statement He ever made, or any word He ever uttered. . . . Book I shows especially the decisiveness and absoluteness of His teaching on the *inviolable truth, thorough trustworthiness, and divine authority of all Scripture."* (*Is Christ Infallible and the Bible True?* p. 5 f.) [16] "Es ist

---

16) M'Intosh is taking issue with those who "declare the indefinite erroneousness and illimitable untrustworthiness of Scripture" (p. 2). Let us have one more quotation on the question whether a Christian can honestly believe and with a clear conscience maintain the erroneousness of Scripture. "If the Bible claims to be true, trustworthy, of divine

einem Christen *unmoeglich,* zu glauben, dass die Heilige Schrift sich selbst widersprechen koenne." (*Proceedings Syn. Conf.,* 1902, p. 19.) [17]

The Apriorism of Faith

Should, then, the Christian judge from the outset, prior to, and independently of, any scientific and critical investigation, that any given statement of Scripture is absolutely true, on the sole basis of Scripture's claim of absolute infallibility? The moderns condemn such a position as due to inadmissible *a-priori* reasoning. The writer of the preface to J. M. Gibson's book *The Inspiration and Authority of Holy Scripture* says: "Dr. Gibson began in the old theory of inspiration, in which he would have remained had his been a metallic, inert, or mechanical mind. . . . He makes a valuable protest against *the vice of apriorism,* which comes down on the Bible with a theory of inspiration really drawn from rationalistic expectations, instead of rising out of the Bible from its inductive treatment as faith and science alike must do." (P. XV.) [18] J. De Witt, too, has no use for the *a-priori* argument.

---

origin and authority, — the Word of God, — it necessarily follows either that the Scriptures, as originally written, were so and cannot be indefinitely erroneous and untrustworthy, or that the Bible is untrue in its root doctrine and that its fundamental claim is false. It cannot be the Word of God, but must be merely the word of not only fallible, but untruthful or incredible men. . . . If the Bible claims in the name of God to speak the truth, and if it, as alleged, is erroneous or unreliable, then manifestly its root claim is false. . . . It cannot be the product of divine inspiration; for every idea of inspiration would be violated by the supposition that men writing under the power of the Holy Ghost should make a false claim." (Pp. 361, 363.)

17) "Holy Scripture *cannot* contradict itself. The Christian is sure of that, sure in advance, even before investigating the 'contradictions.' For (1) Scripture, being the Word of God, is true. . . . (2) Holy Scripture is inspired. . . . (3) Otherwise Scripture could no longer be the norm and rule of the Christian faith and life. . . . These considerations leave no room for argument; it is impossible for the Christian to think that Scripture could contradict itself." (Pp. 14—19. Get these *Proceedings* and study the full argument.)

18) Dr. Gibson writes: "I was brought up to believe that the whole fabric of our faith rested ultimately on the foundation of a book which, though written by many different authors, was yet from beginning to end not their work at all but that of God. They were simply God's penmen, and what they wrote was at His dictation." "This is the method which has till quite recently been most popular with the defenders of the authoritative inspiration of the Scriptures: they have postulated as a necessity of the case the emancipation of all the writers of Scripture from the effects of human weakness and limitation." The proper method is to "form a theory of inspiration not at the beginning but at the end of the inquiry." "According to that preconceived theory of inspiration it was supposed that men inspired of God . . . could speak with absolute scientific precision on every subject they touched." "Those who find rest in the conviction that they have in their possession a book every line and word of which is beyond the reach of error, have an ultimate authority not a whit better than that of the Romanist." (Pp. 4, 32, 36, 90, 115.)

He understands our position quite well: "The *a-priori* argument is very simple and intelligible. No evidence to the contrary is entitled to the slightest consideration. . . . If the *a-priori* argument be valid, all personal deficiency must have been miraculously supplied. There can be no failure of memory or lack of information . . ., no inapt quotation, no dialectic flaw." But he will have none of it. "This beautiful conception must be abandoned." "It must be confirmed by other than *a-priori* reasoning." This is the only proper method: "We shall then be prepared to produce a definition *a posteriori*, reasoning from the effect to its cause, from the consequent to the antecedent, from the revelation that lies before us in the Bible to the principle and method of the originating divine activity" (*What Is Inspiration?* pp. 9, 12, 42.)

Is any particular passage true? The obscurantists say: Since it is inspired, it is true. But "there are not a few passages in the Bible which cannot be regarded by Protestants as in any true sense inspired," declares Hastings, *Encyclopedia*, VII, p. 346. "After a free and fair investigation," applying the *a-posteriori* method, these many passages have been found to be mere human, false statements. "Protestant scholars of the present day, imbued with the scientific spirit, have no *a-priori* theory of the inspiration of the Bible. They do not open any book of the Old and the New Testament with the feeling that they are bound to regard its teaching as sacred and authoritative." And Prof. T. A. Kantonen tells us that, because we fail to apply the *a-posteriori* method, great portions of Holy Scripture become useless to us; we fail to find the truth that shall be revealed to those who reject the story as it is told in Scripture as true. "Relying upon the theory of the verbal inspiration of the Bible, rejecting *a priori* the results of constructive historical criticism, the adherents of this approach have regarded the stories of the Temptation and the Fall as mere historical narratives rather than profound prophetic philosophy of history." (*Luth. Church Quart.*, July, 1935, p. 211.)

Now, do we plead guilty to the charge of apriorism? We certainly do; only we have no sense of guilt about the matter. We are apriorists all along the line. On the general question: Does the Christian accept the Bible as the inspired Word of God because the Bible teaches us that it is inspired or does he accept it as such only after a thorough scientific investigation and demonstration? Theo. Kaftan, speaking for himself and the men just quoted, says: "We do not regard as authoritative what Scripture teaches concerning itself, but our judgment of what is the divine truth is based on the impression which Scripture makes upon us (insofern die Schrift sich bei uns 'durchsetzt')." (See Pieper, *op. cit.*, p. 362.) Dr. Stoeckhardt makes this answer: "What Scripture says con-

cerning itself, its nature and origin, settles the matter for us."
(*Lehre und Wehre,* 32, p. 280.) Dr. Stoeckhardt is an apriorist, and
so are we. And we are thoroughgoing apriorists. The special
question: Is a given statement in Scripture true? finds, for us, its
answer in the general statement of Scripture: All Scripture is true.
In approaching any Bible difficulty our mind is made up from the
start: this passage is absolutely true. There may be difficulties
about it, but the question: Is it true? does not present any difficulties to us. Dr. De Witt represents us as saying in this case:
"No evidence to the contrary is entitled to the slightest consideration." Yes, we do say that, only that we say in addition: There
can be no evidence to the contrary. We know *a priori* that
any "evidence" to the contrary that may be adduced is false. And
when Dr. Kantonen charges us with "rejecting *a priori* the results
of constructive historical criticism," we only ask to amend it by
substituting "destructive" for "constructive."

Dr. J. W. Horine is dumbfounded when he hears us say such
things. Reviewing Dr. W. Arndt's book *Bible Difficulties;* "an
Examination of the Passages of the Bible Alleged to Be Irreconcilable with Its Inspiration," he says: "Naturally, the author is a
Fundamentalist, his viewpoint being that of the absolute inspiration
and verbal inerrancy of the Bible in all its parts, which is the
position of the Evangelical Lutheran Missouri Synod. The examination proceeds, and the conclusion is drawn, from the two premises:
Every single statement of Scripture is literally true; the reader
of Scripture must have faith enough to believe it to be true." (*The
Lutheran,* July 28, 1932.) Yes, we take that position.

And we cannot take any other position. It is the only position
befitting the Christian theologian. Let the Unitarians say: "No
statement can be accepted as true because it is in the Bible" (see
Popular Symbolics, p. 402), the Christian theologian cannot say it.
He cannot thus dishonor his Bible. He holds Holy Scripture in
such honor that he firmly believes that not one of the holy writers
ever erred (Augustine), and he holds Holy Scripture in such honor
that he accepts all and any of its statements without demanding
further proof. What, tell Scripture to step aside for a while and call
in some puny historian or scientist and, after hearing his verdict,
tell Scripture: "Now I can accept your statement"? No, no; with
the Christian it is axiomatic: "The Scriptures cannot err. . . .
It is certain that Scripture cannot disagree with itself." "For it is
established by God's Word that God does not lie, nor does His
Word lie." (Luther, XX: 798.) But that is apriorism — God's Word
cannot lie because God's Word says it cannot lie! Of course it is,
and the Christian cannot be anything but an apriorist in this
matter. A Christian is one who believes God's Word; how, then,

can he demand that before he gives credence to any statement of God's Word, its truth must first be established by some other authority? The *ipse dixit* of Scripture suffices for the Christian.

"Philippi had not yet 'attained the Christian attitude towards Scripture when he wrote the words 'One dare not *from the outset* refuse to grant the possibility of the occurrence of minor discrepancies. . . . We therefore would not like to declare with Calov, at least not *a priori:* "No error, even in unimportant matters, no lapse of memory, . . . can anywhere occur in Scripture." ' But he took the right position, the only one befitting a Christian, when he retracted this statement in the third edition of his *Glaubenslehre* and declared Calov's *a-priori* position to be the correct one." (Pieper, *op. cit.,* I, p. 339.) — In the preface to his book *The Modern Use of the Bible,* a book dealing with the many "mistakes" of the Bible, H. E. Fosdick says: "The position represented in this book will of course be distasteful to those bound by a theory of literal inerrancy in their approach to the Bible." Fosdick is right. But he might have used a stronger word than "distasteful." We abominate and hate that approach to the Bible which operates with the possibility of errors in the Bible. And he is right again when he speaks of us as being "bound." We no longer approach Scripture with the "open mind" of the Unitarian, who claims the liberty to accept or reject so much of Scripture as his critical investigation permits or compels him to do. We are "bound," bound by the *a-priori* attitude that "Scripture cannot be broken."

It is a holy bondage. We are bondsmen of Scripture. That is to say that God has bound us. He requires us to accept His Word without questioning. And it is a willing bondage. It is nothing to be ashamed of. Man does not degrade himself by submitting his judgment to the judgment of the Lord God Almighty. And we would not want it otherwise. It is the only safe position to take. We close our eyes and blindly follow the lead of Scripture. Scripture will never deceive us. Following the lead of your critical investigations, you will go astray. We want to remain bondsmen of Holy Scripture.

This attitude is distasteful to Fosdick and the Unitarians and the moderns. They say it is based on prejudice, which does not permit a fair impartial judgment. They speak of our judgments as being biased and warped, they speak of assumptions and prepossessions and partisanship. Well, we are partisans of Scripture, uncompromising partisans. It is impossible for us to be unbiased in this matter. We should consider it sinful not to take the side of Scripture at once. Open mind? Our mind is made up, before the discussion on any passage opens, that Scripture is right and the critics are wrong. In fact, we do not allow any discussion. This is a matter which is not debatable. The apriorists, thank God, are not open to argument. They are a stubborn lot.[19]

In secular affairs, where men deal with men, we are not so stubborn. There we have an open mind. The juryman dare not make up his mind beforehand. He must first examine the evidence produced. It would be dishonest, immoral in the highest degree, if the judge permitted his preconceived opinion to affect his conduct of the trial. We have no use for prejudiced judges. Moreover, we do not open any book written by man with the idea that we are going to subscribe to all of its statements. We do not accept the pronouncement of the philosopher and the finding of the scientist and the judgment of the historian on their mere say-so. They must substantiate their *dicta* by irrefutable proof. But we dare not ask God and God's Book to submit to the same treatment. It is a wicked thing when the Unitarians and the other liberals place God's Book on a level with men's books — both subject to man's criticism. That was a horrible statement we quoted above: "As faith and science *alike* must do." Science is based on induction; faith accepts the *dictum* of God. N. R. Best says: "Predetermination of the outcome takes the honesty out of any inquiry." (*Op. cit.,* p. 131.) That applies where men deal with men, but it does not apply where God's Book is concerned, and just there Best applies it. On the preceding page (130) he declared that those who accept the miracle stories of the Bible as true take a wrong position when they say: "Whatever is told in this book you must believe just because it is found there." He has forgotten the fine statement

---

19) This apriorism is nothing strange in Christianity. It is ingrained in the very faith of the Christian. On no point of the Christian faith are we open to argument. We do not argue the articles of the Christian faith but we assert them. We would lose them if we awaited the assent of reason, logic, science. The right attitude, safe for us and profitable for the unbeliever, is expressed in "the admirable axiom of Dr. C. F. Deems: 'Believe your beliefs and doubt your doubts. Do not make the common mistake of the skeptics, doubting your beliefs and believing your doubts.'" (Quoted in *Many Infallible Proofs,* by A. T. Pierson, p. 26.) Pierson continues: "Or as Goethe says again: 'Give us your convictions; as for doubts, we have enough of them already.'" You do not serve the unbeliever by taking a wobbling position on any question concerning the Christian faith. — It is a pity that men know this principle but refuse to apply it in the matter of Inspiration. N. R. Best cannot believe in Verbal Inspiration and the inerrancy of Scripture because he insists on applying the *a-posteriori* method, and this same writer states that, in appraising the qualities of Scripture, he proceeds "on the *frank assumption* that a revelation of God has become an actuality in the volume of the Bible" and that this "assumption is of course a *premise of faith,* rather than a conclusion of logic. Even if occasion permitted the matter to be argued, argument would never demonstrate it. The ways of God, like the being of God, transcend syllogisms" (*Inspiration,* p. 12). And this assumption is created in us by God. Through Scripture He has established in us this premise of faith. The *a-priori* certainty is God's work and gift.

he made on page 12, concerning the "premise of faith." He has so completely forgotten the truth that faith is above reason that he can write on page 130: "If we have been at all right in arguing that the Bible is not only lawfully open to the investigations of human reason but is divinely calculated to invoke (even provoke) such investigation. . . ." Predetermination of the outcome takes the honesty out of any inquiry as between man and man, but the refusal to take the bare word of Scripture for establishing the truth of its statements dishonors God and disgraces the Christian.

Just by the way, why should the moderns indulge in such violent harangues against the wrong of *a-priori* reasoning, denouncing our attitude as due to prejudice and bias, when they are indeed guilty of this very thing? The liberals are unable to approach the Bible with an open mind. They approach it *with the preconceived opinion* that it is a human book, subject to errors. They meet its claim that it is God's Book *with suspicion*. They set up the *premise* that they know as much about these things as Scripture. They oppose to the premise of faith the premise of unbelief. They oppose the *ipse dixit* of Scripture with the *ipse dixit* of their own reason. H. M'Intosh hits it off pretty well when he writes: "If it should seem that I have severely handled any writers, it is only those who have roughly handled the Word of God and wrongly condemned the inspired writers, . . . who denounce every independent man that, after the example and on the authority of Christ and of His inspired apostles, would dare to uphold the Bible claim or to differ from the false but *oracular assertions* or to refuse to accept the *infallible ipse dixit* of those presumptuous speculators who are vain enough to *claim* for *their own crude, ephemeral productions what they deny to the oracles of God* and to the very words of even the Son of God." (*Op. cit.*, p. IX. — Italics ours.) Read the article by Prof. J. J. Reeve on "The Presuppositions of the Higher Criticism" in *Fundamentals*, III, p. 98 ff. "These presuppositions and assumptions are the determining elements in the entire movement. . . . It is their philosophy or worldview that is responsible for all their speculation and theories. . . . These presuppositions appealed to me very strongly. . . . But upon closer thinking I saw that the whole movement with its conclusions was the result of the *adoption of the hypothesis* of evolution. . . . The use of the Redactor is a case in point. This purely imaginary being, unhistorical and unscientific, is brought into requisition at almost every difficulty. . . . Their minds seem to be in abject slavery to their theory. Their mental attitude being biased and partial, their methods are partial and the results very one-sided and untrustworthy. . . . *They feel instinctively* that to accept the Bible statements would be the ruin of their hypothesis." That certainly is apriorism of the deepest dye!

It was in connection with the question of the reality of the miracles recounted in the Bible that Best charged us with "predetermining the result of the inquiry." Well, Ph. Schaff tells these people: "The reality of the miracles cannot be disposed of by a simple denial from *a-priori* philosophical prejudice." (*Hist. of the Chr. Church,* I, p. 859.) And this is what Philippi tells them: "The furious search for discrepancies is due primarily to the wicked attitude of the moderns, which boasts of having cut out all assumptions and presuppositions (Voraussetzungslosigkeit); they claimed the right to cut loose from the presupposition that Holy Scripture is the Word of God. In place of that, however, they sat down in the temple of God and *presupposed that they were God.*" (See Pieper, *op. cit.,* p. 291.) Professor Reeve adds this: "When one makes his philosophy his authority, it is not a long step until he makes himself his own god. His own reason becomes supreme in his thinking, and this reason becomes his lord." (*Fundamentals,* III, p. 113.)

The moderns, too, as we have just seen, are apriorists. That does not in itself prove that *our a-priori* reasoning is right. But we mentioned it for two reasons. We thought it might cause them to moderate their voice a bit when they are denouncing *our* apriorism. And it gives us occasion to point out that the "assumption" that there can be no errors in the Bible differs *toto coelo* from the assumption that reason has a voice in determining the truth of a given Scripture-passage. The first is a good thing, demanded by God and created by God in us. The other is a wicked thing. It springs from the wicked pride of reason.

One more remark on the subject of the apriorism of the Bible Christian. None but a believer can take this position. We take it because the Bible assures us, and God thereby creates in us the assurance, that the Bible cannot err. One who does not believe that the Bible is God's Word and that every word of the Bible is God's truth cannot agree with us. He cannot but denounce our position as unreasonable and untenable. It is hopeless to argue with him. But we did not set out to argue with him. Our sole purpose, at the present time, is to point out to the Christian that it should be impossible for him to speak of, and think of, errors in the Bible. The vehement asseverations of the moderns to the contrary ought not to make any impression on us. The fact that they cannot grasp our argument must not lead us to doubt the certainty of our position. The attitude of the Christian must be that he meets all objections with the stubborn *a-priori* argument: The Scriptures cannot err. The professor of science may say to the Christian: "The Bible? Why, I didn't suppose that any intelligent person today believed the Bible!" "Oh, yes," answers the Christian with assurance, "I believe it all. You see *I know*

the Author." [20)]   The skeptic cannot say that. But do not permit
his doubts and subtleties to shake *your* assurance. Believe your
beliefs — they are based on God's Word — and doubt your doubts!

The skeptic does not know what to make of such an attitude.
Dr. G. A. Buttrick, president of the Federal Council for 1940, says
the thing is incredible. "Probably few people who claim to 'believe
every word of the Bible' really mean it. That avowal, held to its
last logic, would risk a trip to the insane asylum." (*The Christian
Fact and Modern Doubt*, 1935.) Well, we are of those — and they
are not just a few — who believe every word of the Bible, and
we really mean it. We shall say it as long as we retain our Christian sanity. Sane faith cannot speak otherwise. Faith is the
product of God's Word, and "the faith produced by the Word is
divinely convinced that the Word, every word of Scripture, is the
divine truth" (*Conc. Theol. Monthly*, XI, p. 809).

Faith Repels Rationalism

Faith listens to the voice of God speaking through Holy
Scripture. It will listen to no other voice. *It will not listen to
the voice of rationalism.* It is rationalism which denies the absolute
inerrancy of Scripture, and when the Christian listens to this voice,
he disgraces himself.

We have already pointed out that the rationalist refuses to
trust the bare word of Scripture and must necessarily take the
a-posteriori position. Let us discuss this point more in detail.
We say that the rejection of Verbal, Plenary Inspiration and the
denial of the absolute inerroneousness of Scripture springs from
rationalistic considerations. We say that these men set reason
above Scripture. *We* do not have to say it. They say it themselves.
The Unitarian who told us: "No statement can be accepted as
true because it is in the Bible," proceeds to tell us: "All its teachings must be subjected to the authority of reason and conscience."
Voltaire tells us that he cannot accept the accounts "of God's
strange and supernatural dealings with the Israelites in Egypt and
in the desert" because "they are revolting to reason." (See
D. MacDill, *The Mosaic Authority of the Pentateuch*, p. 15.) [21)]
And it is not only the Unitarian, the rationalist, and Voltaire, the
scoffer, who champion the rights of reason. J. De Witt, too, insists
that reason has the right to correct Scripture. "If, besides the
divine truth that Scripture embodies, it also contains partial truths,
which are sometimes as misleading as falsehood, and moral incon-

---

20) Margaret Bottome gave that answer. See *Lutheran Annual*,
1941, p. 25.

21) E. Lewis: "The motto of rationalism may be said to be: 'Prove
all that you believe by what you indubitably know.'" (*A Philosophy
of the Christian Revelation*, p. 147.)

gruities and monstrosities from which our souls recoil, how shall I separate the gold from the dross? By the use of my reason? Would you have me become a rationalist? Yes, rather than be a sophist or a simpleton, if one becomes a rationalist by making use of his reason, including conscience and every spiritual faculty with which God has endowed him, strengthened and enlightened by the word, and life, and spirit of Christ. . . . Our enlightened moral instinct rejects it" ("the old inspiration") "unreservedly and forever." (*What Is Inspiration?* P. 179 f.) The liberals say with Walter M. Horton: "To rely upon revelation apart from other truth is as bad as to rely upon prayer apart from action or upon providence apart from intelligent forethought. Revelation is no substitute for reason. If reason without revelation is blind, revelation without reason is a dazzling, unintelligible light. What Matthew Arnold said years ago about the *homo unius libri* still holds good: the man who knows only Scripture does not even know Scripture. . . . There are some ancient misunderstandings about revelation which do not seriously threaten us at present, after the debates of the last half century. We are not likely again to identify God's eternal Word with the Book which contains the record of its revealing, or to insist that everything in that Book is infallibly correct and verbally inspired. We are not likely to suppose that the authority of revelation extends into the sphere of fact and law, where natural science is supreme." (Article in *Revelation,* 1937, p. 263 f.)

Why, they even tell us that Scripture inculcates the principles of rationalism and asks us to run its statements through the crucible of reason. S. P. Cadman: "The authority of the Bible is established by divine revelation, but it is also addressed to human intelligence. The Book itself invokes finite reason and appeals to its decisions. . . . Plainly, the Scriptures do not outlaw man's judgment on their contents. Why should we do so?" (*Answers to Every-Day Questions,* p. 258.) And N. R. Best, who writes on "The Mirage of Inerrancy," gives chapter and verse for that statement. "Utterly vain is it to talk of not employing reason on the Bible. . . . When did the Creator ever brand man's reason as unholy — unfit to handle the sacred things of either His deeds or His words? . . . Every page of the Bible might be justly inscribed with the invitation which stands in living letters *on the first page of the Prophet Isaiah:* 'Come now and let us reason together, saith Jehovah.' Reason is God's joy — not His 'black beast.'" (*Inspiration,* p. 117 f.)

A voice from Germany. Baumgaertel: "The refusal to recognize the physical sciences" (as censor of the scientific statements of the Bible) "bars the way to the church for the educated classes. Do not ask the educated man to bring this *sacrificium intellectus.*

He cannot and must not do that." (See Moeller, *Um die Inspiration der Bibel*, p. 35.) A voice from America. R. T. Stamm, Gettysburg, calls this a "false dilemma," an " 'either-or' fallacy": "either submission to the authority of the Scriptures or the assertion of the proud pretensions of human reason," and thus elaborates his thesis: "We must never forget that it is impossible to construct a systematic theology without employing the same human reason which too many of our writers have tried to deprive of all validity at the outset! And such writers are often the proudest of men, claiming to boast only in the Lord, while their self-confident assurance in the completeness and finality of their own dogmatic construction of revelation equals or excels the 'pride' of the most arrogant humanistic or communistic opponents of religion, who call upon the name of reason and modern science to justify *their* dogmatism.[22] It is not a question of revelation or reason, but of revelation given, received, interpreted, and applied through the human reason which is energized and guided by the Spirit of God." (*Luth. Church Quart.*, April, 1940, pp. 124, 129.)

You cannot insult these men — those who operate in the name of reason alone and those who operate in the name of reason *and* revelation; those who appeal to plain reason and those who appeal to "enlightened" reason (see De Witt and Stamm) — by calling them rationalists. When MacDill (*op. cit.*, p. 22) says: "It is true indeed that the leaders among them [the higher critics], those who have thought out their hypotheses to their logical conclusions, are *thoroughgoing rationalists* — veritable infidels, but they prefer not to be recognized as such, at least for the present," they will take exception to "veritable infidels," but not to the phrase "thoroughgoing rationalists." They will tell him: You are right, and we are proud of the title; we only deplore that the rest of our rationalistic brethren are less consistent than we are.

This applies also to the "conservative" theologians who feel bound to reject Verbal, Plenary Inspiration because their study of science and history has convinced them that the Bible abounds in errors.[23] They are not, indeed, "thoroughgoing rationalists."

---

22) We might have omitted this sentence as not touching our immediate subject. But we wanted to give Dr. Stamm a chance to tell us as plainly as he could what he thinks of the *a-priori* theologians, the verbalists.

23) See pertinent statements on this matter, p. 7 ff. Here are some more: "Isolated facts in the statements of Scripture must be corrected by science." (E. Brunner, *The Mediator*, p. 167.) "With the sacred historians the record of fact as fact and apart from its significance in the unfolding of the divine purpose is something very secondary and subordinate. . . . I know of nothing which should isolate them" (these narratives) "and prevent us from judging them as we should other similar narratives." (W. Sanday, *The Oracles of God*, p. 68 f.) — It is sometimes most difficult to decide where to draw the line between "conservative" and liberal theologians.

They do not find as many errors as the plain-reason men and the enlightened-reason men. But they apply the same basic principle. They permit science and history (their knowledge of science and history) and *their* judgment of what is right and proper to correct Scripture. But that is a form of rationalism. We might even say that it is the heart of the creed of rationalism. The case of the conservatives is correctly diagnosed in a letter written by a theologian in Germany to one of them: "You point to contradictions which you cannot solve with your reason, acknowledging at the same time that you realize the limitations of your knowledge. I am in the same case. . . . You take, in spite of the fact that you recognize the limitations and insufficiency of your knowledge, *a rationalistic position;* I, because I dare not trust the judgment of my limited reason in divine matters, submit to the judgment of my Lord and Master Jesus Christ. With you it is a matter of reason, with me a matter of faith." (See *Lehre und Wehre,* 69, p. 305.) Pieper also diagnoses it as a case of the rationalistic disease (*op. cit.,* p. 295). So does M'Intosh: "All theories of indefinite erroneousness legitimately tend to, and naturally end in, rationalism, or the supremacy of reason over revelation. . . . I know that many who hold the less pronounced views of the erroneousness of Scripture will strongly object to be in this respect classified with avowed rationalists and infidels. . . . Nevertheless, it is shown that, however much they may differ from these in many important matters and though they hold with us the core of the Christian faith, yet in this vital and radical matter, which underlies all the other matters, there is no essential difference; that *they are all radically the same in their rationalistic principle;* and that there is no possible resting-place for any clear and thoroughgoing mind between holding the thorough truthfulness, entire trustworthiness, and divine authority of all Scripture and holding explicitly or implicitly the supremacy of reason over revelation." (*Op. cit.,* pp. 29, 38.)

And here is Walther's diagnosis: "If the possibility that Scripture contained the least error were admitted, it would become the business of *man* to sift the truth from the error. . . . The least deviation from the old inspiration doctrine introduces a *rationalistic germ* into theology and infects the whole body of doctrine." (*Walther and the Church,* p. 14.)

"If the *possibility* that Scripture contained the least error were admitted . . ." — that leads us to examine the theological principle of those theologians who are ready to admit that Scripture contains no known error but are reluctant to teach that Scripture *cannot possibly contain* errors. Those theologians who carry around with them long or short lists of alleged errors in Scripture are badly infected with rationalism. But those theologians, too, who find themselves unable to teach the absolute inerrancy of Scripture in all of its statements until science and history, etc., have demonstrated the truth of all of these statements, are suffering with rationalism, with incipient rationalism.

There are theologians, of the conservative group, who refuse to say that Scripture cannot possibly make erroneous statements. We have already mentioned the case of Philippi, who at one time said: "One dare not from the outset refuse to grant the possibility of the occurrence of minor discrepancies." O. Bensow: "We do not know of a single case where it has been conclusively shown that an error has crept in, while we do know of many cases where the alleged error was proved to be the truth." But he adds: "In these peripheral regions errors *might possibly* have occurred, due to the fact that the writers retained their human auto-activity." (*Die Bibel — das Wort Gottes.*) Meusel: "Most of the alleged contradictions and errors may be and have been solved. But a small residuum remains which makes it impossible for us to maintain, after the aprioristic-absolute manner of our old dogmaticians, the literal inerrancy of Scripture and to say: *Nullus error vel in leviculis.* . . . If it should be shown that a geographical mistake had been made or that Matthew's memory was at fault (27:9), that would not destroy the divine and inspired nature of Holy Scripture." (*Kirchl. Handlex., s. v.* Irrtumslosigkeit.) W. Sanday speaks in a similar strain: "If it should be proved that the Law, as we have it, was not written by Moses or that the 110th Psalm was not written by David. . . ." (*Op. cit.,* p. 109.) [24]

"If it should be shown . . .!" These men are living in constant fear that the inerrancy of Scripture might be disproved — by whom? By the scientists and the historians and the philosophers, etc. They are afraid that Scripture cannot hold its own against human scholarship and wisdom. And so they look to human scholarship to *establish* the claim of Scripture to plenary inerrancy. There is something else besides Scripture on which they base their belief in the truthfulness of Scripture, and basing it on the findings of science and the assent of reason is — subtle rationalism. The *Journal of the American Lutheran Conference,* Dec., 1938, says: "*How can we know* the human framework of the Bible is true — the history, the geography, the biography, the science . . . ?

---

24) H. M'Intosh, too, shies at "absolute inerrancy." "That most extreme and unwarrantable, if not unintelligible, title 'the absolute inerrancy' of Scripture"; "the narrow, negative, and at least questionable ground of absolute inerrancy" (*op. cit.,* pp. 14, 442). At the same time he declares: "Even the extremest position of absolute inerrancy is not destitute of an apology, and may offer a valid and apparently irrefutable defense." (P. 21.)

We not only may but we must study these things critically, *to see if the Bible statements are supported or contradicted by known facts from other sources. . . .* It is my growing conviction that it is possible to arrive at a *reasonable* faith in the substantial truthfulness of the human framework of the Bible." (Italics ours.) This Lutheran theologian is not satisfied with the bare statement of Scripture. His faith calls upon critical investigation and human wisdom to help out the Bible. He wants a "reasonable" faith. (See *Conc. Theol. Mthly.,* XI, p. 812.) This is certainly a rationalistic aberration. Men who admit the possibility of errors in Scripture and thus make it the business of man to sift the truth from error and to establish the truth of Scripture are, as Walther said, introducing a rationalistic germ into theology. It is a case of incipient rationalism. If that is not checked, it will develop into the virulent form.

It is rationalism which, as we have shown, denies the absolute inerrancy of Scripture and its corollary, Verbal, Plenary Inspiration. And now we say: When the Christian listens to the voice of rationalism, he disgraces himself. It is unworthy of the Christian to have dealings with such a wicked thing as rationalism.

The wickedness consists, first, in this, that rationalism is engaged in a criminal business. Scripture has outlawed its business. God's Word commands us to "bring into captivity every thought to the obedience of Christ" (2 Cor. 10:5) and to accept Scripture, every statement of Scripture, as God's truth, as authoritative and binding. Carnal reason, however, refuses to do this. It claims supreme authority for its own judgments. It assumes the right to criticize and correct Scripture. And the Christian should find it impossible to listen to the voice of rationalism for one moment. The Christian stands in holy awe of Scripture, the Word of his God and Savior, and shudders at the bare thought of speaking one word against it. He loves Scripture, in which he has eternal life, and burns in holy wrath against those who call its truthfulness in question. When Satan asks him to forsake Scripture and follow reason, he cries out: How can I do this great wickedness and keep company with "Satan's paramour" (Luther, XX:232)? The Christian will not be seen in the company of her who speaks in dishonor of Holy Scripture. If he listens to such a voice, he dishonors himself.

Hear Walther again: "If the possibility that Scripture contained the least error were admitted, it would become the business of man to sift the truth from the error. That places man over Scripture. . . . Human reason is made the *norma* of truth, and *Scripture is degraded* to the position of a *norma normata.*" Carnal reason delights in degrading Scripture. And the Christian, who trembles at God's Word, is horrified when he finds that his flesh, too, holds Scripture in derision.

The Christian should find it impossible to listen to these criticisms and corrections of Scripture because, in the second place, they spring from carnal pride. Pride, arrogance, conceit, is a wicked thing at all times, under any form. That already is wicked pride when men, because of their superiority, real or fancied, speak contemptuously of the others. But when they assume the right to criticize and correct Scripture, they have reached the limit of conceit and arrogance. We shall not say much of the former case. We can easily bear it when these men look down upon us as pre-Kantian obscurantists and call us verbalists, who, as De Witt puts it, cannot take an *"intelligent* view of inspiration" (*op. cit.,* p. 17). We cannot bear it so well when he speaks contemptuously of "the Reformers, who knew nothing of the refinements of exegetical science" (p. 18).[25] But we cannot bear it at all when, in speaking of the Old Testament writers, he says: "We, who have attained *higher forms* in the world-wide schoolroom of the great Instructor of men" (p. 182).

That is insufferable conceit, wickedness beyond expression, when men presume to censor, revise, rectify and improve Scripture. De Witt and all the other critics, liberal and conservative, claim to know more about certain things than the Biblical writers. But what does that mean? Assuming the right to correct Scripture, that, says Walther, "places man over Scripture." [26] And that really means, it places man over — God. The critics may repudiate this charge on the plea that they have found that these portions of Scripture which they eliminate are *not* God's Word. But God is telling them that every word of Scripture *is* His word; and

---

25) The judgment of Dr. H. R. Mackintosh is not quite so coarse, but equally unacceptable. "It does not seem as if the Reformers (who had many other pressing questions to work at) quite realized where the new evangelical thought of Scripture was to lead or what it implied for exact Biblical study. . . . It ought to be said frankly that Luther often clings to the older notion of a verbally inspired Bible. He actually speaks of the Holy Spirit as the *Author* of the books of Moses; he submitted his judgment undoubtingly to Scriptural statements on points of natural science. . . . The same is true of Calvin. . . . This was obviously bound to lead to conclusions which in a Christian writer are strange and unwelcome." (Written for *The Doctrine of the Infallible Book,* by Charles Gore, p. 58.)

26) Walther again, as quoted in *Proceedings, Iowa District,* 1897, p. 36: "The eighth thesis of Superintendent Kier emphatically states that 'it has not pleased God to perform the miracle of having His witnesses speak and write inerrantly.' It thus asserts that what the prophets and apostles preached was shot through with errors and — oh, what Satanic pride! — that the preachments of the moderns which separate the pure Word of God in Scripture from — what blasphemy! — the rubbish, are much better than the discourses of the prophets and apostles."

whether they believe it or not, it remains God's Word, and whether they realize it or not, they are disputing the truth of *God's* Word. They are setting themselves above God. "Self-deification" — that is a hard saying. But here strong words have to be used. Philippi used them: "They presupposed that they were God." Professor Reeve used them: "When one makes his philosophy his authority, it is not a long step until he makes himself his own god." M'Intosh used them. Speaking of "the old and fatal issues of the common rationalistic principle, namely, that every varying man must become a judge and authoritative standard himself," he says: "Having got rid of an infallible Bible and an infallible Christ, he must reach the supreme absurdity — an infallible self, 'Lord of himself that heritage of woe,' as Byron says" (*op. cit.*, p. 32), self-deification. What we say about these men is what they say about themselves. The old rationalist Loeffler said: "Our reason is manifestly God in us." (See *Conc. Theol. Mthly.*, XI, p. 322.) The First Unitarian Church in Cleveland said on its bulletin-board: "Man is greater than any of the Scriptures." (See *Lutheran Witness*, LX, p. 5.) And if you say that a certain statement of Scripture is not true because your knowledge of science says so, you are committing self-deification. Can a Christian, in his sober mind, declare that a certain statement of Scripture contains a discrepancy because his knowledge of science says so?

Now, self-conceited pride and Christianity do not go together. The spirit of the Christian is humble. Particularly in dealing with Scripture he effaces himself. He is nothing; Scripture is everything. If he cannot solve a contradiction, it does not take him long to put the blame on his ignorance. If he cannot square Scripture with science, he puts the blame on his ignorance and the ignorance of the learned scientist. Augustine was a humble Christian and said: "If I come across a passage which seems to conflict with the truth, I do not doubt for a moment that either the copyist or the translator made a mistake or that *I may not have understood the matter.* It would be a sin to have doubts respecting the inerrancy of the apostles and prophets." (Quoted in Moeller, *op. cit.*, p. 56. See also Luther, XV: 1481.) Luther was a humble Christian and declared: "When Moses writes that God made heaven and earth and all that is in them in six days, let the six days stand. . . . If you cannot understand how it could have been six days" (or how the ax-head could float or the fish swallow Jonah), "then accord to the Holy Spirit the honor that He is more learned than you." (III, p. 21.) Luther was a humble Christian; and when he found that he could not straighten out the chronology of Scripture on a certain point ("Bei Abraham verlieren sich sechzig Jahre"), he would not side with "those rash men who in the case of a Bible difficulty are not afraid to say that Scripture is evidently wrong," but said: "I conclude the matter with a humble confession of my ignorance, for it is only the Holy Ghost who knows and understands everything." (I:721.)   God looks for such an attitude in the Christians. Philip Schaff: "The holy awe of Scripture, the sense of its awful majesty (which we more or less miss in the entire Schleiermacher-school) requires that in cases where our knowledge is not able to clear up the difficulty we humbly bring every thought into captivity to the obedience of Christ." (*Geschichte der Apostolischen Kirche.* See Pieper, *op. cit.,* p. 294.) James Bannerman: The rationalist "comes to the Bible and sits over its contents in the attitude of a judge who is to decide for himself what in it is true and worthy to be believed, . . . not in the attitude of the disciple who within the limits of the inspired record feels himself at Jesus' feet to receive every word that cometh out of His mouth." (See B. Manly, *The Bible Doctrine of Inspiration,* p. 16.)   Which attitude will you take?

When a man charges Scripture with unsolvable contradictions and errors, put that down to his self-conceit. It is the part of Christian humility to put the failure to solve the Bible difficulties down to your own limitations and insufficiencies. Long ago Origen said: "If ever, in reading the Scriptures, you happen to stumble on some thought which becomes to thee a stone of stumbling and a rock of offense, *blame none but thyself;* doubt not that this stone of stumbling and rock of offense has some great meaning. . . . When you have been unable to find the reason for that which is written, blame not the holy letters; lay the blame on thyself alone." (See L. Gaussen, *Theopneustia,* p. 327 f.)

De Witt cries out: "Would you have me become a rationalist? Yes, rather than be a simpleton." Luther declares: "We must become fools, complete fools (simpletons) in Christ." (XVIII: 39.) The Christian, in his sober mind, declares himself for Luther, against the rationalist. He is not ashamed of being a simpleton in the eyes of the wise philosopher. He is ashamed of the foolish pride of his rationalizing flesh.

The Christian cannot bear to hear men talking about the mistakes in the Bible, for, in the third place, he is a believer, and the talk about the mistakes in the Bible is plain unbelief. Unbelief — that is a harsh word. Indeed it is; it denotes the greatest crime of which man is capable. But this talk about being unable to accept Verbal, Plenary Inspiration because of suspected errors in the Bible is the voice of unbelief, plain, common unbelief. When the rationalist Harnack declares that he cannot and will not believe that the sun stood still, and when the rationalist Fosdick declares that he finds some of the miracle-narratives of Scripture historically incredible (see quotations, p. 12 f.), conservative theologians are horrified at such ebullitions of unbelief. But when these same conservatives insist that they have found many discrepancies and erroneous statements in the Bible and therefore cannot believe, teach, and confess that all Scripture is given by inspiration, they, too, are, on this point, rationalists, unbelievers. Scripture plainly states that "all Scripture is given by inspiration of God." *They* say: Not all of Scripture is inspired. This particular statement we cannot believe. Scripture states: "Scripture cannot be broken." No, no; we cannot believe that statement to its full extent. "Thy Word is truth." Not absolutely and in all respects, say the conservative rationalists. A thousand times Scripture says that the writings of the prophets and apostles are God's own Word. And the conservative rationalists say a thousand times that they can no longer, at this time and age, teach verbalism. Are they, on this point, believers or unbelievers?

How often must God say a thing so as to get men to say the same thing? Can God say more plainly than He has said that God spoke by and through the prophets and that the Holy Spirit gave the apostles utterance? And when the rationalists say that they cannot accept Verbal Inspiration, could they say more plainly that they are, on this point, unbelievers? Prof. James B. Green says: "The Law and the Prophets, the teaching of Jesus and the preaching of Paul, these are declared to be the Word of God. It has been estimated that the Bible in various ways asserts its own inspiration some three thousand times. How often does the Bible have to say a thing before men will believe it?" (*Studies on the Holy Spirit*, p. 49. See *Bibliotheca Sacra*, Vol. 97, p. 417.)

Luther cries out in holy wrath: "But it is cursed unbelief (der verfluchte Unglaube) and the odious flesh which will not permit us to see and know that God speaks to us in Scripture and that it is God's Word, but tells us that it is the word merely of Isaiah, Paul, or some other mere man, who has not created heaven and earth." (IX: 1800.) And the Christian is filled with dismay when his flesh urges him to criticize Scripture and reject certain statements as incredible. How *can* the believer bring himself to accept the findings of rationalism, of unbelief? Here are two warring, irreconcilable principles. How can faith make appeasement with unbelief? The ideology of rationalism, which sits in judgment on God's Word and refuses to accept what some scientists tell us not to accept, is incompatible with the attitude of faith, which bows to Scripture and believes though it does not see. Let the rationalist conjure the believer by all that holy science and holy philosophy stands for, the believer should say and will finally say: "I believe *all* things which are written in the Law and the Prophets," Acts 24:14. I shall not permit any man to break any one of the words of my Lord.   •

Unbelief is, in truth, the sin of sins, odious to God and odious to the Christian. "Let us ever bear in mind that every one who denies the inspiration of Scripture is *eo ipso* a critic of Scripture, and one who criticizes Scripture — which, as God's Word, will not be criticized but *believed* — comes under the fearful judgment of God described in Matt. 11:25." "The same faith and obedience that is due to God is due to Scripture in all that it says. He who rejects or even only criticizes Scripture insults the Majesty of God. He is committing a *crimen laesae majestatis divinae.*" (Pieper, *op. cit.,* I, pp. 280, 371.)

All objections to the divine inspiration and the inerrancy of Scripture are unworthy of a Christian.

Other Characteristics of the Christian Attitude
The Shame of Rating Secular Writers Higher than the Holy Writers

It is unworthy of a Christian to charge Holy Scripture with errors. — It might be well to emphasize and elaborate some of the points touched upon in the preceding pages. First, it is unworthy of a Christian to let fallible men exercise authority over Scripture. It is a shameful thing for a Christian theologian to revise and correct Scripture on the authority of some historian or some professor of natural history. Theologians are doing just that. What about the statement of Mark that Herodias, the wife of Herod Antipas, had been the wife of Philip, the brother of Herod, Mark 6:17? Dr. Haussleiter of Greifswald (Lutheran) said: "Here, it seems, a historical error has crept in. Josephus, who was fully informed regarding the complicated relationships of the family of the Herodians, names *Herod* [a half-brother of Herod Antipas] as the first husband of Herodias. According to Josephus, Philip was the son-in-law [the husband of Salome] of Herodias and not her first husband." (See *Lehre und Wehre,* 53, p. 426.) So Josephus is a better authority than Mark, and Mark stands corrected. *The Expositor's Greek Testament* indicates the solution of this difficulty: "He, Herod [a half-brother of Herod Antipas], may of course have borne another name, such as Philip," but makes the fatal concession: *"Even if there be a slip,* it is a matter of small moment," etc. Wohlenberg, in Zahn's Commentary, operates in precisely the same way: "Entweder liegt hier bei Markus ein *verzeihlicher Irrtum* vor, oder jener erste Gemahl der Herodias hiess Herodes Philippus." According to these theologians the historical statement of Mark is either false or subject to doubt because of the greater or equal authority of a second-rate secular historian. — A similar case is discussed by Dr. J. C. Mattes in

Kirchliche Zeitschrift, 64, p. 553. He quotes from F. C. Grant's *The Gospel of the Kingdom:* "Mark's story of John's martyrdom (6:17-29), following his rebuke of Herod's unlawful marriage, does not contradict the statement of Josephus and may be accepted as an added detail explaining Herod's antagonism — though the tale has the features of a later legend, and a *motif* completely different from that of the account in Josephus," [27] and comments: "Apparently the gospels on occasion cannot be as reliable as the accounts of a secular historian, even those of one who handles his materials as apologetically as Josephus." Josephus is a *historian;* Mark tells a *tale,* a legend. — What was back of all the trouble about King Belshazzar? The old secular writers Berosus and Herodotus have a different name for the last ruler of the Babylonian kingdom. And Berosus and Herodotus are trustworthier than Daniel. — "Because Herodotus had written: 'There are no vineyards in Egypt,' and Plutarch had declared: 'Kings began to drink wine from the time of King Psammetichus,' the writer of Genesis 40 must be mistaken when he affirmed that the Pharaoh of Joseph's time drank wine." (*Bibliotheca Sacra,* Jan., 1941, p. 117. Other similar cases are recounted there.)

Is the arboriculturist a better authority in his field than Paul? Of course he is, says Dr. R. F. Stamm. The arboriculturist has the right to show that Paul slipped in Rom. 11:17 ff. Paul did not know much about the art of grafting. Having quoted a statement dealing with this matter, the Gettysburg professor comments: "This is an interesting suggestion and a possible explanation; but one has the feeling that Paul, the man of the city, is here involved in his usual difficulty when he attempts an illustration from nature or from agriculture." (*The Luth. Church Quart.,* 1935, p. 320.) On matters biological the word of the professor of biology counts for more than that of Moses or Paul. For, says Dr. A. Traver, "the Bible is not a text for biology or for chemistry." "Bible-writers wrote with the background of their age and scientific belief." (*The Lutheran,* 1939, May 10, Feb. 22.) What about natural history? Professor Baumgaertel says: "If you want information on natural-history matters, go to the natural-history authorities." (See W. Moeller *Um die Inspiration der Bibel,* p. 31.)

And so all along the line. The liberals declare: "Modern historical and literary criticism, not to mention 'science' generally, has rendered it [the doctrine of "the plenary verbal inspiration of Holy Scripture"] increasingly untenable." (*Christendom,* I, p. 243.)

---

27) Josephus, *Jewish Antiquities,* XVIII, 5: Herod feared that John's activities might stir up a revolt and for that reason executed him. Footnote in Demme's translation: "Der Evangelist gibt uns wohl die Ursache richtiger an, warum des edeln Taeufers Haupt fiel." (P. 508.)

And whén the conservative commissioners of the U. L. C. declared that they were "unable to accept the statement that the Scriptures are the infallible truth 'also in those parts which treat of historical, geographical, and other secular matters'" (*Minutes of the 1938 Convention of the U. L. C. A.,* p. 468), they declared that secular scholars are on some points more reliable than the sacred writers.

Must we, then, call in secular scholars to correct a given text before we preach from that text in our pulpits? The liberals of the extreme left are ready to do that. And we can understand why they can do that. They look upon the Bible as the product of men, subject to the criticism of men. Speaking for the liberals of the extreme left, R. Ingersoll declares: "We should read the Bible as we do every other book; and everything good in it, keep it; and everything that shocks the brain and shocks the heart, throw it away." (*Lectures of Col. R. J. Ingersoll,* p. 357.) Dr. Willett agrees with Ingersoll on this point. "These writings were not supernaturally produced" (*The Bible through the Centuries,* p. 254). These liberals feel justified in subjecting the Bible to the criticism and correction of the historian and the scientist. But how can he do it who believes that "all Scripture is given by inspiration of God"? We certainly are not going to tell our Bible class that, when Mark wrote that Herodias had been the wife of Philip, God permitted him to forget his history and to contradict the great historian Josephus. We are certainly not going to read the Christmas Gospel from our pulpit and tell our people that we shall have to omit verse 2 of Luke 2 because Luke blundered concerning Cyrenius, the Governor of Syria, and then tell them that the rest is Gospel-truth. Luther would not do it. Believing that "Scripture has never erred" and "cannot err," "that God does not lie nor does His Word lie" (XIX:1309; XV:1481; XX:798), he would not listen to any historian or any scientist whose story differed from that of the Bible. He studied the historians very closely; but: "I set Scripture above them. I make use of them in such a way that I am not compelled to contradict Scripture. For I believe that in Scripture the God of truth is speaking, but in the histories good people have done the best they could; they strove to be exact, but they were men! Or perhaps the copyists erred." (XIV: 491.) It is inconceivable how one who believes in Inspiration would want to charge Scripture with errors because certain learned men disagree with Scripture. It is the word of fallible men against the word of the infallible God.[28]

---

28) The conservative moderns protest that they are not preferring the words of fallible men to God's words, for the portions of Scripture under consideration are not God's words, but the words of fallible men. Then they will have to say that every once in a while the inspiring

Put it another way: the moderns are actually advising us to tell our people that certain portions of Scripture are not inspired, because otherwise the attacks of the infidels will prove successful. In other words: we cannot uphold the trustworthiness of the Bible unless we admit errors in it. They are actually giving this advice. Professor Evans, quoted with approval by De Witt (*op. cit.*, p. 43), says: "You may be sure that, so long as you hang the infallible authority of Scripture as the rule of faith on the infallible accuracy of every particular word and clause in the Book, . . . the irrepressible conflict between faith and science will go on. . . ." If the Church would only admit at once and unreservedly that the Bible contains the mistakes charged up against it by the historian and the scientist, "the iridescent declaration of Robert Ingersoll in his *Mistakes of Moses* would collapse like a pricked balloon." One cannot trust one's eyes. Surrender parts of the Bible in order to save the rest! By way of appeasement the Church must maintain herself!

What do you think of a theology which is at the beck and call of science and is glad to act as her train-bearer, "Schleppentraegerdienste zu tun"? [29]

The Christian disgraces himself when he asks fallible men to tell him how much of his Holy Bible he may accept. Take the lowest view of the case. We demand that the holy writers, say the Biblical historians, be treated as respectably as secular historians. Why should we take it for granted that in a case of conflict the heathen or the Jew should be right, but Daniel and Mark wrong? Daniel is entitled to at least as much consideration as Herodotus. Why not operate with the hypothesis that Josephus might have blundered? Why say *a priori* that Mark and Luke blundered? Read Dr. Lenski on Luke 2:2: "Luke was charged

---

activity of the Holy Ghost ceased; that every so often — and that was very often — the Holy Ghost left the holy writers to their own devices; that He permitted the Bible, the book of life, to become a conglomerate of truth and error; and that He put it up to the anxious sinner to search the Scriptures in order to separate the truth from the error. Is such a monstrous conception of the work of the Holy Ghost worthy of a Christian? And is it worthy of a Christian to say that the inspired words "*All* Scripture is given by inspiration of God" do not express the full truth?

29) Moeller's phrase. Read the entire paragraph. "Es fragt sich, ob es gut ist, sofort beim ersten Kanonenschuss der Feinde die Aussenwerke zu raeumen, um die Festung selbst halten zu wollen, um so mehr, wenn es sich um einen blinden Schuss und um schwache Feinde handelt. Die heutige Theologie verbeugt sich vor jeder Wissenschaft oder auch oft Pseudowissenschaft und Naturphilosophie, die den Mund etwas voll nimmt, und erklaert sich bereit, Schleppentraegerdienste zu tun. Das ist ein erbarmungs- und unwuerdiger Zustand, der ein Ende nehmen muss!" (*Op. cit.*, p. 36.)

with misdating this enrolment. What helped the matter along were the mistaken statements of Josephus (on which see Zahn in his commentary on Luke). The word of the renegade Jewish priest Josephus, born as late as 37 or 38 A. D., was taken against the word of Paul's faithful assistant, the inspired writer Luke, who was an active member in the church at Antioch as early as the year 40. Recently discovered inscriptions vindicate Luke." [30] Omit the "inspired" and the concluding sentence and get the point we are at present stressing. Dr. Stoeckhardt thus stresses the point: "Who will forbid us, where the testimony of one witness counts for as much as that of the other, to accept the testimony of the Bible?" (*Lehre und Wehre*, 32, p. 316.) Those who say that the testimony of the secular writer has the preference, are swayed by bias. That is unworthy of a "historical critic." And it is unworthy of a Christian.

The matter gets worse when we realize that these fallible men who are set above Scripture are indeed fallible men who have been convicted time and again of making false statements. Josephus is not an absolutely reliable historian. "It should no longer be denied that Josephus contradicts himself in his account of the census under Quirinius as in other accounts, constructs from different accounts of the same facts different facts, and commits other blunders." (Zahn, *Commentary on Luke*, p. 130.) "The testimony of Professor Sayce to the inaccuracy of Herodotus and other ancient writers is as follows: 'Let us now turn to the classical writers who have left accounts of the ancient history of the East. Among them Herodotus and Ktesias of Knidos claim our first attention. Herodotus has been termed "the Father of History." . . . Ktesias had access to the state archives of Persia; on the strength of these he maintained that Herodotus had "lied," and he wrote a work with the object of contradicting most of the older historians' statements. But when confronted with contemporaneous monuments, Herodotus and Ktesias alike turn out to be false guides.'" (D. MacDill, *The Mosaic Authorship of the Pentateuch*, p. 163.) These "good people," says Luther, did their best but could not help blundering. The man on the street knows that the historians of the present day spend much of their time in correcting the mistakes of the historians of yesterday. And still the moderns faulted our fathers for refusing to trust Josephus more than Mark.

---

30) Zahn, page 129: "Es will doch nicht einleuchten, warum, wo es sich um Ereignisse der Zeit zwischen 7 v. Chr. und 7 n. Chr. handelt, geschichtliche Angaben des griechischen Arztes und Christen Lukas, der schon vor dem Regierungsantritt des Kaisers Claudius ein erwachsenes Mitglied der Gemeinde zu Antiochien war, von vornherein misstrauischer angesehen werden sollen als Angaben des ehemaligen Priesters Josephus, der zu Ende 37 oder Anfang 38 geboren ist."

It is unbelievable. Dr. Stoeckhardt tells them: "Will you say that secular history gives the lie to Scripture? . . . Are we to correct the Biblical history on the authority of occasional scraps in the ancient tradition or the obscure language of the monuments, which are partly contradictory . . .? Das waere Wahnwitz," (*Lehre und Wehre*, 32, p. 315.)

This applies to all branches of human knowledge. Are the geologists who would master Moses infallible? Then why do the geological theories change so often, so often that the layman cannot keep count? "Of the eighty (geological) theories which the French Institute counted in 1806 as hostile to the Bible, not one now stands." (A. T. Pierson in *Fundamentals*, 7, p. 63.) And has higher criticism, for our moderns the queen of sciences, established any assured results? Is there any finality there? [31] The science of one epoch is abandoned by the science of the next. (See Gladstone, *The Impregnable Rock of Holy Scripture*, p. 49.) We would invite the critics to spend their time in searching out the discrepancies in the secular writings. They will then feel less inclined to produce them as witnesses against the Bible. — The judge would disgrace himself who consented to try a case where the plaintiff is unable to produce unimpeachable witnesses. And the Christian disgraces himself if he permits fallible men to testify against the infallible Bible. [32]

---

31) In his latest book, *A Philosophy of the Christian Revelation*, Edwin Lewis mentions on page 34 "the reverberations of the bitter controversy of the so-called Documentary Hypothesis of the Pentateuch," the old "symbols J, E, D, and P," and says: "That chapter in the history of criticism may now be regarded as closed." Other theories now have their day — and it will be a short day. The tragic thing, however, is that in the very next paragraph Dr. Lewis assails Verbal Inspiration on the strength of "facts" furnished by higher criticism. He says: "The Church had unfortunately committed itself to a type of verbalism. . . ." He rejoices over "the breaking of the stranglehold of this verbalism." "How mixed-up the message [of the Pentateuch] is with transient and purely human elements can hardly be denied except by a doctrinaire who persists in closing his eyes to facts."

32) A final word on the unscholarly habits of the discrepancy-hunters, as evidenced by Dr. Haussleiter. A later section, dealing with the "Biblical errors," will discuss other instances. What the *Expositor's Greek Testament* and *Zahn's Commentary* say in a half-hearted way we want to express in stronger terms. It is frivolous to charge Mark with a historical error "on the assumption that Herod the Great could have only one son named Philip" (Lenski's *Commentary*). Dr. Haussleiter and his ilk should take the trouble of studying the genealogical table of the Herodians. Herod had two sons named Philip; one (the husband of Herodias) by Mariamne, the other (the tetrarch) by Cleopatra. Even so two of his sons bore the name of Antipas. For two half-brothers to bear the same name in a family like that of Herod the Great is nothing unusual. Haussleiter constructed the "historical error" by ignoring a matter of common occurrence. For his benefit we shall also mention the other historical fact that Salome, the daughter of Herodias and

And now let us take high ground. We shall take our stand on the impregnable rock of Holy Scripture. We take this position: even if the historians and the scientists and the philosophers had never been convicted of a single error, misstatement, or inaccuracy, we would say that in every case where they contradict Scripture they are in error, and Scripture is right. To say less than that is unworthy of a Christian. If all the philosophers and scientists were united in declaring one statement of Scripture to be false, we would tell them that this little verse of Scripture will stand as true in all eternity. The Christian has no difficulty to say with Luther: "God's Word counts for more than all angels and saints and creatures" (XVIII:1322) and historians and philosophers. He encounters insuperable difficulties in saying that in this instance the scientists are right and Scripture is wrong.

We shall tell the philosophers that, where doctrine is concerned, they know nothing of these things and that the declaration of Scripture is conclusive and decisive. And we shall tell them another thing: on these matters we know more than you. You may know a lot more about science than we do. But do not talk to us on matters of faith. "To be able to judge the Bible, a man needs spiritual sense. I would as soon expect a man to appreciate the Sistine Madonna because he was not color-blind as to expect an unspiritual man to understand and appreciate the Bible simply because he understands the laws of grammar and the vocabulary of the languages in which the Bible was written. I would as soon think of setting a man to teach Art merely because he understood

---

the disinherited Philip (the first husband of Herodias), married the tetrarch Philip, her half-uncle. Furthermore, when Josephus named Herod as the first husband of Herodias, he was right; when Mark gave his name as Philip, he was right. The two historians are not contradicting each other. The trouble is not with Josephus (in this instance) and Mark; the trouble is with Haussleiter and the other critics. They misinterpret one of their historians. — Mark was not a shallow examiner; Haussleiter proved himself a superficial reader.

There are other similar cases. Examining the case of the Gadarene swine, Gladstone remarks: "Both Bishop Wordsworth in his *Commentary* and Archbishop Trench refer to Josephus. I am, however, under the impression that both these excellent authors may have insufficiently examined the effect of the passages in Josephus which relate to the subject." (*Op. cit.*, p. 326. These passages listed and examined there.) So we have this situation: to prove the errancy of Scripture, secular writers are quoted. That is inadmissible. Secondly, the secular writers relied upon as witnesses are in many cases shown to be in error. And in the third place, the charge of "errors in the Bible" rests in some case on a misinterpretation of the secular authority. We read this the other day: "As down payment on an automobile, a man in Tarrytown, N. Y., tendered three $50 bills. They were not only Confederate money but counterfeit." The statements of scientists and historians are in this matter not legal tender. Sometimes they are erroneous, counterfeit. And where there is misinterpretation of the secular authority, the counterfeit of the outlawed money is mutilated beyond recognition.

paints, as to set him to teach the Bible merely because he understood Greek and Hebrew and Aramaic." (R. A. Torrey, *Is the Bible the Inerrant Word of God?* P. 46.) See 1 Cor. 2:14. The Christian would be degrading himself and belittling his spiritual faculties if he asked Kant and Fosdick to tell him how many of the Bible doctrines he may believe.

And with regard to secular matters we shall tell them that what Scripture says about creation and the husband of Herodias and the grafting of olive-branches is absolutely true. If they agree, well; if not, they are wrong. "One passage of Scripture has more authority than all the books in the world." (Luther, XIX:1734.) We should hold this one passage even if all the philosophers from Plato down to Santayana and all scientists from Pythagoras to Einstein declared it erroneous. A Christian can say nothing less. "Wir muessen so keck werden, allen Menschenwitz und alles, was von Menschen kommt, mit Fuessen zu treten, sobald es die Worte Christi betrifft. . . . Was kuemmert's mich was dieser oder jener begabte Suender ueber dieses oder jenes denkt, heisse er nun Schleiermacher oder Storr oder Kant oder Swedenborg, oder wie er will." (Hofacker. See *Lehre und Wehre*, 51, p. 137.) Let us be as bold as Walther: "Let science publicize ever so confidently the results of its research as absolutely certain truths, we do not regard science but only Scripture as infallible. When the results of scientific research contradict clear statements of Scripture, we are certain before all investigation that these teachings of science are absolutely not true, even if we are unable to prove this save by our appeal to Scripture. As often as we must choose between science and Scripture, we say with Christ, our Lord: 'The Scripture cannot be broken,' John 10:35, and with the holy apostle: 'We bring into captivity every thought to the obedience of Christ,' 2 Cor. 10:5." (See Pieper, *Christliche Dogmatik*, I, p. 190.)

The Christian, though he be a mere layman, must be bold enough to challenge not only the philosopher but also the erring theologian. Here is a fine Christian manifesto, issued by Der Deutsche Ev.-Luth. Schulverein (150 members): "We maintain the miracle of Inspiration and believe that the Bible is, word for word, God's Word. . . . Over against the testimony of Christ and His apostles the wisdom of the most learned professors and D. D.'s is, for us, nothing but wind. You may look down upon us as unlearned laymen. We shall hold our position in spite of that." (*Lehre und Wehre*, 55, p. 234.)

When the experts discuss scientific matters, we keep our mouths shut. And we are aware that some of these men, many of them, know more Greek and Aramaic than we do. And more than our high-school boy. But we tell this boy that, when his teacher begins to charge the Bible with historical and scientific errors, he should open his mouth in protest. He need not be abashed and apologetic. He should say: In this matter "I have more understanding than all my teachers," Ps. 119:99.

Faith Undisturbed by Unsolved Bible Difficulties

It might happen, of course, and it will happen, that the professor gets the young man in a corner. The young man cannot solve the historical or chronological difficulty. And then perhaps the young man will worry and give up his case as lost. But that would be unworthy of him as a Christian. That is the next point that needs to be emphasized and elaborated: the Christian is not taking the right attitude if he permits the fact that he cannot solve all Biblical difficulties to perturb him overmuch.

Dr. Stoeckhardt had some difficulty with Matthew 27:9: "spoken by *Jeremy* the prophet." It seems that Zechariah should have been named (Zech. 11:12). And Dr. Stoeckhardt freely says: I cannot solve the difficulty, nor could the others solve it. "Instead of exhausting oneself with such vague guesses, it would have been better to confess *Non liquet* and let it go at that. It would not, after all, be the only obscure passage in Scripture which we cannot decipher." (*Lehre und Wehre*, 31, p. 272.) We do not notice that Dr. Stoeckhardt's pen was quivering when he wrote these words. Luther was equally free to confess occasionally that he was baffled. "Here, in the case of Abraham, sixty years are lost." (I:721.) And he never really did find them. But that did not raise the suspicion with Luther that Scripture here made a mistake. On John 2:13-16: "Here the question arises how the statements of Matthew and of John harmonize. . . . Aber es sind Fragen und bleiben Fragen, die ich nicht will aufloesen. Nothing much depends on it. What do I care that there are many sharp and superclever people who raise all kinds of questions and demand an answer on every single point?" (VII:1780 f.) Peter Martyr took the same attitude: "Although obscure passages occur as to chronology, we must beware of pretending to reconcile them by imputing blunders to the inspired books. Therefore it is that, should it sometimes happen that we know not how to account for the number of years, we ought simply to confess our ignorance and consider that the Scriptures express themselves with so much conciseness that it is not always possible for us to discover at what epoch we ought to make such or such a computation to commence." (See Gaussen, *op. cit.*, p. 243.) [33] Here is one fact which is well established: the great theologians of the Church are not able to harmonize all

---

33) "Conciseness" — that accounts for some of the difficulty. Other factors are mentioned in the same paragraph.

"contradictions" in the Bible. Nor are they able to prove, by science, that all the scientific statements in the Bible are true; to demonstrate in all cases that the Biblical historian is right and the secular historian wrong; and to adduce corroborative testimony in all cases from outside sources. "We do not claim that every historical statement contained in the Pentateuch can be proved to be true by external testimony." (D. MacDill, *op. cit.*, p. 89.)

But this fact should not disturb us. It is not worthy of a Christian to let that fact lead him to doubt in any way the trustworthiness of Scripture. It may embarrass some to be forced to make Luther's and Peter Martyr's and Augustine's confession of ignorance, — and it should put those to shame whose ignorance is due to their neglect of serious study of the case. But we have no reason to be embarrassed and perturbed at our inability to solve all Biblical difficulties. We do not, and the most pronounced foes of Verbal Inspiration do not, feel that difficulties about a certain philosophical truth cast doubt upon that truth. When we and the Bible critics find a statement in some secular book which seems to contradict some other statement in the same book, we do not begin to hoot at the writer. "There may be difficulties with individual passages in the Bible that I in my very limited knowledge cannot explain. But a man is not a philosopher but a fool who gives up a thoroughly established theorem because there are difficulties that he cannot explain. No reputable scientist in any department of science does that." (R. A. Torrey, *op. cit.*, p. 22.) Let us give our Bible the same respectful consideration as reputable human writings receive.

And let us give it higher respect. The doubts as to the absolute and all-embracing reliability of the Bible which arise from our inability to solve every difficulty are not worthy of a Christian. God's guarantee means more than our human limitations. Read on in Torrey: "The proof that Jesus is a teacher sent from God who spoke the very words of God is absolutely conclusive; indeed, it is overwhelming, and therefore I unquestionably accept *His* say-so, however difficult it may be to reconcile with some things I seem to know. Therefore, when the Lord Jesus says, as He continually does say, that this Book is the inerrant 'Word of God,' I heartily believe it; I would be an egregious fool if I did not." (*Loc. cit.*)

We accept the *doctrines* of the Bible even though we do not understand them; and when to our finite mind two doctrines seem to be in contradiction, we do not doubt the truth of either of them. Is it worthy of a Christian to deny the universality of God's grace because certain facts of experience do not seem to agree with it? And are you taking the Christian attitude when you permit your inability to solve minor difficulties in the Bible to raise doubts in your mind as to the reliability of the Bible?

Who told you that the Bible, if it is really God's Word, cannot contain difficulties? The Bible does not tell you that. Your Bible tells you, for instance, that in the epistles of Paul there "are some things hard to be understood" (2 Pet. 3:16). So when you meet with a difficulty in *any* part of the Bible, the Bible does not permit you to say that this part of the Bible must be deleted.

You have no cause to worry. Our faith need not suffer in the least from the fact that our mind is not omnisapient. You cannot harmonize the accounts of Matthew and John on the purging of the Temple. Luther tells you: "Let it be as it will, es sei zuvor oder hernach, eins oder zwier geschehen, our faith does not suffer thereby." (VII:1781.) The chronology in the case of Arphaxad seems confused (Gen. 11:11); "one offers this solution, the other another. But, in the first place, it will not hurt us at all if we cannot find a perfectly satisfactory solution. . . . Denn das ist gewiss, dass die Schrift nicht luegt." (I:714.) The unbeliever makes much of the seeming confusion in isolated passages of Scripture; the Christian reader does not let it bother his faith: "Christliche Leser werden sich leichtlich darein finden." (II:1024.) [34]

What we should worry about is that we are worried about our inability to solve all Bible difficulties. The latent distrust of the absolute infallibility of the Bible which lies at the bottom of it is a wicked thing. Another wicked thing is the pride of reason. We think that, if we cannot demonstrate that everything is in order, God's Word will suffer in the estimation of men or our own faith will suffer. Thinking these thoughts we are making our wisdom and learning the measure of the truth of God's Word. That ill befits a Christian. And if you find fault with the occurrence of these difficulties in the Bible, you are faulting the Holy Ghost.

---

34) Study the valuable observations of Luther and Pieper on this point, in *Christliche Dogmatik*, I, p. 340 ff. Read also page 56 in *Proceedings, Western District*, 1865: "Die Weltweisen berufen sich darauf, dass man in neuerer Zeit so viele Entdeckungen gemacht hat, die mit der Schrift nicht stimmen. Nach der Berechnung mancher Weltweisen muesste die Erde schon ueber 100,000 Jahre alt sein u. dgl. Solche Behauptungen moegen nun wohl manchen in Verlegenheit setzen, den Christen aber nicht. Wenn der sie auch nicht erklaeren kann, so laesst er sich dadurch noch lange nicht stoeren in seinem Glauben. Dazu wissen wir ja, wie unsicher die Ergebnisse der neueren Forschung sind: was der eine heute setzt, das stoesst der andere morgen um." (See p. 57.) "Carl v. Raumer, der selbst ein tuechtiger Geologe, aber zugleich ein Christ ist, sagt: 'Ein jeder huete sich vor den Geologen, denn sie geben gern mehr als sie haben.' Wir Christen haben bei allen Einwuerfen der Wissenschaft zunaechst nur *eine* Antwort: Wir glauben an einen allmaechtigen Gott."

He is the Author of the Bible, and just as it was written He wanted it written. He is responsible, for instance, for the variations in the four records of the institution of the Lord's Supper. "The Holy Ghost purposely ordered it so." (Luther, XIX: 1104.) Guard your tongue when wrestling with these difficulties.[35]

All is not well when a Christian takes offense at "insoluble" difficulties. "The fact that you cannot solve a difficulty does not prove that it cannot be solved, and the fact that you cannot answer an objection does not prove at all that it cannot be answered. There are many who, when they meet a difficulty in the Bible and give it a few moments' thought and can see no possible solution, at once jump to the conclusion that a solution is impossible by any one, and so they throw up their faith in the inerrancy of the Bible and its divine origin. It would seem as if any really normal man would have a sufficient amount of that modesty that is becoming in beings so limited in knowledge as we all undeniably are to say: 'Though *I* see no possible solution of this difficulty, some one a little wiser than I might easily find one.'" (Torrey, *op. cit.*, p. 61.)

And all is well even if it is never solved for you. Pastor G. Schulze of Walsleben (Germany) has well said: "We wait for the time when the difficulty may be solved, and we die in good spirits even though this never occurs." (See Pieper, *What Is Christianity?* p. 251.)[36]

---

35) And when you have solved a difficulty, when you have, for instance, established the agreement of science with Scripture on some point, do not be overproud of it. Do not imagine that that alone makes for a stronger faith. "Hence Dr. Smith observes we should not be too much elated by the discovery of harmonies." (Gladstone, *op. cit.*, p. 50.) Philippi utters the same caution. (See Pieper, *Christl. Dogm.*, I, p. 269.)

36) This stubborn refusal to admit that there are errors in the Bible even though the truth of certain statements cannot be *demonstrated* is one of the reasons why the critics charge us with dishonesty and untruthfulness. They say that we close our eyes to the facts. Kahnis makes the strong statement: "Only he will deny that Scripture contains contradictions who lacks the sense of truth." (See page 25 above.) Kahnis again: "To retain the inspiration dogma of the old dogmatics means hardening oneself against the truth." (See *Baier's Compendium*, I, p.43.) V. Ferm uses the term "loss of intellectual integrity." E. Lewis means the same thing when he says: "Once error is known to be error, its perpetuation becomes a menace. If new facts are discovered in the field of history or in the field of science or anywhere else, no respect for tradition should hinder their being made known." (*Op. cit.*, p. 259.) In *The Christian Fact and Modern Doubt* G. A. Buttrick raises the same charge: "It is no use our evading or trying to hide Bible inconsistencies." And if our attitude is not due to intellectual dishonesty, it is, says Buttrick, due to intellectual weakness: "That avowal [literal infallibility of Scripture], held to its last logic, would risk a trip to the *insane asylum*." It is due to a rabbinical *superstition*, declares Hauss-leiter: "Zerstoeren Sie den rabbinischen Aberglauben von der Buch-stabeninspiration!" (See *Lehre und Wehre*, 57, p. 479.) What should

Should the Christian Theologian Plow with Paine's Heifer?

Another point that should be emphasized and elaborated is this: those theologians who operate with the alleged errors in the Bible find themselves in disreputable company. They are working shoulder to shoulder with infidels and Jews and continuing the work begun by the old rationalists and the ancient heathen adversaries of Christianity. The moderns are using the very same arguments which the pronounced foes of the Bible have been employing in the past centuries. Their weapons have been forged in the workshop of infidelity.

Thomas Paine, the deist, and Voltaire, the scoffer, and D. F. Strauss, the skeptic and religious anarchist, and the old rationalists took up the work, and employed the arguments of Celsus. R. Ingersoll, the agnostic, with Bradlaugh in England, "the last of the Old Guard" (avowed enemies of Christianity), drew on Paine and Voltaire. And now spokesmen of the Christian Church are repeating, in some instances word for word, what those enemies of Christianity have been saying against the Bible.

Gaussen: "The Scriptures have in all ages had their adversaries, their Celsuses and Porphyries. . . . Malchus Porphyry, whom Jerome calls *rabidum adversus Christum canem,* wrote fifteen books against Christianity. The first was entirely devoted to the bringing together of all the contradictions which, he maintained, he had found in the Scriptures. From Celsus and Porphyry down to the English unbelievers of the 18th century and from these down to Strauss, *who had hardly more to do than copy them,* unceasing endeavors have been made to discover more. Strauss says himself that in the criticism of the gospels he *had studied and collected from Celsus to Paulus,* and even to the fragments of Wolfenbuettel." (*Theopneustia,* p. 208.) [37] MacDill: "In these two writings of Voltaire we have almost all the points and arguments that are set forth by higher criticism." (*Op. cit.,* p. 18.) R. A. Torrey: "Most of our modern infidels from Tom Paine to

---

be our attitude over against these charges? We shall certainly reexamine our position in the fear of God and carefully guard against any intrusion of carnal stubbornness, any intention of evading the issue. And when we, ever and again, always, come to the same conclusion and are compelled to declare: "Scripture cannot be broken," all evidence of carnal reasoning to the contrary, we shall willingly bear the contumely heaped upon us. If we are charged with dishonesty or insanity because of our championship of the truth of Scripture, the charges leave us unaffected. They are false charges, and the words of Jesus, Matt. 5:11 and Luke 6:22, apply.

37) By the way, Strauss said of his *own* book, *Das Leben Jesu:* "The book praises itself. It is an *inspired book;* that is to say, its author has laid hold of the most powerful of the driving forces of the theological science of the day and so produced the book." (See Meusel, *Kirchl. Handlexikon, s. v.* Strauss.)

Robert Ingersoll, and also the reputed 'scholars' of 'the *modern critical school*,' have for the most part simply echoed and embellished the arguments of that bitter enemy of Christ of the second century Celsus." (*Is the Bible the Inerrant Word of God?* p. 24.) D. F. Burrell: "All the stock arguments against the inerrancy of Scripture were presented in the *Age of Reason*." (*Why I Believe the Bible*, p. 183.) Can these grave charges be substantiated?

We offer in evidence the following excerpts from three scoffers and sceptics and ask the reader to compare them with the statements of the moderns quoted in our first article. Voltaire states: ". . . (7) that the accounts of prodigies and of God's strange and supernatural dealings with the Israelites in Egypt and in the desert, the ten plagues, the crossing of the Red Sea, the destruction of the Egyptian army, etc., are revolting to reason and cannot have been written by Moses." (Is not this the voice of Fosdick?) MacDill, who quotes this, says further: "The testimony of Christ and the New Testament to the Mosaic authorship of the Pentateuch was noticed by Voltaire as by the more modern analysts, and like them, he set it aside as untrustworthy." (P. 19.) "In regard to other books of the Bible, the views of Voltaire are in accord with the analytics; we might better say, their views are in accord with his." (P. 20.) "After stating these reasons, Voltaire proceeds to decry the general contents of the Pentateuch and closes this third section of his article on Moses with these words: 'It is very pardonable in human reason to see in such history only the barbarous rudeness of a savage people of the primitive times. Man, whatever he may do, cannot reason otherwise; but if God indeed is the author of the Pentateuch, it is necessary to submit without reasoning.' " (P. 18.)[38]

The following excerpts will show that the moderns (liberals, semiliberals and conservatives) are plowing with Paine's heifer. Paine exults: "I have now gone through the Bible as a man would go through a wood with an ax on his shoulder and fell trees. Here they lie; and the priests, if they can, may replant them. They may perhaps stick them in the ground, but they will never make them grow. I pass on to the books of the New Testament. . . . And now, ye priests of every description, who have preached and written against the former part of the *Age of Reason*, what have ye to say? Will you, with all this mass of evidence against you, and staring you in the face, still have the

---

38) We find ourselves in accord with this last statement. In the foregoing, p. 39 f., we told those who believe in a real inspiration of the Bible that they must accept its statements *a priori*, "without reasoning." Voltaire tells them that we were right.

assurance to march into your pulpits and continue to impose these books on your congregations as the works of *inspired penmen* and the Word of God?"[39]

From the "mass of evidence" presented by Paine we select the following: "I begin, then, by saying that these two chapters [Gen. 1 and 2] contain *two different and contradictory stories of a creation*, made by two different persons and written in two different styles of expression. The evidence that shows this is so clear when attended to without prejudice that, did we meet with the same evidence in any Arabic or Chinese account of a creation, we should not hesitate in pronouncing it a forgery." (Dr. G. A. Buttrick, repeated this in 1935 and said: "The doctrine of literal infallibility is slain and pursuit is needless.") "This tale of the sun standing still upon Mount Gibeon and the moon in the valley of Ajalon is one of those fables that detects itself. Such a circumstance could not have happened without being known all over the world. One half would have wondered why the sun did not rise, and the other why it did not set; and the tradition of it would be universal, whereas there is not a nation in the world that knows anything about it." (Harnack, Fosdick, and the Archbishop of York, too, think that this disproves Verbal Inspiration.)— "I observed two chapters, 16th and 17th in the First Book of Samuel, that contradict each other with respect to David and the manner he became acquainted with Saul. . . . These two accounts belie each other, because each of them supposes Saul and David not to have known each other before. This book, the Bible, is too ridiculous even for criticism." The moderns have kept this item in their list to this day. Also this one: "If the parts are found to be discordant, contradicting in one place what is said in another (as in 2 Sam. 24:1 and 1 Chron. 21:1, where the same action is ascribed to God in one book and to Satan in the other), . . . we may take it for certainty that the Creator of the universe is not the author of such a book, that it is not the Word of God, and that to call it so is to dishonor His name." — "In the former part of the *Age of Reason* I have spoken of Jonah and the whale. A fit story for ridicule if it was written to be believed, or of laughter if

---

39) *The Presbyterian*, Jan. 16, 1941: "Belief in plenary inspiration of the Bible is being discarded by many today, even among the conservative element in the Church. . . . Some time ago we listened to a scholar of national reputation lecture on one of the gospels. With almost nonchalant carelessness he tore the book to shreds. This part came out; that passage was apocryphal; these verses were by a later and uninspired writer. . . ." Note how a Lutheran theologian tore the Gospel according to St. Mark to shreds (p. 21). Note there how the moderns go through the Bible uprooting one passage after the other. Hear them cry out: The day of Verbal Inspiration is past! Verbal Inspiration is dead!

it was intended to try what credulity could swallow; for if it could swallow Jonah and the whale, it could swallow anything." Dr. Fosdick's list also contains the story of Jonah and the great fish. — Jonah again: "The story of Jonah satirizes also the supposed partiality of the Creator for one nation more than for another." (Repeated, nearly verbatim, by Dr. H. L. Willett. See quotations on p. 21 f.)

The moderns, as we have seen, use the "contradictory" versions of the inscription on the cross as one of their heavy guns. Paine, too. "Not any two of these writers agree in reciting *exactly in the same words* the written inscription, short as it is, which they tell us was put over Christ when He was crucified." The contradiction between the genealogies, referred to by a Lutheran theologian (page 11 above), is handled by Paine thus: "Did these two genealogies (Matt. 1 and Luke 3) agree, it would not prove the genealogy to be true, because it might, nevertheless, be a fabrication; but as they contradict each other in every particular, it proves falsehood absolutely. . . . Now, if these men, Matthew and Luke, set out with a falsehood between them in the very commencement of their history of Jesus Christ, and of whom and what he was, what authority is there left for believing the strange things they tell us afterward? If they cannot be believed in their account of his natural genealogy, how are we to believe them when they tell us He was the Son of God, begotten by a ghost, and that an angel announced this in secret to his mother? If they lied in one genealogy, why are we to believe them in another?"

Paine finds, of course, a lot of contradictions in the resurrection story. We have not the time to particularize. Nor have we given all of his objections. But we have space for two more items. "The Bible says (Jer. 20: 5, 7) that God is a deceiver. 'O Lord' (says Jeremiah), 'Thou hast deceived me, and I was deceived. Thou art stronger than I and hast prevailed.' " (Dr. Dodd operates with the same passage.) — Read what S. P. Cadman says about the rights of reason (see page 43), and then read Paine: " 'Come now and let us reason together, saith the Lord.' This is one of the passages you quoted from your Bible. . . . I requote the passage to show that your *text* and your *religion* contradict each other. It is impossible to reason upon things *not comprehensible by reason;* and therefore, if you keep to your text, which priests seldom do (for they are generally either above it or below it or forget it), you must admit a religion to which reason can apply, and this certainly is not the Christian religion." (Quotations are from *Life and Writings of Thomas Paine,* Vol. 6: *Age of Reason* and other writings.)

The moderns plow with Ingersoll's heifer, too. He says in *Mistakes of Moses:* "Every nation has had what you call a sacred record; and the older, the more sacred, the more contradictory, and the more inspired is the record. . . . Now, they say the book [Bible] is inspired. I do not care whether it is or not; the question is: Is it true? . . . I find in some book that the sun was stopped a whole day to give a general named Joshua time to kill a few more Amalekites. At another time, we read, the sun was turned ten degrees backward to convince Hezekiah that he was not going to die of a boil." And since this involves a stupendous astronomical error, Ingersoll and Paine and Fosdick and the Archbishop of York cannot believe in Verbal, Plenary Inspiration. — "The second account of creation differs from the first in two essential points. In the first account, man is last made; in the second, man is made before the beasts. In the first account, man is made 'male and female,' in the second, only a male is made, and there is no intention of making a woman whatever." The moderns may not agree with Ingersoll's exegesis, but both are agreed as to the general contention.

When you read the following: "Shall we reason, or shall we simply believe? Oh, but they say the Bible is not inspired about those little things. The Bible says the rabbit and the hare chew the cud. But they do not. They have a tremulous motion of the lip. But the Being that made them says they chew the cud. The Bible, therefore, is not inspired in natural history," you might think one of the moderns is speaking. Ingersoll wrote it.

The moderns will not employ the coarse language of Ingersoll, but some of them are with him when he says: "How many did they have when they went to Egypt? Seventy. How many were they at the end of two hundred and fifteen years? Three millions. That is a good many. . . . Is there a minister in the city of Chicago that will testify to his own idiocy by claiming that they could have increased to three millions by that time?" And this: "The whole supplies of the world could not maintain three millions of people in the desert of Sinai for forty years. . . . It would require millions of acres to support these flocks, and yet there was no blade of grass and there is no account of it raining baled hay."

The deadly parallel once more: N. R. Best: "When did the Creator ever brand man's reason as unholy — unfit to handle the sacred things of His words?" (See page 43 above.) Ingersoll: "Do not imagine that there is any being who would give to his children the holy torch of reason and then damn them for following where the holy light led. . . . If God did not intend I should think, why did He give me a 'thinker?' " (Quotations from *Lectures of Col. R. G. Ingersoll,* containing *Mistakes of Moses* and other writings.)[40]

In preparing for their war against the inspiration of Scripture the moderns found munitions to their liking prepared by the ancients. And as they are marching along, the unbelievers cheer them on. When Professor Smith in Cincinnati was being tried in a court of his Church (Presbyterian) for his attacks on Scripture, a Rabbi, a Theosophist, a Buddhist, a Unitarian, a Universalist, and an atheist defended him in the secular press of the city. (See *Lutheraner,* 49, p. 28.)

The moderns are using the same arguments as the ancients and arrive at the same result. And the Liberals of today are talking the language of the unbelievers of yesterday. You cannot think hard of the *Lutheran Herald* (Jan. 21, 1941) for writing the following: "It happened that the editor picked up the current issue of a Lutheran theological quarterly while he was in the midst of reading Dr. Goodspeed's book (*How the Bible Came to Be*). There he read an article dealing pretty much with the inspiration of the Bible and discovered, what he knew more or less directly, that within the Lutheran Church in the United States we have scholars who are nicely along the road which Dr. Goodspeed is following. The book and the article side by side lead to some somber thought. Time was when the most liberal theologians in America would have shuddered to read a book which leaves the guidance of God the Holy Spirit out of the authorship of the Bible as does Dr. Goodspeed's. And here, in a Lutheran quarterly, we are

40) Here are some excerpts from *Origen Against Celsus* which show that Ingersoll and Paine are in accord with Celsus. "Celsus: 'The Son of God, then, it appears, could not open His tomb, but required the aid of another to roll away the stone.' . . . He ridicules the account of 'the angel's visit to Joseph regarding the pregnancy of Mary,' and the birth of God from a virgin" (his words do not bear repeating). "Their cosmogony is extremely silly." "Celsus makes jest also of the serpent, taking the narrative to be an old wife's fable." Writing the story of the Deluge and the monstrous ark, they "imagined that they were inventing stories merely for young children." (*Ante-Nicene Fathers,* IV.) Stories for children — that sounds familiar. See page 9 f. above. — From Porphyry's list: "He objects to the repetition of a generation in St. Matthew's genealogy; to Matthew's call; to the quotation of a text from Isaiah,. which is found in a psalm ascribed to Asaph; to the calling of the lake of Tiberias a sea; to the expression in St. Matthew, 'the abomination of desolation'; to the variation in Matthew and Mark upon the text 'the voice of one crying in the wilderness,' Matthew citing it from Isaiah, Mark from the Prophets; to John's application of the term 'Word'; to Christ's change of intention about going up to the Feast of Tabernacles (John 7:8); to the judgment denounced by St. Peter upon Ananias and Sapphira, which he calls an imprecation of death. . . . The prophecy of Daniel he attacked upon this very ground of spuriousness, insisting that it was written after the time of Antiochus Epiphanes, and maintains his charge of forgery by some far-fetched indeed, but very subtle criticisms." (W. Paley, *A View of the Evidences of Christianity,* pp. 169, 171.)

treated to an exposition of the doctrine of inspiration which, carried to a logical conclusion, might easily lead its author to a view not far short of that held by the most liberal theologians of the day." When we read the *Lutheran Church Quarterly,* Oct. 1940 (see page 21 above), we could not help thinking of the argumentations employed by the old rationalists.

It is a sad spectacle. Christian theologians using the same methods as pronounced enemies of the Church — no, not the same methods! "There is a startling contrast between the former methods and those of today. The assault is now from within the gates: open warfare has given way to strategy. The Trojan horse has been wheeled within the walls of the Church itself, where a body of militant critics have been attempting to draw the bolts of the citadel." (Burrell, *op. cit.,* p. 184.) [41]

Professor Laetsch asks: "Is that honest?" R. Ingersoll asked the same question. "I tell all the churches to drive all such men out, and when he" (a certain professor) "comes, I want him to state just what he thinks. . . . I want him to tell whether he considers the story about the bears a poem or not, whether it is inspired. . . . I had not the remotest idea that the most learned clergymen in Chicago would substantially agree with me — in public. I have read their replies and will now ask them a few questions. Do you believe in the stories of the Bible about Jael and of the sun standing still. . .? Answer [Ingersoll now quotes one of them]: 'They may be legends, myths, poems, or what they will, but they are not the Word of God.'" And so it goes on, from page 356 to page 426, showing that the liberals teach what Ingersoll teaches and still remain in the Christian Church.

Do we, then, classify the moderns as infidels and agnostics? We do not. The liberals believe in God and the conservatives believe in Jesus Christ. But we do say that in this campaign they are fighting shoulder to shoulder with the unbelievers. And we say another thing. They cut a sorry figure when their unbelieving comrades examine them on the consistency of their position. Ingersoll might ask them whether they believe in God and then declare: You have a queer God, who set out to give us revelation and was unable to keep it free from errors. — Do you believe in Jesus Christ, true God? Then why do you not believe Him when He says that "Scripture cannot be broken," and how can you charge Him with sanctioning those erroneous books of the Old Testament?

Gaussen says this: "On hearing such objections, we feel our-

4[1] See *Conc. Theol. Monthly,* Vol. XII, p. 396: "Ingersoll openly professed his agnosticism; modern unbelief chooses to call itself a 'new meaningful way of interpreting old and familiar passages and stories.' Is that honest?"

selves . . . under the impression of sadness, sadness at seeing persons who acknowledge the Bible to be a revelation from God and not afraid, notwithstanding, to bring so hastily the most serious objections against it." (*Op. cit.*, p. 199.)

The moderns are not in good company. And they have to deny their own principles in employing the arguments of their companions. That is unworthy of the Christian.

Dare the Christian Impeach the Authority of the Lord Jesus?

There is one more point that needs to be emphasized. When the moderns invite us to underwrite their list of errors, they are asking us to charge our Lord and Savior Jesus Christ with error and to impeach His authority. That is asking too much of a Christian.

Jesus put His divine authority back of the Bible. He endorsed every statement made by the prophets and by the apostles when He solemnly declared: "The Scripture cannot be broken," John 10:35. He proclaims the absolute irrefragability, inerrancy, of this Book. He assures us that there is no error in the Old Testament, no error in the New Testament (Matt. 10:19 f.; Mark 13:11; Luke 21:14, 15).[42] And just such portions of Scripture as have been put on the black-list have been vouched for by Christ. Did Moses write the Pentateuch? "Moses wrote of Me," John 5:46. Is the creation story a myth and old wives' tale? Read Matt. 19:4. Is the story of the Flood history or mythology? Read Matt. 24:37 ff. Was Abraham a legendary figure? "Your father Abraham rejoiced to see My day," John 8:56. Is the story of Lot's wife true, and the story of Jonah in the whale's belly? Read Luke 17:32 and Matt. 12:40. Every story related in the Bible, every circumstance of it, and every single jot and tittle shall stand. Jesus guarantees the truth of it.[43]

---

42) See P. E. Kretzmann, *The Foundations Must Stand*, p. 38 ff. *Proceedings*, Iowa Dist., 1891, p. 30 f.

43) M'Intosh: "The object and burden of this book is to show that the Bible is, and claims to be, true, trustworthy, and of divine authority, and that Christ endorses and solemnly seals this claim with His divine authority and declares most absolutely the inviolability, solidarity, and organic unity of all Scripture." "The modern distinction between what is true and what is false in the Word of God is unknown to writers of Scripture and would have shocked the apostles and prophets and most of all the Son of God Himself, who set His solemn seal to every jot and tittle of it." (*Op. cit.*, pp. 2, 432.) S. C. Ylvisaker: "This is not the place to show in detail that or how Christ has identified Himself with all doctrines contained in Scripture, with all facts of history, geography, and so forth, which are mentioned there, and with every word written there as being His very own. Who are we to question one word which He has made His own, when He has said: 'The Scripture cannot be broken'; 'till heaven and earth pass, one jot or one tittle shall in no wise pass from the Law'?" (*Report of the 1940 Convention of the Norwegian Synod*, p. 21 f.)

And is His guarantee worth anything? The moderns actually insist on ruling out His authority. Whether they believe in the deity of Christ or not, they are saying with Voltaire that His testimony on this point is untrustworthy. They speak of "the exegetical mistakes" of Jesus. "They say that Jesus committed blunders when in Mark 2:26 He confused Abiathar with Ahimelech and in Matt. 23:35 Barachias with Jehoiada" (*Neue Luth. Kirchenz.,* April 15, 1901). Baumgaertel, in a letter to the *Allg. Ev.-Luth. Kirchenz.,* Nov. 12, 1926: "We know more concerning the origin of the Scriptures of Israel than the Jewish scribes and *Jesus, who got His knowledge of these matters from them.*" Jesus labored under certain limitations; for instance, He had the mistaken viewpoints of His day and age. Says C. H. Dodd: "We need not doubt that Jesus as He is represented shared the views of His contemporaries regarding the authorship of books in the Old Testament, or the phenomena of demon possessions — views which we could not accept without violence to our sense of truth." (*The Authority of the Bible,* p. 237.) Accordingly, "we no longer accept a saying as authoritative because it lies before us as a word of Jesus" (p. 233).[44]

Jesus is divested of His authority also by those who would extenuate His mistakes on the basis of the *kenosis.* W. Sanday opens the discussion of this question with the statement: "The question involved is nothing less than the authority of our Lord Himself." Absolutely true. He then says: "I should be loath to believe that our Lord *accommodated* His language to current notions, knowing them to be false." That, of course, is an impossibility. But then Sanday states: "I prefer to think, as it has been happily worded, that 'He *condescended* not to know.'" (*The Oracles of God,* pp. 103, 111.) *The Luth. Church Quart.,* 1935, p. 255, also operates with this false *kenosis* and, in addition, with the accommodation theory: "Jesus apparently shared the conceptions of His day regarding these things. As far as His speech indicates, He thought as the people of His time thought. At least when He emptied Himself and took upon Himself the form of a man, He accommodated His speech and activity to the concepts of the world in which He lived." That will not do. Scripture, indeed, tells us that Christ did not know the time of the Judgment (Mark 13:32), but that is far from saying that He could *err* in His statements.

---

44) "The question being asked in a recent meeting of evangelical ministers: 'If Moses did not write the Pentateuch, why did Jesus say that he did?' a voice replied: 'Because He knew no better.'" (D. J. Burrell, *Why I Believe the Bible,* p. 116.) Burrell comments: "It is incredible, however, that such views should be entertained by any of the sincere followers of Christ."

Refraining from the full use of His omniscience does not imply the harboring of erroneous ideas. If Christ "condescended" to be subject to error, His authority is destroyed.[45]

Whether the moderns say so in so many words, every one who underwrites the black-list says in effect that Christ was mistaken when He endorsed every word of Scripture. So this is the situation: Either there are errors in the Bible, or there are no errors in the Bible. And they who take the first alternative are confronted by another dilemma. They will have to say either that Jesus did not know that there were errors in the Bible or that He knew it but would not admit it. And whether they accept the first or the second alternative, they refuse to accept Christ's endorsement of all Scripture as worthy of acceptance. They insist that, while they reject certain portions of Scripture as unacceptable, they do accept the teaching of Jesus, that being all that God requires. But, behold, they refuse to accept one of the basic teachings of Jesus — that concerning the inerrancy, absolute trustworthiness, and plenary inspiration of the Scriptures.

And now they ask us to sign their round robin. Dr. Pieper tells them: "All objections to the divine inspiration and the inerrancy of the Bible are unworthy of a Christian because in that case fallible human judgment with respect to Scripture is exalted above the divine judgment of the infallible Christ, the Son of God." (*What Is Christianity?* p. 251.) R. Torrey tells them: "The Pentateuch is the very part of the Bible where the hottest fight has always been waged between those who believe the Bible to be the inerrant Word of God and those who think that much of it is only fable or 'folk-lore.' Here is where you find the two accounts of Creation,

---

45) . They, too, destroy the authority of Jesus who assume that He *might have been mistaken* in some of His views and judgments. James Stalker does that. He subscribes to Tholuck's statement "Although we find in the sayings of Jesus which we possess no formal hermeneutic mistake, yet the impossibility of such cannot be asserted *a priori* any more than the impossibility of a grammatical blunder or a chronological slip." (*The Ethics of Jesus*, p. 277.) — Tholuck, by the way, belongs also in the first group. He held that Jesus labored under the prejudices of His day. "Tholuck, der die Rationalisten vielfach bekaempft hat, ist doch so weit gegangen, dass er sagt, Christus habe auch keine hoehere Erkenntnis gehabt, als er zu der damaligen Zeit bei der Stufe der Erkenntnis, die damals sich vorfand, haben konnte. Man traut seinen Augen kaum! . . . Christus ein gewoehnlicher Mensch, der nicht mehr wissen koenne als die uebrigen Menschen seiner Zeit! . . . Echt nestorianisch!" (*Proceedings, Iowa Dist.*, 1891, p. 29, quoting Walther.) — So the possibility of error quickly turns into the actuality. But we cannot stand even for the "possibility." If, in pronouncing on the authorship of Moses or on any other matter, Jesus *might have been* mistaken, the truth of His judgment would have to be established by some other means. You or I would have to come to the help of Jesus. Is the Christian willing to play such a role?

about which so many superficial and ill-informed readers and teachers of the Bible gabble so much to their own satisfaction and so much to the disgust of all real students of the Bible. Here is where you have the story of the Fall. . . . And in Mark 7:13 our Lord calls the Pentateuch the 'Word of God' in so many words. And Matt. 5:18: 'One jot or one tittle.' " (*Op. cit.*, p. 15 ff.) Dr. Brooks reminds them of "the marvelous fact that those very passages that men are most apt to believe uninspired (Lot's wife, Sodom and Gomorrah, Jonah) are the ones which have received the sanction of Jesus Christ Himself" and tells them plainly: "It is nonsense to say: 'I believe Christ, but not those things.' " (See *Lehre und Wehre*, 57, p. 129.) They are asking too much of us. Can a Christian in his sober mind face Jesus as He endorses the Old Testament and tell Him: "You might be mistaken"? "Shall we side with the critics in opposition to the testimony given in the New Testament by the apostles and even by the Lord Jesus Himself? Were they so circumscribed by the ignorance of the age in which they lived that they did not know the Scriptures of their people as well as the critics do? Was Jesus? . . . This modern view of the Bible insists upon our acceptance of the Christ-dishonoring doctrine of the *kenosis*, vitally maiming our Lord's unique and perfect personality, making Him, as far as His knowledge is concerned, nothing more than a product of His time." (J. Bloore, *Alternative Views of the Bible*, pp. 60, 66.) God forbid that we should side with those who in order to be in harmony with pseudoscience put themselves out of harmony with Christ's sayings! It comes to this: "By these Scriptures Christ stands with a tremendous decisiveness. With them, in fact, as their Author, Fulfiller, and End, He identifies Himself. . . . Men cannot deny or reject them or their claim without denying or rejecting Him and His." (M'Intosh, *op. cit.*, p. 437. — Read, once more, the article in *Lehre und Wehre*, 69, p. 297: *Ein oeffentliches Bekenntnis zur Inspiration der Heiligen Schrift in Deutschland*.)[46]

---

46) We need not point out that Christ not only endorsed all that the prophets and the apostles wrote, but that their words are the very words of Christ. Christ is "the Author of Scripture." To say that Scripture is God's Word is to say that it is Christ's Word. And St. Peter tells us plainly that the prophets spoke by "the Spirit of Christ, which was in them" (1 Pet. 1:11), and St. Paul, that "Christ speaketh in me" (2 Cor. 13:3). It is thus apparent that our present section is merely an emphatic reiteration of the statement that he who criticizes Scripture commits a *crimen laesae maiestatis divinae*. He who says that Scripture has erred and that Scripture can err is saying that God has erred and can err. But we wanted to reiterate and emphasize that in this present section because it has pleased Christ and the Holy Ghost to do that very thing, to reiterate and emphasize it. When the Christian is tempted to tamper with Scripture, the realization that his Lord and Savior Jesus Christ has endorsed it generally and specifically adds weight to the warning: Do not lay unclean hands on this holy thing!

Men cannot deny the claims of Scripture without denying Christ, who endorsed these claims. We are not saying that all who hold that there are errors in the Bible are no longer Christians. Any Christian, as the *Proceedings of the Synodical Conference* of 1902 set forth, may be assailed by doubts on this matter when he reads Scripture or the dissertations of its critics. There are good Lutheran Christians, pastors and laymen, who, though they are convinced in their hearts that Scripture cannot contradict itself, frequently find themselves grappling with the thought that Scripture does contradict itself. (Pp. 21-25.) And on page 20 the old theologian Andreas Althammer is quoted: "Es gibt freilich einige fromme, ehrliche Leute, die aus Unwissenheit und Einfalt die Schrift fuer selbstwidersprechend halten." Even great theologians sometimes get befuddled.[47] Dr. Pieper mentions in this connection even the denial of the Vicarious Satisfaction. He states, first, that through the means of this doctrine the Holy Ghost enters into the heart, "who teaches men to recognize as His Word the Word He spoke through the prophets and apostles." And then he says: "That we do not deny outright, in every case, that he can have the Christian faith who in the security of his lecture-room or in his 'scientific' writings criticizes the *satisfactio vicaria* is due to the fact that we are willing to account for it on the basis of a 'double bookkeeping' or inconsistency, according to which a person does not believe in his heart and before God what he champions *in disputationibus*, as Luther and Chemnitz put it." (*Christl. Dogm.* I, p. 364.)

However, "all such theological thoughts lie outside of the Christian sphere." (Pieper, *loc. cit.*) What we do say is that those Christians — laymen, pastors, professors — who find mistakes in

---

47) We find a case in point in W. Elerts latest book, *Der Christliche Glaube*. Discussing the teaching of the old dogmaticians on Inspiration, he uses, on page 209, the phrase: "Der tiefere Grund dieser *Irrlehre*," referring to the statement of Quenstedt that Inspiration covers also those things which were already known to the holy writers. And then he says: "Wenn manche Dogmatiker . . . folgerten, dass der schreibende Mensch auch an der Bildung des Wortlautes keinen eigenen Anteil mehr habe, so grenzt das an Gotteslaesterung. Denn wie will man den Heiligen Geist dafuer verantwortlich machen, dass Paulus nicht mehr weiss, ob er ausser der Hausgemeinschaft des Stephanus in Korinth noch einen andern getauft hat (1 Kor. 1:16)." To be sure, it would be blasphemy to ascribe Paul's failure to remember certain data to the Holy Ghost. But Dr. Elert has got things badly mixed up here. All that the old dogmaticians — and we — say on this point is that the Holy Ghost caused Paul to set down this statement and supplied the words, too. — We set down this case in order to show that rejection of Verbal Inspiration is not necessarily due to unbelief, but may arise from misconception. Yes, a man may even know what Verbal Inspiration is and reject it *without realizing* what bearing this has on the fundamental question of the authority of Scripture; in that case he certainly could not be charged with *harboring* a fundamental error.

the Bible and for that reason reject Verbal Inspiration are not thinking Christian thoughts. They are thoughts inspired and uttered by the Old Adam. It is the Christian's duty to suppress such thoughts. It should shock him to find them arising in his mind, just, to quote M'Intosh once more, "as the modern distinction between what is true and what is false in the Word of God would have shocked the Son of God Himself, who set His solemn seal to every jot and tittle of it." We deny Him when we make this distinction; and what would the outcome be if one knowingly and persistently denied a word of Christ? [48]

The Christian Horrified at the Evil Results of Breaking Scripture

There is another reason why the Christian abominates the teaching of the erroneousness and errancy of the Bible. This teaching endangers the faith of the individual believer and causes untold harm to the Church. [49]

When the Lutheran professors Volck and Muehlau began their campaign against the inerrancy of the Bible in 1884, it "confused and saddened many in Dorpat. A lady said with tears in her eyes: 'I can no longer read the Bible.'" (See *Lehre und Wehre*, 1886, p. 2.) It is a stubborn fact that, when you persuade a person to believe that there are errors in the Bible, you have filled him with distrust of the Bible. For what H. L. Mencken, who knows little of the Bible but is very bright intellectually, has said: "If the Bible is true, then it is true from cover to cover. . . . Dr. Machen's position is completely impregnable," is absolutely true. (See *Lutheran Sentinel*, Feb. 13, 1939.) It is absolutely true, therefore, what the liberal D. Schenkel said: "If error is admitted at one point, it is admissible at all points." (See Rohnert, *Dogmatik*,

---

48) On this subject Bishop Charles Gore writes: "I am writing in full recognition of the fact that the leaders of criticism, especially on the Continent, have been very frequently rationalists, by which is meant men to whom the idea of the supernatural and the miraculous is intolerable. This sort of rationalism is, of course, incompatible with Christian faith. But many of the 'critics,' and especially those in Great Britain, have been devout believers; and their motive in maintaining 'critical conclusions' has been the conviction that such conclusions are really scientific and that it is disastrous to set religion in antagonism to science or to seek to shackle science, which is bound to be free. I am writing also in full recognition of the fact that almost every science 'sows its wild oats.'" (*The Doctrine of the Infallible Book*, p. 8 f.) Dr. Gore deals too gently with the Christian who is convinced that there are mistakes in the Bible. Such a theologian must be told that his conviction is not befitting a Christian. No Christian theologian is permitted to cultivate "wild oats" on the holy ground of the Bible.

49) We shall treat this matter very briefly at the present time. After we have discussed two further objections to Verbal Inspiration ("the ethical blemishes of the Bible" and "the trivialities"), we shall go into details.

p. 73.) It is absolutely true, therefore, what the scoffer Paine said: "If Matthew and Luke .cannot be believed in their account of Christ's natural genealogy, how are we to believe them when they tell us He was the Son of God?" Get people to believe that these genealogies are contradictory and unreliable, and you have put them on the road to disaster. "Ein frommer Laie," said Alt-hammer, "muesste irre werden an der Schrift. Waere wirklich ein Widerspruch, wie koennte ein Leser der Schrift zu einer Ueber-zeugung kommen, *was* darin fest und gewiss sein soll?" (See *Proceedings, Syn. Conf., 1902,* p. 20.) There are countless numbers whose faith has been shaken by the preachers of Bible errancy, and but for the grace of God countless numbers would have been lost to the Church and — heaven.

It does not help matters that they have words of praise for the Bible and call the untrue portions "holy ground" (Dr. Fosdick, *The Modern Use,* p. 52), "stories which because of their beauty and intrinsic worth should stand" (Dr. Nolde, *Luth. Church Quart.,* 1939, p. 301). Nor is the situation bettered by the claim that, if only the moral and religious truths of the Bible are true, all is well. The stubborn fact remains that "we would lose confidence in Scripture if we found that Scripture actually contains *falsa* and *errata*" (Stoeckhardt, *Lehre und Wehre,* 1886, p. 314). And Schenkel, Mencken, and Paine agree with Stoeckhardt. Luther: "Dess wird mich (achte auch wohl, auch keinen vernuenftigen Menschen) niemand bereden ewiglich, dass ein Mensch (so er anders ein Mensch ist, der bei Vernunft ist) sollt mit Ernst glauben koennen einem Buche oder Schrift, davon er gewiss waere, dass *ein* Teil (schweige denn drei Teile) erlogen waere, dazu nicht wissen muesste, welches unterschiedlich wahr oder nicht wahr waere." (XX: 2275.) Luther is speaking of the Koran. It would apply to the Bible, too, if the moderns had their way.

They say "the claim that the Scriptures are a perfect whole has wrought more mental distress and created more skepticism than any other dogma of Christian or Jewish theology." Under such preaching "poor souls pass off into the outer darkness" (see page 27 above). What actually happens is that the dogma of the errancy of Scripture is raising distressing doubts in the minds of the good Christians, is undermining the only foundation of faith (Walther: "Mit der Behauptung, dass dem goettlichen Inhalt der Heiligen Schrift auch Irriges, Menschliches eingestreut ist, wird nicht nur dieser Teil, sondern die ganze Heilige Schrift wankend und schwankend gemacht" [see *Lehre und Wehre,* 1911, p. 156]), and strengthens the infidel in his unbelief. No man ever lost his faith because of anything that the Bible says; the Holy Ghost takes care of that. But men have lost their faith because of the lie — which under the influence of Satan they believed — that the Holy Scriptures are untrustworthy. For the passing off of these poor souls into the outer darkness the preachers of the errancy of Scripture are responsible.

This teaching is an evil and malignant thing. We say with Dr. W. Dau: "We deplore and denounce the open and the covert attempts which are being made by misguided men to question or to deny the plenary or verbal theopneusty of the Bible or of parts of it. We abhor and abominate the irreverent schemes which unwise learned men have invented for producing a Bible which in their opinion will suit men better than the Bible of the prophets, evangelists, and apostles. We are indignant at the presumption of men who would have us rise mornings and inquire: 'What is the Bible today? How much . . . is still left of the dear old book?' We consider all these efforts abortive, futile, and doomed to utter failure. The last resting-place for all such dreams will be amid the spiritual and moral wreckage and *débris* which since time immemorial is the goal of rationalism." (From an address on the "Inerrancy of Scripture.")

THE INCREDIBLE FATUITY OF THE ERRORISTS

Dr. Pieper says: "The objections to the verbal inspiration of Holy Scripture do not manifest great ingenuity or mental acumen, but the very opposite." When men set out to criticize God's Word, "they lose their common sense and become utterly unreasonable and illogical." (*What Is Christianity?* P. 243.) On the other hand, Dr. Edwin Lewis speaks of "the incredible fatuity on the part of the literalist, who insists on the 'absolute inerrancy' of Scripture" (*A Philosophy of the Christian Revelation*, p. 55), and Dr. G. A. Buttrick declares that "the avowal of the literal infallibility of Scripture, held to its last logic, would risk a trip to the insane asylum." (See *Conc. Theol. Monthly*, XII, p. 223.) Who is right? It is the purpose of this and following sections to show that those who uphold the thesis that Scripture is in conflict with history, other sciences, and even with itself are in conflict with sound reason. The Modernists and the moderns claim that, when once the mind is scientifically trained, it detects a host of errors in the Bible. It will not be hard to demonstrate that, the better a mind is scientifically and logically trained, the more it marvels at the fatuity displayed by the critics of the Bible.[50]

---

50) The faith of the Christian does not need such a demonstration. But the moderns need it. When one who imagines that the rejection of Verbal Inspiration is required and justified by reason realizes that all his objections are unreasonable, he will approach Scripture with a more

The Historical Blunders of the Errorists

The list of "historical errors in the Bible" does not speak well for the historical acumen of its compilers. It evidences a vast amount of historical misinformation. And the misinformation dispensed by the historical critics of the Bible is due to the fact that they have not learned the first principles underlying the science of history. When they took that course, the professor warned them against undertaking to pass final judgment on any historical matter unless they had full knowledge of all the facts in the case. He commits a historical crime who decides historical questions on the basis of partial information. A mind which is scientifically trained shuns hasty, premature judgments. The professor also warned them against the vice of partiality. Unless a man is ready to make use of all the historical material at his disposal, he cannot qualify as a historian or historical critic. He has no right to pick and choose from the sources at his own good pleasure. These and similar rules and canons are dictated by common sense.

Most of the "historical mistakes" are mistakes of the critics. The critics spoke without full knowledge of the subject. In plain language, the items in question are due to ignorance. Consequently the list has a queer appearance. As the list looks today, every other item is marked "Delete!" The earlier critics have been corrected by scholars of a later day, and the later critics are hard put to find new mistakes — or try to salvage some of the old items — in order to give a respectable length to the list. They used to say that Moses could not have been the author of the Pentateuch as we have it because at the time when it purports to have been written people could not write. This item has been deleted. "It was not long ago that certain 'progressives' were wont to affirm boldly that there never was any such person as Moses, because no mention of him can be found in other records; and, anyway, allowing that there was such a man, he couldn't possibly have written the Pentateuch because the art of writing was unknown in his time. Then along came a man with a spade, and, digging among the ruins of Tel-el-Amarna, he unearthed a whole library of correspondence" dating from the time of the

---

chastened spirit. It will shatter his self-confidence to find that on his own principles, on the application of common sense, his position is untenable. So we are not now asking him for the *sacrificium intellectus*. Leave that to the believer as a believer. All that we ask of the objector is the *usus intellectus*. We want him, for the purpose of the present articles, to use it to the full. — The present discussion will be of some use, too, for the believer. His own flesh makes the same objections, and his carnal pride of reason needs the same treatment.

Exodus. (D. J. Burrell, *Why I Believe the Bible*, p. 61.)[51] "Thus, while von Bohlen pictures an analphabetical ancient world and scoffs at the notion of literary activity in the Mosaic era (a position shared also by Reuss, Dillmann, and others), the modern verdict, which rests on a definite historical basis, is not only this affirmation: 'It is probable that at the time of the Amarna letters' (the fourteenth century, or the time of Moses) 'the usual mode of writing in Syria, Phenicia, and Palestine was the alphabetic' (*Am. Journal of Archeology*, Jan., 1926), but also the unavoidable conclusion that the real origin of alphabetic writing lies in the dim past, too far anterior to Moses to be dated definitely. (*Con. Theol. Monthly*, IV, p. 179.)

All right, Moses could write. But he had no right to speak of Abraham and Amraphel, etc., as historical figures. This item, too, has been blue-penciled, and the censor is recognized among the higher critics of today as a high authority — *A New Commentary on Holy Scripture*, edited by Bishop Charles Gore and others (1929): "With the introduction of Abraham we touch real history and are able to compare the narratives of Genesis with Babylonian and Egyptian records. . . . The identification of 'Amraphel, king of Shinar,' i. e., Babylon, with Hammurabi, the sixth king of the first Babylonian dynasty, who reigned c. 2123-2081 B. C., gives us an approximate date for Abraham's migration from Babylon. . . . There is no reason to doubt the existence of the patriarchs (Abraham, Jacob, Israel) as historic personages." (P. 38.) So item two also was the result of a premature judgment, given by an immature historian.

Item three. Somebody declared that "an alliance between Egypt and the Hittites was as improbable as would be one at the present time between England and the Choctaws." "But, alas for the overconfident critic, recent investigations have shown, not only that such an alliance was natural but that it actually occurred." (The writer quotes from monuments of Egypt and the Tel-el-Amarna tablets): "There has been brought to light a Hittite empire in Asia Minor, with central power and vassal dependencies round about and with treaty rights on equal terms with the greatest nations of antiquity, thus making the Hittite power a third great power with Babylonia and Egypt." (*The Fundamentals*, II, pp. 15, 32.)

Next we have the *cause célèbre* based on Luke 2:1, 2. Here the critics were absolutely sure of their case. This census is a fiction! And Quirinius never governed Syria during the life of

---

51) We read on page 187: "Suffice it here to say that not a single record of the slightest importance in the Pentateuch or other historical books of Scripture has ever been successfully impugned, while, on the contrary, the researches of the archeologists are continually verifying them."

Herod! Luke committed a historical crime. "Twesten, the learned rector of the university at Berlin, whom, for his labors and reputation in other respects, we honor, quotes this passage and that of the blind men at Jericho as showing that we throw ourselves into inextricable difficulties in our endeavor to explain them. . . . These cases are among those which the adversaries of a plenary inspiration have seemed to regard as the most insurmountable." (L. Gaussen, *Theopneustia*, p. 208, 210.) All the evidence was against Luke, insisted the prosecutor. The *Proceedings of the Western District of 1865*, page 31, after stating that "not a single Bible statement concerning secular matters has been proved false," goes on to say: "But there remained one passage which could not be straightened out, the passage stating that Cyrenius was governor of Syria at the time of the birth of Christ, for by all accounts he held that position at a later date. The unbelievers were already shouting in glee and telling us: Don't you see that you have a no-account Bible?" But new evidence came in on that point: "A few years ago it was discovered that Cyrenius was governor of Syria twice, and again the Bible won out." Do we have to go into particulars? We shall take at random C. E. Lindberg's summary: "By the investigations of Ramsay and others it has been proved that there was a periodical census system in the Roman Empire. . . . If the first census began 8—7 B. C., it was slow in materializing on account of the situation in Syria and Palestine. . . . A series of inscriptions bearing on the career of Quirinius proves that he was governor of Syria in the first census and governor and procurator in the second, Acts 5:37. The modern findings in stone and papyri vindicate the accurateness of the Gospel of Luke." (*Christian Dogmatics*, p. 392.) Chapter XXVI of G. A. Barton's *Archeology and the Bible* gives some pertinent papyri and concludes: "So far as the new material goes, it confirms the narrative of Luke."[52)]

---

52) Why, the Sunday-school children know all about this. W. T. Ellis, in his lessons published in the daily press, told them in the lesson for Dec. 25, 1927, that Caesar Augustus himself is a witness for Luke. He quotes from an inscription in a temple in Ancyra (Angora), the *Monumentum Ancyranum:* "In my sixth consulship I carried out a census of the Roman people. . . . A second time, in the consulship of C. Censorius and C. Asinius, I completed a lustrum [or census] without the help of a colleague invested with the consular imperium. At this second lustrum 4,233,000 Roman citizens were entered on the rolls." (This was the Christmas census, and the date was about B. C. 8, as we know by the names of the consuls.) "A third time (A. D. 14) I completed a lustrum. . . ." The case against Luke has been thrown out of court. The expert for the prosecution was compelled to make this declaration: "The outcome of the whole controversy is that no one is entitled to laugh at Luke's statement (or perhaps we should say, the statement of the document he quotes), even if it be not perfectly

Our *Synodalbericht* continues: "Eine andere Schwierigkeit, die sich merkwuerdig fein geloest hat. Apostelgeschichte 13 wird naemlich erzaehlt, dass Paulus den Landvogt auf der Insel Cypern bekehrt habe. Nun fanden aber die Gelehrten heraus, dass sich der Kaiser Augustus diese Insel zur eigenen Verwaltung vorbehalten hatte, dass also da kein Landvogt sein konnte. Lange schien die Sache zur Freude der Unglaeubigen unerklaerlich. Aber man fand auf einmal eine alte Silbermuenze, auf der stand in der Mitte 'Cyprische Landmuenze' und am Rande herum 'Geschlagen unter dem Landvogt Comenius Proclus'. Und noch ein wenig spaeter fand man auch bei einem alten griechischen Geschichtschreiber die Nachricht, dass schon Kaiser Augustus die Insel wieder an den Senat zur Besetzung durch einen Landvogt abgegeben habe. Darum lasse sich doch niemand verblueffen, wenn die Unglaeubigen mit solchen Ungenauigkeiten und Widerspruechen der Schrift prahlen; denn besieht man sie beim Licht, so beweisen sie sich als nicht vorhanden".[53] Put Gore's liberal *Commentary* on the stand. "Cyprus was a senatorial province. Therefore the title of proconsul is correct. An inscription bearing the words 'when Paulus was proconsul' has been found in the island." Verdict for Luke.

The critics have not yet conceded that their black-list is mistaken in every case. Some of them persist in charging the Biblical historians with mistakes on the unreasonable principle that in the

---

accurately worded." (Bishop Gore's *Commentary*.) The laughter in the court-room of which the *Synodalbericht* spoke suddenly subsided. This attack on the veracity of the Bible historian, again, was due to lack of information. — Always bear in mind that even when this corroborative testimony was not available, the case of Luke was not in doubt. This additional material shuts the mouth of the prosecution, but it was never needed by the believer. If we should meet a case where the Biblical writer is not "confirmed" by the historian or scientist or is contradicted by him, we know that the Bible is right and the objector wrong — in every case.

53) Let us repeat this in English: "The sixth class of difficulties are those that arise from our defective knowledge of the history, geography, and usages of Bible times. We have an illustration of this in Acts 13:7. Here Luke speaks of 'the deputy,' or, more accurately, 'the proconsul' [see Revised Version]. The ruler of an imperial province was called a 'propraetor,' of a senatorial province a 'proconsul.' Up to a comparatively recent date, according to the best information we had, Cyprus was an imperial province, and therefore its ruler would be a 'propraetor,' but Luke calls him a 'proconsul.' This certainly seems like a clear case of error on Luke's part, and even conservative commentators in former days felt forced to admit that Luke was in slight error, and the destructive critics were delighted to find this 'mistake.' But further and more thorough investigation has brought to light the fact that just at the time of which Luke wrote the Senate had made an exchange with the emperor whereby Cyprus had become a senatorial province and therefore its ruler a 'proconsul,' and Luke was exactly and minutely correct, after all, and the very 'scholarly' literary critics were themselves in error in their criticism. The mistake was theirs and not Luke's." (R. A. Torrey, *Is the Bible the Inerrant Word of God?* P. 81.)

case of a conflict between a sacred and a secular historian the latter is always right. They will even maintain their charge in the face of abundant historical evidence to the contrary. The critics used to poke fun at Daniel for making Belshazzar the last ruler of Babylon. The last king, they said, was Nabonidus, and no historian mentions Belshazzar. In answer to this the *Lutheran School Journal*, Nov., 1936, page 108, quotes from Urquhart's *Archeology's Solution of Old Testament Puzzles* this inscription made by Nabonidus: "As for me, Nabonidus, king of Babylon, from sin against thee, the great Divinity, save me; and a life of remote days give as a gift; and as for Belshazzar, the eldest son, the offspring of my heart, the fear of thy great Divinity cause thou to exist in his heart and let not sin possess him that he be satisfied with fulness of life." It can no longer be asserted that Daniel invented Belshazzar. And why should Daniel have been proclaimed "the *third* ruler in the kingdom" (Dan. 5:29)? Because Nabonidus was the ruler, his son the coruler, and so Daniel was given the next highest position. It is very simple. But the critics will not have it so. They now assert that no tablets have been dated in Belshazzar's reign. And the monuments do not say that Belshazzar was slain at the taking of Babylon. Prof. Joseph D. Wilson rightly says: "That is a quibble unworthy of the scholar who makes it." (*Fundamentals*, 7, p. 96.) And it is unworthy of Gore's *Commentary* to say definitely and positively: "No Belshazzar was king of Babylon so far as is known. . . . The evidence at present available is against his ever having reigned." Since when does the rule hold that unless a historical writer is corroborated by another historical writer, his account may be ignored? [54]

"Further," says Gore's *Commentary*, "Darius the Mede is an entirely unknown person, and history allows no place for him. Cyrus was the immediate successor of Nabonidus, and no other supreme ruler is known." We shall say that Darius the Mede is a well-known figure. The historian Daniel has made him known to us. Let Baumgaertel, Best, De Witt, and Gore keep on saying: "Einen 'Meder' Darius hat es nicht gegeben," we shall

---

54) Gore's *Commentary* ignores not only the statements of the historian Daniel but also the evidence from secular sources. Barton's *Archeology and the Bible* has devoted chapter XVIII to this matter. It gives us the inscription of Nabuna'id quoted above and extracts from two tablets from Erech recently published. "It was customary for Babylonians, in confirming a contract, to swear by the name of the reigning king, and one of these tablets contains a contract dated in the twelfth year of Nabuana'id in which a man bound himself by the oath of Nabuna'id, king of Babylon, and of Belshazzar, the king's son. As Belshazzar is here associated with the king, he must have been slightly lower in rank and power than the king himself." See also *Journal of the A. L. Conference*, Aug., 1940, p. 531, and *C. T. M.*, III, p. 215.

keep on telling them: Darius the Mede did rule over Babylon. We shall not say that he was "the *supreme* ruler," "an independent king." Daniel does not say so. A mind scientifically trained would not have written into Gore's *Commentary:* "Darius the Mede: an unknown figure, possibly by confusion with Gobryas or Ugbaru, the general of Cyrus, who occupied the city and slew the king's son. . . . The writer evidently thought of Darius as an independent king, reigning before Cyrus and presumably for some length of time," "as supreme ruler." Daniel does not call him an *independent* king. And why use the term "by confusion with Gobryas"? Why not say: Darius, known in secular history as Gobryas? There is a great lack of historical objectivity in these historical critics. One trained in the science of history will write in this strain: "He has not been identified with certainty but was probably sovereign of the Babylonian empire *ad interim* until Cyrus, who was pressing his conquests, was ready to assume the duties of king of Babylon." (Davis's *Dictionary of the Bible.*) — "The writer evidently thought of Darius as reigning for some length of time." Anything wrong about that? Barton's *Archeology* says: "The second tablet shows that in the fourth year of Cambyses [*i. e.*, 524 B. C.] Gobryas was still governor of Babylon. If he is the man who in Daniel is called Darius the Mede, he exercised the powers of governor in Babylon for a considerable number of years." — It is puerile, not worthy of an adult historian, to operate with the rule that whenever a person mentioned in the Bible cannot be absolutely identified with a person mentioned by a secular historian, the Biblical statement is subject to doubt.

Another item which some refuse to delete from the black-list is that concerning the first husband of Herodias. Gore's *Commentary* persists in rating Josephus higher than the evangelists. "It is simplest to suppose that Mark or his informant confused Herodias's husband and son-in-law." (On Mark 6:17.) What we have said on this item in the preceding is all that we are going to say.

We are of course not going to take notice of all the historical "mistakes" on the black-list. But just to show to what lengths the critics have gone in order to get a long list, we should like to cite one more example. Bruno Bauer, the skeptic and scoffer, denies "the reliability of Luke's gospel on the ground that it makes a ruler a contemporary of Jesus who had died half a century before. Lysanias, tetrarch of Abilene, has been murdered 34 years before the birth of Christ. 'Da der Evangelist fuer die vierte Tetrarchie keinen andern Namen ausfindig zu machen weiss, so nennt er frischweg Lysanias, ohne dass es ihm einfiele, danach zu fragen, ob dieser Lysanias noch lebte' (Weisse.) . . . 'In spaeteren Zeiten noch,' sagt Strauss (*Leben Jesu*, I, 375), 'war Abilene von dem letzten Herrscher der frueheren Dynastie ἡ Λυσανίου zubenannt, aus welchem Umstande der Evangelist den Schluss zog, dass es auch damals noch einen Herrscher dieses Namens gegeben habe.'" (*Kritik der Evangelischen Geschichte der Synoptiker*, I, p. 130.) — Man is able to doubt and deny anything. Why, the late Nathanael Schmidt of Cornell University made this statement: "It may be affirmed that we have no absolute contemporary evidence preserved in its original form that Jesus ever lived." (See S. M. Zwemer, *The Glory of the Manger*, p. 42.) And if the canon of the historical critics is right (that the historical statements of the Bible need corroboration from secular sources), men like Professor Schmidt can no longer assume that Jesus was a historical personage. Characterizing these and similar objections, H. M'Intosh applies the terms "culpable ignorance or intellectual density," "paltry puerilities and most jejune ideas," "mental opacity," etc. (*Is Christ Infallible and the Bible True?* Pp. 292, 312, 454, etc.)

How the Critics Blunder in Natural Science

These same terms apply to the list dealing with the alleged blunders in natural science. The ants of Prov. 6:8 may serve as a sample case. (See page 9 above.) The scientific skeptic said (1) that ants are carnivorous and so could not store up "meat"; it would spoil. And (2) they do not house grains for future use; Solomon mistook the white cocoon of the ant pupae for such grains. We hate to waste our paper, but in order to put these scientific blunderers in their place, we submit the following. *International Critical Commentary:* "As to the industrial habit spoken of in the verse, the latest authorities hold that some species of ants are granivorous and store up food." *Encyclopedia Britannica:* "Ants exhibit a great variety of food preference: many are carnivorous, others feed upon nectar and honey-dew; some gather in seeds, etc., and some live on fungi which they cultivate. . . . Certain ants resort to collecting, and feeding upon, plant seeds. These harvesting ants collect, husk, and store the seeds in special granaries." [55] *The Pulpit Commentary* reaches the conclusion:

---

55) Additional authorities: Avebury, *Ants, Bees, and Wasps*, p. 61: "Forel asserts that *Atta structor* allows the seeds in its granaries to commence the process of germination for the sake of the sugar." Wheeler, *Ants*, p. 258 f.: "The ancient peoples were undoubtedly familiar with the granivorous habits of these ants (*Messor barbarus* and *Messor structor*) and probably also with those of the third species, *Messor arenarius*. To them refer many allusions in the writings of Solomon and the Mischna, etc. . . . The entomologists of the early portion of the last century, however, failing to find any harvesters among the ants of temperate Europe, began to doubt or even to deny their existence. . . . All doubt was re-

"Hence writers who were ignorant of ants beyond those of their own country have been presumptuous enough to deny the accuracy of Solomon's statement." This is but a sample case. And it fits most cases in the black-list — the objections are based on plain ignorance and clamant with the presumptuous cock-sureness of the smatterer. — Give science a chance! Let the scientist put himself in possession of all the facts in the case, and science will catch up with Scripture.

Periodically the critics set up a great hullabaloo about the multitude of quails mentioned Num. 11:31, 32. Back around 1886 "an infidel paper in Boston devoted a column of ridicule to the 'quail story.'"   (A. T. Pierson, *Many Infallible Proofs*, p. 180.) Last year a suit was brought against Rev. Harry Rimmer, who had offered $1,000 to any one proving a scientific error in the Bible. The plaintiffs — a group of freethinkers — attempted to prove that the story of the quails involved a scientific impossibility. We are wondering what law of nature was broken by that occurrence. The question is not whether the quails have the habit of appearing in such incredible numbers. No army on the march would expect that once a month some species of bird, obeying a law implanted in this species, would relieve the commissary department of its usual duties. Our infidels will have to take the story as Moses relates it, and Moses describes it as a miracle. So our objectors will have to prove that science has discovered a law which makes it impossible for God to have sent this great number of quails to Israel in its need. Of course, there is nothing in nature to tie the hands of the Lord. — The Boston paper, to give point to its ridicule, "estimated the bushels of quail piled up over the country, showing that each of the 6,000,000 Israelites would have 2,888,643 bushels of quail per month, or 69,629 bushels for a meal." That is rather pointless since Moses does not state that the Israelites devoured all the quails. A great many indeed they did eat, so many that it came out at their nostrils and it was loathsome unto them, v. 20. But Moses does not say that God forced them to eat all the birds He sent. Please read v. 32! And the story of the miraculous fall of the manna will help you to understand how God managed this affair. Where is the scientific impossibility?   The court that heard the evidence the freethinkers

---

moved by Moggridge's excellent work in 1871 and 1872. . . .   He opened the nests of these ants and studied their granaries. . . ."   *The Pulpit Commentary* offers a lot of additional material. For instance: "The late Professor Darwin states of the agricultural ant of Texas, which in many features resembles the ant of Palestine, that it not only stores its food but prepares the soil for the crops, keeps the ground free from weeds, and finally reaps the harvest. (*Journal of the Linnaean Society*, Vol. 1, No. 21, p. 27.)"

of our day had to offer — their experts were Dr. John Haynes Holmes and Dr. Charles Francis Potter — decided in favor of the defendant.[56]

We could wish that the Ingersolls might have their day in court who say, "The Bible is not inspired in natural history. For it says (Lev. 11:5) that the rabbit and the hare chew the cud. But they do not." Are you sure? In the first place, the animals mentioned are not yet *absolutely* identified. Davis's *Dictionary of the Bible* will only go so far as to say that the "coney," *shaphan*, is *probably* the rock-badger. As to the "hare," *arnebeth*, the consensus of opinion is that it is an animal like our hare. But might not the *arnebeth* be an extinct species? However, let that go. Let the *arnebeth* be a common hare. And Ingersoll insists that according to the zoologists the hare does not chew the cud. So we ask, in the second place, what does "chewing the cud" mean? It does not mean that the animal performing that operation must have the complex stomach, which is four-chambered, of the true ruminants. Our zoologists use the term "true ruminants" to designate the animals that have a four-chambered stomach, but they classify as ruminants also those whose stomach is imperfectly four-parted, and also those whose stomach is three-parted. And we claim the privilege, with Moses, of classifying as cud-chewers also those animals which, let their stomach be what it will, chew their food a second time. And the hare *is* such an animal.

Ingersoll and those on his side assert that the zoologists deny that. And so we make our third point: It is not true that "the zoologists," all zoologists, are on Ingersoll's side. Reputable zoologists are on Moses' side. "Selbst noch Linné hat den Hasen [hare, *arnebeth*] unter die Wiederkaeuer gerechnet." (Daechsel's *Bibelwerk*.) Professor Ruetimeyer of Basel, according to Bettex

---

56) We do not know just what evidence the defendant offered. Perhaps he pointed out, with A. T. Pierson, that "the Bible does not say any such a thing as that they were piled two cubits high over a territory forty miles broad; it simply means that the wind which brought them from the sea swept them within reach of about three feet above the ground. If you should say you saw a flock of birds as high as a church spire, even an infidel would ridicule any one for supposing they were packed so high." Or he may have insisted that "the text does not say that the quails were heaped up exactly two days' journey in every direction. It does not say that they were heaped up two cubits high on a level throughout that area. Every student of Hebrew will agree that the words simply denote a piling up of birds to two cubits high, and such piles were found within approximately that distance about the camp." (See *Conc. Theol. Monthly*, XI, p. 210.) The thing is not so ridiculous as the freethinkers make themselves believe. But leave that aside; they must prove that God could not have performed this miracle. Their plea that science does not recognize miracles will be answered later, when we take up the chapter of the fatuity of "higher science."

"einer der ersten Wiederkaeuerkenner Europas," cited also by the *Encyclopedia Britannica* as an authority in mammalogy, stated: "Dass der Hase wiederkaeut, ist mir nicht neu. Nur mache ich darauf aufmerksam, dass in der heutigen anatomischen und embryologischen Klassifikation die Sitte des Wiederkaeuens nicht als Einteilungsgrund allein massgebend ist." (*Die Bibel Gottes Wort*, p. 141.)[57]— The judge trying Ingersoll's case would have a hard time deciding in his favor.

And if the judge decided in his favor? He might do that; he might be swayed by the consideration that there is a preponderance of expert testimony on Ingersoll's side. We readily admit that most zoologists deny that the hare chews the cud. But that would not affect us deeply. Why, even if all naturalists were in conflict with Moses, we would insist that the animal mentioned in Lev. 11:6 does perform the operation there predicated of it. The fathers did not lose a moment's sleep when the secular authorities did not seem to agree with Luke in the matter of the census. Neither would we, even if the judge ruled out the testimony of Ruetimeyer and of the professor at that State university. — Ingersoll and the other critics may have a lot of learning on their side; their fatuity consists in their harboring the idea that their learning could make the Christian doubt the truthfulness of any word of God.

What is wrong with the astronomical phenomena recorded Josh. 10:12 ff. and 2 Kings 20:9 ff.? Paine and Ingersoll, Harnack, Fosdick, and the archbishop of York tell us these things could not have happened, and the Bible, which records them, cannot claim plenary inspiration. What is the scientific error involved? The thing is most amusing. Ingersoll, for instance: "I don't believe that the man who wrote that knew that the earth was turning on

---

57) Another authority quoted by Pastor F. C. Pasche in this connection: "The Hebrew word does not imply having a ruminant stomach but simply rechew, or masticate." (See *Lehre u. Wehre*, 69, p. 188.) Jenks and Warhe, *Comprehensive Commentary: "Arnebeth.* That this is the hare is confirmed by the cognate languages. That it chews the cud is proved beyond all doubt. See Michaelis and Linnaeus. Although it wants the four stomachs peculiar to cleft-hoof cattle, yet it returns the food, once chewed, into its mouth by the esophagus, since its stomach has several little cells, divided by partitions, from which the food, while it is too hard, is repelled." Dr. P. E. Kretzmann states: "Careful scientists, even distinguished biologists, such as one at a leading State university whose lectures I attended, have admitted that our knowledge of certain mammals in this class would not warrant our declaring the statement of Lev. 11:6 untrue. While mammals of this class do not have the digestive apparatus of those that chew the cud, there is evidently a process of total or partial regurgitation, together with a second chewing of the food, which fully substantiates the statement found in Scripture. It is not a mere *semblance* of chewing the cud with which we are dealing but an actual chewing of food previously swallowed."

its axis at the rate of a thousand miles an hour, because if he did, he would have understood the immensity of heat that would have been generated by stopping the world. It has been calculated by one of the best mathematicians and astronomers that to stop the world would cause as much heat as it would take to burn a lump of solid coal three times as big as the globe." (*Lectures,* p. 283.) And another catastrophe would have resulted: "It has been said in Germany: 'The most fearless methodist will feel constrained to own that in the system of our globe, were the sun to stop for an instant, or were the earth's motion to be slackened, belligerent armies, and all that is on the earth's surface, would be swept away like chaff before the wind." (See Gaussen, *op. cit.,* p. 246.) Gaussen answers: "The fact is far from being absurd; it is only miraculous."[58] If these things happened at all, they happened as Joshua tells you, because God directly intervened. And if God had a hand in it, He certainly knew how to provide against the dire consequences Ingersoll and the others fear. Gaussen is not wrong in calling the objection absurd.

If Ingersoll and Harnack should reply that we are wrong there, that miracles do not occur, we shall have to tell them that we agreed to discuss here only the "scientific impossibilities" involved. We are here dealing with common, every-day, honest science. If they want to switch the discussion over to higher science, we shall be at their service in due time.

All right, they say, let us remain in the domain of common science, physical science, and the Bible is wrong because science teaches that the earth rotates on its axis, etc., and Josh. 10:13 should have stated: "And the earth stood still." — Wrong again! Copernicanism indeed teaches that; but everybody except the sciolists knows that the system of Copernicus is based on a — hypothesis. The argument that Scripture is not inspired because of its alleged conflict with some hypothetical assumption has a most flimsy basis. And there is no reason in the world why we should decree that Joshua employed phenomenal and not scientific language. His statement "And the sun stood still" is not in conflict with any established fact of science.[59]

---

58) He adds a section to show that the objection is in error. Even by the laws of physics the belligerent armies would not have been "swept away as if by a tempest." Look it up if you care to.

59) Some of us think that if we don't hem and haw about Joshua's language, we'll lose our scientific standing. Dr. A. L. Graebner did not think so. "The present writer happens to have devoted three of the best years of his life chiefly and assiduously to the study of physical sciences and has been in touch with these sciences for many more years. But if he has profited anything by these sciences, it is, besides a few other things, a habit of speaking with more modesty on certain scientific topics than the college sophomore who knows all about them. . . . And

Then there is the story of Jonah and the whale. Paine made sport of it. Pastor Fosdick, like Paine, ridicules it. Pastor Cadman calls it a "fish story." And Prof. W. H. Dunphy runs a close second to Paine when he protests against "the notion that we must accept 'the credibility of the whole of Judges and the edibility of the whole of Jonah' as revealed truths. Fortunately the Holy Catholic Church of Christ has never committed herself to any such absurdity." (*The Living Church*, Feb. 18, 1933.) However, men who object to this Biblical story in the name of science do not know much about natural science. "There are many skeptics today who are so densely ignorant of matters clearly understood by many Sunday-school children that they are still harping, in the name of 'scholarship,' on this supposed error in the Bible. One of the most popular of 'modernist' preachers trotted this out in an address last October 23, 1921." (R. A. Torrey, *op. cit.*, p. 78.) In the first place, the Bible does not say that a "whale" swallowed Jonah. It was a "great fish," "a sea-monster." And Sunday-school children know that the tarpon, for instance, can swallow a man. There was a tarpon caught weighing 30,000 pounds, and it had in its stomach, whole, one fish weighing 1,500 pounds, besides a large octopus. (See *Lutheran Church Herald*, Sept. 16, 1930.) In the second place, the whale, too, can swallow a man, if it is the right kind of whale, the sperm-whale, "which can

---

he has learned to rate, not only from a theological but also from a scientific point of view, such assertions as this, that 'the Missouri Church holds that the Bible teaches the Ptolemaic astronomy.' We do not know whether the writers of the *Lutheran* would be bold enough to assert that the General Council held the Copernican theory. But we do know that, considering the elements which constitute a synod, there is no synod on the face of the earth which would not stultify itself if it voted an endorsement of the Copernican or any other system of astronomy." (*Theological Quarterly*, VI, p. 40.) Dr. G. Stoeckhardt is not afraid to "ask: Is the Copernican system, under which the earth revolves around the sun, really an established fact, which no man in his senses, at least no astronomer and mathematician, may challenge?" (*Lehre u. Wehre*, 32, p. 314.) We are not going to rate Dr. Pieper as a back number because he writes: "We should always bear in mind and let others remind us of it that our human knowledge concerning astronomical matters is, from the nature of the case, very limited since we are unable to take a position outside of the globe, needed for a full survey. The geographer Daniel, himself a Copernican, declared: 'All cosmic systems ever proposed are not based on experience, for this would require a position beyond the earth, but on deductions and combinations. All of them therefore are and remain hypotheses.'" (*Chr. Dogmatik*, I, p. 577.) When Oberkonsistorialrat Twesten characterized this position as due to "stubborn stupidity," "Borniertheit" (*l. c.*), he lost the calm balance of the mature scientist. — Let us bear in mind, too, that Joshua is charged with a scientific error not so much on the basis of the teaching of Copernicanism but because of the basic statement that daylight lasted twenty-four hours. Even if Joshua had been a Copernican and had written: "And the earth stood still" (the *pedantic* Copernican would have employed that phraseology), Ingersoll and Fosdick would object with the same vehemence.

swallow two men at one gulp without a struggle" (*The Living Church*, Apr. 5, 1930), and, in the third place, a man swallowed by a whale was found in its stomach unconscious but alive after two days (*Princeton Review*, October, 1927); and, in the fourth place, a certain whaler "learned from observation that the great sperm-whale has power to empty his stomach voluntarily" (*The Living Church*, March 22, 1930).

We know, of course, that the whale or any other sea-monster is not in the habit of putting in its appearance at the time and at the place called for by some exigency, of swallowing the man, and vomiting him out, at the right time and place — and keeping him alive for three days. "Diese Historie des Jonas ist so gross, dass sie fast unglaublich ist und ungereimter [scheint] als irgendeine Fabel der Dichter. Wenn es nicht in der Bibel waere, wuerde ich es durchaus als eine Luege verlachen. Denn wenn man ihm will nachdenken, wie er drei Tage in dem grossen Bauch des Walfisches gewesen sei, da er doch in drei Stunden verdaut, Fleisch und Blut des Walfisches haette werden sollen." (Luther, XXII, p. 1424.)[60] "Wenn es nicht in der Bibel waere!" Professor Dunphy and Thomas Paine and Professor Horine, all of whom *believe that there is an almighty God*, have reached the summit of absurdity when they ridicule the story of Jonah as an absurdity. — This objection, in all its phases, reminds one of the man who tried to do business the other day with counterfeit Confederate money.

Prof. R. T. Stamm charges St. Paul with an arboricultural error. Do we have to go into that? Another professor, who was a confirmed infidel, triumphantly asked: "How about that cytological error that Paul the Apostle made in the fifteenth chapter of First Corinthians?" Read the fine answer given him by one of the students, Harry Rimmer. (*The Harmony of Science and Scripture*, p. 109 ff.) Ingersoll gloats over the biometrical blunder committed by Moses. "The Jewish people stayed in Egypt 215 years. How many did they have when they went to Egypt? Seventy. How

---

60) One can hardly trust one's eyes when one reads in an article written by Prof. John W. Horine in the *Lutheran*, March 18, 1937, these words: "Jonah 2:1-9. The writer of this remark is frank to say that he cannot accept as matter of fact the literal statement that Jonah in the fish's belly — in that smelly, suffocating place — had the clearness of mind to order his thoughts and compose the metrical lines of this Hebrew psalm. And there is another difficulty, thus stated by the outspoken Luther: 'It [the story of Jonah] is exaggerated beyond the possibility of belief. If it were not in the Bible, I would laugh at it. For how could Jonah remain in the belly of the whale three days when he would have been digested in three hours.' . . . The book is considered to be not literal history but parable or allegory." In all fairness Professor Horine should have added: While I cannot believe this story because of its absurdity, Luther believed it in spite of its absurdity.

many were they at the end of 215 years? Three millions, for there were 600,000 men of war. Is there a minister in the city of Chicago that will testify to his own idiocy by claiming that they could have increased to three millions by that time?" (*Lectures:* "Mistakes of Moses," p. 291 f.) The ministers of Chicago are not so idiotic as to accept Ingersoll's false premise. They accept the figures which Moses gives. Israel sojourned in Egypt *430 years.* See Ex. 12:40. That gives us eight generations, allowing a little more than 50 years for a generation. "Even if we allow, to be conservative, but four sons for each family, the seventh generation would have numbered 835,584 males." (W. Arndt, *Bible Difficulties,* p. 53.) Nothing idiotic about that computation. And we are going to allow more than four sons for each family. "The children of Israel were fruitful and increased abundantly and multiplied and waxed exceeding mighty, and the land was filled with them," Ex. 1:7.

We conclude this section with L. Boettner's statement: "Today scarcely a shred of the old list remains. . . . Not so much as one single error has been *definitely proved* to exist anywhere in the Bible. . . . There is every reason for believing that with additional knowledge they, too, will be cleared up." (*The Inspiration of the Scriptures,* p. 50.) And if some are never in this life cleared up, that will not keep the Christian from dying in good spirits.

"Unfulfilled Prophecies" and "Misquotations"

The men who prepared the list of "unfulfilled prophecies" did not know their Bible well. Let us examine two samples. Fr. Baumgaertel and C. H. Dodd declare that Ezekiel withdrew his forecast of the fall of Tyre. Ezek. 26 and 29. (See page 17 above.) Hear Dr. Th. Laetsch's statement: "In Ezek. 26 the fate of Tyre is foretold in three sections. a) Vv. 3-6 in general, 'many nations': complete destruction without indicating time or person. b) Vv. 7-14, a destruction by Nebuchadnezzar is prophesied. Note, however, the change from 'he,' v. 8, to 'they,' v. 12, and 'I,' vv. 13, 14, which indicates that others will finish what Nebuchadnezzar began. c) Vv. 15-21. The final complete destruction at which 'the isles shake,' v. 15; again no time or person is named. Where is the proof that Nebuchadnezzar did not take Tyre after the thirteen years' siege? In Ezek. 29:17-20 the Lord does not promise 'Ersatz' for an enforced withdrawal but wages for services rendered by Nebuchadnezzar in the destruction of Tyre. Either the riches of Tyre had been destroyed, or else they were insufficient reward for Nebuchadnezzar's service. Besides, how could Ezekiel withdraw in the tenth year (29:1) a prophecy spoken in the eleventh year (26:1)? Finally, Tyre's later restoration had been prophesied already by Isaiah, chap. 23:15-28, one hundred and fifty years before Ezekiel's prophecy." For one thing, these men have no conception of the prophetic perspective. (See further *Conc. Theol. Monthly,* I, p. 115.)

Second sample. Thomas Paine: "God is a deceiver, Jer. 20:5, 7." Paine was only a layman, and an unbeliever at that. But C. H. Dodd repeats it. "Jeremiah at one time wondered if he had really been deceived, Jer. 20:7." (*The Authority of the Bible,* p. 15.) Dodd is professor of exegesis at Oxford. Have they not studied their Moffatt? "Eternal One, Thou didst persuade me, and I let myself be persuaded," Jer. 20:7. We once heard a man on the street-corner scoff at Matt. 9:17. Does age, he said, contribute to the fragility of glass bottles? He and Paine and Dodd did not study the original.

The charge of "misquotations" is based (a) on the assumption that quotations must give the *ipsissima verba* of the author quoted. No such rule obtains in the realm of literature. Unless the writer declares that he is quoting verbatim, he is quoting correctly if he gives the true sense of the text. The discrepancy-hunters are quick to charge the apostles for their manner of applying statements from the Old Testament[61] with a lapse of memory or with plain ignorance. But all fair-minded men will agree with Luther in saying that as long as the meaning of the text is faithfully reproduced, the charge of misquoting must not be raised.[62]

The substitution of "A body hast Thou prepared for me" in Heb. 10:5 for "Mine ears hast Thou opened" in Ps. 40:6 does not alter the sense. "Bei beiden Fassungen ist der *Gehorsam* das von Gott geforderte Opfer; nur tritt an die Stelle des Ohres als des Organs zur *Aufnahme des goettlichen Willens* der Leib als das Organ zur *Erfuellung desselben."* (Riggenbach, in *Zahn's Commentary.*) "The Hebrew means literally: 'Mine ears hast Thou bored,' an allusion to the custom of pinning a slave to the doorpost of his master by an awl driven through his ear, in token of his complete subjection. The sense of the verse is therefore given in

---

61) "The deviations in form from the wording of the Old Testament text are of various kinds. In some cases the New Testament writers have *expanded* the Old Testament text (*e. g.,* Is. 61:1; Luke 4:18), in many cases *contracted* it (Is. 8:22; 9:1; Matt. 4:15), in some instances the order of sentences has been *inverted* (Hos. 2:23; Rom. 9:25), frequently several passages are *blended into one* (Jer. 32:6 ff.; Zech. 11:12, 13; Matt. 27:9)." (Pieper, *Chr. Dogm.,* I, p. 298.)

62) Luther: "You must know, first, that the evangelists are not concerned about citing every last word of the prophets; they are content with retaining the *sense* and showing the fulfilment. . . . We shall later on see again and again that the evangelist adduces the prophet in a somewhat altered form, but always without prejudice to the sense and meaning." (XI, p. 12.)

the epistle: 'Thou hast made me Thine in body and soul — lo,
I come to do Thy will.'" (A. Strong, *Systematic Theology*, p. 110.)
Would you charge the scribes with misquoting Micah 5:2: "Though
thou be little among the thousands of Judah" by letting the prophet
say: "Thou Bethlehem art not the least among the princes of
Juda" (Matt. 2:6)? The evangelist does not raise that charge
against them. They reproduced very exactly the sense of Micah's
statement: Bethlehem apparently the least, but because of the
great Ruler arising out of it the greatest. (See Stoeckhardt, *Lehre u.
Wehre*, 30, p. 164.) [63]

The charge of "misquotations" is due (b) to the critics' ignorance of the true situation. The outstanding fact in the case is
that the Holy Ghost is the Author of Scripture, of the New
Testament as well as of the Old Testament; and when He through
the apostles quotes the prophets, He is quoting Himself. The
liberals of course do not admit this. But that does not change
the fact. And we cannot help it that on account of their ignorance
the form of the Old Testament quotations constitutes a stumbling-
block to them. But they should, in common fairness, not expect
us, who know better, to rail with them against the alleged inep-
titude and ignorance of the apostles. "They forget," says James
M. Gray, "that in the Scriptures we are dealing not so much with
different authors as with one Divine Author. It is a principle
in ordinary literature that an author may quote himself as he
pleases and give a different turn to an expression here and there
as a changed condition of affairs renders it necessary or desirable.
Shall we deny this privilege to the Holy Spirit?" (*The Fundamentals*, III, p. 33.) [64] "Strange hallucination this! As if the
same truth could not be expressed in somewhat different words;
as if God could not alter or add to, modify or use a part of, give
fresh application to, or light on, His own earlier Word! . . . The

---

63) Would you charge us with misquoting Moeller: "'Verbalinspiration!' *Jeder* Theologe schaudert bei dem Wort ordentlich zusammen,"
by translating: "'Verbal Inspiration!' The bare word sets *our* theologians a-trembling"?

64) Dr. Pieper expresses these same thoughts, *op. cit.*, pp. 297
to 303. They are Scriptural thoughts. 1 Pet. 1:10-12! The same Holy
Spirit who spoke through the prophets spoke through the apostles,
and He may quote Himself as He pleases, express the same truth in
different phraseology, omit or add words, etc. He may even take over
translations from the Septuagint which might have seemed faulty to us
and thus make them an authorized translation, expressing the true
sense. At first glance — and the critics seldom get beyond the first
glance — undue liberties were taken when Is. 61:1 was expanded in
Luke 4:18 and "body" (Septuagint translation) substituted for "eyes" in
Heb. 10:5. The simple "explanation for this treatment, often so bold, of
the wording of the Old Testament passages in the New Testament"
(Pieper), is this: the Holy Ghost is, as Luther expresses it, making
"a new text," explaining the meaning of the old text.

flimsiness and untenableness of the other reasons given for such criticism (the alleged inexact quotations) only show how unscientific and unreasonable their methods are and how easily, when it suits their theories, they accept and use as proof what no sensible man would accept or act on in common life." (M'Intosh, op. cit., pp. 314, 635, 689.) The ultraliberals, of course, will not admit the force of this argument. We are not responsible for their ignorance as to the authorship of Scripture. And the conservative Liberals, who profess that Scripture is inspired of God, are enmeshed in a hopeless self-contradiction.

The charge of "misquotations" is based (c) on the assumption that the apostles were rather ignorant theologians. Bishop Gore assumes that. "The writers of the New Testament often positively give the texts meanings which they cannot bear. I would ask any one to consider St. Paul's arguments in Gal. 3:16 and in Rom. 3:11-18 and in Rom. 9:25. Is it possible to maintain that the particular texts which St. Paul cites really, when legitimately interpreted, support his argument? . . . Can we say that the texts cited in Matt. 2:15-18 are legitimate proofs?" (The Doctrine of the Infallible Book, p. 29.)[65] Let the reader look up, for instance, Rom. 3:11-18 and wonder at the acumen of the critic. — We are glad to see that Gore does not include H. L. Willett's charge of wilful misquotation (see page 18 above) in his list.

Will the critics (d) deny to the Holy Spirit the right to elucidate in the New Testament what He said in the Old Testament? to reveal to the apostles and through the apostles that certain texts of the Old Testament carried a meaning which we should not have discovered without His interpretation? He does not give these texts a new meaning. The Holy Ghost, in quoting Himself, never corrects Himself. Human authors sometimes refer to earlier statements of theirs in order to modify or retract them. The Holy Ghost never.[66] But He certainly may unfold to us the meaning of a certain text. Critics like Gore would do well to realize that the Holy Ghost has a better understanding of the texts quoted Rom. 9:25 and Matt. 2:15-18 than they. Yes, He knows better than Hosea himself what Hos. 11:1 meant. And no doubt Matthew would not have interpreted it as he did of his own knowledge.

---

65) Gore even believes that "inspiration" did not safeguard the apostles against a stupid misinterpretation of Scripture. "Their inspiration did not make them unerring in their interpretation of particular texts. They used them in a way which we should call quite uncritical; and we do not want to feel ourselves bound by their methods."

66) The language of M'Intosh, Grey, and others is not always correct. They speak of the "progress of truth" in a way as though certain truths have been superseded.

Dr. Gore is virtually — though he does not realize it — accusing the Holy Spirit of perverting His own words.[67]

In some instances (e) the alleged misquotation is no quotation at all. The words "And gave gifts unto men" in Eph. 4:8 may well be the apostle's own words. See Stoeckhardt, *Epheser-Kommentar*, p. 191.

Our list operates (f) on the principle that, when we cannot account for a certain statement of the writer, the writer must have made a mistake. The critics would not want to father this principle in this bald form, but they are applying it when they give Matt. 27:9 a prominent place on the black-list. "Spoken by Jeremy." Why, it was spoken by Zechariah (11:13)! — Go easy! In the first place, Matthew *is* quoting Zechariah. But he is *also* quoting Jeremiah! See Jer. 32:6-15. Then, why does he not name both? We shall say, in the second place, that we do not know the answer. "Some have thought that the words quoted were originally spoken by Jeremiah, or that they were taken from a lost writing of Jeremiah (Origen), or that an oral statement of Jeremiah had been handed down and accepted by Matthew (Calov), or the abbreviation of the name of Zechariah had been mistaken for the abbreviated name of Jeremiah (Flacius),[68] or the evangelist suffered a lapse of memory (Augustine, Meyer, Keil, and most moderns)." (Stoeckhardt, *Lehre u. Wehre*, 31, p. 272.) Stoeckhardt proceeds: "These explanations are pure conjectures, and are, in part, in conflict with the Scriptural concept of Inspiration. Instead of exhausting ourselves with vague guesses, it would have been better to confess a *non liquet* and let it go at that." We are willing to confess that we cannot explain why Matthew did not name both prophets. But go easy! Do not be guilty of unscientific haste. Your lack of information does not prove Matthew wrong.

Finally the critics do not see that this free manner of quoting from the Old Testament is (g) a strong proof for Inspiration; merely a rational argument indeed, but we are here arguing on the basis of reason. If the apostles had been writing purely as human writers, they would not have dared to take such liberties with the quoted texts, to make additions of their own, for instance, and to offer the result as a statement of the prophet. It is impossible for us to conceive of the apostles, acting as human writers only, as too indolent to look up the text and get the exact

---

67) We ask our readers to reread, in this connection, Dr. G. Stoeckhardt's series on "Weissagung und Erfuellung," *Lehre u. Wehre*, 30, p. 42 ff.; 31, p. 220 ff.

68) See Gaussen, *op. cit.*, 217: "The copyist, having noticed on the margin the letters Ζου, mistook them for Ιου."

wording. "We are of the opinion that even human reason, if it be reasonable, must refrain from explaining the deviations of New Testament quotations from the Old Testament text by assuming 'mistakes' or 'slips of memory' in the holy writers. There is but one explanation: the Holy Ghost is speaking through the apostles and 'taking liberties' with His own word." (Pieper, *op. cit.*, p. 302.)

The Sad Story of the Discrepancy-Hunters

The list of "contradictions" is a sorry affair. Its compilers operate with a number of hermeneutical laws which are outlawed by reason and common sense. And they disregard the principles of interpretation established by reason and observed by sane interpreters.

They have (a) set up the queer rule that diversities in the accounts of the same event or fact constitute a contradiction. Paine finds that "not any two of these writers agree in reciting, *exactly in the same words,* the inscription on the cross," and the Episcopalian rector repeats it and cries out: "What, then, of verbal inspiration?" (See page 21 above.) The *Lutheran Witness,* 43, p. 185, comments: "Is this not evincing a superficiality which almost beggars description? . . . The shallowness of the modern critic!" If one evangelist gives a fuller account of the inscription than the others, are the others wrong? Gore's *New Commentary* does not find any contradiction here but has no right to say that the fuller form in John 19:19 "is probably the most *correct.*" No, all four are absolutely correct. Accounts of the same event must not differ in the details? If the managing editor should establish such a rule, all of his reporters would go on a strike. A. Strong, quoting from the *Princeton Review:* "One newspaper says: President Hayes attended the Bennington centennial; another newspaper says: the President and Mrs. Hayes; a third: the President and his cabinet; a fourth: the President, Mrs. Hayes, and the majority of his cabinet." (*Systematic Theology,* p. 108.)

N. E. Best asks us "to note the differences between the recital of the Ten Commandments in Ex. 20 and Deut. 5." We have read the two recitals, noted the differences, but were unable to find contradictions. We have also read the article "What was Written on the Two Tables of the Covenant — a Study of the Methods of Modern Critics" in *Conc. Theol. Monthly,* IX, p. 746 ff., and noted other follies committed by Goethe and the other critics in this matter. — Kahnis applies rule *a* to the fourfold account of the words of institution of the Lord's Supper. We object. We insist that the Lord *did* say: "This is My blood of the new testament," Matt. 26:28, and that He *did* say: "This cup is the new testament in My blood," Luke 22:20. And He could say both without contradicting Himself. Read Pieper, *Chr. Dog.*, III, p. 408 ff. — Rule *a* is responsible for many of the alleged contradictions found by Celsus, Paine, Lessing, and modern theologians in the accounts of Christ's resurrection and of His appearances to His disciples. Read *Lehre u. Wehre*, 39, p. 198 ff., and 32, p. 321: "Es gehoert wahrlich nicht viel Verstand dazu, um sofort bei Lektion und Betrachtung der vier evangelischen Auferstehungsberichte zu begreifen, dass gar leicht das eine, was der eine Evangelist mitteilt, unbeschadet des andern, was der andere berichtet, sich habe zutragen koennen." See also *Conc. Theol. Monthly*, XI, 661 f. — Better operate with Augustine's rule: "*Locutiones variae, sed non contrariae; diversae, sed non adversae.*"

Can you believe that men would operate with the absurd rule (b) that, when one evangelist fails to mention a fact mentioned by another evangelist, he is *correcting* this second evangelist? Mark 2:26 mentions Abiathar. "Matthew and Luke both correct Mark at this point by omitting the name. Neither of them thought that Mark was 'errorless.'" (Dr. H. C. Alleman's) Manifesto. See p. 21 above.) That has no basis whatever in reason.[69] Gore's *Commentary* takes the reasonable view. "That Matthew and Luke agree in omitting the note of time is not in the least likely to be due to their detection of the supposed error." In his *Doctrine of the Infallible Book*, however, Bishop Gore forsakes the reasonable view. Why does the fourth gospel record things not treated by the synoptic gospels? "The evangelists plainly differ in details quite freely; and one purpose of the fourth gospel appears to be *tacitly to correct* the earlier tradition in important respects. . . . Criticism seems to be tending steadily to reaffirm that where the writer of the fourth gospel seems deliberately to correct the tradition of the earlier evangelists, his correction should be treated with the highest respect." (Pp. 40, 45.) Name some of these corrections! Fr. Buechsel speaks of "divergencies, unreliable records," in the gospels, but he names only this one "contradiction": "The preexistence of Jesus is clearly taught in John's gospel. . . . However, the synoptic gospels say nothing about it. This *disagreement of the record* therefore permits us," etc. (*Die Offenbarung Gottes*, p. 10.) Now, the earlier gospels do teach the preexistence of Jesus. See Matt. 1:20-23; 16:13-17; 22:42-45. But even if they did not, do they *deny* it?

The "conflicting creation accounts" of Paine and Ingersoll belong in this category. Here is the latest variety of this item.

---

69) Dr. Th. Graebner: "Dr. Alleman is arguing from a premise quite generally condemned by the text-books of logic — an argument *e silentio.*" (*Conc. Theol. Mthly*, XI, p. 886.)

"We recently had a contender who objected to the doctrine of inspiration . . . because there were two accounts of creation and that they were in vital conflict with each other. In the second chapter the woman is mentioned, in a separate and conflicting story of creation, differing altogether from the account in chapter one. We pointed out to him that his error was a lack of intelligent reading of the text. . . . The second chapter of Genesis is but an *addition to the details* of the first chapter. . . . How marvelously this illustrates the ability of the keen mentality that would contradict the Book that God has written!" (Harry Rimmer, *Modern Science and the Genesis Record*, p. 350.)

Applying rule *b*, Bruno Bauer points out that according to Luke 2 Joseph and Mary returned to Nazareth because that was their home town; but from Matt. 2 it appears "dass Joseph erst durch eine Engelsbotschaft nach Galilaea und Nazareth gewiesen wird. Der Widerspruch ist so hart, wie er nur sein kann." (*Op. cit.*, I, p. 120.) We do not like this rule. We would not want to be forced to charge Bauer and the others with not knowing or denying all those things which their books do not relate. Better stick to Augustine's rule: "You must most carefully guard against finding contradictions between the holy evangelists in the fact that one often relates what the others do not relate or that one is silent on matters which the others tell." Supplementing an account is not correcting or contradicting it.

Rule *c*: When similar events are recorded in the gospels, you are usually safe in assuming that such an event occurred only once; but somehow or other the writer or writers made two events out of it. We read, for instance, that Christ cleansed the Temple twice. But the critical schools say it occurred only once, and so there is a contradiction between the synoptists, who place the event at the end of Christ's public ministry, and the fourth gospel, which places it at the beginning. Gore's *Commentary* is rather cautious: "Conceivably the incident happened twice." But it blandly adds: "More probably they are two records of one event." (On John 2:13-22.) Our commentary is not bothered by the consideration that this would involve a contradiction. We do not know why *The Expositor's Greek Testament* should add to the statement "The synoptic gospels insert a similar incident at the close of Christ's ministry" the words: "And there alone," nor why the statement "It is easy to find reasons for such action either at the beginning or at the close of the ministry" should be accompanied by the insinuation: "On the whole it seems more appropriate at the beginning." B. Weiss is outspoken: "Die abstrakte Moeglichkeit, dass derselbe Vorfall sich am Ende der Laufbahn Jesu wiederholt, . . . kann in der Tat wissenschaftlich nicht in Betracht kommen. Die Annahme, dass die synoptische Ueberlieferung, die ueberhaupt nur *eine* Festreise Jesu erzaehlt, den unvergesslichen Vorfall irrtuemlich in diese versetzt habe, ist so einleuchtend." (On John 2:17.) The *Daily News* which reported a police raid on the gambling joints in 1940 and a similar one, by the same captain, against the same joints, in 1941, would not like to be told that it is ignorant of rule *c.* — Luther: "Es kann auch wohl sein, dass der Herr solches mehr denn einmal getan hat." (VII:1781.)

Did Jesus feed a multitude miraculously on two occasions? See rule *c.* Gaussen lists this case under the heading "Another Source of Precipitate Judgment" and speaks of the "utmost rashness . . . whereby people have imagined that the facts they read of were identically the same." And then he hears them railing at Scripture for the resulting contradiction: "What! In the one, five thousand men fed with five loaves; in the other, four thousand men fed with seven loaves! What disagreement!" (*Op. cit.*, p. 234.) Hear D. F. Strauss: Die Sache ist so "zu erklaeren, dass der Verfasser unsers ersten Evangeliums dieselbe Geschichte in verschiedenem Zusammenhang vorfand, um dieser Abweichungen willen die doppelte Erzaehlung derselben Geschichte fuer zwei Geschichten nahm und arglos nebeneinander stellte." (*Das Leben Jesu*, II, p. 227.)

Bruno Bauer charges St. Matthew with breaking rule *c* in making the Pharisees demand a sign from Jesus twice, Matt. 12:39 and 16:1. The thing could have occurred only once! He concludes his investigation thus: "Lassen wir aber das abstrakte *Raesonnement*, es habe dasselbe mehrere Male 'geschehen koennen.' . . . Es ist ueber allem Zweifel erhaben, dass der Schriftsteller, der frei aus der idealen Anschauung ein geschichtliches Ganzes schafft, sich nicht wiederholt." (*Op. cit.*, II, p. 391.) — We stick to the old axiom: *Distingue tempora et concordabit Scriptura.*

A lot of contradictions are fabricated by insisting (d) that in a given case the two writers recording the same event are both observing a chronological order, leaving out of consideration that one of them may have, and has, chosen the topical arrangement or some other logical sequence. In this easy way A. W. Dieckhoff (Rostock), a noted discrepancy-hunter, has bagged quite a number of contradictions in the field of the synoptic gospels, seven of which are examined in *Lehre u. Wehre*, 39, p. 32 ff. For example, since in the story of the temptation of Christ, as told by Matthew and by Luke, the last two temptations are not listed in the same sequence, there is a glaring contradiction — *if* both writers wrote chronologically. As it happens, "Luke is not reporting the temptations in their historical order. . . . He follows the order of places: desert, mountain, Temple." (Lenski, on Luke 4:1-13.)[70]

Augustine, Luther, and Chemnitz insist that the evangelists do not bind themselves to the chronological order but "anticipate and recapitulate" on occasion. Most modern exegetes agree that they combine the chronological and topical order. But Dieckhoff protests against that. He will not grant the evangelists the privileges of secular historians. Well, he can appeal to Bruno Bauer as authority. Bauer quotes Augustine's rule: "What is related at a later place did not necessarily occur later. The evangelist may certainly supplement any of his previous statements," and ridicules it in his ribald way: "Luft! Luft! Wir kommen um!" (*Op. cit.*, I, p. 277.) — We repeat: *Distingue tempora et concordabit Scriptura!* Luther: "The evangelists do not observe the same order; what one places first the other sometimes brings later." (VII:1781.)

In addition to this, the contradictionists fail to observe certain rules and laws which are based on reason and are recognized by all thinking men. Rule *1* is: A real contradiction occurs only where the same thing is asserted and denied of the same object with reference to the same time and place and under the same relation. The high-school sophomore has learned that it involves no contradiction to say that man is mortal and that man is immortal. Man is mortal with respect to his body, immortal with respect to his soul. When Dr. H. E. Fosdick found a contradiction between Eccl. 3:19 ("Death befalleth man and beast") and 1 Cor. 15:53-55 ("This mortal must put on immortality"), he forgot rule *1*. — The devout Bible-readers, says J. M. Gibson, find "this strong and very definite declaration: 'A man hath no preeminence over the beast,' Eccl. 3:19. They turn to a more familiar place and read: 'Fear not; ye are of more value than many sparrows.' Are they troubled? Not at all. How do they settle it? By the exercise of higher criticism." (*The Inspiration and Authority of Holy Scripture*, p. 182.) They do nothing of the kind. They do not discard one of the two statements. They settle the matter by applying rule *1*. — 1 Cor. 10:8 states that 23,000 fell in the plague. Num. 25:9 states 24,000 died in the plague. And Professor Volck (Dorpat) notes down: Another contradiction! Rule *1* asks him: Is the same *time* involved? Paul says they fell in *one* day. Moses does not say that. (See Pieper, *op. cit.*, I, p. 295 f.)

---

70) Lenski, on Luke 4:16: "By starting with this incident, Luke abandons the chronological order from the very start, so that we cannot depend on him for the exact sequence of events. He is concerned more with the inner significance and connection of what he presents than with the order of time, although in a general way he also adheres to that."

Examine Dr. H. L. Willett's contradiction, page 21 f. above. "Moses wrote the words of the Law, Ex. 24:4; 34:28; Deut. 31:24." Right (in part). "Jahve Himself wrote them, Ex. 31:18." Right again. But entirely wrong, since the "same object" of Rule 1 is overlooked. The Lord wrote the words of the Decalog, and He wrote them on stone tablets. Moses wrote the words of Ex. 20:22-26 and "the judgments," Ex. 21:1 ff., and wrote them in a book. — We said: Right, *in part*, because Willett's reference to Ex. 34:28 is entirely wrong. "*He* wrote upon the tables" does not refer to Moses but to the Lord. See v. 1 and Deut. 10:1-4. Moses ought to know whom he meant in Ex. 34:28.

The contradiction discovered by Thomas Paine and Dr. Buttrick ("The Lord moved David to number Israel and Judah," 2 Sam. 24:1, and Satan provoked David to do it 1 Chron. 21:1), ignores the provision of Rule *1*, that the same thing must be asserted and denied. It is asserted that the Lord moved David. 1 Chron. 21:1 does not deny that, and *vice-versa*.[71]

It gets worse and worse. They fabricate contradictions by *inventing* one of the two "contradictory" statements. Willet (p. 21 f. above) finds the Book of Jonah opposed "to the narrower nationalism of Ezekiel." Paine found the same contradiction. Paine and Willett *invented* "the partiality of the Creator for one nation." — Rule 1 pronounces the peddling of "contradictions" of this kind a swindle. That is Dr. Pieper's phrase. (*Op. cit.*, I, p. 296.)

In common fairness the contradictionists should (2) reckon with the possibility that some of their alleged contradictions may be due to mistakes made by the copyists. They make much of these variant readings (as being destructive of the reliability of the Bible). Then let us, too, make something of these mistakes. Luther thus accounts, for instance, for the seeming contradiction between Acts 13:20 and 1 Kings 6:1: "The Greek text is corrupted through an error of the copyist, which could easily occur by his writing τετρακοσίοις for τριακοσίοις." (XIV:600.) Thus also Beza. In another connection Luther says: "Or perhaps the copyists erred." (XIV:491.)[72] There is no need to adopt Luther's conjecture of an error of the copyist in our passage. A number

---

71) For further information consult *Does the Bible Contradict Itself?* p. 40: "God permitted Satan to influence David in such a way that he proudly ordered a census. . . . God punishes evil-doing by permitting sin to beget sin. . . . He withdrew His hand and let the devil have access to the heart of David."

72) See *Conc. Theol. Mthly.*, II, p. 679 ff.: "*Schreibfehler in den Buechern Samuels*", for instance, on 1 Sam. 13:1: "Saul reigned one year." Probably the numeral dropped out. Thus also R.V.: "Saul was [forty] years old when he began to reign." Note: "The number is lacking in the Hebrew text and is supplied conjecturally."

of other solutions have been offered.[73] But our purpose was to show that as long as the possibility of an error on the part of the copyists in a given case remains, no real contradiction can be established.

That brings up Rule 3. Unless you can show conclusively that the solutions of the seeming contradictions which present themselves are absolutely impossible, you have no right to assume a real contradiction. In the words of the Broadus-Robertson *Harmony of the Gospels*, p. 232: "In explaining a difficulty, it is always to be remembered that even a possible explanation is sufficient to meet the objector. If several possible explanations are suggested, it becomes all the more unreasonable for one to contend that the discrepancy is irreconcilable. It is a work of supererogation to proceed to show that this or that explanation is the real solution of the problem. Sometimes, owing to new light, this might be possible, but it is never necessary. And by reason of the meager information we have on many points in the Gospel narrative, it may always be impossible in various cases to present a solution satisfactory in every point. The harmonist has done his duty if he can show a reasonable explanation of the problem before him."

Take the case of the healing of the blind men at Jericho, Matt. 20: 29 ff., Mark 10: 46 ff., and Luke 18: 35 ff. Oberkonsistorialrat Twesten, rector of the university at Berlin, names this and the matter of the census taken under Cyrenius as the two cases presenting insurmountable difficulties. De Witt names as the first difficulty the "two blind men" and "a certain blind man." (See page 20 above.) That comes under Rule 4, which calls for the exercise of common sense. If two blind men were healed, one blind man was healed. The evangelist does not say: Only one was healed. "Das ist ja gar kein Widerspruch, sondern nur eine Vervollstaendigung. . . . Hier ist eben nicht Subtraktion, sondern nur Addition anzuwenden." (*Proc. West. Dist.*, 1865, p. 45.) Second difficulty: "The healing took place as Jesus *went out* from Jericho; as He *drew nigh* to that city." Here we have, to be sure, a real difficulty. But several solutions present themselves. (1) "The older harmonists assumed that there were two miracles: that one blind man was healed at the entrance and two at the departure of Christ." (*Lange-Schaff Commentary*.) Or (2) the Lord might have kept blind Bartimaeus waiting till the next day to test him. And Luke anticipated the result by a prolepsis not uncommon in

---

73) One is given in *Lehre u. Wehre*, 67, p. 149: "It is possible that Paul begins the 450 years with the exodus. Add to the time of the judges the forty years under Moses, the five under Joshua, and the thirty-eight under Samuel, and we get 352+45+38=435 years, 'about (ὡς)' 450 years."

Scripture. See Luke 3:19—23. We have, in Scripture and in secular histories, *anticipation* and *recapitulation*. (Lange-Schaff.) [74]

The seeming contradiction between Mark 2:26 (Abiathar) and 1 Sam. 21:1 (Ahimelech) also presents difficulties. But a solution is possible. A. Hovey: "Some suppose that Abiathar was already assistant to his father at the time of David's visit and was present when he came." Luther: "Sie waren zu *einer* Zeit Priester." (See *Weimar-Bibel.*) Or: "The two names Ahimelech and Abiathar were borne by the father as well as the son." (Lenski, on our passage.) — This is more reasonable than the solution offered by the contradictionists: "It may be a pure slip of memory on the part of the evangelist" (Gore's *Commentary*), i. e., Mark was a slip-shod writer, who either did not report Jesus correctly or did not take time to consult his copy of 1 Samuel.

The discrepancy-hunters find irreconcilable contradictions between statements of Stephen and the Old Testament record. (See page 20 above.)   For instance, Stephen names Sychem as a burial-place, Acts 7:16, and the Old Testament, they say, names Hebron in this connection. Here is *one* solution of the alleged contradiction, and Rule 3 calls for only one possible solution: "Stephen, and with him St. Luke, tells us that the *brothers* of Joseph were buried in Sychem. He thus *supplements* the story of the Old Testament. . . . The further item that Abraham bought land in Sychem from the sons of Hemor is also to be regarded as a supplement to the Old Testament record." (Dr. Stoeckhardt, in *Lehre u. Wehre*, 32, p. 318.)   Can the critics prove, as required by Rule 3, that this assumption involves an impossibility? — The fuss made by the critics over Acts 7:4 would stop if they would quit assuming that Abraham was the first-born son of Terah. They cannot prove it. He may have been the youngest son. Particulars are given in *Lehre u. Wehre*, 70, p. 183 f., and in *Theol. Monthly*, IV, p. 33 ff.: "Some Difficulties in the Speech of Stephen, Acts 7." More than two "discrepancies" are there discussed and disposed of.

We insist that Rule 3 be applied. "The irreconcilability must be demonstrated not only not reconcilable with our present knowledge,

---

74) A. Hovey, *An American Commentary*, mentions another possibility (3): the healing occurred at a point between the old and the new city and so could be described as occurring either when He went out from Jericho or drew near. Hovey says that these explanations seem labored, but adds: "Either explanation is entirely possible. It will not do to say that the accounts are irreconcilable and therefore involve inaccuracy. . . . The present example and a few others would probably be plain if we knew some slight circumstances not mentioned." And, says *The Expositor's Bible* (Gospel of St. Matthew): "How small must be the minds or how strong the prejudices of those who find support for their unbelief in discrepancies of which this is acknowledged to be one of the gravest examples!"

but necessarily and essentially irreconcilable." (M'Intosh, *op. cit.,* p. 636.) "So long as the proof is not furnished that the two reports are in direct opposition, the demand made by the scientific theology of our day that an absolute contradiction be acknowledged is nothing less than a scientific swindle." (Pieper, *op. cit.,* I, p. 296.)

What to do in case no solution offers itself? Canon 4: Refrain from hasty judgments; exercise scientific caution, moderation, and sobriety. Can the statement of Mark 15:25 "It was the third hour, and they crucified Him" be reconciled with the statement of John 19:14"? One solution is that Mark employs the Jewish way of reckoning the time of day, indicating nine o'clock in the morning, while John uses the Roman computation of time and so tells us that the trial of Jesus began at six o'clock. That seems a satisfactory solution. But here is a commentator (Lutheran, strictly conservative) who declares: "No solution has yet been found." Similarly Jerome pronounced the difficulty connected with Acts 7:4 a *questio indissolubilis.* What should we do if we found ourselves in such a case? Dr. Walther says: "When our old Christian theologians were confronted with a difficulty which they could not solve, they humbly doffed their little doctor's hat, bowed before Holy Scripture, and declared: This difficulty will be fully solved, if not before, then certainly in heaven." (*Lehre u Wehre,* 57, p. 157.) And the mature scientist, be he a Christian or a non-Christian, takes the same general position; whether he meets difficulties in astronomy or in the Bible, he does not settle the matter in a moment but defers his final judgment. He unhesitatingly subscribes to Torrey's formulation of Canon 4: "Let us deal with any difficulty we meet in the Bible [or in any sphere of human study] with that humility that becomes all persons of such limited understanding as we all are. Recognize the limitations of your own mind and knowledge and do not for a moment imagine that there is no solution just because you have found none. There is, in all probability, a very simple solution, even when you can find no solution at all." (*Op. cit.,* p. 69.) — The Lutheran exegete we quoted above took that position: "We may not always be able to clear up that difficulty because of our ignorance, but one thing is certain — the Scriptures are inerrant in every case." (Lenski, on Mark 2:26 and John 19:14.)

Rule 5: Exercise your common sense! If Professor Baumgaertel had done that, he would not have read into the text Gen. 7:17 that the Flood *lasted* only forty days. It took forty days for the Flood to reach its crest. — Paine: "The reason given for keeping the seventh day is, according to Exodus, that 'God rested on the seventh day'; but according to Deuteronomy, that it was the day on which the children of Israel came out of Egypt." (*Age of*

Reason, I, p. 120.) N. R. Best seconds Paine. But why could not
the Sabbath be made to commemorate both events? Best exercises
his common sense when he states: "It may be held that God
named both reasons." (*Inspiration,* p. 73.) But he loses it when
he concludes: "The form in which we have the Ten Commandments cannot possibly be shown to be inerrant." — Best further
declares that a great amount of labor would have to be spent to
explain how it happened that King Saul did not recognize David.
(See page 20 above.) He goes on to say that we are "spending
hours" at the task. Jamieson-Fausset-Brown spent two minutes
at it: "The growth of the beard and other changes on a now full-
grown youth prevented the king from recognizing his former
favorite minstrel."

Ingersoll finds himself unable to harmonize the genealogies of
Christ. "Is it not wonderful that Luke and Matthew do not agree
on a single name of Christ's ancestors for thirty-seven generations?"
The Rev. L. A. Lambert (Catholic) reminds Ingersoll and others of
Rule 5 in these words: "It is wonderful only to those who are
ignorant of the fact that Matthew gives the ancestors of Joseph,
while Luke gives the ancestors of Mary, the mother of God.
Are your ancestors on your mother's side all Ingersolls? Must
your maternal and paternal ancestors necessarily have the same
name? A careful study of Christian writers on these subjects
would save you a great deal of ignorant blundering." (*Notes on
Ingersoll,* p. 159 f.) — Bishop Gore: "If our Lord had announced the
Trinitarian formula, as is recorded in Matt. 28:19, so explicitly,
it is hard to believe that it could have made so little impression on
the earliest preaching and practice as recorded in the Acts." (*Op.
cit.,* p. 41.) Better study Pieper, *Chr. Dog.,* III, p. 297 f. and 303 f.
He points out "the logical absurdities" on which Gore's statement is
based. When Gore records that he baptized such and such a person,
does he have to record that he baptized "in the name of the Father
and of the Son and of the Holy Ghost"?

Professor Dieckhoff declared that no man can harmonize the
statement recorded Mark 14:30: "Before the cock crow twice,
thou shalt deny Me thrice" with that recorded by the other evangelists: "This night, before the cock crow, thou shalt deny Me
thrice." Professor Stoeckhardt asked him to apply his knowledge
of ornithology. "Einem von Gott ihnen eingepflanzten Instinkt
zufolge pflegten die Haehne im Altertum und pflegen die Haehne
auch heute noch, in der Neuen Welt wie in der Alten Welt, doch
wohl sicherlich auch in Mecklenburg, kurz ehe der Morgen graut,
ein lautes Geschrei anzustimmen." These cocks also crow at
midnight, as Stoeckhardt tells us; but when men say that they
will do this or that "before the cock crows," they have in mind
the *gallicinium matutinum, the* ἀλεκτοροφωνία κατ' ἐξοχήν, which

announces the break of day. (See *Lehre u. Wehre*, 39, p. 134 ff.) "Before the cock crow, thou shalt deny Me thrice" refers to the *gallicinium matutinum*, and so everybody (except Dieckhoff and his party) understood this statement. In no wise do the three evangelists deny that the cock crowed twice before Peter's three-fold denial. Only they do not record the *two* cock-crowings. It was sufficient that Mark recorded that. Gore's *Commentary* agrees with Stoeckhardt: "The second cock-crowing is mentioned as a note of time in various classical writers. Aristophanes, Cicero, Juvenal, Animianus Marcellinus, are cited. [Stoeckhardt cites additional ones.] It was this second cock-crowing, somewhere about 3 to 4 A.M., which was technically known as *gallicinium*." — "Are not two sparrows sold for a farthing?" (Matt. 10:29.) How, then, could the same Lord say: "Are not five sparrows sold for two farthings?" (Luke 12:6.) He should have given the latter price as two and a half farthings. Yes, indeed, "some have fancied a contradiction here," Harry Rimmer tells us. And he asks the contradictionists to exercise their common sense: "In our modern markets apples may be five cents apiece, but at the same time sell six for twenty-five cents." (*Modern Science*, p. 303 f.)

Other contradictionists complain: Saul's companions heard the voice (Acts 9:7), and they did not hear the voice (Acts 22:9)! Poor Luke! But Luke knew his Greek. They did not hear τὴν φωνήν, but they did hear τῆς φωνῆς. They heard the sound, but did not hear the words and did not get the sense of the sound. (See Lenski, *The Expositor's Greek Testament*, etc.) — B. Bauer knows his Greek, but that does not keep him from the discrepancy-hunt. Luke 7:2 uses the term "servant," δοῦλος, Matt. 8:6 the term "servant," παῖς. Bauer: The Greek word παῖς means both son and servant." Good! But: "Das Kategorische aber, wie der Haupt-mann sagt: 'Mein Knabe,' das Dringende und Flehende seiner Bitte um Hilfe beweist, dass Matthaeus von uns verlangt, wir sollen an den *Sohn* des Mannes denken." (*Op. cit.*, II, p. 26.) And there's your contradiction, as plain as day! — We wish Bauer would exercise common sense and not imagine that his readers will not notice at once that his sole interest in the matter is to find a contradiction. His common sense should have told him that his readers are in possession of common intelligence. — It's a most unscientific swindle.

Epiphanius of old († 407) said of the discrepancy-hunters of his day that they "are not sound in the faith, or else they are weak intellectually." The level of intelligence has not risen since then. — The fatuity displayed in this branch of human knowledge is so great that it calls for additional chapters. It is amusing — and instructive — to see how the will to break Scripture leads men to break down logic and common sense.

SOME MORE INCREDIBLE FATUITIES

"The objections to the verbal inspiration of Holy Scripture do not manifest great ingenuity or mental acumen, but the very opposite: they serve as a shining example of how God inflicts His just punishment upon all critics of His Word — they lose their common sense and become utterly unreasonable and illogical." (F. Pieper, *What Is Christianity?* p. 243.) Will any one, after studying the preceding sections, still think that Dr. Pieper's judgment is too harsh? If so, here is further material. The black-list enumerating the fatuities and puerilities, sophistries and logical absurdities, evasions and misstatements, with which the critics operate is a long one. We shall have to restrict ourselves to reviewing twenty-three additional ones, more than enough to make you subscribe to Pieper's statement "None of us, even though he were a doctor in all four faculties, can deny the inspiration of Holy Scripture without suffering an impairment of his natural mental powers. . . . All opposition to the divine truth, and that includes the opposition to the *satisfactio vicaria* and to the inspiration of Scripture (verbal inspiration), is, as can be clearly shown, irrational." (*Chr. Dogmatik,* I, pp. 280, 614.)

The Errorists Appealing to Scripture

Assertion No. 1: Holy Scripture was written by divine inspiration; yet this same Holy Scripture contains many errors. The conservatives among the moderns make this assertion. The liberals refuse to utter such nonsense. The liberals assert: The Scriptures are purely human writings and contain many errors. That is a logical assertion; the second statement does not contradict the first one. But the conservative critics are not employing their reason when they declare that all Scripture is given by inspiration of God and still find room in the inspired writings for a host of errors. "The many explicit passages teach, if language can teach anything, that the Bible, '*all* Scripture,' is the Word of God, true, trustworthy, and of divine authority. . . . Nor has the most perverse ingenuity been able to show anything else, far less to favor, or leave room for, the direct opposite. I say the *direct* opposite — the logical contradictory. For when the propositions are 'All Scripture is true and trustworthy' and 'Scripture is untrue and untrustworthy in an indefinite number of things,' then the opposition is direct, the propositions are contradictory; and therefore, according to the inexorable logic of the square of opposition, if the one is true, the other must be false." (H. M'Intosh, *Is Christ Infallible and the Bible True?* p. 596 f.) If the conservatives want to be recognized as logical thinkers, they must openly declare, with the liberals, that 2 Tim. 3:16 is not true and that Christ made a mistake when He asserted that "the Scripture cannot be broken," John 10:35. As long as they remain in the half-way station, they involve themselves in hopeless self-contradictions.

The *Baltimore Declaration* of the U. L. C. A. asserts: "We believe that the whole body of the Scriptures is inspired by God. . . . We accept the inspiration of the Scriptures as a fact of which our faith in God, through Christ, assures us, and this assurance is supported by words of Scripture in which the fact of inspiration is asserted or implied, 1 Cor. 2:12; 2 Tim. 3:16; 2 Pet. 1:21." (*Minutes of the 1938 Convention*, p. 474.) But that does not mean, says the interpreter, Dr. A. J. Traver, that the Bible does not contain errors. He asks: "Does not modern science contradict the Scriptures?" He answers: Yes, indeed; but remember: "God did not inspire the writers of Scripture to know all truth. . . . Bible writers wrote with the background of their age and its scientific beliefs. . . . The Bible is not a text for biology or for chemistry." (*The Lutheran*, Feb. 22 and May 10, 1939.) Dr. Traver interpreted the *Baltimore Declaration* correctly, for the commission responsible for the *Declaration* "was unable to accept the statement of the Missouri Synod that the Scriptures are the infallible truth 'also in those parts which treat of historical, geographical, and other secular matters'" (*Minutes*, etc., p. 468). A man does not have to take a course in logic to see that if one asserts that all Scripture is inspired, he cannot make the second assertion that Scripture is not reliable in all of its statements. A layman wrote a letter to *The Lutheran* of January 18, 1939, and declared: "It would appear to this writer that this position" (the Scriptures contain some erroneous statements) "is contradicted in Section 6, where it is asserted: 'Therefore we believe that the whole body of Scripture in all its parts is the Word of God.'" This layman is faulting his theological leaders for using inexact language, for committing a logical absurdity. He knows that a false statement cannot be called a word of God.[75]

If the statement "We believe that the whole body of the Scriptures in all its parts is the Word of God" means what the words imply, we have the self-contradiction just discussed. If it refers to the *Schriftganze*, the "whole of Scripture" (which we are loathe to be-

---

75) Further details are given in *Conc. Theol. Mthly.*, X, pp. 386, 581. — Did the Omaha convention of the U. L. C. (1940) revise the illogical, self-contradictory *Baltimore Declaration* by accepting the *Pittsburgh Agreement*? Dr. H. C. Alleman fought the *Pittsburgh Agreement* because one of its authors stated that "this explanation concerning the Scripture goes beyond the *Baltimore Declaration*"; he denounced "the doctrine of verbal inspiration as a carry-over from the old heathen conception of inspiration." (*Luth. Church Quart.*, 1940, pp. 348, 352.) What happened at Omaha? A correspondent of *The Lutheran*, March 5, 1941, asserts: "There was one thing on which both the majority and the minority agreed: they both were certain that they were not voting for any changes in the positions or practices of the U. L. C. A."

lieve), it would be dealing with the monstrous conception — a conception which no logical mind can grasp — that the whole differs from its parts, that many of the parts are objectionable, but the "whole" is fine.

Furthermore, those who make assertion No. 1 are not only contradicting themselves, but they are virtually making Scripture contradict itself. Rather, they are putting a lie into the mouth of Scripture. It comes to this: "Since the writers so repeatedly claimed inspiration, it is evident that they were either inspired or that they acted with fanatical presumption. We are shut up to the conclusion that the Bible is the Word of God or that it is a lie." (L. Boettner, *The Inspiration of the Scriptures*, p. 22.)

Assertion No. 2: "There is no assertion in Scripture that its writers were kept from error." Thus the notorious *Auburn Affirmation.* See page 27 f. above, where a number of similar assertions are listed. They are filling the world with the cry: "The Bible itself makes no claim to be infallible, save in one passage, whose meaning is open to dispute." (G. A. Buttrick, president of the Federal Council for 1940. See *Concordia Theological Monthly*, XII, p. 222 f.) They do not like the dilemma: The Bible is either inspired and infallible, or, setting up this claim, it is a lying book. They seek to evade it by asserting that the Bible makes no such claim. We cannot conceive how the Auburn affirmationists and their friends in other circles can make this assertion in the face of 2 Tim. 3:16; 2 Pet. 1:21; John 10:35, and the great number of parallel passages. *Hier steht einem der Verstand still.* If these men said that the statements "All Scripture is given by inspiration of God" and "The Scripture cannot be broken" are not true, since in fact Scripture in many places must be broken and stamped as false, our mind could follow their line of argument. But our logical mind refuses to function when they tell us that these passages are true, but do not claim divine inspiration and infallibility for all Scripture statements. "The Bible itself makes no claim to be infallible, save in one passage, whose meaning is open to dispute"? Is Dr. Buttrick referring to John 10:35? If Jesus wanted to claim infallibility for Scripture, could He have used more simple and direct language than by saying that not a single passage of Scripture is subject to correction? The *Lutheran World* called it "an amazing statement that the Scriptures themselves teach that 'every word' contained in them is inspired by the Holy Ghost. We submit that an assertion so sweeping should have been backed by definite and unambiguous quotations." (See *Lehre und Wehre*, 1904, p. 39.) If any man says that the statement "All Scripture is given by inspiration of God" is an indefinite and ambiguous statement, our mind cannot follow the workings of his mind, and there is no use of further arguing the matter. There would be sense in arguing the matter with the extreme liberal who denies the *truth* of 2 Tim. 3:16; John 10:35; etc. We are ready to argue with Richard Rothe, who admits that the *apostles* certainly taught Verbal Inspiration but declares that "his exegetical conscience forbids him to be bound by the teaching of the apostles on this ponit." (See Pieper, *op. cit.*, I, p. 320. Meusel, *Handlexikon*, III, p. 459.) We might not convince him that it is wicked to refuse to be bound by the teaching of the apostles, but we could at least conduct an intelligent conversation. But if men say that the words "All Scripture is given by inspiration" are ambiguous, we cannot any longer argue with them.

But we can do this much: we can let them present their reasons for finding in 2 Tim. 3:16 and the related passages a sense different from what the words express. These reasons prove that their thesis — Scripture does not claim inspiration and infallibility for all its parts — is untenable. They are reasons inspired and dictated by despair. They say: (a) "2 Tim. 3:16 leaves open the question whether inspired Scripture is infallible. That it is profitable no one would deny." (C. H. Dodd, *The Authority of the Bible*, p. 15.) The argument seems to be: A Scripture can be inspired and still be either true or false; and since Paul does not qualify "inspired" by "true," the question is undecided. That means that when God speaks through a prophet and does not expressly say that He is speaking the truth, we may take it or leave it. (The point that a false statment may be profitable, will be discussed later, as Assertion No. 7.)[76]

They say: (b) that "a moment's study of the text (2 Tim. 3:16) shows that the writer could have had in mind at best only the Old Testament." (H. L. Willett, *The Bible through the Centuries*, p. 282.) The argument is: The verbalists cannot prove with 2 Tim. 3:16 that "the Bible claims its own inspiration" (p. 280); all that they could prove from this text would be that the Bible claims the inspiration of the Old Testament. — We are perfectly satisfied with this concession. Just familiarize yourself with the idea that St. Paul insisted on the inspiration and absolute inerrancy of the Old Testament. If a man once accepts that, we'll have no trouble

---

76) N. R. Best puts the argument thus: "Paul dallied with no such negative and speculative claims as 'The Scriptures contain no mistakes.' He struck for something far more positive and far more vital: 'Every Scripture inspired of God is profitable.' . . . 'No errors' — a man could wrestle with that proposition for a century and not prove it; every logician indeed would warn him beforehand that a universal negative is unprovable. But 'profitable' — that he could prove at every Christian hearthstone, at every Christian altar." (*Inspiration*, p. 80.) Dr. Best is ignorant of the true situation. We do not need to prove, and we do not ask the apostle to prove, that no errors are contained in Holy Scripture. The bare statement of Scripture to that effect is sufficient.

with him as to the New Testament. We have never yet met a critic who attached greater importance to the Old Testament than to the New. So we are going to harp on 2 Tim. 3:16, force him to admit that according to the Bible the Old Testament is inspired, and then he will not balk at conceding the same to the rest of the Bible.[77]

Let us assume that 2 Tim. 3:16 has no bearing on the books of the New Testament.[78] We lose nothing thereby. There are many texts which very distinctly assert the inspiration and inerrancy of the books of the New Testament. 1 Cor. 2:13: the words of the apostle are the words of the Holy Ghost. John 8:31 f.: the principle that Scripture cannot be broken applies to the words of Jesus, which are "the truth," and according to John 17:14 and 17 to the words of the apostles. 1 Pet. 1:10-12: the words of the apostles are placed on a level with the words of the prophets. Again, 2 Pet. 3:2: The "words of the holy prophets" and "the commandments of us, the apostles of the Lord," are of equal authority. It follows that, if Paul ascribes inerrancy and absolute authority to the Old Testament, he must assert the same of the New Testament. 2 Cor. 13:3: Paul presents his writings to us as the words of Christ, and, again, 1 Cor. 14:37: "The things that I write unto you are the commandments of the Lord." Is the New Testament of equal authority, equally inspired and equally inerrant, with the Old Testament? And there is 2 Pet. 3:16! The "epistles" of Paul are put in the class of "the Scriptures." (See G. Stoeckhardt, *Lehre und Wehre*, 1886, p. 254.) "All Scripture is given by inspiration," says Paul, and, says Peter,

---

77) Quoting Mark 7:13, where "our Lord calls the Pentateuch 'the Word of God' in so many words," and Matt. 5:18, R. A. Torrey remarks: "Now of course, these two passages refer primarily only to the Pentateuch. But *if you can accept the Pentateuch, you will not have much trouble with the rest of the Bible*. This is the very part of the Bible where the hottest fight has always been waged between those who believe the Bible to be the inerrant Word of God and those who think that much of it is only fable or 'folk-lore.'" (*Is the Bible the Inerrant Word of God?* P. 16.) Quoting Matt. 1:22; John 10:35; 2 Pet. 1:21; 2 Tim. 3:16, and similar passages, James M. Gray remarks: "Let us reflect that the inspiration of the Old Testament being assured as it is, why should similar evidence be required for the New? Whoever is competent to speak as a Bible authority knows that the *unity* of the Old and New Testaments is the strongest demonstration of their common source. They are seen to be not two books but only two parts of one book." (*The Fundamentals*, III, p. 19.)

78) We need not assume that. "In 2 Tim. 3:16: 'all Scripture' *may* include a Gospel like Luke's (cf. 1 Tim. 5:18) or even Paul's own epistles (cf. 2 Pet. 3:15)." (James Orr, *Revelation and Inspiration*, p. 161.) "Nothing in the text indicates that Paul restricts the term 'inspired Scripture' to the holy books known to Timothy from his childhood. Rather the contrary.'" (Wohlenberg, in *Zahn's Commentary*.) Additional references are given in *Conc. Theol. Mthly.*, I, p. 113. There the proofs offered by Dodd for his thesis "The Bible itself does not make any claim to infallible authority for all its parts" are examined.

the epistles of Paul are "Scripture." The critics will have a hard time to show that these passages are ambiguous.[79]

Some of the critics commit the puerility of saying (c): "The sixty-six books of the Bible certainly do not all claim for themselves to be given by inspiration of God. Very few of them do." (J. M. Gibson, *The Inspiration of Holy Scripture*, p. 24.) — The prophets of the Old Testament spoke and wrote by inspiration of God (Luke 1:70: "as He spoke by the mouth of His holy prophets"; Acts 3: 18, 21: "by the mouth of all his prophets since the world began"); so also the apostles (Matt. 10:19 f.). But, says Gibson, unless a book written by a prophet or apostle says on its title-page: "Written by inspiration," the writer does not claim inspiration for this book. What about Ezra's writings? "We know him as 'Ezra the scribe.' Yet there is no mention of any commission to take in hand either the recording or the editing. The same applies to Nehemiah." (*Op. cit.*, p. 84.) The same applies to Second Timothy and Second Peter, says Dodd: "Neither passage (2 Tim. 3:16 and 2 Pet. 1:21) claims the rank of inspired Scripture for the writing in which it occurs." (*Op. cit.*, p. 15.) Sure enough; we do not find the statement on the title-page: "This epistle is inspired." But Dodd conveniently overlooks the word "apostle" in 2 Tim. 1:1 and 2 Pet. 1:1 and 2 Pet. 3:2. He also leaves out of consideration John 17:14; 1 Cor. 2:13; 1 Thess. 2:13. No, Ezra did not say: "This book is inspired"; but 2 Tim. 3:16 writes it on the title-page of Ezra's writing, and the passages quoted in the preceding section do the same for all the books of the New Testament. Gibson again: "Luke does not say, These other teachers to whom you have been listening are not infallible, but I am. . . . Is there anything about Luke being specially appointed to give an *ex-cathedra* utterance? Not a word of it. Here are the claims he makes on his own behalf: that he has given much attention to the subject and that he has been careful to be accurate in verifying his facts. . . . He does not say: 'The Spirit moved me to write this to you.' He simply says, 'It seemed good to me also.'" (*Op. cit.*, p. 133 f.) Even Charles Gore uses this argument. "The evangelist St. Luke in his preface appears to make no claim to inspiration but only to accuracy." (*The Doctrine of the Infallible Book*, p. 45.) Here the puerility is buttressed with a fallacy. The fact that St. Luke

---

79) One sample to show how hard they try to divest the passages claiming inerrancy for the Bible, including the New Testament, of their force: "In 2 Pet. 3:16 St. Paul's epistles appear" (?) "to be alluded to as 'Scriptures'; but if we deal candidly with the evidence, it would appear that this one book of the New Testament is not by the writer in whose name it is written." (Charles Gore, *The Doctrine of the Infallible Book*, p. 33.) There must be some force in St. Peter's statement; else Bishop Gore would not resort to the desperate expedient of denying its clarity and appealing to the question of the authenticity of the book.

claimed accuracy has no bearing on the question whether he claimed inspiration. The logicians call this the fallacy of the irrelevant conclusion or the *ignoratio elenchi.* Gibson once more: "The prophets had sometimes special directions to write, as when Jeremiah prepared the roll which Jehoiakim destroyed and again, by divine direction, prepared a second roll; but we have no evidence of any special call or commission to record the prophecies for the sake of the ages to come." (*Op. cit.,* p. 84.) For us the evidence of Rom. 15:4 ("Whatsoever things were written aforetime were written for our learning") is conclusive. Furthermore, if prophecies relate future events, — do they not? — what was in the mind of the prophets in writing them down if they did not "record them for the sake of the ages to come"?

S. P. Cadman employs (d) plain sophistry in support of the thesis under discussion. In his *Answers to Everyday Questions* he says on page 253: "Nowhere does the Book itself claim for the entire content of its literature what you assert in its behalf. . . . It is a baseless assumption that every word of Holy Scripture must be regarded as practically infallible." For instance: "Not everything that Genesis, Jonah, and Daniel contain is literally and factually true." (P. 274.) We naturally ask: How can the Bible claim to be God's Word, God's truth, if it actually tells factual untruths? Here is the sophistry: "We have to distinguish between factual truth and moral or religious truth. To say that the Bible is true does not imply that everything it states is fact. It conveys many of its sublimest truths by fiction, poetry, rhapsody, and dream. If you dispute the assertion, read the parables of Jesus, . . . and the Genesis document. . . . Not everything that Genesis, Jonah, and Daniel contain is literally and factually true." It is sophistry to conclude from the fact that Jesus conveyed a spiritual truth by means, for example, of the story of the Ten Virgins, — it being immaterial whether these events actually took place, — that the holy writers had the right to tell the story of the Fall or of Jonah's experience as facts, knowing that these things did not occur. You will get the full import of the equivocation if you read the question which Dr. Cadman is answering. "Question: Why do ecclesiastics ask us to accept the Bible as the Word of God and then tell us that the account of creation is not historic or Jonah's experiences a 'fish story'? . . . How can you blame men if they conclude that the Book is full of errors and that consequently its author or authors are fallible?"

The easiest way to evade the force of 2 Tim. 3:16 is (e) to give the term "inspiration" a new meaning. First say with Dodd that "inspired Scripture" is not the same as "infallible Scripture" (see above) and with Gore: "The New Testament certainly does not warrant our identifying inspiration with infallibility on all subjects."

(*Op. cit.,* p. 46.) And then, when the simple Christian objects that what is God-breathed, what the holy writers expressed in words which God gave them, cannot be fallible; that, if "the holy men of God spake as they were moved by the Holy Ghost" (2 Pet. 1:21), they could not have spoken error and untruth, tell him that he has the wrong conception of "inspiration," tell him that "the inspiration of the Bible is the total spirit and power it reveals. . . . The proof that the book is inspired is its power to inspire." (H. L. Willett, *op. cit.,* p. 288.) Or: "All Scripture is because of the inspiration of God. That does not mean that everything that was written was inspired. It means that men wrote because they were under the inspiration of some divinely given truth." (E. Lewis, *A Philosophy of the Christian Revelation,* p. 260.) Or: "Inspiration does not carry inerrancy. It is the capacity to explore independently the regions of the spirit and to convince others of the reality of that which one has discovered." (C. H. Dodd, *op. cit.,* p. 129.) Or, in the simple language of the vulgar rationalists: Inspiration is "die andaechtige Gemuetsverfassung" (Semler; see Hoenecke, *Ev.-Luth. Dogmatik,* I, p. 352). The trouble with this *quid-pro-quo* operation is that it puts too great a strain upon the credulity of the simple Christian. The words of the apostle cannot bear this alleged meaning. Since "all Scripture" is the subject of which "given by inspiration of God" is predicated, don't begin to talk of a "devout state of mind." Your hearers will not know what to make of the devout state of mind of the Scriptures. And was the apostle really such a bungler that, when he said that "no prophecy of the Scripture is of any private interpretation, but holy men of God spake as they were moved by the Holy Ghost," he actually wanted to say that their teaching was the product of their "capacity to explore independently the regions of the spirit"? — These samples should be sufficient to show that indeed the critics of God's Word lose their common sense and become utterly unreasonable and illogical. But, say the critics, hear our further proofs for the thesis that Scripture does not claim infallibility for all its parts; these additional proofs are irrefutable. We shall hear them, and to give them the prominence which the critics attach to them, we shall treat them as special Assertions.

Summoning Christ as the First Bible Critic

Assertion No. 3: Christ Himself corrected the Scriptures. The argument is: If Christ, the great Teacher (and *we* add: Christ, the Author of Scripture) found it necessary to revise and amend Scripture, to point out the mistakes and false teachings in the Old Testament, you can no longer hold that the Bible claims infallibility for all its parts. Of the various mechanisms employed in the war against Verbal Inspiration some moderns consider this to be the most effective one. They drill their students in its use. A graduate of Union Theological Seminary told his examining board: "The men who wrote our Scriptures were inspired by God, but they mixed some of their own errors in with God's truth. Jesus said: 'It hath been said of old . . .; but I say unto you.' There were some parts of Scripture which Jesus Himself did not accept as God's truth, at least not the whole truth of God." (*The Presbyterian*, Nov. 26, 1936.) It is drilled into the students at Gettysburg, too. Their professor, Dr. H. C. Alleman, declared in his manifesto against Verbal Inspiration: "If Christ can be quoted as saying in John 10:35 (as the verbal inspirationists hold) that 'Scripture cannot be broken,' and if that means that it is without error or contradiction, how are we to square this statement with those instances, particularly in the Sermon on the Mount, in which He deliberately breaks Scripture? For example, does not Matt. 5:39 abrogate Ex. 21:24, and does not Mark 7:19 repeal Lev. 11?" (See p. 21 above.) His colleague Dr. J. Aberly makes the same assertion. And there are many others.[80]

The assertion that Christ corrected the Scriptures does not reveal great mental acumen. It means (a) that Christ contradicted Himself. At one place He says that "the Scripture cannot be broken," and at another place He is engaged in breaking Scripture, revising, censoring, correcting it. In the Sermon on the Mount He solemnly declares that not "one jot or tittle shall pass from the Law" (Matt. 5:18), and three verses later, from v. 21 on, He strikes out whole sentences, passages, and sections. Drs. Alleman and Haenel and the others are asking us to believe that God is reversing, correcting, and contradicting Himself.[81]

---

80) Aberly: "In this total view we must have the Spirit of Jesus to differentiate between what is temporary and what is permanent — this attitude will be found to be that of the New Testament writers and even of Jesus Himself towards that unique revelation of God which we have in the Old Testament. . . . This view of the total purport of the Old Testament determined the corrections made of such teachings as were at variance with it. Illustrations of this will be found in the corrections of the law of retaliation, among others in the Sermon on the Mount, Matt. 5:17-48. (*The Luth. Church Quart.*, April, 1935, p. 119.) Others: *The Expositor's Greek Testament* on Matt. 5:21-26: "Christ's position as fulfiller entitled Him to point out defects of the Law itself." Johannes Haenel: "Die Gegenueberstellung des Zitats und der Erwiderung Jesus' laesst nicht im geringsten den Gedanken aufkommen, dass Jesus nur ein Missverstaendnis der Erklaerer beheben will. . . . Gegen die *Schriftworte selbst* wendet sich Jesus." (*Der Schriftbegriff Jesus'*, p. 180 ff.) Etc.

81) H. M'Intosh: "Those utterances of our Lord — mainly those in the Sermon on the Mount opening with 'Ye have heard that it hath been said by them of old time,' on which they have sought to found their unwarrantable assertions — are directed not against the teaching of Scripture, which *would have been a divine contradiction of Himself.* For it was God who 'in times past spoke unto the fathers by the prophets'; and it was the same God who 'in these last times hath spoken unto us

Nor (b) do we have to exert great acumen to show that the text will not bear Dr. Alleman's interpretation. When Jesus quoted the provision of the Law "Thou shalt not kill" (Matt. 5:21) and then adds: "But I say unto you, . . ." is He revoking the Law? Where do you see in the text the words on which your whole argument hinges: "But I say unto you, You may kill"? Our contradictionists have not mastered the logical law of the contradiction. Jesus indeed says: "Whosoever is angry," etc. But the prohibition of sinful anger, etc., is not a substitution for the Mosaic prohibition of murder. It is not even an addition to it. Ex. 20:13 forbids anger as well as murder. The "but" of Jesus is not directed against Moses but against those who found in Moses nothing but the prohibition of the gross act of murder. In the words of Dr. Lenski: " 'You have heard' means: from your teachers, the scribes and Pharisees, on whom you were entirely dependent for your instruction. They told you that 'it was said,' of course by Moses, 'to the ancients,' to whom he first brought the Law: 'Thou shalt not murder.' . . . But this was all that you heard — nothing but a civil law, to be applied to an actual murderer, by a civil court. . . . Not a word about God and what He by this commandment requires of the heart. Not a word about the lusts and the passions that lead to actual murder and, though they produce no murder, are just as wicked as murder. . . . What the disciples now hear from Jesus is vastly different from what in the past they heard from the scribes and Pharisees. The opposition is not to 'it was said.' Jesus is not contradicting or correcting Moses." (On Matt. 5:21, 22.)   Jesus does not revoke Ex. 20:13. He leaves it in full force. He does not strike out one jot or tittle. And these moderns are telling us: Jesus is here plainly breaking Scripture! [82]

"Does not Matt. 5:39 abrogate Ex. 21:24?" Jesus was *not* a revolutionary; He was not a parlor-communist. He did not ask the civil courts to cease exacting the just punishment from the criminal. "Here again Jesus does not abrogate or change the penal laws as

---

by His Son.' It was the Son who Himself declared, as if to answer by anticipation this very objection, 'Till heaven and earth pass, one jot or one tittle. . . .' (Matt. 5:17, 18; Luke 16:17.) With this He prefaced all His utterances about the teaching of the ancients. So that He could not have directed them against the Scriptures, which were His own Word, but against those misapprehensions, perversions, and misapplications of it with which an unspiritual religiosity and soulless literalism had associated and overcrusted it." (*Op. cit.*, p. 295.)

82) See also G. Stoeckhardt, *Die biblische Geschichte des Neuen Testaments*, p. 92: "Christus setzt das Gesetz Mosis nicht ausser Kraft und Geltung. Christus bestaetigt vielmehr das Gesetz, 'streicht es recht heraus und zeigt *den rechten Kern und Verstand*, dass sie lernen, was das Gesetz ist und haben will' (Luther)." Also Kretzmann, *Popular Commentary:* "Christ *confirms* and *expounds* the Law. . . . The Lord now proceeds to prove His condemning statement by expounding a few of the commandments according to their *full spiritual significance*."

too harsh, as not humanitarian enough, or as needing reform in other respects. . . . But the very God who placed that law and its execution where it belongs, in the hands of the government, places another law and its execution, the law of love, into the hearts of Christ's disciples." (Lenski.)[83] — "And does not Mark 7:19 repeal Lev. 11?" Certainly not! The teaching that it is not food but the evil thoughts of the heart that defile man does not say that there is anything wrong about the Levitical law concerning clean and unclean beasts, but simply corrects the misapprehension and mis-application of Lev. 11, as though Levitical purity in itself constituted moral and spiritual purity. And if anybody should insist that the abrogation of the Ceremonial Law constituted a breaking of Scrip-ture, Jewry, orthodox Jewry, would side with him but not the Christian theologians.

It is interesting to note that Dr. Charles F. Schaeffer, professor at Gettysburg, wrote in *The Lutheran Commentary* (1895): "The Lord does not mean the teaching of Moses himself but the erroneous mode of interpreting his words." More interesting that in the *New Testament Commentary*, edited by Dr. H. C. Alleman, Dr. Henry Offermann writes (p. 169): "When the scribes interpreted the com-mandment, they used to read the words of the commandment and then pointed out to their hearers the punishment for the trans-gressor. That was all. They had no further comment to make. They were satisfied with the letter of the Law, but made no at-tempt to penetrate into its spirit. There is nothing in the text to indicate that Jesus objected either to the commandment or to the words attached to it. What He objected to was that the traditional interpretation did not go beyond the act itself." And there are liberal theologians who would not endorse this part of Dr. Alle-man's manifesto. *A New Commentary on Holy Scripture*, edited by Bishop Charles Gore and others, says: " 'Ye have heard that it was said by them of old times' is a traditional scribal phrase, with the sense of 'you have understood this to mean.' But our Lord em-phasized the divine mind behind this prohibition of murder and teaches that both the harboring of anger and the use of abusive language are included within its scope." And here is the ultra-liberal H. L. Willett, who says: "Furthermore it must be remem-bered that Jesus was bringing no indictment against the Hebrew Scriptures, which He held in the highest reverence. He wished,

---

83) Dr. Graebner's answer to the Alleman-manifesto: "If the Jews of His time justified a passionate and revengeful spirit, Jesus now carries out more fully the spirit and design of the Law by urging the readiness of a true disciple to forgive, to win, to restore. And who is not able to see the difference established between public and official vengeance and the private relationship of men to men?" (*Conc. Theol. Mthly.*, XI, p. 885.)

however, to carry out their spirit to its legitimate ends." (In *The Christian Century*, Oct. 21, 1936.)

Assertion No. 4a: Christ erred in endorsing the whole of the Old Testament. — When we answer assertion No. 3 by pointing out that Christ endorsed the whole of the Old Testament, critics reply: Christ certainly did that, but He was wrong in doing that. They are off on a different tack; but they are still sailing on the sea of un- reason. It is an unchristian assertion, as we have shown in the third article (see pp. 71 ff. above); but it is also unreasonable. To ask us to say that Christ endorsed all of the Old Testament, the authenticity of the Pentateuch and the story of Jonah and the whale, because "He knew no better" is asking too much of a Chris- tian; but it is also asking too much of a thinking man. Oh, yes, it is reasonable enough for Voltaire to declare that Christ's testimony on these points is not absolutely trustworthy, for Voltaire insisted that Christ was a mere man. But a theologian who believes that Christ is true God and still insists that He made "exegetical mis- takes" and false statements is not using his reasoning powers. And we shall go a step farther. Let Jesus be a mere man. But was He a good man, an honest man? The critics, not only the conservatives but also the liberals, insist on that. Only the scoffers, the infidels, may deny it. However, you cannot teach that Jesus was a good, honest man and still claim that He was mistaken on various points, on the point, for instance, of the inerrancy of the Bible. For He claimed to be a teacher sent from God who spoke the very words of God. It is impossible for a mere man to claim absolute infalli- bility and remain an honest man. Use your thinking powers! When you assert that Jesus was wrong in endorsing the Old Testament, this Jesus, who claimed to speak the Word of God in all His state- ments, you are proclaiming Jesus as a fraud. Are you ready to do that? [84]

The critics do not want to do that. And so they are driven to employ various clumsy subterfuges. (Assertion No. 4b.) We have mentioned some on page 71 above. For instance: "Jesus con- descended not to know." Here are some more. Jesus did not

---

84) R. A. Torrey: "Jesus Christ claimed to be a teacher sent from God who spoke the very words of God. He claimed this over and over again, and if He was mistaken about the origin and character of this Book, concerning which He has so much to say, He was a fraud, an unmitigated fraud. If these people are right who tell us that these incidents in the Book of Genesis, for example, which our Lord has so plainly endorsed, are simply 'folk-lore' or inaccurate and unreliable traditions of the day, then, beyond a question, Jesus Christ was a fraud, an unmitigated fraud." (*Op. cit.*, p. 20.) *Proceedings, Iowa District, 1891*, p. 31: "If the Bible were not inspired and consequently infallible, it would not be a good book but a lying book, for it claims divine inspira- tion for itself; then, too, *Jesus would not be good but a deceiver*, for He endorses the Bible as a divine book."

endorse the story of Jonah in the belly of the fish; Luke 11:29 f. does not mention this part of the story; so Jesus never vouched for the truth of it; the account of Matt. 12:40 is not trustworthy.[85] The meaning of this is: You cannot say that we are charging Jesus with an error for endorsing this story, for He never endorsed it! Another subterfuge: "It is said that the language of our Lord about the Old Testament requires us to accept the account of the Flood and the story of Jonah as literally true. . . . However, it seems to me to be even preposterous to suggest that He binds us by His allusion to the Flood (Luke 17:26 ff.) to suppose that it occurred as it is described in Genesis. We should, I think, feel the same way about His allusion to Jonah's resurrection out of the whale's belly, if it were authentic." (Charles Gore, *op. cit.*, pp. 19, 25.) The meaning of this is as above. But where is the proof for this idea? Bishop Gore "thinks" it. Can he make me think it? And why, we ask, did Jesus refer to these incidents if they were not facts? That is easy to answer, say the critics. Christ used these incidents as parables, and so they need not actually have happened. Prof. J. W. Horine: "The book (Jonah) is considered to be not literal history but parable or allegory. . . . Our Lord's reference to this event [Jonah being disgorged from the mouth of the great fish] does not contradict this view. He is simply using it as an illustration. 'Just as *we* refer to the prodigal son or the good Samaritan in precisely the same terms we should use were their adventures historical facts, so may Christ have done here.'" (*The Lutheran*, March 18, 1937.) The meaning of this subterfuge is: Christ knew that this incident never occurred; and so our charge that the critics actually ascribe fallibility to Jesus is groundless. But we ask again: How will Professor Horine prove that Jesus did not consider the history of Jonah literal history?[86] Do not ask

---

85) H. L. Willett: "It would seem that the reference to Jonah's stay in the belly of the sea-monster was no part of the narrative as used by Jesus. There is no reference to this portion of the account in the record of the Gospel of Luke (11:30-32). . . . It seems strange that so important an incident as that of the miraculous deliverance of the prophet should have been omitted from the gospel of Luke if it were an authentic part of the gospel-story." (*The Chr. Century*, Dec. 9, 1936.) See also Gore's statement: ". . . if it were authentic." Willett and Gore could quote D. F. Strauss as their authority. "The continuance of Jonah in the belly of the whale does not seem to have been brought in as a parallel case *until later, subsequently,* that is, at the time when the morning of Sunday had been fixed upon for the resurrection of Jesus." (*A New Life of Jesus*, I, p. 439. *Das Leben Jesu*, I, p. 403.)

86) A writer in *The Living Church*, April 26, 1930, puts it this way: "St. Matt. 12:40 need not carry with it an acceptance by our Lord of the literal and complete historicity of the Book of Jonah, unless one is prepared to assert one's own acceptance of the literal and complete historicity of every parabolic story used by Him to drive home by forceful illustration His teachings. Is your correspondent willing so to

us to accept your Assertions No. 4 b, by which you seek to escape the dilemma into which your Assertion No. 4 a places you, on your mere *dictum.*

Better say at once — Assertion No. 5 — that "Christ never offers a word of Scripture as a final reason for belief," and have done with it. Dr. John Oman (Cambridge) makes this assertion in *Vision and Authority,* page 188: "The method of citing texts is only a second-hand dealing in truth. . . . Christ encourages His disciples to rise above the rule of authorities and investigate till each is his own authority. . . . Christ appeals to the testimony of Scripture but never offers a word of it as a final reason for belief. His final appeal is always to the heart by God." Oman naturally takes this position, for, "whatever the authority of Scripture may be, it is not of the infallibility of verbal inspiration" (p. 94). Oman, of course, makes no serious attempt to prove his assertion by Scripture. "Citing texts is only a second-hand dealing in truth." The proof which he offers in this connection is: " 'All ye are brethren,' He says, 'and one is your teacher,' " and he deduces from this — by what laws of reason we know not —: "Even Christ Himself is not our Rabbi." . . . We are anxious to know what he makes of the passage John 5: 39. Or cf John 8: 31. Or John 10: 35. Or Matt. 4: 4. And Matt. 4: 7 and Matt. 4: 10. Whatever Satan's answer might be, though he might have answered: "It is written? Why, everybody knows chat Scripture is not infallible," Christ declares, first and last: "It is written." (See further *Proceedings, Iowa District,* 1891, pp. 29—31: "Mit der Schrift bewies Christus seine Worte und Lehre.")

ANOTHER FUTILE PLEA

Assertion No. 6: Inspiration and infallibility must be restricted to the Gospel-message in the Bible or, to stretch a point, to the religious and moral teaching of the Bible. — But is that not the same as Assertions 1 and 2? It is, essentially. But the critics — the great majority of them — prefer Form 6 to 1 and 2, because that form has greater appeal. They delude themselves with the idea that nothing is lost if only the infallibility of the great Gospel-message is saved.[87] Assertion 6 has a more specious form than

---

accept, for example, the story of the Rich Man and Lazarus?" Here is confusion worse confounded. The story is a true story. "There *was* a certain rich man. . . . And there *was* a certain beggar." We even know his name: "Lazarus."

87) Discussing a similar case of juggling, the *Proceedings of the Iowa District* say: "Die Leugner der Inspiration fuehren, wenn man ueber ihre greuliche Lehre erstaunt und entruestet ist, immer solche Reden im Munde: 'Wir wollen euch ja nichts von eurem Glauben rauben; denn wenn auch Moses und Jesajas, Matthaeus und Markus, Paulus und Petrus sich geirrt haben, so bleibt uns doch Christus, von dem allein unser Heil abhaengt.' Das sind eitel *Taschenspielerkuenste.*"

the others and is therefore more widely used. For that reason we shall treat it separately, even though we shall have to repeat ourselves somewhat. We shall be adding, however, some new material.

J. M. Gibson takes issue with those "who insist on every part of the Bible being equally inspired"; it is "unfaithfulness to the sacred Scriptures" not to reserve full, real inspiration for "the Gospel, the central theme of the Bible" (*op. cit.*, p. 101). James Orr is satisfied "with a Scripture supernaturally inspired to be an infallible guide in the great matters for which it was given — the knowledge of the will of God for their salvation in Christ Jesus, instruction in the way of holiness and the hope of eternal life" (*Revelation and Inspiration*, p. 217). The *Baltimore Declaration:* "We accept the Scriptures as the infallible truth of God in all matters that pertain to His revelation and our salvation." (*Minutes of the 1938 Convention of the U. L. C. A.*, p. 471.) Dr. A. J. Traver, in his exposition of the *Baltimore Declaration:* "The Holy Scriptures are the infallible truth 'in all matters that pertain to His revelation and our salvation,'" not in secular matters, for "Bible writers wrote with the background of their age and its scientific beliefs" (*The Lutheran*, Feb. 22, 1939). And in *The Lutheran* of Jan. 23, 1936, Dr. Traver says distinctly: "Inspiration includes only the knowledge essential for knowing God and His plan for man." [88]

---

88) "S. Episcopius († 1643), Arminian-Reformed, had already limited inspiration to the so-called essentials." (Guericke, *Symbolik*, p. 172.) So also the Lutheran G. Calixt † 1656. — (See Pieper, *op. cit.*, I, p. 322). J. T. Beck († 1878), conservative: "Auf die goettlichen Reichsgeheimnisse erstreckt die Theopneustie sich; auf das Aeusserliche und Menschliche nur, soweit es mit Ersteren in wesentlichem Zusammenhang steht." (See *Proc., Syn. Conf.*, 1886, p. 22.) Pastor Matschoss of the "Ev. Lutheran Church in Prussia" (Breslau; "Altlutheraner"): "Scripture, being inspired, is the infallible and reliable Word of God in matters that pertain to our salvation. . . . There may be mistakes in non-essential matters." (See *Lehre und Wehre*, 1909, p. 280.) Prof. J. O. Evjen: "To the Reformer (Luther) Scripture was binding to the extent that it proclaimed Christ, the Gospel, or pointed to Christ. Many historical matters in the Bible did not concern Christian life." (*Luth. Church Quart.*, April, 1940, p. 149.) Synod of Maryland (U. L. C. A.): "Article III of the *Pittsburgh Agreement* adds to the *Baltimore Declaration* because it countenances, or seems to countenance, verbal inspiration and inerrancy of the Scriptures and makes the Bible the infallible rule in matters other than faith and practice." (*The Lutheran*, June 12, 1940.) The pronouncement of the *Baltimore Declaration*, by the way, does not constitute an advance from the teaching of the General Council. The *Lutheran Church Review* wrote in 1904: "According to H. E. Jacobs 'the Holy Scriptures are the infallible and inerrant record of God's revelation of His saving grace to men.' . . . The holy writers were not inspired, however, to be 'teachers of astronomy or geology or physics,' and no number of contradictions in this sphere would 'shake our confidence in the absolute reliability of Holy Scripture as the infallible test of theological truth, an inerrant guide in all matters of faith and practice.'" The writer is Dr. Joseph Stump. (See *Lehre und Wehre*, 1904, p. 35 f.)

When the liberals of the extreme left divide the Bible into more-inspired, less-inspired, and non-inspired portions, their reasoning is clear and consistent. They treat the Bible as a purely human writing and their concept of inspiration is different from that of the conservatives. Their "inspiration," being an activity of the human mind, does not connote infallibility. With them the more-inspired portions, too, are fallible, as Willett plainly tells us: "No error has ever resulted in greater discredit to the Scriptures or injury to Christianity than that of attributing to the Bible such a miraculous origin and nature *as to make it an infallible standard of morals and religion.*" (*Loc. cit.*) But when the conservatives acknowledge the divine origin and authority of Scripture and then confine its inspiration to the Gospel-message, they involve themselves in a self-contradiction and are forced either to make the Bible set up extravagant, yes, false, claims or to deny the plain, every-day meaning of common human words.

Nowhere does the Bible say that only certain portions of it are inspired and infallibly true. If any one wants to believe in partial inspiration, he will have to believe it on the authority of the critics. He cannot quote a single passage of Holy Scripture in support of it.[89]

But everywhere the Bible declares that all of it is God's Word, absolutely true. And so the moderns are compelled to twist and torture these passages, divest them of their meaning, and then try to convince us that we have been misreading them. They do not display great theological skill and acumen in their treatment of these passages. The best they can do is to affix footnotes to the text, saying that the text does not mean what it says. "All Scripture is given by inspiration of God." Footnote: That does not mean that all of Scripture is inspired, but only its religious teaching. N. R. Best: "Here, then, in 2 Tim. 3:16, is the Bible's

---

Dr. Stump expresses the same view in his *The Christian Faith*, pp. 318, 320. — H. L. Willett: "The finality and authority of the Bible do not reside in all of its utterances, but in those great characters and messages which are easily discerned as the mountain peaks of its contents. Such portions are worthy to be called the Word of God to man." (*Op. cit.*, p. 289.) Let these samples suffice. Many more could be adduced in support of our statement that the great majority, liberals and conservatives, subscribes to Assertion No. 6.

89) "Wir fragen dagegen: Woher stammt diese Unterscheidung von heilswichtigen, minder wichtigen und unwichtigen Aussagen der Schrift? Oder genauer: Wo macht die Schrift diese Unterscheidung? Und zwar: Wo bringt die Schrift diese Unterscheidung in Verbindung mit der Inspiration, so dass sie diese bei den genannten Nebendingen ganz aussetzen oder doch so stark zuruecktreten liesse, dass den heiligen Schreibern wohl einmal ein Fehler mit unterlaufen konnte, was bei den das Heil direkt beruehrenden Stuecken eben durch die Wirkung der Inspiration ausgeschlossen war?" (*Theologische Quartalschrift*, July, 1931, p. 182.)

standard description of its own qualities, and here surely, if from
the Bible viewpoint a preternatural exactness was essential to
inspired literature, there would have been some tangible hint of
that characteristic. Instead the outlook of the apostle — himself
an undoubted agent of divine inspiration — was entirely in another
direction. Paul had his eyes on the moral dynamic of the book —
its spiritual vitality." (*Inspiration*, p. 97.)[90]   J. A. W. Haas: "It is
this combination of various witnesses, all tending to the unity of
the *saving Gospel* through the illuminating and guiding control
of the Spirit, which constitutes inspiration. *Therefore* every true
Scripture is God-breathed and 'is profitable for doctrine,' etc.,
2 Tim. 3:16. . . . We must not identify the Word absolutely with
the Bible as a book." (*New Testament Commentary*, p. 122.)

John 10:35: "The Scripture cannot be broken." Footnote: What
Scripture says concerning the Gospel is absolutely infallible; what it
says on other matters can be broken. Our footnote to this astound-
ing perversion of the text: Would you classify "the scripture" which
calls the rulers "gods" as a Gospel-message?   Second footnote:
Jesus cannot be made to say here: Some Scripture may be broken.—
Rom. 15:4: "Whatsoever things were written aforetime were written
for our learning." Footnote: *Some* of those things that were written
aforetime were written for our learning. — Acts 24:14: "I believe
all things which are written in the Law and in the Prophets." Footnote: Paul made a mistake in taking everything written in Scripture to be true.[91]

It does not require great intelligence, no more than that of
a child, to understand the force of the universals "all," "whatsoever," of the all-inclusive "*the* Scripture cannot be broken." If
men were not obsessed with the idea that miracles do not occur
(liberals) or that science has found mistakes in Scripture (conservatives), average human intelligence would keep them from
making Asserton No. 6 and basing the assertion on Scripture.
These men have not sufficient acumen and ingenuity to convince us
that Paul said "all" and must have meant "some."

Furthermore, do they not see that they are destroying the
Christian's trust in his Bible? Are they not intelligent enough to
know that, unless they can give the Christian a safe criterion for

---

90) Our own footnote: Why, then, did Paul say: "*All* Scripture"?
If Paul found room in the Scriptures for "the ordinary misunderstandings
and blunders of humanity," as Best declares on the same page, why
did *Paul* not make Best's restriction?

91) J. M. Gibson's attempt to prove Assertion No. 6 is herewith
submitted as an outstanding curiosity. In support of his statement from
which we just quoted he argues: "On the principle of all parts of
Scripture being equally inspired one might preach on the Bible for
fifty years and never once bring the Gospel in." He certainly has a low
opinion of the intelligence of the Christian preachers.

distinguishing between the reliable and the unreliable parts of the Bible, they are rendering the Bible to a great extent useless to the Christians? For such a criterion does not exist. The Bible has no index giving that information. And the critics know of no such criterion. They tell us so themselves. *Hasting's Encyclopedia,* VII, p. 346: "There is in reality no clear dividing line between what is and what is not worthy of a place in Scripture." (See Pieper, *op. cit.,* I, p. 362.) Dr. Fosdick thinks he has a sure criterion. There eternal truth is speaking "where the deeps of the Book call to the deeps of the human heart" (*The Modern Use of the Bible,* p. 61). Your own heart will tell you what belongs to religious truth and what is human error. But it seems this criterion does not satisfy his brother critics. *They* confess that there is no certain rule to be applied.* For instance, R. F. Grau: "Die Grenzen des Goettlichen und Menschlichen in der Schrift koennen ueberhaupt nicht mechanisch und quantitativ bestimmt werden, so wenig wie in der Person Christi." (See *Proc., Syn. Conf.,* 1886, p. 28.) K. Girgensohn: "Die Schrift enthaelt auch fuer den einzelnen das Wort Gottes in keiner feststellbaren Abgrenzung." (*Die Inspiration der Heiligen Schrift.*) Here is what happens in every case where men try to apply Fosdick's formula of finding the deeps of the Book calling to the deeps of the human heart: "Immer wieder beunruhigte mich die Frage: Was ist Kern, was ist Schale? Wo 'treibt die Schrift Christum,' wo nicht? Wo beginnt die Bibelkritik, wo hoert sie auf? Das waren Fragen, auf die mir weder mein Verstand noch theologische 'Wissenschaft' eine klare, befriedigende Antwort geben konnte. Was nuetzt mir die bekannte Kompromissformel 'Die Bibel *enthaelt* Gottes Wort,' wenn mir niemand mit Sicherheit sagen kann, was nun in der Heiligen Schrift Gottes Wort *ist* und was nicht? Diese Formel gestattet schrankenlosen Subjektivismus, der nur relative Wahrheit kennt und darum das Herz nicht wahrhaft fest machen kann." (See *Lehre und Wehre,* 1923, p. 302.) The theory of Assertion No. 6 makes sport of the Christian. He is told to separate the true from the false in Scripture and to wait till some secret voice — deep calling unto deep — tells him how to do it.[92]

---

92) "I now ask my new instructors to tell me what are the things in Scripture that *do* affect faith and life — to speak definitely, not in vague generality — and to set forth in completeness and with unerring certitude, not partially or dubiously, what in Scripture is infallible and of divine authority and what is not. But I find they cannot or do not tell me, nor do they show me how I can surely ascertain this for myself; and thus my whole faith becomes unsettled. . . . Sometimes I may be told the Bible is infallible and authoritative in all that affects faith and life; and when I ask what affects faith and life, I am answered that in which it is infallible; and I thus feel that my intellect is insulted and my soul trifled with by a vicious logic and an impotent evasiveness. At other times certain leading religious and ethical principles are set

These men know little of Scripture. Our Bible is a wonderful, a divine book, able to make us wise unto salvation (2 Tim. 3:15) and achieving this end by means of everything therein written. "Whatsoever things were written aforetime were written for our learning." To be sure, the Gospel is the chief part of the Bible. The Bible stresses the great truth that Christ Crucified is the Center of the Bible, the all-important thing. But everything in the Bible bears on the one theme. The least important thing subserves the one important thing. Rom. 15:4. "So, then, the entire Scripture is throughout nothing but Christ, God's and Mary's Son; all has to do with this Son, that we might know Him." (Luther, III:1959.) "Er ist das Mittelpuenktlein im Zirkel, und alle Historien in der Heiligen Schrift, so sie recht angesehen werden, gehen auf Christum." (VII:1929.) [93] These men have only a smattering of the Bible.

And they know little of the psychology of the Christian. They dare to tell him that great portions of his Bible are unprofitable. They tell him that the comfort he was wont to find in the story of Jonah is based on a fable. They warn him against accepting great portions of the Bible as true. And when the Chrisian asks them how he may know what is true and what is false, lest he lose what is profitable to him, they leave him at sea. We do not say that they are deliberately making sport of the troubled Christian. But Satan is making sport of him. And have they so little understanding that they do not realize that Assertion No. 6 inevitably arouses the holy indignation of the Christian, who feels that not

---

forth as unquestionably matters of faith and life. But when I inquire how and on what principle these were separated from the rest, . . . I am told that by general consent they are received because men's consciousness witnesses to their truth. By this the painful and perplexing fact is forced upon me that even for these no divine or Scriptural, but only a human foundation is given; that these are regarded as authoritative not because they are revealed in the Word of God but because they accord with the consciousness of man. . . ." (M'Intosh, *op. cit.*, p. 606 f.)

93) L. S. Keyser: "How marvelous is the reasoning of these rationalists! . . . We leave it to any one who will use his reason logically whether the first chapters of our Bible separate the *religious* teaching from the sciences with which it is connected. Does this part of the Bible set off religion by itself, as if it were something isolated and alone? Is not this rather the real teaching, the full-orbed and comprehensive teaching, of the Bible, that its primary purpose is religion, but religion set vitally and organically in a scientific and historical environment?" (*Contending for the Faith.* See Kretzmann, *The Foundations Must Stand,* p. 59 f.) Dr. Stoeckhardt: "Nun gut, wir sagen auch, dass Christus A und O, Kern und Stern der ganzen Schrift ist. Das lehrt Christus selbst Joh. 5:39. . . . Wenn die Schrift aber gleichwohl auch etwas von der Weltschoepfung . . . aussagt, so nehmen wir auch solche Aussagen als Gottes Wort und Offenbarung hin und finden, wenn wir naeher zusehen, dass dieselben nicht so isoliert dastehen, sondern mit dem Hauptinhalt, der Geschichte des Gnadenbundes, irgendwie zusammenhaengen." (*Lehre und Wehre,* 1893, p. 329.)

only he himself is being played with but Scripture itself made a thing to be laughed at — a conglomeration of 'truth and error, a guide-book which is unclear, indefinite, and hazy in its instructions.[94)]

God the Original Errorist

Now comes another group of critics who will not subscribe to the thesis that great portions of Scripture are unprofitable. They subscribe whole-heartedly to the thesis that the Bible is full of errors but see the folly committed by their brethren of Class 6. However, since they are minded to uphold the erroneousness of Scripture, they are forced to set up Assertion No. 7 — which is as senseless as No. 6 —: Everything in the Bible, inclusive of the errors, is profitable; *God* put these errors into the Bible; the erring human word is the Word of God. — Prominent theologians, Lutherans and extreme liberals, actually make this assertion. We are not referring to those who insist that these mistakes do not matter much.[95)] We are contemplating the phenomenon that sober theologians are saying that God saw fit, in order to make us wise unto salvation, to give us a fallible Bible. R. F. Grau (Koenigsberg): "Gott hat es zugelassen, ja gewollt, dass sich in der Heiligen Schrift auch Fehler finden. Ich wage es, mit dem groessten Schriftforscher unsers Jahrhunderts, mit Hofmann, zu sagen: Die Heilige Schrift ist etwas Besseres als ein fehlerloses Buch." (See *Lehre und Wehre*, 1893, p. 329.) S. Parkes Cadman: "Not everything related in Holy Scripture (Genesis, Jonah, Daniel) actually happened; nevertheless, actual or imaginative, all was enlisted for

---

94) D. J. Burrell disposes of the matter thus: "But what do you propose? A new Bible? Aye, you tell us that under the clear blaze of your erudition the Bible has come to be 'a new Book.' It is indeed a new book; full of errors on all points within the cognizance of the senses, yet heralded by you as a trustworthy guide in matters beyond sight! The thinking world derides you. Is this the edifice you have been so laboriously constructing? A Bible without ground of confidence? . . . But they say: 'We insist on loyalty to Christ. Our whole system is Christocentric. Back to Christ!' But back to what Christ? To the Christ who affixed His authoritative seal to the so-called 'fables' of the Flood, of Lot's wife, and of Jonah in the whale's belly? To the Christ who called the Scriptures 'truth' and never breathed a word or syllable against their absolute inerrancy? . . . Or, in your process of 'construction,' are you giving the world a new Christ, too? One of your leaders recently said from his theological chair: 'The time has come for a restatement of the doctrine of Christ.'" (*Why I Believe the Bible*, p. 180.)

95) J. A. Cottam: "Such minor discrepancies, or errors, are not worth mentioning as compared with the substantial reliability of the whole records; for it is the whole record, and not microscopic infallibility, about which the Christian faith is concerned." (*Know the Truth*, p. 219.) E. Lewis: "The integrity of the revelation does not stand or fall by the wrappings." (*Op. cit.*, p. 37.)

the service of its spiritual ideals. . . . For millions of believers the Bible is the more divine because of its human elements." (*Op. cit.*, pp. 247, 253.) O. L. Joseph: "Does not the human element, with its limitations and perchance even errors, exalt the wisdom of God in using such an agency to further His gracious plan?" (*Ringing Realities*, p. 217.) Would you call these Biblical statements which are false God's Word? Surely! Generalsuperintendent Dr. Paul Blau: "Wir haben ganz ehrlich zugegeben, dass die Bibel Menschenwort ist, wir koennen ihr nachweisen, dass ihr alle Unvollkommenheit menschlicher Rede anhaftet. . . . Die Schreiber der Buecher sind fehlsame, irrtumsfaehige Menschen gewesen. . . . Aber es ist alles Gotteswort." (*Die Menschwerdung Gottes*, p. 31 f.) Hans Rust, Ph. D., D. D., professor in Koenigsberg: "Wir muessen das Menschenwort der Heiligen Schrift in seiner ganzen Fehlsamkeit, Armseligkeit, Duerftigkeit und Anfechtbarkeit stehenlassen und es Gott zutrauen, dass er auch durch dieses fehlbare Menschenwort sein unfehlbares Gotteswort bezeugt und immer zu bezeugen imstande sein wird." (*Vom Aergernis des Menschenwortes in der Heiligen Schrift*, p. 553.)[96]

"Was ist das doch fuer ein loses und sinnloses Gerede!" That is Dr. Stoeckhardt's reply to Grau's proposition: "Vicious and foolish twaddle!" To be sure, God overrules the errors of man for good; but that is far from saying that God sanctions and glorifies these errors. No man in his senses will say that the God of Truth and

---

96) We should like to submit a few more similar statements. The more, the better — since they carry their own refutation. To save space, we shall use smaller print. K. Girgensohn: The errors in the Bible are due to the special will of God, since nothing, not the least detail, is due to chance and since such errors, understood "spiritually" or "experienced," can result in good and serve our salvation. (*Op. cit.*, p. 113.) J. M. Gibson: "Though we cannot claim perfection for any of the organs or vehicles of inspiration, the result of the whole may be said to be perfect, as adapted to the accomplishment of its end." "So far from finding fault or suggesting difficulty, we should recognize the marvelous grace of God in so lifting up the best legendary literature of the world as to make it a vehicle of high and pure revelation." (*Op. cit.*, pp. 145, 157.) J. De Witt: "We shall learn how important and valuable, if not necessary, the divine sufferance of these blemishes was in the accomplishment of the ruling purpose of revelation." "Even for us they [the enormities in the Bible] have their moral uses, if only by repulsion. (*What Is Inspiration*, pp. 72, 181.) Yea, even the false teaching of the Bible serves a good purpose! Wilhelm Herrmann (Ritschlian): "The doctrine of a double predestination, which, following Rom. 9—11, Luther" (?!) "and Calvin developed even more crudely than Augustine, has no basis in faith. . . . But the fact that the Bible contains such a development of thought as we find preeminently in Rom. 9: 20-23 should also *subserve our salvation*, if it brings us to face the question whether we are prepared to follow Scripture even in that which we cannot understand to be a notion rooted in our faith. If we decide to do this, we are treating the Bible as a law-book which requires from us external obedience." (*Systematic Theology*, p. 134.)

Holiness moved the holy writers to present, for instance, legends and myths as truths.[97] "The thinking world derides you" (Burrell, p. 127) when you claim to be loyal to Christ and still reject as fables what He stamped and sealed as truth; still more will the thinking world deride you when you assert that Christ knew these fables to be fables and still found it profitable to have men deal with them as true. Still more will the thinking world deride Grau when he alleges, in support of his monstrous proposition, that Christ, too, in becoming man, "was made to be sin," was made personally subject to error and sin! "What vicious and foolish twaddle!" (*Lehre und Wehre*, 1893, p. 329.) And when the Barthians declare that the erroneous word of man is in fact the real Word of God, when they refuse to believe that God performed the miracle of giving us by inspiration an infallible Bible but are ready to believe that God daily performs the greater miracle of enabling men to find and see in the fallible word of man the infallible Word of God, the thinking world declares: We cannot think your thoughts; *hier steht einem der Verstand still.*

"Science Does Not Recognize Miracles"

Assertion No. 8: Miracles do not occur; science does not recognize miracles; therefore the Bible, which relates miracle after miracle, cannot be literally inspired; it cannot be inerrant, for its writers put their mistaken notions about miracles into it. — That is the argument advanced by the extreme liberals among the moderns, and they consider it unanswerable. Our answer is that the argument constitutes a flagrant fallacy.[98]

These liberals are convinced that the miracle-stories of the Bible are myths or old wives' tales, because, said A. Harnack, "miracles, of course, do not occur. That an ass spoke, that the tempest was stilled with one word, we do not believe that." Science forbids it, said R. Seeberg; "the world-view of the Biblical writers was, as we all know, different from ours. They did not possess the exact knowledge of the cosmic laws which we have. In those days it was easy to believe in miracles. Every one feels at once how far we have advancd beyond the naïve views of the men of antiquity." (See *Lehre und Wehre*, 1908, p. 373.) H. E. Fosdick: "We used to think that God created the world by fiat. . . . Our ideas of the method of

---

97) Dr. Stoeckhardt: "Der Geist Gottes, der Allwissende, so sehr er sich an die Eigenheit der menschlichen Organe akkommodiert hat, kann doch nun und nimmer einen menschlichen Irrtum sanktionieren." (*Lehre und Wehre*, 1886, p. 314.)

98) We are herewith redeeming the promise made in a preceding section: "Their plea that science does not recognize miracles will be answered later, when we take up the chapter of the fatuity of 'higher' science." (P. 87.)

inspiration have changed." "What happened to the idea of miracle when this onrush of inductive science overtook it is clear." What happened? We do not want to live in "a land of topsyturvy, where axes float, dry sticks change to serpents, bedeviled swine run violently into the sea." No, no, "to be a Bible Christian must we think, as some seem to suppose, that a fish swallowed a man, or that the sun and moon stood still at Joshua's command, or that God sent she-bears to eat up children who were rude to a prophet, or that saints long dead arose and appeared in Jerusalem when our Lord was crucified?" (*Op. cit.*, pp. 30, 141, 53, 181.) Jonah, says Prof. J. W. Horine, was not swallowed and disgorged by the fish; that "is not literal history but parable or allegory." (*The Lutheran,* March 18, 1937.) The Biblical miracle of Creation did not actually occur, declares Prof. O. F. Nolde; "pupils may later discard the scientific import of the story." (*Luth. Church Quart.*, July, 1939, p. 299.) Evolutionism has discarded that miracle with all the others, said E. H. Delk in the *Luth. Quarterly.* "The belief in organic evolution, including the appearance of man, . . . has become the working theory of science. . . . The Hebrew tradition of how man was made has been modified by later scientific research. . . . As to the *method* and duration of the creative process, the origin of man's sinful nature, . . . modern thought through science, historical criticism, philosophy, and ethics has a modifying and illuminating word to say." (See *Lehre und Wehre*, 1913, p. 149 ff.) And "Prof. G. B. Foster goes so far as to declare that a man can hardly be intellectually honest who in these days professes to believe in the miracles of the Bible." (See *Fundamentals*, IV, p. 93.)

The pupils of higher criticism and the professors of evolutionism cannot believe in miracles. The miraculous contents of the Bible and of the Christian religion is offensive to them.[99] On that account they abominate Verbal, Plenary Inspiration. "No miracles" — that is one of the chief articles of the theology of higher criticism.[100] And the critics are persuaded that the discussion is closed

---

99) The miracles belong to "the intellectual stumbling-blocks over which many young people are falling when they read the Bible." (Fosdick, *op. cit.*, p. 59.)

100) "The whole of the modern critical school of Germany is actuated by a fierce hatred of the supernatural. The ruling principle in their criticism is denunciation of the miraculous. Whatever cannot be brought under their *scientific canons* is to be rejected as mythical or fabulous." (R. A. Redford, *Studies in the Book of Jonah*, p. 6.) — Professor Redford goes on to say: "The critic will not follow us into the *innermost sanctuary* of Christian faith. Let us, then, remain with him for a while in the *outer court* of human judgment and reasoning." That is the method we are applying. We have set forth the Christian's attitude pp. 30 ff., 52 ff. Now we are asking the critics to apply nothing more than human judgment and reasoning.

and the debate won when they proclaim: Science has ruled out the miracles.

Not so fast, we say. Science does not rule out miracles. We are speaking of common, honest, every-day science. Real science does not teach that miracles are impossible. We have never found such a statement in any text-book on physics or chemistry or any other science. We have not yet heard that science has discovered a law which kept the Lord from sending such a great number of quails. Good, common, honest science knows better than to make such a statement. For it knows nothing of the miraculous, the supernatural. It sticks to the natural. It is well equipped for that. It is able to observe natural phenomena, and it busies itself with studying the natural causes of them. But it has no facilities for studying the supernatural. It has no laboratories for testing creative powers. Its lenses cannot detect what is behind the miracles. "Mit *Wundern* weiss die Wissenschaft nichts zu machen" (E. Muehe, *Biblische Merkwuerdigkeiten*, p. 90.) [101] When a common, honest, bona-fide scientist is asked by Harnack and Fosdick: What do you make of the Biblical miracles, he straightway answers: That is beyond my ken and province.

But the "higher scientists" are quick to answer: We know, through science, that miracles cannot occur. — Men who say that do not think logically. They are operating with a crude fallacy. It is known as the μετάβασις εἰς ἄλλο γένος. It consists in applying the principles ruling one realm of science to a different realm of science. But everybody knows that the rules of geometry do not apply in psychology. And everybody ought to know that what is true in the realm of the natural has no bearing whatever on what is possible and true in the supernatural sphere. Dr. Walther says on this point: "We will have nothing to do with a science which . . . wants to sit in judgment on Scripture and correct it on the basis of science; which, instead of remaining in its sphere, wants to elevate the laws that happen to apply in its domain into universal laws and force them on Scripture. We regard such a μετάβασις εἰς ἄλλο γένος both as idolatrous and *unscientific*. We agree fully with Melanchthon when he writes: 'As it would be insanity to say that the Christian doctrine could be judged by the rules of the cobbler's trade, so also they err who invest *philosophy* with the right to sit in judgment on theology.'" (See Pieper, *op. cit.*, I, p. 189.) On this *metabasis*, this incursion into a foreign field, called in German "Grenzueberschreitung," a theologian wrote in the

---

101) "Human science as such deals only with such things as man can prove by what his five senses observe and experience, only with what his reason can grasp and understand. What is beyond that it treats as an unsolved enigma. . . . Science has no place for *miracles*."

Deutsche Lehrerzeitung, as quoted in *Lehre und Wehre,* 1923, p. 301: "Gewiss ist es wahr, dass die Wissenschaft gewaltige Fortschritte gemacht hat. . . . Gewiss ist es auch wahr, dass Gott dem Menschen den Verstand gegeben hat, damit er ihn gebrauchen soll. Aber die Wahrheiten, des christlichen Glaubens liegen jenseits der Grenzen des menschlichen Verstandes, also auch der exakten Wissenschaft. Und darum ist es unmoeglich, dass Glaube und Wissenschaft (im Vollsinn des Wortes) jemals in einen unueberbrueckbaren Gegensatz treten koennten. Wo er vorzuliegen scheint, da hat auf der einen oder andern Seite eine *Grenzueberschreitung* stattgefunden, da verwechselt man die Wissenschaft mit Glauben oder den Glauben mit Wissenschaft." Indeed, "we must learn," says the professor of natural history J. A. Thomson, "to render unto science the tribute that is its due, and to God the things that are *His.*" (*Science and Religion,* p. 4.)

Among thinking men it is not permissible to apply the laws which obtain in physical science to divine science which deals with miracles. Thinking men will not permit you to say: Since science knows only natural causes, there is no room left in this world for the operation of supernatural causes. Thinking men will not permit you to depart from the realm of observed facts and pass judgment on things that lie beyond the area of observation. Thinking men subscribe to the statement of *The Presbyterian* (July 12, 1928): "There are two great realms of existence — the natural and the supernatural. Science deals only with the natural. Revelation deals . . . with the supernatural and its manifestation in the natural. *When science minds its own business* and confines its teaching to the natural, there is no conflict between revelation and science. But *when science leaves its own proper field* and tries to rise up into the supernatural or the origin of the natural, then it always has come in conflict with the revelation and its facts. When men theorize about the origin of natural things and teach evolution, then they leave science and take up *spurious philosophy,* and this means conflict and false teaching." And it means that they are committing a logical crime.

And it is not only the Bible-theologian who stigmatizes this *metabasis* as irrational and illogical.[102] There are plenty of liberal

---

102) To quote a few more conservatives. R. A. Torrey says: "It is both amazing and ludicrous the way in which the enemies of the Bible call in as expert witnesses men who have never given any attention whatever to that line of study. They do it *in no other branch of study in the world.* They would be considered fools if they did. But they do it constantly when it comes to questions about God and the Bible. This method is thoroughly unscientific, illogical, and irrational." (*Op. cit.,* p. 42.) W. E. Gladstone: "Finding in the Mosaic story various statements which he deems to be irreconcilable with natural laws, Professor Huxley protests, not against those particular statements, but

theologians whose logical mind forbids them to measure the super-natural with the natural. To quote just one of them: "This is in substance what is being pleaded for here. It involves the distinction between something we know and something in which we can only believe. But it also involves that no increase in what we know will ever dispense with that in which we believe or will make it an object of indubitable scientific knowledge. . . . Identify the infinite with the creative, and we have the field into which faith may take us, but which *can never be the object of scientific knowledge.* 'A scientific knowledge of the Creator' is an utter contradiction in terms; indeed it savors of sheer *intellectual arrogance,* to say nothing worse." (Edwin Lewis, *op. cit.,* p. 171.) And it does not require Christian knowledge to see the absurdity of the reasoning which rejects miracles on "scientific" grounds. The heathen and the Jew can see it, too. "It is most absurd for one to pretend that he believes in God and in the same breath deny the supernatural belief that God steps in and changes the course of nature." [103) Prof. A. Einstein, who does not believe in God, may think logically when he denies the possibility of miracles. But one who admits the supernatural has no right to deny the miracles, and he reaches the height of absurdity when he denies them because science cannot explain them. Dr. Einstein is our authority for such a statement. He says: "The doctrine of a personal God interfering with natural events could never be refuted in the real sense by science, for this doctrine can always take refuge in those domains in which scientific

against the entire relation; and he casts aside without more ado not only the whole tale as it is given in Genesis but the large mass of col-lateral testimony, from every quarter of the globe, which supports it. Is this a scientific, is it a philosophical, is it altogether a rational method of proceeding?" (*The Impregnable Rock of Holy Scripture,* p. 304.) And consider also this: "True science does not start with an *a-priori* hypothesis that certain things are impossible, but simply examines the evidence to find out what has actually occurred. It does not twist its observed facts to make them accord with *a-priori* theories, but seeks to make its theories accord with the facts as observed. To say that miracles are impossible, and that no amount of evidence can prove a miracle, is to be supremely unscientific. . . . The fact of the actual and literal resurrection of Jesus Christ from the dead cannot be denied by any man who will study the evidence in the case with a candid desire to find what the fact is, and not merely to support an *a-priori* theory." (*The Fundamentals,* V, p. 105.)

103) Rabbi Baron told the Milwaukee Council of Churches: "I believe in science and natural laws. Miracles are based on belief in the supernatural, on belief that God steps in and changes the course of nature. I cannot reconcile them with reason. I cannot believe in them." In an open letter Rabbi Sharfman gave this reply: "If a minister, priest, or Rabbi doesn't believe in the Bible-story of the Creation or in miracles, he has no business to be a spiritual leader. It is most absurd, etc. . . . I say, in the language of the Bible: 'Is there anything impossible for the Lord?' . . . Were Moses and all the elders of Israel impostors?" (See *The Northwestern Lutheran,* Feb. 9, 1941.)

knowledge has not yet been able to set foot." (See *The Christian Beacon,* Sept. 19, 1940.) Who, then, are the real obscurantists? L. Gaussen: "If your wisdom makes bold to constitute itself the judge of what is found contained in the Bible; if it drags the book of God to the seashore of science, in order to collect in its vessels what it sees in it to be good and to throw out what it finds in it to be bad . . ., then it is necessary that it should be reproved; it is guilty of revolt; it judges God. *Here there is no longer science,* there is fascination; there is no longer progress, there is obscurantism." (*Theopneustia,* p. 325.)[104] He is certainly an obscurantist who would make the ignorance to which science confesses the source of knowledge.

But, say the critics, it is not in the name of common, every-day science that we are ruling out the miracles; we are doing it from the higher reaches of science. We are applying "inductive science" (Fosdick), "the processes and the technique of science" (Delk); forsaking "pre-Kantian conceptions" (Kantonen), we operate with "the thought of our time," the present "scientific era" (A. G. Baldwin). (See *Conc. Theol. Mthly.,* XII, p. 395.) But these high-sounding names and titles cannot hide the *metabasis* of which "higher science" is guilty. In fact, the very name "*inductive* science" unmasks it. The claim is made that, while common science deals only with observed facts, the philosopher has the right to draw deductions from these observations, and these deductions, they say, rule out miracles. But investigation and induction are different matters.[105] We are ready to listen to you when you present the results of your investigation. And we are willing to hear your inductions — as long as they are logical. But in the present case your inductions are based on a fallacy. We willingly grant you that science deals with nothing but natural causes; but when your "inductive science" infers from this that every effect must have a natural cause, it no longer deserves the name of science; and the philosophy back of it is weak in logic.

---

104) Dr. Pieper's statement applies here. "One who appeals to natural reason in matters of the Christian religion and would make it, in whole or in part, the source and norm of the Christian doctrine commits a μετάβασις εἰς ἄλλο γένος and is enthroning human unreason in place of the Word of God as master and teacher." (*Op. cit.,* I, p. 238.) It is an absurdity of the first rank to teach that there is an almighty God and then to reject miracles as absurdities.

105) "Many a man who is very safe in the department of investigation and perfectly trustworthy so long as he confines himself to the simple results of observation and experiment is as unsafe whenever he ventures into the department of philosophy or logic and attempts to draw inferences from his investigations; his conclusions may be as inaccurate and unsound as his experiments are careful and exact. The fact is, investigation and induction belong to different departments; and we are not always to adopt the inferences of the most accurate investigator." (A. T. Pierson, *Many Infallible Proofs,* p. 142.)

We have noted above that the liberals have logic on their side when they refuse to subscribe to the self-contradictory thesis of the moderate critics that the Bible, inspired, contains mistakes. But whatever credit they have earned on this score they lose when they reject the miracles of the Bible for "scientific" reasons. They are breaking one of the fundamental laws of logical thinking. Do you know what this *metabasis* really is? The handbooks of logic list as one of the material fallacies the converse fallacy of accident. And *metabasis* is a species of this common fallacy. The logician will not permit you to say that "a statement which is true when certain conditions are present is true generally." What did you think of the scientists, mentioned in the preceding section, who deduced from the fact that the ants of their locality do not do certain things that the ants of Palestine did not do these things? And now we are being told in the name of "inductive science" that, because science has not discovered and cannot observe supernatural forces, supernatural forces are non-existent.

"Kurzum, es ist so albern, so laecherlich, was die Bibelfeinde ueber solche geringfuegige Verschiedenheit des Berichts sagen, dass es einen anekelt, nur noch mehr darueber zu reden." (*Proc., Western District*, 1865, p. 46.) That applies to all of their arguments. *"Anekelt"* — it is nauseating. So we had better pause a while. We must not discuss too many of their fatuities at one time.

FATUITIES AND ABSURDITIES AD NAUSEAM

"The vast majority of the difficulties and objections arise from erroneous preconceptions and false presuppositions, untenable assumptions and unfounded assertions, strange misconceptions and persistent misrepresentations, by mistakes and misstatements of the questions — with all the fallacious inferences therefrom. . . . The prevalence of errors in Scripture is proclaimed *ad nauseam* in many of our current reviews, both theological and general; in periodicals, both religious and secular; and in many of the recent books bearing on the question." (H. M'Intosh, *Is Christ Infallible and the Bible True?* Pp. 473, 621.) At the risk of nauseating the reader we shall discuss a few more of the sophistries and absurdities with which the moderns assail the verbal inspiration and the infallibility of the Bible.

Another Case of Miracle-Phobia

Assertion No. 9: The production of an absolutely infallible book by human writers, through divine inspiration, would constitute a miracle, and, as we have just told you, miracles do not occur. — We have here a special application of the principle responsible for Assertion No. 8. An ax-head cannot swim; the laws of physics forbid that. And the holy writers, being fallible men, cannot be made to produce an infallible book; the laws of psychology forbid that. We are not surprised when men who reject the plenary inspiration, the infallibility, of the Bible because of the many miracles it records, will become the more vehement in their protest when they are told that the Bible is itself a miracle, of miraculous origin, the result of a direct, immediate, unique operation of God. Consistency and logic is on their side, to that extent. But their premise is false. Assertions 8 and 9 are produced by the same logical fallacy, the same μετάβασις εἰς ἄλλο γένος.

The liberals among the moderns assert that God could not have given us through fallible men an infallible book. That would constitute a miracle. The conservatives among them do not deny that God performs miracles. They aim to remove the offense which the "errors" in the Bible present to carnal reason by claiming that God did not perform the miracle of giving to mankind an infallible Bible.[106] What we said under Assertion No. 2 takes care of that. What we are now dealing with is the assertion that "a human book divine" is an impossible concept.

Just that is asserted. Kahnis (Lutheran) said: "The presupposition that the gospels contain no erroneous statements and contradictions flouts the eternal laws to which the Creator subjected the human mind." (See Proceedings, Syn. Conference, 1902, p. 24.) True, the knowledge of any man is limited and his reasoning subject to error. But when Kahnis uses the term "eternal laws" to describe this situation, he is asserting that it is not possible for the power of God to intervene and change the situation. J. M. Gibson agrees with Kahnis, emphasizing the thought that, if a man were given the power to utter the eternal wisdom of God and write down absolute truth, he would be unmanned, dehumanized. "The defenders of the authoritative inspiration of the Scriptures have postulated as a necessity of the case the emancipation of all the writers of Scripture from the effects of human weakness and limitation. They have said that, if we cannot have the guarantee that every word these holy men of old have written expresses accurately and only the mind of God, the whole thing is useless, because, if these people who are the vehicles of revelation cannot be trusted in everything, they can be trusted in nothing. . . . According to this theory it was supposed that men inspired of God

---

106) Superintendent Kier: "It has not pleased God to perform the miracle of having His witnesses speak and write inerrantly." (See Proceedings, Iowa District, 1897, p. 36.) S. Goebel (Reformed): "Our Bible nowhere and nowise makes the claim that it was produced by a miraculous, immediate act of God. The Bible records miracles. But it does not assert that it owes its origin to a special miracle by which the Bible-text was supernaturally produced" (Allg. Ev.-Luth. Kztg., 1926, No. 40).

must be *so completely unmanned, as it were, so thoroughly deified,* that they could speak, like supermen, with absolute scientific precision on every subject they touched. . . . The treasure is in earthen vessels. . . . We cannot claim perfection for any of the organs or vehicles of inspiration. . . . We see no grounds for believing that God has wrought a continual miracle for the purpose of preserving from all possible error every line and word of the Bible." (*The Inspiration and Authority of Scripture,* pp. 32, 90, 123, 144.) Gibson cannot conceive the thought that God could endow the prophets and apostles, while writing under inspiration, with immunity against all error — a quality which no other mortals ever possessed or will possess. That would be making *supermen* of them! It would *unman* them! Psychology vetoes such ideas. So says Dr. T. A. Kantonen. Writing in *The Lutheran* on "The Canned Goods of Past Theology," he asserts that we must "abandon once and for all the *unpsychological* and mechanical theories of inspiration and unhistorical views of verbal inerrancy which the application of scientific and historical methods to the study of the Bible has rendered obsolete." (See *Conc. Theol. Mthly.,* VII, p. 223.) That means: To ascribe inerrancy to anything written by men flouts the laws of psychology. Could God do that? And would He do it sixty-six times?[107] Summing up. we quote J. De Witt's declaration that the miraculous element must be removed from inspiration. "The conception of those who believe in the inerrancy of all the contents of the Bible implies a divine energy that so completely absorbs and controls the human composer as to insure absolute truth in the least important details, rendering the slightest inaccuracy impossible. . . . All personal deficiency in the prophet must have been *miraculously supplied.* Must this beautiful conception be abandoned or even modified? We answer, however reluctantly, that it must surely be put aside." (*What Is Inspiration?* Pp. 9, 12.) L. Gaussen is surely right in stating: "The plenary inspiration of the Scriptures is, in spite of the Scriptures, denied (as the Sadducees denied the resurrection) *because the miracle is thought inexplicable.*" (*Theopneustia,* p. 37.)[108]

---

107) N. R. Best puts that question. He repudiates "the thought of a Bible planned and composed as a unique religious unity under influences that have affected no other writing of men," "the belief that in a way altogether unparalleled by any human experience elsewhere the Holy Spirit presided over the mind of each writer until he had finished the stint of authorship assigned him." That would imply "sixty-six separate miracles of supernatural control wrought for the production of the Bible's sixty-six documents." (*Inspiration,* p. 36.)

108) The argument that God could not give us an infallible Bible through men who are by nature fallible is sometimes extended in this way: "Some people suppose that with His limitless resources God would surely have found it easy to give a perfect revelation to the most imperfect people. But have these friends ever in seriousness raised the question

Gaussen continues: "But we must recollect the answer made
by Jesus Christ: 'Do ye not therefore err, because ye *know not
the Scriptures, neither the power of God?'* (Mark 12:24)." The
believer has no difficulty here. He accepts the miracle of inspiration as all the other miracles God graciously performed. The
laws of psychology do not bother him in this connection. He
does not fear that the holy writers were dehumanized by being
kept free from error, as little as the friends of Daniel were unmanned by being made immune to the scorching flame. "Wenn
nun diese Ansicht mit irgendwelcher Psychologie nicht stimmt,
so ist zu antworten, dass die Inspiration eben ein Wunder ist."
(A. Hoenecke, *Ev.-Luth. Dogmatik*, I, p. 344.)[109] But the critics
are in a bad way. They will not take their stand on Scripture.
They appeal to reason and science. But reason forbids them to
deny the miracle of inspiration on scientific grounds. Reason tells
them that they are committing the fallacy of the *metabasis* when

---

how it could have been done? Let us suppose it possible that a document
could have been constructed in heaven which would have been a perfect
revelation of the truth, the whole truth, and nothing but the truth
desirable for man to know on all the subjects which concern him here
and hereafter. What mortal could have read it? For it must have
been in a perfect language; and there never has been any such language
upon earth; so it must have been in an unknown language. And even
if that difficulty had been overcome, which of the sons of men would
have been capable of seeing and understanding and appreciating the
authentic product of heaven's high literature? There would need to
have been not only a miraculously constructed book, but a miraculously
reconstructed humanity to take it in; and wherein would that have been
different from the annihilation of the human race as it is and the creating
of another? Etc., etc." (J. M. Gibson, *op. cit.,* p. 147.) Prof. R. W. Nelson
repeats the human-language argument: "Of the earth earthly, human
language simply cannot be a literal vehicle for conveying God's infallible
will and wisdom to men," and he extends it still farther: "How can
divine absoluteness come to men through any medium so long as it is
a fact that, even if God Himself, in all His sublimity and glory, should
appear in my study at this moment, I should be able to see and hear
Him by no means other than my most fallible powers of perceiving
and understanding? Confronting God thus immediately, I should still
be human. In a word, we have now discovered that an infallible revelation, by whatever means it might come through an authority however
absolute, presupposes and requires infallible readers in order to render
its own infallibility any more than a deceiving fiction. . . . We have
found that, if God should supernaturally reveal Himself and His teaching
to men, this revelation could not be absolute or infallible to any finite
man." (*Christendom*, IV, p. 400 ff. See *Conc. Theol. Mthly.*, XI, p. 308.) —
We shall make some remarks on these notions under No. 14.

109) "Die Heilige Schrift ist nicht durch Entwickelung des Geistes-
lebens in den vom Geiste Gottes erleuchteten Menschen entstanden,
sondern sie ist diesen durch ein Wunder gegeben; das heisst mit andern
Worten: der Ursprung der Heiligen Schrift ist ein Geheimnis. . . .
Dabei ist es aber auch wahr, dass Gott durch diese Maenner geredet hat
und dass sie, solange sie inspiriert waren, nur Gottes Wort redeten, frei
von allem Irrtum und aller Truebung. Dass dies bei suendigen Menschen
moeglich war und geschehen ist, das ist eben das Wunder der goettlichen
Eingebung." (*Kirchenblatt* [A. L. C.], Sept. 10, 1932.)

they do so. The laws of natural science are not applicable to the domain of the supernatural. If the Bible were a human product, you would be justified in applying the laws of psychology. But "Holy Scripture did not grow on earth. Die Heilige Schrift ist nicht auf Erden gewachsen." (Luther, VII: 2095.) The liberal critic, of course, will deny that; but when he denies it on scientific, psychological grounds, he becomes guilty of committing a gross fallacy. The scientist has no right to speak on the question of the miracle. He has no instrument for measuring creative, miraculous powers. "Mit Wundern weiss die Wissenschaft nichts zu machen." We are repeating ourselves. Yes, but it seems to be necessary. So we shall repeat Dr. Einstein's statement that there are "domains in which scientific knowledge has not yet been able to set foot." And for good measure we call the attention of the critics to the statement of the scientist Dr. Pank: "Die Wissenschaft forsche in Freiheit, wissenschaftlich und exakt, aber so exakt, dass sie Dinge, die ueber ihre Grenze gehen, *ex actu* laesst, und so wissenschaftlich, dass sie nicht durch subjektive Beimischungen sich selbst unwissenschaftlich macht." (See *Lehre und Wehre*, 1908, p. 125.) And to the article in the liberal *Christian Century*, Sept. 14, 1938, on "The Pretensions of Science": "Furthermore, science is limited to a secondary role in human destiny because it can deal only with quantities, with things which can be measured. . . . Man lives in terms of good and evil, beauty and ugliness, right and wrong. These things evade the tools and technique of science as air passes through the meshes of a net. This has been said several times before, but it will stand having a riveting-machine applied to it." [110] When the critics rise to speak on the question whether God could perform the miracle of inspiration, they are called out of order.

N. R. Best raises the objection: "At all events, not one Bible-writer furnishes the least clue to let us know how it felt to be writing, under God's inspiration, works sacred to later ages. . . . They did not analyze their own psychology." (*Op. cit.*, p. 19.) All right; let us go over the same ground again. The Bible-writers did not attempt to explain the act of inspiration in terms of human psychology. Of course not. They knew better than to commit the μετάβασις εἰς ἄλλο γένος. It is impossible to describe a miracle in scientific terms. The holy writers themselves, who experienced

---

110) "This has been said several times before." Dr. W. Dau, for instance, said it before: "Science does not operate with such concepts as infinity, eternity, omnipotence, omnipresence, which are current terms in theology. The Deity and its divine attributes are unknown quantities in science; but science cannot rule them out of existence." (*The Testimony of Science*, p. 38.) And now the liberal *Christian Century* wants a riveting machine applied to this statement of a Bible theologian.

the miracle, were unable to explain it. And if they could not describe and explain it, why should the critics waste their time in telling us that, since they cannot understand this miracle and reduce it to psychological formulae, we must give up our belief in Verbal Inspiration? We shall not do so. The psychological difficulties do not bother us. "*How* this was possible is indeed beyond our intellectual cognition, just as the *unio personalis* of God and man, and particularly *that* fact that the Son of God condescended to die on the cross without laying aside or merely reducing His deity, remains an impenetrable mystery for us." (Dr. Pieper, *Chr. Dog.*, I, p. 282.) We do not know the manner of inspiration, but we know the blessed fact. With that our faith is satisfied.[111] The critics will not accept the fact until they have satisfied reason and science as to the process. The result is that they deprive themselves of the blessing of the fact — and are doing it in the service of unreason and pseudoscience.

---

111) "What is inspiration? Inspiration is a *miracle*, or a miraculous process; and, like all miracles, there is much about it which we cannot fully understand. . . . The exact manner in which the minds of the inspired writers of Scripture worked when they wrote we do not pretend to know. Very likely they could not have explained it themselves. . . . We *know the result*, the effect, but we do not understand the process. The result is that the Bible is the written Word of God; but we can no more explain the process than we can explain how the water became wine at Cana or how five loaves fed five thousand men or how a word raised Lazarus from the dead." (*Proceedings, Southeastern Dist.*, 1939, p. 12.) Let us hear a few more refreshing statements of this kind. B. Manly: "So, too, the inspiration is not explicable by us any more than the condition of the withered hand at the instant that it was healed and restored to activity by supernatural power. If the change in the hand or arm was properly supernatural, no explanation as to how it was done can make it more intelligible, no lack of explanation more incredible. Just so as to the inspiration. We have no reason to suppose that it was understood as to the nature or mode of operation even by those who enjoyed it; much less can it be intelligible to others who never experienced it; and certainly those who had it never undertook to explain its nature for our enlightenment." (*The Bible Doctrine of Inspiration*, p. 62.) *Watchman-Examiner*: "It is also evident that inspiration describes a result rather than a process. How God could control a man so that what he wrote would be the very Word of God is an inscrutable mystery, and I venture to say it will remain so. But why should such a question concern us? What we need to know is not, 'How did God breathe forth the Scripture?' but, 'Did He do it?' When we are hungry, the thing that interests us most is that there is food on the table. . . . So to the Christian it is enough to know that Scripture is God-breathed. We will feed upon it as the living Word of the living God, and let the doctors wrangle over how it came to be so. . . ." (See *Theol. Mthly.*, 1923, p. 361 f.) G. Stoeckhardt: "This matter presents an incomprehensible mystery which human reason cannot clear up. That the Holy Ghost is the real author of Scripture and spoke through the prophets and apostles we believe and confess according to Scripture. The *How*, however, is hidden. The process of inspiration, the manner in which the Holy Ghost transmitted His thoughts and words to the holy men, is beyond our research. No man has ever looked into this workshop of the Holy Ghost. All we need to care about is the final result: .

Trying to Break Scripture with a Broken Reed

Assertion No. 10: It is the part of wisdom to apply science as a corrective to the Bible. — No greater folly could be committed. Christian wisdom vetoes such a procedure. See preceding sections. And common human wisdom protests against such folly. It is foolish — to elaborate just one point — because what goes by the name of science is seldom sure of its findings. Its systems are changing continually. The science of today is the corrective of the science of yesterday. Much of what is held to be absolutely true today will be discarded by the scientists of tomorrow.[112] The article: Day-To-Day Philosophy in the *Reader's Digest* of July, 1932, contains this statement: "Physics, mathematics, and especially the most advanced and exact of sciences, are being fundamentally revised. Chemistry is just becoming a science; psychology, economics, and sociology are awaiting a Darwin, whose work in turn is awaiting an Einstein."[113] Einstein — the name has become

---

we are satisfied to know that the word of the prophets and apostles is indeed God's Word. That is essential for our faith, our salvation. Our faith does not need to trace step by step the way leading to this result; that has nothing to do with our salvation. Men think they must find a 'scientific' explanation of inspiration; and losing themselves in bootless speculations, they lose the fact of inspiration." (*Lehre und Wehre*, 1886, p. 283.)

112) C. E. Macartney, in the *Princeton Theological Review:* "What we are so sure is experimental and established fact today, may assume a different aspect tomorrow, and the last word will be God's." (See *Theol. Mthly.*, V, p. 296.) The statement "The last word will be God's" belongs in one of the preceding sections, but it will do no harm to keep harping on it. — "The science of one epoch is to a large extent a help which the science of the next uses and abandons." (Dr. Smith of the University of Virginia; quoted in W. E. Gladstone, *The Impregnable Rock of Holy Scripture*, p. 49.)

113) A few examples. "A third great fact emerges when we inquire into the origin of all these forms of power that are familiar to us upon the earth. Till recently the scientific answer to this question was in the one word 'sun.' . . . But to this answer, that we owe all our powers of doing work to the sun, we must add another, which dates from Becquerel's discovery of radioactivity in 1896. . . . We have spoken of the source of our earth's energy in the parent sun, and of the newly discovered fountain of power which was unknown till the twentieth century, namely, the liberation of the energy locked up in the nucleus of the atom." (J. A. Thomson, *Science and Religion*, p. 83 ff.) — The scientific idea for years has been, as Dr. Richard C. Tolman, of the California Institute of Technology, lately told the National Academy of Sciences at Yale University, that inevitably creation is bound some day to freeze up, a form of universal death not only for earthly life but for all forms of energy. But — under the new thermodynamic principles the old law of conservation of energy, which seems to require that the universe shall ultimately freeze up, works differently." (*Associated Press*. Caption of the article: "New Mathematics Indicates Earth May Last Forever.") — "The science of physics is also studying the composition of matter. The *Encyclopedia Britannica*, in the article on 'Matter,' relates the history of this investigation: 'First came the molecular theory of matter. Matter was made of molecules. Then came Dalton's theory

the symbol for Science in Revolution against Itself! Discussing Einstein's Theory of Relativity, J. A. Thomson writes: "Some of the consequences of the theory are nevertheless understandable enough. At a stroke it gets rid of the mysterious old hocus-pocus of 'action at a distance' which gravity was supposed to exert. As Professor Eddington has said, we need no longer speak of the earth as being attracted by the sun, but rather of the earth as trying to find a way through a time and space *tangled up* by the presence of the sun." (*Op. cit.*, p. 253.) The next great man will of course upset Einstein's theory. And how much upsetting has gone on in the field of historical science! The historians have to spend a great deal of their time in correcting the mistakes of their teachers. Need we cite instances?

---

that molecules were made of atoms. Finally, in atoms particles have been found that are called corpuscles, or electrons.' I was taught the atomic theory in my boyhood days, even in such a succint formula as this: Two atoms make one molecule. This is now *antiquated gibberish.* . . . J. M. Macfarlane: 'No one can predict what the ultimate views as to the constitution and relation of matter and energy may be.'" (Dr. W. Dau, *op. cit.*, p. 17 f.) From an article in *Allg. Ev.-Luth. Kztg.*, Nov. 15, 1940: "Wir wollen im folgenden versuchen, in ein paar grossen Zuegen die Wandlung im Weltbild der Physik zur Darstellung zu bringen. . . . Es ergibt sich die merkwuerdige Situation, dass die Physik in den letzten Jahrzehnten, zu Erkenntnissen gefuehrt wurde, die alles das, worauf sich die Naturforschung als selbstverstaendliche Voraussetzungen stuetzte, in Frage stellen. . . . Man kann also mit von Weizsaeker sagen: 'Der Begriff des unveraenderlichen Elementarteilchens beschreibt die Erfahrungen nicht mehr adaequat.' Oder mit andern Worten: Der alte Substanzbegriff, das staerkste Bollwerk der materialistischen Natur- und Weltauffassung, laesst sich in der neuen Physik nicht laenger aufrechterhalten." — Astronomy: "Noch stand fuer Kopernikus und Kepler die Sonne fest. Und noch fuer zwei Jahrhunderte die 'Fixsterne.' Heute ist auch unser Milchstrassensystem nur einer unter den Sternennebeln, die alle im 'Werden' sind — und alle dem zweiten thermodynamischen Hauptsatz unterliegen: Sie geben bestaendig Waerme an den eiskalten Weltraum ab." (W. Elert, *Morphologie des Luthertums*, I, p. 379.) — Geology: Let it be repeated: "Of the eighty theories which the French Institute counted in 1806 as hostile to the Bible, not one now stands." (*Fundamentals*, VII, p. 63.) — Anthropology: "Die Anthropologie hat nach mancherlei Umwegen zu frueheren Auffassungen zurueckgefunden. Bald nach der Jahrhundertwende hat der Breslauer Professor Klaatsch schwerwiegende Einwaende gegen Darwin und Haeckel erhoben und nachgewiesen, dass sowohl die fuenffingrige Hand des Menschen als auch sein ueberaus urtuemliches harmonisches Gebiss Bildungen sind, die den entsprechenden der Menschenaffen gegenueber nicht als Abkoemmlingsformen gedeutet werden duerfen. . . . Dr. Herbert Fritsche, der in der 'Wache' ueber den heutigen Stand der Wissenschaft berichtet, schliesst: 'Der Mensch als Eigenlinie und, recht verstanden, als sein eigener Vorfahr steht heute als der grosse Universalist vor uns. Er steht der Tierheit gegenueber. Er ist wieder zur Mitte der Schoepfung geworden und damit auch zum zentralen Sinn alles lebendigen Werdens. Weder ist er der enthaarte Schimpanse noch der 'geschlechtreif gewordene Affenembryo' der Darwinischen Aera, sondern er ist ein Eigener, ein dem Herzen der Schoepfung nahe gebliebenes Kind.'" (*Allg. Ev.-Luth. Kztg.*, Feb. 21, 1941.)

We shall let Professor T. V. Smith of the Philosophy Department of the University of Chicago sum up: "For science is today and always has been — and always will be — 'in flux,' in a condition of incessant change. Science has never yet settled anything by probing into the origin of things. Witness the contradictory theories of contemporary scientists *in every field of knowledge*. The essence of science is theory and hypothesis. But who can live by such uncertain speculations? Who can continue to live on the 'dry dust' of conjectures?" (Quoted in *The Sovereignty of God*, p. 109.) Professor Smith is not a Christian theologian. He has no use for the "religious way of life." He is a pure hedonist. The moderns cannot charge him with partiality. And his unbiased judgment is that science is "in flux." At no period can men absolutely rely on its findings. The young scientists are kept busy weeding out the "wild oats" (Bishop Gore's phrase) which the old scientists sowed.

Common science is "in flux." Is higher science, "inductive science," particularly higher criticism and the philosophy of evolution, in a better way? "The essence of it is theory and hypothesis." All the world knows that there is nothing so evanescent and unreliable as the findings of the higher critics and the evolutionists. Their systems and hypotheses go with the wind.[114]

---

114) "The criticism of the beginning of the twentieth century will be an anachronism before the next century opens." (Dr. H. E. Jacobs, *A Summary of the Christian Faith*, p. 274.) "The older document hypothesis. Fragment hypothesis. Myth hypothesis. Supplement hypothesis. New document hypothesis. . . . One hypothesis tears down the other." (Dr. L. Fuerbringer, *Introduction to the Old Testament*, p. 27 ff.) "They talked of 'Elohist,' 'Jehovist,' and 'Priest's Code' and caused cabalistic capitals, E, J, P, to dance across their pages, in token of mysterious literary wisdom. They fashioned a 'polychrome Bible,' wherein the words of differing documents were printed in different colors. It was a weird book, dazzling the eyes like Joseph's coat. But its rainbow flash was too much for the Christian world, and the 'documentary theory' sank into oblivion. It was a wild orgy while it lasted, but most of its living devotees are busy hoping that it is forgotten." (*The Presbyterian*, Oct. 17, 1940.) See "the autopsy, or post-mortem examination of the mortal weaknesses of that school of 'higher criticism' which dominated theological thinking nearly fifty years (Wellhausen's system)" in *Bibliotheca Sacra*, Jan. 1941, p. 99. Page 57 above gave Edwin Lewis's autopsy: "Other theories now have their day — and it will be a short day." These theories could not live; they contained too many extravagances and absurdities. Absurdities? The term is used in the foreword to Dr. Fosdick's *A Guide to Understanding the Bible*. In the introduction to this book Paul Elmer More writes: "There are heavy sins of commission to be charged against the so-called higher criticism, that, from its lair in Germany, raged over the world in the nineteenth century — many extravagances of conjecture and not a few absurdities.'" (See *Journal of the Am. Luth. Conf.*, June, 1939, p. 76.) "Extravagances of conjecture" — are you acquainted with the system called Form Criticism and the one called *Schallanalyse*? Concerning a book advocating this ultra-

Now, we are not reproaching science for always being "in flux." We honor it for that. We would have little respect and little use for it if it remained static. Science could not achieve its high and noble purpose if its servants were not constantly at work in eliminating the mistakes of former generations. It takes honesty and requires much labor and intelligence to get rid of erroneous systems and to construct better systems. We admire these honest, painstaking scientists. (We are speaking of *real* science, the common kind.) The world owes much to them. We would be in a bad shape if the scientists refused to acknowledge the mistakes of the older science and kept on cultivating the wild oats their fathers

---

modern theory of New Testament criticism Dr. W. Arndt says: "Wenn man dieses Werk liest, wird einem zunaechst fast unheimlich zumute. Gibt es tatsaechlich Leute, die das Gras wachsen hoeren koennen?" (*Conc. Theol. Mthly.* III, p. 713.) — As to biological evolution, which theory is correct, Darwin's or the theory of 1941? Or are those scientists right who cannot find any true relationship between man and the beast? And what has become of evolution as the way of life with its proud claim of the innate power of man to achieve high and higher levels of moral excellence? The horrors of the present era have given it the lie, and it is reaching the stage of disintegration. "At a conference in the fall of 1937, President Mackay of Princeton Seminary spoke on the 'terrifying fact of disintegration.' He spoke of disintegration in the realm of thought: the international public had believed in evolution, which was felt to guarantee a flowering, developing progress, with much better days ahead; but now conflict and tension are the great words. . . . Disintegration in both individual and universal ethics, in the social realm, etc., etc." (W. T. Riviere, *A Pastor Looks at Kirkegaard*, p. 56.) Let us repeat it: "The evolutionary hypothesis today stands discredited not only as a means of comprehending origins in the field of natural history and biology, but also in its more modern re-creations of philosophy, ethics, and religion. The Christian element that followed evolutionary religion is exhausted by world facts and is now returning to revelation and to faith. The vapid, incomprehensible philosophy that evolutionists fed to the world twenty years ago is discounted, and philosophy is now being rewritten." (*The Watchman-Examiner*, June 19, 1941.) *The Lutheran* of Aug. 6, 1941, makes a similar statement. In an article captioned "A Scientist's Confession" Prof. G. G. Peery, biologist, states: "During most of the second half of the nineteenth century, science was almost entirely under the influence of materialism. As scientists delved more deeply into the secrets of the molecule, the atom, the electron, they came rather generally to the conclusion that there were sufficient forces in matter itself to account for all life. Thus scientists, as philosophers, accepted the doctrine of materialism and denied the existence of God. Life was fully explainable, in its origin and in its continuity, in terms of chemistry and physics. The beginning of the twentieth century found the pendulum of thought swinging in the opposite direction. Today one may say that the philosophy of materialism has almost completely broken down. The beginning of the end came when scientists realized that blind force, inherent in matter, could never possibly account for consciousness, intelligence, and design in nature." And whatever new philosophy is emerging will also go with the wind, unless it is absolutely oriented in God's Word. The true philosopher must be a Christian philosopher, and he cannot be a Christian philosopher who denies all or some of the truth of the Bible.

sowed. It is the part of wisdom for science to change its position.[115]

But it is the height of unwisdom to make fallible, shifting science the corrective of God's Word and to base the Christian faith on "the narrow, fragmentary phases of ephemeral human opinion." It is not reasonable to ask a man to evaluate spiritual things according to changing standards and to base his hope of eternal life on teachings which admittedly may be found false tomorrow. The liberals, indeed, find nothing unreasonable in this. They *want* their theology and religion to be "in flux." They call that progressiveness. They are perfectly satisfied to preach that life came to the earth from some distant planet and after a few years to reverse themselves and preach that life originated on this earth from non-living

---

115) By the way: theology, too, derives *some* benefit from this ability of science to discover new truths — new to science. We are not now referring to the fact that science — physics, astronomy, medicine, history, etc. — is day by day confirming, or rather bearing witness to, the truth of various Bible statements. (At one time the Bible statement that the stars cannot be numbered was thought to be an unscientific statement. Had not Hipparchus, the Greek astronomer, found the number of stars to be exactly 1,022? Now that science has advanced and procured modern telescopes, it tells us that the stars truly cannot be numbered.) What we have in mind is a certain benefit accruing to us through the revolutionary findings of Prof. A. Einstein. Whether his theory is fully true or not, "the results which have been elaborated from the Einstein theory of relativity must be called staggering. These results mean nothing less than that from the standpoint of the latest philosophical thought the Ptolemaic system (which makes the sun move around the earth) is as valid as the Copernican (which makes the earth move around the sun)! A. Sommerfeldt writes in *Sueddeutsche Monatshefte* (Vol. 18, 1921, No. 2) concerning the effect of Einstein's theory on astronomy as follows: 'Hereafter none must be prohibited from saying: The earth is stationary, and the firmament revolves around the earth, or: The sun moves, and the earth stands in a focus of its orbit. According to Einstein's theory a firmament revolving around a stationary earth develops the same centrifugal forces in the earth that according to Newton are developing in a revolving earth, and this has been demonstrated mathematically by Thirring. It will always be more convenient, and for the purpose of astronomical computation more practical, to work from the basis of the Copernican system. But it is not unreasonable to accept the Ptolemaic. Indeed, the theory of relativity has been able to make its conquest just because it has shifted its standpoint regarding this question.' In *Unsere Welt* (1920, No. 3) Doctor H. Remy discusses 'The Physical Principle of Relativity' and says: 'From this point of view the usual conflict between the Copernican and Ptolemaic systems finds its definite solution. We cannot deny that it is senseless to call one of these systems the only correct one and to designate the other as being false.' It seems as if the world do move." (Dr. Th. Graebner, in *The Lutheran Witness*, 1924, p. 149.) See *Christliche Dogmatik*, I, p. 578 (1924): "By the way, the newspaper-men threatened about a year ago that Einstein's theory of relativity would knock Copernicanism on the head."

materials.[116]   They are not ashamed to say that last year they taught (with the Bible) that this earth will come to an end but that now they must preach that this earth will last forever. They are proud of the fact that they no longer believe with their fathers in the resurrection of the body, proud of it that science has destroyed that monstrous conception. They tell us: In the prescientific age, theologians taught the resurrection of Jesus and His deity; such teachings have, thank God and science, gone by the board. The liberals see nothing wrong in correcting the teachings of the Bible according to the findings of what they call inductive and we call speculative science. They are satisfied to have their spiritual wealth affected by the fluctuations of secular values.

The conservatives among the moderns do not care to go so far. They do not want to make science the *ultima ratio* of faith. But they do demand that large portions of the Bible be rewritten, adjusted to the latest findings of science. What they, then, are asking for is, first, that in every generation, or perhaps in every decade, Christendom be presented with a new, revised edition of Holy Scripture. The first edition made Cyrenius governor of Syria at the birth of Christ. The second edition eliminated that portion. The third edition has now restored it. Who knows, some historian may appear on the scene tomorrow whose great renown will cause the semiliberals to get out a fourth edition to correspond with the second one. (Among the ultraliberals a Bible may then be circulating which omits the main fact of the first edition — the birth of Christ.) The ants of Prov. 6:8 must go or can stay, all depending on which entomologist has the greatest following. How often will Josh. 10:12 ff. have to be revised? Einstein tells the conservatives it may stay as originally written. But these semiliberals may choose to follow some other authorities and retain their revised Holy Scripture.

However, this contemptuous treatment of Holy Scripture has, in the second place, fatal consequences. No, it does not concern our salvation directly whether Cyrenius was governor at the time fixed by Luke. But it does concern our salvation directly whether the Bible is trustworthy or not. These men who are assailing Verbal Plenary Inspiration on scientific grounds are de-

---

116) "It has been suggested by some distinguished men of science that minute and simple forms of life may have come to the earth from elsewhere. They may have traveled in the crevices of a meteorite, sufficiently well wrapped up to withstand extreme cold in the journey through space and great heat as they approached the earth. . . . The hypothesis most in accord with evolutionary thinking is that of the occurrence of abiogenesis in the dim and distant past. That is to say, simple living creatures may have arisen long ago by a process of natural synthesis from non-living materials — from some colloidal carbonaceous slime activated by ferments." (J. A. Thomson, *op. cit.*, p. 106.)

stroying the foundation of faith. Casting doubt on portions of Holy
Writ, they are causing men to doubt all of Holy Writ. And, as to
our present particular point, under their ministration men will
never know whether to accept Plenary Inspiration; men will not be
permitted to accept it till science has spoken the final word on
every passage. Today men will be inclined to believe that all
Scripture is given by inspiration of God because some great
scientist endorsed a particular passage; tomorrow's developments
in the field of science may shatter their trust. These conservatives,
too, are making science the *ultima ratio* of faith. They give science
an authoritative voice in the Holy of Holies. And we say again: It
is insane folly to measure spiritual, eternal values by secular standards, fluctuating, fallible secular standards.

Speaking of "theologians who believe that they may retain
their self-respect only by reconstructing their universe according
to the shifting vogue of speculation," Dr. Theodore Graebner says:
"Could theology make another new departure and come safely to
terms once and for all with these new teachings of the other
sciences? Not so, because these have just gone into the melting-
pot again. The author of a recent scientific work writes: 'Since
I began writing this essay, there has been a striking increase in
critical activity, inspired by the new quantum mechanics. . . . The
change in ideas is now so rapid that a number of statements of this
essay are already antiquated, as expressions of the best current
opinion.' How mistaken, therefore, to base theology on the shifting foundation of natural science, which, for all its merits and
marvels, is temporary and imperfect in its conclusions." (*God and
the Cosmos*, p. VIII f.) That applies not only to the liberals but
also to the conservative critics. And both classes should ponder the
question of the ultraliberal philosopher T. V. Smith: "But who can
live by such uncertain speculations? Who can live on the 'dry
dust' of conjectures?" [117)

---

117) Miles H. Krumbine (a semiliberal or liberal himself) contributes the following to the present chapter of the gullibility of our
moderns: "The current passion of the pulpit for a word from Eddington
and a line from Jeans has conferred on scientists an authority out of all
proportion to the inherent importance of their utterances. . . . Rather
than religion being endangered because it makes too much of prescientific assumptions as to the nature of the universe and of man, it is
actually threatened with contempt for accepting too uncritically the
latest word of science as final. Obscurantism may have been religion's
ancient vice; *gullibility* is rapidly supplanting it, at least among the
so-called liberals." (*Ways of Believing*, p. 39.) On the same subject
Prof. C. C. Rasmussen (Gettysburg) says: "Of two ministerial friends
of mine, one twitted the other for the assiduity with which he repeatedly
hurried back to consult the savants, 'He is going back this year to find
out that what he learned last year is not so.' The thrust was good-
natured; but it was unforgettable, because it was uncomfortably close
to the truth. . . . There is room to question the prophet, the 'speaker

Scientific and Theological Counterfeiting

Now, having answered ten assertions, let us on our part make a few assertions and await the answer of the moderns. Statement No. 11: The Bible critics lack the scientific mind and spirit. — They have been telling us that "Protestant scholars of the present day, *imbued with the scientific spirit*," are forced to reject the verbal inspiration and inerrancy of the Bible (Hastings, *Encyclopedia*); the authors of the Bible were "living in a prescientific era" (see *Conc. Theol. Mthly.*, XII, p. 395 f.); they would not have spoken of miracles if they had known anything about "inductive science" (Fosdick); they lived in a pre-Kantian age and this same "pre-Kantian conception of truth" (Kantonen) molded the old theology; one who "knows the processes and technique of science" must reject the Bible account and cast away Verbal Inspiration (Delk). The moderns are obsessed with the idea that they cannot accept every teaching and every word of the Bible because their scientific sense is so highly developed.

Let us lay this ghost. The moderns are laboring under a delusion. They cannot qualify as scientists. For the true scientist is — to mention only a few characteristics — humble, honest, and unprejudiced.

The true scientist has a very humble mind. As he studies scientific matters, he becomes increasingly aware of the great limitations of science. He is ever compelled to make confession of his ignorance. The pursuit of science does not engender a boastful spirit. *"Ignoramus, ignorabimus,"* said Du Bois Raymond at a congress held in 1872 and listed seven world-mysteries: the nature of matter and force, the origin of motion, of life, of consciousness, of rational thought and speech, the question of design and purpose in nature, and the nature and origin of free will. (See *Lehre und Wehre*, 1900, p. 237.) Eddington concludes a survey of the latest theories in physics thus: "We have turned a corner in the path of progress, and our ignorance stands before us, appalling and insistent." (See *God and the Cosmos*, p. VII.) [118] The result is that

---

for God,' if that speaker's message is conspicuous for its 'variableness and shadow of turning.' The Master has said: 'Heaven and earth shall pass away, but My Word shall not pass away.'" (*Luth. Church Quarterly*, Jan., 1941, p. 45.) C. A. Lindberg uses the term "childish simplicity": "Some who reject the plenary inspiration of the Bible have never attempted to investigate any contradiction, but nevertheless have greater demands on Scripture than on science itself, whose results they are ever ready to accept with childish simplicity, even though science is frequently compelled to change its dogmatic assertions." (*Christian Dogmatics*, p. 395.)

118) Let a few more scientists speak on this subject. Laplace: "What we know is but little; what we do not know is immeasurable." (See *Lehre und Wehre*, 1913, p. 24.) Huxley: "The mysteries of the

"the average scientist is humble in his attitude and cautious in his claims. In such measure as he shows humility and caution, he will be impatient of the cock-sureness and arrogance of the scientific propagandist" (*loc. cit.*). Men who look deep into science learn modesty.

And when they look beyond science, their humility grows a hundredfold. When they deal with supernatural matters, their knowledge of the limitations of man keeps them from passing any judgment. They declare themselves incompetent to discuss miracles and infinity and omnipotence. Hear once more the statement of Edwin Lewis, liberal: " 'A scientific knowledge of the Creator' is an utter contradiction in terms; indeed, it savors of sheer *intellectual arrogance*, to say nothing worse." It is not only Luther and Walther who realize that "the Holy Spirit is more learned" than they are and humbly "doff their little doctor's hats" to Him. The great scientists — the humble scientists — do the same. Pascal, the great mathematician and philosopher, declared: "The last step of reason is to acknowledge that there are many things which transcend reason. Reason is weak as long as it does not take this step. ... If there are natural things which reason cannot comprehend, what shall we say concerning supernatural things?" (*Pensées*, II, p. 248.) Even the *Christian Century* said: "Science is limited to a secondary role in human destiny, because it can deal only with quantities, with things that can be measured. . . ." There are values "which evade the tools and technique of science." Realizing that

---

Church are child's play compared with the mysteries of nature." (*Loc. cit.*) J. A. Thomson: "We have to take for granted a certain number of irreducibles, such as electrons and protons. We are not sure that we know more than a few of the real laws of nature. There are large questions concerning human destiny, large questions as to the beginning and ending of the world, on which science sheds no light. . . . The limitations and ignorances of science. . . ." (*Op. cit.*, p. 199 f.) Sergius P. Grace, himself a scientist, inventor, and research specialist, told his audience in St. Louis: "The scientist will keep pressing forward, but he will never find the ultimate meanings of his world, energy, space, matter, life. That will remain locked forever in the mind of the Creator." (*Globe-Democrat*, March 4, 1931.) W. Dau: "Honorable scientists have favored the world with confessions of ignorance and hopeless inability that were wrung from them by nothing else than their own studies and researches. The confessions are valuable, not only for their contents, but also for their candor and sincerity." *The Testimony of Science*, which contains this statement (p. 10), fills twenty-six pages with such confessions. Two samples. The Marquis of Salisbury: "If we are not able to see far into the causes and origin of life in our own day, it is not probable that we shall deal more successfully with the problem as to how it arose many million years ago." (*Evolution*, p. 37.) In *European Thought in the Nineteenth Century*, p. 399, there is a deserved rebuke of sciolists who pose as scientists by Merz, who says: "There is a popular philosophy founded upon *the unknown principle of matter* and the *equally unknown principle of force* by second-rate *scientists in Germany.*"

the mysteries of science are child's play compared with the mysteries of faith, science is willing to play a secondary role, yes, play no role at all in establishing spiritual values. The mature scientist is modest. The late Dr. Adolph Lorenz, the world-renowned Austrian surgeon, said: "Does medical science, or any other science, tend to destroy belief in God? My friend, you are young. I am old. Science, truly pursued, does not tend to destroy belief in God. *The pursuit of scientific knowledge makes an honest man humble.* It makes him realize how little he knows. It makes him believe in God." (See *The Lutheran,* Sept. 3, 1931.) In his treatise "Die Denkweise der Physik und ihr Einfluss auf die geistige Einstellung des heutigen Menschen" (1937) the physicist Prof. Gustav Mie shows that the choice is not between being "a man scientifically trained" and "a believing Christian," but that "one must choose to be either a prideful man who places himself beside God or a truthful man who realizes that he is infinitely beneath God." (See *Allg. Ev.-Luth. Kztg.,* Nov. 29, 1940.) Science trains its pupils in modesty.

Science warns its pupils against appraising science too highly and appealing to its findings as the *ultima ratio. Science for the Elementary-School Teacher,* by G. S. Craig, says in the preface: "Too frequently we assume that we are living in an age of science, when in reality science has been applied to only a small fringe of society's problems." Again: "In a very real sense the scientific method may never be fully mastered by the individual." Why, it takes a man a lifetime to master only one of the many branches of science, and such a man will not use the term "master." And we have been told that Prof. Edwin E. Aubrey (liberal) told his class in this year's summer course at the University of Chicago: "The purpose of this course is to destroy your faith in the omnicompetence of science."

Furthermore, the fact that science has made so many mistakes keeps its true disciples in a modest frame of mind. Reread the preceding section. How often has science been compelled to reverse itself! The "Mistakes of Science" is an important *locus* in the Prolegomena of General Science, and the teacher makes use of this *locus* to instil modesty into the pupils. The class is asked to write a paper on "The Confession of a Scientist" and this Confession embraces two parts: He confesses his great ignorance in many matters of science, and he confesses his many mistakes. He declares in the name of science both: *"Ignoramus, ignorabimus,"* and: *Erravimus, errabimus.* The pupil who has mastered this *locus* continues his study of science in a very chastened spirit. If he is minded to continue his work in science in the spirit of presumptuous dogmatism and arrogant cock-sureness, he will not be permitted to graduate. Modesty is one of the outstanding characteristics of a scientist.

Next, the true scientist is honest. He is always ready to acknowledge and to correct the mistakes of science, his own mistakes and the mistakes the fathers of science made. His scientific conscience will not permit him to perpetuate theories which have been proved false. We admire science for this quality of honesty and candidness. And without it science would never have made its great advances.

Furthermore, the honest scientist is extremely cautious. He is not hasty in his judgments. He will not utter a final judgment until all the facts in the case are assembled and closely examined. Science deals with facts, with facts alone; and when a man enters the order of scientists, he takes the solemn obligation to gather all the facts relating to his particular province, even if it takes his lifetime to complete what his predecessors began, and, if he dies before that is completed, to leave the judgment to his successors. We admire these patient, plodding scientists; and we admire the scientific restraint they exercise: no judgment except on the basis of established facts. They may put out certain hypotheses as possible explanations of certain observed facts. But their scientific conscience will not permit them to label these hypotheses as facts, as established truths.

Do the Bible-critics, as a class, measure up to the humility and honesty that characterizes the scientists as a class? It is not an indication of modesty when Dr. Fosdick declares that "no *well-instructed mind*" can believe in Verbal Inspiration. And it is not only the liberals but also the conservatives who make the monstrous assertion — and believe it! — that the Bible theologians are ignoramuses. Scientific moderation and broad-mindedness should have kept the critics from indulging in such supercilious self-conceit. Mature scientists do not assume a superior attitude towards those who cannot agree with them.[119] What is worse, the critics assume a superior attitude towards the Biblical writers. It is agreed by most men that these writers were men of no mean attainments. But our critics do not hesitate to stigmatize their books as a catch-all of all manner of puerilities, imbecilities, contradictory statements, and silly anecdotes. Why, one of them even says: "We who have attained *higher forms* in the world-wide

---

119) "There is a class of men, of no mean intellectual caliber, who say that 'the Bible is not the inerrant Word of God,' and they are cocksure that it is not, and they have a very supercilious contempt, or, at least, a great patronizing pity, for the preachers and other people, whom they characterize as 'reactionaries' or 'obscurantists' or 'medieval' or 'archaic' or 'antediluvian,' who still hold to the belief that 'the Bible is the inerrant Word of God.'" (R. A. Torrey, *Is the Bible the Inerrant Word of God?* p. 39.) Torrey adds: "The fundamental trouble with these men is set forth by God Himself in a remarkable sentence in Rom. 1:22: 'Professing themselves to be wise, they became fools.'"

schoolroom of the great Instructor of men" than the Old Testament writers. (De Witt, *What Is Inspiration?* P. 182.) Worse than that, they have the arrogance to pass judgment on matters of which they know absolutely nothing. The scientist does not presume to draw the supernatural into the realm of his investigation; he is too modest for that; but the critics deny miracles, deny the *creatio ex nihilo,* deny the resurrection, because their smattering of science knows nothing of these things. We are not speaking of Christian humility. We are speaking of scientific humility, and that keeps men from sitting in judgment on God.

Again, it does not reveal humility when men reject certain teachings because of certain unsolvable difficulties connected therewith. It is a mark of self-conceit when men imagine that, because *they* cannot solve the problem, nobody else can. It is the height of arrogance and vanity when men ask tc have their ignorance made the deciding factor on the question at issue. That is not the scientific spirit. "The prime truth of science — universal gravitation — is not yet free of difficulty. . . . But reasonable men are not by these" (difficulties) "kept from believing in gravitation." (H. M'Intosh, *Is Christ Infallible and the Bible True?* P. 651.) It is unreasonable to doubt a truth because of certain difficulties connected therewith, and it is contrary to scientific modesty.[120] Oh, yes, there are a few Bible difficulties, in connection with seeming contradictions and certain historical and scientific statements, which have not yet been solved. But only the conceited critic will say: There is no solution possible; else I would have found the solution; therefore the Bible is full of errors. Yes, miracles transcend the puny minds of Harnack and Fosdick; but the scientist will tell them: Withhold your judgment! And will they reject Inspiration because "the processes and technique of science" cannot explain it? Are they really asking us to take our cue from their ignorance?[121]

---

120) Torrey's words will bear repeating: "Let us deal with any difficulty we meet in the Bible with that humility that becomes all persons of such limited understanding as we all are. Recognize the limitations of your own mind and knowledge and do not for a moment imagine that there is no solution just because you found none. . . . It would seem as if any really normal man would have a sufficient amount of that modesty that is becoming in beings so limited in knowledge as we all undeniably are to say: "Though *I* see no possible solution to this difficulty, some one a little wiser than I might easily find one.' . . . A man is not a philosopher but a fool who gives up a thoroughly established theorem because there are certain difficulties that he cannot explain. No reputable scientist in any department of science ever does that." (*Op. cit.,* pp. 22, 61, 69.)

121) M'Intosh: "If we were not to believe anything till it was entirely free of difficulty, or plausible objections, then we should believe nothing. The prime truth of science — universal gravitation — is not yet free of difficulty. And the first truth in religion — God is Love — is by no means free of difficulty; and plausible objections have been urged

Then, there is such a thing as scientific honesty. The scientists, as a class, are ever ready to admit the mistakes of science. Are the Biblical critics ready to admit the many mistakes of Biblical criticism, apologize for them, and openly declare that the charges of the errancy of the Bible are unfounded? That these charges are entirely unfounded has already been demonstrated on page 78 ff. Science, the most painstaking investigation, pursued on scientific lines, and all the advances of science have not overthrown a single teaching of Christianity or discredited a single statement of Scripture.[122] But they are still harping on the charge that the Cyrenius passage contains a glaring blunder and that the story of the healing of the blind men at Jericho contains an outright contradiction. In spite of the fact that reputable scientists have agreed that the Ptolemaic theory might be true, they are still filling the land with the cry that only the Copernican theory can be true and that therefore Joshua was weak in science. The least that we can ask of the moderns is the candid confession that many, most, of the counts in their indictment of the Bible have been disproved. When will they issue a manifesto to that effect?

Science is honest. It shows no partiality. The moderns who are pleased to attach greater weight to the statements of the secular historian Josephus than to those of the Biblical historian Luke have not the scientific mind.

The honest scientist refuses to judge before he has assembled

---

against it from terrible and staggering things in nature, providence, and life. But reasonable men are not by these kept from believing in gravitation or in God; and why, then, should they in believing the *Bible claim* when, like these, it is established on its own proper evidence?"

122) Edwin Lewis: "Christianity contradicts no *known* facts. Its falsity can at no point be logically demonstrated." (*The Faith We Declare*, p. 126.) *America* (Roman-Catholic) recently wrote: "Between the years 1749 and 1941 the progress of scientific research was phenomenal. Voluminous information was gathered concerning the times of Christ, the contemporaries of Christ; and enemies of the Savior strove to use the fresh knowledge to weaken the historicity of the Gospel-story. Each attempt not merely failed to shake that story but actually ended up by adding additional confirmation to it. Knowledge of the complex forces of nature experienced an enormous increase during the 1749—1941 period, and foes of the God-man sought to employ this accumulated learning to assail the miracles and other features of the Gospel. Every attack petered out in failure. In this year of 1941, when mankind knows more about the science of history and the laws of nature than it ever knew before, the Gospel-story is still going strong. If such multitudes of big-name leaders of science, of history, of 'liberal theology,' had hurled the concentrated and persistent attack at any other book that they hurled at the gospels, that book would have been discredited long ago. . . ." (See *Conc. Theol. Mthly.*, XII, p. 630.) And that applies not only to the doctrines and the outstanding facts of the Bible but also to the least details. Of the geographical statements of the Bible "not one has been proved false" (*Proc., Western Dist.*, 1865, p. 31). "A real contradiction, precluding any solution as unthinkable and impossible, has not yet been discovered." (*Lehre und Wehre*, 1898, p. 107.) Etc.

and studied *all* the facts in the case. Many of the statements of the Bible are ruled out by critics who are bound to confess that many of the circumstances that would shed light on these statements are unknown to them.

Occasionally even such dishonesty is practised as Lindberg stigmatizes in the words quoted above: "Some who reject the plenary inspiration of the Bible have never attempted to *investigate* any contradiction." A. W. Pink speaks in a similar strain: "There are no real discrepancies. The harmony existing between them does not appear on the surface, but often is only discovered *by protracted study*." (*The Divine Inspiration of the Bible*, p. 60.) Most discrepancies vanish when honest, thorough scientific investigation is applied to them, such as is evidenced, for instance, in the articles "The Chronology of the Two Covenants" (Gal. 3:17 cp. with Ex. 12:40) and "The Alleged Contradiction between Gen. 1: 24-27 and 2:19" in *Conc. Theol. Mthly.*, XII, p. 606 ff., 652 ff. We are not, of course, speaking of all moderns, but of that class of glib critics who do not find the time for scientific study of the case, but fill their time with denouncing the Bible for its contradictions and mistakes.

Again, will an honest scientist undertake to speak with authority in a matter of which he is absolutely ignorant? Here are the Bible-critics who deny the truth of the Creation in the interest of evolution and consequently charge the Bible with a grave mistake, and this in spite of the fact that "the ultimate nature of matter not only remains unknown, but also unknowable" (*Theological Forum*, Jan., 1931, p. 40). And still they pretend to know all·about the origin of matter! (See the entire article: "Creation of Matter.") Recall the statement of the Marquis of Salisbury: What do you know about the origin of life in our day? And do you presume to tell us all about how life originated in the dim ages of the past? The evolutionary critics of the Bible are not scientists; they are charlatans.

And when a preacher tells his congregation that the account of Gen. 1 must be rejected because science has established that evolution produced the plants and the animals and man, he is saying what is not true. A scientist loses caste when he falsifies the record in order to prove his point. But the evolutionary critics of the Bible are operating with manufactured evidence.

What is the explanation of these unscientific tactics? The Bible-critics are, as a rule, swayed by prejudice. And such an attitude does violence to another principle of pure science. Science is unprejudiced. Its disciples are not permitted to carry any preconceived opinions into their investigations. But our moderns are constantly doing this very thing. Here are those who are so thoroughly convinced of the truth of the assumptions of higher criticism, including the hypothesis of evolution, that they will not listen to any contrary statement, the contrary statements of the Bible. "These presuppositions and assumptions are the determining element in the entire movement. . . . Their minds seem to be in abject slavery to their theory. . . . They feel instinctively that to accept the Bible statements would be the ruin of their hypothesis." (See p. 40 above.) "Dr. Fosdick," says the *Journal of the Am. Luth. Conf.* (June, 1939, p. 76), "is also in the grip of the evolution *fixation.*" These men cannot read the Bible with a scientific, impartial, objective mind.

Here are those who are obsessed with the idea that the finding of a scientist carries more weight than any statement of Scripture, that Scripture must yield to science. In the case of a conflict between a secular writer and a Biblical writer the secular writer is always right. These men are unable to investigate the matter with scientific calm and objectivity.

Here are those who have a horror of the supernatural. They have the *idée fixé* that science has ruled out the miracle. It is impossible to convince these men of the truth of the Bible teaching on this point. It is useless to argue with "criticism that is inspired by a dogmatic denial of the supernatural" (Bishop Gore's phrase; see *The Doctrine of the Infallible Book,* p. 28), with those who dispose of the reality of the miracles by the "simple denial of them from *a-priori* philosophical prejudice" (Ph. Schaff's phrase).[123]

And here are those who hate the Bible. The sole object of their Bible-study is to discredit the Bible. The more items they can add to the black-list, the better pleased they are. Can you believe that B. Bauer, for instance, who finds a contradiction between Luke 7:2 and Matt. 8:6 (Luke speaking of the "servant" and Matthew, allegedly, of the "son") and has Luke invent the ruler "Lysanias," is not actuated by prejudice, that he is able to treat the Bible fairly?

The fact of the matter is that, as long as a man cannot accept the Bible as the Word of God and as the supreme and only authority, he cannot treat the Bible fairly. A man who in these matters is guided, entirely or in part, by his natural mind and reason will be prejudiced against the Bible as God's Word. "There is no such thing as a neutral reason" (*The Sovereignty of God,* p. 16), for "the carnal mind is enmity against God," Rom. 8:7. The

---

123) And what can you expect of those whose attitude is thus described by Dr. Wm. Robinson: "Then, we also have in American universities an unmistakable tendency to deny the supernatural. For a man really to believe the miracles of the New Testament is tantamount to surrendering his academic standing." (See *The Sovereignty of God,* p. 159.)

unbelieving critic cannot but take an antagonistic position towards God's Word. And unless the believer is constantly on his guard, his flesh will ever and again influence him in the same direction. There is much prejudice and animosity evident where men discuss the authority and inerrancy of the Bible. A candid discussion is a rare thing.[124]

Prof. G. L. Raymond declares: "The science of the day trains the mind to be candid and logical; and theology is inclined to be neither." (*The Psychology of Inspiration*, p. VI.) If he is speaking of common science as being candid, we fully agree with him. If he is speaking of the science pretended by the critics of the Bible, he will be hard put to it to make good his claim.[125]

No. 12: The moderns deal largely in hypotheses. — We have already touched upon this subject. We shall now, partly by way of recapitulation and partly by way of supplement, add a few more remarks.

1) Hypotheses are guesses. The handbooks say: "The hypothesis is a tentative theory or supposition provisionally adopted to explain certain facts and to guide in the investigation of others; frequently called a *working hypothesis*." The hypothesis — unless it be one of the wild kind which has no scientific justification whatever — serves a good purpose. But all men are agreed that, as long as it remains a hypothesis, it is not an established truth; it remains, in unscientific language, a guess. "Science, as the term is mostly used, is made up largely of learned guesses, but it is seldom that scientists have a concrete thing like the comet to try their guesses on." (*Detroit News*.)

2) Copernicanism, the various theories with which higher criticism has been and is operating, and the doctrine of evolution are hypotheses. (We are specifying these theories because the moderns are fully convinced that these teachings have given the

---

124) Here is an extreme case of bigoted prejudice. "Some will then ask, Well, why don't more men believe in the resurrection, especially some of our outstanding scholars? I think the reason they do not believe is because they do not want to believe, that they have determined not to believe. . . . Prof. C. E. M. Joad of the University of London declared as late as 1933 that he will not believe in such an event, no matter what the evidence. These are his own words: Even if the evidence were far more impressive than the tatter of inconsistencies, divergencies, and contradictions which is in fact available, I should probably still refuse to credit the fact which it purported to establish.' No matter what the evidence is, because of his own convictions regarding what ought to be in the universe, Professor Joad frankly states that he will never believe, 'no matter what the evidence.'" (*The Supernaturalness of Christ. Can We Still Believe in It?* p. 221 f. See *Conc. Theol. Mthly.*, XII, p. 235.)

125) And science trains the mind "to be logical." Absolutely. But the moderns do not show that they have been sufficiently trained in this particular technique of science. Other sections of this essay have demonstrated that.

death-blow to the plenary inspiration and the inerrancy of the
Bible.) All the world knows, the scientists know, and the moderns
dare not gainsay it, that they are pure hypotheses. T. H. Huxley
designates evolution, for instance, as a hypothesis; he calls it that
four times in seven lines of a page in the *Encyclopedia Britannica.*
E. Haeckel says: "It is self-evident that our genealogical history is
and ever will be a fabric of hypotheses." (See *God and the Cosmos,*
p. 306.) J. A. Thomson: "The *hypothesis* most in accord with evolutionary thinking is that of the occurrence of abiogenesis in the
dim and distant past." (*Op. cit.*, p. 106.) And the moderns, as a rule,
unhesitatingly use the same designation. F. Baumgaertel: "The
hypotheses which natural science today sets up regarding the origin
of the world *are indeed hypotheses,* but one thing is absolutely
sure: Creation did not take place as the Old Testament describes it."
(See W. Moeller, *Um die Inspiration der Bibel,* p. 31.) E. Brunner:
"It is a well-grounded hypothesis that a more or less continuous
pedigree traces the origin of humanity far back into the animal
sphere." (*The Word and the World,* p. 99.) H. E. Fosdick: "It may
be that the *evolutionary hypothesis* is dangerous to the religious
faith of many folk who welcome it today, as some conservatives
think, but, for all that, the more facts we know, the better founded
does the hypothesis appear." (*The Modern Use of the Bible,* p. 51.)
Well-grounded [126] or not, a hypothesis it is, and a hypothesis it
remains, by their own admission. Since the days when Huxley
and Fosdick used the term hypothesis, nothing has occurred in the
world of science to justify men to speak of evolution as an established truth. We have not heard of the jubilations which would
have been held, we have not seen the bonfires which would have
been blazing on the campuses of the universities and the liberal
seminaries, if those long-hoped-for facts had been finally discovered. The teachings which are relied upon to demolish the
Bible are mere guesses; in military slang, duds. These duds are
certainly not going to break Scripture.

3) The pathetic thing is that the moderns believe in these
hypotheses with a heroic faith. They accept them as established
truths and as precious truths. In one breath they speak of evolution as a hypothesis and as a fact: "well-grounded hypothesis."
H. Spencer and Huxley said: "This hypothesis may be expected to
survive and become established." (See *Lehre und Wehre,* 1913,
p. 71.) And when you hear the high-school teacher and the university professor talk on this subject, when you hear the liberal
preacher base his rejection of Gen. 1 on the assured results of
science, on the teaching of evolution, you notice that they are con-

---

126) "It is a *well-grounded* hypothesis" — founded on what — facts
or speculations?

vinced that they are living in the day of the fulfilment of Huxley's prophecy. Though no conclusive facts have been adduced, they believe that evolution is a fact.

We cannot understand how Dr. Delk could pen the following: "It is true that this theory was once a hypothesis. Every scientific truth was once held as a mere hypothesis. The belief in organic evolution, including the appearance of man, for the overwhelming majority of scientists has passed out of the stage of hypothesis and become the working theory of science." (See *Lehre und Wehre,* 1913, p. 149.)   More than this; it is certainly a strange psychosis that could induce Haeckel to declare that evolution is indeed a hypothesis, but one that has been elevated to the rank of a fact. The situation has been adequately described by the statement: "Dr. Fosdick is in the grip of the evolution *fixation.*" The human mind has the faculty of persuading itself of the truth of a thing which in its sane moments it refuses to accept as proved. "Unable to prove the theory, the scientists decided to declare it a certainty anyway." [127)   And it has become a veritable article of faith to them. They feel aggrieved if you presume to doubt it. They claim the right to cherish it and fight for it. A man once told us indignantly: "We let you believe what the Bible teaches; you ought to let us believe what science teaches." It is a fixation.

---

127) Statement by *America,* April 19, 1941. The entire paragraph reads: "The theory of evolution is still only a theory. Despite the world-wide efforts of untold millions of scientists, it has never been proved. Unable to prove the theory, the scientists decided to declare it a certainty anyway, somewhat after the fashion in which printing-press money is declared to be real money when it is not. And thus into the text-books, into the lecture-halls, into the anthropological sessions, stepped the theory disguised as a fact. This modern age, which regards itself as so enlightened, ridicules the theories which passed for facts in former epochs. For example, the Ptolemaic theory, which assumed that the earth was the central body around which the sun and planets revolved is today the butt of countless witticisms. It is quite possible that some future epoch will pour on the theory of evolution the same stream of sarcasm that this age pours on the theory of the Alexandrian astronomer. We may imagine a gathering of scientists three centuries hence and the newspaper dispatches describing the proceedings." We may as well give the next paragraph, too: "Dispatch. April 12, 2341 A. D. The American Association of Super Scientists opened their annual convention yesterday. In the afternoon session, Prof. B. A. Stufchert read a scholarly paper entitled: 'The Gullibility, Self-Deception, Stupidity, and Fatuity of Former Ages.' Professor Stufchert blasted the unscientific methods of premodern eras. 'In the period between 1850 and 1975 A. D., the unscientific orgy reached its peak,' Professor Stufchert stated. 'In these years, instead of following the facts wherever they led, it became the custom to make the facts fit in with preconceived ideas. For example, consider the now forgotten monkey-descent theory. A world-wide build-up and conspiracy favored this theory, and when the proof for it was not forthcoming, the so-called scientific circles felt, if it wasn't true, it ought to be and taught it anyway. As a consequence, several generations believed they were descended from monkeys and acted accordingly' "

Science does not teach evolution. It admits that evolution cannot be proved. And there is irrefutable proof that man did not descend from the ape or from any other animal or from dead matter. Speaking of the hypothesis of abiogenesis, J. A. Thomson writes: "As we have said, there is no evidence in support of this view." (*Op. cit.*, p. 107.) See the quotation above from the *Allg. Ev.-Luth. Kztg.*, Feb. 21, 1941. Oswald Spengler writes in *Der Untergang des Abendlandes*, II, p. 35: "Not the slightest trace of a development of the race towards higher structure has been found. Man has come as the result of a sudden change, of which the whence, how, and why will be an unfathomable mystery. . . . The origin of the earth, the beginning of life, the introduction of animated beings, are mysteries which we must accept as such." *The Lutheran Witness*, which quotes this and more, comments: "The statements quoted from Spengler, a philosopher whom the entire world acclaims as one of the greatest thinkers of the day, are a blow to the pseudoscientific cock-sureness of the evolutionists." (1924, p. 149.) But cock-sure they, as a class, remain. They will not, they cannot give up their faith.

It is too precious. What is back of this faith? No doubt, with many it is the misguided scientific conscience. They honestly believe that science has established evolution. But there are also those whose thoughts are motivated by their abhorrence of miracles, by the pride which will not submit to God as the Creator and Lord of all, and the resulting antagonism to His Word, the Bible. E. Muehe says: "Dem christglaeubigen, frommen Kopernikus ist es nie eingefallen, an der Wahrheit der biblischen Erzaehlungen zu zweifeln. Aber viele der heutigen Naturforscher sind nicht Nachfolger seines Christenglaubens, sondern Anbeter seiner Wissenschaft geworden. *Wenn das kopernikanische Weltsystem in der Bibel stuende, so wuerden sie es sicherlich nicht annehmen;* nun es aber nach ihrer Meinung gegen die Bibel zu sprechen scheint, machen sie es zu ihrem ewigen Evangelium und glauben, der persoenliche Gott und seine Bibel sei dadurch ueber den Haufen geworfen." (*Biblische Merkwuerdigkeiten*, p. 91.) Yes, there are those who accept certain hypotheses as truth because they are determined not to accept God's Bible as the truth. E. Haeckel was one of them. He was brazen enough to confess: "Gentlemen, if you refuse to accept the hypothesis of spontaneous generation, you are thrown back on the miracle of a supernatural creation." (*Lehre und Wehre*, 1913, p. 359.) A. Harnack had to be told by W. Walther that he took the very same position. (See *Lehre und Wehre*, 1902, p. 30.)

4) This, too, happens that some men parade these hypotheses without a real acquaintance with them. They will even trot out dead hypotheses against the Bible. W. T. Riviere writes: "In 1920

... evolution was popularly understood, even by the learned, to be a scientifically proved doctrine of inevitable progress. This misunderstanding was so general and so serious that I worked out a standard treatment for my young University of Texas freshmen when they returned to Cleburne for the Christmas holidays. It was based on student reaction to a certain lecture about evolution which impressed all my freshmen. During a drive in my little coupé it was easy to start the student into a speech on evolution; and without fail the well-taught lecture came point by point from the eager youth." Pastor Riviere goes on to tell how he would take the student into the manse, open the text-book on evolution, show the student where he and his instructor were mistaken, and adds: "Of course I had little concern about apes or about anything more than a general awareness of current changes in Darwinian theory; but perhaps it was healthy for young and growing minds to remember, from this bookish correction, that small-town pastors are bachelors and masters of art who may happen to know some of the faculty's lore, and that a preacher may have the right to speak with authority in his own field." (*Op. cit.*, p. 53 f.) It does happen that some do not know exactly what Darwin's hypothesis was and do not know that this particular hypothesis is dead. Another case of dealing with counterfeit confederate money.[128)]

---

128) *Science for the Elementary-School Teacher,* copyrighted 1940, has this: "Despite the fact that man is similar in some respects to the apes, the popular idea that man is 'descended from a monkey' is not held to be true by biologists. It may be true that in the course of evolutionary development both man and the apes had a common ancestor, from which both are descended; but the various families of monkeys, apes, and man have been distinct for a long time." (P. 373.) — In reading this handbook of elementary science we came across a curious phenomenon. It leaves the teacher in the lurch at a critical point. Chapter XVIII: "Man Is an Animal," starts out with the statement: "The human species is composed of individuals which have many of the characteristics of other animals." The phrase occurs repeatedly: "*Like any other animal,* man is affected," etc. Surely, being descended from some sort of animal, man is an animal. However, the boys and girls must be told — they know it already — that man greatly differs from the other animals. "Man's intelligence gives him an advantage in the struggle for existence. . . . How has man managed to survive? The answer is obvious. The human species possesses a brain which is of such a nature that it gives man an advantage over all other living things. He is able to reason. . . . The thinking processes are complemented by his ability to make his ideas known to his associates through the medium of speech," etc. (P. 375.) And the preface states: "One of the most recent species to make its appearance on the earth is modern man, a living being, *uniquely endowed with intelligence."* The boys and girls will accept that. But now the bright members of the class will ask: Where did man's intelligence come from? Why is reason and speech not found in the apes and cats? How did the human species acquire reason and speech? The handbook suggests no answer to the poor teacher. It cannot, of course, suggest an answer. St. George Mivart says: "The origin of consciousness remains shrouded in inscrutable mystery." (*Origin of Human Reason,* p. 212.) Discussing the origin of speech, he quotes

5) These hypotheses, the old abandoned ones and those which are in vogue now, mean nothing to the theologian and to the scientist. The Bible theologian attaches no value to them. Bishop Manning, indeed, declared that "the evolutionary theory has been accepted by all schools of theologians for the last fifty years." (See *The Christian Century*, Jan. 26, 1938.) But that statement lacks scientific precision. The Bible theologians — the true theologians — do not dream of accepting this hypothesis. They refuse to let the evolutionary or the Copernican or any other hypothesis correct Scripture. As Dr. Pieper says: "It is unworthy of a Christian to force Holy Scripture, which he knows to be God's Word, into agreement with human opinions (hypotheses), with the so-called Copernican cosmic system and similar hypotheses, or to accept such forced interpretations by others." (*Op. cit.*, I, p. 577.) And Dr. Hermann Sasse describes the Christian position thus: "The Lutheran Church, today as formerly, has greater respect for the Word of God than for the hypotheses of modern science." (See *Allg. Ev.-Luth. Kztg.*, 1938, p. 82.)

However, at present we are not concerned with the reaction of theologians towards the demand to accept these hypotheses as truths. We are asking just now how much value the scientist attaches to them. The answer is: None, as far as their value as proofs is concerned. As the *Watchman-Examiner* (June 19, 1941) puts it: "You are not in the absolute realm of science when you are hypothetical. You must go outside its door when you take up a hypothesis, and you can come back in only when you have established your facts."

Facts! From the first chapter on the moderns have been telling us that "the facts" disprove Verbal Inspiration. We ask them to produce these facts — and here they are offering us hypotheses! That is counterfeiting, theological and scientific counterfeiting.

THE LIST OF FATUITIES CONTINUED

Robert F. Horton is "smitten with amazement at the unobservant and unintelligent treatment of Scripture which alone has rendered the old theory of Inspiration possible for thinking men." (*Revelation and the Bible*, p. 120.) F. Pieper finds that "the objections to the verbal inspiration of Holy Scripture do not manifest

---

Romanes to this effect: "Any remark which I have to offer upon this subject must needs be of a wholly speculative, or unverifiable, character. I attach no argumentative importance to any of these hypotheses." See *The Testimony of Science* for many similar statements. And so the handbook is silent on this question. What shall the teacher do? Should he suggest to the pupils that there is such a thing as Creation? If he dare not do it, the bright pupils will think of that anyway.

great ingenuity or mental acumen, but the very opposite" (*What
Is Christianity?* P. 243). Who is right? Let us examine a few
more of the absurdities and sophistries employed by the moderns
in their polemics against Verbal Inspiration.

A Lot of Romancing

No. 13. The moderns deal largely in bare assertions and bland
assumptions. — These assumptions do not deserve to be classed
with the hypotheses. Both lack proof, but while the legitimate
hypothesis at least makes an honest attempt to support itself by
pointing to certain facts, the assertions now before us have nothing
back of them but the word of their proponents. — We are not now
concerned with disproving these assertions. We are simply listing
them as unsupported assertions. — Those that have been discussed
above are set down here again for the purpose of proper classifi-
cation; and a few new specimens are added.

1) "God cares not for trifles." That is N. R. Best's assertion.
"There is a great maxim dear to the most just and most enlightened
legal minds — a maxim drawn from ancient Rome, the mother of
the world's jurisprudence: The law cares not for trifles.' It is
a maxim which theology ought to adopt in honor of the heavenly
Father, whose infinite mind is the native home of law as well as
of revelation, and whose love desires for mankind no petty securi-
ties within tight-closed corrals but abundant life along the wide
ranges of a free universe. 'God cares not for trifles.' Certainly it
is an intellect childishly restricted which is able to imagine Him
who 'upholdeth all things by the word of His power' sitting in the
central rulership of the universe with concern in His thought about
the possibility that Matthew, Mark, Luke, and John would not get
it straight whether Peter denied his Lord to two or only to one of
the high priest's serving maids." (*Inspiration*, p. 79.) We will
grant that "the law cares not for trifles." But we are asking for
proof that, because the law cares not for trifles, God does not care
for these so-called trifles of contradictions and errors in the Bible.
None is offered. Nothing but rhetorical declamation is offered.
We have nothing but Best's word for the axiom: "God cares not
for trifles."

2) Best's negative assertion declares in the positive form: Inspiration covers only the Gospel-message, or only the important
doctrinal declarations of Scripture. The moderns consider this one
of their strongest arguments against Verbal Inspiration. Both the
liberals and the conservatives make much of it.[129] But, as a rule,

---

129) For instance: H. L. Willett (liberal): "The finality and authority
of the Bible do not reside in all of its utterances, but in those great
characters and messages which are easily discerned as the mountain

they offer no proof for it. The Bible nowhere makes the statement that inspiration must be restricted to the truths of salvation. But the moderns take it to be a self-evident truth. They do not care to waste words on proving an axiom. So we have to tell them that we are not minded to accept such a far-reaching statement on their bare word, on the strength of their subjective conviction.

3) We need not be surprised that the moderns who deal with bare assumptions in the most important matters should be guilty of the same presumption with regard to less important, comparatively less important, matters. For instance, the story of Jonah is not a true story but, as H. L. Willett tells us, "is given the mold of a novel. . . . The incidents of the storm, Jonah's deliverance by the great fish (perhaps intended as a symbol of Israel's engulfment and restoration), are the dramatic embellishments of a story with a very definite purpose." (*Op. cit.*, p. 110.) Where is the proof for the statement that a novelist invented the story of the great fish and hid a comforting truth in it? No proof is offered. Prof. J. W. Horine writes in the *Lutheran*, March 18, 1937: "The book [Jonah] is considered to be not literal history but parable or allegory. . . . So Jonah (Israel) was disgorged from the mouth of the great fish (Babylon)." Where is the proof that the writer of this book did not expect his readers to take these occurrences as facts but knew that they would find an instructive parable in it? Pure romancing on the part of the moderns, and they want us to accept *their* romance as true. And Professor Horine goes on to tell us that the Lord's reference to this story does not prove it to be a true story. "He is simply using it as an illustration. . . . Just as *we* refer to the Prodigal Son or the Good Samaritan in precisely the same terms we should use *were their adventures historical facts*" (our italics), "so may Christ have done here." Where does Christ indicate that He is treating this story as a parable? We are certainly not ready to accept the mere *dictum* of men as valid proof. Another statement by Willett: "There are three books in the Hebrew Scriptures which have the appearance of works of fiction written with a definite bearing on current thought and intended to be tracts for the times. They are Ruth, Jonah, and Esther. . . . These are

---

peaks of its contents. Such portions are worthy to be called the Word of God to man." (*The Bible through the Centuries*, p. 289.) Joseph Stump: "The holy writers were inspired with a supernatural knowledge of God and of His will, and on these subjects their words are final and infallible. On scientific matters they neither knew, nor professed to know, more than other men of their day." (*The Christian Faith*, p. 319.) *The Lutheran*, Feb. 22, 1939: "The Holy Scriptures are the infallible truth 'in all matters that pertain to His revelation and our salvation,'" but on secular matters the "Bible writers wrote with the background of their age and its scientific beliefs."

Biblical romances." (*Op. cit.*, pp. 102, 107.) To us they do not appear to be romances. Whose word counts for most?

4) They do indeed offer proofs for the unhistorical character of the Book of Jonah, but these proofs, too, consist of nothing but bare assertions and assumptions. First, in answer to our objection that the Hebrews would hardly admit a book of fiction into their sacred canon, they remind us of "the inveterate love of romance common to the ancient Jews with the other nations of the East." Granted that the ancient Jews and the other nations of the East had an inveterate love of romance,—the nations of the West have it, too,— that has no bearing on the question. Love of romance will not permit a religious people to justify a pious fraud in sacred matters.[130] And then they point out, as corroborating the theory that the story is a parable, that "the belly of a sea-monster is actually used in Jeremiah (51: 34, 44) as a figure for the captivity of Israel." Again: "The myth of the sea-monster is preserved not only in the story of Jonah, but in fragmentary allusions to the leviathan, Rahab, and the dragon, in Job 3: 8; 26: 12, 13; Is. 51: 9; cf. 27: 1." Is the reader able to see the connection? Redford says: "A theory of this kind is based upon so many assumptions that it demands almost implicit faith in those who put it forth." (P. 39.) "We protest against the random assertions of the critical school." (P. 66.)

5) The Bible-stories of the Creation, of the Temptation, and the Fall get the same treatment as the story of Jonah. It is said to be against the spirit of the Bible to take these stories literally; they are myths indeed, but myths which teach important spiritual lessons. They speak of "the *majestic* creation myth" (Georgia Harkness). "For myself, I think it (Gen. 1) holy ground" (H. E. Fosdick, *Modern Use of the Bible*, p. 52). "They declare that what has been called the fall of man, original sin, and the devil, these are, at best, *great* mythological theories." (J. S. Whale, *The Christian Answer to Prayer*, p. 35.) "Gen. 3 is a *didactic* poem." (See *Religion i. G. u. G.*, *s.v. Suende*.) "The *explanatory* myth of Eve and the apple." (S. McDowall, *Is Sin Our Fault?* P. 234.) J. M. Gibson asks men to "recognize the marvelous grace of God in so lifting up the best legendary literature of the world, such as the story of the Garden of Eden or of the Fall, as to make it the *vehicle of high and*

---

130) R. A. Redford: "Mr. Cheyne remarks (in *Theol. Rev.*, XIV, p. 213) that 'ordinary readers, especially when influenced by theological prejudice, are unable to realize the inveterate love of romance common to the ancient Jews with the other nations of the East.' Yet surely, if that were so, it would make the fact of the admission of a mere book of fiction into the canon all the more inexplicable, for the compilers of Scripture, knowing the prevailing tendency, would be careful to exclude such a book. . . . Thirdly, there is the difficulty of reconciling such a legend about a great prophet, given in his name, with his character, unless it were true." (*Studies in the Book of Jonah*, p. 36.)

pure revelation"; and T. A. Kantonen chides those who "have regarded the stories of the Temptation and the Fall as mere historical narratives rather than *profound prophetic philosophy of history"* (see p. 16 above). Indeed? Where does the Bible say or indicate that? Once more we are asked to take their word for it.

6) Higher criticism, which is responsible for 3), 4), 5), is made up almost entirely of bare assertions and mere assumptions. There is, for instance, the great Redactor. We are supposed to believe in his existence and work on their mere word. Their *fiat* created him. And how do you know that the various documents which were finally fused into the documents that make up the Bible really existed? Ask the higher critics.[131]

7) Higher criticism again: "It is probably due to the influence of Q that Mark locates the temptation at the beginning of Jesus' ministry, omitting details; but from Matthew it is evident that the story is a piece of apocalyptic symbolism, evidently 'literary' in conception, though doubtless originally oral in form. . . . This [the Transfiguration] is either an account of a resurrection appearance which has been antedated and shifted back into the Galilean ministry, or it is the account of some ecstatic experience born of exalted faith, told and retold in terms similar to the accounts of the Resurrection and hence influenced by the latter." (Quoted from Frederick C. Grant's *The Gospel of the Kingdom,* in *Kirchliche Zeitschrift,* 1940, p. 553.)

8) Some more higher criticism romancing. The writer of the article "The 'Cursing' of the Fig-Tree" in the *Luth. Church Quarterly,* April, 1936, assumes the role of the Redactor of Mark. "The condition of the story is singularly chaotic. . . . In some instances it becomes possible to reconstruct with a fair degree of probability an earlier form of a given incident than the one which Mark presents. . . . It is obvious that, if food had been lacking in Bethany, the dis-

---

131) Read again Prof. J. J. Reeve's statement. "These presuppositions and assumptions are the determining element in the entire movement. . . . The use of the Redactor is a case in point. This purely imaginary being, unhistorical and unscientific, is brought into requisition at almost every difficulty." (*Fundamentals,* III, p. 98.) And hear Prof. W. H. Green, *The Unity of the Book of Genesis* (p. 572): "The alleged diversity of diction, style, and conception is either altogether fictitious or is due to differences in the subject-matter and not to a diversity of writers. The continuity and self-consistency of Genesis, contrasted with the fragmentary character and mutual inconsistencies of the documents, prove that Genesis is the original of which the so-called documents are but several parts. The role attributed to the Redactor is an impossible one, and proves him to be an unreal personage. And the arguments for the late date of the documents and for their origin in one or the other of the divided kingdoms are built upon perversions of the history or upon unproved assumptions" (See Dr. L. Fuerbringer's article on this point in *Lehre und Wehre,* 1898, p. 206 ff.)

ciples would have been hungry, too, and the story would almost
certainly have disclosed the fact in some way. There is no such
indication. Apparently Jesus was the only one who 'hungered.' . . .
Nothing is said in the story about the owner of the tree. . . . Jesus
is now said, to have deprived the owner of his tree, not only without due process of law, but apparently without a thought." The
Redactor then tells us how Matthew edited the original story and
that "it is possible that this parable of Luke's (13:6-9) may have
been the kernel from which Mark's story sprouted," and that the
true story is simply this, that Jesus saw a dying fig-tree and said it
would soon wither away, and so it did; the next morning it *was*
withered away, and "Peter saith unto Him: Rabbi, behold, the fig-
tree is withered away."

9) H. E. Fosdick asserts: "It is impossible that a book written
two or three thousand years ago should be used in the twentieth
century A. D. without having some of its forms of thought and
speech translated into modern categories." (*Op. cit.*, p. 129.)   One
of these antiquated forms of thought is the belief in the resurrection of the flesh. Another is the "ascription of many familiar ailments to the visitation of demons" (p. 35); as S. Cave puts it:
"Where Paul speaks of 'demons,' we speak of 'neurosis,' 'complexes,'
and 'repressions' " (*What Shall We Say of Christ?* P. 55). For the
purposes of the present section it will be sufficient that we match
Fosdick's assertion with the counter-assertion: It is possible for
men of the twentieth century to employ the Biblical forms of
thought. In addition, we point out that the proof offered by Fosdick and Cave for their assumption is also nothing but an assumption: where is the proof that the "demons" Paul speaks of were
common ailments?

10) True, these assumptions are frequently introduced with
a "perhaps." "Jonah's deliverance was *perhaps* intended as a
symbol." Mark's Redactor speaks of "a fair degree of probability."
H. L. Willett answers the question "What is the Q on which the
gospels are said to be founded?" thus: "It is one of the documents
which scholars *have assumed* as a source, . . . *perhaps* in Aramaic,
. . . *possibly* from the hand of Matthew himself." (*The Christian
Century*, March 2, 1938.)[132]   We give due credit to the honesty

---

132) *Kirchliche Zeitschrift*, 1940, p. 551, quotes from *The Gospel
of the Kingdom:* "If, as also seems probable, the Marcan pericope is
based upon, or at least echoes, a section in Q, then perhaps the later
evangelists were really justified in both these assumptions, viz., . . ."
and comments: "Providing we admit several 'ifs,' 'editors,' 'later hands,'
'as is probable,' plus 'glosses,' and 'copyists making errors,' with a few
hasty generalizations thrown in, we can arrive at any conclusion we
want, preserving at the same time an appearance of great critical
acumen." H. M'Intosh: "Professor Schmiedel's article in *Encyclopaedia
Biblica* abounds with his 'may be,' 'might be.' 'possible.' The alleged

which inspires the cautious "if" and "perhaps." But we have to point out that the higher critics are making these hypothetical assertions with a purpose. They are thereby paving the way for later dogmatic assertions. And they are certainly asking for some sort of credence for their suggestions. — Whether they introduce their assertions with an "if" or a "verily," they are asking us to subscribe to their guesses.

This, then, is the situation: we are denounced as obscurantists for believing the *dictum* of God and are invited to accept as true the *dictum* of men. We are asked to discard the oracles of God on the strength of the oracular assertions of men.[133] The result would be that men treat great stories of the Bible as romances and accept the romancings of the critics as true.

So we have this situation: the moderns have been telling us that the facts in the case are against Verbal Inspiration. We ask them to produce these facts. And here they are offering us a lot of assumptions! And they really believe that they breaking down Verbal Inspiration!

A Lot of Sophistries

No. 14. The moderns operate quite a bit with sophistries. We have already noted a number of cases of fallacious reasoning. Some of these, with a few additional ones, are set down here for a more particular examination.

The moderns operate with this argument: Not all parts of Scripture are of equal value; it follows that not all parts of Scripture are inspired or, as they sometimes put it, equally inspired. J. M. Gibson declares that they "who insist on every part of the Bible being equally inspired" fail in their "duty of giving the Gospel its due place of prominence" (*The Inspiration and Authority of Holy Scripture*, p. 101). S. P. Cadman wrote in the *Herald*

---

occasions of utterance *may really have been* confusions of two or more occasions. . . . Some of the words *may not have* proceeded from Jesus directly.' . . . If such hallucinations and ratiocinations were to be tolerated, then, *anything may be,* and verily the world *may* rest on an elephant, the elephant on a tortoise, the tortoise on nothing, as Schmiedel *in vacuum* certainly does. . . ." (*Is Christ Infallible and the Bible True?* p. 408.)

133) L. Gaussen: "Critical science does not keep its place when, instead of being a scientific inquirer, it would be a judge; when, not content with collecting together the oracles of God, it sets about composing them, decomposing them, canonizing them, decanonizing them; and when it gives forth oracles itself!" (*Theopneustia,* p. 324.) We shall not blame M'Intosh for dealing severely with the "writers who denounce every independent man that, after the example and on the authority of Christ and of His inspired apostles, would dare to uphold the Bible claim or to differ from the false but oracular assertions, or to refuse the infallible *ipse dixit,* of those presumptuous speculators who are vain enough to claim for their own crude, ephemeral productions what they deny to the oracles of God." (*Op. cit.,* p. IX.)

Tribune of New York: "Do not regard the books of the Bible as infallible in every particular or of equal value in all their parts." (See *The Presbyterian*, July 12, 1928.)   The Alleman manifesto makes the defenders of Plenary Inspiration say: "All Scripture is on the same level. . . . One word is as important as another." (*Luth. Church Quarterly*, 1940, p. 354.)   The meaning of these declarations is that, if a man believes that all parts of the Bible are inspired, he will have to teach that all parts of the Bible are on the same level of importance. — There is a fallacy in the argument, for the relative value of a statement has no relation to the fact of its inspiration.   The argument is a prize *non sequitur*.   And this is the consequence of the sophistry: Verbal Inspiration is made ridiculous.   Gibson carries the ridicule so far as to pity the poor preacher who "might preach on the Bible for fifty years and never once bring the gospel in," "on the principle of all parts of Scripture being equally inspired" (*loc. cit.*).   Somebody is certainly taking a ridiculous position.[134]

Next: Paul himself said that Inspiration did not keep him from human error; he said: "We have this treasure in earthen vessels."[135] — But St. Paul is not referring to Inspiration here.   When

---

134) M'Intosh: "Nor does the advocacy of inerrancy require or imply holding the equality in value of all parts of Holy Writ, as has so often falsely been averred. . . . In actual fact and in habitual conception they hold them to be equally true and inerrant, but not equally important. . . . The simple-minded earnest Christians regard the Scriptures, and the Church has ever regarded them, as of almost infinitely diversified value, — *just as Creation is, though every part and particle of it is nevertheless the product of God.*"   And now pay attention to the further remark: "Yes, it is because they hold it to be all inspired of God, and therefore all inerrant, that they hold all to be of real though not of equal value; which the others do not and cannot." (*Op. cit.*, pp. 463 f.)

135) J. M. Gibson: "The defenders of the authoritative inspiration of the Scriptures have postulated as a necessity of the case the emancipation of all the writers of Scripture from the effects of human weakness and limitation."   But "the treasure is in earthen vessels. . . . We cannot claim perfection for any of the organs or vehicles of inspiration." (*Op. cit.*, pp. 32, 144.)   G. L. Raymond: "'We have this treasure,' says Paul in 2 Cor. 4:7, 'in earthen vessels.' . . . Now, if all other earthen vessels — crystals, flowers, and animals — leave some of their material influence upon the evident divine plan to shape them in accordance with a divine law, why should not the human mind also leave some of its more powerful mental influence upon the truth which the mind receives, transmits, and, to a certain extent, interprets?" (*The Psychology of Inspiration*, p. 154.)   The following statement shows that the moderns make use of St. Paul's words to support not only the thesis that the Bible contains mistakes but also their thesis that the imperfections and mistakes in Scripture enhance the value of Scripture (Assertion 7).   W. Sanday: "We do not think it likely that God would allow the revelation of Himself to be mixed up with such imperfect materials. But we are no good judges of what God would or would not do. *His ways are not our ways.* Out of the imperfect He brings forth the perfect. It is so in the world of nature, and it is so in the world of grace. *We have our treasure in earthen vessels.* The vessels may be earthen, but the treasure which

Paul speaks of inspired words, he tells us that they are supplied by the Holy Spirit, not by man's wisdom; they are unaffected by human frailty; they are words absolutely true. Here he is praising God for carrying on the work of the ministry of grace through weak vessels, frail men.[136] It is contemptible sophistry to make out of a true statement of Paul a statement which he would denounce as false. The pettifogger employs such tactics. He tries to make the witness say that black is white.

Note the sophistry contained in the following statement: "I am not overlooking the passages of Scripture quoted by Calvinistic theologians in suppport of their doctrine of Scriptural infallibility. . . . The point here that is relevant to our thought is that even such supernatural guidance would not render these written reports any more certain than human language can be. . . . Of the earth, earthy, its words carried by men to facilitate their understanding, description, and cooperative control of earthly things, human language simply cannot be a literal vehicle for conveying God's infallible will and wisdom to men. . . . We have found that, if God should supernaturally reveal Himself and His teaching to men, this revelation could not be absolute or infallible to any finite man. (R. W. Nelson, in *Christendom*, IV, p. 400 ff.)[137] The sophistry consists in the subtle mixing up of the terms "absolute," perfect, and "infallible," "true." True enough, the infinite cannot be compressed into, and expressed by, the finite. Human language cannot express the *full* meaning of divine things. But only the unwary reader will be led by Professor Nelson to conclude therefrom that God is unable to give us, by means of the human language, a *true* knowledge of divine things. In the words of Dr. Pieper: "We have not, indeed, a full, complete, perfect knowledge of God, but we do have a *correct* knowledge, such as befits the weakness of the earthly life. . . . The 'absolute knowledge of God' belongs to the *sine mente soni* [sounds

---

they contain is divine. . . . If the Bible had been so [more perfect than it is], it could never have been in such close contact with human nature. Its message could never have come home to us so fresh and warm as it does. As it is, it speaks to the heart, and it does so because, according to a fine saying in the Talmud, *it speaks in the tongue of the children of men.* . . . The body, the outward form, may be of the earth, earthy, but the spirit by which it is pervaded and animated is from heaven." (*The Oracles of God*, p. 29.) — Italics in the original.

136) See Kretzmann's and Lenski's commentaries. Luther: "Our hands and tongues are indeed perishable and mortal things, but through these means, through these perishable and earthen vessels, the Son of God wants to exhibit power." (VI: p. 144.)

137) G. L. Raymond has a similar statement: "The exact fact seems to be that the spiritual, which is infinite in its nature, necessarily becomes finite when limited, or — what is the same thing — made definite by being expressed — and too often *suppressed* — in terms applicable only to material conditions." (*Op. cit.*, p. 308.)

without sense] with which the vocabulary of certain philosophers and philosophizing theologians abounds." (*Chr. Dog.*, II, p. 40.) When God gave man his language, He took care to supply it with all the terms needed to express so much of the divine wisdom as we need to know at present, to know with absolute certainty. Gibson's quips about the heavenly language, the "perfect language" in which a "perfect revelation" would have to be written, and the "miraculously reconstructed humanity" called for by this "unknown language" (see footnote 108 on page 137 f.) reveal his ignorance of the distinction between *full* knowledge and *correct* knowledge. Note also the equivocation in his use of the term "whole truth." The Bible does not reveal the whole truth; we know only "in part"; and there are divine mysteries which we shall never fathom. On the other hand, the Bible *does* reveal the whole truth, all and everything we need to know for our salvation.

It should also be pointed out that, in elaborating his statement that "such supernatural guidance would not render these written reports any more certain than human language can be," Professor Nelson confines himself to the discussion of whether spiritual things can be revealed in human language. But "the Calvinistic [Lutheran, Biblical] doctrine of Scriptural infallibility" covers not only what Scripture says concerning God's will and wisdom, concerning divine things, but also what Scripture says concerning earthly things, scientific, historical matters and the like. Many, perhaps most, of the attacks against the inerrancy of Scripture are directed against the latter class of statements. And now Professor Nelson makes the *general* statement that inspiration would not render *these written reports* any more certain than human language can be. The statement is too sweeping. Whether anything certain can be said about divine things we have just discussed. But will any one question, will Professor Nelson question, whether human language is capable of expressing earthly things in exact language? Whatever the limitations of human language are, the holy writers, the Holy Ghost, found very exact words to set forth the fact that Jesus was born while Cyrenius was governor of Syria. Here is the statement that heaven and earth were created in six days. Human language has no words, indeed, to *define* "created," but it has the facilities to express the fact that in six days God created heaven and earth in exact terms. The ax-head did not sink. Any doubt in the mind of any linguist about the meaning of these words? No human words can explain the miracle, but the inspired language on this point is not subject to the least doubt. The least that Professor Nelson could do was to say in a footnote: "My statement is too sweeping. I should have said that on many points in dispute between the inerrantists and the errorists the written records speak a language which is certain and exact."

The sophistry hidden — clumsily hidden — in the assertion that Luke's statement concerning his careful historical investigations proves that he did not claim inspiration for his writing has received sufficient attention. See Assertion No. 2, c. The same with regard to the distinction made between "factual truth" and "religious truth" (parables, etc.). See Assertion 2, d and Assertion 4, b. But our task is not yet finished. Other sophistries need attention. And because these are put forth with particularly loud clamor and receive great popular acclaim, we shall discuss them in separate sections.

No. 15. The statement that the Bible is out of harmony with science finds wide acceptance. It is bandied about as an axiomatic truth.[188]. But it is not a true statement. It is a sophistry, and men accept it so readily only because they fail to see the equivocation with which it operates. (1) The term "science" is used as equivalent to the term "scientists." What the scientists say, or rather, to use precise language, what some scientists say, is labeled as the findings of science. And many are enmeshed by the sophistry. They know that science does not lie. What is established as a fact — and the sole business of science is to establish facts — must remain a fact. The Bible cannot deny facts, cannot be out of harmony with science. And now certain "findings" of renowned scientists which the Bible does deny are presented to them as the findings of science, and thoroughly bewildered, they conclude that the Bible is out of harmony with science and cannot be the inerrant Word of God. Scripture is broken down!

What they should say to the moderns is this: "We must wait for science to have reached a settled conclusion before any legitimate argument or any well-grounded objection to the Bible can be fairly deduced from it. How opposite to this and how inconsistent with candor and common sense the course usually pursued by opponents of revelation, we need scarcely pause to describe. As soon as any idea has been started by some scientific man which seems to conflict with the received view of Christians, — an idea thrown out, perhaps, as a mere conjecture, or a theory, novel, peculiar to himself, and as yet untested, — some are ready to exclaim, and to trumpet it in all the newspapers: 'Ah, Moses was mistaken! The Bible is in error! The learned Professor So-and-so

---

138) H. L. Willett: "Nor were the writers of the Bible safeguarded supernaturally or in any other manner from the usual historical and scientific errors to which men of their age were liable." (*The Bible through the Centuries*, p. 284.) A. J. Traver: "Does not modern science contradict the Scriptures?" (*The Lutheran*, Feb. 22, 1939.) Clarence Darrow, at a forum conducted in St. Louis, May, 1931: "The various parts of the Bible were written by human beings who had no knowledge of science, little knowledge of life, and were influenced by the barbarous morality of primitive times."

has just discovered it. There can be no mistake about it *this* time. Science never lies!' True, science never lies. And so, figures never lie; but they often deceive, they are often misinterpreted and misapplied. Our inference, our understanding, our observation of the facts, or our induction from the facts may have been fallacious." (B. Manly, *The Bible Doctrine of Inspiration*, p. 239.) The Bible does not contradict a single established fact of science. The statement that the Bible is out of harmony with science should read: The Bible is out of harmony with pseudoscience. What Solomon says about the ants is declared to be false by a certain number of scientists, not by science.

2) While some cite certain spurious facts against the Bible, others operate with spurious findings deduced from facts, alleged or real facts. In the statement "The Bible is out of harmony with science" the term "science" is sometimes used as an equivalent with speculative science; "inductive science." But that is an equivocation. Science deals only with the truth; the conclusions of "inductive science" are in many cases false. They are the result not of observation but of reasoning, and the reasoning of the scientific philosopher is often at fault. Since the Fall the reasoning power of man is greatly impaired.[139] And we are certainly not going to accept some of the deductions and all of the speculations of fallible scientists as absolute truth. But these speculations are being labeled as "science," and playing upon the respect we have for science, the sophists hope that we will buy their goods as having real scientific value. Surely we know that what real science teaches is true and cannot be in conflict with the Bible.[140] But science *in concreto*, that including the theories and guesses of the scientists, cannot claim the dignity and authority of true science. We will not be duped by the identification of these two terms attempted by the moderns.

We tell them, in the words of Dr. S. G. Craig: "It is one thing to say that the Scriptures contain statements out of harmony with the teachings of modern science and philosophy and a distinctly different thing to say that they contain proved errors. Strictly speaking there is no modern science and philosophy, but only modern scientists and philosophers — who differ endlessly among

---

139) "Freilich, liebe Freunde, wenn die Vernunft noch waere, wie sie Gott den Menschen anerschaffen hat, dann waere sie ein Licht, das uns leuchten koennte." (*Proc., Western Dist.*, 1865, p. 56.)

140) Dr. Walther: "*We know for certain that there is no contradiction and that there can be no contradiction between Christian theology and TRUE science, science in abstracto.*" Walther adds, of course, that "nevertheless we do not by any means regard it as the task of the theologian, nor as possible at any time, to bring our Biblical theology into harmony with science as it exists *in concreto*" (*Lehre und Wehre*, 1875, p. 41. See Pieper, *op. cit.*, I, p. 191).

themselves. It is only on the assumption that the discordant voices of present-day scientists and philosophers are to be identified with the voice of science and philosophy that we are warranted in saying that the Bible contains errors because its teachings do not always agree with the teachings of these scientists and philosophers. Does any one really believe that science and philosophy have already reached, even approximately, their final form?" (See L. Boettner, *The Inspiration of the Scriptures*, p. 62.) When they reach their final form, — in heaven, — they will agree with the Bible.

3) The statement that Scripture is out of harmony with science is applied to a special case when the moderns declare that the advanced scientific knowledge of our age has rendered the belief in miracles ridiculous. We have examined the statement that "science does not recognize miracles" under Assertion No. 8 and found that it operates with the fallacy of the μετάβασις. We are now pointing out that it operates with the fallacy of equivocation. Recall R. Seeberg's statement "In those days it was easy to believe in miracles. Every one feels at once how far we have advanced beyond the *naive* views of the men of antiquity. . . . The Biblical writers did not possess the exact knowledge of the cosmic laws which we have." Hear H. E. Fosdick seconding him: "An ax-head might usually sink in water, but there was no reason why God should not make it float if He wished to do an extraordinary thing. It was surprising when He did it, but it presented no intellectual problem whatever. No laws were broken, because no laws were known. No Hebrew had ever dreamed of such a thing as a mathematical formula of specific gravity in accordance with which an ax-head in water ought invariably to sink." (*Op. cit.*, p. 137.) Right, says A. Harnack in his *Wesen des Christentums*: "Als Durchbrechung des Naturzusammenhangs kann es keine Wunder geben." (See *Lehre und Wehre*, 1902, p. 31.) Others ridicule, on the same grounds, the belief that God rules sickness and health and at times directly intervenes for the good of His people. A. G. Baldwin: "The attributing of the various plagues to the direct intervention of a God offers difficulty to any one whose knowledge of modern science gives him a different concept of cause and effect. But we must remember that these stories were not written in a scientific era." (*The Drama of Our Religion*, p. 49.) J. S. Whale: "The view that God antecedently wills the lightning stroke, shipwreck, cancer, cannot save itself, especially in a scientific age. It is a matter of common observation that 'Streams will not curb their pride The just man not to entomb, Nor lightning go aside To give his virtues room; Nor is that wind less rough That blows a good man's barge.'" (*The Christian Answer to the Problem of Evil*, p. 33.) Now, when these men claim that science discredits the miracles of the Bible and the miraculous

interventions of God, they are making the same equivocal use of terms as we noted under (1) and (2). It is a *spurious* philosophy, a spurious science, which they call in as witness for their side. And their witness cannot qualify as an expert.

Besides, the statement under consideration operates, like all sophistries, with a truth which becomes a half-truth and with fallacious deductions. It is true that science has made great advances. But it has not advanced quite so far as Seeberg's argument calls for. J. A. Thomson told us that we know "only a few of the real laws of nature." Dr. A. Lorenz informed us that the farther the medical scientist advances in his studies, the more he "realizes how little he knows." Our medical men confess that they do not know exactly how the plague originates and how it spreads and ends. A thousand questions of sickness and health have them baffled. So Seeberg and Whale are operating with half-truths.

And it is less than a half-truth when Fosdick declares that the action of the ax-head and the other miracles "presented *no intellectual problem whatever*" to Elisha and the other prophets. The prophets and the apostles were not quite so "dumb."

But we will grant that the Biblical writers knew less than we do with regard to such things as the mathematical formula of specific gravity. (Be careful, however, even here; you know little on the question of how much less they knew.) What does that prove for Seeberg's and Fosdick's contentions? Nothing. All the advances that science has made and will make have no bearing on the question of miracles and any other direct intervention of God. What you know about the cosmic laws — even if you had a full knowledge of all the cosmic laws — does not give you the right to ask for the floor when this question is debated. The miracle is not a problem of science. — By the way: if the prophets' belief in miracles had been due to their lack of scientific knowledge, how will you account for the fact that leading men of science today find it possible to believe in the direct intervention of God? — Do not appeal to science in order to make the prophets ridiculous! You are making yourself ridiculous by committing the fallacy of citing the cosmic laws against the miracles. In a court-room you would be stopped by the objection: "Irrelevant!"

The second fallacy is committed when they use the "cause and effect" argument. To be sure, every effect has a cause, but every effect does not have a *natural* cause. The fact that the rising streams in Whale's poem usually entomb the careless traveler — that is a law of nature — does not prove that supernatural causes cannot nullify the natural effect of the torrent. The argument used by Whale and the others is called the fallacy of accident.

4) Practical application. We shall not revise the Bible for the

purpose of harmonizing it with "science." We are asked to do that. Charles Gore says "it is disastrous to set religion in antagonism to science or to seek to shackle science, which is bound to be free." (*The Doctrine of the Infallible Book*, p. 8.) But that does not appeal to us. It would not be scientific. For the assertion that Scripture is not in harmony with science rests, as we have seen, on an equivocation. There is no room in true science for equivocations, untruths. And it would not be the Christian procedure. We heard Dr. Pieper say that it is unworthy of a Christian to let human opinions correct the Word of God (*op. cit.*, I, p. 577). It is, therefore, as we heard Dr. Walther say, not the task of the theologian to bring theology into harmony with science, as it exists *in concreto*. That would be disastrous. Those who make the practical application of the false theorem under consideration and attempt to harmonize Scripture with science by deleting what some scientists do not like suffer a terrible loss. "Modern theology, fearful for the future of the Church, has made an appeasement with science. It has agreed to retain and maintain only so much of Scripture and the Christian doctrine as will pass the test of 'science.' . . . The result is that modern theology has lost the divine truth. It has renounced Holy Scripture as the infallible truth and the sole authority and corrupted all the chief articles of the Christian doctrine, taking the very heart out of them." (*Proceedings, Delegate Synod*, 1899, p. 34.) If you think that the Bible-theologian Pieper is here using immoderate language, hear Georgia Harkness: "Then liberal theology came to terms with science, purging religious thought of much error" (a liberal is speaking), "but moving so far in the direction of capitulation to the scientific method that it almost lost its soul." (*The Faith by which the Church Lives*, p. 142.)

No. 16. The quibble: "The Bible is not a text-book of science" is used to buttress the contention that the Bible does not claim exactness and infallibility for everything it states, that inspiration covers only spiritual matters and does not extend to scientific matters. Dr. A. J. Traver: "The Bible is true in all matters that pertain to religion. It is not a text for biology or for chemistry. It knows nothing of electricity or of airplanes. There is no reason that it should. These are matters for the investigation and discovery of the human mind." "It is not necessary that men should know how to fly in order to be saved from their sins. Bible-writers wrote with the background of their age and its scientific beliefs. *The one thing that they were called to do was to reveal God to men.*" "Inspiration includes only the knowledge essential for knowing God and His plan for man. It would seem absurd to turn to the Bible for knowledge of electricity or biology or chemistry or any of the sciences. In this field of human knowledge, men can discover truth by searching after it." (*The Lutheran,* Jan. 23, 1936; Feb. 22, 1939; May 10, 1939.)[141]

The moderns make much of this argument. They never fail to use it. You can hardly find a modern treatise on the inspiration and fallibility of Scripture in which the author does not, sooner or later, produce the clinching argument "The Bible is not a text-book of science." Here the conservatives use the same language as the liberals. "Nor were the writers of the Bible safeguarded supernaturally or in any other manner from the usual historical and scientific errors to which men of their age were liable. Their work is not a text-book on either of these subjects. . . . They referred to the facts of nature as they were known in their day. But the themes with which they were concerned were not in these areas." A liberal wrote that, H. L. Willett. (*Op. cit.,* p. 284.) But J. Stump might have written it. He did write the equivalent. H. E. Jacobs might have written it. "According to H. E. Jacobs," says Stump, "'the Holy Scriptures are the infallible and inerrant record of God's revelation of His saving grace to men.' The holy writers were not inspired, however, to be 'teachers of astronomy or geology or physics.'" (See *Lehre und Wehre,* 1904, p. 86.) — They present the argument in various forms. . For instance: "Nobody in his senses ever went *to Jesus* for the latest news in physics or astronomy," says H. E. Fosdick (*Op. cit.,* p. 269), and Prof. J. O. Evjen: "Christ came not to teach science. . . . The Bible is not an authority on geology, surgery, agriculture, law" (*What Is Lutheranism?* P. 24), and Prof. F. Baumgaertel: "Christ never claimed that His knowledge of scientific matters was infallible, and science has a perfect right, in judging historical questions and matters connected with the origin of the Old Testament, to disregard the judgment of Jesus" (see W. Moeller, *Um die Inspiration der Bibel,* p. 50). — They set up the acceptance of this axiom with its implication .as

---

141) Similar statements. J. Stump (U. L. C.): "It must be borne in mind that the Bible is a religious book, and not a text-book on science. The holy writers were inspired with a supernatural knowledge of God and of His will; and on these subjects their words are final and infallible. On scientific matters they neither knew, nor professed to know, more than other men of their day." (*Op. cit.,* p. 319.) R. F. Grau (Lutheran, Koenigsberg): "If the morality of the Old Testament is imperfect, how can we attribute perfection to things which have much less relation to the kingdom of God, such as its cosmological, astronomical, chronological ideas? These things must rather be judged by the canon which Jesus set up in the words: 'Man, who made me a judge or a divider over you?' (Luke 12:14.) Jesus would ask you, and I ask you: Who has given you the right to look for cosmology, astronomy, etc., in the Bible, which is the book of salvation, of faith? Here the rule applies: Render unto science and cultured progress the things which belong to science, and to God and faith the things that belong to faith." (See *Lehre und Wehre,* 1893, p. 327.)

the mark of genuine Lutheranism. C. A. Wendell: "Lutheranism means three things: . . . (2) Faith in the Holy Scripture, not as a fetish, on the one hand, nor a mere human document, on the other, nor as an arsenal of theological polemics nor as a text-book of history and natural science, but as the inspired Word of God, whose purpose it is to make us wise unto salvation." (*What Is Lutheranism?*, P. 242.) A. R. Wentz: "Neither will the Lutheran theologian regard the Bible as a text-book on any subject except the special revelation of God in Jesus Christ. . . . The spirit of essential Lutheranism does not rime with the literalism of the Fundamentalist, which makes the Bible a book of oracles, a text-book with explicit marching orders for the 'warfare between science and religion.'" (*What Is Lutheranism?* P. 91.) W. Elert: "Die orthodoxe Dogmatik nahm die Schrift trotz ihres Inspirationsdogmas — oder auch dadurch verfuehrt — als Lehrbuch ueber alle darin vorkommenden heterogenen Inhalte. . . . Immerhin war hier aus der Bibel, die Luther als Gesetz und Evangelium las, ein naturwissenschaftlicher Kanon geworden." (*Morphologie des Luthertums,* I, pp. 51, 377.) — They cannot get along without it. They need it for their own peace of mind. Having established to their own satisfaction that the Bible is not reliable in its scientific statements, they quiet their apprehensions as to the general reliability of the Bible by taking refuge in their dogma: The Bible does not claim plenary inspiration and full inerrancy. Examine Dr. Stump's statement "The holy writers were not inspired to be 'teachers of astronomy or geology or physics (Jacobs), *and no number of contradictions in this sphere would 'shake our confidence in the absolute authority of Holy Scripture as an inerrant guide in all matters of faith and practice* (Jacobs). " They think, too, that they need it in order to save the reputation of the Bible and keep men from skepticism. The article "Is the Bible a Text-Book on Science?" in *The Presbyterian* of July 19, 1928, speaks of "the oft-asserted apology so timidly spoken in the hope of saving the Bible from the ruthless destruction wrought by the critics and the scientists, an apology which runs thus: 'We do not accept the Bible as a text-book on science, but we do accept it as a guide to religion and life.' When in the presence of higher critics, these same religionists admit: 'We do not accept the Bible as a text-book on history, but we do accept it as a guide to religion and life.'" That describes the situation correctly. Hear, for instance, J. M. Gibson. Speaking of "the theory that Scripture was given to acquaint people with astronomy, geology, history, and everything else under the sun, and above it, too," he warns us that that "raises a host of difficulties which no ingenuity can completely remove and men like Tyndall and Huxley are forced into skepticism. . . . Make the demand that it must be a scientific revelation, and you put innumerable weapons into the hand of the enemy" (*op. cit.*, pp. 91, 169 ff.). — Indeed, they make much of this axiom of theirs. W. Sanday sums up for the moderns: "The Biblical writers were not perfectly acquainted with the facts of science: is it certain that they would be more perfectly acquainted with the facts of history?" But be of good cheer: "It is coming to be agreed among thinking men that the Bible was never meant to teach science and that the Biblical writers simply shared the scientific beliefs of their own day." (*Op. cit.*, pp. 25, 27.)

But all of this is sophistry. The reasoning is fallacious. The fact that Scripture is not a text-book of science has no bearing on the question whether its scientific statements are true. We are not now considering the fact that Scripture claims infallibility for all of its statements. We are examining the statement of the moderns that, since Scripture does not present itself as a text-book of science, it cannot be permitted to claim accuracy for its scientific statements. And we shall say that that statement is devoid of logic and common sense. No man in his senses will say that the historical data presented by a reputable historian are, of course, reliable (so far as a human writer can claim reliability) but that, when he trenches upon the domain of natural science, he is under suspicion, for he is merely a historian. When a statesman writes a paper on the international situation, will you say that, however right he may be on political questions, his historical references are *eo ipso* less reliable than those of a historian? Dare you presume that, however careful he is in his political statements, he permits himself to become careless in stating historical facts? Moreover — and this is addressed to the conservatives among the moderns — how are you going to prove your thesis that, because the purpose of Scripture is to make us wise unto salvation, not to give us a course in astronomy, etc., the Holy Ghost was careful about matters of doctrine but on scientific matters left the prophets to their own devices and permitted all sorts of inaccuracies and errors to mess up His Holy Scriptures? You must prove — not merely assert — that such a mode of procedure was naturally to be expected of the Holy Ghost. We say it is unreasonable to expect that. Dr. Pieper: "It is a foolish objection against the inspiration of Holy Scripture when modern theologians state that the Bible is no text-book of history or geography or natural science and that for this reason it is self-evident that inspiration could not pertain to the historical, geographical, and natural-history statements. . . . It is indeed 'no text-book of the natural sciences.' Its true purpose is rather to teach the way to heaven by faith in Christ, 2 Tim. 3:15; John 17:20; 20:31; Eph. 2:20-22. But where it does, even though only in passing, teach matters of natural history, its statements are incontrovertibly true according to John 10:35." (*Op. cit.*, pp. 265, 384, 577.)[142] And there is no reason in the world why John 10:35 should not apply to *all* of Scripture. There is no known law of reason that compels us to say that, because the Bible is not an astronomical treatise, its astronomical statements are subject to doubt. Dr. Stoeckhardt's judgment on Grau's argument is: "Was ist das fuer ein Wirrwarr! Und was ist das fuer eine Logik!"

Notice the sinister sophistry. Through an ambiguous use of terms the statement "The Bible is not a scientific treatise" is made to mean, "Its statements are not scientifically correct," and the mind of the simple is confused. The thought is suggested: A text-book of science uses exact language; does it not? The Bible is not such a text-book, is it? Therefore you need not look for exactness in the Bible on some subjects — and Plenary Inspiration must be given up. Verbal Inspiration, and with it Scripture has broken down!

Examine, too, the argument that "in this field of human knowledge, men can discover truth by searching after it," or, as N. R. Best puts it: "When, pray tell us, did God ever make to man a gratuitous present of information which man could by any pains search out for himself?" (*Op. cit.*, p. 82.) That is beside the question. What is there, pray tell us, to hinder God from putting, through inspiration, His divine authority behind the scientific statements in question? The holy writers may have known some of these things (not all of them, by any means) through observation. But it pleased God to guarantee the truth of it to us.

Again, the employment of caricature always betrays a sophistical intent. When Gibson speaks of the "theory that Scripture was to acquaint people with astronomy, geology, history, and *everything*

---

142) Dr. L. S. Keyser: "Sometimes you hear men say that the Bible was not written to teach science. That is true when properly qualified, but it is not sweepingly true. The Bible was not meant to teach science as a scientific text-book, but even the lay mind can see that, wherever the Bible makes statements that belong to the scientific realm, its statements ought to be correct, to agree with what is known to be true in scientific research." (In the *Luth. Church Review*, quoted in *Lehre und Wehre*, 1905, p. 140.) Dr. M. Reu: "Scripture is no text-book on history or archeology or astronomy or psychology. But *does from this follow* that it must be subject to error when it occasionally speaks of matters pertaining to that field of knowledge?" (*In the Interest of Lutheran Unity*, p. 70.) We call special attention to the following paragraph from D. J. Burrell's *Why I Believe the Bible* (p. 52) because it points out the fatal consequences of the contention under discussion. "It is a common thing to hear it said: 'The Bible was not intended to be a scientific book,' giving the impression that it makes little difference, therefore, whether its scientific affirmations are correct or not. This, however, is not a matter of small moment. If the book is not veracious in this particular, what ground have we for committing ourselves to its spiritual guidances? . . . The question is not whether the Bible was intended to be a scientific book or not, but whether the Bible is true. It is not true unless it is true and reliable every way."

else under the sun, and above it, too," and Best asks: "Can three
pages of duodecimo print (this Genesis prolog) be a compendium
of universal origins?" (*Loc. cit.*), and Prof. W. H. Dunphy states
that "the worshiper of the letter insists on treating them as an
encyclopedia of universal information" (*The Living Church,* Feb. 18,
1933), they misrepresent our position. The Bible does make some
scientific statements but does not claim — nor do we claim for it —
that it gives universal information. These men are befogging the
issue.

They argue, furthermore, from unproved premises. They
assume that the Bible is concerned only with religious truths, not
with scientific truths. While they are trying to prove this assumption (against the explicit declaration of Scripture that *all* Scripture
is inspired and true), we shall go a step further and tell them that
what Scripture says on historical, scientific matters, and the like,
subserves its religious teaching.[143]

And finally, back of it all is the *assumption* of scientific errors
in the Bible. The entire discussion runs around a mistaken notion.
All the energy expended in trying to show why the Bible is little
concerned about the exactness of its scientific teaching is wasted
effort. As long as the premise is not proved, they are engaged in
idle discussions.

If anything more should be said on this subject, we'll say this:
No, the Bible is no text-book of science; it is something infinitely
better than any text-book of science. All of its scientific statements
are reliable. Scientific text-books have to be rewritten every few
years. But not a single paragraph of the Bible needs to be revised.
If any statement in the text-books is confirmed by the Bible, then
you can absolutely rely on it. Again: the Bible supplements these
text-books most helpfully. *Science for the Elementary-School
Teacher* brought up the question about the origin of human intelligence and speech, but was unable to give the teacher the

---

143) Dr. Stoeckhardt: "These seemingly extraneous matters are
throughout put by Scripture into relation with faith, are matters that
belong to God and faith. . . . Does not the account of Gen. 1 touch the
specific Christian faith? Do the Gentiles and the Turks confess together
with us Christians the first article of the Christian faith?" (*Loc. cit.,*
pp. 327, 332.)   J. A. Cottam: "In the first chapter of Genesis the Bible
speaks with authority, clearly, and finally on a matter of biology . . . as
a matter of the greatest religious importance" (*Know the Truth,* p. 69).
J. G. Machen: "People say that the Bible is a book of religion and not
a book of science, and that, where it deals with scientific matters, it is
not to be trusted. . . . I should like to ask you one question. What do
you think of the Bible when it tells you that the body of the Lord Jesus
Christ came out of the tomb on the first Easter morning nineteen hundred
years ago? . . . Account would have to be taken of it in any ideally
complete scientific description of the physical universe. . . . Is that one
of those scientific matters to which the inspiration of the Bible does not
extend? . . ." (*The Christian Faith in the Modern World,* p. 54 f.)

needed information. The Bible gives it. J. Stump is wrong when he says that the holy writers did not know more on scientific matters than other men of their day. On some things they knew, by revelation, much more. On the origin of this world Moses knew more than the men of his day and many men of our day. — And here they are filling the world with the cry: The Bible is not a text-book of science! [144)]

The Trump Card

No. 17. The variant-readings sophistry. The contention is that we have no reliable Bible text and that, consequently, Verbal Inspiration must go by the board. Theodore Kaftan: "The number of the variant readings is legion; there is no fixed text; it must give the verbal-inspirationist quite a jolt when he realizes that no one, not even he himself, is able to say which text is the one that is verbally inspired." (See Pieper, *op. cit.*, p. 287.) N. R. Best: "On the hypothesis here outlined the revelation of God perished from the earth ages ago — being destroyed by the incompetence of those who transcribed it from one manuscript to another and rendered it out of its original languages into the tongues of the nations. The logic of this is that we today have no Bible at all to which any divine authority can be attributed." (*Op. cit.*, p. 78.) J. Aberly: "If it was necessary to eliminate all such errors from the original records, would it not seem to be just as necessary to guard against their creeping in through their transmission? . . . 'God in His wisdom may have given to His people in early ages an absolutely inerrant book, but that His providence has failed to preserve.'" (*The Luth. Church Quarterly*, 1935, p. 125.) Lyman Abbott presents the case thus, and it could not be better presented: "An infallible book is a book which without any error whatever conveys truth from one mind to another mind. In order that the Bible should be infallible, the original writers must have been infallibly informed as to the truth; they must have been able to express it infallibly; they must have had a language which was an infallible vehicle for the communication of their thoughts; after their death their manuscripts must have been infallibly preserved and infallibly copied; when translation became necessary, the translators must have been able to give an infallible translation; and, finally, the men who receive the book must be able infallibly to apprehend what was thus in-

---

144) Luther: The only book in which no historical [or scientific] errors *can* occur is the Bible. See XIV:491. — Dr. A. Graebner: "The Bible is not a text-book of zoology or biology or astronomy, claiming for itself the authority secured by the most careful and extended human investigation, observation, and speculation. Its claims are infinitely higher. The authority of human scientists is never more than human; that of the Scriptures is everywhere divine. The omniscient Creator knows more about His handiwork than any created mind. Etc." (*Theological Quarterly*, VI, p. 41.)

fallibly understood by the writers, infallibly communicated by
them, infallibly preserved, infallibly copied, and infallibly translated. Nothing less than this combination would give us today an
infallible Bible; and no one believes that this infallible combination
exists. Whether the original writers infallibly understood the truth
or not, they had no infallible vehicle of communicating it; their
manuscripts were not infallibly preserved or copied or translated;
and the sectarian differences which exist today afford an absolute
demonstration that we are not infallibly able to understand their
meaning." (*Evolution of Christianity*, p. 36 f. Quoted in Foster,
Modern Movements in American Theology, p. 99 f.)

Now, the appearance of a legion or legions of variant readings
does not jar our belief in Verbal Inspiration in the least. According
to the first form of the present argument the condition of the copies
renders the alleged inspiration of the originals doubtful or even
illusory. It certainly does not. The fact that our copies offer a
multitude of variant readings has no bearing on the Scriptural
thesis that everything written by the holy writers was verbally
inspired and remains verbally inspired. We insist that these two
matters be kept separate. Let it be that the copyists did not do
their transcribing by inspiration; nobody claims that. But the
question before us just now is: Were the originals written by inspiration? And the fallibility of the copyists certainly does not
affect the infallibility of the prophets and the apostles.

No modern will deny this self-evident truth, put in this bald
form. When pressed, the moderns produce the second form of the
argument. We notice, however, that their discussion of the variant
readings has a tendency to get back to the question of *the inspiration of Scripture.* By implication and insinuation doubt is being
cast on the verbal inspiration of the original documents. Charles
Hodge makes the statement "Many of them [the discrepancies] may
fairly be ascribed to *errors of transcribers*" (*Systematic Theology*,
I, p. 169), and the former owner of my copy of the book at once
wrote on the margin: "What in these cases becomes of *verbal inspiration?*" And when Hodge states on the next page that "the
writers were under the guidance of the Spirit of God . . . and the
Sacred Scriptures are so miraculously free from the soiling touch
of human fingers," our annotator points to the "errors of transcribers" and asks: What, then, becomes of verbal inspiration? The
same idea is put into print by Dr. H. C. Alleman: "*At best* the
theory of a mechanical verbal inspiration can apply only to the
original manuscripts of the authors themselves and not to copies,
and surely not to translations. Now, we do not have the original
manuscripts; the Holy Spirit did not preserve them. What we do
have in the original languages are copies, manifestly faulty. Crit-

ical scholars have found ten thousand diversities in the preserved manuscripts of the Old Testament and 150,000 in the New Testament, a total of 160,000 in the Bible. So the theory of a mechanical verbal inspiration simply falls to pieces." (*The Luth. Church Quarterly*, 1936, p. 247.) Note the *"at best,"* italicized by us, and note that "the theory of a mechanical verbal inspiration" which has "fallen to pieces" is the teaching that the originals were written by verbal inspiration. Note also the "if" in Dr. Aberly's statement: *"If* it was necessary to eliminate such errors from the original records. . . ." Dr. J. A. Singmaster writes: "Another startling fact contradicts the dictation theory, and that is the numerous various readings in the several manuscripts. While these do not vitiate the Scriptures in the least, they do show that God did not seem to require that every word must be miraculously preserved as originally written." (*Handbook of Christian Theology*, p. 67.) What is the "dictation theory"? The teaching that the words written *by the apostles and the prophets* were verbally inspired; and, says Dr. Singmaster, the various readings in the copies prove that this teaching cannot stand. Dr. J. A. W. Haas uses pretty plain language. "The early position of Protestant doctrine put an infallible Bible over against an infallible organization. *It is supposed"* (our italics) "that the original manuscripts of the books of the Bible were without error in every detail. No one ever saw or can prove such an infallible set of books, but their existence is made an article of faith. Actually Christians have always had a Bible that contains many variant readings." (*What Ought I to Believe*, p. 28 f.)[145] The subtle suggestion is that somehow or other the legions of variant readings must cause doubts as to the verbal inspiration of the originals. So let us settle this point once for all. The fact that a copyist misspelled a certain word or substituted a different word does not make the original word uninspired. The fact — and this is an apt analogy — that human nature is now corrupt does not alter the fact that man was created perfectly holy. You know this; you concede it when pressed for a definite statement. And we shall hold you to your concession. You have lost

---

145) The same idea was expressed and applied not only to Verbal Inspiration but also faith in Christ, by Prof. E. W. E. Reuss of Strasbourg, who, when a student had handed in an essay in which he maintained his faith in the plenary and literal inspiration of Scripture, told him: "My dear friend, the arguments of science do not affect you because the subject in question is in your eyes a matter of faith. Well, allow me to say to you in the name of the faith you propose to defend that the ground on which you have taken your stand is an extremely dangerous one. To identify faith in Christ with the historical belief that is bound up with Biblical documents is to enter on a path which may lead you very far. The least weakening of your theory of the Canon will shake the whole superstructure of your Christianity, and the reaction may be as subtle as it will be radical." (Quoted, with approval, in R. F. Horton, *Revelation and the Bible*, p. VI.)

the right to mix up with your discussion of the faulty copies any
discussion of the originals. All "ifs" and "buts" based on the
copies are ruled out by mutual agreement.

Furthermore, we are not ready to discuss the faulty copies
with any one who does not admit the infallibility of the originals.
When Dr. Abbott presents his list of "infallibilities" to us, we stop
him after the first item: "In order that the Bible should be infallible, the original writers must have been infallibly informed as
to the truth; they must have been able to express it infallibly."
Surely; but do you, Dr. Abbott, believe that they did write by inspiration? When he says No, and when others say: "God *may have
given* to His people in early ages an absolutely inerrant book," we
refuse to continue the discussion. First the question of the verbal
inspiration and infallibility of the Bible must be settled between us.
Unless that is settled, our conversation on the errors of the copyists
and translators and printers can reach no satisfactory conclusion.
It is evident that, when one party accepts the inspiration of the
Bible as an established truth and insists that the errors in the
copies cannot overthrow that fact, while the other party insists on
constructing the doctrine of inspiration from the condition of the
copies, the two parties are talking along different lines, and the
talk will go on interminably. And there are practical considerations behind our insistence on settling, first and before anything
else, the question of the infallibility of the holy writers. Much is
gained, everything is gained, when a man has been convinced, by
Scripture, that all Scripture is given by inspiration of God. Such
a man will stand firm when the shock-troops — the legions of
various readings — are unloosed upon him. And only such a man
is in a position to take up the study of these variants (textual
criticism) profitably. A man who takes a negative attitude towards
the inspiration of Scripture will hail these legions as helpful allies;
he who takes a doubting attitude will quickly surrender to them.

Our first concern is to get men to listen to what Scripture
says on Verbal Inspiration. To that we devote most of our time.
We do not, of course, absolutely refuse to discuss anything else.
If men insist on constructing the doctrine of inspiration from the
condition of the copies, we shall devote some little time to that
angle. We'll do that presently. But all along we shall keep on
stressing the main points, first, that Scripture teaches Verbal Inspiration and, second: the fact that the copies are somewhat
faulty does not prove and does not indicate that the originals
were faulty.[146]

---

146) Dr. A. Hoenecke: "A further objection: Since we certainly do
not possess the original text throughout, verbal inspiration cannot be
predicated of the Bible throughout. Ein wirklich toerichter Einwand!
They must have a poor case if they have to resort to such subterfuges.

The moderns, in general, admit that. As a rule, they put their variant-reading argument in this form: there are legions of variant readings; it follows that we have no fixed, no authentic, no reliable text; and from that it follows that Verbal Inspiration is a dead issue. Dr. A. E. Deitz puts it this way: "Manifestly, we cannot be guided by a book which is no longer available, however perfect and inerrant and infallible it may have been." (*The Luth. Ch. Quarterly*, 1935, p. 130.) Another modern puts it still more bluntly: "We have been dwelling in the traditional text as in an ancient, comfortable house; the spirit of our fathers ruled there and made it comfortable and cozy. Now comes the building inspector, condemns the building, and demands that we move out." The old house is "rotten, rickety, in a tumble-down condition." (See Pieper, *op. cit.*, I, p. 414.)

Let us examine this second form of the argument. We shall find that it is an unwarranted generalization to say that on account of the legions of variant readings our present Bible text is doubtful and unreliable. Note, in the first place, the tendentious overstatement, the sophistical exaggeration in the argument. These legions of variant readings consist, as the textual critics tell us, for the greater part, by far the greater part, in variations in the spelling and the like, which do not in any way affect the sense, things about which no serious man would make a fuss. Such for instance, are "the variations in the spelling of proper names: Ναζαρέτ — Ναζαρέθ. . . . Among other insignificant variations may be mentioned the presence or absence of ν final in verbs: ἔλεγε — ἔλεγεν," and so *ad infinitum*. (A. B. Bruce, *Exp. Gr. Test.*, I, p. 52 f.)[147] This class of variant readings does not jolt us. These legions make

---

They fail to distinguish between the inspiration and the preservation of the inspired Scriptures. . . . Even though we admit that in several passages we do not have the inspired text, that disestablishes the inspiration of the original Scriptures as little as the present corrupt condition of man does away with the creation of the first man in the image of God." (*Ev.-Luth. Dog.*, I, p. 386.) Dr. W. Dau: "If in a copy of the Bible that should fall into the hands of Pastor Montelius one leaf were missing, the *Bible* would not on that account be defective. If in the translation which we have something should have been rendered incorrectly, the *Bible* would not on that account be faulty. If the manuscripts that have been preserved till our time should in some cases be undecipherable, or some mistake of a copyist should be found in it, the *Bible* would not on that account be erroneous." (*Theol. Mthly.*, 1923, p. 75.)

147) "The miracle of inspiration is not perpetuated in those who have copied and translated the Scriptures, though the accepted translation is so entirely free from fundamental error that fairness must conclude that God has wonderfully preserved the purity of the original text in the transmission. Prof. Moses Stuart, one of the ablest scholars of modern times, says: 'Out of some 800,000 various readings of the Bible that have been collected, about 795,000 are of about as much importance as the question in English orthography is whether the word *honor* or *Savior* should be spelled with a *u* or without it." (*Proc., Southeastern Dist.*, 1939, p. 27.)

a great din, but as they come closer, we find them to consist of tin soldiers. What the moderns say of the havoc wrought by these armies is of the same value as some of the war-bulletins being issued by the high commands.

Next, some of these variants do indeed affect the sense. Some — a few. Do not keep up your sophistical practice of exaggerating! There are only a few that affect the sense, as the textual critics tell us. "It is reckoned that of the seven thousand nine hundred and fifty-nine verses of the New Testament there hardly exist ten or twelve in which the corrections that have been introduced by the new readings of Griesbach and Scholz. as the result of their immense researches, have any weight at all. Further, in most instances they consist but in the difference of a single word, and sometimes even of a single letter." (L. Gaussen, *op. cit.*, p. 190. — Examine the exhaustive lists given in that chapter.) Ten or twelve verses — and our war-bulletin writers speak of "legions"! And now mark well: these few variants which do affect the sense in no case affect any Scriptural doctrine. For instance, the variant ὅς or ὅ for θεός in 1 Tim. 3:16 are certainly not equivalents. But reading "who" for "God" in no wise affects the doctrine of the deity of Christ. This doctrine is abundantly established by the host of the other *dicta probantia.* Let 1 John 5:7 be an interpolation; does that fact give the doctrine of the Trinity the least jolt? Some important manuscripts omit the clause ὁ ὤν ἐν τῷ οὐρανῷ in John 3:13. Delete it, and Scripture still teaches that the Son of Man is and was in heaven. "There are instances where, if a certain variant is accepted, the passage no longer proves a certain doctrine. But the remarkable thing is that these instances occur only in cases where this doctrine is firmly established by many other passages." (*Proceedings, Synodical Conf.*, 1886, p. 66.) The fact is that "the wonderful divine providence so held its protecting hand over the Bible text that in spite of the *variae lectiones* not a single Christian doctrine has become doubtful." (Pieper, *op. cit.*, p. 290.)[148] The text

---

148) Prof. Moses Stuart: "Of the remainder some change the sense of particular passages or expressions or omit particular words or phrases; but not one doctrine of religion is changed, not one precept is taken away, not one important fact is altered, by the whole of the various readings collectively taken." (*Loc. cit.*) "Richard Bentley, the ablest and boldest of the earlier classical critics of England, affirmed that even the worst of manuscripts does not pervert or set aside 'one article of faith or moral precept.' . . . And Dr. Ezra Abbot of Harvard, who ranked among the first textual critics and was not hampered by orthodox bias (being a Unitarian), asserted that 'no Christian doctrine or duty rests on those portions of the text which are affected by the differences in the manuscripts; still less is anything *essential* in Christianity touched by the various readings. They do, to be sure, affect the bearing of a few passages on the doctrine of the Trinity; but the truth or falsity of the doctrine by no means depends upon the reading of these passages.' " (B. Manly, *The Bible Doctrine of Inspiration*, p. 224.)

of the Bible is in such a condition that in every instance where we need a plain, direct, clear statement of doctrine or important fact, the text is there — clear and uncorrupted. The bombs which the legions of the variant readings discharged against the certainty of the text are duds. This talk about the dilapidated condition of our Bible home is justly characterized by Dr. Pieper as "frivolous talk, flowing from ignorance."

Note, in the second place, the fallacy in the generalization: The Bible text, as we have it, is not reliable because of the variant readings. There is doubt, to be sure, about the reading of some passages. But we shall never grant that that fact casts doubt on the reliability of the ten thousand passages about which there is no doubt. The textual critics — and they need not be verbal-inspirationists — will not stand for such insinuations of the moderns. They do not speak of *the* Bible text as unreliable. *They* speak of an established, authentic, accepted text. And so shall we. The moderns are unreasonable. Take a reasonable view: God certainly wanted the churches of today to have the same advantage as the first churches, which had the original manuscripts, written by the apostles. God wants all churches of all times to have a certain, sure Word, expressed in a certain, sure text. Now, if the fact that there are variant readings would deprive us of a reliable Bible text, would God have permitted these variants to occur? Is this rationalizing? Well, then listen to Christ's own guarantee that the Church of later days shall have a good text, perfectly good and reliable. John 17:20 guarantees that the word of the apostles will remain in the possession of the Church, the word of the apostles as transmitted to the Church in a reliable text. And when Christ asks His disciples of the later days to continue in His Word (John 8: 31, 32) and to teach all things He commanded (Matt. 28:20), He promises them a good, reliable, absolutely reliable text; else they could not know His Word. And He has kept His promise.[149]

---

149) The Lord took special care of this matter. No, He did not endow the copyists with miraculous infallibility, but we are going to say that it is a miracle before our eyes that the text has been so faithfully preserved. We speak of "the wonderful, miraculous divine providence guarding the text." "We truly stand before a miracle of divine providence." (F. A. Philippi. See Pieper, *op. cit.*, p. 409.) "God has wonderfully preserved the purity of the original text in the transmission." (See above.) "Very wonderfully and very graciously," says J. G. Machen, "has God provided for the preservation, from generation to generation, of His holy Word. . . . You do not have to depend for the assurance of your salvation and the ordering of your Christian lives upon passages where either the original wording or the meaning is doubtful. God has provided very wonderfully for the transmission of the text and for the translation into English." (*The Christian Faith in the Modern World*, p. 43 f.) "The Lord has watched miraculously over His Word," says Gaussen (*op. cit.*, p. 167), who asks us to compare the Bible in this respect with any other book of antiquity ("the comedies

The broad statement that the Church of today must get along with a corrupted, unreliable Bible text does not express the truth. It does not agree with the facts.[150] And it does not proceed from the Christian way of thinking, from Christ's way of thinking. In spite of the variants found in the Old Testament Christ said: "They have Moses and the Prophets" (Luke 16:29); they have a reliable text. And when He appealed to the *text as written*, "we do not read," says Dr. Pieper, "that the devil brought up the matter of 'various readings'" (p. 288). *Summa summarum*, "what the Church lacks in our day is not a reliable te..t of the Bible, but the faith in the sufficiently reliable text" (p. 410. — Be sure to read the two sections in Pieper on this subject, I, pp. 286 ff. and 408 ff.).

No, the few variants — by now we are agreed that the various readings which amount to anything are but few in number — jolt us as little as the obscure passages in the Bible disturb our faith. The Bible contains some *cruces interpretum*, but we have never permitted the Romanists to adduce this fact as a proof for their dogma of the obscurity of Scripture. We cannot be absolutely sure whether the ἐϱευνᾶτε in John 5:39 is the indicative or the imperative. Does that justify any man to deny the clarity of Scripture? And the occurrence of a few variants is not a sane argument against the integrity of *the text* of the Bible. The Protestants among the moderns will not receive a jolt if the Romanist should argue: Since there are some obscure passages in the Bible, the whole Bible is obscure. Then they should not try to jolt us by employing the same line of argument: Since the text in some instances has been corrupted, the Bible text is unreliable.[151]

---

of Terence alone have presented thirty thousand variant readings; and yet these are only six in number, and they have been copied a thousand times less often than the New Testament") and to meditate on the saying of Bengel: "Thou mayest, then, dismiss all those doubts which at one time so horribly tormented myself. If the Holy Scriptures — which have been so often copied and which have passed so often through the faulty hands of ever fallible men — were absolutely without variations, the miracle would be so great that faith in them would no longer be faith. *I am astonished, on the contrary, that the result of all those transcriptions has not been a much greater number of different readings.*" (*Op. cit.*, p. 196.)

150) These are the facts: "The best of the present-day Hebrew and Greek scholars assert that in probably nine hundred and ninety-nine cases out of a thousand we have either positive knowledge or reasonable assurance as to what the original words were; so accurately have the copyists reproduced them, and so faithfully have the translators done their work." (L. Boettner, *The Inspiration of the Scriptures*, p. 19.)

151) Prof. J. P. Koehler: "Es moegen in einzelnen Stellen Unklarheiten entstehen, so dass man die Stellen gerade nicht bestimmt auslegen kann. In den meisten Faellen bezieht sich das auf aeussere sprachliche Dinge, oder es betrifft feine Schattierungen der Gedankenverbindung, auf deren Feststellung wenig ankommt, soweit es die Lehre betrifft. Man wird die Stellen dann zu den sogenannten dunklen Stellen rechnen,

Here is a variation of the second form of the argument: We no longer have the original manuscripts; *they* may have been — or were — inerrant by virtue of Verbal Inspiration; but since we possess only copies, made by fallible men, it is a waste of time to discuss Verbal Inspiration; it has no practical value. — The examination of this argument will take us over the old ground, indeed, but it will do no harm to *emphasize* some of the old points.

We heard Dr. J. A. W. Haas say: "No one ever saw or can prove such an infallible set of books," and heard Dr. A. E. Deitz repeat it: "Manifestly we cannot be guided by a book which is no longer available, however perfect and inerrant and infallible it may have been." Let us hear Dr. E. H. Delk repeat it. Discussing the statement by Dr. W. A. Maier: "I challenge any one within the range of my voice to show that the Bible, as originally inspired by God, contains even a minute mistake," he says: "This is a retreat to an impossible citadel in order to defend an unnecessary point of view of what is essential to Christianity. If we had the Bible 'as originally inspired of God,' this challenge might be of some force." (*The Luth. Church Quarterly*, 1936, p. 426.) This slur about an "impossible citadel" is played up by W. M. Forrest in this wise: "No one can attack a non-existent fortification. The autographs [of the Bible] are nowhere; no man living can prove what was in them, and no man dead has left us any record of what they were like when he read them. . . . All we have is our existing Bible. If it needed to be inerrant, why did God allow it to become errant after having gone to the trouble of getting it all miraculously written out without error? . . ." (*Do Fundamentalists Play Fair?* P. 55 f.) The commissioners of the U. L. C. A. played it up in their report to the

wenigstens in dieser Hinsicht. Aber der Klarheit der Schrift, soweit es sich um die Lehre handelt, tut das deshalb keinen Eintrag, weil die betreffende Lehre entweder schon in solcher Stelle oder sonstwo in der Schrift klar vorliegt. . . . Es kann der urspruengliche Text durch die Abschreiber verdorben sein, dadurch dass sie Woerter absichtlich oder unabsichtlich einschoben. Da entsteht wieder die Frage, ob diese Tatsache uns den *vorliegenden* Bibeltext nicht zweifelhaft mache. . . . Manche Leute meinen, es sei nicht noetig, auf dem Wortlaut zu bestehen, weil er ja doch nicht gewiss ist. Doch das folgt nicht. Das bleibt stehen, Gott hat sein Wort durch den Heiligen Geist eingegeben, so dass kein Tuettel davon hinfallen kann, und wir bestehen darum bei der Auslegung auf dem Wortlaut, wo er feststeht. In andern Faellen aber geben wir uns wiederum nicht mit Wortklauberei ab, sondern lassen solch aeussere Dinge dahingestellt, um so mehr, als die Wahrheit der Lehre doch nicht davon abhaengt. Dass es mit der aeusseren Gestalt der Schrift so steht, das gehoert mit zu ihrer menschlichen Niedrigkeit. die von Gott jedenfalls damit zugleich sozusagen in Kauf genommen wurde, dass er seine Offenbarung in menschliche Rede durch Menschen kleiden liess. Es ist daher eine unverstaendige Ueberschaetzung solcher rein menschlichen Dinge, wenn sich jemand dadurch in seinem Glauben an die Unfehlbarkeit der Schrift in jedem Wort, das geschrieben ist, wankend machen laesst." (*Der Brief Pauli an die Galater*, p. 37 f.)

convention of 1938: "The disagreement [on the doctrine of verbal inspiration] relates, furthermore, to a matter of theological interpretation, which, in addition, applies only to a non-existent original text of the Scriptures." (See *The Lutheran*, Oct. 5, 1938.) And the presidential address at the same convention stated: "The crucial difference developed in recent discussions rests in the matter of the verbal inspiration of an original text of the Scriptures (which, of course, does not exist)."

These flippancies call for a few remarks. (1) "No one ever saw such an infallible set of books." Neither did any one of us see Christ. Does it follow that our knowledge of Christ is faulty? We know as much of the power and love and beauty of Christ as those who saw Him with their physical eyes. If you admit *that*, you will no longer argue that, because you have not seen the original manuscripts, you cannot know whether they were without error in every detail.[152]

2) "*What is the use* of affirming inerrancy of an 'original autograph' which is not in existence?" The question has only academic interest. — No, it is a question of great importance, of the utmost importance. We want to know whether the words that Paul wrote down were (and are) the very words of God, by virtue of verbal inspiration. We want to know that today. For if the words of the apostles, in the original autographs, were not God's words, words of power, life, and salvation, then the copies, written or printed, could not transmit to us divine words. In the article "Have We the Original Text of the Holy Scriptures?" (*Conc. Theol. Mthly.*, X, p. 105 ff.) we read: "If the original manuscripts of the holy writers were inerrant, then it was at least possible for scribes to transmit an inerrant message to posterity. If the original writings were (and not merely contained) the Word of God, then the copies transmit to us the Word of God in the degree in which they are faithful to the original. If the original manuscripts were not, but merely contained, the Word of God, accuracy of transcription did not avail to render that divine which was not divine. Yes, a great deal depends on the nature of the original." (Be sure to read the

---

152) D. J. Burrell: "We have heard the higher critics saying: 'What is the use of affirming inerrancy of an "original autograph" which is not in existence? The theory that there were no errors in the original text is sheer assumption, upon which no mind can rest with certainty. We must take the Scriptures as we have them, without reference to a hypothetical original which no living man has seen.' It is a poor rule, however, which cannot be made to work both ways. No living man has ever seen the incarnate Word. There is no accurate portrait of Him in existence — certainly not if the Scriptures are unreliable. Nevertheless we do believe that the original Christ, who for a brief period of thirty years lived among men and then vanished from sight, was 'holy, harmless and undefiled'; precisely as it is claimed the Scriptures were in their original form." (*Op. cit.*, p. 122.)

entire article!)[153] The moderns think they can get along with
an errant Bible. But to us the question of the verbal inspiration
and inerrancy of the Bible, the Bible as originally written, is a
matter of vital importance. — It is of some importance, too, to the
textual critics. They are devoting much time to the labor of
restoring the original text. For many of them it is a labor of love.
And they have more than a literary interest in it. They would lose
their real interest if they knew that, after they had improved the
faulty copies, they got nothing but a faulty Bible.

3) "No man dead has left us any record of what they [the
autographs] were like when he read them." — That is a contemptible statement. The earlier copyists left a record.

4) Now for their real argument: the original manuscripts have
disappeared, and since we have only copies of them, the value of
the original is lost. — Do they really mean to say that? That
would mean, of course, that, if God wanted us to have His real,
authentic, authoritative Word, Paul would have had to write out
a hundred million original manuscripts of his epistles, so that
every Christian congregation could have them in Paul's handwriting or in the handwriting of his thousand amanuenses. Or, as
the *Conc. Theol. Mthly.* article referred to above suggests, God
would have had to engrave His sacred Word on gold plates,
deposit them in a specified spot, entrust them, say, to the officials
of the Congressional Library in Washington "to be inspected and
copied by anybody that desired to do so." Copied? No; that would
not do either. For where is the guaranty that he copied correctly?
We cannot believe that the moderns seriously mean that a document
loses its value when it is copied. The Church at Rome did not
say that the only worth-while epistle they had was the Epistle to
the Romans. They did not say that they did not have the Epistle
to the Galatians because they had only a copy of it. They did
not demand that the autographs circulate in all congregations
of that day down to all congregations of the last days. How many
of our moderns have laid their eyes on the manuscripts which

---

153) Dr. James M. Gray: "Some would argue speciously that to
insist on the inerrancy of a parchment no living being has ever seen
is an academic question merely and without value. But do they not
fail to see that the character and perfection of the Godhead are involved
in that inerrancy? Some years ago a 'liberal' theologian, deprecating
the discussion as not worth while, remarked that it was a matter of
small consequence whether a pair of trousers were originally perfect
if they were now rent. To which the valiant and witty David James
Burrell replied that it might be a matter of small consequence to the
wearer of the trousers, but the tailor who made them would prefer
to have it understood that they did not leave his shop that way. . . .
The Most High might at least be regarded as One who drops no stitches
and sends out no imperfect work." (*The Fundamentals,* III, p. 11.)

contain the proclamations of the President or of the Leader of Germany? All they see is the printed copy. And they know exactly what these men said. Do our lawyers ask to have the original engrossed documents embodying the legislative acts of Congress in their hands before they make use of them? Have done with this talk about copies not being as good as the originals. The Bible did not lose its force, its authority, the divine power of its words, through its transmission to us by way of written or printed copies.

5) If the moderns should now say that they were not referring to the copies *as such*, but only to faulty copies, we shall tell them that in that case they should not have used such general terms. And since they have used general terms ("a non-existent original text"), we shall not go on till they have definitely conceded that a good copy is as good as the original. If that is conceded, we shall have no further trouble with them. We, too, concede the variant readings. We have conceded right along that in some instances the original text has not yet been established. But we do not concede that the faulty transcription or faulty translation of a few passages vitiates the entire transcription. Some few passages have become doubtful. That gives no man the right to cast doubt on all the other passages whose reading is not in doubt. Reasonable men do not thus treat other, human documents. Have done with this vicious trifling! Since you have admitted that you are not arguing against the *copies as such*, accept the copies where there are no various readings as being just as good as the original, the words you read in the copies as having the same inerrancy and the same divine power as the words which were written by Paul's own pen. In the words of the *Watchman-Examiner:* "Certainly, it must always be remembered that, when we speak of the inspiration of the words of Scripture, we logically mean those words that were written by Paul, Moses, and others. To this it has been replied that the documents written by Paul and Moses have perished. Why contend for the inspiration of something we do not possess? Here it is well to remind the objector that the same question might also be asked of those who believe in any kind of Biblical inspiration. But there is an answer. Granted that the original documents are lost, the words of those documents are still with us through copies made before their loss. And in so far as we have these words, we have a verbally inspired Bible today. The whole science of textual criticism proceeds upon the assumption of an inspired original. And we cannot honor too highly that company of godly scholars who have labored to lead us back to this original." (See *Theol. Mthly.,* 1923, p. 363.)

Finally (6) the moderns ought to realize that in arguing

against Verbal Inspiration on the basis of the alleged non-existence of the original, they are cutting their own throats. They stand for, say, Partial Inspiration, the inspiration of the doctrinal contents of the Bible; they insist that these doctrines are true because the sections presenting them were written by inspiration. We ask them: What do you know of these doctrines? You do not have the original text! You cannot prove the *gratia universalis* with John 3:16 because the original which is supposed to have contained these words is no longer in existence. "Here it is well to remind the objector that the same question might also be asked of those who believe in any kind of Biblical inspiration." [154]

Now let us take a last look at Abbott's "infallibilities" phalanx. It looks formidable. But the argument is based on a fallacy. The first statement: "In order that the Bible should be infallible, the original writers must have been infallibly informed as to the truth; they must have been able to express it infallibly," is a true statement. But the next statement: "After their death their manuscripts must have been infallibly copied" is not true. It employs the sophistical generalization discussed above. The mistakes which the copyists made render a few passages doubtful but do not make all the rest fallible. It is simply not true that a message, a teaching, a statement, of the Bible loses its infallibility, its power, its divine character, when a fallible human being copies it, transmits it, preaches it. Will the condemned criminal doubt the validity of the pardon because a lowly messenger, and not the governor himself, brings and reads to him the pardon? And if the messenger mispronounces a word or two, is the pardon invalidated? — Enough has been said on this matter above. We shall add only one more remark. It is conceivable that, when we offer our main proof to Abbott — Christ's promise that He would preserve His infallible Word to the Church — he might reply: How do you know that Christ spoke those words? The original writers may have set them down infallibly, but the faulty copies, etc., etc. Our final remark is this: We go our way rejoicing and thanking God for the precious boon of an infallible Bible; let the others, if they must, wallow in the bog of doubt and uncertainty, a bog of their own making.

The argument under consideration (No. 17) is born of despera-

---

154) Dr. Pieper: "Theodore Kaftan is so set on doing away with Verbal Inspiration that he asserts two things which cancel each other. On the one hand he asserts that, as all theologians know, 'there is no fixed, firm text,' 'since the number of variant readings is legion.' On the other hand, he (Kaftan) is sure that he can determine on the basis of Scripture what in Scripture is and what is not the objective Word of God. That this would be impossible on the supposition that 'there is no fixed, firm text' did not dawn on him." (*Op. cit.*, p. 366.)

tion. The case of those who deny the verbal inspiration and reliability of the Bible must be desperate if they have to bring in the unrelated matter of faulty copies. And this desperate argument, if upheld, leads to despair. If there is no reliance on our Bible as we have it, we get religious nihilism.

A FINAL INSTALMENT OF FATUITIES, SOPHISTRIES AND FALSIFICATIONS

There is no end to the sophistries, misstatements, and puerilities which the moderns marshal against Verbal Inspiration. But there is an end to the readers' patience. So we shall bring our examination of the first objection to an end.

Fallacies, Psychological and Logical

No. 18. When the moderns ask us to yield up Verbal Inspiration, frankly to admit that the holy writers made many mistakes, in order to give the infidel less cause to be offended and keep men from being forced into skepticism, they commit a psychological fallacy. — The moderns actually make this proposal. "Take the utterances which trench on the domain of science," insist that these utterances are true, "and men like Tyndall and Huxley are forced into skepticism. . . . Because there are some things in the Bible he cannot be quite sure of, he gives it all up." (J. M. Gibson.) We must "shorten our line of defense," give up the teaching that "the very words of Scripture are the Word of God," if we would gain men whose "*Weltanschauung,* or philosophical outlook, is different" (J. Aberly). See pages 25 ff. and 55 above for these and other similar statements. "Seelenmordende Verbalinspiration" is the term used by Dr. Johannes Meinhold (*Pastoralblaetter,* 1933, p. 443). R. F. Horton formulates the appeasement proposal thus: "If we feel called upon to invent an unfounded dogma that this book is, as it were, written by God, or at least guaranteed against all errors, scientific, chronological, historical, or literary, we must remember the responsibility which we incur; the attacks on revelation which are made on the ground of that fictitious theory are attacks of our own creation. If, on the other hand, we will allow this Book of Genesis to be precisely what it is, without claiming for it anything more than it evidently claims for itself, we shall find that the quibbles of Infidelity will fall silent. . . . It is quite possible that the Book of Jonah may by its obvious inspiration reach the conscience of a reader and turn him to God; but if you start with the demand that the episode of the fish is a matter of faith, you at once close the book and its message to the modern mind. . . . The frank surrender of that hurtful dogma — of the worm-eaten dogmatism of the guardians of the letter of Scripture — will be the beginning of a new era of faith in the Bible and its revelation." (*Revelation and the Bible*, pp. 59, 259, 262, 405.)

This demand that the Church surrender the teaching of Verbal, Plenary Inspiration, of the infallibility of Scripture, as being a hurtful dogma originates in fallacious thinking. The demand operates, for one thing, with a logical fallacy. This is the demand: The Bible contains many mistakes; therefore honesty and wisdom require that the Church no longer insist on the infallibility of Scripture. That would be a perfectly good argument if the premise were correct. But the premise is false, as we have demonstrated *ad nauseam*. So we need not discuss this logical fallacy any longer. What we are going to discuss is the psychological mistake the appeasers are making.

1) They do not understand the psychology of the Bible-theologian, the Bible-Christian. We cannot surrender one word of Holy Scripture. We are convinced that every word of Scripture is a word of God. We should be guilty of high treason if we gave up one jot or tittle of the oracles of God, if we would try to gain the good will of the infidel or unbeliever by surrendering certain provinces of the holy land. So, when the moderns hold their appeasement conferences, they need not ask the Bible-Christians to attend. Their passionate appeal to us to save the Bible and the cause of the Church by yielding up parts of the Bible makes no impression upon us. The only impression it makes upon us is that we are filled with indignation for being asked to do such a thing.

We can understand why the liberals attend the appeasement conference. *They* look upon the Bible as a purely human book. They feel at liberty to censor and edit it to the liking of themselves and the others. And we can somewhat understand the attitude of the conservatives among the moderns. They have convinced themselves that those portions of Scripture which offend them and others are not God's Word. And so they feel free to delete them in order not to offend the unbeliever. What we cannot understand is that they should think for one moment that those who have a holy awe of Scripture as being throughout God's Word would make common cause with those who set out to ravage and despoil it.

Are the moderns really asking the Bible-theologians to become their allies? They are not, indeed, going to put it in these bald terms: We know that you believe in Verbal Inspiration, but we are asking you to sacrifice your conscience. But they do expect that their loud cry that the educated classes cannot accept the Bible as it is will make some impression on us, raise the

thought in our minds whether it might not be better not to hold
out so stubbornly for Verbal Inspiration.[155] And they hope to
soften our resistance with the argument that these "mistakes"
are, after all, matters of minor importance. They used that argument on themselves; they argued themselves into the belief that
matters which do not directly concern salvation lie outside of
Inspiration. They hope that such considerations will influence
our attitude, too. Do they know so little of the psychology of
the Bible-Christian?

They misjudge us and (2) they misjudge the unbeliever.
If they think they can win the doubter and unbeliever by making
concessions, they betray their ignorance of the psychology of the
skeptic. His mind is so constituted that, if he gains the right to
repudiate one statement, one teaching of Scripture, he will claim
the right to repudiate two and more statements and teachings. And
you cannot blame him for that. If any man is given the right to
reject that which does not agree with his "scientific" mind or with
his reason, he is not going to stop at the "mistakes" of the Bible,
but will repudiate anything that is offensive to him. How are you
going to stop him from deleting the doctrine of the deity of Christ
and of the vicarious satisfaction and all other teachings which are
offensive to his carnal reason? Start out to appease the skeptic,
and you will have to yield one province after the other. Those
who think that, if they yield one half of the Bible to the unbeliever,
he will gladly accept the other half do not know the workings of
the unbelieving mind.[156]

You aim to win the doubting, skeptical mind for the Bible by
making these concessions? You are turning it against the Bible!
By all the laws of psychology the man who has learned (from you!)
that half of the Bible is untrustworthy will conclude that the other
half is not much better. "The clever skeptic can ask such awkward questions as these: 'If, as you allege, there are errors in the
Bible in some things, why not in others — why not in all? If it has

---

155) These tactics *have* proved effective. Dr. Pieper: "The threat is
uttered that the Church will lose its influence in the world, fall into
contempt, and drag out a miserable existence if it will not submit to
so-called science as the supreme authority and permit it to purge and
certify the Christian doctrine. . . . This threat has intimidated the entire
modern so-called 'confessional,' 'conservative' theology. Modern theology
has made an appeasement with science." (*Proc., Delegate Synod*, 1899,
p. 34.)

156) H. M'Intosh: "Their [the moderns'] theory of indefinite erroneousness, by setting reason above revelation and making man's own
individual consciousness the standard and judge in the ultimate issue
of what is true and what is false in Holy Writ, warrants every man in
accepting or rejecting just as much or as little of it as he thinks fit, or
none at all should he think best." (*Is Christ Infallible and the Bible
True?* P. 456.)

erred in an indefinite number of things, why should I believe it in others or be asked to receive it as true in anything?'" (M'Intosh, *op. cit.*, p. 471.) He will be filled with suspicion of the Bible; yea, he will come to the inescapable conclusion that the Bible is a lying book. The skeptic does not have to be particularly clever to make this deduction. Common sense tells him that, "if the Bible is not God's book, it is a book of miserable lies. Why? It claims to be the Word of God. But one who assumes a name to which he is not entitled is a swindler and cheat." (*Proc. Iowa Dist.*, 1891, pp. 26, 31.) The skeptic who reasons thus has logic on his side, and because of his bad psychology he is quick to operate with this good logic; he thanks the moderns for the concession they are making; they are catering to his innate hatred of the Bible.[157]

These men surely are adepts in the arts of sophistry. They know how to mix up truth and falsehood for the purpose of proving a lie. It is certainly a fact, an undeniable truth, that many intellectuals take occasion to stumble at the Word because of the "mistakes" in the Bible. That is mixed up with the lie that Scripture is mistaken in many of its statements and with the lie that the theologians invented the dogma of verbal inspiration. And that is done in the interest of the lying delusion that men can be won for the truth, for the Church, by the suppression of the truth.[158]

3) The moderns should study and apply the psychological approach and method which the Holy Ghost employs. He does not appeal to the thinking of the natural mind, which is and remains enmity against God and His Word. He creates a new way of thinking — the psychology of the Christian which bows before every word of God. And He creates this new psychology simply

---

157) And if he is lost, the appeasers will be held accountable. N. R. Best cries out: "Only God knows how many souls that folly [the doctrine of plenary inspiration] has ruined!" The truth of the matter is that "the price of a lowered and unsettling view of Scripture has been, and is being, paid for by the eternal loss of countless souls" (H. M'Intosh, *op. cit.*, p. 457). The price is paid by those who permit the objections of carnal wisdom to uproot their faith or strengthen them in their unbelief. But God will demand their blood at the hand of those who nourished their doubt or unbelief. (See pages 76 f. above; also *Conc. Theol. Mthly.*, VIII, p. 348.)

158) It *is* a delusion. Dr. Walther: "We are firmly convinced that it is not possible to better the present apostate world through the lie that the divinely revealed truth is in fine accord with the wisdom of this world; its only help lies in this, that the divine foolishness, the old unadulterated Gospel, be preached to it." (*Lehre und Wehre*, 1875, p. 41. See Pieper, *Chr. Dog.* I, p. 191.) It is a delusion to think that faith can be really helped by establishing harmony between the Bible and science (see Walther's statement, *loc. cit.*); and a wicked and cruel deception is being practiced when this harmony is established by canceling Scripture statements. Can a lie serve faith?

by preaching the Word. Let us win the skeptic and confirm the doubting Christian through the testimony of the Bible itself! The divine power inheres in the words written in the Bible; and when we confront the doubter and unbeliever with the bare, simple statements of Scripture, we have the power and persuasiveness of God on our side. Let that work on the doubter. That will, by the grace of God, win the consent of men despite the protest of their old way of thinking. — And here are the appeasers laying aside the sword of the Spirit, the quick and powerful Word, and trying to win the battle by retreating before the enemy, by conceding the partial erroneousness of Scripture. It is unspeakable folly, and it must be "paid for by the eternal loss of countless souls."

No. 19. We must take the time to examine one more sophistry. We have promised, in footnote 10, that we would sometime look into the *"tu quoque"* argument, and though the sophistry back of it is so bald that it seems a waste of time and paper further to uncover it, we must keep our engagement.

In support of the thesis that reason has the right to sit in judgment on Scripture and to reject any statement which is "unreasonable"[159] this argument is advanced: Since God has given men reason, He wants them to use it as their guide through Scripture; and when you Bible-theologians employ reason in studying Scripture, you are supporting the thesis that reason has the right to judge Scripture. N. R. Best: "It may seem a jesting 'tu quoque' to say of the literally orthodox in Bible-studies that they are more inveterate rationalists than the higher critics, whom they so unanimously condemn. But it is not a jest; it is the easily observable fact. Confronting two seemingly disagreeing portions of Scripture, the conservative weaves a great net of cross references by which he drags the questioned paragraph or chapter into a decidedly different orientation. . . . The result reached is the product of a purely human exercise in the art of rationalizing the varied materials of the Bible. . . . He puckers his brow for hours at a time attempting to range all the data of the story in one consistent chain. He has a perfect right to. But it's reason he's using; he's an undeniable rationalist. . . . Certainly the reflective and the scrupulous among students using these methods of exposition cannot pretend to abide by the dictum that men have no right to invade the realm of divine revelation with reason's readjustments. . . . The very nature of reason, as God has embedded it in the intelligence of men, gives it a houndlike scent for what is not

---

159) R. F. Horton: "The dead are not raised; and such magical prodigies as the transportation of a body through the air are dishonoring to the general tone, the high and spiritual tone, of the narrative. . . . Faith must not be encumbered with demands which *strain the reason.*" (*Op. cit.*, p. 284 f.)

plain, for what is apparently altogether non-understandable. It is preposterous to put all this artificial enmity between reason and revelation. God gave both, and He prepared the one that it might receive the other. He has fitted each to each." (*Inspiration,* pp. 117—121.) [160)

That is sophistry. It is certainly true that we employ our reason in studying Scripture. God certainly wants us to use our intelligence in order to understand the meaning of the words He speaks to us. You must be able to think logically in order to get the import of any statement in Scripture or any other book. That is the God-pleasing *usus rationis ministerialis,* or *organicus.* But it is a transparent fallacy to deduce from the fact that a certain use of reason is required that any other use of reason is permissible, the *usus rationis magisterialis,* by which reason is permitted to criticize and correct Scripture. People ought to be able to understand that there is a great difference between saying that we must use our reason in order to get the meaning and sense of a Scripture statement and saying that reason has the right to label that statement as nonsense. [161)] Scripture does not authorize the *usus magisterialis* by calling for the *usus ministerialis* (see Col. 2:8; 2 Cor. 10:5), nor does reason itself justify it. Reason being the judge, Best's and Stamm's argument is based on a fallacy. To use harsher language, it is a sophistical argument. It operates with an ambiguous term. When these men say: Is not the Bible addressed to human intelligence? we shall not go on with the argument till they specify very exactly what the Bible, according to their view, expects human intelligence and reason to do.

They go so far, by the way, as to contend that Scripture itself

---

160) Similarly S. P. Cadman: "The Bible is addressed to human intelligence. . . . The Scriptures themselves do not outlaw man's judgment on their contents. Why should we do so?" (*Answers to Everyday Questions,* p. 258.) G. L. Raymond: "The very acceptance of revelation as a guide to life involves the use of reason." (*The Psychology of Inspiration,* p. 319.) R. T. Stamm: "We must never forget that it is impossible to construct a systematic theology without employing the same human reason which too many of our writers have tried to deprive of all validity at the outset." (*Luth. Church Quart.,* April, 1940, p. 129.) Ingersoll: "If God did not intend I should think, why did He give me a 'thinker'?" (*Lectures,* p. 383.)

161) Quenstedt understood the difference: "Theology does not condemn the use of reason, but its abuse and its affectation of directorship, or its magisterial use, as normative and decisive in divine things." (See H. Schmid, *Doctrinal Theology,* p. 35.) So did Pieper: "Human reason must indeed be employed in interpreting Scripture, never, however, as *principle,* but always only as *instrument.*" (*Lectures on "The Lutheran Church,"* p. 50.) So did L. S. Keyser: "Reason is a God-given faculty; surely it must be intended to be used, though not abused. . . . We dislike rationalism, which sets human reason above the Bible." (*A Reasonable Faith,* p. 24 f.)

submits its teaching to the judgment of reason. They quote Is. 1:18! Best: "Every page of the Bible might be justly inscribed with the invitation which stands in living letters on the first page of the prophet Isaiah: 'Come now and let us reason together, saith Jehovah.' Reason is God's joy — not His 'black beast.'" (*Loc. cit.*) Paine, too, cites this Scripture: "'Come, now, and let us reason together, saith the Lord.'. . . It is impossible to reason upon things not comprehensible by reason; and therefore, if you keep to your text, . . . you must admit a religion to which reason can apply, and this certainly is not the Christian religion." (*Life and Writings of Thomas Paine*, Vol. 6: "Age of Reason.") Another case of sophistry — twisting the meaning of a word, and, as it happens, of a word which does not occur in Scripture in the sense here attached to it. Our word does not really mean "to reason," but it means to judge, to establish the right of a case. The English translation has misled many. But let that go. We are willing to accept Moffatt's translation: "Come, let me put it thus, the Eternal argues," and to interpret: "God deigns to argue the case with us, that all may see the just, nay, loving principle of His dealings with men" (M. Henry), and to admit the conclusion: God does appeal to man's reason, to his sense of right and wrong. But we do not admit the argument: Because in one case God appeals to man to use his reason and his sense of justice; man's reason is in every case fit to judge divine things. That is called the fallacy of arguing from a special case and applying it generally. And it is sophistry to build up the case for rationalism on the fact that the English Bible happens to use the word "reason" in Is. 1:18. You might as well harp on the words "reasonable service" in the translation of Rom. 12:1. And that, too, is actually being done. G. L. Raymond says: "The third test of truth was said to be conformity to the results of logical inference, or reasoning. 'Let us reason together,' says Isaiah; let us give a 'reasonable service,' urges Paul in Rom. 12:1." (*Op. cit.*, p. 166.)

Bound to make the verbal-inspirationist a *particeps criminis* and thus estopping him from denouncing their rationalistic mishandling of Scripture, these moderns elaborate the *"tu quoque"* argument by charging that the doctrine of verbal inspiration is constructed on rationalistic principles. "Frank nennt die traditionelle Inspirationslehre, das, was unsere alten Dogmatiker aus der Schrift ueber die Schrift gelehrt haben, *schlecht-rationalistische* Konsequenzmacherei." (*Lehre und Wehre*, 1890, p. 145.) J. Stump: "The dogmaticians were led to maintain it (the Verbal Inspiration) by the exegencies of the times and the *stress of their severe dialectics.*" (*Lehre und Wehre*, 1904, p. 86.) P. T. Forsyth "protests against the vice of apriorism, which comes down on the Bible with a theory of inspiration really drawn from *rationalistic expectations*" and calls it "the rationalism of orthodoxy."[162] The charge is not based on truth. We ask the Bible what it says of itself, and only because the Bible says that every word in it is given by inspiration do we teach Verbal Inspiration. W. Sanday is not well acquainted with what the Bible theologians have written on the subject of Verbal Inspiration; else he would not have administered this lecture to them: "The fundamental mistake that is too often made is to form the idea of what Inspiration is from what we should antecedently expect it to be. . . . We do not think it likely that God would allow the revelation of Himself to be mixed up with such imperfect materials. But *we are no good judges of what God would or would not do*. His ways are not our ways. Out of the imperfect He brings forth the perfect." (*The Oracles of God*, p. 29.) That is certainly a surprising charge. *We* have been telling the rationalists that men are "no good judges of what God would do or not do." And now that charge is hurled at our head! But the charge is false. We form our idea of what Inspiration is from Scripture. We say that God does not allow the revelation of Himself to be mixed up with errors because, first and foremost, Scripture says that. We do show, too, that that accords with reason, but we base our faith not on the reasonableness of it but on the declaration of Scripture. So, then, while the first form of the *"tu quoque"* argument operates with a fallacy, the second form is based on misrepresentation.[163]

And, would you believe it, these men are making the verbal-inspirationist not only a *particeps criminis* but the arch-criminal. Gibson declares that the moderns "proceed on a humbler method, . . . on the modest principle of sitting at the feet of the inspired writers and especially at the feet of Christ Himself, the great Master, and *accepting what they find there*" (*loc. cit.*). Best insists

---

162) Forsyth writes that in the preface (p. XIV) to J. M. Gibson's *The Inspiration and Authority of Holy Scripture*. Gibson himself says: "The defenders of the authoritative inspiration of the Scriptures have postulated as a necessity of the case the emancipation of all the writers of Scripture from the effect of human weakness and limitation. This is what may be called the *rationalistic method* of proceeding, for it starts with a theory framed in accordance with what the theorist regards as reasonable and deals with all the facts in the case in the light of that theory." (P. 32 f.)

163) Dr. J. H. C. Fritz: "We know and believe that 'all Scripture is given by inspiration of God.' We believe this not because we have arrived at this truth by a process of reasoning but because of the testimony of the Holy Spirit, who by His very Word has wrought this divine conviction in our heart. The Verbal Inspiration is an *article of faith*. Though we can prove to any one that it is *not even reasonable* to deny this Verbal Inspiration, yet we can *argue* no one into believing it; that faith must be wrought by the Holy Spirit Himself." (*Proc., Texas Dist.*, 1939, p. 12.)

that "the liberal scholar is usually content to *let the text stand
undisturbed and even unexplained, just as it is,* while the "conservative weaves a great net of cross references," etc.; . . . "he's an
undeniable rationalist, trying by reason to establish something *not
said in the Bible.* . . . The literally orthodox are more inveterate
rationalists than the higher critics" (*loc. cit.*). We read in *Lehre
und Wehre,* 1895, p. 292: "A prominent professor says that the
doctrine of inspiration as formed by our dogmaticians does not
spring from the true comprehension and humble acceptance of
Holy Scripture but is the product of rationalistic cogitations; it is
a deduction from true presuppositions falsely applied." Any comment necessary? *Lehre und Wehre* comments: "Things have
reached such a pass that a rationalist accuses the Bible Christians
of indulging in rationalistic cogitations, while he plays the role of
true orthodoxy."

Misstatements, Misinterpretations, Mistranslations

No. 20. The moderns deal very largely in misstatements and
misrepresentations. That is their chief stock in trade. The basic
untruth that the Bible contains many mistakes has spawned a
countless number of other untruths. Would you want to give the
exact score of only those misstatements which have been listed
here from page one on down, some of them under the heading of
"bare assertions" and "sophistries"? Instead of that let us add
a few new ones; the examination of these and of some of the old
ones will exemplify and illustrate the dishonest polemics of the
moderns against Verbal Inspiration.

There is the assertion of H. E. Fosdick "that at the beginning
Hebrew religion had no hope of immortality." Proof-texts cited
are Eccl. 9: 4-6 and 3: 19. Consequently there is a contradiction
between these passages and 1 Cor. 15: 53-55. "No ingenuity of
exegesis can make these two agree." (*The Modern Use of the
Bible,* p. 25.) However, in Job's days Hebrew religion had the hope
of immortality, Job 19: 25 ff.! Those who say that this book was
written in or after the exile might ponder Gen. 15: 15: "Thou shalt
go to thy fathers in peace." If these words are not plain enough,
read Matt. 22: 31 f. The statement of Jesus stamps the assertion of .
Fosdick as a misstatement. You have the choice of charging either
Fosdick or Jesus with making a misstatement.

Fosdick states further that the Bible does not really teach the
resurrection of the body. Read Matt. 22: 31 again: "as touching
the *resurrection* of the dead." The only way of clearing Fosdick
of having made a misstatement is to employ the sophistry of C. H.
Dodd: "On this occasion Jesus dismisses with cool contempt the
crude notion of a renewal of *physical* existence." (*The Authority
of the Bible,* p. 219.)

How much truth is there in the statement that Biblical "tradition" is nothing more than an adapted form of specifically Babylonian folk-lore and tradition and in that other statement that God in His marvelous grace so lifted up the best legendary literature of the world, the story of the Creation, of the Fall, etc., as to make it the vehicle of high and pure revelation? .(See p. 15 f. above.) The statement that the writer (or writers) of the Pentateuch borrowed from Babylonian sources is a misstatement of the rankest kind. One who knows these Babylonian tales will never make such an assertion. There is a faint resemblance, but too great a difference in the essentials. The Babylonian account of "creation" knows nothing of a *creatio ex nihilo.* Further, "according to the pagan story the gods were not existent from eternity but were either created or begotten, the myth does not say by whom or in what way" (L. S. Keyser, *op. cit.,* p. 87 ff.). Another essential difference lies in the puerile and repulsive conceptions that characterize the pagan myths. That is the judgment of H. E. Fosdick.[164] And it is the judgment of the experts, the assyriologists. When Friedrich Delitzsch went before the public, in his *Babel und Bibel,* with the assertion that the Bible in many of its portions is simply a reproduction of Babylonian myths and legends, they discredited him. "Einstimmig ist *Babel und Bibel* von der fachmaennischen Kritik zurueckgewiesen worden," said the periodical *Der Alte Glaube* and named Cornill, Koenig, Strack, Kittel, and many others as repudiating him. (See *Lehre und Wehre,* 1903, p. 16 ff., 90 f.) But the myth (that the Biblical writers were borrowers) persists. R. H. Malden, Dean of Wells, to mention just one instance, still believes it and spreads it. "The Babylonian version of the Flood is much older than the version in Genesis, but the two correspond so closely in many points of detail that there is no room for doubt as to the source of the Biblical narrative. . . . Eden is fairy-land. A sacred tree appears frequently on Babylonian gems. . . ." (*The Inspiration of the Bible,* pp. 54, 56.)

Moses did some more borrowing, said Delitzsch in *Babel und Bibel;* he got the Decalog and the rest of the Pentateuchal code from Hammurabi. Wrong again; just read the 282 regulations of this Babylonian code and compare them with the Mosaic code. Barton's *Archeology and the Bible* lists them and comes to the

---

164) "Folk call them parallels [to the Bible account], but I do not see how they can do it if they have read them. They are full of the quarrels of gods, the fear of primeval dragons, the war of Tiamat and the hosts of chaos against Marduk and the gods of light. They do, indeed, give us the same cosmology, but Marduk builds it up by slitting Tiamat like a flat fish and making the firmament of her upper half and the earth of her lower. . . . This welter of mythology, . . . these miasmic marshes." (*Op. cit.,* p. 52.)

conclusion: "The Mosaic code was not borrowed from the Baby-lonian. A comparison of the code of Hammurabi as a whole with the Pentateuchal laws as a whole, while it reveals certain sim-ilarities, convinces the student that the laws of the Old Testament are in no essential way dependent upon the Babylonian laws. Such resemblances as there are arose, it seems clear, from a sim-ilarity of antecedents and of general intellectual outlook; the striking differences show that there was no direct borrowing." (P. 340.) Barton is liberal, as some of his phrases indicate, but honesty compels him to denounce this charge of borrowing. The liberal *Independent* does the same and points out that the Baby-lonian code contains no trace of the Decalog and no Sabbath legislation. (See *Lehre und Wehre*, 1903, p. 60; 1913, p. 172, in the series of articles "Die Assyriologie und das Alte Testament.") Above all, in the Babylonian code Hammurabi is speaking; in the Mosaic code God is the Lawgiver. No wonder that the assyriol-ogists called Delitzsch out of order on this point, too.

The purpose of the charge that the sacred writers were bor-rowers is to show that the Bible is a purely human product, a poor product at that. Delitzsch: "The thought that the Bible is the personal revelation of God constitutes a mental aberration of the gravest type." The Bible comes from Babel! — What Delitzsch proved is that he knew very little of the Bible. The Babylonians knew nothing of the essential teachings of the Bible — salvation by grace, through the Messiah. And the Bible originated in Babel!

The other contention, that God made "the best legendary literature of the world" the vehicle of pure revelation, operates with the same untruth that the Bible account of creation, etc., is of one piece with the Babylonian legends. Moreover, it gives expression to the hideous untruth that God induced the prophets to tell these myths as facts of history, and to the further hideous untruth that Jesus and the apostles, who endorsed the history related by the prophets, either were mistaken in accepting myths as true stories or, knowing better, hoped that the Christians would soon advance far enough to discover "the profound prophetic prophecy" hidden in them.

A few samples of scientific blunders committed by those who charge the Bible with scientific blunders. H. E. Fosdick cannot believe in Verbal Inspiration because Gen. 1 states that light ex-isted before the sun existed, three days before. (*Op. cit.*, p. 34.) *A New Commentary on Holy Scripture*, edited by Charles Gore and others, states: "There can be little doubt that the writer of P based his account on cosmological ideas current in Babylon; and in their close material resemblances both accounts are at variance with the conclusions established by modern scientific research. For example, we notice at once that light is created and day divided from night before the creation of the luminaries; and, moreover, plant-life appears before the sun, a manifest impossibility." These men do not seem to know that even today the sun is not the only source of light.[165]

Those who deny the inspiration of Scripture because of their firm belief in atheistic evolution should read the article "The Great Deception" in the *Journal of Theol. of the A. L. Conf.*, Aug., 1941, with the addendum in the September issue, p. 796. That tells them what arrant blunderers they are. "To assume that beginningless inorganic matter, without intelligence of course, after countless myriads of light-years should have chanced to be so influenced by other inorganic forces as to change into organic matter which after new myriads of light-years have produced intelligence in man, is so monstrous a thought that we prefer assuming a beginningless transcendental intelligence, which at least can account for the phenomena." Again: "The species are so persistent in preserving themselves that they revert to type when man's efforts cease." Conclusion: "To ascribe such powers to senseless matter is itself utterly senseless. . . . Materialism finds itself in conflict not only *with the nature of natural phenomena* and with human reason but also *with its own postulates.*"

Here is a "scientific" blunder of a somewhat different kind. Liberals believe that the hope of the moral and spiritual advance of man rests not in the Bible and its teachings but in the new science and the new philosophy based on the new scientific outlook. They even go so far as to say with Prof. H. E. Barnes, at a regional meeting of the American Association for the Advancement of Science, in December, 1928, that "this newer view of God must be formulated in the light of contemporary astrophysics, which completely repudiates the theological and cosmological outlook of the Holy Scriptures." This has nothing to do with science; it is the "higher science" discussed above. But since they call it "science," we are going to list it among the "scientific" blunders. It is a colossal blunder. This new science has utterly failed of its purpose. President Robert M. Hutchins of the University of Chicago said in his address at the December, 1933, convocation of the university: "We do not know where we are going, or why, and we

---

165) See H. Rimmer (*Modern Science and the Genesis Record,* p. 43 ff.) on "the contention of semiknowledge that there could be no light before the creation of the sun. The criticism of Gen. 1 is not scientifically tenable. There are many sources of light apart from sunlight itself. . . . The *aurora borealis.* . . . The brilliant gleaming light that at night transforms the dark depths of the sea into a luminous highway . . . phosphorus. . . . Another source of light is the radioactive glow that comes from those particles which Sir Oliver Lodge defines as cosmic light."

have almost given up the attempt to find out. We are in despair because the keys which were to open the gates of heaven have let us into a larger but more oppressive prison-house. We think those keys were science and the free intelligence of man. They have failed us. We have long since cast off God. To what can we now appeal? The answer comes in the undiluted animalism of the last works of D. H. Lawrence. . . ." President Mackay of Princeton Seminary records the same experience: "The international public had believed in evolution, which was felt to guarantee a flowering, developing progress with much better days ahead," but this new philosophy has failed in lifting the poor depraved human race to a higher level. (See footnote 114, p. 143 f.) But when men stick to a theory which has fallen down, they are committing a scientific blunder. And they are sticking to this false theory. The *Christian Century,* for instance, discusses President Hutchins's statement in an article published Jan. 24, 1934, with the heading "The Revolt against Science," chides President Hutchins for giving aid and comfort to "the dogmatists in religion," derides Verbal Inspiration, and insists that science will save the race: "The revolt is not in the interest of reaction, but of liberty and progress. It is not out to discredit science, but to save it, to expand it, to put purpose in it, to build a sky over it, and to call its attention to the stars. It has no wish to return to a culture from which science is banned, nor to a cultus that is too sacrosanct to submit to criticism. It looks forward, not backward — toward the emergence of a culture which will embody excellencies impossible in any previous culture which lacked science." Is a scientist speaking or a visionary?

We next submit a few samples of the great lot of misrepresentations. There is the claim "that all scholarship is arrayed against the credibility of the Scriptures," or, toning it down a bit, "that the *leading* scientists of recent times are all arrayed against the Book." (See D. J. Burrell, *Why I Believe the Bible,* p. 184.) That misrepresents the situation. Some, indeed of the leading scientists, yes, many of them, or perhaps most of them, deny the inspiration and the infallibility of Scripture, but the statement that all the leading scientists are arrayed against the Book is an untruth. Many of the leaders in science believe the Bible.[166] The list of

---

166) In the Bodleian Library at Oxford you will find the original of a manifesto signed by 617 leading scientists of the time (Balfour, Bently, Bosworth, Sir David Brewster, and 613 others), who deeply deplore that men pursue scientific studies for the purpose of raising doubts concerning the truth and authority of Scripture and declare: What God has revealed in nature cannot contradict God's revelation in Scripture. (See *Proc., Iowa Dist.,* 1892, p. 67.) Gladstone: "The older I grow, the more confirmed I am in my faith and religion. I have been in public life 58 years, and 47 in the cabinet of the British government, and during

those who accept the Bible as God's Word is a long one. Read the list given in *Conc. Theol. Mthly.*, X, p. 255, Sir William Dawson, M. A., L. L. D., F. G. S., and others, who refuse to fault the Bible because of the teaching of evolution, "which is a theory founded on ignorance." Add the name of R. A. Millikan — and many others. Why should we name them? Our moderns know them as well as we do. And mark well: *a goodly number of them stand for Verbal Inspiration.* Let Dr. Howard A. Kelly, professor in the Johns Hopkins University, holding academic degrees from the leading universities of America and Europe, speak in their name: "I believe the Bible to be the inspired Word of God. . . . I can trust God, though I shall have to stand alone before the world in declaring Him to be true."[167] Many of the leading scientists are on our side. We are not citing this fact as a support of our faith. Nor shall we, on the other hand, permit the fact that many scientists are against us to disturb our faith. Let the majority be against us. Majorities do not decide questions of religion and faith. They do not even decide questions in science. We are calling attention to the fact that many scientists are believing Christians and that not a few of them stand for the full inerrancy of Scripture simply in

---

those 47 years I have been associated with 60 master minds of the country, and all but five of the 60 were Christians." Gladstone did not find that he had to "sacrifice his intelligence" (Baumgaertel's phrase) in accepting the teachings of Scripture. After naming seven scientists, among them Isaac Newton, whose intelligence did not compel them to charge the Bible with mistakes, D. J. Burrell quotes the "last words of Professor Dana to the members of my class at graduation: 'Young men, you are going out into a world where you must meet an unceasing assault upon your faith. Let me ask you to remember, as my parting counsel, that, whenever you are in doubt amid the confused voices of scientific controversy, you may always with perfect confidence affix your faith to the statements of the Word of God.'" (*Loc. cit.*) *The Lutheran Witness*, 1931, p. 370: "For every scientist who denies the hereafter and calls the religion of the Christian Church 'bunk' I will quote you a scientist who declared himself a believer in the Bible. Make the test. Against Edison, for one, I quote Lord Kelvin, one of the giants of nineteenth-century physics, who, when asked what he considered his greatest discovery, said, 'When I discovered my Savior in Jesus Christ.'"

167) "I was once profoundly disturbed in the traditional faith in which I was brought up, by inroads which were made upon the Book of Genesis by the higher critics. I could then not gainsay them, not knowing Hebrew nor archeology well, and to me, as to many, to pull out one great prop was to make the whole foundation uncertain. So I floundered on for some years. . . . One day it occurred to me to see what the Book had to say about itself. . . . I now believe the Bible to be the inspired Word of God, inspired in a sense utterly different from that of any human book. I believe Jesus Christ to be the Son of God. . . . I can put God's assertions and commands above every seeming probability in life, dismissing cherished convictions and looking upon the wisdom and reasoning of men as folly opposed to Him. . . ." (See *Watchman-Examiner*, Nov. 10, 1932.)

order to show up the dishonesty of the polemics against Verbal Inspiration.[168]

Another misrepresentation: the men of Bible times had little knowledge of science; the Biblical writers were not trained thinkers; because of that they could harbor such superstitious notions and pen such unscientific nonsense. Recall the statement of Clarence Darrow that "the human beings who wrote the Bible had no knowledge of science," and that of H. E. Fosdick: The floating ax-head "presented no intellectual problem whatever. No laws were broken because no laws were known. No Hebrew had ever dreamed of such a thing as a mathematical formula of specific gravity" (*op. cit.*, p. 136). — The ancients were not so rude and witless as all that. They did not know quite so many things as we do, but they knew quite a lot, and their intellectual faculties were quite well developed. "Do not forget that the gospel-facts occurred in the age of Caesar, Augustus, Tacitus, Pliny, an age of ripe scholarship and keen criticism. The gospel-facts do not belong to a period in the hazy past wherein fact and fancy blend. They transpired before a wide-awake, intelligent, cultured citizenship. Nothing could convince them unless supported by the strongest

---

168) A few side-lights on this dishonesty. Some scientists are dishonest. *Der Alte Glaube* said: "Man klagt in unserer Zeit mit Recht darueber, dass in der Wissenschaft so viel Schwindel, so viel Betrug, so viel Falschmuenzerei getrieben wird, . . . dass man den sonst verpoenten 'Probabilismus' offen und ungescheut als gangbare Muenze verwertet." (See *Lehre und Wehre*, 1913, p. 310.)   When E. Haeckel was charged with committing falsifications in the interest of the doctrine of evolution and was convicted of it, he said: "I find some comfort in the fact that hundreds of accomplices are sitting with me in the dock; die grosse Mehrzahl naemlich von allen morphologischen, anatomischen, histologischen und embryologischen Figuren, welche in den besten Lehrbuechern verbreitet sind, sind alle nicht exakt, sondern mehr oder weniger zurechtgestutzt oder konstruiert" (*loc. cit.*). That is a matter which concerns the scientists. But since these "facts" are being adduced as proofs for the errancy of Scripture, the matter comes within the scope of the present discussion. Prof. J. J. Reeve calls attention to another dishonest practice. Having stated: "I was much impressed with their boast of having all scholarship on their side. But some investigation and consideration led me to see that the boast of scholarship is tremendously overdone," he adds: "A striking characteristic of these people is a persistent ignoring of what is written on the other side. They think to kill their opponents by either ignoring or despising them. They have made no attempt to answer Robertson's *The Early Religion of Israel;* Orr's *The Problem of the Old Testament;* Wiener's *Studies in Biblical Law;* and *Studies in Pentateuchical Criticism*, etc.. They still treat these books which undermined the very foundations of their theories with the same magnificent scorn." (*The Fundamentals*, III, p. 111 f.)   Again, some act on the assumption that only the higher critics count as authorities. Once more, we hear them loudly proclaiming that the advance of science has discredited the Bible; but when the progress of scientific research corroborates the Bible, all is silent. The tactics employed by these men is to make such a loud noise that the innocent public gets the false impression that all the leading scientists and theologians are arrayed against the Bible.

evidence." (F. S. Downs, *The Heart of the Christian Faith*, p. 113.)
Going farther back, we find that Solomon was not a mean scientist.
He knew his botany. And "his copper-refineries at Ezion-geber
used methods rediscovered less than a hundred years ago in the
Bessemer process" (statement by Prof. Nelson Glueck; see *Lutheran Witness*, 1941, p. 114). Jacob knew something about the
science of genetics and had observed the results of cross-breeding.
And "an ancient Babylonian frieze from the year 800 B. C. shows
a man putting pollen on a fig flower, plainly indicating an act of
artificial cross-pollination." The *Lutheran Church Herald* quoted
this from the *Journal of Heredity*.[169] Ask the schoolchildren
about the scientific attainments of the ancient Egyptians. Moreover, the holy writers knew certain things which the scientists
could not tell them, knew them by inspiration. "He hangeth the
earth upon nothing!" Job 26:7. The writer may not have known
that it is "gravity" which holds the earth in place (if our present
assumptions are correct; the thing is becoming doubtful). But
they did know — what their contemporaries did not know — that
the earth rested on nothing. Since inspiration does not work
"mechanically" and does not produce unconsciousness, the holy
writers knew what they had written and those that read these
statements were intelligent beings.[170]

Other misrepresentations: The Bible theologians invented the
doctrine of the plenary inspiration of Scripture.[171] That is a
slanderous misstatement. They got their doctrine of verbal inspiration in the same way as Dr. H. A. Kelly got it: they went to
the Bible to see what it had to say about itself, and they believed
what they heard the Bible say. — Cremer: "Diese Inspirationslehre
[der Dogmatiker] war ein schlechthinniges Novum." And a writer
in the *Congregationalist*: "The Fundamentalist theory of a verbally

---

169) The *Herald* adds the remark: "The theory of evolution has so
blurred the thinking of many men that they cannot see how it could be
otherwise than that the ancients were primitive, childlike men in point
of intelligence and were incapable of solving the problems of us moderns.
. . . There are many evidences that in matters of astronomy, principles
of building and architecture, artwork, literary expression, the ancients
were the equals, if not the superiors, of men today, who have all the
advantage of building on what the pioneers before them have learned."

170) It has been said that the Biblical account "anticipates modern
scientific discovery." That means: "The Bible has been so written that
in the fierce light of the latest science its truthfulness has stood the test
of the most searching investigation by the keenest antagonists — the
highest scientific authorities themselves being witness." (H. M'Intosh,
op. cit., p. 626.)

171) R. F. Horton: "At last the poor and insufficient answer is forced
to come out: We have no reason to give except the arbitrary dogma of
the Church, and we suppose the dogma was invented as a security for
the truth of Jesus. . . . The belief in its inspiration rests only on an unsupported dogma." (*Op. cit.*, pp. 235, 240.)

inspired Bible was unheard of in the Church until the post-Reformation period." That is a falsification of history. The ancient Church taught exactly what Luther and the later dogmaticians taught.[172] — "Others have affirmed that the seat of authority is to be found in the [infallible] Bible. This was particularly the contention of the later reformers, who felt the need of some authority to oppose to the Roman Catholic doctrine of the infallible Church." (*The Bible Through the Centuries*, p. 290.) Dr. J. Stump seconds Willett: "The dogmaticians were led to maintain it (the Verbal Inspiration) by the exigencies of the times and the stress of their severe dialectics." One cannot fault Dr. F. Bente for saying: "Stump flunkert hier; die Dogmatiker hatten das Interesse, *die klare Lehre der Schrift* ueber die Inspiration vorzulegen." (*Lehre und Wehre*, 1904, p. 86.) — H. C. Vedder: "The followers of Luther developed an extreme theory of the verbal inspiration and absolute authority of the whole canon." (*Op. cit.*, p. 326.) Not true! Luther had the same "extreme" doctrine as the dogmaticians. Charles Gore knows his Luther and says: "Luther actually speaks of the Holy Spirit as the *author* of the books of Moses; he submitted his judgment undoubtingly to Scriptural statements on points of natural science; and in a famous controversy he appealed to a New Testament verse as an infallible oracle, to be accepted with the purest literalism." (*Loc. cit.*) Any "extreme" statement adduced from the dogmaticians can be matched by one from Luther just as "extreme." — "How sternly would Luther have rebuked the rash and baseless dogmatism which says that to question a part of the Scriptures is to shake the authority of the whole." (R. F. Horton, *op. cit.*, p. 342.) Do not try to make people believe that! Luther had no occasion to say anything like that. One who declares "The Scriptures have never erred"; "Scripture cannot err" (XV: 1481; XIX: 1073), is not going to extenuate

---

172) H. C. Vedder, who does not believe in Verbal Inspiration, quotes statements of the earliest writers (Justin, Irenaeus, and others) to that effect and then adds: "It would seem also that there was early developed as 'high' a doctrine of inspiration as that held by modern theologians. Gaius, rather earlier than later, had said: 'For either they do not believe that the divine Scriptures were dictated by the Holy Spirit, and thus are infidels; or they think themselves wiser than the Holy Spirit, and what are they then but demoniacs?'" (*Our New Testament. How did We Get It?* pp. 48—50.) — The term "dictated" will be examined later on. — Charles Gore: "It ought to be said frankly that Luther often clings to the OLDER notion of a verbally inspired Bible. He actually speaks of the Holy Spirit as the *Author* of the books of Moses." (*The Doctrine of the Infallible Book*, p. 58.) — The *Proceedings* of the Iowa District, 1892, p. 19 ff., submit voluminous quotations from the Church Fathers which prove that they taught Verbal Inspiration. See also P. Kretzmann, *The Foundations Must Stand*, p. 69 ff. — Dr. Pieper is right in saying: "It is evident that Cremer had entirely lost control not only of the historical facts but also of himself when he wrote the above." (*Op. cit.*, I, p. 280.)

the occurrence of mistakes in the Bible. Horton's interest in this is to find support for his contention that the occurrence of errors in the Bible need not create doubt as to the trustworthiness of the divine parts of the Bible (*op. cit.*, p. 289). Do not ask Luther to back up this idea! Luther would say: "No man will take stock in a book or writing parts of which are untrue, particularly if he cannot tell which parts are true and which are untrue." (XX:2275.) When Professor Frank (Erlangen) applied the same tactics, claiming that Luther found the Bible to be a mixture of divine and human elements, of truth and error, and was not much disturbed thereat, Professor Stoeckhardt commented: "Das kann Frank nur einem Ignoranten, der Luther nicht kennt, einreden." (*Lehre und Wehre*, 1890, p. 145.) — Anything to discredit Verbal Inspiration!

No. 21. A large part of the misstatements with which the moderns operate consists of misinterpretations of Scripture. Of the texts which suffer much at their hands 2 Tim. 3:16 is the chief sufferer. They use it to support their favorite thesis that only the Gospel-message or only the religious teachings are inspired, true and trustworthy. As a rule, they offer no proof for this thesis. We have noted this under No. 13 (2): "The moderns deal largely in bare assertions." But the bare assertion becomes a false assertion, a misstatement, when they use 2 Tim. 3:16 or any other text to support it. We have come across this misinterpretation several times already; but since it is such a glaring maltreatment of Scripture, it ought to receive one more treatment.

It seems incredible that a theologian would attempt to prove the thesis that not all of Scripture is inspired by quoting the text that "all Scripture is given by inspiration." But here is, for instance, James Orr (conservative), who writes in the *International Standard Bible Encyclopedia* (*s. v.* Bible): "Marks of Inspiration. — This is the ultimate test of 'inspiration' — that to which Paul likewise appeals — its power to 'make wise unto salvation through faith which is in Christ Jesus' (2 Tim. 3:15) — its profitableness for 'teaching, for reproof, for correction, for instruction which is in righteousness' (v. 16) — all to the end 'that the man of God may be complete, furnished completely unto every good work' (v. 17). Nothing is here determined as to 'inerrancy' in minor historical, geographical, chronological details, in which some would wrongly put the essence of inspiration; but it seems implied that at least there is no error which can interfere with, or nullify, the utility of Scripture for the ends specified. Who that brings Scripture to its own tests of inspiration will deny that, judged as a whole, it fulfils them?" [173]

---

173) Similarly J. M. Gibson: " 'Every Scripture inspired of God is also profitable for teaching. . . .' That is perhaps the *locus classicus* on the subject of inspiration. . . . Almost every one in our day is *willing to have the scope of Scripture teaching limited to the spiritual and the*

We shall restrict ourselves to three remarks. (1) In no known language can the statement that all Scripture is profitable for doctrine, etc., be made to mean that some parts of Scripture are not profitable. (2) The text does not propose to give the "marks of inspiration." What the text does is to name the purpose and benefit of inspiration. (3) If this *were* the mark of inspiration, that "it is profitable for doctrine," etc., St. Paul should have given us the mark by which we can tell what is profitable for doctrine. Since he did not give such a mark, men will have to depend on either your or my or their own judgment of what is profitable. But a mark which has no objective certainty is useless as a mark. — The moderns are setting 2 Tim. 3:16 topsy-turvy.

They do the same with many other passages. Numerous instances have been given above, such as the maltreatment of: "Let us reason together," "reasonable service," "treasure in earthen vessels," "Rahab and the dragon" (Is. 51:9), etc. Add, as samples, the following monstrosities, taken from *Revelation and the Bible*, by R. F. Horton: "We certainly misunderstand the apostle when we give to the moral teaching with which his writings abound that note of finality and that suggestion of infallibility which would preclude the free operation of the Spirit in revealing other things to us as the ages roll by." (P. 302.) And the proof-text offered for this statement is — Phil. 3:13-16! Look it up. — "The epistle of James distinctly disclaims the infallibility which a foolish dogmatism has attached to it. See chap. 3:2: Πολλὰ γὰρ πταίομεν ἅπαντες." (P. 349.) — "Whoever wrote 2 Pet. 3:1-7 was under the unscientific impression that the heavens were *a solid substance* capable of being destroyed by fire." (P. 362.) — "It was the complaint of our Lord against the men of His own day that they searched the Scriptures because they thought that in *them*" (italics in the original) "they had eternal life, but would not come to Him that they might have life, John 5:39; the R. V. gives the obvious sense of the original. It is not a little significant that the passage most frequently quoted as an authority for Bible-study is indeed a warning against the

---

practical." (*Op. cit.*, p. 90.) Dr. N. R. Melhorn in the *Lutheran* of July 16, 1941: "The testimony of three apostles (Paul, Peter, Jude) affirms the Bible's reliable authority. 2 Tim. 3:16. . . . The process of delivery of truths to prophets and apostles is termed inspiration. Inspiration, while beyond human understanding of its nature, can be defined as that action of God whereby certain chosen servants of Him were protected from error in recording *revelation*." (Italics in original. Inspiration, accordingly, covers only so much of Scripture as deals with the truths of revelation.) — In this article Dr. Melhorn remarks: "It is not surprising that at least once in every generation of the Christian Church the question of the Bible's authority has been raised." Very true! It has been raised in the present generation. That is why we are discussing it just now. And as long as men persist in curtailing the authority of Scripture, the discussion will have to go on.

substitution of Scripture, which is a mere witness, for the Savior to whom it is meant to bear witness." (P. 406.) Anything to get rid of Verbal Inspiration! [174]

Why, they even resort to mistranslations. Horton writes: "Because this is the Book of God, we have no reason to say that everything said about God in the Book is true. The historical and *progressive* character of the Book gives no foothold for such unintelligent and slumberous dogmatism. Cf. Deut. 4:19, where Jahveh is spoken of as allotting the various objects of false worship unto all nations under the whole heaven, but retaining Israel for Himself." (P. 10.) That is a misinterpretation of Deut. 4:19. And to support this misinterpretation, Moffatt perpetrates this bald mistranslation: "The Eternal, your God, has allotted them *for worship* to all nations under the broad sky." "For worship" is not found in the Hebrew text. Putting it in the translation is falsifying the text. It amounts to the same when Gore's *A New Commentary* says: " '*divided,*' i. e., allotted to be worshiped by them."[175] — Another sample. Moffatt translates the לְמִינוֹ and לְמִינָהּ of Gen. 1:11 and 24 with: "of every kind," "every kind of." That is an impossible translation. The only possible translation is "after his kind." What is the purpose of this falsification? Is it to ward off the smashing blow which the phrase "after his kind" gives to evolution?[176] Better stick to the old tactics and say: Because evolution is true, Moses made a mistake by teaching the contrary and using the phrase "after his kind."

---

174) That is the purpose of Horton's book. It ends with these statements: "We have exalted the Scriptures above our Lord so as to make Him Himself seem to be dependent upon them: with a mistaken zeal we have given them the very title, *viz.*, the Word of God, which is His own ineffable name. In our blindness we have attached such sacred significance to everything which is contained in the Biblical literature that. . . . This dangerous and, in the last resort, idolatrous perversion of Christianity. . . . And if even one soul is led out of the comfortable but suffocating prison-house of the received dogma into the open air of the true revelation, the author will not have toiled in vain." (Pp. 406, 407.)

175) See Koenig, *Theologie des Alten Testaments*, p. 249: "Erst in der neuesten Zeit hat man ja auszusprechen gewagt, dass die Voelker ausser Israel 'von Jahve selbst der Gottlosigkeit und dem Goetzendienst preisgegeben' worden seien. (Delitzsch, *Babel und Bibel*, II, p. 36.) Und wie kommt er zu dieser furchtbaren Anklage? Nun, wie soeben aus seinem Buch angefuehrt worden ist, soll es 'mit nackten Worten' in Deut. 4:19 ausgesprochen sein. . . . Deut. 4:19 sagt also nur dasselbe aus wie viele andere Stellen (Ps. 19:2; Jes. 40:26 usw.), dass Gott den Nichtisraeliten bloss, aber auch wirklich die allgemeine Offenbarung geschenkt hat, die aus Natur und Weltgeschichte herausleuchtet."

176) L. S. Keyser: "The so-called translation of Dr. James Moffatt cannot be trusted, because he so frequently misconstrues the Hebrew text in the interest of his higher criticism and evolutionary conceptions. . . . Moffatt has 'doctored up' the Hebrew text of Gen. 1:12. 'Every' is not in the text. And the pronominal form for 'his' is ignored." (*Op. cit.*, p. 113.)

Crowning Absurdities

No. 22. The following assertions and arguments might have been discussed under the head of "bare assertions" or "misstatements," but the reader will see at once why we put them in a lower bracket and label them as *ludicrous*. Here are nine samples, all taken from writings which ridicule Verbal Inspiration. Others have been noted above.

There is (1) the allegorizing nonsense. H. E. Fosdick and the others condemn the allegorizing interpretation employed by Church Fathers in the strongest terms and thank God that this arbitrary and fanciful method is no longer in vogue.[177] They are right in condemning the allegorizing of the Fathers, but the queer thing is that they are doing the very same thing; only they call it by a different name. Fosdick calls it "change in mental categories." The Bible speaks of miracles, of the floating ax-head and the dead rising, of angels and devils, etc., but these "forms of thought and speech must be translated into modern categories." (P. 129.) The others speak of "didactic poems" and "apocalyptic symbolism," call the "legends of the Garden of Eden and of the Fall the *vehicle* of high and pure revelation," and try to find "the profound prophetic philosophy of history" hidden in these stories. Another queer thing is that these moderns believe, and would have us believe, that it requires great acumen and deep spiritual insight to establish which stories of the Bible are history and which are myths and fables. The truth of the matter is that they apply a very simple canon: any story which contains miraculous or unheard-of elements must be treated as a fable. The story of the Fall, for instance, is, on the face of it, a fable. R. F. Horton: "A serpent that speaks proclaims itself to be in the region of fable." (*Op. cit.*, p. 38.) R. H. Malden puts it this way: "Nor do I think that God ever created a serpent which spoke with a human voice." (*Op. cit.*, p. 54.) Franz Delitzsch, prominent Lutheran exegete, came to the same conclusion: "Das Reden der Schlange steht auf gleicher Linie mit dem Reden der Tiere in der Fabel," and you have the choice, he says, of dismissing it as a pure myth or trying to find some deep symbolic import in it. And the sun, of course, could not literally do what the Book of Joshua says it did. Nor could a real fish have swallowed

---

177) H. E. Fosdick: "Allegorizing appeared everywhere. . . . By allegory Origen supported allegory. . . . We have outgrown allegory. . . . In the modern Church this old method of interpretation is largely discredited." (*Op. cit.*, pp. 65—96.) Charles Gore: "In the great Alexandrian teachers, Clement and Origen, this allegorical method runs riot again. Origen held that the literal meaning of the text is constantly allowed to be such as we cannot believe to be true, just in order to force us to consider the spiritual, or hidden, meaning. Most of the Fathers held fast to both the literal and the hidden meaning. To us their allegorical interpretations appear utterly arbitrary." (*Op. cit.*, p. 51.)

and disgorged a real man. It is the old canon of the allegorist Origen: when we cannot believe the literal meaning to be true, we must resort to allegorizing. The only difference is that these moderns apply the canon in the spirit of "vulgar" rationalism. Discussing the statement of Delitzsch, Dr. Stoeckhardt says: "Von solchen Saetzen zum *rationalismus vulgaris* ist nur ein kleiner Schritt." (*Lehre und Wehre,* 1890, p. 204.) It really harks back to the old vulgar rationalist Celsus, the pagan. "Celsus makes jest also of the serpent, taking the narrative to be an old wife's fable." (See footnote 40.) Were the "vulgar" rationalists possessed of deep spiritual insight?

Furthermore, it strains our powers of belief too much when the moderns ask us to believe that the writers of these Biblical poems and fables believed that their readers would possess such a high degree of intelligence that they would not mistake these poems and fables for actual history though they are presented as actual history and would find the intended meaning though not a hint of the intended meaning is given by the story-teller. The story of Jonah does not hint at any hidden meaning, but the readers of the story, at least the readers in the centuries of Enlightenment, would find that here the story of Israel's captivity and deliverance was being told. As we said above, "Fosdick is able to believe that when the writer of Josh. 10:12 wrote: 'Then spake Joshua,' etc., he did not mean to say that Joshua actually spoke or that the sun actually stood still, but that he was writing a poem and hoping that in the last days a man would arise who would be able to interpret the mysterious words 'And the sun stood still.' "

And finally, when you hear how the moderns interpret these poems, myths and fables, you will understand why we had to have a ludicrous section in our black-list. For instance, what was the real story clothed in the poetic language of Josh. 10:12 f.? Why, simply this, say some of the interpreters, that Joshua asked for, and received, the strength and ability to do two days' work in one day.[178] Or, what is back of the legend of Abraham? Why, says the

---

178) Ernst Muehe: "Theologen der Neuzeit meinen, die Stelle muesste als eine *bloss dichterische Darstellung* des Ereignisses aufgefasst werden: Josua habe erkannt, das Werk dieses Tages sei so gross, dass fuer die bloss menschliche Kraft der Tag noch einmal so lang sein muesste als ein gewoehnlicher, sonst koenne er es nicht zu Ende bringen. In heiligem Eifer betend, haette er diese Ueberzeugung in die dichterischen Worte gekleidet: Sonne, stehe still usw. Damit haette er aber nur gemeint: HErr Gott, verleihe uns auf ausserordentliche Weise doppelte Kraft, dass wir in *einem* Tage vollbringen, wozu sonst die Anstrengung zweier Tage noetig ist. Dies Gebet haette der liebe Gott auch erhoert und ihnen doppelte Kraft gegeben. . . . Ein wirklicher Stillstand der Sonne und des Mondes sei dabei gar nicht behauptet, sondern das waere nur bildliche Redeweise. Seitdem selbst der grosse Gottesgelehrte Hengstenberg leider diese willkuerliche Meinung behauptet hat,

Dean of Wells, "Abraham should perhaps be regarded as representing a tribe or clan rather than as a single historic figure" (*op. cit.*, p. 11). Please give us the meaning of particular incidents in the legend; for instance, what does the laughing of Sarah mean? We cannot tell you that, say the interpreters of the Biblical story-tellers, that is an immaterial embellishment; but we can tell you what the marriage of Abraham and Sarah means. — Tell us! — Why, it was "the symbol of the political union of a southern Israelitic clan with a non-Israelitic tribe south of Hebron. And Abraham's relations with Hagar represent the intimate intercourse between Egypt, Palestine, and Arabia." Etc. Thus the *Encyclopaedia Biblica*. (See *Lehre und Wehre*, 1902, p. 25.) Then there is Fosdick's allegorizing which translates the Biblical forms of thought and speech into modern categories. The women at the tomb never really saw angels. Then what did they mean when they told the disciples that they really did see some? In his examination of the *Modern Use of the Bible* John Bloore deals with this puzzle: "How, then, shall we explain what these categories, which the modern man discards because of his superior intelligence, meant to those who could and did use them? . . . The category of demonology and angelology is nothing more or less than 'a transient phrasing of abiding experiences' (Fosdick). . . . The modern man is virtually denying that the Biblical writers meant what they said when they described angelic visitation, ministry, and communication as being commerce with actual spiritual beings." And now: "Did the Lord mean that the Father would send Him twelve legions of 'spiritual experiences'? And what can He mean when He speaks of joy in the presence of the angels [of spiritual experiences] over a repentant sinner?" (*Alternative Views of the Bible*, p. 94 f.) — These are some of the "facts" which keep the moderns from accepting Verbal Inspiration! — Indeed, if the Bible-stories were of such a nature that we had to go to these interpreters to find out their meaning, we, too, would turn our backs on Verbal Inspiration.[179]

2) Speaking of myths, we want to say that we are unable to accept and believe the myths which the moderns present to us.

---

sind ihm darin viele gefolgt." (*Biblische Merkwuerdigkeiten*, p. 93.) Muehe then goes on to point out that the poem is somewhat askew, since it tells the story in such a way that not only additional strength but also additional *time* was needed.

179) By the way, Gore makes a most illogical deduction from the fact that he and we condemn Origen's allegorical interpretation. In the passage quoted above he continues: "Hardly any one now can be found really to rely upon it. I mention this only because those who would force us to retain the ancient literalism without the ancient allegorism seem to be behaving unreasonably." That is certainly a queer canon: if a man is wrong in one thing, it must be presumed that he is wrong in everything. — Anything to bring Verbal Inspiration into disrepute!

We cannot believe in the existence of the Redactor. He is nothing but a mythical character. We are loathe to believe that a man worked on the Bible in such a clumsy fashion that it takes the higher critics years and decades and centuries to unravel his work. And that is another myth which we cannot accept — that the higher critics possess the uncanny ability to take up a book written centuries ago and tell us with unfailing accuracy which sections were written by P and which by J, and even to split up a single verse, assigning each half to a different source. You are asking too much of us if you want us to invest the higher critics with these supernatural powers.[180] You cannot expect us to keep a sober face when we hear the modern redactors telling us the true story of the Cursing of the Fig-tree (see No. 13, 8) and pretending that they can tell the story of Christ's life and death better than the eye-witnesses. It is too ludicrous; says H. M'Intosh: "He [Professor Schmiedel in *Encycl. Biblica*] fitly crowns these feats, on this assumption, by what is perhaps the most ludicrous of all — that these critics are able two millenniums away to know and tell what Jesus was, said, and did, better than the men who lived with Him, and died for Him, and were especially chosen and inspired of God for the express purpose of giving to the world for its salvation God's record of His Son and revelation of Himself." The crowning absurdity appears from the next sentence: "And that, too, from these assumed to be 'utterly untrustworthy' writings." (*Op. cit.*, p. 711.)

On a par with this conceit of the higher critics is the claim of the evolutionists that they can give us the authentic account of the origin of this world. Far removed from the scene of activities, they act and speak as though they had been present, and, ignorant though they are of the inner working of the forces of nature today, they claim to know all about their operation "millions of years ago." When a Christian hears these claims, he says: "Das glaube

---

180) J. Bloore: "Its acceptance requires us to believe that the critics possess unparalleled literary keenness and an acumen which indeed must be accounted stupendous. In fact, could anything short of the supernatural account for their mysterious, uncanny skill in dismantling documents? . . . The critics of Scripture go at their task with neither doubts nor qualms. They even split up the text of a document into such minute fractions that a single word is sometimes assigned to another source than that of the rest of the verse. Resort must be had to that which their highly developed historical sense requires them to discard — the supernatural and miraculous — as well-nigh the only adequate explanation of this extraordinary ability to analyze, dissect, sift, and piece together the different documents in so complete a mass of literature as the Old Testament must be, according to their views. It is really too much to ask of any one not already committed to it as a corollary of their peculiar view of the Bible." (*Op. cit.*, p. 64.)

ich noch lange nicht."[181] And the scientist declares: "If we are not able to see far into the causes and origin of life in our day, it is not probable that we shall deal more successfully with the problem as to how it arose many million years ago." (Marquis of Salisbury. See footnote 118.) — Anything to discredit Verbal Inspiration — even if they have to credit the higher critics with supernatural faculties.

3) The higher critics take great credit for having discovered a simple way of disposing of the Biblical difficulties. H. L. Willett: "Higher criticism has destroyed the doctrine of verbal inspiration. . . . It has made faith easier and more confident. . . . Most of all, it has explained the seeming contradictions and conflicts of Biblical statements which were in former periods the target of captious and often successful attack." (*Op. cit.*, p. 264.) Yes, Paine attacks, for instance, the accounts that Saul knew David and that Saul did not recognize David, and declares: "These two accounts belie each other." How do the higher critics relieve the situation and explain the conflict of these two statements? N. R. Best has told us that, while "the conservative puckers his brows for hours attempting to range all the data of the story in one consistent chain and weaves a great net of cross references by which he drags the questioned paragraph or chapter into a decidedly different orientation," the liberal scholar has found an easy way out of the difficulty: "The higher critic says: 'Two traditions' — and lets it go at that." (*Op. cit.*, p. 120 f.)[182] Very simple; but Paine would say that that does away with Verbal Inspiration. Surely, say the higher critics, Verbal Inspiration must go; we are one with you there. And so Paine is satisfied. And the higher critics actually believe that they have accomplished great things for the cause of the Bible and Christendom. H. L. Willett can solve many other difficulties. Ingersoll finds

---

181) Dr. E. A. W. Krauss: "Wie, fragt ein Christ, die Heilige Schrift soll den Naturwissenschaften widersprechen? der Astronomie? Und wenn sie es'tut, wer hat dann recht? Gott, der Sonne, Mond und alle Sterne selbst erschaffen hat, . . . der soll in seinem Wort nicht besser und zuverlaessiger reden koennen vom Lauf und Gang dieser Himmelskoerper als diese Menschen, deren nie einer auch nur einem dieser Koerper nahe gekommen ist? Das glaube ich noch lange nicht." (*Proc. Sym. Conf.*, 1902, p. 7.)

182) R. F. Horton: "How is it that in the story of Saul and David we find David, in 1 Sam. 16:18, introduced to Saul as 'a mighty man of valor and a man of war,' and yet, at the end of chapter 17, Saul inquires of Abner whose son David was, as if he had never seen him before, and can get no information from Abner about him?" Answer: "Criticism has solved the difficulties and given us a genuine explanation of the apparent flaws and imperfections. . . . Criticism has, in one word, revealed the nature of these historical compositions, showing approximately the materials which go to their making and the period of their compilation." (*Op. cit.*, pp. 91—94.) Higher criticism says: "Two traditions" and lets it go at that.

the story of Jonah difficult to believe. Willett tells him: "The miraculous features of the narrative present no difficulties to one who approaches it in the spirit of a student of history and tradition." The thing did not happen in real life! (*Op. cit.*, p. 110 f.) And so Ingersoll is satisfied. But he is not going to give the higher critics credit for having discovered a new and ingenious way of solving the difficulty. He will insist that he knew that right along. Professor Kantonen tells us that "the application of scientific and historical methods to the study of the Bible" will relieve us of the "handicaps" which "the mechanical theories of inspiration" place upon exegesis. (See *Conc. Theol. Mthly.*, VII, p. 223.) All very simple, but what we are objecting to at present is that the higher critics want us to look upon their proposed solution as indicative of great acumen.

4) We can credit the higher critics with great resourcefulness. First they said that Moses could not have composed the Pentateuchal code; such an elaborate code could have been produced only in the ninth century. Then it was found that the code of Hammurabi was written about 850 years before Moses. What now? Why, Moses copied from Hammurabi. (See *Lehre und Wehre*, 1903, p. 60; 1913, p. 306.) — "A few years ago it was customary for criticism to deny that these plagues ever happened. Classifying them among the reputed folk-lore of the Hebrews and relegating them to the realm of the purely mythological, the critic calmly and boldly denied that they ever occurred at all. But these past years of research and study have so established the historicity of the record that this procedure is no longer possible; so the new attack has been made on the basis of naturalism. It is plainly stated that *Moses* himself brought about these plagues upon the Egyptians, and that he did so by the use of his own superior knowledge. In a word, he was a bacteriologist, three and a half thousand years before Pasteur! That in itself is a greater miracle than the plagues could ever have been! No microscope, no instruments of research, yet he not only anticipated the discoveries of Lister and Pasteur, but he also applied *germ warfare* to the redemption of Israel and 'bent the Egyptians to *his* will.'. . . The present writer of this refutation is not utterly ignorant of the science of bacteriology, but he humbly confesses that he does not know of any pathogenic micro-organism that would bite everybody except a Hebrew. . . ." (H. Rimmer, in *Christian Faith and Life*, April, 1937, pp. 91, 98.)

5) The critics display great ingenuity in extenuating the pious frauds practiced upon God's people. How did the Book of Jonah, a romance, a fable, get among the sacred books of Israel? That was due to "the inveterate love of romance common to the ancient Jews." (See No. 13, 4.) Or, it is due to the queer working of the

Oriental mind. Dealing with ·the question whether "the story of Eden is to be called history or allegory," N. R. Best says: "The difficulty felt by so many modern Christians in accepting allegory as an inspired vehicle of God's truth is strictly an occidental diffi- culty. No Oriental would feel it. It is a hindrance imposed on faith by the unimaginative matter-of-factness that is more or less characteristic of the Anglo-Saxon mind everywhere, and especially of that strain in Anglo-Saxondom which draws inspiration from the rigid and literal Puritans. To them the exercise of mental inven- tion to create a tale of what never happened on sea or land was a wilful excursion into thé realm of that Evil One who was a liar from the beginning. Of course, they could not dream of such a piece of wicked impertinence existing within the covers of ·the Bible." (*Op. cit.,* p. 88.)[183] We have ·strong doubts whether the Oriental mind is so constituted that it condones the telling of myths *as true history.* Furthermore, the Bible is meant for the Occidentals as much as for the Orientals. On Best's and Malden's theory God would have had to give the world two Bibles, an Oriental and an Occidental Bible. Above all, the normal (the Christian) Oriental mind feels on this point the same as the normal (the Christian) Occidental, Anglo-Saxon, Puritan mind: it feels and knows that *God could not have inspired* the prophets to present myths and romances as history.

6) Some more "pious fraud." By what right did the anonymous writer of the Pastoral Epistles sign Paul's name to them? "It seemed legitimate in that age to put words on the lips of a man whose mind was being interpreted." (Prof. W. C. Berkemeyer in *New Testament Commentary,* p. 582.) This flimsy apology is elaborated by R. F. Horton thus: "Supposing this conjecture of the origin of these letters be accepted — that they are not a composition of St. Paul in the literal sense of the word — what difference does it make to our idea of the revelation contained in them? It must be owned, very little. The truths are not less true because they are incorporated in a com- position which had the origin we have supposed. . . . We have here

---

183) The Dean of Wells on the Oriental mind: "We always think first of truth of fact; Orientals are said always to think first of truth of value. . . . We must remember that the Old Testament was written by Orientals, who did not contemplate any but Oriental readers. We are likely to miss a great deal of its meaning unless we can learn to read it with Oriental eyes." On the legends in Numbers, Exodus, and the latter part of Genesis: "The Oriental attitude towards fact is not the same as our own, and in the Old Testament the center of interest is not in the facts narrated but in the construction put upon them." "The stories of Abraham passing off Sarah as his sister and Jacob's deception of Isaac are legends or pieces of folk-lore. Orientals have never regarded duplicity as we do, but have always admired it (when successful) as a mark of superior intelligence. They do not appear to feel strongly against treachery." (*Op. cit.,* pp. 8, 31, 61.)

an example of religious writing common in antiquity but unknown among us." (The Oriental mind works differently from the Occidental mind, and the mind of the ancients differently from that of the moderns!) And "the author of the Second Epistle of Peter" (which purports to be a writing of St. Peter) "had no intention to deceive when he wrote in the name of his august master. To call him a *falsarius* is a very gratuitous condemnation. . . . This humble disciple had no intention whatever of imposing on his readers, who knew as well as he did that Peter was dead years ago." (*Op. cit.,* p. 310 f., 360 f.) Was the Chronicler a *falsarius?* "In 1 Kings 5: 13-15 Solomon sends a levy of 30,000 men out of Israel to do the work, while the Chronicler (2 Chron. 2:17 f.) insists on it that these hewers of wood, etc., were *strangers,* and he gives their number exactly as the same as the passage in Kings, which suggests that he purposely corrects the impression that native-born Israelites would be employed on such *corvée*-work." (P. 131.) He was not a *falsarius* but a *corrector!* But some of his statements must be taken *cum grano salis.* "A comparison between 2 Sam. 24:9 and 1 Chron. 21:5 illustrates afresh the Chronicler's habit of *raising the figures.*" (P. 129.) The Chronicler committed a falsification, and he did it from chauvinistic motives. What about the pious fraud committed by the writer of Heb. 11? "We are not at liberty to accept the statements there made about Abraham and the other worthies as additional historical facts." But the writer of Hebrews presents them as historical facts — is that not a falsification? No, indeed, "our author is simply treating the subject *homiletically;* he is reading into those early records a rich spiritual or theological significance." (P. 130.) — We thought that the era of Bruno Bauer, who made Luke invent historical figures (Lysanias) to suit his purpose, was past. We were mistaken.

7) Occasionally the Biblical writers make false statements in good faith. They are not *falsarii;* their fault is incompetence. We must remember that the authors of the books of Judges, Kings, Chronicles, wrote in the days when "the habits of exact chronology and accurate chronicling had not been cultivated." (R. F. Horton, *op. cit.,* p. 104.) "The Chronicler — in perfect good faith, but without any historic justification — reads into the story of the ancient monarchy the ideas and practices of his own time. It is idle and foolish to bring the charges of dishonesty against a writer because, in the manner of all authors in antiquity, he felt at liberty to dress the story of by-gone and ancient days in the garb and coloring of his own surroundings and his own preconceptions." "For example, when the older historian says that Solomon gave to Hiram twenty cities in the land of Galilee (1 Kings 9:11) and the Chronicler speaks of the cities which Hiram had given to Solomon

(2 Chron. 8:2), we are to conclude that the later author, dazzled with the glory of the great king, could not credit the story that Solomon had handed over cities in his own land to a stranger and assumed that the transaction had been precisely the other way." (P. 134 f., 124.)[184] Was Luke one of these authors of antiquity who had not cultivated the habits of exact chronology? Yes, indeed, says Gore's *A New Commentary*, on Acts 7:6-11: "Luke's defective sense of time, which is one of his limitations as a historian, appears here." Luke was honest enough, but he lacked the exactitude of the modern historian.[185]

8) When we saw the statement by F. Bettex: "These critics say that God, not being a man, cannot speak; consequently there is no word of God!" (*Fundamentals*, IV, p. 82), we were inclined to think that he might have overstated the case. But we later found that, for instance, C. H. Dodd, professor of exegesis at Oxford, declares in all seriousness: The Epistle to the Romans cannot be, strictly speaking, "the Word of God." For "in the expression 'the Word of God' lurks an equivocation. A word is properly a means of communicating thought through vibrations of the vocal cords, peculiar to the human species. The Eternal has neither breath nor vocal cords; how should He speak words?" (*Op. cit.*, p. 16.) It is an undeniable fact that God has no vocal cords; and this is one of the "facts" over against which Verbal Inspiration cannot stand — one of the facts which breaks the Bible claim to be the Word of God!

---

184) Gore's *A New Commentary*: "A remarkable rewriting of history; the Chronicler dismisses such a tradition as unworthy of a great king and reverses the transaction." — See *Commentary* by Jamieson, Fausset, Brown or *Weimar Bibel*: "Die Staedte, die Hiram Salomo wiedergab, weil sie ihm nicht gefielen."

185) R. F. Horton: "This opening passage of *Acts* gives us a clear indication that the author lays no claim to infallibility. In the simplest and most natural way *he corrects himself.*" (Italics in original.) "When he wrote the gospel, he had been under the impression that the ascension had taken place immediately after the resurrection. . . . The author looked on these events as compressed into a few hours. When he approached his second treatise, he was better informed and knew that for six weeks after the resurrection the risen Lord manifested Himself to His disciples. . . . When an author thus corrects himself, we certainly learn to trust him more as an honest writer, but we feel at once the absurdity of ascribing the qualities of infallibility and inerrancy to his work." (*Op. cit.*, p. 260 f.) — Lenski on Luke 24:50: "Intolerable is the claim, which boasts as being the genuine exegesis, that in his gospel Luke tells us that Jesus ascended to heaven on the very day of His resurrection, while in the Acts the same Luke tells us that Jesus ascended forty days later. This preposterous claim calls it genuine exegesis when it decrees, 'He led them out' must mean that very Easter night. So the ascension took place at night, in the moonlight! First Luke got hold of one tradition and followed it; then he discovered another and again followed it, with never a word of explanation — and he sent both documents to 'the same man, Theophilus!'"

9) We listed a number of misinterpretations under No. 21. The following ones are listed here because of their outstanding absurdity. Paine: "I begin by saying that these two chapters [Gen. 1 and 2] contain two different and contradictory stories of a creation." Name one of these contradictions! Gore's *New Commentary:* "Gen. 2: 4 b-25: J's Narrative of Creation. . . . Man is formed before plants and animals." Name one more! Ingersoll: "In the first account, man is made 'male and female'; in the second only a male is made, and there is no intention of making a woman whatever." Any more? Yes. "In the first chapter of Genesis, Adam alone is mentioned and the woman is left out." We have already listed this particular blunder of a nameless discrepancy-hunter (see page 99),[186] but set it down here again for the purpose of comparing his lack of intelligent reading of the text with that evidenced by the *New Commentary* of the well-known Bishop Gore. The writer of the statement: "Man is formed before plants and animals (Gen. 2: 4 b-25)" did not read *this* text intelligently. — R. H. Malden: "Eden is fairy-land. . . . It was fairy-land to Ezekiel when he wrote of the king of Tyre of his own day: 'Thou wast in Eden, the garden of God, . . . thou art the anointed cherub," chap. 28: 13, 14." (*Op. cit.,* p. 53.) "I doubt whether justice is, as a general rule, done to the episode of the burning bush, Ex. 3. Knowledge of another person's name was, and probably still is, in some parts of the world, supposed to give the possessor some power over him." (P. 33.) "The prayer of Jonah does not fit the circumstances which are said to have given rise to it. 'Out of the belly of *hell* cried I' — not of *the fish."* Best of all: "Jonah was angry at the success of his own mission to Nineveh, but in spite of its repentance it had long been desolate. (In fact, it had been destroyed some three centuries before the book was written.)" (P. 57 f.) So the story is evidently a fabrication, and in the face of these "facts" Verbal Inspiration cannot stand! — R. F. Horton: "On the old and orthodox idea of revelation the Epistle of Jude would be discredited; for it is impossible that apocryphal works like the *Book of Enoch* and *the Assumption of Moses* (v. 9) are worthy of credit." (*Op. cit.,* p. 364.) Who told Horton that Jude is quoting from these apocryphal books? But aside from that, on Horton's theory St. Paul's writings would be in worse condemnation, for Paul even quotes from pagan writers. — It seems incredible that Marcus Dods (a conservative modern), in listing "irreconcilable

---

186) H. Rimmer "pointed out to him that his error was a lack of intelligent reading of the text" (Gen. 1: 27). And, "Moses adds later details that he did not use in the broad outline. . . . How marvelously this illustrates the ability of the keen mentality that would contradict the Book that God has written!"

discrepancies," should offer this: "According to Mark, Luke, and John the women found the stone already rolled away from the entrance to the tomb; according to Matthew this was accomplished by an angel *in the presence of the women.*" (*The Bible, Its Origin and Nature,* p. 136.)   Matthew does not say that the women saw the angel rolling away the stone and seating himself on it.   For one thing, he has ἐκάθητο and not ἐκάθισεν.   See Zahn's *Kommentar* on Matt. 28:1-3. — We have not the space to display any more samples.

No. 23.   Some of the assertions and arguments are more than ludicrous; they are grotesque.   We submit three samples.   Arthur Brisbane (who would classify himself as ultraliberal) thus proves that the Bible-story is not true: Jesus said, "*Today* thou shalt," etc.; but "if the soul travels at the speed of the radio rays, which in less than one second pass around the globe seven times, it would take it 300,000,000 years to reach the limits of the universe."

H. E. Fosdick (very liberal) and Ingersoll find that the Sinaitic wilderness could not possibly have sustained the 600,000 men and their families, 3,000,000 persons.   So Fosdick solves the difficulty by suggesting, in the *Ladies' Home Journal,* that the Hebrew word *alaf* be here translated "a family."   "All our trouble comes from translating it 'a thousand' here."   Num. 1:34, 35 would thus state that the tribe of Manasseh numbered not 32,000 but had thirty-two *families,* making 200 people altogether.   So a total of only about 5,500 made the Exodus.   "At least that fits the possibilities."   No miracle was needed to sustain such a vast host.   It is not necessary to assume that Moses "stretched the statistics."   And Ingersoll can no longer gloat over the biometrical blunder committed by Moses in letting the seventy increase to three millions in such a short time.   However, if Fosdick's suggestion is adopted, Ingersoll will have to charge Moses with a bad arithmetical error.   Add the 46 "families" of Reuben, the 59 of Simeon, and all the others, and we get 598 "families."   But the census officials whose figures Moses accepts, get the sum of 603 "families" (Num. 1:46).   Computing a family at 6, the census official for Gad should have reported 270 persons.   He padded the figures and reported 650.   The national official tried to rectify these mistakes, and in verse 46, where he was entitled to 3,618, he put down only 550.   These men were poor in arithmetic.   If Israel numbered 603,550 men, the figures given Ex. 38:25, 26, as to the sum raised by taxation, are correct.   If Fosdick's suggested figure, 5,500, is correct, the sum given in verse 25, at half a shekel for every man, cannot be correct.   Or else they were taxed to death. (See further *Theol. Mthly.,* 1928, p. 299 ff.)

H. C. Alleman: "Matt. 21:7 says the disciples placed their garments upon *them* (the ass and the colt), and He sat on *them.*   Does that mean that Jesus sat upon both animals?" (*Luth. Church*

Quart., Oct., 1940, p. 356.)[187] Dr. Alleman goes out of his way to give the sacred story a farcical twist. Before him David Friedrich Strauss did it. He says that "the evangelist makes Jesus slavishly and unreasonably carry out the prophetic description by riding at once upon both animals." The Lange-Schaff Commentary calls it a "frivolous criticism," "to which it is sufficient to reply that Matthew knew as much Hebrew and had as much common sense as any modern critic of his gospel."

"Wir sind Wirklichkeitsmenschen!" — Gentlemen, your facts have turned out to be fictions and Scripture still stands, the Impregnable Rock, unbroken, unbreakable!

---

187) Similarly Gore's *A New Commentary:* "Matthew's misunderstanding of Zechariah leads him into *absurdity.* He speaks . . . of the Lord as riding on both animals." He does not. Just "refer the second αὐτῶν (them) to the garments" (*Exp. Gr. Test.*). According to Greek grammar it fits perfectly.

CHAPTER II

Has the Bible Moral Blemishes?

The second objection to Verbal Inspiration is based on the so-called unethical portions of the Bible. The mistakes of the Bible are to the moderns a small matter compared with the ethical blemishes they see in the Bible. These alleged immoralities and indecencies scandalize them beyond expression. That is what arouses their most violent protest.[188] The moderns, both conservatives and liberals, join with the unbelievers and infidels in loudly protesting that the Bible as it stands contains much that outrages their moral sensibilities. What the present age needs is an expurgated Bible; and since Verbal Inspiration stands for an unexpurgated Bible, Verbal Inspiration must be done away with.

THE MODERNS HORRIFIED AT THE BAD ETHICS OF THE BIBLE

The black-list produced by the moderns in support of their objection is black indeed. The God of the Bible, of the Old Testament part of it, is painted in black colors. "Yahweh was a selfish, tribal god, not unlike the other gods of the peoples surrounding the Hebrews, a cruel god, a god of war, who demands the sacrifice of children and hates his enemies." (See *Luth. Church Quart.*, Jan., 1941, p. 79 f.; the charge is there refuted.) J. De Witt: "Especially shocking are the moral blemishes of the Bible. Acts are recorded in the Old Testament which exhibit a low standard of morality. . . . Take for example the butcheries in Canaan under Joshua. . . . In this connection the black treachery of Jael comes to mind, violating the sacred laws of hospitality. . . . The inspired books are more vulnerable here than at all other points. The boldest scoffer of our times in flaunting *The Mistakes of Moses* has declared that there are laws in the Mosaic code that would disgrace any modern statute-book, and his assertion cannot reasonably be disputed. . . . Enough has been given to discredit the whole volume, unless a broader definition can be found for the inspiration that

---

188) H. M'Intosh: "The ethical and religious teaching is now usually first and most strongly urged in proof and illustration of the erroneousness and untrustworthiness of the Bible." (*Is Christ Infallible and the Bible True?* p. 4.) That is correct, says C. H. Dodd. "It long ago became clear that in claiming for the Bible accuracy in matters of science and history its apologists had chosen a hopeless position to defend. Much more important is the fact that in matters of faith and morals an unprejudiced mind must needs recognize many things in the Bible which could not possibly be accepted by Christian people in anything approaching their clear and natural meaning." (*The Authority of the Bible*, p. 13.)

produced it than any that has yet been advanced." Verbal Inspiration must go! (*What Is Inspiration?* Pp. 60 f., 68, 120, 183.) De Witt refers us to Ingersoll. Let us hear him. "The Bible is full of barbarism. . . . I call upon Robert Collyer to state whether he believes the Old Testament was inspired, whether he believes that God commanded Moses and Joshua or any one else to slay little children in the cradle. . . . I want Prof. Swing to tell whether he believes the story about the bears eating up children, whether that is inspired. . . . Everything that shocks the brain and shocks the heart, throw it away." (*Lectures,* p. 298 ff.) [189] H. E. Fosdick agrees with Ingersoll on this point. "Those deeds in the Old Testament which from our youth have shocked us by their barbarity — the ruthless extermination of the Amalekites, . . . the ninth chapter of Esther, where the writer rejoices in a vengeful massacre . . ." (*The Modern Use of the Bible,* pp. 14, 26). The Lutheran R. F. Grau declared: "The morality of the Old Testament is imperfect" (see *Lehre und Wehre,* 1893, p. 324), and Dr. H. C. Alleman draws the inevitable conclusion therefrom: "When we read Old Testament stories of doubtful ethics and *lex talionis* reprisals, with their cruelty and vengefulness, their polygamy and adultery, it is difficult for us to sympathize with the theory of verbal inspiration, however much we may sympathize with the motives which led to it." (*The Luth. Church Quart.,* July, 1936, p. 241.) H. L. Willett, too, has no sympathy with Verbal Inspiration, for "the book thus produced should be a clear and unvarying record of the divine mind, with no suggestion of mistake in matters of fact and norms of conduct." But: "The Bible is not a perfect book. . . . It is not final in its morality." And the verbal-inspirationists should be silenced. "No error has ever resulted in greater discredit to the Scriptures or injury to Christianity than that of attributing to the Bible such a miraculous origin and nature as to make it an infallible standard of morals and religion." (*The Bible through the Centuries,* pp. 3, 283, 289.) Verbal Inspiration is an evil thing and must go, declares C. H. Dodd, pointing to "the harm that has been done to the general conscience by allowing the outworn morality of parts of the Old Testament to stand as authoritative declarations. . . . The old dogmatic view of the Bible therefore is not only open

---

189) Similarly the scoffer Thomas Paine: "Whenever we read the cruel and torturous executions, the unrelenting vindictiveness, . . . with which more than half of the Bible is filled, it would be more consistent that we called it the word of a demon than the Word of God. It is a history of wickedness that has served to corrupt and brutalize mankind. . . . As to the book called the Bible, it is blasphemy to call it the Word of God." (*Age of Reason,* I, p. 21.) Similarly the scoffer Clarence Darrow: "The various parts of the Bible were written by human beings who . . . were influenced by the barbarous morality of primitive times."

to attack from the standpoint of science and historical criticism, but, if taken seriously, it becomes a danger to religion and public morals. A revision of this view is therefore an imperative necessity" (*loc. cit.*). The times call for an expurgated Bible.[190]

One of the blackest sections of the black-list before us deals with the imprecatory psalms, Pss. 35, 55, 59, 69, 79, 109, 137, and others. Says Ingersoll: "I want Prof. Swing to tell whether the 109th psalm is inspired." H. E. Fosdick: "Read the closing words of the 137th Psalm, which even Gounod's glorious music cannot redeem from brutality." (*Loc. cit.*) R. H. Malden, dean of Wells:

---

190) We submit a few more statements which show how deeply the moderns are scandalized at our unexpurgated Bible, how bitterly they resent the claim that all Scripture is given by inspiration. S. P. Cadman: "Slavery, polygamy, incest, needless wars, cruel massacres, and other non-moral acts and crimes can all be justified by the baseless assumption that every word of Holy Scripture must be regarded as practically infallible and then literally construed. It is not too much to say that this dogma has been prolific of skepticism upon an extended scale." (*Answers to Everyday Questions,* p. 253.) G. L. Raymond declares that "the earlier books of the Bible manifest in places the influences of comparatively low domestic, social, ethic, and religious standards," points to "the wholesale slaughter committed by Joshua and David," and concludes that "it is not necessary to affirm that men must accept every phrase of the Bible as infallibly correct" (*The Psychology of Inspiration,* pp. 145, 153, 189). Dr. E. G. Homrighausen (Princeton Theological Seminary): "Few intelligent Protestants can still hold to the idea that the Bible is an infallible book; that it contains no linguistic errors, no historical discrepancies, no antiquated scientific assumptions, not even *bad ethical standards.*" (*Christianity in America,* p. 121.) F. Baumgaertel: "It is a fact that certain traits in the character of Yahweh are offensive to us Christians: in his name people steal. [Ex. 11:2.] In his name blood was poured out like water: the butchering of the first-born in Egypt, the command to massacre whole populations, the slaughtering of the prophets of Baal, Samuel cutting down with his own hand the king of the Amalekites." (See W. Moeller, *Um die Inspiration der Bibel,* p. 21.) H. F. Baughman: "The ethics of the Bible are controverted by modern sociology. Its morals are questioned by modern psychology. . . . It is interwoven with the ethics of an ancient day, which have long since been displaced by the onward march of human knowledge." (*The Luth. Church Quart.,* July, 1935, p. 254 f.) At the Washington Debate, in 1937, Dr. H. W. Snyder, representing the U. L. C., declared that "the Lutheran Church, outside perhaps of the Missouri Synod, has never subscribed to a verbal theory of inspiration," and told why he cannot accept Verbal Inspiration: "As one writer on this question says: 'It [the Bible] has carried with it the husk as well as the kernel,' and in illustration of his meaning he quotes some stories of vengeance, cruelty, *lex talionis,* polygamy, adultery, which it relates." (See the *Journal of the A. L. Conference,* March, 1938; CONC. THEOL. MTHLY., IX, p. 359.) In view of these facts the Christian reader must expurgate his Bible before he can get any benefit from it. In the words of Georgia Harkness: "The Bible has one great theme — the obligation of man to God and of God to man. More than once this obligation was crudely conceived, for man's own vindictiveness and passion have a way of getting mixed with his idea of holy things. If we would *sort out the humanly crude from the divinely pure* in the message of the Bible, we would have an authoritative measure — the mind of Christ." (*The Faith by Which the Church Lives,* p. 70.)

"What are we to make of the fierce prayers for vengeance on the enemies of the writer, whether personal or national, which are to be found in some of the psalms? They belong to a more primitive state of society and were written by men who had little belief, if any, in life beyond the grave.... The ethical standards of more than two thousand years ago cannot be expected to be the same as our own." (*The Inspiration of the Bible*, p. 61 ff.) E. F. Keever, writing on "The Imprecatory Psalms" in *The Luth. Church Quart.*, April, 1940, p. 131 ff., does not agree with Henry Ward Beecher, who is reported to have said that "David seems to have been inspired at times by the spirit of the Lord, and at other times by the spirit of the devil"; but he agrees with Dr. Malden. He says: "Let us not look for Christian ethical concepts in the primitive morality of ancient tribes. If we study the religion, the ethics, the culture, and the national traditions of ancient Judaism; if we sense the madness of the everlasting wars that sacked their cities, ... what other appeal could these ill-starred tribes make than utter frenzied cries to all the powers in the upper and nether world to curse the bloody, idolatrous hordes that almost brought them to extinction?" In the article "Some Thoughts on Inspiration" in the *Journal of the A. L. Conf.*, May, 1939, Hjalmar W. Johnson says: "The *human element* appears also with sad realism in the imprecatory psalms. In these passages (Ps. 109: 8, 9, 10; 137: 9) the human, or shall I say inhuman, element is sadly evident." And that proves, they say, that there was no Verbal Inspiration. In the words of R. W. Sockman: "If every word of Scripture were thought of as dictated by God to sacred penmen preserved from error, how would the reader reconcile the cruel explosiveness of the imprecatory psalms with the tenderness of Isaiah's fifty-third chapter or Paul's fifteenth chapter of First Corinthians? How would he harmonize the cynicism of Ecclesiastes with the buoyant hopefulness of Revelation?" (*Recoveries in Religion*, p. 61.)

They tell us further that these immoral sentiments vitiate the morals of the Christian people. People will make use of the imprecatory psalms to give expression to, and justify, their carnal hatred. C. H. Dodd: "Many people found that the imprecatory psalms so perfectly expressed what they felt about the enemy that they could join in the services with a fervor and reality they had never known. Yet as they look back upon that state of mind they probably do not regard it as the high-water mark of their religious life.... The old dogmatic view ... becomes a danger to religion and public morals." (*Loc. cit.*) These psalms must be expunged from the Christian Bible. They are not fit to be read in Christian services. "Give us Christian responsive readings! To be sure, there are some heart-warming, soul-lifting passages in the Psalter. But what place should there be in our responsive readings for ancient Jewish tribal teachings which Jesus Himself set aside?" (*Western Christian Advocate*, Jan. 19, 1928.) These psalms must be put on the *index locorum prohibitorum.* F. Baumgaertel asks that: "Ps. 137:9 duerfte doch nicht im Psalmbuch stehen."

Next on the black-list are the "filthy stories" and the records of gross sins committed by great men of the Bible. "Old and modern theologians have spoken of 'filthy stories' in the Scriptures· and insist that you dare not charge the Holy Ghost with telling them." (F. Pieper, *Chr. Dog.*, I, p. 338.) There is Gen. 38 (Judah and Tamar) and Ezek. 23! Ingersoll is scandalized at these portions of Scripture: "A great many chapters I dare not read to you. They are too filthy. I leave all that to the clergy." (*Op. cit.*, p. 368.) Paine is scandalized: "The obscene and vulgar stories in the Bible are as repulsive to our ideas of the purity of a Divine Being as the horrid cruelties and murders it ascribes to Him are repugnant to our ideas of His justice." (*Reply to the Bishop of Llandaff*, p. 33.) The Lutheran W. F. Gess ·is scandalized: "It is disgusting to burden *God's* Word with the record of such horrible sins. Reverence should forbid that. It does not take a keen eye to see that *Schmutzgeschichten* such as the story of Judah and Tamar and of the foul deed of Gibeah have no place in God's Word." (See *Proc., Syn.·Conf.*, 1909, p. 45.) Dr. H. C. Alleman, too, feels that "the pure Scriptures must be separated from their filth." (See *The Lutheran*, Jan. 14, 1937.) "Furthermore,' asks R. H. Malden, "what are we to make of the conduct of David in the matter of Bathsheba and Uriah the Hittite?" (*Loc. cit.*) R. F. Horton: "Did we not even as children wonder how Gideon, who had received a direct revelation from God, could encourage the idolatry of the ephod, or how Samson, whose strength came from the Spirit of God, should practice immoralities? . . . Granted that the crimes recorded in the book are not entirely approved, yet how comes it that they are not more emphatically condemned if the writing comes in any sense from God? . . . When the simple truth of the matter is perceived, the idea that the Book of Judges is · inspired in that sense [in the sense of Verbal Inspiration] will be maintained not, as now, by the friends but only by the enemies of divine revelation." (*Revelation and the Bible*, pp. 92, 100.) — Some years ago a book was published in New York which contained all the "filthy stories" the compiler could find in the Bible, and only those. The purpose of that black-list was to ridicule the idea that the Bible is a "holy" book. — The point of the present argument against Verbal Inspiration is that the Holy Ghost would not and could not record these "filthy" stories and

He would not do it for the further reason that the reading of them would harm public morals.[191]

A special point is given the argument by anathematizing the idea that the Holy Ghost would speak by the mouth and write by the hands of men who had committed great sins. (See W. Lee, *The Inspiration of Holy Scripture*, pp. 217, 221 ff.)

Sections of the New Testament, too, are put on the black-list. H. L. Willett lists "the anger of Paul at the high priest who ordered him smitten in court and his advice to Timothy about taking a little wine," also "the summary punishment of Ananias and his wife." "In other words, the Bible is not an authority to us on all the questions with which it deals." (*Loc. cit.*, p. 291.) Even Jesus Himself, *as the Gospels present Him*, is not free of moral obliquity. He infringed on the property rights of His neighbors. By what right did He destroy the fig-tree which was not His and deprive the Gadarene pig-owners of their property? Unless Verbal Inspiration is discarded, unless the Gospel accounts are set right, Jesus appears in a bad light. H. L. Willett: "Even in the life of Jesus the same difficulties appear. So difficult are the narratives of the demons sent into the swine and the cursed fig-tree that many who hold without hesitation to the inspiration and authority of the Book wonder if there has not been some error in the record at these points." (*Loc. cit.*) [192]

---

191) "Long passages are adduced about the sins of leading historical characters, such as the drunkenness of Noah, the incest of Lot, . . . the murder and adultery of David, the dissoluteness of Solomon, and all the evil-doings of the times of the judges, the kings of Israel and Judah, down to the close of the Old Testament; as also not a few kinds of things in the New Testament. 'There,' it is said with something akin to scorn and ironical triumph, — 'there are your famous saints! — There is your trustworthy, infallible, and divinely inspired, and authoritative Bible!'" (H. M'Intosh, *op. cit.*, p. 318.) "Another objection raised against the divine origin of the Bible and the doctrine of inspiration is: The sins of the saints as recorded in the Bible must necessarily have an evil effect on the morals of its readers. . . . Do not Christian preachers continually protest against books. . . which present to the eyes and ears of men human foibles, passions, illicit sexual relations, and crimes in all their shameful reality? If this must also be said of the Bible, how can this book be inspired by God Himself? Has it not thereby forfeited all claims to being God's own Book?" (*Theol. Mthly*, 1925, p. 333: "The Bible and the Sins of the Saints.")

192) "Mr. Huxley observes that the evangelist has no 'inkling of the legal and moral difficulties of the case,' and adds, the devils entered into the swine 'to the great loss and damage of the innocent Gerasene or Gadarene pig-owners.' Further: 'Everything that I know of law and justice convinces me that the wanton destruction of other people's property is a misdemeanor of evil example.'" (See W. E. Gladstone, *The Impregnable Rock of Holy Scripture*, p. 298.) After the writer of the article "The 'Cursing' of the Fig-tree" in *The Luth. Church Quart.*, April, 1936, has given us the true story of this incident (the evangelist had garbled it), he states: "As to the matter of ownership, there is

Finally, the moderns are scandalized at certain doctrines of the Bible, doctrines taught not only in the Old Testament but also by the apostles and Jesus. Hear Ingersoll: "I would rather that this thrilled and thrilling globe, shorn of all life, should in its cycles rub the wheel, the parent star, on which the light should fall as fruitlessly as falls the gaze of love on death, than to have this infamous doctrine of eternal punishment true; rather than have this infamous selfishness of a heaven for a few and a hell for the many established as the word of God." (*Op. cit.*, p. 311.) Hear H. E. Fosdick: "Bible categories that shock the modern conscience — miracles, demons, fiat creation, apocalyptic hopes, eternal hell." (*Op. cit.*, p. 5.) R. F. Horton: "The writer of Heb. 6:1-8; 10:26, 27 is throughout imbued with the stern spirit of the old Law. . . . This doctrine seems at variance with the idea of God given to us elsewhere in the New Testament. We must treat it as a judgment passed by the writer, a judgment which, however sincere, can claim no more infallibility than other judgments which are passed by good and earnest men." (*Revelation and the Bible*, pp. 332, 335.) C. T. Craig: "Despite its majestic insights, the Epistle to the Hebrews has not been an unmixed blessing. It is more responsible than any other book of the New Testament for the retention of the idea that a bloody sacrifice was necessary in order to make possible the forgiveness of men's sins." (*The Study of the New Testament*, p. 111. — See the stinging rebuke administered to this writer in *Kirch. Zeitschrift*, 1940, p. 555.) A writer quoted by L. Gaussen: "St. Paul speaks of 'having delivered an incestuous person over to Satan,' 1 Cor. 5:5. Could this passage (fanatical no doubt) have been inspired? . . . He tells them, further, 'that in Adam all die,' 1 Cor. 15:22. Judaical superstition! It is impossible that such a passage can be inspired." (*Theopneustia*, p. 202.) And it is impossible that Verbal Inspiration, according to which these passages and all other passages are inspired, can be true. This doctrine, too, is immoral and harmful. The moderns have been telling us that from page one on. Verbal Inspiration, "if taken seriously, becomes a danger to religion and public morals." (C. H. Dodd, *loc. cit.*)

This, then, is the situation: while the common folk throughout Christendom call the Bible "the good Book," the intellectuals declare it to be a book which is in parts bad, so bad that it needs to be expurgated before it can be placed in the hands of the common people. "A possible reason for the crime wave may be

---

now no need of invoking the eminent domain of the Son of God in order to legitimize His behavior towards the property of other people. For Jesus did not kill the tree, and He had no thought of so doing." (P. 191.)

the teachings of the Sunday-school, says a Cleveland, Ohio, pastor in *Scribner's*. . . . If the lives of these men (the brigands of the Old Testament) are to be told the children, they must be greatly cut and told as stories of half-mythical characters." Just as censors are appointed for expurgating the plays presented to the public, so the moderns are calling for a Board of Censors for Certain Books of the Bible. The Bible needs most careful editing and pitiless expurgation. (See *Theol. Mthly.*, 1927, p. 181.) The vicious doctrine of Verbal Inspiration must be broken down!

THE MORAL SENSE OF THE CHRISTIAN OUTRAGED BY THE CALL FOR AN EXPURGATED BIBLE

Sections of the Bible outrage your moral sensibilities? The trouble with you is that you have permitted your carnal feelings to blunt your Christian sensibilities. In the first place, the moral sense of the Christian forbids him to charge God and God's Word with immoralities. The Christian trembles at God's Word, Is. 66:2. He believes that "every word of God is pure" (Prov. 30:5). He declares: "Thy Word is very pure," Ps. 119:140, and his Christian feeling is outraged when men speak of moral blemishes in God's Word. When the atheist and the infidel declare that their ethico-religious consciousness forbids them to respect the God of the Bible, the God who ordered the extermination of the Canaanites and inspired the imprecatory psalms;[193] all Christian theologians tell them: Do not appeal to your ethico-religious consciousness; you have none; you are uttering blasphemy. It is a *crimen laesae maiestatis divinae* to criticize God, and it is blasphemy to charge God's Word with sanctioning immoralities. — And the moderns agree with us that we cannot charge God with sanctioning immoralities; they, too, denounce such a charge as blasphemy.

• But the moderns are themselves doing this very thing. To be sure, they resent the charge that they are criticizing the *inspired Word*. They insist that these objectionable portions of the Bible belong to the "human side" of the Bible, are not inspired, are not God's Word, do not belong in the Bible. But pleading thus, they are pleading guilty. What right has the skeptic to treat the Bible as a human book? And what right has the modern to treat it as partly divine and partly human? Both, the moderns no less than

---

193) The infidels clothe their objection in just this form. "Regarding these things (the slaughter of the Canaanites, the ferocious and vindictive expressions in many of the psalms) the argument of skeptics is a brief one: This book professes to be divine, but it represents *God as approving of immoral actions*, and therefore it cannot be divine. Its claim is false, and we must disregard it." (Marcus Dods, *The Bible, Its Origin and Nature*, p. 87.)

the skeptics, claim the right to criticize that book of which God has solemnly declared: "All Scripture is given by inspiration of God." The moderns are not ashamed to say openly that the Bible is subject to their censorship. "It belongs to the Church in every age to examine the sacred writings by the light both of tradition and of its own spiritually illumined self-consciousness. . . . By the light of its own spiritually illumined consciousness it discerns the Word of God within those Scriptures. . . . The Church has the right of rejecting from this Word whatever does not satisfy the demands of its ethico-religious consciousness." (G. T. Ladd, *The Doctrine of Sacred Scripture*, II, pp. 502, 508.) [194] They are actually arrogating the right to sit in judgment on God's Word. And we tell them: You are committing the *crimen laesae maiestatis divinae*. When Professor Grau declared that "the morality of the Old Testament is imperfect," Dr. Stoeckhardt wrote: Das ist ein "blasphemes Urteil ueber die Sittlichkeit des Alten Testaments." (*Loc. cit.*) It is blasphemous to say that the writers of the Old Testament expressed unethical judgments, for, whether the moderns accept it or not, they wrote by inspiration of God. How is it possible that Christian theologians can speak disparagingly of the sacred writings? The skeptics do it because they are lacking the ethico-religious consciousness. The moderns are doing it because they have permitted their carnal sense of what is right or wrong to dull their Christian sense. Their Christian heart has not bidden them to separate the "chaff" from the wheat, the "filthy" from the

---

194) Exercising his ethico-religious consciousness, Professor Ladd "finds various passages, and even some entire books of the Old Testament, which manifest a relatively low moral tone and contain relatively many moral imperfections. Still others of these proverbs show so much of mere shrewdness as scarcely to escape the charge of being immoral when considered from the Christian point of view (see Prov. 17:8; 18:16; 21:14). We can go only a certain distance in company with the spirit of the imprecatory psalms: thence our path and theirs lie in different levels and lines." (*Op. cit.*, I, pp. 464, 472.) Similar statements by others: "If, besides the divine truth that it embodies, the Bible also contains . . . moral incongruities and monstrosities, from which our souls recoil, how shall I separate the gold from the dross? . . . If anything agrees not with these words of Christ in the Gospels — polygamy, slavery, revenge, and barbarity of every kind — we renounce and denounce it as evil. Our enlightened moral instinct rejects it unreservedly and forever." (J. De Witt, *op. cit.*, p. 179 f.) "Who whispers to us as we read Genesis and Kings: This is exemplary; this is not? Who sifts for us the speeches of Job and enables us to treasure as divine truth what he utters in one verse, while we reject the next as satanic raving? 'The spiritual man — the man who has the spirit of Christ — judgeth all things.' This, and this only, is the true touchstone of Scripture by which all things are tried." (Marcus Dods, *op. cit.*, p. 160 f.) "The Spirit-wrought faith applies a sifting process to the Bible-word. Through this sifting process it gets the Word of God, the Word of Christ, to which it pneumatically adheres." (E. Schaeder, *Theozentrische Theologie*, II, p. 69.)

pure. The suggestion that God's Word contains filthy elements outrages the Christian's sensibilities.[195]

Let us repeat this. When the moderns call for an expurgated Bible, they are judging God. And that is the height of immorality. L. Gaussen did not go too far when he denounced the arrogance of the moderns in these strong terms: "You do not, it seems, comprehend the divinity, the propriety, the wisdom, the utility of such or such a passage of the Scriptures, and on that account you deny its inspiration! Is this an argument that can have any real value, we do not say in our eyes, but in yours? *Who are you?* 'Keep thy foot when thou goest into the house of God,' feeble child of man, 'and be more ready to hear than to give the sacrifice of fools, for they consider not the evil that they do. Be not rash with thy mouth; God is in heaven and thou upon earth,' Eccl. 5:1, 2. *Who art thou, then, who wouldst judge the oracles of God?* Hath not the Scripture itself told us beforehand that it would be to some a stumbling-block and to others foolishness, 1 Cor. 1:23; that the natural man receiveth not the things of the Spirit of God and that he cannot even do so and that they are spiritually discerned, 1 Cor. 2:14? . . . Man must first return to his place as a weak, ignorant, and demoralized creature! He cannot comprehend God until he has humbled himself. . . . It is thus that people strike their own defective knowledge, like an impure hook, into the Word of God and drag to the public dung hill whatever they have been unable to understand and have condemned!" (*Op. cit.*, p. 204.) Instead of complaining that the Bible outrages their moral sensibilities, these men should recognize with fear and terror that they are suppressing, dulling, outraging their own ethico-religious, Christian consciousness, which trembles at God's Word.

Once more: if the moderns are right in placing the Bible on the *Index Expurgatorius*, Christ was wrong in underwriting the whole of Scripture. "It does not take a keen eye,'" said Gess, "to see that filthy stories . . . have no place in God's Word." Was, then, Paul dim-sighted when he did not find a single statement of Scripture offensive to his moral sense but declared that "whatsoever things were written aforetime, were written for our learning" (Rom. 15:4)? And did our Lord endorse all of Scripture (see John 10:35) because His eyes were not so clear as those of the moderns? When they take offense at what was not offensive to Jesus, they are virtually discrediting the good judgment of our

195) "All objections to the divine inspiration and the inerrancy of the Bible are unworthy of a Christian." (F. Pieper, *What Is Christianity?* p. 257.) The objection which is based on the alleged moral incongruities in the Bible is unworthy of the Christian.

Lord and Savior. Reverence for God — the first of all ethical demands — should make such an attitude impossible.[196]

But, say the moderns, Jesus *did* repudiate the imperfect morality of the Old Testament and stood for a more perfect ethics. "Jesus set aside the ancient Jewish tribal teachings." (*West. Chr. Advocate.*) "We go fearlessly to the old inspiration, approving or rejecting, as it may be. . . . Whatever in the Old Testament revelation is not in accord with the revelation of His righteousness or purity or love or truth *in the words and life of Christ*, has been annulled and superseded." (J. De Witt, *op. cit.*, p. 180.) "The task of harmonizing such ethical conceptions (the vengeful massacre of the ninth chapter of Esther, the brutality of the closing words of the 137th Psalm) with the Sermon on the Mount surely is too much for human wit or patience. . . . The method of Jesus is obviously applicable: 'It was said to them of old time, . . . *but I say unto you.*'" (H. E. Fosdick, *op. cit.*, p. 27.) [197] Now, Jesus *did not* repudiate the ethics of the Old Testament. Where did He, for instance, disavow the imprecatory psalms? And do not quote Jesus' command "Love your enemies" as proving that Jesus repudiated

---

196) "If the Mosaic cosmogony is fabulous, how is it that Jesus uttered no word against it? And why did He not denounce those imprecatory psalms which are 'too horrible to be read' in some of our modern pulpits? . . . Is it possible that His eyes were not as clear, in this particular, as those of our recent Biblical scholars? Or was His soul not so sensitive as theirs with regard to these dreadful things in Scripture? We are in a dilemma. Was He unscrupulous or merely ignorant? . . . To question the teaching of Jesus with respect to the Scriptures is not merely to doubt the statement of one who was subject to human limitations; it is to call in question the veracity of the living God." (D. J. Burrell, *Why I Believe the Bible*, p. 117 f. — By the way, Burrell is not a kenoticist. "His limitations, whatever they may have been, were certainly not such as to expose Him to the liability of error or to the danger of uttering an untruth." P. 116.)

197) Similar assertions: Marcus Dods: "There are actions recorded in the Old Testament which seem to have the divine sanction and yet *are condemned by the New Testament code.*" (*Op. cit.*, p. 87.) Dr. J. Aberly: "In this total view of Scriptural teaching we must have the Spirit of Jesus to differentiate between what is temporary and what is permanent. . . . This view of the total purport of the Old Testament determined the corrections made of such teachings as were at variance with it. Illustrations of this will be found in the *correction of the law of retaliation*, among others, in the Sermon on the Mount, Matt. 5:17-48. (*The Luth. Church Quart.*, April, 1935, p. 119.) Dr. H. C. Alleman calls attention to "Old Testament stories of doubtful ethics and *lex talionis* reprisals" and insists: "Does not Matt. 5:39 *abrogate* Ex. 21:24?" (*The Luth. Church Quart.*, 1936, p. 241; 1940, p. 356.) "Will you please explain the meaning of Ps. 129:21: 'Do not I hate them, O Lord, that hate Thee?'" The editor of *The Christian Herald* answered in the issue of March, 1940: "In reading this verse, we must remember that those words were spoken under the Old Dispensation — the dispensation of wrath and before the advent of Christ. Jesus said: 'Love your enemies.'"

the Moral Law of the Old Testament. He would ask you to quote
His statement recorded Matt. 22:39. And when you quote: "But
I say unto you," to prove that Christ revoked the *lex talionis* as
permitting and sanctioning private revenge, you misinterpret the
words of Jesus. Enough has been said on this subject in the first
chapter of this essay, under Assertion No. 3, p. 115. What needs to
be said now is this: Those who insist that Jesus repudiated parts
of the Old Testament teaching put Jesus in a bad light. They make
Him contradict Himself. He said that not one jot or tittle of the
Law shall pass away, Matt. 5:18. He said that Scripture cannot be
broken, John 10:35, and the moderns make Him break Scripture
again and again. Did Jesus, then, not know His own mind?
Do the moderns not see that they are questioning the veracity of
God? Reverence for God — the first of all ethical commands —
should make such an attitude impossible.

THE DISTORTED MORAL SENSE OF THE CRITICS

In the second place, the ethico-religious consciousness which
is offended at the morality taught in the Old Testament (and in
the New Testament), its alleged cruelty, barbarity, etc., is not the
ethico-Christian consciousness. It is a distorted moral sense. The
ethics of God's people stems from the ethics of God. Our sense of
right and wrong is formed on God's judgments of what is right
and wrong. We know something of love because we know the
love of God. And we have a sense of holiness and justice because
we have somewhat realized the majesty of God's eternal righteousness and holiness. The moral sensibilities of the moderns are
shocked by the Scripture story of the extermination of the
Canaanites. That is because their moral sense is warped. They
have no sense of the awful justice of God. Dr. H. E. Fosdick well
says: "The trouble with many folk is that they *believe in only
a part of God.* They believe in His *love.* They argue that because
He is benign and kindly He will give in to a child's entreaty and
do what the child happens to desire. They do not really believe
in God's *wisdom* — His knowledge of what is best for all of us —
and in His *will* — His plan for the character and career of each
of us." (*The Meaning of Prayer*, p. 56.) Apply that here: the
moderns believe in only a part of God; they do not believe in His
holiness. Their moral sense is not fully developed. The extermination of the Canaanites was an act of the outraged holiness of God.
The measure of their loathsome crimes and unspeakable depravity
was filled up. They needed to be swept away from the face of the
earth. God's holiness could tolerate them no longer. Their extermination had an ethical reason. And those who charge the

executors of God's judgment with inhumanity (charging God, in effect, with ungodliness) have no sound ethical sense.[198]

They say this story reflects the low morality of Old Testament times, the cruelty of "Yahwe, the tribal god," and of His servants. No, indeed, the God of the New Testament, Jesus Christ Himself, executes the same justice and vengeance. Jesus pronounced and executed a terrible judgment against Israel, man and woman, father and child. What befell Pompeii? Who has been scourging the nations that have gone their own evil way with the sword, with hunger, with pestilence? And what will happen on the dread Day of Judgment? The Lord Jesus shall be revealed from heaven, in flaming fire taking vengeance on them that know not God, and shall punish them with everlasting destruction, 2 Thess. 1:7-9. The moral sense of the Christian does not rebel against the divine justice exhibited in damning the wicked [199] and exterminating the

---

198) W. E. Gladstone: "They [the Hebrew race] were appointed to purge and to possess the land of Canaan on account of the terrible and loathsome iniquities of its inhabitants. The nations whom they were to subdue had reached the latest stage of sensual iniquity, which respects neither God nor nature. The sensual power within man, which rebelled against him when he had rebelled against God, had in Canaan enthroned its lawlessness as law, and its bestial indulgences had become recognized, normal, nay, more, even religious and obligatory." (Op. cit., p. 128.) L. Boettner: "The Old Testament teaches that not only certain individuals but sometimes whole towns and tribes were so degraded that they were a curse to society and unfit to live." (The Inspiration of the Scriptures, p. 58.)   James Orr: "Extermination, where commanded, had always an ethical reason. If the Canaanites were condemned, it was because, after long patience of God, the cup of their iniquities was full to overflowing. 'After all,' says Ottley, quoting Westcott, 'the Canaanites were put under the ban, not for false belief, but for vile actions.' Nor was there any partiality in this. To quote what has been said elsewhere: 'The sword of the Israelite is, after all, only a more acute form of the problem that meets us in the providential employment of the sword of the Assyrian, the Chaldean, and the Roman to inflict the judgment of God on Israel itself." (Revelation and Inspiration, p. 105.)

199) "Our emotions are not trustworthy. People say, 'I do not feel that God would condemn the wicked,' and therefore they refuse to believe that He will. But what have our feelings to do with God? What warrant have we to imagine that an infinitely holy God 'feels' about sin as we do and has the same shallow tolerant view of it as we have? No warrant whatever. The only way in which we can know how God looks upon sin is by what He says, and in the Bible we have the record of what He says." (J. H. McComb, God's Purpose in This Age, p. 67.)   "These things, reason will still say, are not becoming a God good and merciful. . . . Reason wants to feel out and see and comprehend how He can be good and not cruel. But she will comprehend that when this shall be said of God: He damns no one, but He has mercy upon all; He saves all, and He has so utterly destroyed hell that no future punishment need be dreaded. It is thus that reason blusters and contends, in attempting to clear God and to defend Him as just and good." (Luther, XVIII:1832.)

Canaanites. It is a warped ethico-religious consciousness that is offended at these things, a sickly sentimentalism, begotten by carnal reasoning. Dr. J. Aberly is right in declaring "that God reveals Himself not only in mercy but also in judgment. There is a severity as well as a goodness of God. . . . That easy-going sentimentalism which often is made a synonym for the Christian spirit certainly omits this sterner side, which must be regarded as inseparable from a religion that has the cross at its center." (*The Luth. Church Quart.*, April, 1935, p. 120.) A man who says of the ninth chapter of Esther and of the 137th Psalm what H. E. Fosdick said of these passages "believes in only a part of God" and has no true conception of the holiness and justice of God. His moral sense is distorted.

The same applies to those whose moral sensibilities are shocked by the so-called imprecatory psalms. The moral sense of the Christian is not shocked when God manifests His hatred of sin and pours out His consuming wrath upon the rebellious sinner, inflicting upon him woe temporal and eternal. The mind of the Christian is formed on the mind of God and reflects the divine hatred of sin. The Christian cannot remain indifferent when he sees men rebel against God; their machinations against God and His Word and His people arouse his indignation and holy wrath. For that reason he looks upon these psalms as holy psalms. He does not denounce them. He prays them. For in them holy men of God voiced their hatred of sin, denounced God's severe judgment against the enemies of God and His Church, and threatened them with temporal and eternal woe. They did that in God's name. Yea, God gave them the very words by which to express their and His wrath; He inspired these psalms. God made the psalmists able preachers of His holy Law. If these psalms called for personal revenge and voiced carnal hatred, we, too, would say that "David was inspired by the spirit of the devil." But they do nothing of the kind. They flow from, and give expression to, the stern, inexorable justice of God. "There is not one of these passages which tampers with truth or justice; they are aimed only at sin, to blast and wither it. 'Lead me, Lord, in Thy righteousness because of mine enemies,' Ps. 5:8. This is the universal strain. All these passages are strokes delivered with the sword of righteousness in its unending warfare with iniquity. Nor is there one among them of which it can be shown that it refers to any personal feud, passion, or desire. Everywhere the psalmist speaks in the name of God, on behalf of His word and will." (W. E. Gladstone, *op. cit.*, p. 180.) Luther: "The prayers in the psalms are directed either against the devil as a liar or against the devil as a murderer, that is, either against pernicious doctrine or against the tyrants and persecutors." (IV:1753.) [200]

The offense which men take at the so-called imprecatory psalms is due to two defects in their moral sense. They are, in the first place, deficient in the sense of the enormity and hatefulness of sin, of the rebellion against God, of false doctrine. They refuse to let God's wrath against the evil-doer make its full impression on their ethico-Christian consciousness. "If so many people now-adays find the language of the psalms we are discussing strange and offensive, it is largely due to indifference toward the sacred teachings which God has given us in His Word." (W. Arndt, *Bible Difficulties*, p. 40.) And, secondly, their moral sense lacks too much of the fear of God. They dare to lay down rules of behavior for the almighty, all-holy God. They tell us that it would be unseemly if God had inspired the imprecatory psalms. The rebuke which W. E. Gladstone administers to such presumptuousness is

---

200) The essay "The Imprecatory Psalms," by Prof. H. Hamann, in the *Proceedings of the New South Wales District*, 1940 (and in *Lehre und Wehre*, 1924, p. 292 ff.) fully covers the subject. We quote: "They reveal the holy and righteous will of the God of Sinai; they are the expression of His stern and inexorable justice; they make known to men God's fearful wrath against sin and ultimately also against sinners, if they do not repent, so that all may stand in awe and tremble before His outraged majesty. . . . The imprecatory psalms belong to the Law and represent the Law at its strictest and sternest, and no one should be offended at them who knows that God is a 'jealous God,' who will not abate one jot of His holy and immutable Law. . . . McClintock and Strong's *Cyclopedia*, VIII, p. 755: 'The truth is that only a morbid benevolence, a mistaken philanthropy, takes offense at these psalms; for in reality they are not opposed to the spirit of the Gospel nor to that love of enemies which Christ enjoined. Resentment against evil-doers is so far from sinful that we find it exemplified in the meek and spotless Redeemer Himself, Mark 3:5.' . . . I do not believe that the psalmist would have written those fearful words in Ps. 137:9 if he had not known that terrible prophecy uttered by Isaiah against the same proud city long before: 'Their children shall be dashed to pieces before their eyes; their houses shall be spoiled and their wives ravished,' Is. 13:16. The psalmist simply pronounces his beatitude upon him who will carry out the doom foretold by the just and holy God. . . . Let us think of our Savior: what hard sayings, what words of flaming indignation did He utter when He opposed the malice and stubbornness of His enemies, who were at the same time the enemies of God, of God's people, and of true religion and who hardened themselves more and more in their iniquity! Seven times He pronounces the woe upon the scribes and Pharisees. . . . We recall the words of St. Paul in 1 Cor. 16:22: 'If any man love not the Lord Jesus Christ, let him be Anathema,' i. e., accursed. . . . Not only according to the Old Testament but also according to the New Testament there is such a thing as righteous wrath against sin and, in a certain relation, also against sinners who persist in their sin; there is such a thing as legitimately calling upon God to punish and to avenge, when His glory and the welfare of souls demands it; there is such a thing as holy acquiescence and joy in His righteous and perfect judgment." See also the remarks by Dr. J. T. Mueller in Conc. Theol. Mthly., XII, p. 470. (This also takes care of "the anger of Paul," which H. L. Willett has set down as a moral blemish.)

much too mild: "With respect to their severity[201] I suggest, and if need be contend, that we, in our ignorance and weakness are *not fit judges* of the extent to which the wisdom of the Almighty may justly carry the denunciation, *even by the mouth of man,* and the punishment of guilt." (*Op. cit.,* pp. 178, 180.) Because the sentiments expressed in the imprecatory psalms are offensive to the moderns, they will not believe in Verbal Inspiration. Because we believe in Verbal Inspiration, we know that those sentiments express the mind of God; and while some of the expressions *may* seem too harsh to us, we bridle our thoughts. We know that, while now we see only through a glass darkly, the light of glory will reveal to us that every word of the imprecatory psalms is in full accord with the eternal Holiness.

Believing in Verbal Inspiration, we know, too, that it was the Holy Ghost who recorded what the moderns are pleased to call *Schmutzgeschichten,* the stories of revolting crimes and heinous sins, and set them down in plain, unvarnished language. If God had asked Ingersoll and Gess to record the shameful story told Gen. 38, the shame of Judah and Tamar, they would have been horrified, would have indignantly rejected the proposal as coming from an unclean spirit. Moses had no such prudish scruples. And if we would "listen to what St. Paul says, Rom. 15: 4: 'Whatsoever things were written aforetime' etc., if we firmly believed that the Holy Ghost Himself, and God, the Creator of all, is the true Author of this book" (Luther, II: 469), we should know *a priori* that these stories contain nothing improper, unchaste, smutty.[202] "It is true, this is a rather gross chapter [Gen. 38]. However, it is found in Holy Scripture, and the Holy Spirit wrote it, whose mouth and pen are as clean as ours. . . . If He was not ashamed to write it, we should not be ashamed to read and hear it." (III: 559.) There is nothing about it to cause a modest person to blush and, much less, to corrupt his morals. Convince yourself of that *a posteriori.* Read these chapters in the fear of God. You will see at once that "the most pure mouth of the Holy Spirit" here depicts sin in such colors that the reader's heart is filled with horror and detestation of sin. And all the coloring needed is to present sin in its own

---

201) He is speaking of the imprecatory psalms: " 'I hate them with a perfect hatred; I count them mine enemies,' Ps. 139: 22. This brings the objection to a point. It is that this immeasurable detestation and invocation of wrath by man even upon God's enemies cannot be justified, and is not to be referred to divine inspiration."

202) L. Gaussen: "We have been asked, finally, if we could discover anything divine in certain passages of the Scriptures, too vulgar, it has been said, to be inspired. We believe we have shown how much wisdom, on the contrary, shines out in these passages as soon as, instead of passing a hasty judgment on them, we would look in them for the teaching of the Holy Ghost." (*Op. cit.,* p. 355.)

color, in its nakedness and frightfulness. These so-called "filthy stories" do in the moral sphere what is done in the dissecting-room where a wretched body is cut up and laid bare in order to show how the disease had ravished it.[203] Will the students be filled with lascivious thoughts when they see the dissector handling the nude corpse and uncovering the hideous filth produced by the disease? Not if they are normal men. The moral sense of one who cannot distinguish between the story of David's great sin and the current sex-novels is distorted.

These men do not serve the cause of Christian morals by demanding that the stories of the great sinners and of the extermination of the Canaanites, together with the imprecatory psalms, be deleted from the Bible. They are there for a good purpose. The sinner needs them, and the saint, who is a sinner, needs them. They warn us, 1 Cor. 10:11, and they comfort us, Rom. 15:4; 2 Tim. 3:16. "Why does the most pure mouth of the Holy Spirit stoop down to such low, despicable things, aye, things which are unchaste and filthy, yea, damnable, as if such things should serve to instruct the Church and congregation of God? How does that concern the Church?" Read on in Luther, II:1200 (and I:628 ff. — on the sins of Noah and of Ham), and thank God that He has shown you here the vileness of human nature, in the sinner and in the saint, the terrible wrath of God against the transgressor, and the wonderful grace of our Lord and Savior towards the vilest

---

203) Dr. Thomas De Witt Talmage (pastor of the Brooklyn "Tabernacle"): "Mr. Ingersoll declares that there are indecencies in the Bible which no one can read without a blush of shame. . . . I can go into the office of any physician here in Brooklyn and find magazines on the table and books on the shelves which the physician would not indiscriminately read to his family; yet they are good, valuable, necessary, morally pure books. A physician who did not have them would not belong in the profession. Even so there are passages in the Bible which form the anatomy of sin, showing what a lazar-house of iniquity the heart is when unrestrained. . . . When you read these passages, you will not be like one that has been infected with the evil, but like one that comes out of the dissecting-room and is much wiser than before he entered; he is in no wise enamored of putrefaction. There is a description of sin (as you will find it in the poems of Byron) which is seductive and corruptive, but the Biblical painting of sin warns and saves." (See *Lehre und Wehre*, 1882, p. 226; Weseloh, *Das Buch des Herrn und seine Feinde*, p. 121.) "Mayor Gaynor of New York said before a conference of Lutheran ministers that, when on a certain occasion he had put a Bible into the library of a city, a friend wrote him that he could not understand how Mayor Gaynor would put a book in a public library which he himself would not be willing to read from cover to cover in his family circle. The mayor said that the argumentation of the writer did not impress him at all; for, while it was true that the Bible speaks of shocking crimes, it never treats them as the present-day salacious literature deals with such matters, but always refers to sin and wrong-doing in such a way that a person is warned." (See *Luth. School Journal*, 1936, p. 106.)

sinner. All of us need to take these stories to heart. The pride of
Israel needed to be laid low.[204] Our nation would do well to study
the reason for the extermination of the Canaanites. "What are we
to make of the conduct of David in the matter of Bathsheba and
Uriah?" asks the Dean of Wells. This: we are to make much of
the fearful power of Satan over our sinful flesh, much of the fierce-
ness of God's wrath in punishing sin, and very much of the grace
of Jesus which forgives us our sins and crimes. "May these psalms"
[and the story of David, etc.] "work in us what God designed them
to achieve — teach us the heinousness of all sin and wickedness and
the stern reality of God's righteous anger toward all who remain in
sin, so that we may flee for refuge to the Savior, Jesus Christ, in
whose wounds alone are to be found righteousness, life, and salvation." (*Proc., New South Wales.*) And here are the moderns
declaring that these sections of Holy Scripture were not fit to be
inspired, not fit to be read! Christian ethics would suffer thereby!
These moderns do not know the first thing about Christian morals.
Christian morality springs from the sense of the heinousness of
sin and of the wondrous grace that saves from sin.

UNETHICAL TACTICS

In the third place, some of the moderns stoop to unethical
manipulations of the facts. F. Baumgaertel misrepresents the situation when he writes: "Den Propheten Elisa hoehnen spielende
Kinder; sie haben ihre kindliche Ungezogenheit mit dem Tode zu
buessen, 2 Koen. 2: 23." Moeller calls that "eine Einschmuggelung
in den Text" (*op. cit.*, p. 11). Anything goes if it serves to vilify
the prophets and Scripture and Verbal Inspiration.[205] — Verbal
Inspiration, says Cadman, would make God responsible for "slavery,
polygamy, incest, needless wars, cruel massacres." Note the
sinister lumping together of what God commanded, what He

---

204) Robert Haldane: "The pride of the Jews, who vaunted their
descent from Abraham and even imagined that God had chosen them
as His covenant people because of the high virtues of their forefathers,
could not have been humbled in a more effective way than by reminding
them of the sins of the patriarchs. The sins of Abraham, Isaac, Jacob,
and Judah are set down to warn Israel not to seek salvation through
the works of the Law." (*The Verbal Inspiration of the Old and New
Testaments Maintained and Established.* German edition, p. 197.)

205) "The unconverted man loves objections as the condemned
man at court is glad to detect a flaw in the argument which is directed
against him, though the flaw may not at all affect his guilt or the real
conclusiveness of the testimony. A man disposed to skepticism opens
the Word, if at all, not to find moral beauty, but to hunt for something
on which to hang a new objection." (A. T. Pierson, *Many Infallible
Proofs*, p. 179.) We had discrepancy-hunters, and here we have im-
morality-hunters. We are not judging individuals. But we want the
man who is set on finding ethical blemishes in the Bible to ask himself
what his motive is.

tolerated, and what He absolutely prohibited. Incest is mentioned in the same breath with slavery and the extermination of the Canaanites. One would expect Dr. Cadman to differentiate between these things and tell his readers that the Bible nowhere sanctions incest, lest they get the idea that God, who did order these wars, took a tolerant view of the horrible crime of incest. And what about polygamy and slavery? The objectors like to harp on these subjects as constituting a flagrant case of moral obliquity. Ingersoll: "I have no love for any God who believes in polygamy. . . . I call upon Robert Collyer to state whether he believes that God was a polygamist. . . . God believed in the infamy of slavery." Now, God did not institute polygamy; he permitted it but never sanctioned it. See Gen. 2:24. "From the beginning it was not so," Matt. 19:8. Nor did God institute slavery. He tolerated it, for good and sufficient reasons (study statecraft!), provided for the humane treatment of slaves (see, for instance, Ex. 21:26 f.; 21:2; Lev. 25:39 ff.) and their Christian treatment (see, for instance, Col. 4:1; the Epistle to Philemon). Do not slander God and Holy Scripture! — R. F. Horton asked: "How comes it that the crimes recorded in the book are not more emphatically condemned if the writing comes in any sense from God?" That comes near being an outright falsehood. Did God use soft words in condemning the adultery and murder David committed? Or does Horton really mean to say that because Moses did not conclude Gen. 38 with the statement "These people committed a horrible crime," the moral sense of Moses was dulled? — Professor Baumgaertel: "Der angebliche Befehl Gottes zur Ausrottung der Kanaaniter ist ein misslungener Versuch einer Rechtfertigung fuer die grausame Landeseroberung." (See Allg. Ev.-Luth. Kztg., No. 45, 1926, on this charge of Baumgaertel.) Can Baumgaertel and associates prove that God's command to exterminate the Canaanites, as recorded in the Bible, was a fiction, invented for the purpose of clothing the "crime" with divine authority? If not, they are guilty of the infamous slander of charging the holy writers with fraud, hypocrisy, and blasphemy. These things are not ethical.[206]

---

206) In the spirit of Baumgaertel Prof. W. M. Forrest writes: "The account in Samuel says God tempted David to make a census of the people. That was before Jewish theology had invented the devil. When Chronicles was written centuries later, the inspired writer had no such notion of a verbally inerrant Bible as the Fundamentalists have. Hence he boldly changed the record and said Satan did the tempting. But in either case and in many others showing God cruel and vindictive we have a picture of God so alien to Christ's teaching that it is unfair to hold it as a part of Christian faith." (Do Fundamentalists Play Fair? p. 77.) — Some do not go so far as Baumgaertel and Forrest, will not charge the holy writers with wilful fraud. Marcus Dods explains and excuses the alleged moral blemishes in the Old Testament with the theory of the "progressive revelation." He says: "The best men among

Not all the items in the black-list before us are due to a defective moral sense. Some are the product of ignorance and defective reasoning. We offer a few samples.

Ex. 11:2: "Let every man *borrow* of his neighbor," etc. Accordingly "the Israelites stole in the name of God" (Baumgaertel), "defrauded" their neighbors (Marcion). This charge springs from ignorance of the Hebrew language. שאל does not mean borrow, but *petere*, as in Luther's translation: "fordern," and in the R. V.: "Let them ask," and in Moffatt's translation: "ask," and in Gore's *Commentary*: "demand," and in Kretzmann's *Popular Commentary*: "demand." Did the Lord have the right to demand and take from the Egyptians whatsoever He pleased? (See *Lehre und Wehre*, 1908, p. 308; *Proc., Minn. and Dak. Dist.*, 1898, p. 34.) [207)]

"A mind disposed to hunt for something on which to hang a new objection" is, says A. T. Pierson, glad to come upon 2 Sam. 12:31. "This has been violently assailed as a proof of the cruelty of David — the man after God's own heart, who nevertheless took the people of Rabbah and sawed them in twain or drew them over iron harrows or clove them with axes òr roasted them in brick-

---

the Jews *misunderstood* God." (*Op. cit.*, p. 88.) Fosdick has the same explanation: "The Old Testament [the ninth chapter of Esther, the 137th Psalm] exhibits many attitudes indulged in by men and ascribed to God which represent early stages in a great development. . . ." (*Op. cit.*, p. 27.) James Orr had men like Dods and Fosdick in mind when he wrote: "The writers of the Bible, it is said, attributed to Jehovah their own defective, semibarbarous conceptions." (*Op. cit.*, p. 104.) Dods and Fosdick do not make the vile insinuations of Baumgaertel. They look on Moses and David as honest men. But they involve themselves in a difficulty of another kind. They represent God as being not quite honest. On their theory God permitted David to think that he was speaking the mind of God ("The Spirit of the Lord spake by me," 2 Sam. 23:2) when he wrote his imprecatory psalms; God took no steps to keep the writers of the Bible from attributing to Him their own semibarbarous conceptions; it was according to God's plan ["progressive revelation"] that men had in the initial stages false ideas of God; David thought that God was a semibarbarous Being because God planned it that way.

207) G. L. Raymond has a typically modern explanation of this "fraudulent" transaction. It does away with Verbal Inspiration, naturally, but clears God of fraud. He wants the passage interpreted in a *literary* sense, meaning that the words "The Lord said unto Moses" "need not be interpreted literally." God did not really say: "Let every man borrow," but Moses *thought* that the Lord meant that. "For this reason, when we come to consider the discrepancy indicated between what we conceive to be the character of God and the advice to do evil that good may come, we may conclude that these passages, interpreted in a *literary and not a literal sense*, mean no more than that Moses was inspirationally impressed with the conception that he should lead the people out of Egypt and obtain funds for the purpose in the best way he could, in which circumstances the natural promptings of a descendant of Jacob as well as of an enslaved race impelled him into advising the subterfuge of the false pretense of borrowing." (*The Psychology of Inspiration*, p. 139 ff.) In the same way Horton gets rid of the moral blemish presented by the imprecatory psalms.

kilns. But *what if it refers only to the work at which he set them?*
(Angus' *Bible Hand Book.*)" M. Henry condemns this as a sinful
act of cruelty. Be it so — it has as little to do with inspiration as
the other sinful acts of David. R. Jamieson calls it "an act of
retributive justice." Gore's *Commentary,* however, has: "Read as
R. V., margin. The theory that the passage refers to various forms
of torture is not supported either by the language or by the construction of the Hebrew." Moffatt: "He also brought away the
townsfolk, whom he set to work with saws and iron picks and iron
axes and made them labor at brick-making." Our old *Weimarische
Bibelwerk* suggests a similar translation: "Er hiess das Volk
bringen auf Saegemuehlen und in die Eisenbergwerke. . . ." Be
sure that you know the exact translation of this passage — *a crux
interpretum* — before you tell the world that you have bagged one
more ethical blemish.

H. L. Willett's contention that "Paul's advice to Timothy about
taking a little wine" proves that "the Bible cannot be taken as
inerrant in all its parts, is not an authority to us on all the questions
with which it deals," reveals the prohibitionists' misapprehension of
the teaching of the Moral Law on this question. See Pieper, *Christ.
Dog.,* I, p. 305, on 1 Tim. 5:23.

Jesus broke the Law, illegally deprived the owners of the swine
of their property, says Prof. Huxley; and He had no right to kill
His neighbor's fig-tree. The higher critics Willett and *The Luth.
Church Quart.* exculpate Jesus by denying that He ever did these
things. Both Huxley and the moderns are ignorant of the simple
truth of natural and revealed religion which declares that the Lord
is the absolute Owner of the earth and of man's possessions. They
virtually deprive the Lord of the right of eminent domain. "The
earth is the Lord's and the fulness thereof," Ps. 24:1. Luther:
"Why did Jesus permit the devils to enter swine which belonged to
other people? Answer: Christ is Lord of all, and there is nothing
that does not belong to Him; the pigs, too, were His." (VII:
p. 44.) [208]

---

208) Gladstone: "I find the answer to it in the reasonable and
(as it seems to me) almost necessary supposition that the possession of
the swine was unlawful and therefore was justly punishable by the
ensuing loss. . . . The punishment inflicted upon the owners did not
constitute a breach but rather a vindication of the Law; as a law would
be vindicated if casks of smuggled spirits were caught and broken
open after landing and their contents wasted on the ground." (*Op. cit.,*
pp. 300, 303.) Lenski gives the same answer: "Swine were an illegal
possession for Jews." Luther is willing to consider it: *"Vielleicht
konnte auch* Christum das Gesetz Mosis dazu bewogen haben, und er
mag sie darum als Veraechter des Gesetzes gestraft haben." (*Loc. cit.*)
But the answer given Ps. 24:1 is sufficient and all-conclusive. — The
solution offered by the higher critics would, if accepted, deprive us of
what is infinitely more precious than all earthly possessions — of the
trustworthiness of Scripture.

O. Bensow (*Die Bibel — Das Wort Gottes*) on the authorship of the imprecatory psalms: "Die menschlichen Gedanken sind gegen die goettlichen Gedanken zu scharf hervorgetreten." We cannot conceive of a more grotesque concept of Inspiration than this. The Holy Ghost set out to utter His thoughts through David; but off and on the carnal feelings of David interfered, and the thoughts of the Holy Ghost could not get full expression. David should not have said: "My tongue is the pen of a ready writer," Ps. 45:2. According to the moderns he should have confessed: I bungled my psalms.

The moderns imagine that they are giving Verbal Inspiration the death-blow when they bring up the fact that the holy writers were sinful men. This argument, however, is the result of defective reasoning and of the failure to realize the profoundest truth of the Christian religion. The moderns point to the dissimulation practiced by Peter at Antioch, the doubting of Moses, the crimes of David. "David," they say, "was a wicked man," unfit to be God's mouthpiece and "incapable of writing these praises (in the Psalms) to the God of righteousness" (*Fundamentals*, II, p. 63). Note, first, the defective reasoning. It is based on the false premise that inspiration means sinlessness or, more precisely, that, if the holy writers were absolutely inerrant in their teaching and writing, they must also have been perfect in their lives. How will you prove that? Scripture does not say it. What St. Paul wrote in Rom. 7 concerning his great sinfulness did not keep him from saying that he spoke and wrote the words of the Holy Ghost. Nor does reason tell us that God can reveal His will only through sinless angels.[209] But how can God make sinners His mouthpieces? Learn the basic truth of Christianity! Will you set a limit to the infinite grace of God? Surely Peter and David were not worthy to be chosen by God to be His spokesmen, His mouthpieces. David was amazed at this mark of divine favor. The adulterer and murderer, made "the sweet psalmist of Israel," exults: "The Spirit of the Lord spake by me, and His Word was in my tongue." "My tongue is the pen of a ready writer," 2 Sam. 23:1, 2; Ps. 45:1. And how he loved to sing the praises of the God of grace! "Thou art fairer than the children of men; grace is poured into Thy lips," Ps. 45:2. Do you abhor the thought that God received back into His favor the murdering adulterer? Then why should you abhor the thought that God could use David's tongue to utter forth His wondrous

---

209) "Christ Himself distinguishes between the doctrine of the apostles and their life. We are bound to what they taught, not to what they did. They were not moved by the Holy Ghost in all that they did, but when they spoke, they were moved by Him. This objection thus confuses things which Christ strictly dissociates." (*Proc., Syn. Conf.*, 1886, p. 63 f.)

grace? Moreover, the sinner who has been pardoned is best fitted, psychologically, to become the mouthpiece of the God of grace. Do not criticize the wisdom of God's choice! Briefly, "whoever says that the Spirit of God cannot convert again the fallen Christian and cannot produce noble thoughts in him, knows nothing either of Christian theology or of psychology." (*Lehre und Wehre,* 1913, p. 216.) This objection is so preposterous that the *Neue Luth. Kztg,* No. 10, 1901, dismisses it in one sentence: " 'Weil Petrus einen sittlichen Irrtum begangen habe, koenne er nicht von intellektuellen Irrtuemern frei gewesen sein': das ist eine sehr voreilige Schlussfolgerung. Doch das sei fuer diesmal genug."

Dr. Pieper: "None of us, even though he were a doctor in all four faculties, can deny the inspiration of Holy Scripture without suffering an impairment of his natural mental powers. . . . All opposition to the divine truth, and that includes the opposition to the *satisfactio vicaria* and to the inspiration of Scripture (verbal inspiration), is, as can be clearly shown, irrational." (*Op. cit.,* I, pp. 280, 614.)

CHAPTER III

Does the Bible Deal in Trivialities?

The moderns have a third grievance against the Bible as God gave it to us. They are scandalized at the many "trivialities" incorporated in it. Those portions of the Bible, they say, which treat of purely secular matters, common household affairs, petty concerns of men, and the like, do not belong to the Word of God. God's Word is too high and holy a thing to have these *levicula* mixed up with it. It is inconceivable that, when the Holy Ghost inspired the saving Word, He should have bothered about the marital affairs of Isaac and Rebecca. The moderns are complaining that their sense of the fitness of things is outraged when they are asked to believe that it was by divine inspiration that Paul wrote to Timothy about his cloak. And Verbal, Plenary Inspiration, which requires them to believe just that, is an intolerable thing.

Thomas Paine thus voices his indignation: "When I see throughout the greater part of this book scarcely anything but a history of the grossest vices and a collection of the *most paltry and contemptible tales,* I cannot dishonor my Creator by calling it by His name." (*The Age of Reason,* I, p. 28.) Paine is right, says R. F. Horton: "To suppose that there is any divine revelation in the command of Paul to bring the cloak and the books and especially the parchments which he left at Troas is a *reductio ad absurdum* of the unreflecting view which dogmatism has taken. Or the fatherly counsel to Timothy to take a little wine for his stomach's sake: it is a kind of *travesty of inspiration* to maintain that St. Paul was the mouthpiece of God in giving such advice." (*Revelation and the Bible,* p. 304.) Similarly Prof. W. F. Gess: "It would be irreverent to burden the Holy Ghost with such trifles and insignificant *minutiae* as Paul's forgotten cloak, barren statistics (Neh. 7:6, 7 ff.), dry genealogies, and the like." (See *Neue Luth. Kztg.,* 1901, No. 6.) And Professor Kahnis: "The home-spun philosophy of Solomon's Proverbs dictated by the Holy Ghost? There can be no such thing!" (See *Baier,* I, p. 103.) And Dr. H. C. Alleman has the same idea when he asks us to "look upon the divine truths in one light and the trifles of men in another." (*The Lutheran,* Jan. 14, 1937.) [210]

---

210) "Meanwhile another evasion is made in order to except a part of the Scriptures from the *Theopneustia.* If this is not the most serious objection, it is, at least, one of those that are most frequently advanced: 'Was it suited to the dignity of inspiration to accompany the thoughts of the Apostle Paul even in those vulgar details to which we see him descend in many of his letters? Could the Holy Ghost have gone so far

. THERE ARE NO TRIVIALITIES IN THE BIBLE

The moderns find fault with our Bible on account of these trivialities. The Bible-Christians take a different attitude. We thank God for the "trivialities" in the Bible. — There are no trivialities in the Bible! For (a) is this a triviality: "God loves men in all their smallness"? That truth is worth more to us than all the wealth of the world. Blessed is the man who has learned it. And we learn it from this, that the Holy Ghost has filled His Bible with these "trivial" records. He moved the holy writers to describe in detail the common every-day activities of the patriarchs, their labors in the field and house, their little worries and cares. Paul was solicitous about the state of health of his friends; he missed the parchment he needed for study: would the Holy Ghost, the High and Holy One, care to provide Paul with the words in which to clothe his directions about these matters? The Holy Ghost did that very thing. And that proves absolutely that our petty affairs are not beneath the notice of the Lord of heaven. Our gracious Lord shares our troubles. Whether we are engaged in some great work for the Church or are concerned about some small family matter, we are the objects of God's solicitude. If you want to know how much God thinks of you, study the "trivialities" recorded in the Bible. The fact that the Holy Ghost recorded these mundane matters invests them with supermundane importance. There are no trifles in the Bible.

Let us repeat this in the words of Luther: "Are you wondering and asking how it could please the Holy Ghost to describe such common and contemptible things? Listen to what the holy Paul writes Rom. 15: 4: 'Whatsoever things were written aforetime were written for our learning, that we through patience and comfort of the Scriptures might have hope.' If we firmly believed, as I believe, albeit weakly, that the Holy Ghost Himself and God, the Creator of all things, is the *true author of this Book,* and of such mean, despicable things, — mean and small to our carnal eyes, — we should, as St. Paul says, derive the greatest comfort therefrom. . . . This is what the Holy Ghost would teach us when He condescends to write about the saints and their petty affairs: the lowliest works of the saints please God. *Behold the glory and worth of a Christian man: there is nothing so small about him but that it pleases God."* (II: 469, 471.)

We are well aware that the moderns will not admit the force of the argument that, since the Holy Ghost directed the holy writers

---

as to dictate to him those ordinary salutations with which they close? or those medicinal counsels which he gives to Timothy with respect to his stomach and his frequent infirmities? or those commissions with which he charges him with respect to his parchments and a certain cloak?' " (L. Gaussen, *Theopneustia,* p. 305 f.)

to write about these trifles of men, these trifles are important in His sight. The moderns say that this argument is based on a *petitio principii* and reject it as an apriorism. They prefer to apply their own *a priori* method and to deal with the Bible on the principle that what they consider trivialities cannot be the subject of inspiration. As long as they uphold this principle, there is no use of arguing with them. We shall have to let them go their own way. Let H. E. Fosdick ridicule us, to whom, because we believe in "verbal dictation, the Scriptures become so exalted that nothing in them can be trivial, and so holy that to doubt them becomes blasphemy" (*The Modern Use of the Bible*, pp. 30, 68); we shall go our way, reverently study the "trifles" in the Bible and rejoice in the truth of the statement in which Dr. Pieper's discussion of this subject culminates: "God loves men in all their smallness." (*Chr. Dog.*, I, p. 307.)

We thank God for the "trivialities" in the Bible. These are precious portions of the Bible. Unfolding the precious truth that God loves men in all their smallness and has a tender regard for their petty cares and troubles, we gain (b) the profitable knowledge that our prayers to God are acceptable and pleasing to Him. Is it worth anything to you to know that when you bring your financial difficulties and your family troubles to the notice of the Lord of heaven He will not turn away from you in disdain? to know, in other words, that the gracious providence of the Ruler of the world watches over the affairs of such an insignificant creature as you are? Then study the "trivialities" recorded in the Bible. If we would learn the Christian art of confident prayer, we must learn that God really does take an interest in such insignificant creatures as we are. "Prayer does involve confidence that God takes interest in the individual who prays." H. E. Fosdick says that, and here he is right.[211] And now God not only assures us that

---

211) Let us have the entire passage. "When a man, making earnest with prayer, sets himself to practice communion with God, he is likely to awaken with a start some day to a disturbing reflection. 'This thing that I am doing,' he well may say, 'presupposes that the almighty God takes a personal interest in me. I am taking for granted, when I pray, that the Eternal is specially solicitous on my behalf. Prayer may seem a simple matter, but on what an enormous assumption does it rest!' Now, this reflection accords entirely with the facts. Prayer does involve confidence that God takes interest in the individual who prays. . . . He knows all the stars by name, Ps. 147: 4; He numbers the hairs of our heads, Matt. 10: 30; of all the sparrows 'not one of them is forgotten in the sight of God,' Luke 12: 6. . . . How can we make it real to ourselves that He who sustains the milky way, who holds Orion and the Pleiades in his leash, knows us by name? . . . For one thing, we seem too small and insignificant for Him to know. If God cares for each of us, that presupposes in us a degree of value and importance surpassing imagination; and as one considers the vastness of the physical universe, it seems almost unbelievable that individual men can be worth so much. . . .

He is solicitous about our affairs but also confirms our assurance
by making the recording of these petty concerns of His saints
a matter of inspiration. If you believe that it was by divine inspiration that Paul wrote about Timothy's stomach ailment and
Moses about the golden earring and two bracelets given to Rebecca, you will gain the assurance that the great God is interested
in our trifles. And if He is concerned about our trifling ailments,
we shall certainly dare to bring our heavy troubles before Him.
Study these "trivialities" in the Bible with reverence, and you will
say with Robert Haldane: "If we regard these passages not as the
word of men but as God's Word, we shall discover their beauty and
importance. God Himself is here speaking. The High and Lofty
One that inhabiteth eternity comes down to the weakness and the
needs of His servants. Nothing that concerns them escapes His
attention." (*The Verbal Inspiration of the Old and New Testaments
Maintained and Established.* German edition, p. 182.) Do you
want to learn to pray with confidence? Then let Fosdick tell you
that God is concerned about man in all his pettiness. And do not
listen to him when he ridicules the idea that an inspired record
would deal with the trifles of men.

Does it comport with the dignity of God to speak and write
about a cow's hoof? God will do just that if the mean hoof plays
into the affairs of His people. And if God is willing so to "demean"
Himself, He must certainly think highly of His Christians. Let us
hear Luther on this point: "How now? Has God nothing else to
do than to count the tears and wanderings of David (Ps. 56:8)?
Hasn't He enough to do in ruling the world and listening to the
choirs of the angels praising and lauding Him without ceasing?
Can there be anything more wondrous than that? And still it
remains true that God is occupied with counting the tears and
wanderings of David. . . . Yes, and Moses says to Pharaoh, Ex.
10:26: 'Our cattle also shall go with us; there shall not an hoof
be left behind.' Not only are the men, women, and children, and the
cattle to leave Egypt, but we shall leave nothing behind, not even
one mean hoof. Therefore, say I, not only the mighty, knightly
virtues are highly prized by God; . . . but also the meanest hoofs
have value in His sight. Yes, and hear what Christ says, who uses
stronger language: 'The very hairs of your head are all numbered,'
Matt. 10:30, telling us that we shall not lose one hair. Friend,
what can be meaner and of less account on the body of man than

God gives to our lives the dignity of His individual care. The eternal
God calls us every one by name. All great pray-ers have lived in the
power of this individual relationship with God. . . . Indeed, prayer is
the personal appropriation of this faith that God cares for each of us."
(*The Meaning of Prayer*, p. 46 ff.)

a hair or nail? But they all are counted, and the Father in heaven
is concerned about them. . . . Therefore this is of great, immense
comfort to the believer. . . . This is what the Holy Ghost would
teach us when He condescends to write about the saints and their
petty affairs. . . . It shows that God loves these small affairs."
(II: 469 ff.) And now apply this to prayer. Luther does so when,
continuing the story of Jacob and Rachel, he says: "The Holy
Ghost so guides and rules the pious wives that He shows that they
are His creatures, whom He would govern not alone according to
the spirit but also according to the flesh, that they should call on
Him, pray, thank Him for the children, be obedient to their hus-
bands, etc." (II: 540.)

We thank God for the "trivialities" in the Bible. We have
learned two important lessons from them. There is still more spiritual wealth contained in them, as we shall see when we (c) study
some of the individual passages in question. The moderns spurn
them as useless trash. They cannot or will not see the wealth, but
"in these 'trivialities' in the Bible there are important lessons for
eyes that are able to see. Whoever imagines that these *levicula* are
unworthy of the Holy Ghost, knows little about the Holy Ghost or
about the Christian life and conduct" (F. Pieper, *op. cit.*, p. 306).

Let us begin with 2 Tim. 4:13. The moderns usually begin
with this passage. The Anomoeans of old, the extreme group
among the Arians, started it, within the Christian Church.[212] And
R. Seeberg is sure that the Anomoeans were right, on this point.
He has Paul's cloak among the first items on the black-list. "The
theory that the words are inspired is disproved by a cursory glance
at the peculiarities of the Biblical writers. Each of them writes in
his own style and has his own favorite thoughts and favorite
phrases. *Trivial events are mentioned,* for instance, that Paul left
his cloak and his books at Troas. Timothy is advised to drink wine
instead of water for his stomach's sake. . . ." (*Revelation and In-*

---

212) From the earliest time, when the Church has had to engage in
controversies with heretics, both parties recognized the divine authority
of the Bible. The Anomoeans were the first to take a different attitude.
"Of this party S. Epiphanius tells us, and he mentions it as an offense
unheard of in any previous controversy, that, when pressed by arguments from Scripture, its defenders replied, either: 'The apostle made
that statement merely as a man,' or: 'Why do you quote the Old Testament against me?' It is generally believed, too, that the objection noticed
by St. Jerome in his Preface to the Epistle to Philemon proceeded in
like manner from the Anomoeans. This seems to me the earliest allusion
to the vulgar objection against Inspiration, founded upon the apostle's
words 'The cloak which I left at Troas,' etc. On such passages the
heretics founded the conclusion, as stated in Jerome's Preface: '*Non
semper apostolum, nec omnia, Christo in se loquente dixisse.*'" (W. Lee,
The Inspiration of Holy Scripture, p. 79 f.)

spiration, p. 26.) [213) The Anomoeans and Seeberg and the rest
insist that the Holy Ghost could not have written these words,
seeing that they contain nothing of spiritual value. But it does
not require much spiritual insight to discover great wealth in them.
Grotius was not a hide-bound dogmatist, but he would not pass by
our verse as unworthy of notice. He calls attention to "the poverty
of the apostle, who could not afford to lose this cheap thing which
he had left in a distant town" as teaching us a valuable lesson.
Erasmus was not a hide-bound dogmatist, but he, too, prized this
verse highly: "Whatever kind of parchment this was, Timothy
knew for what purpose Paul wanted it, and that will serve as
a further example of the tireless zeal of the apostle in the work
of the Lord. We learn this lesson, too, that even those who were
endowed with such great gifts were not relieved of the necessity
of using common means for acquiring further knowledge and
proficiency; how much more must it be our duty to use all means
to retain and increase our knowledge of divine things!" (Quoted by
Walther in *Lutherstunde;* see *Proc., Iowa Dist.*, 1892, p. 66.)
Is there any spiritual value here? Ask those who, when they suffered hardships and deprivations in the service of the Lord, found
comfort in the thought that they had for their companion the great
apostle. Ask those who, when they found their zeal lagging, drew
inspiration from the example of the apostle who, imprisoned and
facing trial and death, was concerned with his studies and the needs
of the Church. Useless rubbish? A triviality when the Holy Ghost
presents to us this picture of a man about to leave this life and
still devoting his thoughts and time to the performance of his
duties here on earth; subjected by his Lord to great hardship and
still using all his energies to serve his dear Lord? L. Gaussen
"quotes the noble words of the venerable Haldane on this verse
of Paul: 'Here, in this solemn farewell address, of which the verse
before us forms a part, the apostle of the Gentiles is exhibited in
a situation deeply calculated to affect us. We behold him standing
upon the confines of the two worlds — in this world about to be

---

213) R. Seeberg goes on to overhaul the other familiar objections to
Verbal Inspiration, the alleged errors and contradictions in the Bible,
etc., and pronounces the coroner's verdict: Verbal Inspiration is dead.
"The last few decades have witnessed the overthrow of a time-old wall,
which for centuries had surrounded and protected the city of Protestant
Christendom. Crumbling stones were removed, one after another. . . .
It was resolved to remove the wall; some set to work with sighs, others
with joy. The wall to which I refer was the *Verbal Inspiration of the
Bible*, the conviction that every word of Holy Scripture was given by
inspiration of the Holy Spirit. It has disappeared as if in one night.
No theologian of any repute now upholds it; it is no longer taught in
the schools. . . . The theory of verbal inspiration has fallen. . . . Not
only theology but also the Church has abandoned the old theory of
verbal inspiration." (*Op. cit.*, pp. 1, 3, 35.)

beheaded, as guilty, by the emperor of Rome; in the other world
to be crowned, as righteous, by the King of kings; here deserted by
men, there to be welcomed by angels; here in want of a cloak to
cover him, there to be clothed upon with his house from heaven,'"
and adds: "Ah, rather than bring forward these passages in order
to rob the Scriptures of their infallibility, one should have owned
in them that wisdom of God which so often by a single stroke has
contrived to give us instructions for which without that long pages
would have been necessary." (*Op. cit.*, p. 311.) No, no; "we cannot
notice any interruption in this verse of inspiration" (Erasmus), we
cannot see and cannot say that the sublime words of verse 1 and
the glorious statement of verse 8 were written by inspiration, but
that at verse 13 the Holy Ghost withdrew into heaven and left
Paul to deal with trifles. Says Gaussen: "Ah, unhappy he who
feels not the sublime humanity, the tender grandeur, the provident
and divine sympathy, the depth, and the charm of such a mode of
instruction! But more to be pitied still, perhaps, is he who declares
it to be human because he does not comprehend it!" (*Loc. cit.*) [214]

Is 1 Tim. 5:23 a barren waste? And would the Holy Ghost
concern Himself with dietetics? R. Haldane (*op. cit.*, p. 172 f.) cultivated this "waste" and harvested eight golden sheaves. For instance: it is the Christian duty of the pastor — and all others —
to take care of his health lest he impair his usefulness in the
Church. — Use the ordinary means to preserve your health. Substituting prayer for these God-given means is sinful, a form of
enthusiasm. Why did Paul not try the faith-cure on Timothy?
Because he was not a fanatic. And why did he not restore Timothy
and Epaphroditus (Phil. 2:27) to health by means of a miracle?
Because he was not a fanatic and because he used his miraculous
gift only as the Spirit led him. — "Thine often infirmities," "thy
frequent attacks of weakness" — it is well for the servant of God

---

214) Some readers may have time to read B. Manly on this verse.
"Consider the case about this much-complained-of cloak. Here is a man
who some thirty years ago renounced ease, fortune, popularity, brilliant
prospects — all for Christ, in order to do good to the souls of men. He
has had his reward all along from the world and from his nation in
stripes, in rod-beatings, in stonings, in imprisonment, in treachery and
deadly conspiracy, in unblushing falsehoods, in unassuaged malice. And
now his end is near. He is advanced in years, in his last prison, his
usefulness accomplished, his course finished. He is just awaiting the
sentence of death. Bravely, cheerfully, triumphantly, he writes his last
letter to his dearest friend, his son in the Gospel. Not a note quivers,
not a word hints at gloom or threat. — But he is shivering with cold.
Winter is commencing. He is in want of clothes. And in that prison
he is lonely. . . . Only Luke is with him. . . . He has come to stand
by Paul to the last. But the good man wants his books, especially certain beloved precious parchments. They would cheer his lonely hours.
He needs his cloak; he wants his manuscripts. Is there nothing touching
nothing affecting in this?" (*The Bible Doctrine of Inspiration*, p. 253 f.)

who is handicapped by some ailment to know that his is not an exceptional case. — By anticipation the apostle here condemns the teaching of various sects that the use of wine is sinful. (Pieper: "The apostle here warns us against imposing Prohibition, a law of men, upon the *Church* as a law of God." *Op. cit.*, p. 305.) — Finally, and mainly, says Haldane, notice the deep concern and tender solicitude of the apostle for his fellow-laborer. The Holy Ghost has set this down as an example for us. Will it be profitable for you to study it? — We are wondering whether this was one of the passages which J. M. Gibson had in mind when he wrote: "If the Bible was all equally the Word of God, why should I not be able to use even the least promising parts of it? It was only by sad experience that I was compelled practically to admit that it was not all on the same level. . . . On the principle of all parts of Scripture being equally inspired one might preach on the Bible for fifty years and never once bring the Gospel in. . . . In my early ministry I wasted many precious hours in trying to make sermons out of quite impossible texts." (*The Inspiration and Authority of Holy Scripture*, pp. 5, 101.)

Or was Dr. Gibson thinking of the salutations in Rom. 16? We love Paul for sending those greetings; we are glad to know that the Holy Ghost recorded these marks of Christian friendship. "But for these affectionate greetings to beloved friends, we should have lacked evidence of the genuine tenderness of the apostle's soul, and we might have been told that Christianity left no room for the virtue of friendship." (B. Manly, *loc. cit.*) [215]

---

215) L. Gaussen: "People often object to those greetings which close the epistles of Paul and which, after all, we are told, are of no more importance than those ordinary compliments with which we all usually conclude our letters. Here, then, is nothing unworthy of an apostle, no doubt; but no more is there anything inspired. Here the Holy Ghost has allowed Paul's pen to run on, as we ourselves would allow a clerk to conclude by himself, in the usual form, a letter the first part of which we had dictated to him. Is it not evident that here the apostle surrenders himself, in the course of sixteen verses, to the purely personal reminiscences of friendship? Was there any need of inspiration for the dry nomenclature of all those persons? These verses require no inspiration." Gaussen replies: "We are not afraid to avow that we delight to recall those sixteen verses; for, far from furnishing any ground for objection, they belong to the number of passages in which the divine wisdom recommends itself by itself. . . . Listen first, with what affectionate interest the apostle recommends to the kind regard of the church of Rome that humble woman, who, it would appear, undertook the voyage from Corinth to Rome for the sake of his temporal affairs. . . . Have we not here (in verse 13) the very Christian politeness which he recommends to these same Romans in the 12th chapter of this epistle, verse 10?" — For yet another reason, Gaussen points out, this list of names is valuable. "We find Paul taking care to salute by their names all the most eminent among the believers at Rome, even among the women, . . . without saying a single word about its Pope, or about Peter, or about a vicar of Jesus Christ." (*Op. cit.*, pp. 316—321.)

You do not know what to do with those dry genealogies? Ask the Israelites, who were much interested in knowing that Jesus is the son of David, the son of Abraham, and the Gentiles, who are vitally interested in knowing that Jesus is the son of Adam. Ask the good woman who was much comforted when she found the names of Rahab and of David, great sinners, listed among the ancestors of Christ. (See *Lutheraner,* 1889, p. 84.) Ask the man who was led to repentance when he studied the genealogy in Gen. 5: "And he died," "and he died." (See *Proc., West. Dist.,* 1868, p. 24.) "No part, not even a list of names, could be taken from the Book without doing violence to it or causing loss to us. Nothing must be taken from, or added to, its perfect unity." (J. Bloore, *Alternative Views of the Bible,* p. 152.) [216)]

We thank the Holy Spirit for the letter Paul wrote to Philemon, for its contents and for its style, for the courtesy and consideration of Paul, which pleased Philemon and pleased God. "There is a universal admiration for Paul's letter to Philemon. Even the critics have found no fault with it. Luther sees in it 'a masterfully lovely example of love,' like the love of Christ for us. . . . The whole letter is of pure gold." (Lenski's *Interpretation of Philemon,* Introduction.) But Kahnis has a grievance against it. "Would you have us believe that, when the apostle Paul wrote that tender urbane letter to Philemon, tinged, as it is, with some humor [!], he set down what the Holy Ghost dictated to him?" We can easily believe it. We are glad to know that Paul practiced what he preached: "Let your speech be alway with grace" (Col. 4: 6); and when we ask the Holy Spirit to give us the graces of a Christian

---

216) One more remark concerning the genealogies — those set down 1 Chron. 1—9. W. Lee points out that, compared with the genealogies of the tribe of Judah and of the house of David, the genealogical notices relative to Simeon, Reuben, Gad, and Manasseh are exceedingly brief, and that these again are followed by the particularly copious genealogies of the Levites, to which the writer comes back once more in chapter 9. Here "these two important features present themselves: (1) We know that on the return from the exile in Babylon all persons were excluded from the sacerdotal office who were unable to prove their Levitical descent (Ezra 2: 61 f.; Neh. 7: 64 f.). . . . Josephus also tells us that to this chosen family was committed the custody of the Sacred Books. . . . (2) We can at once perceive how the family annals of David's line are inseparably connected with the whole scheme of redemption. . . . 'In the period that followed the Exile the Messianic hopes, awakened by the subjection of the people, were again excited. . . . It must have been a matter of importance for the writer's contemporaries to find collected here the names of the still remaining descendants of the ancient reigning house; who, although little celebrated, were yet to be the ancestors of the longed-for Deliverer. . . .' " (*Op. cit.,* p. 394.) Matthew and Luke, too, knew the importance of this section of Chronicles.

gentleman, He will tell us to study this little epistle and mold our speech and behavior on Paul's. And even indulge in pleasantries? What are these pleasantries to which Kahnis objects as beneath the notice of the Holy Ghost? Is it the business language in which Paul clothed his request? "Charge this to me. . . . I myself will duly pay." What is wrong with that? "It is," says Dr. Pieper, "a concrete way of expressing the universal Christian obligation of love: 'Bear ye one another's burden and so fulfil the law of Christ,' Gal. 6:2." (*Op. cit.*, p. 316.) And Paul's fine way of thus reminding Philemon of his duty went to Philemon's heart. Or is it the phrase "Receive him (the runaway slave) as myself"? Paul liked this phrase. See Rom. 16:13: "Salute Rufus and *his* mother *and mine.*" God likes this phrase. It expresses the precious Christian fellowship, precious because of the blood of Christ. Do you want to call it a pleasantry? Do so, it is pleasant beyond expression, this God-given pleasure of Christian companionship. Or did Kahnis have reference to the play upon words, the paronomasia, of verse 20: "I would like to make a profit off thee in the Lord"? ("Ὀναίμην is a play on the name Onesimus." *Expositor's Greek Testament.*) The *thought* cannot be objectionable to Kahnis. Paul's profit is his happiness. "His happiness is what he desires, happiness in seeing these two converts and spiritual children of his joined in truest Christian fellowship. A nobler sentence has seldom been written." (Lenski.) But Kahnis objects to the form in which this divine thought is expressed. It smacks too much of wit and humor. Well, our little epistle teaches us that wit is not displeasing to God. God endowed Paul with the happy faculty of stating important truths in a striking, taking way, and Paul here puts it to a spiritual use. "Es ist 'ein feiner, geistlicher' Scherz." And as concerning common, every-day humor, God does not frown upon the laughter of His children. Their innocent merriment and good-natured humor springs from a spiritual source. They are at peace with God; all is well with them; they are in good spirits, in high good humor. They, and they alone, are in a position to enjoy all earthly gifts of God, not the least of which is humor. And in this innocent mirth they praise God. — To sum up, the Holy Ghost here teaches us how to treat *res civiles ex principiis altioribus* (Bengel). But Kahnis insists that such a way of teaching would be discreditable to the Holy Ghost. Anything to discredit Verbal Inspiration!

Kahnis once more: "The home-spun philosophy of Solomon's Proverbs dictated by the Holy Ghost? There can be no such thing! Will you make of these rather dubious rules of conduct — they must be taken with quite a grain of salt — laws of the Holy Spirit?"

G. T. Ladd, R. F. Horton, and others agree with Kahnis.[217] We are not now concerned with the assertion that some of Solomon's maxims are objectionable (the preceding chapter dealt with such matters) but with the assertion that many of them are so commonplace and platitudinous that the Holy Ghost would not stoop to find a place for them in His Book. We are glad that He did that, glad to hear again that God holds little things, for instance, the homely virtues of the common man, common honesty and common prudence, in high regard. And while it is true that these maxims are taught by human philosophy, — the moral philosopher Marcus Aurelius or Confucius might have written most of them, — we are happy to know that God has put His stamp upon them. If they came to us as the wisdom of a mere Solomon or a mere Confucius, we could not be absolutely sure of their moral worth. Our ethico-religious consciousness, by which Ladd and the others would test Scripture, is not a safe guide. But now we know that they are God's truth. And we shall keep on using them. Everyone of them. This one, too: "Though thou shouldest bray a fool in a mortar, yet will not his foolishness depart from him."

The moderns have little use for the minute portrayal of the domestic affairs of the patriarchs. We have much use for it. We have learned from it that great and comforting truth that God cares for His children and is concerned with their worries, small and great. Now let us learn two ethical lessons. First, when we are performing the common tasks of the household, we are doing truly good works and serving God in holiness. If you are looking for God's saints, you will find them not only in church but also in the kitchen and the stable. Luther on Gen. 29 (Jacob and Rachel): "Thus the holy fathers, I say, are depicted in a rude and carnal way, in the low estate of this life, than which in the mind of the Papists there can be nothing more unclean and worthless. They say that here nothing better is presented to us than that they took

----

217) G. T. Ladd: Only some of "these wise sayings may be regarded as inspired writing. . . . Others of these proverbs are commonplace and fall even below the average of an Oriental wise saying: such, to our judgment, appear in instances like 14: 20, 23; 18: 23; 19: 6, 7; 11: 26: 'He that withholdeth corn, the people shall curse him; but blessings shall be upon the head of him that selleth it.'" (*The Doctrine of Sacred Scripture,* I, p. 465 f.) R. F. Horton: "Great indeed is the responsibility of teachers who have led ignorant people to suppose that all the prudential maxims of the Proverbs . . . are to be considered, as a matter of faith, the specific words of God. . . . If these Wisdom Books are merely human philosophy, what place have they in a book of divine revelation? . . . We are able to hear the voice of God speaking to us in such places as 10:29 . . . without perplexing tender consciences by telling them that 27:22 ('Though thou shouldest bray a fool in a mortar among wheat with a pestle, yet will not his foolishness depart from him') is a word of God, that 30:15, 16 is an inspired utterance, or that 31:6, 7 is a precept emanating from the lips that spake the Sermon on the Mount." (*Op. cit.,* pp. 193, 195.)

wives, begat children, milked the cows and goats, etc., which are altogether worldly and pagan works. . . . God would glorify not only their knightly virtues but also the filthy and mean works, and this description adorns them as with gold and gems." (II: 459, 469.) Again, on Gen. 30: "The Holy Ghost, who is the Author of this book, delights to describe, *dass er also spielen und scherzen moege*, these trivial, puerile things, these worthless things. . And He sets them down here because He wants them preached about in the Church, for instruction in righteousness. . . . We should glory and rejoice in these common works of the household, since the Holy Ghost condescends to expatiate on them." (II: 566, 569.) Secondly, we need to learn the lesson of faithfulness in small things. He is not a faithful servant who is willing to do great things for his master but slights the smaller things. And no man can do great things if he neglects the details. And when the Holy Ghost pays such close attention to insignificant details in the lives of the saints of the Old Testament and of the New Testament, He is teaching us the lesson that minor matters must not be slighted. Pieper: "The Holy Ghost is of the opinion that faithfulness in small matters is decidedly proper and necessary. We read Luke 16: 10: 'He that is faithful in that which is least is faithful also in much; and he that is unjust in the least is unjust also in much.'" (*Op. cit.*, I, p. 304. — "He who is dishonest with a trifle is also dishonest with a large trust.") And so, when the moderns disdainfully turn away from the "trifles and filth" in the Bible, we turn away from the moderns in disgust and listen to Luther, who, with a reverent spirit and a full sense of the spirituality of the Bible, speaks thus concerning the ornaments Rebecca received from Isaac's father: "What is here related is adjudged by reason to be a most carnal and worldly affair; and I myself often wonder why Moses expends so many words on such trifling things, since he was so brief on much more important things. But I do not doubt that the Holy Ghost wanted these things written down for our instruction. For nothing is presented to us in Scripture that is trifling and useless; for all that is written was written for our learning, Rom. 15: 4." (I: 1712.)

Nor is it unbefitting the Holy Ghost and out of keeping with the majesty of the Bible that it contains regulations concerning the treatment of the domestic animals ("Thou shalt not muzzle the ox when he treadeth out the corn," Deut. 25: 4) and touching the robbing of a bird's nest (Deut. 22: 6 f.), and the like. Such regulations have ethical value. See the literature sent out by the humane societies. And they are big with comfort for the worrying Christian. The truth that the Lord preserves "man and beast" (Ps. 36: 6) may help us in our deepest spiritual afflictions. (See *Proc., Northern Ill. Dist.*, 1909, p. 43. D. J. Burrell, *Why I Believe the Bible,*

p. 29.) [218] "He giveth to the beast his food and to the young ravens which cry," Ps. 147:9; and shall He forget me? "Behold the fowls of the air; . . . your heavenly Father feedeth them." Learn this comforting lesson: "Are ye not much better than they?" Matt. 6:26. We thank God that regulations concerning such small matters as muzzling the ox and robbing the bird's nest are incorporated in our Bible.

Trivialities in the Bible? There are none. Pastor E. L. Arndt: "Der *Liebe* ist keine Kleinigkeit zu klein. Eben weil sie so gross ist, kuemmert sie sich um alles." (*Proc., Mich. Dist.*, 1895, p. 32.)

Every single word of Scripture is important, every single statement profitable, 2 Tim. 3:16. Yes, and everything bears on Christ, the central, the one theme of Scripture. Luther: "So, then, the entire Scripture is throughout nothing but Christ, God's and Mary's Son; all has to do with this Son that we might know Him." (III: 1959.) To be sure, not everything set down in Scripture is of the same importance.[219] Nor do we in the present state of our knowledge see the importance of every statement the Bible makes. Nor do we always see the full importance of every statement. The Jews saw the importance of Deut. 25:4. It taught them humaneness. But there is more to it. See 1 Cor. 9:9, 10 and 14. The apparently trivial command concerning the ox is "written for our sakes." God is taking care not only for oxen. In Deut. 25:4 the Holy Ghost is impressing upon the Church its duty to provide for

---

218) H. E. Fosdick on God's care for the whole and for every part of His creation, for beast and for man: "When one believes in God at all, he must believe that God has a purpose for the universe as a whole . . . 'Nothing walks with aimless feet,' says Tennyson. 'There are no accidents with God,' says Longfellow. . . . Can God have a purpose for the whole and not for the parts? . . . God calls us everyone by name. As an Indian poet sings: 'The subtle anklets that ring on the feet of an insect when it moves are heard of Him.' . . . Of course, it is not God's will that 'one of these little ones should perish,' Matt. 18:14." (*The Meaning of Prayer*, p. 51 f.) Why this same man should ridicule those who believe that "nothing in the Scriptures can be trivial" is beyond our comprehension.

219) Must we bring evidence to show that the Bible-theologians do not say that? This is what they say: "Whilst everything in the Scriptures is for man, it does not follow that every part is equally valuable to every man. The Bible is framed with reference to the average want of a whole race. Everything in it is there for somebody, although it may not be specially meant for you. And yet the parts which seem to the individual least adapted to his wants, may have even for him a priceless value; they may inspire him with a sense of new necessities, may enlarge his mind and heart and lead him out of himself in a wider sphere." (Krauth, *The Bible a Perfect Book*.) It is not our fault that J. M. Gibson "wasted many precious hours in trying to make sermons out of quite impossible texts." There are many verses in the Bible which are there for a very good purpose but not for the purpose of making sermons out of them. (We are, of course, not referring to texts like 2 Tim. 4:13.)

its ministers.[220]   Go slow! This and that passage which you are about to cast on the rubbish-pile may contain great wealth.

Not a single statement made by any of the holy writers is useless, worthless. We believe in Verbal Inspiration, and we are not going to say that the Holy Ghost, the real Author of Holy Scripture, is a hack writer, merely concerned with filling the prescribed space. (Luther's phrase: "Der Heilige Geist ist kein

---

220) Why, this insignificant little passage even bears on the weighty matter of Inspiration. Is the Old Testament the inspired Word of God? No doubt of that. 2 Tim. 3:16 says it plainly. But is the New Testament, too, the inspired Word of God? The cavilers say you cannot prove it from 2 Tim. 3:16. But "St. Paul puts the New Testament on a level as God's Word with the Old Testament: 'For the *Scripture* saith: "Thou shalt not muzzle," etc., and: "The laborer is worthy of his hire," 1 Tim. 5:18' — putting a text from Luke, 10:7 on a level as *Scripture* with one from Deut., 25:4." . . . (H. M'Intosh, *Is Christ Infallible and the Bible True*, p. 402.) "It may be observed that the apostle here (1 Tim. 5:18) combines the Old and the New Testament under the title γραφή when addressing the same person to whom he subsequently writes: πᾶσα γραφὴ θεόπνευστος, 2 Tim. 3:16." (W. Lee, *op. cit.*, pp. 111, 240.) — A second question answered by other triviality-passages is: Was Inspiration a mechanical process? "The very passages just mentioned [1 Tim. 5:23 and 2 Tim. 4:13], which seem so trivial in themselves, are of prime importance for the doctrine of inspiration. They prove that the apostles were not dead machines under inspiration, that the Holy Ghost did not, in the process of inspiration, ignore the personal and brotherly relationship of the holy writers but operated with it in the inspirational act." (A. Hoenecke, *Ev.-Luth. Dogm.*, I, p. 350.) — R. Haldane calls attention to still another point. If the holy writers had not written by inspiration but out of their own wisdom, various sections of their writings would certainly have taken on a different form. "Would the combined genius of all the sages of the world have led them to tell the story of the Creation in one chapter and of the building of the Tabernacle in thirteen, as Moses actually did? . . . The world was created for the Church. By the Church the glory of God is made known, Eph. 3:10. . . . The Church (of which the Tabernacle was a type), where God is truly worshiped, is more precious and of more importance in the sight of God than all the rest of the world." (*Op. cit.*, p. 203 f.) — One more point, contributed by Dr. Th. Graebner: Similarly the topographical notes in the Pentateuch and in Joshua have been characterized as having only paltry worth and of being entirely insignificant so far as spiritual values might be concerned. Bible students of better discernment have found in these long lists of place names much to instruct and confirm their faith. It was Major Conder who in his *Tent Work in Palestine* announced that "of all the long catalog in Joshua, there is scarce a village, however insignificant, which does not retain its desolate heap or modern hovels with the Arab equivalent to the old names." Any modern Bible atlas, as that of G. A. Smith, confirms this tribute to the minute exactness of the Old Testament. A closer study of the original confirms this impression of an exact contemporary record. Sometimes, as in Josh. 15, both the old name and the newer name are listed. There are many technical words, used by ancient surveyors and by none else. Hence we have so many references to points of the compass, to drawing lines, to sides, shoulders, corners, edges, ravines, cliffs, ascents, ends, fountains, valleys, and stones. Many of these technical points are more clear in the Revised Version than in the Authorized, all testifying to the truth that the story of God's people is firmly anchored in the soil of authentic history.

Narr noch Trunkenbold, der *ein* Tuettel, geschweige *ein* Wort sollte vergeblich reden." III:1895.) Be sure that every phrase and every clause is there for a purpose. The Author knows why He wants to tell the story in just that way.[221]

And what is the ultimate purpose of that particular story and of every narrative set down in Scripture? Luther tells us, as St. Paul told us before Luther: "Christ is the center of the circle, and all stories in Holy Scripture, viewed aright, have to do with Christ." (VII:1924.) See Rom. 15:4; 1 Cor. 2:2. Everything in the Bible is of great importance. We have said all that needs to be said about the distinction between lesser and greater and greatest importance. We are now interested in stressing the fact that the all-important story of Christ lends its weight to all the rest. "Thou shalt not muzzle the ox" — God cares for us because of Christ! "Use a little wine" — Paul's concern for Timothy sprang from the love of Christ! — There are no trivialities in the Bible.[222]

The moderns do not like to hear that, will not say it. But Paul liked to say it. Rom. 15:4! Luther liked to say it. What Paul said of the prophets, Luther said of Paul: "It is impossible that there is a single letter in Paul" (not even in 1 Tim. 5:23 and 2 Tim. 4:13) "which the entire Church should not follow and observe." (XIX:20.) We shall keep on saying with H. E. Jacobs: "Would you say, then, that some things in Scripture are unimportant and may be readily surrendered? By no means. Even the accidents of Scripture, if we may so speak, are important in their own place. Chrysostom: *In sacris Scripturis nil est supervacuum*" (*A Summary of the Christian Faith*, p. 282), and with Prof. J. P. Meyer: "All Scripture, even in the most casual remark, is given to make us wise unto salvation. As highly as we prize our salvation, so sacred must be to us every word of our God." (*Theol. Quartalschr.*, Jan., 1942, p. 62.) We heartily subscribe to Thesis

---

221) "And he, casting away his garment, rose and came to Jesus," Mark 10:50. Origen on this passage: "Shall we venture to say that these words have been inserted in the Gospel without a purpose? I do not believe that one jot or tittle of the divine instruction is in vain." (*Comm. in Matt. 16:12.* — See W. Lee, *op. cit.*, p. 88.)

222) R. Seeberg does not know Luther too well. In the chapter "Luther's Views of the Bible," written to prove Luther's so-called "liberal" attitude towards the Bible, we read: "When Luther refers to Scripture, he is thinking of the Gospel of Christ and His kingdom, of sin and grace, in short, of the religious content of Scripture, of 'Christ and the Christian faith.' . . . Everything else in the Scriptures is for Luther comparatively indifferent." (*Op. cit.*, p. 18.) What has Luther just been saying about all stories having to do with Christ? In the light of that statement we shall say that Luther did not read anything in the Bible without thinking of the Gospel of Christ, of sin and grace, of "Christ and the Christian faith"; for Luther the entire content of the Bible was religious, everything in Scripture was to him highly important.

XVII of Walther's *The Lutheran Church the True Visible Church:*
"The Ev. Lutheran Church accepts the whole written Word of God
[as God's Word], deems nothing in it superfluous or of little worth,
but everything needful and important." (See the discussion of this
thesis in *Proc., West. Dist.,* 1868, p. 18 ff.) We thank God for the
"trivialities" in the Bible.

The moderns are unwilling and unable to do that. They take
the position that God—or whoever the author of the Bible may be—
would have produced a better book if he had omitted these trivialities. And they are proud of their position. They feel superior
to the obscurantists who still treasure every bit of the Bible, every
jot and tittle. We shall have to tell them that they have nothing
to be proud of. There are two reasons for that.

THE TRIVIALITY-CHARGE INDICATES LOW INTELLIGENCE, SPIRITUAL DULNESS, AND WICKED SELF-CONCEIT

First, it is not a mark of high intelligence to scoff at small
things. It is only the fool who feels that bigness is the measure
of importance. The philosopher knows that great events often —
perhaps always — originate in small things. The scientist knows
that grandeur is built up on specks; the painter employs slight
touches to create beauty. Why do we use the microscope? The
Watchman-Examiner (Jan. 16, 1941) says: "The microscope tells
us that bigness is but the multiplication of littleness. . . . The
gigantic suns and nebulae of outmost space have their laws, and
so also do the microscopically visible crystals of the inorganic world
and the microscopically invisible electrons of the atom. The
mathematics of the telescopic world are the mathematics of the
microscopic world. . . . As Browning says: 'We find that great
things are made of little things. And little things go lessening till
at last comes God behind them.' The great canvases of the sky,
more beautifully colored than any Rembrandt and changing with
each passing moment, gladden the eye only because of the possibilities of beauty that inhere in the tiniest of things. . . . Now,
it is certainly characteristic of the saints not to regard bulk as
a criterion of value." And that is not a specifically Christian
philosophy. The veriest tyro in science knows it.[223] Not only
the Bible but also common sense teaches what Booth Tarkington
heard in his boyhood days from his uncle: "I don't know anything

---

223) The scientists tell us: "Inside any common pin as marvelous
an activity is going on as ever was present among the stars. Here are
electrons so many and so small that the race in a million years could
not count them, and yet not one electron touches another." (H. E. Fosdick, *op. cit.,* p. 48.) We cannot vouch for the exactness of this statement,
but it proves that the scientists insist that infinitesimal things play
an important part in the universe.

at all that wouldn't be important if we could get at the whole truth of it. We spend a great deal of our lives in excitements over what we think are the big things, whereas, if we carefully examined what we pass over as negligible trifles, we might improve our conceptions of the universe and consequently our conduct and contentment." To all of which the moderns say yea and amen; and then they display their black-list of trivialities in the Bible and argue against Verbal Inspiration on the principle that God would not concern Himself with trifles. There is a lack of acumen here.

So much in general. Now a few particulars. Most men hold that faithfulness in small matters is a great virtue. No business man would entrust an important matter to a clerk who pays no attention to details. And the general who overlooks "trifles" is guilty not only of stupidity but also of a moral wrong. One does not have to be a Christian to know that. "Even the unbelieving world," says Pieper, "when it uses its reason, pays tribute to this virtue; it recognizes the great man by his trustworthiness in small matters." (*Op. cit.*, I, p. 304.) But when the moderns come across 2 Tim. 4:13, they forget to use their reason and insist that it would be unworthy of the Holy Ghost to concern Himself about such trifles and to record Paul's worry about those few books and parchments.[224)]

The moderns like to read *The Cotter's Saturday Night*. We do not blame them for that. In fact, one who is unable to see the beauty and grandeur of this portrayal of the simple, happy, godly life of the common folk — "the lowly train in life's sequestered scene — the toil-worn cotter frae his labor goes — And, 'Let us worship God,' he says, with solemn air — the cottage leaves the palace far behind" — would be considered an uncultured boor. Where, then, does he stand who turns up his nose at the Biblical story of Abraham and Sarah, of Isaac and Rebecca, of Jacob and Rachel? — He may say that Burns's classic is all right but that it would be unseemly for the Holy Ghost to write about the domestic life of the patriarchs. We shall take care of that in a moment.

Again, the moderns do not display much intelligence when they are willing to accept the story of the human birth of the Son of God, but are offended at the idea of God dealing in His Book with human trifles. We are now speaking of the conservatives among

---

224) A short digression will not be out of place here: Philippi (quoted in Pieper, *loc. cit.*) in speaking of "the books, parchments, and cloak, and the wine mentioned 1 Tim. 5:23, which always raises the ire of the critics," remarks: "We should not be surprised if our modern naturalists, who set such great store . . . by books, especially their own, as being absolutely necessary for the welfare of the human race, would one of these days make a complete about face and rate *only these* passages as inspired."

the moderns. They believe with all their heart that God condescended to be born of a woman and to take upon Himself the weaknesses of the human race. But they cannot bring themselves to believe that God would condescend to *speak* of human weaknesses and trifles. God can do the greater, but must not do the lesser! These moderns are taking a self-contradictory position. They are unreasonable.[225]

And so are the liberals among the moderns. Let us now reason with *them*. They do not believe in the Incarnation. But they do believe in Creation. Those among them who believe in a personal God will praise Him for creating not only the stars but also the grain of sand and the snowflake. They admire the wisdom which creates and preserves the life of the little birds and the lowliest insects and utilizes them for the preservation of the human race. They resent the idea that their God looks only at big things and would debase Himself by caring for the petty things on earth. H. E. Fosdick does not hesitate one moment to write these words: "So far as physical nature has any testimony to bear on the matter at all, she says: 'There is nothing too great for the Creator to accomplish, and nothing too small for Him to attend to. The microscopic world is His as well as the stars." (*Op. cit.*, p. 48.) On this point they are in full accord with the Bible-theologian. They will say with Philippi: "Was ist vor Gott klein, vor dem nichts gross ist?" But as soon as the question of Verbal, Plenary Inspiration comes up, they completely reverse themselves and indignantly declare: God could not have rcorded these trivialities found in the Bible; God would not debase Himself by writing about muzzling the ox and having Paul speak about the diet of Timothy. — These moderns are unreasonable men.[226]

---

225) "He who talks as though it were beneath the dignity of the Holy Ghost to refer to such small matters as eating, drinking, clothing, etc., in the Scriptures must have completely forgotten that the eternal Son of God did not consider it beneath His dignity to assume a true human nature from the Virgin Mary into His divine person, to be wrapped in swaddling-clothes and laid in a manger. He who stands in adoration before the miracle in the manger at Bethlehem will not consider it strange, but altogether in order, that mention is made in the Scriptures, which are *God's* Word, of *human* trivialities." (Pieper, *op. cit.*, p. 307.)

226) G. Stoeckhardt on 2 Tim. 4:13: "May the Holy Ghost not speak to men of small things as well as of great things, of seemingly unimportant as well as important matter, just as He chooses? Shall we prescribe to Him what He may say and how to say it and teach Him what befits Him and what does not? In that case we ought to find it equally objectionable that the great God, infinite in majesty, created the worms and midges." (*Lehre und Wehre*, 1886, p. 287.) R. Haldane: "1 Tim. 5:23 and 2 Tim. 4:13, they think, are too unimportant for inspiration. Such a conclusion, even if we did not see the importance, is altogether unreasonable. On that basis we would have to discard many other sections of Scripture whose purpose and meaning we do not understand, but that

Indeed, our moderns are deficient in the knowledge of the ways of the divine wisdom. Let them study the great truth revealed 1 Cor. 1:23 ff. The wisdom of God — which is foolishness to the Greeks — chooses foolish and weak and base things to accomplish His great purposes. In the words of A. G. Rudelbach: "How many thousand times since the days of the Anomoeans has the cloak which Paul left at Troas been trotted out as yielding one of the strongest proofs against Verbal Inspiration; this cloak, think the modern unbelievers, can do greater things than the mantle of Elijah! . . . But as the unfathomable love of the Son took upon Himself the deepest humiliation, so the Holy Ghost also deeply humbled Himself: the place of His self-humiliation is Holy Scripture; He did not disdain to make what is the meanest and lowliest in the eyes of men the object of divine presentation and preservation. . . . It is of a piece with what the Apostle Paul describes as the *plan of God* in His entire revelation, that 'He hath chosen the foolish things of the world to confound the wise,' 1 Cor. 1:27. This standard the wise men of the world know not; so they naturally pounce upon these things which seem petty to them and do not see that their occurrence in Scripture militates against the wisdom of the divine plan as little as the circumstance that we do not know what useful purpose certain animals serve permits us to doubt the wise design in creation." (*Zeitschrift fuer die ges. Luth. Theol. u. Kirche*, 1840, Erstes Quartalheft, p. 8 f.) And these moderns will not permit the Holy Ghost to demean Himself by having Paul mention his threadbare cloak in an inspired passage!

A fatuity of another sort is committed by those who argue that, since Paul of himself knew all about the forgotten mantle and parchments and his need of them, and of the medicinal value of a little wine, 1 Tim. 5:23 and 2 Tim. 4:13 were not written by inspiration of God. O. Bensow: "It would be preposterous to look upon these passages as having been dictated by the Holy Ghost. Paul did not need the help of the Holy Ghost in giving these counsels and commissions. If the Holy Ghost had dictated these passages, He would have done something entirely superfluous." (*Die Bibel — das Wort Gottes*, p. 27.) Kahnis has the same notion, when he says: "Since the Proverbs of Solomon are based not on revelation but on experience," what a foolish thing it is to present this homespun philosophy as being dictated by the Holy Ghost! Similarly G. T. Ladd, when he argues against Verbal Inspiration by pointing out that some of these Proverbs are "commonplace,"

---

would be as absurd and irreverent as the contention of a presumptuous infidel that the worm or fungus cannot be God's creature because they seem too insignificant to him, or that the entire earth could not have been created by God because it contains so much desert and unproductive land, for which he can see no use." (*Op. cit.*, p. 166.)

known to everybody. Obsessed by the notion that only those
sections of Scripture can be the inspired Word of God which contain revelations of unknown matters, Kahnis thinks he has clinched
the argument against Verbal Inspiration when he asks: "If Luke
the Evangelist wrote down only what the Holy Ghost dictated,
why does he adduce tradition and his own research?" (*Op. cit.*)
Similarly Seeberg: "If Luke knew that the Holy Spirit would
direct him, why did he make the careful study of which he tells
us chapter 1:3?" (*Op. cit.*, p. 30.) The entire argument of these
men is, as Gaussen puts it: "These verses require no inspiration."
But therein they completely miss the point of the whole argument
about Verbal Inspiration. The verbal-inspirationists do not say —
as the Bible does not say — that everything that is written by
inspiration had to be supernaturally revealed. All that the Bible
says is that whatever a holy writer wrote he wrote by direction
of the Holy Ghost and in the words chosen by Him. The moderns
should learn the distinction between revelation and inspiration.
But they are everlastingly confusing the two concepts.[227] And,
consequently, much of their fighting against Verbal Inspiration is
aimed at a straw man. They need not tell us that Paul did not need
a divine revelation in order to write about his cloak. What they
should prove is that the statement of the Bible that *all* Scripture
is given by inspiration refers only to the revelation of unknown
matters. — When the moderns once learn the basic difference between revelation and inspiration, they will drop the argument
under consideration.[228]

---

227) Look up the statement by Horton quoted above: There is no
divine *revelation* in the command to bring the cloak; it is a travesty of
inspiration to maintain that Paul was the mouthpiece of God in giving
the fatherly counsel to Timothy.

228) Dr. Joseph Stump (U. L. C.) is one of those who hold that
revelation and inspiration cover the same ground. "Inspiration has to do
with matters of religion and the communication of the divine revelation.
. . . The holy writers produced (by inspiration) a correct and inerrant
record of God's revelation of Himself to men. . . . The Bible is the inspired record of all that God has supernaturally revealed to men concerning the way of salvation." (*The Christian Faith*, p. 318 f.) We are
calling attention to Dr. Stump's view at the present time because of the
specific treatment he gives to 2 Tim. 4:13 and 1 Tim. 5:23. "This inspiration permitted the Apostle Paul to include in his epistle matters of
a purely personal nature, such as the request to Timothy to bring his
cloak from Troas and his personal advice to Timothy regarding his health.
His inspiration had to do with matters of 'religion and the communication
of the divine revelation; and he was none the less an inspired man even
though he was *forgetful enough* to leave his cloak at Troas and concerned enough about Timothy's health to give him dietetic advice, which
*may or may not be regarded as good advice by modern medical authori-
ties.* The inspired nature of what he wrote is not affected by such purely
personal statements. These things belong to the human side of the
Scriptures. . . . The purpose of Paul's inspiration was to give us an in-

Some moderns use more diplomatic language. Instead of declaring that the secular sections (including the triviality passages) are not inspired, they say that some parts of the Bible are more inspired and others less inspired. This is the famous degrees-in-inspiration theory. Some passages are the result of the application of the full power of inspiration; others — mainly the triviality passages — got only a slight touch of it. A classical statement to this effect is by A. D. C. Twesten (disciple of Schleiermacher), who called it an "excess of the mechanical theory" to extend the exer-, cise of the divine influence in an *equal degree* "to all and everything in Scripture," to "history" as well as to "doctrine." (See W. Lee, *op. cit.*, p. 335.) C. Gore: "A new science of historical criticism has arisen, . . . which does not seek to diminish our reverence for the Scriptures, but it would have us recognize grades of inspiration." (*The Doctrine of the Infallible Book*, p. 61.) Dr. H. E. Jacobs: "There are few theorists who would assign the same degree of inspiration to the statistics and rolls in Ezra or Chronicles as to those parts of the New Testament for whose reading the dying ask when all other earthly words have lost their interest." (See F. Bente, *American Lutheranism*, II, p. 220.) Delitzsch calls it "abgestufte Geisteswirkung." We heard J. M. Gibson declare that the Bible "is not equally the Word of God — it is not all on the same level." And O. Bensow specifically mentions Paul's forgotten cloak when he says that the "breath of the Spirit" is not the same in all passages (*op. cit.*, p. 46 ff.). Three remarks on this: (1) There are degrees in the importance of the individual passages of the Bible. We are agreed on that with the most liberal of the moderns. But we know of no law of human thought which requires that degrees of importance presuppose degrees of inspiration. (2) Do not ask us Bible-Christians to assign anything less to the triviality passages than full inspiration, full trustworthiness. We have found much comfort and much wholesome admonition in them. Don't tell *us* that the Holy Ghost had little, if anything, to do with that. (3) The moderns get into trouble with their intelligence when they try to reconcile this degree theory with 2 Tim. 3:16 and the other passages of the same import. We assume that they would count this passage as one

---

fallible knowledge of the revealed will of God." (*Loc. cit.*) We are here calling attention to the fact that while some of the moderns argue against Inspiration on the basis of the "trivialities," others, like Dr. Stump, want to uphold Inspiration but feel uneasy about their theory that a lot of unimportant statements are mixed up with the inspired statements of the Bible. They feel the incongruity and the need of explaining it. — The idea underlying Stump's theory — that occasional mistakes and similar phenomena in the Bible do not affect its trustworthiness in religious matters — will be discussed in the next chapter.

written under the full influence of inspiration. But it declares that
"*all* Scripture" is *inspired.* It adds no restriction to the effect that
some Scripture is fully inspired, other Scripture less fully, hardly
perceptibly. Have done with this nonsense. If the Holy Ghost
spoke a word, He spoke it. He did not half speak it. Speaking
John 3:16 in a distinct voice, did He mumble when He came to
2 Tim. 4:13? The moderns will, of course, say that they understand the word "inspiration" in 2 Tim. 3:16 to mean simply eleva-
tion of the mind, illumination, or something like that. We tell them
that then they are making the apostle speak nonsense. "The mind
of all Scripture is enlightened"? Using our intelligence, we know
that 2 Tim. 3:16 states that every word of Scripture was spoken,
written by God. And common intelligence protests against the idea
that some of these words were fully spoken, some only half spoken.

There is a second reason why the moderns cannot pride themselves on their treatment of the triviality passages. From the
point of intelligence their boasting is vain. But there is something
worse. When men say that God could not have written these
passages, they are doing a wicked thing. Criticizing the Bible, they
are judging God. They presume to judge God by their own
standards of propriety. They are telling God that He permitted
things to go into His Book which jar their refined sensibilities.
They consider it their sacred duty to improve that Book which
God declared perfect. They insist that the Bible will be a better
book after they have chiseled off its imperfections and given it the
finishing touch. It is a wicked thing, this damnable pride, which
induces creatures to judge and condemn the ways of the Creator.
It is a wicked thing when men, weak in intelligence, call in question
the wisdom of God in giving His Church the Bible as He gave it.
Are they indeed judging God? What else are they doing when
they tell us that it was proper for Burns to write *The Cotter's
Saturday Night* but that such a thing would not befit God? That
it was all right for Confucius to set down his maxims but that
these commonplaces have no place in God's Book? They are certainly laying down rules for the guidance of the Holy Ghost.

Are they really judging God? They will tell us that what they
are criticizing are the words of men which somehow or other
found their way into God's Book; if the Timothy passages and
Proverbs, etc., were really God's Word, they would keep silence. —
No, no, you are deceiving yourselves. In the first place, it is, all
of it, God's Word and remains God's Word despite your refusal
to acknowledge it as such. And, in the second place, on your own
presentation of the matter, you are judging God. You are holding
Him accountable for the "trivialities" in the Bible. You say that
God directed Paul to give the Church the great Timothy epistles.

You say — and you are right in saying it — that, when Paul wrote: "Jesus Christ came into the world to save sinners" (1 Tim. 1:15) and: "He called us with an holy calling," etc. (2 Tim. 1:9), he wrote by inspiration of God. But then you say, when Paul came to the matter of the cloak and the wine, the Holy Ghost lessened His inspiration or even suspended it. However, we point out to you that the Holy Ghost in no wise intimated that His operation was now ceasing and that it was only Paul who was now speaking, writing. You are the men who are saying that the Holy Ghost could not have continued speaking. You are indeed laying down rules for the Holy Ghost to observe.

Or will you say that there was no need for the Holy Ghost to mark off the objectionable passages, since God knew well enough that in time theologians would arise in the Church whose advanced knowledge and refined sensibilities would at once detect those flaws, re-edit the Bible, supply the inspiration mark for 1 Tim. 1:15 and 2 Tim. 1:9, but caution against 1 Tim. 5:23 and 2 Tim. 4:13 and thus give the Church a perfect Book? Do not say that. It would be the height of overweening self-conceit. — The truth of the matter is, of course, that long before the moderns came on the scene, pagans and infidels had already taken the Bible to task for these "improprieties." The moderns have not improved on the pagans.

And the conservative moderns are not much better than the liberal moderns. The liberals are saying that all of the Bible is merely man's word; it would not befit the great God to speak to us in lowly human words — and the conservatives chide the liberals for such a judgment. And now they are doing the very same thing. They say it would not have befitted God to write *some* of the things in the Bible.

Men who are offended at the triviality passages should realize that their attitude springs from wicked pride and constitutes a *crimen laesae maiestatis divinae*. We repeat here the solemn warning given by L. Gaussen: "You do not, it seems, comprehend the divinity, the propriety, the wisdom, the *utility* of such or such a passage of the Scriptures; and on that account you deny their inspiration. . . . Who are you? 'Be not rash with thy mouth. God is in heaven and thou upon earth,' Eccl. 5:2. Who art thou, then, who wouldst judge the oracles of God?" (*Op. cit.*, p. 204.)

THE CHRISTIAN ATTITUDE

Such an attitude outrages the Christian sensibilities. It goes against the grain of the Christian mind to conceive of Holy Scripture as a mixture of important and trifling matters. With that observation Hollaz closes his discussion of the *levicula*. In answer to the objection that "Scripture contains matters of such little importance that they are not worthy of divine inspiration, e. g., *baculus Jacobi*, Gen. 32:10, *penula Pauli*, 2 Tim. 4:13," he points out first that, since God considered such insignificant things worth creating, He certainly considered them worth mentioning in His inspired Book, and, secondly: *"Nemo interim Deum reverenter colens in Scripturis pro levi aut vili habebit, quod sapientissimo Dei consilio ipsis est insertum."* (*Examen Theo. Acroa. Prol.*, p. 93 f.) Do you hold God in high reverence? Do you adore His wisdom? Then you will not treat that as trifling, vile, and worthless which was set down in Scripture by His all-wise counsel; you will not want to break the least Scripture.

We, too, are apt to stumble when we read these Biblical "trivialities." Let us heed the warning of Luther: "I beg and faithfully warn every pious Christian not to take offense at the simple language and ordinary stories which he frequently finds here. Let him not doubt that, however mean it all appears, these are the very words, deeds, judgments, and history of the high majesty and wisdom of God; for this is the Scripture which makes fools of all the wise and prudent and is open only to babes and fools, as Christ says Matt. 11:25. Away with your overweening conceit! Think of Scripture as the loftiest and noblest of holy things, as the richest lode, which will never be mined out, so that you may find the divine wisdom which God places before you in such foolish and mean form. He does this in order to quench all pride. Here you will find the swaddling-clothes and the manger in which Christ lies, to which the angels directed the shepherds, Luke 2:11. Mean and poor are the swaddling-clothes, but precious is the treasure, Christ, lying in them." (XIV: 3, 4.)

"Blessed Lord, who hast caused *all Holy Scripture* to be written for our learning, grant that we may in such wise hear them, read, mark, learn, and inwardly digest them, that by patience and comfort of Thy holy Word we may embrace and ever hold fast the blessed hope of everlasting life, which Thou hast given us in our Savior, Jesus Christ, who liveth and reigneth with Thee and the Holy Ghost, ever one God, world without end." (*The Lutheran Hymnal*, p. 14.)

CHAPTER IV

The Disastrous Results of Criticizing and Correcting Scripture

(A RÉSUMÉ)

Before examining three further objections against Verbal Inspiration, it will be well to pause a while and survey the disaster wrought by the contention of the moderns that the Bible contains a lot of (1) errors, (2) immoralities, and (3) trivialities. Amplifying previous remarks on this subject, we would here present a comprehensive view of the frightful consequences of the denial of Verbal Inspiration. The moderns do untold harm (1) to the Church and (2) to themselves.

LOSING HALF OF THE BIBLE

In the first place, the moderns would rob the Church, and do rob their disciples, of a great part of the Holy Bible. They ask the Church to discard half of it. Thomas Paine figured that the useless and harmful portions of the Bible would amount to at least that much. The moderns accept his figure. The historical and scientific errors, the unethical episodes and teachings, and the trivialities take up much space in the Bible. More than that, they put the historical and secular matters in general in the uninspired section of Holy Scripture. Recall how they account for the "historical mistakes" and the other "blemishes" of the Bible: when the prophets and apostles recorded history, they did not write by inspiration. It follows that also that part of their history and science, etc., which happens to be true is a purely human product. A. D. C. Twesten insists that inspiration does not extend in an equal degree "to all and everything in Scripture without distinguishing between *doctrine and history*, between the religious contents and the garb in which such contents are presented to us." (See W. Lee, *The Inspiration of Holy Scripture,* p. 335.) The moderns have decreed that only those portions of Scripture which reveal the saving truth are inspired; what the holy writers said besides that is purely their individual opinion — you may take it or leave it.[229]

---

229) W. Sanday: "I know of nothing which would mark off these narratives, especially in the earlier books, from others of the same kind outside of the Bible. I know of nothing which should isolate them and prevent us from judging them as we should similar narratives." (*The Oracles of God,* p. 69.) J. O. Evjen: "To the Reformer [Luther] Scripture was binding to the extent that it proclaimed Christ, the Gospel, or pointed to Christ. Many historical matters in the Bible did not concern Christian life." (*Luth. Church Quart.,* April, 1940, p. 149.) A. J. Traver: "The Holy Scriptures are the infallible truth 'in all matters that pertain to His revelation and our salvation,' not in secular matters." (*The Lutheran,* Feb. 22, 1939.)

On that basis much more than half of the Bible is not the Word of God. Besides, many of the moderns look askance at the entire Old Testament as being, at best, the product of an imperfect inspiration. Accordingly, much more than half of the Bible belongs in the uninspired section of the Bible.

And the moderns deplore the fact that there are still men in the Church who receive the whole Bible as the Word of God. They consider it their duty to warn all Christians against this delusion. R. Seeberg: "No one who knows the history of the Church can doubt that the fall of the theory of Verbal Inspiration is an event of first-rate importance. . . . But in ecclesiastical practice men often involuntarily talk as if Verbal Inspiration still held its ground. . . . Consequently it is a matter of importance for every Protestant Christian to form for himself a reasoned judgment upon this question and . . . attempt to discover what substitute Protestant Christendom can accept in its place." (*Revelation and Inspiration,* p. 2. — The substitute offered by Seeberg will be examined later.) The laymen, says B. Steffen, must be informed that much of the Bible is unreliable. "While in point of fact Verbal Inspiration has long ago been overthrown by Biblical science, our laymen are tenaciously clinging to it. That is an intolerable situation which cannot continue. . . . God has given us His Word in a book which, taken literally, is full of contradictions. Too long has that been denied and hushed up." (*Zentralinspiration,* opening paragraphs.) That intolerable situation, says W. Sanday, must be remedied: "To assume this necessary task, I must first point out how it is probably true that the human element in the Scriptures is larger than many good people now, and nearly all good people not long ago, supposed it to be." (*Op. cit.,* p. 18.) And so we have this frightful situation: the Church is asked by many of her teachers to discard half of her Bible.

Those that listen to the voice of the seducers are the poorer for it. Everything that God put into the Bible enriches us. St. Paul, the faithful guardian of the Church's wealth, tells us: "Whatsoever things were written aforetime were written for our learning" (Rom. 15:4). Luther raises his warning voice when the children of the Church make ready to yield up this or that passage: "Sintemal kein Buchstabe in der Schrift vergeblich ist." (X:1018.) Stress, by all means, the Gospel truths. They are all-important. But heed Sasse's warning: "The necessity of bringing into prominence as the essential revelation that part of the Scriptures which contains a direct declaration of the Gospel's promise of grace to the believing sinner, can result in failure to recognize the importance of other parts of the Scriptures." (*Here We Stand,* p. 117.) "We could not afford to dispense," declares Spurgeon, "with one verse of

Holy Writ. The removal of a single text, like the erasure of a line of a great epic, would mar the completeness and connection of the whole. As well pluck a gem from the high priest's breastplate as erase a line of revelation." You may not know why God selected a particular incident for incorporation into Scripture and told it in just that particular way. Do not delete this portion of Scripture; the time may soon come when you need it for your nourishment. All that God presents to us in Scripture is nutritious. Strike out Gen. 1 as mere history? There are days when we find rich comfort in the truth that God created us and keeps us — created us for eternal life. Strike out the Imprecatory Psalms and the teaching of eternal damnation? The secure sinner absolutely needs to hear these passages. "We must have the whole Christ of the whole Bible if we want to have a whole salvation." (L. Keyser, *A Reasonable Faith*, p. 50.) We need and want the whole Bible. It is an unbreakable, indivisible whole. If you break a piece from it here and a piece there, you lose the full blessing the whole Bible offers. The moderns are impugning the wisdom of God when they hold up half of the Bible to ridicule as constituting excess baggage, for, in the words of Bengel, "not only are the various writings, when considered separately, worthy of God, but they together exhibit one complete and harmonious whole, unimpaired by excess or defect," and when they induce Christians to relinquish portions of the life-giving and life-sustaining Word, they are by so much sapping the Church of her strength and influence. Would the moderns have the Church live by a fraction of the truth God gave her?

LOSING ALL OF THE BIBLE

Worse than this, they will not even let the Church live on and enjoy the fraction of the truth which they have left her. They concede that that part of the Bible which deals with the truth of God is the inspired, infallible truth. They tell their people: You lose nothing by giving up these erroneous and unimportant sections of the Bible; the main part of it, the Gospel, is errorless; stick to that and all is well.[230] — To be sure, the Gospel is the

---

230) Which is the inspired part of the Bible? "What I am trying to show is that it is in true thoughts about God, and true principles of life, that the truth of the Bible must be sought rather than in accuracy of detail." (E. Grubb, *The Bible, Its Nature and Inspiration*, p. 20.) Be more specific! Well, that which contains the essentials. Lewis F. Stearns: "The Bible never claims an infallibility in non-essentials. We [the American Congregationalists] are coming more clearly to understand the great purpose of the Bible . . . and so to discern what is essential and non-essential for the attainment of that purpose." (See G. P. Fisher, *History of Christian Doctrine*, p. 548.) And where do we find the essentials? N. R. Best: "In its *loftier* portions

heart of the Bible. All is well with him who sticks to the Gospel. But all is not well when the moderns tell the Christians that the blessed Bible, which contains the Gospel, is half wrong and only half right. Get a man to believe that a given page of the Bible contains unreliable matter, and you cannot get him to believe that the next page, containing a Gospel message, is reliable. We have said this before (see page 196 f., No. 18, 2), but it must be repeated again and again. It is an inexorable law of psychology that the man who has been made to distrust half of the Bible will become suspicious of all of the Bible. For it is the fundamental claim of the Bible that it is infallible in all its parts. If, then, I am sure that it is wrong in only one of its statements, I shall no longer accept its claim to infallibility in any of its parts. Walther: "When you assert that the divine contents of the Bible is mixed up with human elements and false statements, you make not only this part of the Bible but the entire Bible unreliable and untrustworthy." (*Lehre u. Wehre*, 1911, p. 156.) The moderns are keeping men from putting their full trust in the Gospel truth revealed in the Bible. They get them to throw away one half of the Bible and keep them from enjoying the other half. — There are men who do reject parts of the Bible but put their full trust in the Gospel message. They will not believe that God created heaven and earth in six days, but they do believe John 3:16. There a miracle of grace has been performed — a double miracle of God's infinite grace. It is not the doing of the moderns. If God did not intervene, the Christians who hearken to the moderns would doubt the absolute truth of John 3:16. Men who dally with the thought that it is all right to decimate or even halve the

---

it soars to elevations of sublimity well worthy of an ultimate authorship in the mind of God" (*Inspiration*, p. 13); in those portions, says Charles Gore, which contain "spiritual value." (*The Doctrine of the Infallible Book*, p. 13.) Be more specific! R. Tuck: "In all matters not directly bearing on *morals and religion* there is the ordinary human element in the Bible records" (*Bible Difficulties*, p. 402), "in the sphere of morals and religion, where man is especially weak, there is pressing need for an infallible Divine revelation. . . . It is unreasonable for man to expect an infallible revelation on matters of science, observation, philosophy, or history." (*A Handbook of Bibl. Difficulties*, p. VII.) More precisely, it is only the saving truth, the Gospel, which is inspired and infallible. The *Baltimore Declaration:* "We accept the Scriptures as the infallible truth of God in all matters that pertain to His revelation and *our salvation.*" Joseph Stump: "Thus the Bible is the inspired and inerrant record of all that God has supernaturally revealed to men concerning Himself and the *way of salvation.*" "According to H. E. Jacobs 'the Holy Scriptures are the infallible and inerrant record of God's revelation of His *saving grace* to men.'" (*The Christian Faith*, p. 319. The *Lutheran Church Review*, 1904, p. 38.) H. C. Alleman: "What is infallible in the Bible? The good news, or the *Gospel of God* which God revealed in the prophets and fulfilled in the Christ." (*The Lutheran*, Jan. 14, 1937.)

Bible if one only retain the Gospel passages, are playing with their salvation.[231]

The moderns, indeed, are wont to tell their people that the "errors in the Bible" do not affect, or detract from, the value of its religious content. J. Stump assures them: "No number of contradictions in this [secular] sphere would 'shake our confidence in the absolute authority of Holy Scripture as an inerrant guide in all matters of faith and practice' (Jacobs)." (See *Lehre und Wehre,* 1904, p. 86.) Dr. James Martineau (Unitarian) has, says Marcus Dods, "cut away from the Gospels ten times more than a sober criticism warrants; still he is constrained to say: 'No one can affect ignorance of what Jesus was; *enough is saved to plant His personality in a clear space,* distinct from all that history or even fiction presents.'" (*The Bible. Its Origin and Nature,* p. 155.) Dods himself adds this: "Suppose we yield the stories of the childhood, suppose we admit — as indeed we must — that some of the things recorded are questionable, . . . our esteem of the Gospels is not lessened by finding in their narrative events which perhaps never happened." (*Op. cit.,* p. 180 f.) And Prof. J. O. Evjen reassures the Church: "Fallibility in dates or names does not invalidate its religious contents." (*What Is Lutheranism,* p. 24.)[232] To be sure, the question whether the cock crowed once or twice has, in itself, no bearing on any religious truth. The value of Christ's death would not have been affected if God had created heaven and earth in six periods and not in six days. And if a preacher of the Gospel gets his dates mixed, that does not invalidate his message. But the question before us is whether the Bible which claims infallibility for *all* of its statements would remain trustworthy if it were wrong in its dates. The question is whether the

---

231) Our *Lutheraner* (1942, p. 19) thus sounds the alarm: "Wenn die Bibel nicht mehr in allen ihren Teilen das von Gott eingegebene Wort der Wahrheit ist, . . . dann ist damit der Anspruch der Bibel auf unfehlbare Offenbarung der Wahrheit hinfaellig geworden. Dann waere es toerichte Anmassung und leere Prahlerei, wenn wir mit dem Apostel ruehmen wollten: 'Ich bin gewiss, dass weder Tod noch Leben . . .', Roem. 8:38, 39. Denn diese Zuversicht koennen wir nur auf Grund der Schrift haben, und ist die Schrift nicht in allem, was sie sagt, zuverlaessig, so koennen wir uns schliesslich auf keine ihrer Aussagen verlassen, da wir nicht gewiss sein koennen, ob sie auf Wahrheit beruht. Dann muessen wir wieder ohne Steuer und Kompass auf dem unruhigen Meer menschlicher Meinungen und Ansichten, menschlichen Schwankens and Zweifelns einer ungewissen, dunklen, trostlosen Zukunft entgegenfahren."

232) Even Arthur T. Pierson declares: "We are therefore to judge the Word of God by its professed purpose, and if, in the unfolding of moral and religious truth, scientific errors or inaccuracies appear, which have no relation to spiritual truth, they may not make the Bible unworthy of acceptance as a guide to the knowledge and practice of duty." (*Many Infallible Proofs,* p. 114.)

Christian who holds that the evangelists garbled the story of Peter's denial will not question the accuracy of the Gospel message in John 3:16. He cannot help doing that. Thomas Paine knew more about this point than the moderns. "If Matthew and Luke cannot be believed in their account of Christ's natural genealogy, how are we to believe them when they tell us He was the Son of God?" H. L. Mencken: "The instant they [the modernists] admit that any part of the Bible may be rejected, if it be only the most trifling fly speck in the Pauline epistles, they admit that any other part may be rejected. *Thus the divine authority of the whole disappears.*" And your own G. T. Ladd has said: "For the overthrow of this dogma [that every jot and tittle of Scripture is inspired and authoritative], in its principle, one instance of fallibility, when proved, is as good as a thousand." (*The Doctrine of Sacred Scripture*, I, p. 13.) You say yea and amen to that. And it is true. How, then, after you have proved to the satisfaction of your people that the Bible is a fallible book, will you get them to put their trust in any of its statements? Your bare assurance that somehow or other certain statements still are absolutely reliable will not reassure them. And Satan is quick to seize upon your arguments against Plenary Inspiration to raise the fear in the heart of the Christian who would rely upon John 3:16 that he is relying upon an unreliable book.

Once in a while a modern will offer proof for the assertion that the Biblical "errors" in secular matters need not shake the Christian's reliance on the Gospel statements of the Bible. Marcus Dods offers this proof: "The rule '*falsus in uno, falsus in omnibus*' is valid in the law courts as applicable to a witness who is found intentionally distorting truth. But the maxim has no application to ordinary life or to the writing of history. For there is no man who has not occasionally stumbled into error. . . ." (*Op. cit.*, p. 154.) That is plain sophistry. It does not touch the point at issue, *viz.*, whether one error in Scripture would not invalidate Scripture's fundamental claim of absolute infallibility, and it will not allay the fear raised in the Christian's mind by the errorists. Dods again: "And, secondly, if it be said, Is not all error important where divine truth and eternal interests are concerned? we answer, No! else God would have provided for the absence of all error." (*Loc. cit.*). That is a *petitio principii* in *optima forma*. N. Best offers another proof: "There is a great maxim dear to the most just and most enlightened legal minds — a maxim drawn from ancient Rome, the mother of the world's jurisprudence: 'The law cares not for trifles.' It is a maxim which theology ought to adopt in honor of the heavenly Father. . . . '*God cares not for trifles*.' Certainly it is an intellect childishly restricted which is able to imagine Him who 'upholdeth all things by the word of His power' sitting in the central rulership of the universe with concern in His thought about the possibility that Matthew, Mark, Luke, and John would not get it straight whether Peter denied his Lord to two or only to one of the high priest's serving maids." (*Op. cit.*, p. 79.) The bare assertion that "errors" in the Bible do not invalidate the Bible's fundamental claim is proved by the bare assertion that God considers it a trifle that His statement "All Scripture is given by inspiration" is not borne out by the facts in the case. These fallacies are not going to allay the fears you have raised in the hearts of the believers. Break Scripture at one point, and all of it breaks down.

The matter becomes worse, a thousand times worse, when the troubled disciple of the moderns asks how he can distinguish the religious truth in the Bible from the errors mixed in with it and his teachers tell him that an exact criterion does not exist. We heard Grau tell him: "The boundaries between the divine and the human elements cannot be definitely fixed in a mechanical way. No one knows how much is divine, how much human." He goes to E. Lewis and hears: "What is of the *form* of revelation, and what is of the *substance?* It may be that an infallibly exact criterion has not been given us." (*A Philosophy of the Christian Revelation,* p. 140.) We know, and Dr. Lewis knows, that God has not given us a special revelation on this matter, and we know of no theologian who has drawn up two such lists: "A. Truth in the Bible. B. Errors in the Bible" and dared to label them as absolutely correct. It seems as though the moderns are making sport of the Christians when J. Paterson Smyth warns his readers against accepting all statements of Holy Scripture as true; goes forth "to do battle, for the sake of our disquieted brethren, against the foe who teaches that the Bible is infallible in every detail"; rejoices that "Verbal Inspiration is now recognized by most educated people as a theory entirely unsupported by facts, and is fast being thrown to the moles and the bats with the rest of the world's old, discarded mind-lumber"; points out the need of distinguishing between the human elements in the Bible, the historical and ethical errors and other human shortcomings, and the divine elements; and then blandly tells his disquieted brethren: "We cannot draw a line between the divine and the human. We cannot say of any part, 'This is divine,' or, 'That is human.' " (*How God Inspired the Bible,* pp. 56, 116, 131.) The moderns actually operate with the canon: "What the extent of the Inspiration was in each case we need not, indeed we cannot, determine. . . . Where nature ended and Inspiration began, it is not for man to say." (Bishop Daniel Wilson, in *The Evidences of Christianity* [1828], p. 506. See W. Lee, *op. cit.,* p. 34.) The moderns are actually telling their brethren that the Bible is an *indistinguishable* compound of truth and error.

Grau tells us that we cannot draw the line between the divine and the human components of Scripture in a *mechanical* way. Have the moderns some other way? Oh, yes. Ladd declares that "the Church discerns the true Word of God," finds the "inner Bible by such a *living* process as implies the possession and growth of an ethico-religious consciousness which is spiritually illumined and spiritually guided. . . . By the light of its own spiritually illumined consciousness it discerns the Word of God within those Scriptures" (*op. cit.,* II, pp. 501, 502). S. P. Cadman's way: "There are other matters in the Bible which you are not required to believe. . . . But wherever it commands the approval of *your conscience* and the assent of your heart, it is undeniable." (*Answers to Everyday Questions,* p. 268.) R. Seeberg puts it this way: "We need not analyze the experience further. The result is enough. The thoughts of revelation become so active in our soul that we *feel them immediately* as the expression of the divine will, operative and present." (*Op. cit.,* p. 48.) But your own individual experience or ethico-religious consciousness is not enough, says B. Steffen. The infallible criterion "ist das einmuetige Zeugnis der Glaubensgemeinschaft aller echten Bibel-Christen aller Zeiten" (*op. cit.* p. 95). He does not tell us who gathered this unanimous testimony or where it is recorded. Try to apply the rule which W. A. Brown offers: "How can we tell what part of the Bible is revelation and what is setting? There is one very simple and effective way to do this. It is to bring everything the book contains into touch with the central personality in whom the story culminates — the Lord Jesus Christ." (*Beliefs That Matter,* p. 226.) But how does Jesus let you know whether He reacts favorably towards any particular passage or unfavorably? And how can you tell whether your reaction towards this passage is Jesus' reaction? Or would you care to be guided by Matthew Arnold's "literary intuition" in order to find "the Secret of Jesus"? [233] Whatever guide you follow, whether it be Arnold's literary and

---

233) H. M'Intosh: "Matthew Arnold repudiates everything distinctive of the Christian faith; yet he professes to have found by literary intuition a something in Scripture that is true, which he calls the 'Secret of Jesus,' but which had eluded the discovery of all the theologians and churches until now, when he by a unique literary and moral intuition has been able to discover it, as a vein of golden ore among the crude and misleading mass of Jewish superstition and apostolic delusion. And when we inquire what this wonderful secret is, it simply amounts to that veriest platitude of natural theology, the merest elementary dictate of conscience, that there is a power outside ourselves that makes for righteousness." (*Is Christ Infallible and The Bible True?* p. 357.)

moral intuition or Ladd's ethico-religious consciousness, you are following a will-o'-the-wisp. It will lead you anywhere. And it will lead you nowhere. Anywhere — give your ethico-religious consciousness, your subjective judgment, the right to sit in judgment on Scripture, and it will reject the purest gold as dross and get you to take its own dross as Scripture gold. And it will get you nowhere. This allegedly infallible standard is not fixed. It fluctuates. This ultimate authority — the individual mind — varies with each individual. Must I take your subjective judgment as to what is true in Scripture as infallible or must you be guided by me? [234] And the same individual will today reject as false what he yesterday received as true. The disciples of the moderns are left at sea. They are set adrift on the sea of doubt and uncertainty. The compass with which they are furnished points in different directions. These disquieted disciples can never come to rest and peace. They would find comfort or instruction in this and that passage, but their masters tell them that these passages *may* be dross, human opinions that do not belong in the Word of God.[235]

---

234) M'Intosh: "Since different minds will and do have different ideas and come to different, often opposite, conclusions as to what is true and what false in Scripture, witness Dr. Ladd and Dr. Martineau. . . . Professor Ladd finds, as the result of adopting and applying the rationalistic principle, which assumes the right and function of reason to sit in judgment on Scripture to ascertain what in it is true, that the only reliable elements therein, besides the ethical principles common more or less to it with other religions and philosophies, are the Messianic elements connected with redemption. But he, as usual, leaves us in blissful ignorance as to what these specifically are and where explicitly they are recorded and how we can inerrantly find them amid the mass of erroneous and unreliable materials with which they are surrounded. Assuming and applying the same rationalistic principle of the supremacy of reason over revelation, Dr. Martineau finds that the elements which above all others are to be rejected as false and pernicious are just those Messianic and redemptive elements that Dr. Ladd holds to be true and of divine authority. . . . His reason, sitting in judgment on Scripture, rejects as superstitious, pernicious, and intolerable what Dr. Ladd's reason in the same attitude and on the same principle receives as true, trustworthy, and authoritative." (*Op. cit.*, pp. 449, 346 f.)

235) We do not know how those who claim to have an infallible criterion for distinguishing between the human and the divine parts of the Bible and then regularly fail in arriving at an absolute conclusion can keep up their claim. They ought to listen to J. P. Smyth and the rest of their brethren, who tell them: "We cannot say of any part, 'This is divine,' or, 'That is human.'" We cannot understand how Ladd can ask us to rely upon the discriminatory judgment of the ethico-religious consciousness, when he himself states: "The inquiry is now raised and anxiously made: Who or what rule will teach me to distinguish between the Bible and that divine Word which the Bible contains but is not identical with? If this inquiry means, Who or what rule shall make me *infallible*" (italics by Ladd) "in making this distinction? then the reply must be: No such person or rule exists." (*What Is the Bible*, p. 419.)

This is the unspeakable hurt which the moderns inflict on the Church: they are undermining the Christian's trust in God's Word, the Bible. They are laying waste the fair land. The despoiled inhabitants are crying: "We can no longer read the Bible." (See Luther's warning and the collect on p. 272.) J. P. Smyth quotes a university student: "There are hundreds of young fellows like me who do not want to lose their grasp of the Bible, but we can no longer view it as we have been taught to do. If there is any way by which we can still hold it and treasure it, do our teachers know it; and if they do, why do they not tell us?" Another one who "heard of the discrepancies, the contradictions, and the crudeness of the early moral teaching of the Bible" declared: "I was brought up in the traditional beliefs about the Bible, and I have suffered the exquisite pain of finding my Bible slipping from me." Smyth consoles these men by telling them that these imperfections are the human parts of the Bible and do not belong to God's Word. And when the disquieted Christians ask him: Which is the unreliable and which the reliable part of the Bible? he shrugs his shoulders and tells them: "We cannot say of any part, 'This is divine,' or, 'That is human.'" (*Op. cit.*, pp. 8, 15.) The moderns are filling the city of God with doubt and fear and despair.[236] Breaking Scripture, they are breaking men's hearts.

FOMENTING TREASON

Further, the fifth columnists are aiming to entice Zion away from her allegiance to her Lord. They succeed in individual cases. Under their solicitations many have deposed the Word of God as the sole authority and enthroned human authority. They are giving the theologian the right to decide which parts of the Bible must be recognized as man's word and which parts may be accepted as God's Word. And they are telling the Christians to assume and exercise the same right. Who whispers to us which parts of the Bible are objectionable and which are acceptable? asks M. Dods, and answers: "'The spiritual man' — the man who has the spirit of Christ — 'judgeth all things.'" (See footnote 194.)[237] The

---

236) *Ev.-Luth. Gemeindeblatt*, 21. Maerz 1937: "Wer findet denn Gottes Wort aus diesem Wirrwarr heraus? Der Theolog. Wie weiss er aber, was in der Bibel Gottes Wort ist? Wenn ein Wort auf ihn einen tiefen Eindruck macht, das ist ein Gotteswort. Wie aber, wenn morgen dasselbe Wort auf ihn keinen Eindruck macht? Dann muss er sagen: Es war doch kein Gotteswort. Und kommt ein anderer Theolog hinzu und sagt: Auf mich macht dieses Wort keinen Eindruck, dann haben wir die verzweifelte Lage, dass, was einer fuer ein Gotteswort haelt, der andere nicht dafuer haelt! Wehe jeder Kirche, in der solche Theologen regieren!"

237) E. Lewis: "What is of the *form* of revelation and what is of the *substance*? It may be that an infallibly exact criterion has not been given us. It may be that provision is made for the exercise, at the

disciples of the moderns are being systematically trained to exercise authority over Scripture or to accept the authority of the theologians. *Christianity Today* thus describes the horrible situation created in the Church by the modernists: "If the Bible only *contains* the Word of God, as even the modernist is willing to admit, then certainly it may lack a great deal of being infallible, and we are then left to the mercies of 'higher criticism' or to our own individual opinions as to just which elements are the words of God and which are only the words of man." There is treason abroad in the good land. Men are seducing God's people from their sworn allegiance.

In other words, the moderns are educating their pupils along rationalistic lines. The human authority which they enthrone is the authority of reason. Ladd calls it the authority of the ethico-religious consciousness, but M'Intosh is right in identifying that "with the rationalistic principle of the supremacy of reason over revelation." (See footnote 235.) It is plain carnal reason which induces men to reject parts of the Bible on scientific grounds or because of the protest of the moral sensibilities of the natural man. It is plain carnal reason which guides Ladd's ethico-religious consciousness in rejecting or accepting divine revelation. But the entrance of the rationalistic germ into the Church is disastrous. It endangers her very life. The germ will spread and grow. Fully developed, it kills all Christian doctrine. [238] By the infinite grace

---

supremely critical moment of decision, of that *moral freedom*" (italics by us) "which must never be entirely overwhelmed. It may be that wavering evidence is our divinely given opportunity for *self-assertion*, so that when we do decide, it is our *deepest self* that is uttered." (*Loc. cit.*) H. L. Willett tells an inquirer, in the question-box of the *Christian Century:* "It is evident that it is not only the privilege but the duty of the student of Scripture to exercise his right of judgment regarding the statements of the Bible, remembering the origin and character of the record and the fact that the freedom to estimate the historical and moral value of all parts of the book, the right of private judgment, is the foundation stone of Protestantism."

238) Walther: "The least deviation from the old inspiration doctrine introduces a rationalistic germ into theology and infects the whole body of doctrine." (*Walther and the Church*, p. 14.) M'Intosh: "The theory which sets reason above revelation and makes man's own individual consciousness the standard and judge in the ultimate issue of what is true and what is false in Holy Writ, warrants every man in accepting or rejecting just as much or as little of it as he thinks fit, or none at all should he think best." (*Op. cit.*, p. 456.) It is, for instance, a natural development when J. P. Smyth, who on page 118 "throws Verbal Inspiration to the moles and bats," declares on page 124 that "James, the saintly Judaist, . . . insisted, like another Baptist, on the *central truth* of all religion, that '‘tis only noble to be good.'" (*Op. cit.*) *The Life and Morals of Jesus of Nazareth*, by Thomas Jefferson, known as *The Jefferson Bible*, is widely advertised and extravagantly praised. In the Foreword D. E. Lurton says that "within this brief and sublime story are the authentic words of Christ which give life to the Bible. They are its essence." Jefferson edited the Bible by eliminating every-

of God it has not reached that stage throughout visible Christendom. But even there where it is only in the incipient stage it works disaster. It enfeebles the Church. By so much as our faith rests on reason, it is deprived of its divine strength. By so much as it loses hold of God's Word, its virility wanes.

The moderns, like all fifth columnists, pooh-pooh the danger. Reporting on the Omaha convention of the *United Lutheran Church* a secular paper employed the caption "Lutherans Dispute over a Single Word," the single word being the word *errorless*. (See *Lutheraner*, 1940, p. 378.) That was to be expected. But here is a church paper which indulges in the same ridicule: "For any of us, in such times as these, to quibble over theories of Inspiration. . . is no less a disaster than was the session of the synod of the Russian Orthodox Church which met in Petrograd in 1917 to discuss the color of vestments at the very time when, six blocks away, the Kerenski revolution set the stage for atheistic Communism." (*The Lutheran Standard*, March 22, 1941. — In *Kirchliche Zeitschrift*, October, 1941, Dr. Reu takes this *Lutheran Standard* writer severely to task.) It seems incredible that a Christian theologian should voice the idea that there is not much difference between Verbal, Plenary Inspiration and Partial Inspiration. That little word "errorless" is all-important. It expresses the difference between a strong and a weak Church, yea, between a living and a dying Church. Our spiritual strength comes only from God's Word, and the whole Bible gives the Church her full strength. "How is it possible for a preacher to be a power for God, whose source of authority is his own reason and convictions?" (*Fundamentals*, III, p. 111.) — The Church is engaged in a life-and-death struggle. And while the liberals are assaulting the wall from the outside, the conservative moderns within the Church are breaking down the morale of the people and sabotaging the Bible.[239]

---

thing but the four Gospels and reducing these to "the very words of Jesus," and, finally, says the *Lutheran Herald* of Aug. 5, 1941, "paring away everything from what remained that did not fit in with Jefferson's own religious preconceptions. The result may be imagined: gone is the Incarnation; gone are all the miracles; gone is the Resurrection. The Gospel according to Jefferson ends with the words 'There laid they Jesus and rolled a great stone to the door of the sepulcher and departed.' Nothing left but 'morals.'"

239) The Church is harmed in other ways. For instance, the outsider, the unbeliever, will have no respect for the Bible of the Christians when Christian theologians tell him that the Fourth Gospel had to correct the Synoptic Gospels and Christ had to correct the Old Testament, and that the writers of the New Testament were not quite sure just what Jesus did say, and that the Bible contains many things not fit to be read in the churches and homes. The outsider will lose his respect for the theologians of the Church when he hears that it took them centuries to discover what the Anomoeans (Arians) and the pagan

IMPAIRING THEIR MENTAL FACULTIES

In the second place, the crusade against Verbal Inspiration proves disastrous to the crusaders themselves. They lose great parts of the Bible and the blessings connected therewith, as has been shown. But they harm themselves also in other ways. One of the evil consequences of the denial of Verbal Inspiration is the impairment of the natural mental powers which inevitably sets in when men undertake to disprove the infallibility of Holy Scripture. Dr. Pieper did not overstate the case when he declared that no man "can deny the inspiration of Holy Scripture without suffering an impairment of his natural mental powers." Those who assert either that Scripture does not claim infallibility or that this claim is a false one must fly in the face of the facts in order to prove their assertion, must suppress their natural acumen, must resort to all kinds of inanities and puerilities to bolster their claim. Glance over the long list — and it is only a partial one — tabulating the false assertions and fallacious arguments of the moderns, and you will realize that these men are not using the intelligence that God gave them. Men with a normal historical sense would not ridicule the statement of Luke that Lysanias was tetrarch of Abilene at the time of Christ, as Bruno Bauer and Strauss did, on the ground that "Lysanias had been murdered 34 years before the birth of Christ." They would ask themselves whether there might not have been a second Lysanias of Abilene, instead of charging that Luke simply invented this person. Strauss, indeed, in order to substantiate his charge against Luke declared that "neither Josephus nor any author of that time alludes to the existence of

---

Celsus already knew about the mistakes in the Bible, and that they discovered it only on being prodded by Paine and Ingersoll. And the Christian layman cannot understand what the theologians are about when he is confronted by the score of "theories of inspiration" which circulate in the theological world. We are wondering what the layman Thomas E. Finegan, editor of *Winston's Encyclopedia and Dictionary*, thought of the theologians when he wrote the article on "Inspiration." "All orthodox theologians agree in ascribing divine assistance to the Scriptural writers but differ widely as to the degree, extent, and mode of inspiration. The advocates of Plenary Inspiration assert that every verse of the Bible, every word of it, every syllable, every letter, is the direct utterance of the Most High. In opposition to this theory" (we shall not blame the layman for using the term "theory") "some writers confine Inspiration to all that is directly religious in the Bible, to all that is matter of direct revelation, leaving out of the question all that can be known by ordinary intellectual application. Other authorities attribute inspiration only to the spirit, ideas, or doctrines of the Bible, exempting the strict form or letter. Some go yet further and include in the fallible sections the mode of argument and expository details." This man did not have time to list all the other theories, but as he listed and studied these few contradictory teachings, he no doubt thought: Either the Bible uses confusing language, or the theologians cannot understand simple language.

a second ruler of Abilene who bore this title." "Ebrard, however, proves that this entire objection is nothing more than a historical blunder on the part of Strauss himself." Strauss did not know his Josephus and did not translate correctly. Submitting the Josephus passages in question, W. Lee concludes: "Hence, therefore, Josephus *does* make mention of a later Lysanias and, by doing so, fully corroborates the fact of St. Luke's intimate acquaintance with the tangled details of Jewish history in his day." (*Op. cit.*, p. 361.) A historical critic of normal intelligence does not rush into print before he has thoroughly examined the available sources. And remember, this is not an exceptional instance. Dozens of similar blunders are found in the black-list we have furnished. Or take this case: J. P. Smyth, the man who has "thrown Verbal Inspiration to the moles and bats," argues that "St. Paul uses such words as 'I speak as a fool,' which, though quite natural and fitting for a human writer, would hardly be the words dictated by the Holy Spirit" (*op. cit.*, p. 116). This man has not the faintest idea what the doctrine of Verbal Inspiration is and still insists on being heard in the case. He also "detects traces of human prejudice and passions [in the Biblical writers], as when St. Paul, quoting a Greek poet, dubbed the whole race of Cretans as 'evil beasts and liars' " (*op. cit.*, p. 121). A normal mind would not charge Paul with prejudice unless it were proved — and Smyth makes no attempt to prove — that the Cretans did not have these national characteristics. And remember, our black-list furnishes a whole lot of similar cases. Or see how N. R. Best's mind works: "Four persons who read respectively the four separate accounts of Peter's tragic denial of the Lord would have in mind four quite different groups of incidents. The best reconciling which the inerrancy dogmatists can do with this case is to infer that Peter actually denied the Lord *seven*" (our italics) "times — which disagrees with what the Lord predicted." (*Op. cit.*, p. 77.) The desire to ridicule Verbal Inspiration rushes men into all sorts of extravagances. Dr. Best does not realize that men of normal intelligence will not seriously consider these caricatures. And, remember, the stock charges of the moderns do not rise to any higher level. If you doubt this, you will have to read the preceding chapters once more.

And it is not only the second-rater that loses his acumen when he sets out to demolish Verbal Inspiration. The theological giants, too, operate with the same puerilities. Here is R. Seeberg: "The theory that the words are inspired is also disproved by a cursory glance at the peculiarities of the Biblical authors. . . . Paul declared that he baptized certain persons in Corinth, but that he did not remember others beside these, 1 Cor. 1:16. No one would regard such a confession of ignorance as inspired by the Holy Spirit." (*Op. cit.*, p. 27.) That statement springs from the same ignorance that dictated J. P. Smyth's comment on "I speak as a fool." On page 103 Seeberg asserts: "Paul's teaching with regard to the righteousness attainable by Christians differs from that of James (2:21 ff.) and John (1 John 3:7)." That is bad enough, but the next sentence reads: "But on both sides Christian ideas are represented." Two ideas conflicting with each other — and yet both are Christian! Seeberg even goes so far as to assert: "There can be no doubt that the Biblical authors could certainly draw conclusions intrinsically false from inspired truths"! ! (p. 102). Again: "Matt. 8:28 speaks of two possessed in the territory of the Gadarenes; according to Mark 5:2 there was only one. Without question, in these instances one of the authors is wrong." (P. 29.) Seeberg has a low opinion of the intelligence of his readers. Some of his readers will look up Mark 5:2, and when they fail to find there the "only" ("there met Him *only* one man with an unclean spirit"), on which the whole argument hinges, they will wonder how an intellectual giant like Seeberg could permit his mind to be tricked by such a palpable sophistry.

Let us examine Professor Edwin Lewis. "The author of the Fourth Gospel is not particularly interested in chronology. Any attempt to 'harmonize' his story with that of the synoptic Gospels is doomed to hopeless failure. Some scholars, it is true, claim that in his account of the Passion Week he is deliberately *correcting* the Synoptic chronology; but that is a question. Even if he is, we may still believe that his motive is that which controls him throughout, namely, a desire to emphasize *spirit*. In the Synoptics, the last supper is represented as the Passover meal. A belief consequently arose in the early Church that Christ had the same significance as the paschal lamb. In the Fourth Gospel, the last supper is eaten the *evening before* Passover. By a single stroke, therefore, the author breaks the connection. . . . He breaks it — so it would seem — because he is afraid of crass literalism. Paul's saying expresses him perfectly: 'The letter killeth, but the spirit giveth life.' " (*A New Heaven and a New Earth*, p. 156.) We are not now interested in the harmony of the four Gospels on this point.[240] Nor are we much interested in noting the un-

---

240) A scholar should not make such a wild statement that any attempt to harmonize the four Gospels is doomed to hopeless failure. See *Bibliotheca Sacra*, January, 1940, p. 63 ff.: "The Chronology of the Holy Week." (The closing paragraph reads: "In conclusion we must admit that we are uncertain and even ignorant of some points concerning the chronology of Holy Week. On the other hand, it is only fair for us to credit the Gospel writers with full knowledge of the subject. And it is only reasonable to go a step further and say that, having full knowledge of the subject of the chronology of that last

warranted *assumption* that a contradiction exists, and the further bland *assumption* that if the early Church had had only the synoptic Gospels, it would have become a prey of crass literalism. What arouses our interest just now is the fact that Dr. Lewis really expects the Christians to feel safe with having so much unsafe material in their Bible. He has a strange conception of the psychology of the Christian.

Consider the case of R. Tuck. He presents this "elucidation of Jonah 1:17 to our very careful consideration": "The Chaldee word *dagah*, which has been rendered a *fish*, was meant by the sacred writer to signify a *boat* or *skiff;* and the word *lebalang*, which has been rendered *to swallow*, literally means to *remove* from place to place. The verse reads then, agreeably to reason, as it is in the original, without supposing impossibilities, thus: 'Now, the Lord had prepared a great barge to remove Jonah, and Jonah was in the belly (hold) of the barge three days and three nights." (*Op. cit.*, 412.) — Those who do not like Tuck's interpretation might consider the following ones: "Some have affirmed that the entire narrative was a dream which Jonah had while asleep in the sides of the ship. . . . Quite recently another interpretation has been suggested. It is stated that the name Nineveh is no other than Ninua, or Nunu, which means 'fish,' and as the city was called the great city, its old Assyrian name was simply the Great Fish or the Fish City. To this day, it is said, the name on the monuments is represented by a fish in a basin or tank. This view would make Nineveh itself the 'great fish' that swallowed Jonah, and in crying to the Lord for deliverance, he gave the city its old Assyrian name, praying to be delivered from the 'great fish.'" (R. S. MacArthur, *Bible Difficulties*, pp. 441, 443.)

Testing Professor Ladd, we find that he, too, does not rise above the level of the minor theologians. The minor theologians have been telling us that Jesus either did not know that the story of Jonah was fiction or did not think it worth while to inform His hearers that He did not believe in it. Professor Ladd sides with them! "We should be very careful not hastily to commit the

---

week, we may trust the faithfulness of each man that he has transmitted to us exactly as much of that knowledge as was in keeping with his own purpose of writing. . . . All alleged chronological difficulties vanish into nothingness in the light of verbal inspiration. 'Thy Word is truth.'") See also *Kirchliche Zeitschrift*, 1940, p. 342 ff., *Conc. Theol. Mthly.*, XI, p. 634. A. Fahling, *A Harmony of the Gospels*, pp. 180-182: " 'The first day of the feast' (Matt. 26:17). 'Strictly speaking, the Passover Festival began on the evening of this day. But because by noon, the fourteenth of Nisan, or Abib, all traces of leaven had to be removed, . . . it was already called 'the first day of the feast' [f. n. 2.]. — 'Before the feast of the Passover' (John 13:1). This expression refers to the whole festival, in this case to the whole remaining festal week."

authority of Christ to trivialities now in dispute among Biblical critics and commentators. Because He refers to Jonah, for example, without apparently questioning the historical nature of the narrative of the transaction of this prophet, it does not follow that His authority may be pledged to one of several theories as to the nature of the book in which the narrative occurs." The reason why Ladd cannot accept the story of Jonah as a true story is stated as follows: "A narrative in which a man is represented as composing a poetical prayer, surrounded with water, his head bound with seaweed, and drifting with marine currents while inside a monster of the sea, was surely never intended by its author to be understood as literal history. The book of Jonah was written as an allegory." (*What Is the Bible?* pp. 76, 84.) Ladd's reasoning is in the best tradition of *rationalismus vulgaris*. And we are asked to assume that our Lord Jesus reasoned in the same way. And our question why Jesus did not enlighten His hearers on this matter is thus disposed of: "Shall it be claimed that, if Jesus knew the story to be allegorical, He must distinctly aver it to be so when speaking amidst a people whose daily speech dealt in allegory? Or that, if not for the sake of hearers of His own time, at any rate for the sake of readers in this Occidental and unfigurative age, He must have given full notice of His opinion of the Book of Jonah? . . . The commentator may not help out the *dullness*" (our italics) "by the support of Christ's infallible authority." (*The Doct. of S. Scrip.* I, p. 66.) — "So in Job [38:4 ff.] it is implied that the stars were made *before* instead of (as here in Genesis) after the founding of the earth." (*What Is the Bible?* p. 138.) — Interpretation of John 5:39: "The Jews were caught and entangled in the form. . . . Christ does not find fault with them for diligent study of their Sacred Scriptures; He does accuse them of *folly and sin in idolizing the written word* while neglecting its ideal contents of truth." (*Op. cit.,* I, p. 51.) — "Is the Christian Church *absolutely* dependent upon the authority of the Bible?" Certainly not, says Ladd. Proof? "For true Christian faith and character existed before the Bible. . . . The Church was founded before the canon of the New Testament was formed." (*What Is the Bible?* p. 443.) — One more item: "The propriety of making a distinction between the Bible and the Word of God has always been virtually admitted by the Christian Church. To charge this distinction with heresy or regard it with suspicion, can only be due, in the case of honest inquirers, to ignorance of history as well as of the facts of the case. . . . Luther himself and the other great reformers expressly insisted upon this distinction. These all speak rather of the Bible as 'containing' or 'embracing' or 'conveying' the Word of God." (*Op. cit.,* p. 445.) We cannot under-

stand how Professor Ladd can make this statement that the phrase
"The Bible *contains* the Word of God" as opposed to the phrase
"The Bible *is* the Word of God" is a good Christian phrase, employed
by Luther, always employed by the Church. Read any history of
dogma. Read W. Lee, *op. cit.*, p. 400 f.: "The two leading representatives of the views of those who changed the formula 'The
Bible *is* the Word of God' into 'The Bible *contains* the Word of
God' are Le Clerc and Grotius. Le Clerc's writings reflect the ideas
of Spinoza, and Spinoza introduced into Christian theology the
speculations of the medieval Jews, and more particularly the
philosophy of Maimonides. Grotius openly avows the source of
his opinions: Maimonides." [241)]

---

241) Ladd puts Luther into the class of those who made a distinction between the Bible and the Word of God. It is one of the
mysteries of the ages how theologians who claim to be conversant with
Luther's writings can give credence to the myth that Luther did not
teach Verbal, Plenary Inspiration. A hundred years ago Rudelbach
dealt with this phenomenon. The myth, which has no basis in Luther's
writings — as Rudelbach conclusively shows — will not die. "Man weiss
wohl, wie schwer es in Deutschland haelt, einen fuer ausgemacht
geltenden Schulsatz, wie jener sich gibt, aufzugeben." (*Zeitschrift f. d.
gesm. Luth. Theol. u. Kirche*, 1840, zweites Quartalh. p. 6.) Now, after
a hundred years, the moderns are still singing the same song: Luther
did not identify Scripture and the Word of God. J. P. Smyth: "Luther
gives no countenance to the notion of Verbal Inspiration and repeatedly
emphasizes the great truth that the Holy Spirit is not confined to a book
of the past ages, but dwells and speaks in the conscience of every
Christian man." (*Op. cit.*, p. 88.) E. Brunner: "He who identifies the
letters and words of the Scriptures with the Word of God has never
truly understood the Word of God. A better witness than Martin Luther
we can scarcely call up. . . . And Luther would never have approved
the opinion of later orthodoxy that everything in the Scriptures just
because it *is* in the Scriptures is equally inspired by the Holy Spirit."
(*The Theology of Crisis*, p. 19. *The Word and the World*, p. 94.) R. Seeberg also asserts that Luther had this "low" view of inspiration. See
footnote 222. C. A. Wendell chimes in: "The nervous anxiety to prove
the 'complete inerrancy' of the Bible 'from cover to cover' may be good
Fundamentalism but hardly good Lutheranism, for Luther was not of
that type. . . . Luther did not fret and fuss to prove its 'alleged inerrancy from cover to cover.' He did not claim inerrancy for it."
(*What Is Lutheranism?* p. 235.) And in 1940 Prof. J. O. Evjen wrote, in
The Lutheran Church Quarterly, p. 149: "It was heresy for Ockham not
to believe every single word of the Bible. For Ockham the Bible was
inspired, word for word. . . . Luther had a different conception of
heresy. To the Reformer, Scripture was binding to the extent that it
proclaimed Christ, the Gospel, or pointed to Christ. Many historical
matters in the Bible did not concern Christian life." The moderns
persist in ascribing to Luther a "liberal" attitude toward the Bible, to
Luther, who said: "The Holy Ghost . . . is the Author of this book"
(II: 566); who said: "The Holy Scriptures are the Word of God, written
and (as I might say) lettered and formed in letters" (IX: 1770); who said:
"Scripture, *or* the Word of God" (VIII: 1111, 1129; XIV: 413), ". . . purum
Verbum Dei, *hoc est*, Sancta Scriptura" (see IX: 87); who said: "Also

When we study this long list of aberrations, these baseless assertions, illogical conclusions, and exhibitions of plain ignorance — this comedy of errors — we cannot refrain from setting down once more Dr. Pieper's judgment: "The objections to the verbal inspiration of Holy Scripture do not manifest great ingenuity or mental acumen, but the very opposite: they serve as a shining example of how God inflicts His just punishment upon all critics of His Word — they *lose their common sense* and become utterly unreasonable and illogical." (*What Is Christianity?* P. 243.) The comedy of errors presents a tragedy.

---

gibt man dem Heiligen Geist die *ganze* Heilige Schrift" (III:1890); who said: "The Scriptures have never erred" (XV:1481); who said: *"All stories of Holy Scripture have to do with Christ"* (VII:1924); and who said these things not once but a thousand times. Ladd demands that "the reader who wishes to know certain of the real views of Luther must consult the *unexpurgated*" (italics in original) "editions of his works, especially of his Vorreden (Walch, XIV) and not what Reuss has called 'die cursierenden von frommen Gesellschaften castrierten Special-Ausgaben'" (*The Doctrine*, II, p. 166). Exactly. We insist on that, too. Do not read merely those emasculated selections put out by the moderns but read the entire Luther. Read only volumes I—IX and XIV, and, says Pastor W. Bodamer in the article "Luthers Stellung zur Lehre von der Verbalinspiration" (*Theologische Quartalschrift*, 1936, p. 240 ff.), you will find "more than a thousand statements" of Luther which unequivocally assert Verbal Inspiration and identify Scripture and the Word of God. A hundred or so of such statements are there quoted. "Hoeret, ihr Herren, Papst und Kaiser, ist denn die Bibel Gottes Wort oder nicht?" (VII:1089). *Princeton Theol. Review*, 15, p. 502: "We may begin our synthetic presentation of Luther's views with the obvious and all but universally admitted remark that the Reformer, following the custom of the medieval Church and of his own opponents, commonly uses Scripture and the Word of God as synonymous and interchangeable terms." But the moderns cannot rid themselves of the hallucination that Luther did not equate Scripture and the Word of God, did not teach the absolute inerrancy of Scripture. The thing is inexplicable. Ladd reads his unexpurgated Luther, reads these two thousand plain statements and declares: Luther could not have meant that! For "Luther holds that the Gospel of John is far to be preferred to the other three and that the epistles of Paul and Peter much surpass the three Evangelists Matthew, Mark, and Luke." (*Op. cit.*, II, p. 154.) We ask Ladd to prove his assertion that "Luther holds the distinction between the Biblical writings and God's Word" (*What Is the Bible?* p. 48), and his proof is that Luther held some books of the Bible to be more *important* than others. That is not normal argumentation. Consider C. A. Wendell's proof. "Luther did not claim inerrancy for the Bible. 'Johannes macht hie eine Verwirrung,' 'John is confused here,' in other words, makes a mistake, he says in one of his sermons "(VIII:884)." Wendell bases his proof on a mistranslation! Luther did *not* say: "Johannes ist hier verwirret." What he does say is that this is one of the many instances where the parallel accounts in the Gospels are *seemingly* contradictory. The statement "Johannes *macht* hier eine Verwirrung "cannot be made to mean: "Johannes *ist* verwirret." But Wendell and others make it to mean that and triumphantly exclaim: Luther did not teach the inerrancy of Scripture! (A writer in the *Journal of the Am. Luth. Conf.*, March, 1936, p. 9 ff., argues along the same lines. — These and similar arguments are examined Conc. Theol. Mthly., I, p. 868 f.; III, p. 306 ff.; VIII, p. 443 f.) The moderns are going to believe the myth till doomsday.

THE SORRY SUBSTITUTES FOR PLENARY INSPIRATION

Another thing that does not speak well for the acumen, theological and otherwise, of the moderns is the matter of the substitutes they offer for Verbal Inspiration. After Seeberg expressed his sorrow or joy over the "fall of Verbal Inspiration" ("Verbal Inspiration has disappeared as if in one night. No theologian of any repute now upholds it. . . . The theory of verbal inspiration has been of incalculable service to the Church. . . . How simple and clear must have been the inner life of our forefathers with this theory of verbal inspiration!"), he looked around for a substitute. "Every Protestant Christian must form for himself a reasoned judgment upon this question. This object may be achieved by . . . attempts to discover what substitute Protestant Christendom can accept in its place. If that theory (Verbal Inspiration) falls, as fallen indeed it has, the question then confronts us, How shall a substitute be found?" (*Op. cit.*, pp. 1—4.) "The whole volume will be discredited," said J. De Witt, "unless a broader definition can be found for the inspiration that produced it than any that has yet been advanced." (*What Is Inspiration*, p. 68.) The moderns have found a lot of substitutes. It seems impossible to list them all. They can be roughly divided into two classes. The ultraliberals deal with the no-inspiration-at-all theories. These follow the pattern of Father Semler's definition of inspiration as "die andaechtige Gemuetsverfassung" of the holy writers. The substitutes offered by the more-or-less conservatives come under the general head of Partial Inspiration; to these we shall confine our present discussion. The partial-inspiration men offer their wares under different labels. Some prefer to call the Bible "the *record* of revelation."[242] The most popular trademark seems to be: Only the Gospel portions are inspired. That is, says P. T. Forsyth, "the saving distinction of the Bible and the Gospel" (Foreword to J. M. Gibson's *The Insp. and Auth. of H. Scripture*). R. H. Malden puts it this way: "When we call the Bible inspired, we mean (or at least I mean) that it is of unique and permanent religious value." (*The Inspiration of the Bible*, p. 4.) That is what the United Lutheran Church of America means when it speaks of Inspiration. See Baltimore Declaration, above. That is exactly the substitute which Seeberg found: "The Gospel is both the revela-

---

242) Luthardt: "Scripture is not in itself the revelation, but only a report of the revelation." Volck: "Die Bibel ist die Urkunde der Heilsgeschichte." Hofmann: "Die Schrift ist ein Denkmal, eine Urkunde der Heilsgeschichte." Werner Elert at Lausanne (1927): "We believe with all Christians that the Holy Scriptures hold divine authority for us as the true record and historical revelation of God." (See *Theol. Mthly.*, VII, p. 363.) The meaning of this label is: Scripture *contains* the Word of God.

tion given by Christ and the special understanding of this revelation. In the latter sense it is given by a special, personal gift of grace by God, or, as we say, *by inspiration*. . . . When Luther refers to Scripture, he is thinking of the Gospel of Christ." (*Op. cit.*, pp. 68, 18.) These theories vary much in detail, but are one in restricting Inspiration to scattered portions of the Bible.[243)]

---

243) Their discoverers like to give them big names. B. Steffen calls his theory "*Zentralinspiration*"; it means what Seeberg and the Baltimore Declaration mean. W. Sanday calls it "*Vital Inspiration*" but means the same thing: "In all that relates to the revelation of God and of His will, the writers assert for themselves a definite inspiration." (*Op. cit.*, pp. 46, 74.) G. L. Raymond has told us that, if we want to know which portions of the Bible are inspired, we must be able to distinguish between their "literary" and their "literal sense." What does that mean? See footnote 207. And, says Raymond, we must make a further distinction: there are in man "two minds, namely, the conscious and the subconscious, which latter term is used to indicate a mind of the results of which we are conscious, but of the processes of which we are unconscious. . . . It has been shown that, when a man is inspired, the very conditions necessitate that whatever is revealed should affect first the inner or subconscious realm of his mind; that whatever may be received in this inner or subconscious region influences both it and the outer, or conscious, realm, by way of suggestion; and that whatever influences by way of suggestion must, from its very nature, leave the outer or conscious realm free to express itself according to methods dominated by its own inherited or acquired intelligence." What is Raymond driving at? Why, he is showing that not everything in the Bible is inspired. "Specific details can never be supposed to be a necessary part of that which is merely suggested. They are not logically attributable to the spirit that inspired it." (*The Psychology of Inspiration*, pp. 56, 307.) R. F. Horton's theory: "We best serve the cause of truth by trying accurately to distinguish what is divine truth and what is human imperfection. . . . According to the simpler and, we may add, saner view of inspired writings these references (Gal. 3:19; Acts 7:53; Heb. 2:2; and Heb. 11:31, 32) only show that the writers were acquainted with the Jewish tradition on the subject and alluded to it without any intention of passing a critical verdict on its veracity. . . . They are simply treating the subject *homiletically*." (*Revelation and the Bible*, p. 329 f.) J. P. Smyth: "Inspiration is the result of contact between the Spirit of God and the spirit of man." (*Op. cit.*, p. 119.) That definition is broad enough to take care of any accident that might befall a holy writer. Bishop Gore: "The Anglican reformers of the sixteenth century devised a question to be answered by those just to be ordained deacons. 'Do you unfeignedly believe all the canonical Scriptures of the Old and New Testaments?' To which the answer was required: 'I do believe them.' But our bishops of today have proposed an *addition* to the question, so that it should run: 'Do you unfeignedly believe all the canonical Scriptures of the Old and the New Testament *as conveying to us in many parts and in divers manners the revelation of God*, which is consummated in Jesus Christ?' And the answer they proposed is: 'I do so believe them.'" (*Op. cit.*, p. 63. Italics ours.) Bishop Gore asks the Church to accept this substitute. — The following definitions might perhaps be assigned to Class I: No real inspiration at all. But giving the writers the benefit of the doubt, we shall put them into Class II: Partial Inspiration. G. T. Ladd: "At no time, except during the dominance of the *post*-Reformation dogma, has the 'inspiration' of the authors of sacred Scripture been regarded as specifically different in kind from that possessed by other believers, or as given to them solely for the purpose of fitting them to compose an infallible Bible."

The moderns have thrown Verbal Inspiration to the bats and moles; and what is this that they have brought in instead? It does not look respectable. It has no scientific respectability. This theory presupposes such an unaccountable behavior on the part of the Holy Ghost and prescribes such an unworkable use of the Bible that the scientists would unanimously vote to throw it out. This theory of a partial, intermittent, sporadic, spasmodic, and erratic inspiration asks us to believe that the Holy Ghost constructed His Bible, the Book of Life for man, in such an awkward manner that on one page He breathed His words into the minds and hearts of the apostles, on the next page He permitted them to set down their own ruminations, and in the middle of the page He interrupted them to speak His own words. This stop-and-go theory places the holy writers, too, in a bad light. If that is true, that at times "the human thoughts predominated over the divine thoughts" (Bensow), we must assume that every so often the writer got the signal to go on his own, every so often he was ordered to stop and let the Holy Ghost speak, but occasionally the psalmist refused and kept on speaking his own thoughts. We much prefer the theory of the ultraliberals: No inspiration at all. That is a clean-cut affair. But the inspiration-in-spots theory is too awkward and clumsy to get serious consideration. H. Kraemer speaks of "the clumsy form of the literal inerrancy of the document in which God's revelation is told" (*The Christian Message in a Non-Christian World*, p. 218), Horton of "that crude dogma of infallible inspiration" (*op. cit.*, p. 25). We are willing to let any scientist, any philosopher, decide which is the crude and clumsy form, Plenary Inspiration or intermittent inspiration.[244)]

(*Op. cit.*, p. 75.) E. Lewis: "All Scripture is because of the inspiration of God. . . . That means that men wrote because they were under the inspiration of some divinely given truth." (*A Philosophy*, etc., p. 261.) M. Dods: "Inspiration is the indwelling of the Divine Spirit. All Christians believe that they themselves enjoy this indwelling, but they are not conscious of becoming infallible." (*Op. cit.*, p. 145.)

244) Speaking of the theory that "certain portions of Scripture have resulted from the unaided exercise of human judgment or of human faculties, . . . that the writer has but partially or imperfectly handed down the communication from heaven," W. Lee observes: "If we had never heard of the difficulties which have been urged against Inspiration, could the suspicion have ever occurred to any fair mind that God may have thus left to all the chances of human fallibility the history of that revelation which (it is assumed) He has given to His creatures, instructing them in their duties and unfolding to them His decrees?" (*Op. cit.*, p. 237.) G. Stoeckhardt: "It is difficult to form a conception of a self-activity of the Holy Ghost — the moderns grant, in theory, that in the recording of God's thoughts concerning salvation this self-activity took place — which was interrupted every few moments. . . . It is at bottom a most unreasonable idea, this modern distinction between essentials and non-essentials, which recognizes the former as God's Word but finds the latter fallible. That is a 'mechanical' construction.

The inspiration-in-spots men become still more unreasonable when they assume that God gave the world a Bible which is a medley of truth and error, of wisdom and folly, but left it to us fallible men to find the dividing line between truth and error. And these same moderns who tell us that we must find this dividing line tell us in the next breath that there is no such dividing line. See Lewis' and Smyth's statements above. Here are some more. Prof. A. E. Deitz: "We may liken the teaching of the Bible to a large circle at the center of which we place Christ and the cross. Around that center there is a large region of certainty which includes all the great teaching of the Bible about religion and morality. Out at the circumference we may place those unessential matters about which for any reason there may be some doubt, such as historical inaccuracies, numerical errors, etc. Now, if we inquire how far out toward the circumference does the region of certainty extend, answers may differ. . . . The realm of certainty gradually fades out into the uncertain and unknown just as it does in every department of human knowledge." (*The Luth. Church Quart.*, 1935, p. 131 f.) W. Sanday corroborates that: "What is the relation of the natural to the supernatural, of the human to the divine in the Bible? They *shade off* into each other by almost *insensible degrees*." (*Op. cit.*, p. 74.) Just try to trace the line on the basis of the directions given by Raymond; find out where the conscious mind and where the subconscious mind of the writers was working. Were the writers themselves able to apply Raymond's test? No; the Bible which the stop-and-go-inspiration men give us does not work. We should not know how to use it. Nay, it works disaster. A man might cast aside the divine as being human and lose his

---

On this theory the Holy Ghost sometimes, when unimportant matters were being recorded, rested and slept, as Homer sometimes nodded, and the human pen just kept on writing and, no longer guided by the Holy Spirit, often wrote down nonsense (hat vielfach gefaselt)." (*Lehre und Wehre*, 32, pp. 257, 313.) Discussing the idea that "here the Holy Ghost has allowed Paul's pen to run on," L. Gaussen points out: "What idea can a man have of the sacred writers, when he would impute to them the mad audacity of mingling their own oracles with those of the Most High? That would be similar to the case of the man who was engaged by a Geneva minister to transcribe his sermons, and 'had thought it his duty to enrich all the pages with his own thoughts.'" (*Theopneustia*, pp. 271, 317, 322.) F. Bente: "Verbal inspiration in *theologicis* but in all *non-theologicis* no verbal inspiration, on the same page of the Bible, yes, in one and the same sentence about ten per cent of the words verbally inspired by the Holy Ghost and ninety per cent not inspired, or *vice versa*, ninety per cent of the words by the Holy Ghost and ten per cent by the writer — that is an inconceivable concept and a theory which is as unreasonable as it is antiScriptural." (*Lehre und Wehre*, 1904, p. 87.)

soul. The highway constructed by the moderns has the sign: Travel at your own risk! [245)]

The partial-inspiration men reach the height of unreason when they attempt to square their theory with 2 Tim. 3:16. It is pathetic to see how their greatest men, Ladd and Orr and others, labor to make this passage prove Partial Inspiration and bring forth nothing better than this: the apostle means to say that that part of Scripture is inspired which is profitable for doctrine.[246)] "Das sind eitel Taschenspielerkuenste," and clumsy ones at that. They are forcing Paul into an embarrassing situation. Paul tells Timothy to study "the Holy Scriptures, which are able to make thee wise unto salvation." Timothy begins at Gen. 1. Paul interrupts him and points out that that·chapter deals with secular matters and is not inspired. Timothy: "But you said that *all* Scripture is given by inspiration." Paul: "I did not express myself clearly. I meant that *some* Scripture is given by inspiration, that *some parts* of Scripture are profitable." Timothy: "But Jesus, too, said: "The Scripture cannot be broken, John 10:35." [247)] Paul: "Jesus did not express himself clearly. He meant that only the doctrinal portions of Scripture are authoritative." — No, no; either Jesus and Paul and Peter (2 Pet. 1:21) used misleading language, employing universal terms without any restrictions, or the moderns are guilty of employing violent, unreasonable exegesis.

The moderns fighting Verbal Inspiration in the name of reason

---

245) "Again we must press the question, the all-important question: If the Bible is inspired only in spots, which spots are inspired? Who is to decide? Who has the wisdom to tell us with satisfying certainty? We have read after Graf, Wellhausen, Cheyne, Driver, and Robertson Smith down to Kent, Foster, Bade, Fosdick, Faunce, Merril, and the rest and do not feel that we can trust either their logic or their judgment. Then, who can point out to the world the parts of the Bible that are inspired and the parts that are not inspired? The world ought to have certainty on this matter." (*Bible Champion*, 1923, p. 599.)

246) James Orr: "This is the ultimate test of 'inspiration' — its power to 'make wise unto salvation.' " (See what has been said under No. 21, p. 211 ff.) Ladd, too, insists that "the *post*-Reformation theology" garbled "that one passage in the New Testament to which the appeal is sometimes most confidently made — 2 Tim. 3:16." The apostle never intended to say that all Scripture, being inspired, is profitable for doctrine; what he impressed upon Timothy was that only portions of Scripture are inspired — those that are "morally useful in perfecting a righteous character." (*What Is the Bible?* p. 95.)

247) "Now what is the particular thing in Scripture for the confirmation of which the indefectible authority of Scripture is thus invoked? It is one of the most casual clauses — more than that, the very form of its expression in one of its most casual clauses. This means, of course, that in the Savior's view the indefectible authority of Scripture attaches to the very form of expression of its most casual clauses. It belongs to Scripture through and through, down to its most minute particulars, that it is of indefectible authority." (B. B. Warfield, *Revelation and Inspiration*, p. 86.)

do not have reason on their side. Their vaunted substitutes can get no scientific rating.[248] And when we examine the long array of arguments which they so confidently marshal against Verbal Inspiration — these baseless assertions, these plain sophistries, these unbelievable fatuities — we think of Luther's word: "Scripture makes fools of all the wise" (XIV:4). When men set out to subvert a divine truth — in this case the divinity, infallibility, and inviolability of Holy Scripture — they cannot but stultify themselves. "They lose their common sense and become utterly unreasonable and illogical."

SPIRITUAL DECAY. OBDURATION

And a greater loss than that of common sense is involved. The hurt touches a more vital spot. One who has come under the influence of God's Word and still presumes to criticize it, risks the impairment and the loss of his spiritual faculties. He who takes offense at Scripture and rails at its "errors" and "immoralities" and "trivialities" may fall under the dread judgment of obduration. God will not be mocked, and He will not have His Word mocked. If a man persists in stifling the glad response to Scripture's testimony, to its majesty, infallibility, and inviolability, which this testimony would create or has created in his heart, he will lose the faculty to respond. He will be given over to an obdurate mind.

No man may set himself in opposition to God's Word with impunity. Ponder the dread truth set down in 1 Pet. 2:6-8. ". . . and a stone of stumbling and a rock of offense, even to them which stumble at the Word, being disobedient; whereunto also they were appointed." Stoeckhardt: "The unbelievers, who absolutely refuse to obey the Word, are, by God's just judgment, set and appointed to that lot that they are yet more and more embittered and hardened through the Word, that the Word of salvation becomes to them a savor of death unto death. God gives them up to their perverse, obdurate mind." That applies not only to those who take offense at the Gospel, but also to those who stumble at Scripture in general. H. Weseloh thus applies it: "If men *will* not permit the heavenly light to enlighten them, . . . if they *will* run against the Word, then they *shall* do it. For God will not be mocked. . . . Christ is set for the fall and rising again of men — for the rising

---

248) That is the verdict of Dr. C. E. Macartney: "Those who have departed from faith in an infallible Bible have made desperate but utterly vain efforts to secure a suitable substitute. . . . But as time goes by, the pathetic hopelessness of this effort is more and more manifest." (See L. Boettner, *The Inspiration of the Scriptures*, p. 81.) You may think that Dr. Macartney is biased. Then hear Dr. Ladd: "The post-Reformation theory has tottered and fallen — a ruin complete so far as its own compacted and well-cemented structure is concerned. But no equally elaborate and *self-consistent* doctrine of Sacred Scripture has arisen to take its place." (*Op. cit.*, p. 69.)

again of the contrite and humble, but for the fall of the proud and
self-righteous. Even so Scripture, coming to us in the lowly form
of a servant, is set for the fall of the haughty and self-satisfied, but
for the rising up of those who know how deeply they have fallen.
Face to face with Scripture, men's hearts are revealed" (*Das Buch
des Herrn und seine Feinde*, p. 130 f.). When Scripture comes to
a man and asks to be received as the Word of God and he, following
the reaction of his natural heart, refuses to acknowledge the claim;
when Scripture, speaking with divine power, warns him that this
offense, this stumbling at the Word, proceeds out of the evil heart
and pleads with him to suppress it, and he keeps on treating God's
Word as the common word of man, such a man faces the dread
judgment of obduration, and it is only because of the wondrous
grace of God that in a given case the judgment has not yet been
executed. "One who criticizes Scripture — which, as God's Word,
will not be criticized but *believed* — comes under the fearful
judgment of God described in Matt. 11:25." (Pieper, *Chr. Dog.*, I,
p. 280.) "Thou hast *hid* these things from the wise and prudent
and hast revealed them unto babes." Will men, following their
carnal wisdom and conceit, persist in treating parts of the Bible as
the word of fools? Then Scripture *shall be* to them a stumbling
block and the wisdom of God foolishness! "This is the Scripture
which makes fools of all the wise and prudent and is open only
to babes and fools, as Christ says Matt. 11:25." (Luther, XIV:4.)
You refuse to be a babe and simply believe, you refuse to be
Christ's fool? Then be your own fool. Be blinded, utterly unable
to see, shut out from all spiritual light.

It is a wicked thing to charge the Bible, written by inspiration
of God, with errors and unethical teachings and puerilities — and
there are men who are not able to see this wickedness. Augustine
writes in his *Harmony of the Gospels* (Book I, chap. 7): "Those
sacred chariots of the Lord, however, in which He is borne
throughout the earth and brings the peoples under His easy yoke
and light burden, are assailed with calumnious charges by certain
persons, who, in impious vanity or in ignorant temerity, think to
rob of their credit as veracious historians those teachers by whose
instrumentality the Christian religion has been disseminated all the
world over. . . . They still strive by their calumnious disputations
to keep some from making themselves acquainted with the faith,
while they also endeavor to the utmost of their power to excite
agitations among others who have already attained to belief, and
thereby give them trouble. . . . We have undertaken in this work
to demonstrate the errors or the rashness of those . . . who are in
the habit of adducing this as the palmary allegation in all their
vain objections, namely, that the evangelists are not in harmony
with each other." And there are men who say: Augustine is talk-

ing foolishness! Eusebius said: "I deem it wicked presumption when a man is brazen enough to say that Scripture has erred." And there are men who say: Eusebius is talking foolishness! They are *unable* to see the wickedness. Again, men are actually unable to see the wickedness of declaring that the testimony of Christ concerning the Old Testament is unreliable because Jesus lacked the critical acumen! [249] Once more, men are actually able to apply the warnings against obduration to those who believe every word of the Bible and charge *them* with harderning themselves against the truth.[250] If a man will not see, he shall not see.

A dread judgment is pronounced Matt. 11:25 and 2 Cor. 2:16. What is, in itself, the savor of life unto life can become the savor of death unto death. All that is written in Scripture is written for our learning, and much of it has become to "the wise and prudent" an occasion for stumbling. Passages such as the imprecatory psalms and Paul's instruction concerning his mantle and Timothy's ailment, which should serve to strengthen our spiritual life, must now serve to strengthen their determination to tear apart the Sacred Volume.

"There has come to us a crisis in the history of the Bible," says J. P. Smyth, "a crisis through which our generation must pass — amid strife and heartburnings, it may be — amid doubts and fears for the future of religion — but whose results will ultimately be the enthroning of the Bible in a position firmer and more lasting than it has ever held before in the hearts of the Christian people." (*Op. cit.*, p. 6.) Every generation must pass through this crisis. Yes, and every individual who deals with the Bible. Shall I accept the Bible as being throughout the Word of God? Shall I believe that "all Scripture is given by inspiration of God"? The question must be answered. The Bible presses for a decision. What will our answer be? Our flesh insists that we throw Verbal Inspiration to the bats and moles. That is Smyth's advice. He is convinced that that will enhance the glory and influence of the Bible. Scripture itself urges us to give a different answer. Two forces are meeting in your heart and struggling for dominance. You must decide for one

---

249) R. Rothe: "The Redeemer never claimed to be an infallible, or even a generally precise, interpreter of the Old Testament. Indeed, He could not have made this claim. For interpretation is essentially a scientific function, and one conditioned by the existence of scientific means; which, in relation to the Old Testament, were only imperfectly at the command of Jesus as well as of His contemporaries." (See Ladd, *op. cit.*, I, p. 28.)

250) J. P. Smyth, who has thrown Verbal Inspiration to the moles and the bats, says: "If Christ had to say, why should not the Bible have to say, too, 'Blessed is he who shall not find occasion of stumbling in me.'" (*Op. cit.*, p. 135.) R. Seeberg: "The old theory can only be retained against the monitions of conscience, or the sense of historical truth must be devitalized in order to save the hypothesis." (*Op. cit.*, p. 62.)

or the other. Is every chapter and verse of the Bible inspired and true or not? Has science, evolution, etc., the right, for instance, to correct the first chapter of Genesis? You must answer the question. Your faith is being tested.[251] Will you decide in favor of your unbelieving, supercilious flesh or in favor of Scripture? The decision may be hard to make. There will be heartburnings. Will you break with your flesh and the popular theology of the moderns, or will you break with Scripture? And if I break with Scripture, against its powerful pleadings to remain true, there looms before me the dread judgment of obduration. The struggle will be hard and heartbreaking. But God has given us the strength to pass through the crisis safely. There is that in the Christian heart which responds to the voice of Scripture and rejoices in the truth that "all Scripture is given by inspiration of God." [252] Do not stifle that response. "Blessed is he," says Christ, "whosoever shall not be offended in Me," Matt. 11: 6. Blessed is he who shall not be offended at My Word, at Scripture!

In asking us to delete one half of the Bible, the moderns assure us that there is no cause for alarm. The other half remains! And that is the important part; if the Gospel message is inspired, all is well. — But the moderns are not through with us. They have additional objections against Verbal Inspiration. And if these are well founded, there is *nothing* left of the Bible; the words in which the Gospel message is brought us are worthless.

---

251) Dr. N. R. Melhorn writes in *The Lutheran,* Sept. 24, 1941: "*A Test of Believing.* The first chapter of Genesis, indeed the first eleven chapters of that beginning of revelation, has been throughout the Christian era something by which scholars and common people alike tested the character of their faith. One might almost suspect that the attitude which is assumed toward this plain and simple story of the beginning of things is an illustration of that which is described as the basic sin of our first parents. They yielded, it will be remembered, to the plea of the devil that, if they should eat of the tree of knowledge of good and evil, they should become as gods. Man has never been distinguished by his humility with reference to the search for truth, and from time to time the Christian world has been harassed, even aggravated, by attacks upon the verity of the revelation of our world's beginning and continuance. . . . According to learned men who have accepted Darwinism or some development thereof the declarations of Genesis 1 are altogether unsatisfactory. . . . For them Moses was a most unsatisfactory scientist."

252) These two truths that the Christian has the capacity to see, and rejoice in, the light of Scripture and that the glorious light of Scripture *blinds* those who refuse to respond, are expressed in Rudelbach's observation: "Bei dieser Fuelle des Erweises waere es fast unerklaerlich, wie diese Stelle (2 Tim. 3:16) von so vielen seit du Perron und Grotius bis auf Semler und manche Neuere herab so schmaehlich gemisdeutet worden ist, wenn man nicht wuesste, dass auch die groesste Klarheit eine *congeniale* im Geiste des Auslegers voraussetzt, um nicht zu *blenden.*" (*Zeitschrift fuer die gesm. Luth. Theol. u. Kirche,* 1842, Zweites Quartalheft, p. 9.)

CHAPTER V

Is Verbal Inspiration Mechanical Inspiration?

The moderns have many more objections against Verbal Inspiration. To three of these they attach special importance. They denounce Verbal Inspiration as "a *mechanical* theory of inspiration"; they abhor it as "resulting in an *atomistic* conception of the Scriptures"; they abominate it as establishing "the *legalistic* authority of the letter." — The old evil Foe means deadly woe. The appeasers have up till now been telling us that nothing is lost if the Church gives up half of the Bible, seeing that they are willing to let her retain the important half, the Gospel message; if only the saving truths be inspired, all is well. And now they are insisting that not even this portion of Scripture is inspired, verbally inspired. They would have us believe that the words in which the saving truth is clothed are purely human — human words which are not absolutely reliable, human words which do not carry divine authority. — They are out to break Scripture; they will not have men receive it as the very Word of God.

DENOUNCING VERBAL INSPIRATION AS A MECHANICAL OPERATION

Verbal Inspiration is a detestable thing in the eyes of the moderns. They express their detestation of it in the horrified exclamation: "Mechanical Inspiration!" and stigmatize us as "mechanical inspirationists." Some of them call it a heathen conception. G. P. Mains: "Many have believed in its verbal inspiration as literal as though God dictated every word, using the human writer only as an automaton. This view, however, is distinctively neither Hebrew nor Christian. From immemorial times it has been shared by the heathen seers concerning the utterances of their oracles." (*Divine Inspiration,* p. 71.) R. Seeberg: "We must also be careful not to regard the situation as if the theory of verbal inspiration were 'really' Christian. . . . That kind of inspiration in which the prophet in ecstatic fervor forgets himself and the world and becomes only the pen or tongue of a deity, was far from unknown in the ancient world, and was then introduced into Jewish and Christian thought by the theories of Plato and Philo." (*Revelation and Inspiration,* p. 31 f.) Dr. H. C. Alleman supports Seeberg's protest against the heathen doctrine of verbal inspiration: "The doctrine of verbal inspiration . . . is foreign to the genius of our Confessions. It is, in fact, a carry-over from the old heathen conception of inspiration: a man who was possessed by a god lost self-control and became but a mouthpiece of the deity."

[301]

(*The Luth. Church Quart.*, Oct., 1940, p. 352.)   M. Dods, whom
Alleman calls in as a corroborating witness, describes "the mechanical or dictation theory as the theory of complete possession, in
which the divine factor is at its maximum, the human at its min-
imum. What is human is suppressed; the indwelling God uses
the human organs irrespective of the human will. The man is the
mere mouthpiece of the God. This view has always been popular
outside of Christianity." (*The Bible: Its Origin and Nature*, p. 107.)
S. P. Cadman voices his protest in these words: "It is conceivable
that God possessed the power to reduce the authors of this sacred
literature to the level of mere automata acting under hypnosis. . . .
God inspired selected personalities to transmit His will to their
fellows, but in so doing He did not obliterate their individuality
nor thereby make them speak like puppets in a Punch-and-Judy
show." (*Answers to Everyday Questions*, p. 253.)   Dr. J. A. Singmaster puts it this way: "Various theories of inspiration have been
advocated. The most popular and fallacious of these is the dictation
theory, which holds that the writer is merely an instrument which
the Spirit used as a player does the organ or that he is merely the
stenographer of God. . . . The apostles were not unconscious
media for the Spirit." (*Handbook of Chr. Theol.*, p. 67.)   The
moderns are up in arms against the idea of putting the prophets
and the apostles on a level with the pythoness of Delphi.

As a rule, the moderns use more moderate language. They
will not use the terms "heathen doctrine," "mantic divination,"
"hypnosis," but use the milder term "mechanical" to express the
same idea: the holy writers must not be made automata.[253]   Dr. R.
V. Foster inveighs against "the mechanical theory," "which holds
that the sacred writers were as mere machines, or amanuenses;
mere passive recipients and recorders of what was dictated by the
Holy Spirit." Dr. T. O. Summers takes·Musaeus, Baier, and Quenstedt to task for teaching "that the Holy Spirit acted on men in a
passive state; that those who were under the power of the inspiring
Spirit were acted upon as mere machines, mechanically answering
the force which moved them." Dr. M. S. Terry takes "the leading
churches of the Reformation, which accepted the Calvinistic creed"
to task for teaching that "the normal powers of the holy writers
were suspended or neutralized in the process of their writing";
that they were "impassive machines, controlled by another per-

---

253) Cremer: "The dogmaticians taught a doctrine of inspiration
which was an absolute *novum*. True, it lacked only the concept of ecstasy
to be a renewal of the mantic doctrine of inspiration as taught by Philo
and the old apologetes, which had been universally rejected by the
Church in its opposition to Montanism. But the very absence of this
concept only made the situation worse, for it reduced the mantic inspiration to a mechanical one." (Pieper, *Chr. Dog.* I, p. 279.)

son." [254]   Dr. A. H. Strong: "The dictation theory holds that inspiration consisted in such a possession of the minds and bodies of the Scripture writers by the Holy Spirit that they became passive instruments or amanuenses — pens, not penmen, of God. . . . Representatives of this view are Quenstedt, Hooker, Gaussen. . . . We cannot suppose that this highest work of man under the influence of the Spirit was purely mechanical." (*Systematic Theology*, p. 102.)   Dr. G. Drach: "One theory of divine inspiration is that of mechanical verbal dictation.   According to this theory the human writers under the influence of the Holy Spirit were in a passive state of receptivity, similar to that of a stenographer who takes dictation. . . .   Zwingli's spirit led his followers to incline toward the dictation of words as well as to the inspiration of the contents of the Sacred Scriptures, and this theory found its way into some of the Reformed confessions, and also influenced some of the Lutheran theologians of the seventeenth century." (*The Luth. Church Quart.*, 1936, p. 244 f.)   Dr. A. J. Traver: "There can be nothing mechanical about it.   God did not dictate to the writers of the Bible as to a stenographer." (*The Lutheran*, Jan. 23, 1936.)   Dr. J. A. W. Haas: "In the problem of inspiration the facts of course refute any mechanical theory of verbal inspiration in minute detail." (*The Lutheran*, Jan. 23, 1936.)

The moderns denounce Verbal Inspiration as a dangerous and horrible thing.   Dr. T. A. Kantonen, in the article "The Canned Goods of Past Theology," published in *The Lutheran*, Dec. 12 ff., 1935: "Lutheran exegesis will be seriously handicapped unless it abandons once and for all the unpsychological and mechanical theories of inspiration and unhistorical views of verbal inerrancy which the application of scientific and historical methods to the study of the Bible has rendered obsolete."   Dr. E. E. Flack: "Is not the inspiration of Scripture too high and holy a reality to be defined in terms of stenography?   Does one exalt the Word of God by dehumanizing it?" (*The Luth. Church Quart.*, 1935, p. 417.)

The moderns are demanding that this foolish, wicked theory be abandoned once and for all.   A. Deissmann is glad to note that

---

254) See *Theological Quarterly*, 1913, p. 2 ff.; 1914, p. 79.   The article containing these references is entitled: " 'Mechanical Inspiration' the Stumbling-Block of Modern Theology."   Are the terms "mechanical inspiration" and "verbal inspiration" synonymous?   Not with us.   But the moderns use them so.   See footnote 1.   When the moderns denounce "mechanical" inspiration, they mean verbal, plenary inspiration. Ladd: "Theories of verbal or mechanical operation."   Sanday: "Mechanical and verbal inspiration of the Bible."   Evangelischer Oberkirchenrat in Stuttgart: "Die evangelische Kirche betrachtet die Bibel als Wort Gottes; nicht im Sinne einer *mechanischen Verbalinspiration*, sondern als das in Menschenwort gekleidete Zeugnis Gottes von seinem Wesen und Walten." (See *Conc. Theol. Monthly*, VII, p. 719.)

"this dogma of verbal inspiration of every letter of the New Testament, which rightly can be called mechanical inspiration, is now abandoned in all scientific theology." (*The New Testament in the Light of Modern Research*, p. 234.) And they want the Lutheran Church, together with the entire Christian Church, to abandon it because it is not Biblical. H. E. Jacobs wrote in the introduction to *Biblical Criticism*, by J. A. W. Haas: "If the verbal theory of inspiration means that every word and letter is inspired, so that the writer was purely passive and performed a merely mechanical office, as 'the pen of the Holy Ghost,' this, we hold, is an assumption for which we have no warrant." (See F. Bente, *Was steht der Vereinigung im Wege?* p. 50.) W. Sanday: "The mechanical and verbal inspiration of the Bible may be questioned, but its real and vital inspiration will shine out as it has never done." (*The Oracles of God*, p. 46.) Christ did not teach it, says G. T. Ladd: "The germinal doctrine of Sacred Scripture given us in these words [of Christ] is as far as possible from the rabbinical view of His own day. Nor does it afford a root for a growth into any theories of verbal or mechanical inspiration or of the infallibility of the Old Testament. . . ." (*The Doctrine of Sacred Scripture*, I, p. 38.) And the Lutheran Church should not teach it any longer, says E. E. Fisher: "It is more consistent with Lutheranism to believe that the writers of the Holy Scriptures were truly human in the way in which they accomplished their tasks than to believe that they were automatons who served as 'secretaries' to take down the dictation of the Holy Spirit. For one thing, what we know of the way in which the writings have come to assume their present form precludes any conception of dictation. But more important is Lutheranism's conviction that the human personality may be made the vehicle of the divine without the loss or destruction of human freedom." (*The Luth. Church Quart.*, 1937, p. 196.) If the Lutherans want to get together, they must get rid of Verbal Inspiration, says *Folkebladet*, Nov. 23, 1938: "Students of Scripture are more and more getting away from the theory of verbal inspiration, a theory which has brought more confusion among Christians than perhaps anything else. It is an impossibility to imagine that the prophets and apostles could have intended that their words should be considered as a dictation by the Holy Spirit and that they as almost unconscious automatons were the Holy Spirit's pencils. When a subjective theory is elevated to the status of an objective primary truth, then hubbub [*virvar*] surely will ensue in the Church. And that has most certainly been the case." — This, then, is the grievance of the moderns against Verbal

Inspiration: it degrades the writers to the level of machines! [255] They resent the idea that the apostles had to submit to be made into dead writing machines. They ask the "mechanical-inspirationists": How dare you make the prophets undergo the horrible experience of Verbal Inspiration? Summoned by the cry of Cadman: Let us not reduce the authors of our sacred literature to the level of mere automata acting under hypnosis! they are determined to drive the foul spook out of the Church.[256]

---

[255] *Fundamentals*, III, p. 13: "The inspiration includes not only all the books of the Bible in general but in detail, the form as well as the substance, the word as well as the thought. This is sometimes called the *verbal* theory of inspiration and is vehemently spoken against in some quarters. . It is too mechanical, it degrades the writers to the level of machines, it has a tendency to make skeptics, and all that."

[256] Queerly enough, the charge that the later dogmaticians, such as Quenstedt, and those who accept their phraseology are "mechanical inspirationists" is made by some who themselves believe that every word of Scripture is divinely inspired and absolutely true. For the sake of a complete record we submit the following references. W. Lee declares that "it seems impossible to reconcile this phase of the purely organic, or as it has of late years been termed, *mechanical*, theory of Inspiration with the highest aim of religion" and quotes these words of Quenstedt (*Theol. Didactico-Polemica, cap. IV, sect. II*) as proving him a "mechanical inspirationist": "All and each of the things which are contained in the Sacred Scriptures . . . were not only committed to letters by divine, infallible assistance and direction but are to be regarded as received by the special suggestion, inspiration, and dictation of the Holy Spirit. For all things which were to be written were suggested by the Holy Spirit to the sacred writers in the very act of writing and were dictated to their intellect as if unto a pen (*quasi in calamum*), so that they might be written in these and no other circumstances, in this and no other mode or order." Lee adds: "For the present, I shall merely observe that, while I can by no means accept this system as correct or as consistent with the facts to be explained, it will be my object in the present discourses to establish in the broadest extent all that its supporters desire to maintain; namely, the infallible certainty, the indisputable authority, the perfect and entire truthfulness, of all parts and every part of Holy Scripture." (*The Inspiration of Holy Scripture*, pp. 33, 37.) B. Manly quotes this same statement of Quenstedt as proving that Quenstedt held "the theory of mechanical inspiration, or, as it has been termed, the dictation theory." Manly himself says: "Who said these words [Gal. 3: 8]? God, personally. The manner of the quotation can only be explained on the principle that the Scripture is so identified, in all that it says, with God Himself, that what Scripture says, God says; and so a personal utterance of God and a saying of Scripture are simply equivalent." (*The Bible Doctrine of Inspiration*, pp. 44 f., 130.) Quenstedt could not have used stronger language. One more example. We read in *The Luth. Church Quart.*, 1940, p. 353: "It is only fair to Dr. M. Reu to say . . . that he disclaims the doctrine of mechanical verbal inspiration. In his brochure *In the Interest of Lutheran Unity*, in the chapter 'What is Scripture?' he says: 'The mode (of inspiration) was a mystery and will remain a mystery for this life. It is always a mystery how the Spirit of God works on human personality.' (P. 65.) 'There is a theory of Verbal Inspiration which degrades the authors of the Biblical books to dead writing machines.' (P. 68.) But with that limitation he proceeds to claim

FIGHTING AGAINST A STRAW MAN

What is all this about? In the first place, the moderns are fighting against a straw man. And as they unfold this particular grievance of theirs against Verbal Inspiration, we notice, in the second place, that they are waging war against Scripture.

The lusty strokes which the moderns deliver against "verbal, mechanical inspiration" hit a straw man. The advocates of Verbal Inspiration have not taught and do not teach that the holy writers, uttering the words of the Holy Spirit, were thereby deprived of their intelligence and consciousness. The moderns cannot produce a single statement by the dogmaticians of the early Church or of the seventeenth century to the effect that the Holy Ghost could not speak through the prophets without turning them into dead machines or putting them into a state of coma or forcing them to act as vacuous stenographers. All that we can find in these statements about Verbal Inspiration is to the effect that the holy writers wrote what was given them to write consciously and rationally, that they fully used the powers of their mind and their special gifts, that their hearts were filled with horror of the sins which their words denounced and with joy and wonderment at the grace of God which their pens described. Quenstedt is held up by the moderns as the *exemplum horribile* of the mechanical-inspiration aberration. Have they read Quenstedt through? Have they read page 82 ff. of the offensive chapter in his *Theol. Didac.-Pol.?* There he repudiates the idea "as though the holy writers had written without, and contrary to, their will, without consciousness and unwillingly." No; "they wrote uncoerced, willingly, and knowingly; *sponte enim, volentes scientesque scripserunt*. . . . The holy writers were said to be φερόμενοι, *acti, moti, agitati a Spiritu Sancto,* by no means as though they were out of their mind . . . or as though they did not understand what they were to write." [257] Were the old Church Fathers "mechanical inspira-

---

that the Scriptures themselves demand verbal inspiration." The entire passage reads: ". . . dead writing machines, who without inner participation wrote down word for word what was dictated to them by the Spirit. We meet this doctrine in the Lutheran Church occasionally already during the sixteenth century, more frequently in the seventeenth century, although it can hardly be called the earmark of the presentation of all orthodox dogmaticians; later it is limited to popular writers, and today it is found only in some fundamentalist camps."

257) Presenting a detailed examination of Quenstedt's position, the article in the *Theol. Quart.* ("'Mechanical Inspiration' the Stumbling-Block . . .") states: "There is not a single place to which his modern critics can point that would prove that Quenstedt regarded the inspired penmen of God as 'impassive instruments,' 'machines,' 'dehumanized or superhuman humans.' This is a turn which Quenstedt's critics have given to Quenstedt's thought. This thought Quenstedt himself declines."

tionists"? "Epiphanius urges against Montanus 'that whatsoever the prophets have said, they spake with understanding'; he refers to their 'settled mind,' their 'self-possession,' and their 'not being carried away as if in ecstasy.' So also Cyril of Jerusalem, alluding to this question, says of the true Spirit: 'His coming is gentle; most light is His burden; beams of light and knowledge gleam forth before His coming.'" (W. Lee, *op.cit.*, p. 85.) And which one of the present-day verbal-inspirationists makes of the prophets and apostles vacuous stenographers or even senseless machines? Not A. L. Graebner: "The Bible was written by divine inspiration, inasmuch as the inspired penmen performed their work as the *personal organs* of God," etc. (*Outlines of Doctrinal Theology*, p. 4.) Not F. Pieper: "The inspired authors were not dead or mechanical, but living instruments, endowed with intelligence and will, and employing a definite style, and using a peculiar mode of expression (*modus dicendi*)." (*What Is Christianity?* p. 242.) "God did not first kill or dehumanize Isaiah, David, and all the holy prophets in order either to speak or write His Word *through* (διά) them; but He carefully kept them alive and preserved them in their genuine human way of expressing themselves, in order that they might speak and write so as to be understood by men." (*Chr. Dog.*, I, p. 277.) Not R. C. H. Lenski: "'God-inspired' means 'breathed by God,' the very word 'breathed' referring to His *Pneuma*. Is that mechanical? Peter says: '. . . borne along by the Holy *Pneuma*,' like a vessel on its true course by the gentle wind. This is neither a theory nor something dead and mechanical. God made the mind and heart of man, and His Spirit knows how to guide them. He does not move them about like blocks, but fills them with light, guides them with light, guides them in word and thought." (On 2 Tim. 3:16.) Not H. M'Intosh: Mechanical inspiration "was never taught in its usual sense by any intelligent upholder of the Bible claim. But while we disown this, we hold that the words of Scripture are *not merely* the words of man, but also the words of God — the Spirit's inspired words, as well as the writer's *spontaneous* words." (*Is Christ Infallible and the Bible True?* p. 658.)[258]

---

258) A few more statements might prove welcome. They will convince the honest opponent that the upholders of Verbal Inspiration do not teach a mechanical inspiration. A. Hoenecke: "The passages just mentioned (1 Tim. 5:23 and 2 Tim. 4:13) prove that the apostles were not dead machines under inspiration, that the Holy Ghost did not, in the process of inspiration, ignore the personal and brotherly relationship of the holy writers but operated with it in the inspirational act." (*Ev.-Luth. Dog.*, I, p. 350.) G. Stoeckhardt: "Das Diktieren des Heiligen Geistes war kein mechanisches Vorsprechen, dem ein mechanisches Nachschreiben zur Seite gegangen waere. The holy men of God were not sleeping or dreaming as they spake and wrote, moved by the Holy Ghost. The

We have not read every book and article and remark that was written by a verbal-inspirationist. But as far as we have read, we have not found a single statement to the effect that divine inspiration put the holy writers into a state of coma. Neither did Dr. W. T. Riviere ever find such a statement. He writes: "Fundamentalists and Bible-believers are accused of holding what may be called a Typewriter Theory. . . . I do not recall ever hearing this theory advocated, but something of the sort is often attributed to conservatives. It makes a nice target for ridicule." (*Bibliotheca Sacra*, July, 1936, p. 298.) And even if the moderns could dig up

_____

powers of their soul, their will, and intellect were active. It was a real speaking and writing. And that is an intellectual activity of rational beings. . . . The Holy Ghost put this entire apparatus, this human research, meditation, study, and composing into action, applied it to His purpose, made it the medium of His activity, His speaking. The prophets and apostles themselves, these living persons with their will and thoughts, their searching and composing, were pens, *calami*, of the Holy Ghost. . . . While they were searching, meditating, writing, the Holy Ghost supplied His heavenly wisdom, His eternal, divine thought, and also the right words; He gave them the words *gleichsam unter der Hand*. That is what the fathers described with the phrase *suggestio rerum et verborum*. . . . Thus the Holy Ghost in no way did violence to the will and thought of His human organs. He swayed and actuated their will and their thinking, but θεοπρεπῶς; *suaviter, leniter*, as the fathers expressed it, *gleichsam unvermerkt, wie unter der Hand*. He poured His divine wisdom, spiritual thought, spiritual words into their mind and heart. The mind of the holy authors moved freely, according to its natural bent; freely it expressed itself in the sacred writings. At the same time it was altogether swayed and controlled by the Holy Ghost. What the mind, the mouth, the pen, of the prophets and apostles produced was not their own, not human wisdom and human words, but from beginning to end it was of the Holy Ghost. From the first conception of the thought to its finished expression it was all the product of the Spirit of God." (*Lehre und Wehre*, 1886, p. 282 f.) *The Lutheran Teacher*, Feb. 13, 1938 (Norwegian Lutheran Church): "One of the tenets of our Church is belief in the verbal inspiration of the Bible. . . . Now, if God really did not guide these men in the choice of words but left this matter to the discretion of the writers, we could never feel free from the suspicion that these fallible human beings might have erred in the selection of their phraseology. Yet, on the other hand, God did not dictate to a dictaphone, which is a machine for reproduction void of all personality. The holy writers were not mere machines. . . . They knew what they were writing, though it might be true that they did not at all times realize to the full the deep significance of all they said. . . . They found expression for their personality in their own individual habits of style. . . ." Let us hear a few representatives of the Reformed Churches. J. Bloore: "In those who wrote the Bible, the emotions of the soul, the energies of the spirit, and even the infirmities of the body are made use of under the control of the divine Spirit, always, of course, in a manner according to the purpose in view. The individuality, peculiarity, and distinctive qualities of these writers find expression in their work, so that the Book is one of ever-living interest from the human side, while from the divine it proves itself in every part to be 'the word of God, living, active, and sharper . . .' (Heb. 4:12, 13). . . . This is not mere dictation — far from it, for all the powers of the mind and heart

such a statement, that would not justify them in characterizing the old doctrine of verbal inspiration as "the mechanical theory of inspiration," in charging Luther and Quenstedt, Pieper and Warfield, with making the holy writers vacuous stenographers. "It ought to be unnecessary," says B. B. Warfield, "to protest again against the habit of representing the advocates of Verbal Inspiration as teaching that the mode of inspiration was by dictation." (*Revelation and Inspiration,* p. 173.) Warfield utters his protest in connection with his statement: "The Church has always recognized that the Spirit's superintendence extends to the choice of the words by the human authors (verbal inspiration). It ought to be unnecessary. . . ." We protest against the insinuation that Quenstedt and Luther, Warfield and Pieper, ever intimated that the Holy Spirit dictated to Moses and Paul as to vacuous stenographers.

We protest against it in the name of reason. Reasonable men refrain from "fighting against windmills." — We are back on our old subject. It seems that in every phase of their attack on Verbal Inspiration the moderns are doomed to display a lack of acumen. — There is no sense in taking the old dogmaticians to task for something they never said. There is no profit in setting

---

of the instrument are engaged and wrought upon so that a divine impress is left upon the whole man." (*Alternative Views of the Bible,* pp. 148, 150.) *Bibliotheca Sacra,* Jan., 1941, p. 72: "It is of interest to compare Peter's declarations here (1 Pet. 1: 10, 12) with his claim in the second epistle (2 Pet. 1: 20, 21) that men spake from God as they were carried along by the Holy Spirit. Here the passivity of the prophets seems to be emphasized, and yet in the first epistle we are introduced to the most intense kind of mental activity. There is no conflict, provided we understand that the reflection of the prophets followed the revelation of the Spirit to them and did not enter into the prophetic message. . . . Hence the prophets, though passive in the sense that they did not contribute the message apart from the Spirit's moving, yet were so far from being mechanical instruments that they had all their powers of thought aroused and taxed by the disclosures granted to them." L. Boettner: "Instead of reducing the writers to the level of machines or typewriters, we have insisted that, while they wrote or spoke as they were moved by the Holy Spirit, they nevertheless remained thinking, willing, self-conscious beings whose peculiar styles and mannerisms are clearly traceable in their writings. . . . Hence we see that the Christian doctrine of inspiration is not the mechanical lifeless process which unfriendly critics have often represented it to be. Rather it calls the whole personality of the prophet into action, giving full play to his own literary style and mannerisms, taking into consideration the preparation given the prophet in order that he might deliver a particular kind of message, and allowing for the use of other documents or sources of information as they were needed. If these facts were kept more clearly in mind, the doctrine of inspiration would not be so summarily set aside nor so unreasonably attacked by otherwise cautious and reverent scholars." (*The Insp. of the H. Scr.,* pp. 37, 44.)

up a straw man and then knocking him down.[259] Philippi is right in calling these tactics *"senseless ridicule"* and Boettner in calling it an *"unreasonable* attack." The attack springs from ignorance. "When modern theologians declare that our orthodox dogmaticians had the conception of a purely mechanical inspiration, this must be condemned as outright fiction or else lack of acquaintance with the old dogmaticians." Thus Pieper (*What Is Christianity?* p. 242.) It is one of the "groups of confusions and misconceptions, misrepresentations, and caricature which . . . have confused the issues." Thus M'Intosh (*op. cit.,* pp. 8, 312). It is a sorry spectacle. M. S. Terry attacks the dogmaticians for teaching that the holy writers spoke "with the mantic frenzy of sibyls and soothsayers," and that, when Jeremiah dictated to Baruch, "his normal intellectual activity was temporarily arrested or neutralized by divine power." (See *Theol. Quart.,* 1913, p. 2.) Terry is fighting a bogey. S. Bulgakoff enters the fray: "I assume that no one can any longer, in our time, advocate the theory of a mechanical inspiration of sacred books. This theory either regards the writers as passive instruments in God's hands or interprets the process of writing as dictation from the Holy Spirit." And he asseverates: "Inspiration is not a question of *deus ex machina.* It is not an act of God which coerces man and to which he is subjected apart from his own will." (In *Revelation,* by Baillie and Martin, p. 153.) Bulgakoff is wrestling with a specter which he himself created. There is no point in A. H. Strong's quoting Locke: "When God made the prophet, he did not unmake the man." (*Op. cit.,* p. 103.) Professor Ladd is wasting his energy when he declares: "Nor is man made most fit for this office when rendered passive like a pen to write, or a tablet on which to write, the dictated message from God." (*What Is Scripture?* p. 430.) What do you think, in the light of what the dogmaticians really taught and actually did not teach, of W. Elert's strong language: "Wenn manche Dogmatiker . . .

---

259) J. G. Machen: "This doctrine of 'plenary inspiration' has been made the subject of persistent misrepresentation. Its opponents speak of it as though it involved a mechanical theory of the activity of the Holy Spirit. The Spirit, it is said, is represented in this doctrine as dictating the Bible to writers who were really little more than stenographers. But of course all such caricatures are without basis in fact, and it is rather surprising that intelligent men should be so blinded by prejudice about this matter as not even to examine for themselves the perfectly accessible treatises in which the doctrine of plenary inspiration is set forth. It is usually considered good practice to examine a thing for one's self before echoing the vulgar ridicule of it. But in connection with the Bible such scholarly restraints are somehow regarded as out of place. It is so much easier to content one's self with a few opprobrious adjectives, such as 'mechanical,' or the like. Why engage in serious criticism when the people prefer ridicule? Why attack a real opponent when it is easier to knock down a man of straw?" (*Christianity and Liberalism,* p. 73.)

folgerten, dass der schreibende Mensch auch an der Bildung des Wortlautes keinen eigenen Anteil mehr habe, so grenzt das an Gotteslaesterung" (*Der Christliche Glaube*, p. 209.)? It is nothing less than bathos when Dr. Flack exclaims: "Is not the inspiration of Scripture too high and holy a reality to be defined in terms of stenography? Does one exalt the Word of God by dehumanizing it?"

Again, it seems such a waste of paper when the moderns pen statements like these: "This is one of the chief reasons why the doctrine of verbal inspiration has been discarded as incapable of proof and *incompatible with the evident fact*. If the divine mind dictated to the writers the substance and form of the writings, there could not be the individuality that characterizes these documents. There is a striking unity of purpose disclosed in them; but their style, vocabulary, and point of view are as various as their names." (H. L. Willett, *The Bible Through the Centuries*, p. 284.) The facts disprove a mechanical inspiration! Dr. E. H. Delk: "That the oracular and dictation theory of writing has disappeared . . . goes almost without saying. The note of individualism is so strong in the synoptic writers that no theory of verbal inspiration is longer tenable." (*Luth. Church Quart.*, 1912, p. 568.) F. Buechsel: "Selbstverstaendlich kam die alte Inspirationslehre in Widerspruch zu den einfachsten Tatsachen in den Schriften der Bibel. Die individuellen Eigentuemlichkeiten, die diese Schriften stilistisch zeigten," etc. (*Die Offenbarung Gottes*, p. 113.) Similar statements have been set down above. *But the verbal-inspirationists, the so-called "mechanical-inspirationists," have been making the same statements.* Find examples above. We, too, have discovered these facts and cheerfully accept them. Why should the moderns waste paper by repeating what the dogmaticians have long ago set down? Every statement of theirs dealing with the difference of style and the individuality of the writers can be matched with one by Pieper and Hoenecke and Warfield. The moderns are beating the air. They are proving to us what none of us denies. Have done with this nonsense.

The moderns will reply to this that we are inconsistent; that, if we concede the difference in style, etc., and with them reject mechanical inspiration, we shall have to reject verbal inspiration, too. And here lies the root of the trouble. The moderns will admit that Quenstedt and Warfield and Pieper never said, in so many words, that the holy writers became dead machines and vacuous stenographers. But they insist that anyone who declares that every word written by the apostles was given them by the Holy Ghost to write necessarily teaches a mechanical inspiration: verbal inspiration *cannot but be* mechanical inspiration. This objection reveals the ignorance on the part of the moderns of an essential feature of inspiration: its miraculous nature. We have treated of this matter in chapter I of this treatise, under Assertion No. 9, p. 135 ff. We say with Luther: "Die Heilige Schrift ist nicht auf Erden gewachsen." (VII: 2095.) Every miracle presents a mystery, and we are ready to admit that we cannot solve the mystery how the holy writers wrote exactly what the Holy Spirit gave them to write and still wrote with perfect freedom. We are not presumptuous enough to deny either one of these revealed truths because we are unable to solve the psychological difficulty that confronts us here. Will you say that it was impossible for God to make Paul His mouthpiece without destroying the personality and freedom of the apostle? "It is in vain," says Charles Hodge, "to profess to hold the common doctrine of Theism and yet assert that God cannot control rational creatures without turning them into machines." (*Syst. Theology*, I, p. 169.) Do not quote to us the laws of psychology — "the *unpsychological* and mechanical theories of inspiration and unhistorical view of verbal inerrancy" (Professor Kantonen). The handbooks of psychology certainly do not contain a section explaining the mystery of Verbal Inspiration. But God is not bound by our psychological wisdom.[260] And it is not for us to form judgments on this matter on the basis of our very limited knowledge of psychology; the less so, as we do not know from personal experience what inspiration is. "We who have never ourselves experienced this act of the Spirit cannot penetrate the mystery of it; we doubt whether the holy writers themselves did." (Lenski, on 2 Tim. 3:16.) At any rate,

---

260) F. Bettex: "But just here we are amused at those weak-minded critics who, with hackneyed phrases, talk so glibly about 'mechanical instruments' and 'mere verbal dictation.' Does, then, a self-revelation of the Almighty and a making known of His counsels, a gracious act which exalts the human agent to be a co-worker with Jehovah, annihilate personal freedom? Or does it not rather enlarge that freedom and lift it up to a higher and more joyous activity? Am I, then, a 'mechanical instrument' when with deep devotion and with enthusiasm I repeat after Christ, word for word, the prayer which He taught His disciples? . . ." (*The Fundamentals*, IV, p. 77.) H. M'Intosh: "Psychological difficulties. . . . A similar presumptuous and inane objection is that such a control or influence over men's minds as would secure the truth and divine authority of the Bible is inconsistent with the mental freedom of man — as if God the Holy Ghost could not so act on the human mind as to ensure this without violating its free action — and must be confined within the narrow grooves of the oracular dictates of such audacious but unveracious speculation." (*Op. cit.*, p. 623.) Der Deutsche Ev.-Luth. Schulverein: "Wir halten fest an dem Wunder der Inspiration, und das ist, was die modernen positiven Theologen 'mechanisch' schelten. . . . Wir lehnen jede Erklaerung des Vorgangs der Inspiration ab. . . . Gegen das Zeugnis Jesu und seiner Apostel ist uns die Gelehrsamkeit der gelehrtesten Professoren und Doktoren lauter Wind." (See *Lehre und Wehre*, 1909, p. 234.)

they gave us no explanation of it. And here are men who are not afraid to declare *ex cathedra:* Verbal Inspiration must be mechanical inspiration! — If their reasoning is correct, then pity the blessed in heaven, who are incapable of thinking any but God's thoughts and cannot but speak in God's own words; they have lost their personal freedom! We thank God that He knows how to work in men in ways that are beyond the laws of common psychology. We thank Him that He converted us by His gracious power. We contributed nothing of our own towards our conversion. We were *pure passivi.* And yet we were not coerced. In the moment that faith was created in us we gave joyous consent. We were converted willingly — God made us willing.[261] We do not find it impossible to accept the teaching of Scripture that God · spoke through the prophets and apostles, made them His mouthpieces, without making them insensible machines.

The moderns keep harping on the term "dictation." Did not the dogmaticians state that the Holy Spirit "dictated" the contents and words of Holy Scripture to the holy writers? And is not "dictation" a mechanical affair? We have promised (footnote 172) to shed some light on this plaguing term and now tell the moderns that they are misquoting the fathers. Oh, yes, the fathers employed the word "dictation" and called the holy writers "amanuenses." B. Mentzer actually wrote: *Tanta est S. Scripturae auctoritas, quanta est* DICTANTIS *Spiritus Sancti, cuius illi fuerunt* AMANUENSES." But are the moderns not acquainted with the common law of all language that where metaphors are employed the point of comparison must be scrupulously observed lest the writer be made to utter nonsense? No man dreams of saying that when Jesus called Herod a fox He had the idea that Herod was a four-footed animal. Herod was a fox *in a certain respect.* It is the cheapest kind of ridicule to make the fathers who compared the holy writers to stenographers *in a certain respect* say that the holy writers were vacuous stenographers. Use common sense! When the fathers call the apostles amanuenses, they give expression to the truth that they spoke and wrote not by their own right, in their own wisdom, but by the authority of God. The words of John 3:16 are so truly the very words of the Holy Ghost as

261) Quoting some more from Stoeckhardt (*Lehre und Wehre,* 1886, p. 283): "Verbal Inspiration presents an incomprehensible mystery, which the human mind cannot elucidate. . . . We may perhaps find an analogy in the miracle of conversion. The conversion of the sinner is *in solidum* the work of the Holy Spirit; not the least part of it is effected by man's own powers. Still conversion is not effected by way of coercion; it does not change man mechanically; but it is a mysterious, inscrutable working of God on the will, the mind of man, which so influences his will and mind that he now wills, and gladly wills, what is God's will and thinks that which is godly."

though He had dictated them into the pen of St. John, as though we heard the Holy Ghost proclaim them today from heaven in His own majestic voice. The fathers never intended to convey the thought that the holy writers were lifeless machines. Again and again they disavow such ideas. G. P. Mains got the right idea when he used the phrase "*as though* God dictated every word," but falsified the idea of the fathers when he added: "using the human writer only as an automaton." The moderns are quoting the dogmaticians correctly as far as the bare word "dictation" is concerned, but are misquoting as far as the context is concerned. In the words of Dr. Pieper: "God used the holy writers as His *organs*, or *tools*, in order to transmit His Word, fixed in writing, to men. In order to express this relation between the Holy Ghost and the human writers, the Church Fathers as well as the old Lutheran dogmaticians call the holy writers *amanuenses, notarii, manus, calami,* secretaries, notaries, hands, pens, of the Holy Spirit. It is a well-known fact that these expressions are very generally derided by modern theologians. But Philippi justly calls this 'senseless ridicule.' The expressions are altogether Scriptural if only the *point of comparison (tertium comparationis)* is not lost sight of, namely, the *mere instrumentality.* The expressions state neither more nor less than the fact that the holy writers did not write their own word but τὰ λόγια τοῦ θεοῦ, the Word of God, and that, as we have seen, is the authoritative judgment of Christ and of His apostles. These expressions therefore should not be made the butt of ridicule; people ought to realize that they are in conformity with Scripture." (*Op. cit.,* I, p. 276.) The moderns are fighting a straw man.[262]

---

262) Dr. Stoeckhardt: "Ganz sachgemaess haben daher die alten Lehrer der Kirche diese Taetigkeit des Heiligen Geistes ein Diktieren und Propheten und Apostel Haende, Handlanger, Notare, Griffel (*manus, amanuenses, notarii, actuarii, calami*) des Geistes Gottes genannt. Es ist Unverstand und boeser Wille, wenn man deshalb den Alten vorwirft, dass sie eine ganz aeusserliche, mechanische Vorstellung von der Inspiration gehabt haetten. Das *tertium comparationis* liegt auf der Hand. Man wollte mit jenen Vergleichen nur recht stark hervorheben, dass Propheten und Apostel hier dem Geist Gottes nur als Organe gedient haben, um seine Gedanken den Menschen kundzutun, dass sie in keiner Weise Mithelfer waren, dass sie alles, was sie geschrieben, auch alle Worte und Ausdruecke empfangen, nichts aus sich selbst herausgenommen haben. . . . Ihr ganzes Herz war bei dem, was sie schrieben. Hieronymus schon bezeugt: '*Neque vero prophetae in ecstasi locuti sunt, ut nescirent quod loquerentur.*' Die Propheten haben, wie er weiter ausfuehrt, ihres Amtes nicht gewartet '*instar brutorum animalium.*' Der Geist hat ihnen nicht nur das aeussere Hoeren ('*quod in auribus resonat*'), sondern auch das feinere geistliche Gehoer ('*secretiorem auditum*') gegeben, kraft dessen sie nicht nur die Rinde, sondern auch das Mark zu erfassen vermochten." (*Lehre und Wehre,* 1892, p. 327 f.) — We cannot permit men to charge those who use the term "dictation" with being "mechanical-inspirationists." Dr. R. Watts upheld Verbal Inspiration in

The terms "dictation," "amanuensis," "mouthpiece," are not bad, said Pieper. They express the Scripture truth that God spoke by, *through*, διὰ τοῦ προφήτου, Matt. 1:22; διὰ στόματος Δαυίδ, *by the mouth* of David, Acts 1:16. The moderns should not blacklist the term "mouthpiece," seeing that the Lord said: "My words which I have put in thy mouth," Is. 59:21. David liked the term: "The Spirit of the Lord spake by me, and His Word was in my tongue," 2 Sam. 23:2. Luther liked it: "Ein Prophet wird genannt . . ., dem der Heilige Geist das Wort in den Mund legt." (III:785.) "Darum sind diese Worte Davids auch des Heiligen Geistes, die er durch seine Zunge redet." (III:1891.) "Pen" is not a bad word. Ps. 42:1: "My tongue is the pen of a ready writer." [263] Then read Rev. 2:1 ff. and Lenski's comment: "Jesus dictates the letters; John takes the dictation. . . . Despite those who taboo the word, the Lord here *dictated* those seven letters to John." St. John did not protest against serving as an amanuensis in a somewhat literal sense. And all the apostles and prophets were glad to serve as amanuenses in the higher sense in which the fathers use the term.

These terms are very good terms. They express the all-important truth that the holy writers were not the real authors of the Sacred Writings, but that these Sacred Writings are throughout the very Word of God. Blessed is he who will say with Luther: "The Holy Scriptures are written *by* the Holy Ghost" (IX:1770); "Diese Worte Davids sind des Heiligen Geistes Worte." And this truth, that what was spoken διὰ τοῦ προφήτου, through the prophet, was spoken ὑπὸ κυρίου, *by* the Lord (Matt. 1:22), is strongly and strikingly expressed in the good old terms "dictation," "mouthpiece." And so we say: "The Christian minister of the right sort, who simply repeats what he hears Scripture saying, will instruct his congregation on the question: Given by inspiration of God — what does that mean? about as follows: That does not mean that

his book *The Rule of Faith and the Doctrine of Inspiration.* Dr. Pieper praised this book highly, but was constrained to say: "Dr. Watts takes exception to the use of the term 'dictation.' To be sure, you can force the metaphor and make it express preposterous notions. But the old *Lutheran* theologians, for example, who used this term, did not conceive of inspiration as given 'by an external audible utterance.'" (*Lehre und Wehre*, 1886, p. 233.) So, when Hoenecke, for instance, writes: "We can compare the writers with various instruments. Harp and flute have different tones; yet he who can play both instruments can perfectly produce through both the same melody. The holy writers are animated, living harps and flutes," etc. (*op. cit.* I, p. 346), do not rush to the conclusion that that is "mechanical inspiration" — something which Hoenecke repudiates. See his statement quoted above.

263) Prof. J. P. Meyer: "Wer darf unseren Dogmatikern den Vorwurf machen, dass sie eine mechanische Auffassung der Inspiration verrieten, weil sie in Anlehnung an den Ausdruck des 45. Psalms die heiligen Schreiber als 'Griffel' des Heiligen Geistes bezeichnen, die ein 'Diktat' des Heiligen Geistes niederschrieben?" (*Theol. Quartalschrift*, 1931, p. 189.) See also P. E. Kretzmann, *The Foundations Must Stand*, p. 24.

God dictated the Bible to men after the fashion of the teacher who dictates something to little boys and girls or that God called out these words and the holy writers wrote them out thoughtlessly. But it does mean that God really inspired all the words of Scripture, infused them into the minds of the holy writers, gave them into their heart and pen, spoke and pronounced to them inwardly what they should write and did write. Just look at the text! It is written: 'All Scripture given by inspiration of God.' Any child can understand these words, and we must understand them to mean what they say." (Dr. Stoeckhardt, quoted in *Freikirche*, Oct. 22, 1939; *Lutheraner*, 1941, p. 325.)

FIGHTING AGAINST SCRIPTURE

The moderns are with us when we reject mechanical inspiration. They are glad to hear that we disavow it. They may be glad to learn that they were mistaken in ascribing such a teaching to the fathers. Is, then, the issue settled? It should be. Theologians should not keep on quarreling after the misunderstanding has been cleared up. But we notice that the moderns are not yet satisfied. They will not let the matter rest with our disavowal of mechanical inspiration. They heartily subscribe to the first part of Dr. Stoeckhardt's statement. But the second part of it raises their ire. We are as far apart as ever. The fact is that the point at issue is not so much the question of mechanical inspiration but rather the question of the truth of Scripture. Their real grievance is that the old dogmaticians taught the verbal inspiration and absolute inerrancy of Scripture. Our grievance against them is not their fight against the straw man — we could easily forgive and forget that — but their fight against Scripture. That is a serious charge. We submit the proof for it under three heads.

1) The fight against the "mechanical theory of inspiration" is a fight against the truthfulness of Scripture in that it denies one of the chief teachings of Scripture, the doctrine of Verbal Inspiration. You will remember that the moderns identify verbal inspiration and mechanical inspiration. Recall Deissmann's statement: "This dogma of verbal inspiration of every letter of the New Testament, which rightly can be called mechanical inspiration." [264]

---

264) Sanday: "Mechanical and verbal inspiration of the Bible." Alleman: "The doctrine of verbal inspiration . . . the old heathen conception . . . a man became but a mouthpiece of the deity." Add this, by Dr. J. A. W. Haas: "There has been a misinterpretation of the following words in 1 Cor. 2:13: 'Words which the Holy Ghost teacheth.' The term 'words' is taken to mean every single word down to the minutest 'and.' . . . It was unfortunate that our early dogmaticians developed a *mechanical, verbalistic* theory of inspiration of the Word. . . . Our early

Recall the claim of the moderns that verbal inspiration *cannot but be* mechanical. But Scripture teaches Verbal Inspiration, and we raise the charge against the moderns that they are in direct opposition to Scripture; when they stigmatize the teaching of the old dogmaticians as un-Lutheran and unchristian, as mechanical, they are ridiculing the Word of God. Let Dr. Reu elaborate this. "During the last years a hot pursuit was started against this theory [the mechanical theory] in some quarters of our Church. . . . Alas, not seldom this pursuit *aims at Verbal Inspiration* in every form, and thus the combat becomes a fight against the testimony of Scripture concerning itself. We do not want to emphasize the fact that without Verbal Inspiration we lack every guarantee that the divine content is expressed in Scripture correctly and without abbreviations; we rather stress the fact that Scripture itself demands it. It is demanded by the form of the quotations 'The Holy Spirit speaks,' 'God says'; furthermore, it follows from the fact that Jesus as well as Paul draw important conclusions from the wording of Old Testament passages, a few times even from a single word, as *elohim* in Ps. 82:6 or σπέρμα in the story of Abraham; and in particular does it follow from 1 Cor. 2:12, 13: 'Of these we also speak — not in words which man's wisdom teaches us, but in those which the Spirit teaches — interpreting spiritual (things) by spiritual (words).'... Even the formation of the word was taught by the Spirit." (*In the Interest of Luth. Unity*, p. 68 f.) Scripture clearly teaches Verbal Inspiration, and the moderns, denouncing that as mechanical, are in the open, fighting not a straw man but Scripture.[265]

---

theologians were really Calvinistic in their verbalistic conception. . . . It is a mere fiction to uphold the infallibility in every statement and not merely in the essentials of faith." (*The Luth. Church Quart.*, 1937, p. 280 f.)

265) There are those among the moderns who admit that Scripture teaches Verbal Inspiration but insist that Scripture is wrong on this point. Warfield writes: "Among untrammeled students of the Bible it is practically a matter of common consent that the writers of the New Testament looked upon what they called 'Scripture' as divinely safeguarded in even its verbal expression and as divinely trustworthy in all its parts, in all its elements, and in all its affirmations of whatever kind. . . . It is also the judgment of all those who can bring themselves to refuse a doctrine which they yet perceive to be a Biblical doctrine. . . . Let us pause long enough to allow Hermann Schultz, surely a fair example of the 'advanced' school, to tell us what is the conclusion in this matter of the strictest and coldest exegetical science. 'The Book of the Law,' he tells us, 'seemed already to the later poets of the Old Testament the "Word of God." For the men of the New Testament, the Holy Scriptures of their people are already God's Word in which God Himself speaks.' This view, which looked upon the Scriptural books as verbally inspired, he adds, was the ruling one in the time of Christ, was shared by all the New Testament men, and by Christ Himself." (*Op. cit.*, p. 61 f.) "Thus, for instance — to confine our examples to a few of those who are

2) The moderns repudiate "mechanical" inspiration, by which they mean verbal inspiration, because of the alleged errors in the Bible. Convinced that the Bible teems with imperfections, mistakes, ethical aberrations, they refuse to teach that the Holy Ghost is the real Author of the whole Bible and offer the substitutes "dynamical inspiration," "concept inspiration," and the like, which leave room for these "errors." Professor Kantonen would have us "abandon the unpsychological and mechanical theories of inspiration *and* unhistorical views of *verbal inerrancy*." He believes that "the Bible has the same limitations that bound any historical process.... Or, as one of the Biblical writers themselves, Paul, said: 'We have this treasure in earthen vessels.'... The scientific opinions which the Biblical writers shared with their contemporaries. . . . The Bible is a magnificent cathedral, . . . well preserved, although today we may perhaps detect here and there a crack in the walls or a loose brick." (*The Message of the Church, etc.*, p. 103 f.) The thesis is that, since Scripture contains mistakes, it cannot have been mechanically (verbally) inspired. M. Dods: "If we should find on examination that much of what is human — discrepancies or inaccuracies — enters into the Bible, we must expand our theory to include this" and therefore reject "that which has been known as the mechanical or dictation theory" (*op. cit.*, p. 106 f.). W. Sanday: "The writers and teachers of the early church doubtless held a high view of it (Inspiration), but it was not by any means a mechanical view. They would not have hesitated to admit what we might call slips of the pen. Take, for instance, Matt. 27:9, where

---

not able personally to accept the doctrine of the New Testament writers — Archdeacon Farrar is able to admit that Paul 'shared, doubtless, in the views of the later Jewish schools on the nature of inspiration. These views . . . made the words of Scripture coextensive and identical with the words of God.' . . . The writer of an odd and sufficiently free Scotch book published a few years ago (James Stuart) formulates his conclusion in the words: 'There is no doubt that the author of Hebrews, in common with the other New Testament writers, regards the whole Old Testament as having been dictated by the Holy Ghost, or, as we should say, plenarily and, as it were, mechanically inspired." (*Op. cit.*, p. 175 f.) This is what actually happens: commenting on Jer. 1:9 ("I have put My words in thy mouth") C. H. Dodd declares: "That this is direct imaginative experience does not admit of question. We may readily suppose that the words and the touch on the lips were actual *hallucinations*." (*The Authority of the Bible*, p. 79.) Most moderns will not go that far. They prefer to say with *Folkebladet*: "It is an impossibility that the prophets and apostles could have intended that their words should be considered as a dictation by the Holy Spirit" (dictation = verbal inspiration). These men say that Jeremiah and Paul did not mean "verbal" inspiration. But that does not alter the fact that they refuse to accept a clear teaching of Scripture. They will not, indeed, charge the holy writers with having hallucinations. But they will have to charge them with using misleading language. They will have to say that, when Paul declared that all the words of Scripture are inspired, he did not mean what he said.

a saying which really belongs to Zechariah is attributed to Jeremiah." (*Op. cit.*, p. 18.) Dr. G. Drach: "The theory of a mechanical verbal inspiration simply falls to pieces. . . . This theory holds that the prophets and apostles were inspired . . . in all that they wrote. . . . So we must settle on a theory of inspiration which while it avoids mechanical verbal inspiration . . . does not overexalt the apostles as infallible mouthpieces all the time. . . . We repudiate the absolute infallibility of the apostles and others who wrote the Sacred Scriptures." (*The Luth. Church Quart.*, 1936, pp. 247 to 251.)[266]

---

266) A few more statements to show that what is back of the fight against "mechanical" inspiration is the conviction that the Bible is an imperfect book. Dr. A. J. Traver: "By its very nature, inspiration is spiritual. There can be nothing mechanical about it. God did not dictate to the writers of the Bible as to a stenographer. . . . Inspiration includes only the knowledge essential for knowing God and His plan for man. . . . Inspiration of the kind necessary for the knowledge of God is not necessary for scientific knowledge." (*The Lutheran*, Jan. 23, 1936.) Since in Dr. Traver's opinion the Bible made several false scientific statements, he naturally refuses to say that these were direct statements of the Holy Spirit. And so the moderns operate with the dynamical theory of inspiration, which nicely takes care of the errors. "Die Schrift verdankt ihre Entstehung zwei Faktoren, einerseits der freien goettlichen Selbstbetaetigung. . . . andererseits der freien menschlichen Selbstbetaetigung gegenueber der goettlichen Offenbarung. . . . Die goettliche Selbstbetaetigung bestimmt die menschlichen Organe zur Selbsttaetigkeit und verklaert sie zu freien Organen des goettlichen Geistes. Auf Grund solchen Zusammenwirkens des goettlichen und menschlichen Geistes nennen wir die Heilige Schrift das gottmenschliche Wort. . . . Wir bemerken nur noch (4), dass eine *Irrtumsfaehigkeit* der Schrift in bezug auf solche Dinge zuzugeben ist, was entweder gar nicht in das Gebiet der Heilsgeschichte faellt oder als ganz unwesentlich die Substanz der Heilsgeschichte in keiner Weise beruehrt." (Zoecklers *Handbuch der Theol. Wiss.*, I, p. 747 f.) Similarly Luthardt-Jelkes *Kompendium der Dogmatik*, p. 111, quotes Quenstedt's statements *"Nulla falsitas, nullus vel minimus error, sive in rebus, sive in verbis"* and comments: "Dass diese Saetze viel zu weit greifen, liegt auf der Hand. . . . Dieser Fehler besteht darin, dass das Verhaeltnis des Heiligen Geistes zur Schrift nicht durch die *eigene geistige Aktivitaet* der biblischen Schriftsteller, sondern nur aeusserlich durch die Hand der Schreibenden vermittelt gedacht ist." The mistakes are there — you must charge them to the self-activity of the holy writers — and so you will have to abandon Verbal Inspiration. Quoting a number of similar statements, one, for instance, by William Adams Brown, who protests against "making the Bible the result of immediate divine dictation," the *Theol. Quart.*, 1914, p. 77, states: "The plenary, or verbal, inspiration is denonunced as 'mechanical inspiration' for this additional reason that such an inspiration would make the inspired penmen inerrant." The moderns have the idea that, if the dogmaticians had only known about these errors in the Bible, they would not have taught verbal (mechanical) inspiration. Dr. J. A. W. Haas puts it this way: "It was unfortunate that our early dogmaticians developed a mechanical-verbalistic theory of inspiration of the Word. . . . Out of the minute verbalistic conception grows the problem of the infallibility of the Word. Extreme verbalism demands . . . an original perfect text for all the books of the Bible. . . . The whole idea of a completely infallible Word in every historical and geographical detail is

Every blow which the moderns aim at the "mechanical, verbalistic inspiration," repudiating it because of the alleged errors in the Bible, hits Holy Scripture. They are fighting a straw man inasmuch as Verbal Inspiration is not mechanical; but inasmuch as they identify the two concepts, they are really engaged in a warfare against Scripture. The reason they give for their inability to accept Verbal Inspiration is a terrible indictment of the Word of God. They are saying that the Bible is not true in every respect. Study the following pronouncement by the editor of *The Christian Century*, March 30, 1938, and ask yourselves whether he is serving the cause of the Bible. "The writers of the Bible were men like ourselves — like E. St. Jones and Kagawa, if you wish. . . . I cannot imagine what added authority the Bible would have if it were conceived as having been dictated by God to a stenographer. Its value would be no more precious. Its meaning would be no more clear. Its truth would be no more authoritative. Indeed, I fear it would subtract from its authority if God had so dictated it, for *I would be at a loss to account for the obvious errors in it.*" I should not care to have a friend who, when men calumniate me, takes it for granted that I am guilty and then tries to find excuses for me. When enemies of the Bible posed the question: "Hat nicht das Neue Testament neben der reinen Lehre Jesu *manches stoerende Beiwerk?*" the Evangelische Oberkirchenrat in Stuttgart hemmed ånd hawed and finally said: "Die Evangelische Kirche betrachtet die Bibel als Gottes Wort; nicht im Sinne einer mechanischen Verbalinspiration, sondern als das in Menschenwort gekleidete Zeugnis Gottes von seinem Wesen und Walten." Yes, it contains "some incongruous trappings," but that does not hurt the chief contents of it, etc. — The Bible deserves better apologists, better friends. God protect the Bible against its friends who declare: "Christian faith affirms the presence of both the divine element and the human factor in inspiration. We have the heavenly treasure in earthen vessels. 'God used men — not machines.' . . . 'Discrepancies do exist. Matt. 27:9 quotes Zechariah, but credits Jeremiah with the words. There seems to be a disagreement in the Synoptists on the number of times the cock crew, etc.' (Dr. C. J. Sodergren.) . . . The human

---

due to the position which John Gerhard took in his *Confessio Catholica*." (*The Luth. Church Quart.*, 1937; p. 280 f.) Dr. Joseph Stump: "The seventeenth-century dogmaticians of the Church, impelled by a laudable desire to maintain the supreme authority of the Bible, formulated a very definite theory of inspiration. The sacred writers were regarded as mere amanuenses who wrote down what God dictated. Consequently in their view no human element entered into the writing of the sacred books. God alone is the author of Holy Scriptures. . . . Hence it followed that the Holy Scriptures in the original text are to be regarded as completely free from errors of any kind." (*The Christian Faith*, p. 315.)

element may also be recognized as we observe the fact that sometimes the strong feeling of the writer blinds him to qualities of purity and mercy. . . . In these passages (Ps. 69:24; 58:6,10; 109:8,9,10; 137:9) the human, or shall I say inhuman, element is sadly evident." (Hjalmar W. Johnson, in the *Journal of the Am. Luth. Conf.*, May, 1939, pp. 18—21.)

BREAKING EVERY WORD OF SCRIPTURE

3) The moderns do something worse to the Bible. They not only cut away great parts of it — the alleged errors and indecencies — but they emasculate all of it. In their fight against the "mechanical-verbalistic" inspiration they are fighting against the reliability and divinity of every word of the Bible. That is a serious charge. But their own words prove it. They have been telling us right along that inspiration does not extend to the letter, the words of the Bible. Dr. H. E. Jacobs assured us that, "if the verbal theory of inspiration means that every word and letter is inspired," he will have none of it. A. Deissmann told us that he is glad that "this dogma of verbal inspiration of every letter of the New Testament, which rightly can be called mechanical inspiration, . . . is now abandoned." "What is the extent of inspiration?" asks G. L. Raymond; "does it apply to the style and the words or only to the substance and the sense?" He answers: "The inspired element is underneath the phraseology rather than in it. . . . We have no reason to expect to find evidence of inspiration in the specific details of the expression, except so far as, indirectly, they may indicate the general trend of that which is expressed." (*The Psychology of Inspiration*, pp. 154, 187, 307.) Do we hear correctly? Are the moderns saying that the *words* of the Bible are not inspired words? The editor of *The Lutheran* (June 21, 1928) *is* saying: "For every essential issue there is divine truth at hand; that *its verbal expression is of human origin* can be frankly recognized." H. Wheeler Robinson: "The confident appeal to the Scriptures as affording an infallible direction of faith and conduct is made impossible if that is sought in the *letter*" (italics by author) "of the Word of God to men. . . . The fuller recognition of the principle of mediation . . . throws us back on the inner content of the revelation *instead of its literary expression and record.*" (*The Chr. Experience of the Holy Spirit*, p. 175.) H. F. Baughman: "Its authority is not to be identified with the form of language which announces the truth of God but must be found in the light of experience through which the Word of God came to the soul of a man." (The *Luth. Church Quart.*, 1935. p. 260.) J. A. W. Haas: "Men were never saved by a Bible that was mechanically perfect in its verbality." (*What Is Revelation?*

p. 16.) Not perfect in its verbal expression? Did not the Holy Spirit choose the words? Or was that left to fallible men? The Holy Spirit did not choose the words, say the moderns. G. T. Ladd: "Inspiration is not 'verbal' in the technical sense of the term; that is, it does not consist in, or involve, the selection and dictation, by the Holy Ghost Himself, of all the words employed by the writers." (*What Is the Bible?* p. 436.) G. Drach: "Zwingli's spirit led his followers to incline toward the dictation of words as well as to the inspiration of the contents of the Sacred Scriptures, and this theory . . . also influenced some of the Lutheran theologians of the seventeenth century. . . . Gerhard went from the inspiration of the impulse to write to the inspiration of the contents and then to the inspiration of the choice and use of words." (The *Luth. Church Quart.*, 1936, pp. 245, 247.) And so, of course, since fallible men made the choice of words, "we do not know," says Luther A. Weigle, "whether the words of the Bible given us are true or accurate." (See *Conc. Theol. Mthly.*, XIII, p. 151.) — As we read Gen. 1:1 or John 3:16, the moderns warn us not to be too sure that we are dealing with God's Word. God's Word may be contained in these words, which transmit to us the ideas of the writers, but that must be established in some other way. What Moses and John wrote may be true or it may be false. There can be no absolute reliance on any verse of Scripture. — The moderns are fighting Scripture in that they deny one doctrine of Scripture, as we saw under 1). But that means, as we now see, that they are fighting all of Scripture.

The moderns do not want to have inspired *words*. Is further proof required? Then examine the substitutes they ask us to accept in place of the old doctrine which they have thrown to the moles and bats. There is the concept-not-words theory. Dr. Drach has defined it for us as "the inspiration of the contents, not the dictation of words." J. De Witt: "It simply means that truth as inspired by God is of such quality and nature that invariable verbal accuracy is not needed. It may be expressed with great freedom and in various forms without impairing its substantial value. It is the thought that is inspired." (*What Is Inspiration?* p. 41.) *Suggestio rerum?* Yes; *suggestio verborum?* Never![267]

---

267) See footnote 255. — Warfield: "This may be called the rationalistic view. . . . It affirms that . . . the Bible is inspired only in its *thoughts* or *concepts*, not in its words. . . . This legacy from the rationalism of an evil time still makes its appearance in the pages of many theological writers . . .; but it has failed to supplant in either the creeds of the Church or in the hearts of the people the church doctrine of the plenary inspiration of the Bible, *i. e.*, the doctrine that the Bible is inspired not in part, but fully, in all its elements alike, — things discoverable by reason as well as mysteries, matters of history and science as well as of faith and practice, *words as well as thoughts*." (*Op. cit.*, p. 59.)

Then there is the dynamic theory, the popular theory of the day. Nine out of ten opponents of Verbal Inspiration cry out: Not mechanical, but dynamical! Professor Ladd will tell us what it is. "Inspiration may be said to be 'dynamical,' as distinguished from what is mechanical. Its general conception is that of a divine influence coming like breath or wind into the soul of man and producing a transformation there. . . . The influence is dynamical — a divine force dwelling and working in the human soul. It therefore involves the highest activity of all the normal powers. . . . Inspiration is not 'verbal.'" (*Op. cit.*, p. 434.) C. E. Lindberg: "The orthodox dynamic theory . . . sets forth the divine activity but also places proper emphasis on the human side. . . . The holy writers were not merely mechanical instruments, such as pens or amanuenses, there was an *auto-activity* analogous to the new life that succeeds the new birth, when the regenerated soul cooperates with the Holy Ghost." (*Christian Dogmatics*, p. 389.) In German they say: "Die Inspiration ist Entfachung der menschlichen Selbsttaetigkeit." (F. Buechsel, *op. cit.*, p. 113.) Just how this "dynamic inspiration" worked when the holy writer penned a sentence, just how the divine dynamics and the human dynamics balanced each other, they will not tell us.[268] But one thing they tell us plainly: the dynamic theory does away with the inspiration of the words. A. H. Strong: "The dynamical theory, the true view, holds . . . that the Scriptures contain a human as well as a divine element, so that, while they constitute a body of infallible truth, this truth is shaped in human

---

268) *Fundamentals*, VII, p. 21: "Fifth, 'dynamic inspiration.' But the efforts of those who hold to this view to explain what they mean by the term are exceedingly vague and misty." M'Intosh: " . . . what has been contemptuously called the mechanical, as distinguished from the dynamical, theory of Inspiration — though what mechanical or dynamical can precisely mean in such matters the users of these misleading phrases have never yet attempted to make plain." (*Op. cit.*, p. 463.) Nor does M. Dods (who does not believe in Verbal Inspiration) think much of the dynamic theory: "This theory has been found to introduce confusion into the subject." (*Op. cit.*, p. 120.) Professor Ladd sees the difficulty of pointing out just where, say in John 3:16, the divine force gave way to the human force or in which word human fallibility was overcome by the divine infallibility. After describing the "dynamical," he is forced to add (on p. 437): "In all inspiration, the exact place where the divine meets the human and is limited by it, as well as the precise mode of the operation of the Spirit, remains concealed and mysterious." He employs the analogy of "the ordinary Christian experience" — no Christian "can draw a line in the working of his thoughts and emotions and say: 'This is of God, and this other is my own.'" The confusion grows when Lindberg, for instance, finds it necessary to oppose the views of "the old dogmaticians who held to the mechanical theory of inspiration," insists on operating with the dynamic theory and the auto-activity of the holy writers, and finally arrives at the position of the old dogmaticians, declaring with them that "the holy writers imparted the divine truth as to thought *and expression*," "that *every word* in the original text is inspired" (*op. cit.*, pp. 395, 401).

molds. . . . Inspiration did not always, or even generally, involve a direct communication to the Scripture writers of the words they wrote. . . . They were left to the action of their own minds in the expression of these truths." (*Op. cit.*, p. 102 f.) Archdeacon Farrar's definition is quoted as classical in R. Tuck, *A Handb. of Bibl. Diff.*, p. V: "The *dynamic*, or power, theory. It holds that Holy Scripture was not 'dictated by,' but 'committed to writing under the guidance of,' the Holy Spirit. While recognizing the divine energy, it does not annihilate human co-operation. The truths are inspired by the Holy Spirit, the words and phrases are the result of the writer's own individuality; the material is of God, the form is of man." [269] It seems that, on this point, the dynamic-

---

269) A word, in passing, on the monstrosity of the concept: thoughts without words. They have been telling us that Verbal Inspiration is "unpsychological." Well, we are unable to grasp the psychology underlying the theories which they offer as substitutes for Verbal Inspiration. They say that God inspired the thoughts but not the words. Did you ever discover yourself thinking a definite thought without clothing that thought in definite words? In *speaking* and *writing*, thoughts are expressed in words, and the *mind* cannot but follow the same process. Stoeckhardt grappled with the problem posed by the "concept theory," gave it up, and declared: "In jeder vernuenftigen Rede haengen Gedanke und Ausdruck so eng zusammen, wie Leib und Seele." (*Lehre und Wehre*, 1886, p. 256.) Nor could A. A. Hodge grasp the idea: "The line can never rationally be drawn between the thoughts and words of Scripture"; nor Canon Westcott: "The slightest consideration will show that words are as essential to intellectual processes as they are to mutual intercourse. . . . Thoughts are wedded to words as necessarily as soul to body. Without it the mysteries unveiled before the eyes of the seer would be confused shadows; with it, they are made clear lessons for human life." (See *Fundamentals*, VII, p. 23.) *The Expositor's Greek Testament* refuses to subscribe to the laws of this new psychology. On 1 Cor. 2:13: "In an honest mind thought and language are one, and whatever determines the former must mold the latter." Lindberg: "If we believe that the thoughts were inspired, we must also believe, logically, that the words were inspired as well. Some persons, who do not have clear conception concerning inspiration and boast that they are liberal, say: We believe in the inspiration of the idea, but not of the words. Even the best modern psychology holds that there cannot be an idea without form or words. Man thinks in words." (*Op. cit.*, p. 396.) Lenski: "Erase the words, and the thought disappears. . . . The thought cannot be separated from the words which are its vehicles." (On 2 Tim. 3:16.) And: "This distinction between content and words is an illusion. Of what is Holy Scripture composed? Merely of words! Page after page of words, and then some more words. And what are these words? They are the vehicles of thought. Without words, there is no thought or content. Take out the words, and what do you have left? Nothing! That is the fatal feature for all who do not want to admit Verbal Inspiration and still would like to believe in an inspiration of content. The bird flies out of their hand, and they retain only a few feathers. If only one could take a knife and go into the Bible, and cut out the words entirely, and then after all the words have been removed, hold it up and say, 'Behold this is the bare thought.' But after such an operation is completed, what is left? The empty pages of the Bible! Beautiful content and thought!" (Quoted in *The Pastor's Monthly*, 1935, p. 261.) — Another point: If the inspiration of *words* would have to be mechanical, the same objection would hold as to the inspiration, a real inspiration, of *thoughts*.

theory men teach the same as the concept-theory men. Well, that is no affair of ours. All that we are interested in is to show that the moderns have a horror of the *suggestio verborum*. They leave us in no doubt that they will not have the words of Holy Scripture proceed out of the mouth of the Lord. — Note that the purpose of these theories is not merely to take care of the alleged errors in the Bible. See 2). They cover also those parts and passages which are accepted as true. The words of John 3:16, too, are not inspired. John 3:16 is broken.

The words are not inspired; they are not God's own words, but the writers' own words — if you still doubt that the moderns say that, ask them for further elucidation of their dynamic theory. They will tell you to consult Zoeckler's *Handbuch*. "Two factors produced Holy Scripture. One is the free self-activity of God. The other is the free human self-activity over against the divine revelation. . . . The human organs are *free* organs of the divine Spirit. . . . Holy Scripture is thus a divine-human word." "Nach der modernen wissenschaftlich vermittelten Umbildung des Inspirationsbegriffs ist nicht sowohl ein unbedingt *goettlicher* als vielmehr ein *gottmenschlicher* Ursprung und Charakter der Schrift zu lehren." Dr. Stump continues the elucidation: "In the view of the seventeenth-century dogmaticians no human element entered into the writing of the sacred books. God alone is the Author of the Holy Scriptures." That is wrong, for "there is a human as well as a divine factor to be taken into account in considering the writing of the Holy Scriptures." (*Loc. cit.*) "The Bible," said Professor Volck, "is the product of two factors, a divine and a human factor"; "the Bible was composed by men"; "the holy writers," said Th. Harnack, "exercised absolute self-activity (selbststaendigste Aktivitaet)"; acting independently, they expressed their own thoughts in their own words, and Thomasius insisted that "the sacred writings were not dictated by the Holy Ghost, but were — produced by the self-activity of their authors." (See *Lehre und Wehre*, 1886, p. 168; *Proceedings, Syn. Conf.*, 1886, pp. 31, 36.) " 'The human side' of Scripture, as the moderns use the term, means that the holy writers were *causae efficientes*, not only the writers but indeed the authors of Holy Scripture." (Dr. Walther. See *Proc., Iowa Dist.*, 1891, p. 54.) Why, they even use the phrase "eigene produktive Geistestaetigkeit." They do not want to have the Holy Spirit to be the sole Author of Scripture. Only in a restricted sense will they call Him the *real* Author. They refuse to call the words of Scripture "the very words of God." And we say that he who makes out of these divine words human words is fighting Scripture, is striking at its very heart.[270]

---

270) Was not Moses the *author* of the Pentateuch and St. John the *author* of the Fourth Gospel? — Do we have to go over the same old

Bound to let us know that in their opinion the Bible is the product of a joint authorship, a divine-human book, the moderns even use the very expressive term "synergism" in this connection. For instance: Dr. M. S. Terry, who does not believe in the inerrancy of the Bible, characterized the "mechanical inspiration" as monergistic and declared: "The synergistic theology is the opposite of this and the only tenable alternative." (See *Theol. Quart.*, 1913, p. 4; 1914, p. 79.) As in synergism conversion results from the collaboration of God and man, so Scripture has been produced by

---

ground again? Certainly the holy writers were not dead machines. They wrote as rational, intelligent writers write. They searched for the right word, and they chose the fitting word. But when the moderns use this same phraseology in order to say that the words of Scripture are not the very words of the Holy Ghost, seeing that they are the writers' own words, they are not speaking our language, the language of Scripture. The holy writers were not "the originators but the receivers and announcers" of their message, and the Holy Ghost supplied not only the substance but also the form (the words) of the message. Did the holy writers cooperate? Yes, as instruments; no, if that means that they produced anything of their own. Two factors? Yes, one the instrument of the other; no, if it means independent factors. May Moses and St. John be called authors? Stoeckhardt does not hesitate to call them "the holy authors." (See above.) But when the moderns call them co-authors of the Bible, meaning that God is the Author of the thought and the apostles the originators of the words, they are not speaking the language of Scripture and of the Church. The Church does not state on the title page of her Book: "The Bible, the Word of God and of the holy writers." What would Paul have put on the title page? See 1 Thess. 2: 13. — Stoeckhardt: "Die Weissagung der Schrift (2 Petr. 1: 21), die Heilige Schrift, ist kein Produkt der Menschen, des menschlichen Willens. Jene 'selbstaendigste Aktivitaet' der heiligen Schriftsteller wird ausdruecklich verneint. Die Position lautet: Die heiligen Menschen Gottes haben geredet, getrieben von dem Heiligen Geist. Freilich jene heiligen Maenner, die Propheten, waren es, die da redeten; aber da sie die Weissagung niederschrieben, wurden sie vom Heiligen Geist getrieben, bewegt, getragen (φερόμενοι). Sie standen ganz und gar im Dienst, waren Werkzeuge des Heiligen Geistes. Der Heilige Geist war es, der hier in der Weissagung seine Gedanken, seine Weisheit kundgab und die Propheten und ihr Reden, Schreiben als *medium* gebrauchte, das, was er wollte, den Menschen zu wissen zu tun. Der Heilige Geist, kein anderer ausser oder neben ihm, ist der Autor der Schrift, der Weissagung. Die Schrift ist Produkt des Heiligen Geistes, und zwar ausschliesslich Produkt des Geistes, kein 'von Menschen verfasstes Gotteswerk'." (*Lehre und Wehre,* 1886, p. 214.) Warfield: "The Church has held from the beginning that the Bible is the Word of God in such a sense that its words, though written by men and bearing indelibly impressed upon them marks of their human origin, were written, nevertheless, under such an influence of the Holy Ghost as to be also the words of God, the adequate expression of His mind and will." "Here [Acts 1: 16] the Holy Spirit is adduced, of course, as the real Author of what is said, but David's mouth is expressly designated as the instrument (it is the instrumental preposition that is used) by means of which the Holy Spirit speaks the Scripture in question." "The things which they spoke under this operation of the Spirit (2 Pet. 1: 19-21) were therefore His things, not theirs. Though spoken through the instrumentality of men, it is, by virtue of the fact that these men spoke 'as borne by the Holy Spirit,' an immediately divine word." (*Op. cit.*, pp. 83, 97, 173.)

two factors, God contributing the ideas, man the words. It would be well if all the moderns, all those who speak of the "two factors" and the "free self-activity," would, without more ado, call their teaching the "synergistic theory of inspiration." It is what they mean. They do not want to call Scripture exclusively the product of God. Scripture makes that claim.[271] Scripture wants us to receive all its words as words chosen by God and therefore expressing the thought so perfectly and infallibly as only God can express it. But the moderns will not have it so.

To sum up, the moderns abominate and loathe Verbal Inspiration. The ridicule which they heap on "mechanical inspiration" is intended to discredit Verbal Inspiration and turn men against it.[272] And discrediting Verbal Inspiration, they are discrediting Scripture. They are destroying the Christian's faith in the absolute reliability of the words of Holy Scripture. They are breaking all of Scripture.

CAN THE CHRISTIAN BASE HIS FAITH AND HOPE ON THE WORDS OF FALLIBLE MEN?

We face a frightful situation. Uncertainty, doubt, and fear are sweeping through the land. The stop-and-go theory of inspiration is bad enough. According to it only half of the Bible is inspired. And now the moderns apply to the rest their half-and-half theory, and all is lost. The passages dealing with the

---

271) Dr. Pieper: "Where Scripture speaks of the *causa efficiens* of Scripture only one factor is recognized, the divine factor. Scripture does not say: 'All Scripture is given partly by inspiration of God, and partly it is produced by men,' but only: 'πᾶσα γραφὴ θεόπνευστος.' The holy men that took part in this matter are characterized as *instruments through* whom God spoke. What resulted was not a writing which is half man's word and half God's, but Scripture, which is nothing but God's word (cf. Matt. 1: 22; 2: 15, etc.; Heb. 10: 15) and cannot be broken (John 10: 35)." (*Lehre und Wehre*, 1892, p. 197.)

272) Pieper: "To discredit Verbal Inspiration among the public, the assertion is rather generally made that the dogmaticians had entirely 'mechanical conceptions' of the inspiration of Scripture." (*Op. cit.* I, p. 365.) M'Intosh: "They have sought to heap ridicule upon the true and Scriptural position by associating with it foolish fancies excluded by it"; "they have found it a much easier thing first to misrepresent and then to caricature the position of the real defenders of the claim of Scripture than honestly to face their proof." (*Op. cit.*, pp. 8, 268, 312.) Machen: "If we say: 'Yes, we do believe in Verbal Inspiration,' then they hold up their hands in horror. 'How dreadful, how mechanical!' they say. 'If God really provided in supernatural fashion that the words should be thus and so, then the writers of the Biblical books are degraded to the position of mere stenographers, indeed, even lower than that . . . of mere machines. . . .' Such is the hole into which we are thought to be put. . . . How can we possibly escape? Well, I think we can escape very easily indeed. Yes, I believe in the verbal inspiration of the Bible; but I do insist that you and I shall get a right notion of what the word 'verbal' means." (*The Christian Faith in the Modern World*, p. 46 f.)

saving truth are, they tell us, half divine and half human; the words in which the divine thought is expressed are the words of men. But the only way in which we can receive the divine truth is through words — and can the Christian base the hope of salvation on the words of fallible men? Dr. Haas told us that the Bible is not mechanically perfect in its verbality. Dr. Weigle told us: "We do not know whether the words of the Bible given us are true or accurate." Dr. Seeberg told us, in addition: "There can be no doubt that the Biblical authors could certainly draw conclusions intrinsically false from inspired truths." (Op. cit., p. 102.) When you must make fallible men your authority, there is an end to Christian assurance. Beware of this "Dictated-but-not-read theory." That is what W. T. Riviere calls this concept theory. "A busy man dictates a letter to his stenographer and tells her to transcribe and mail it without waiting for his final inspection and signature. Since there is large opportunity for mistakes to occur, this procedure is rarely followed with important letters. The addressee, warned by the notation 'dictated but not read,' does not hold his correspondent responsible for all details of expression or even of matter." (Bibliotheca Sacra, 1936, p. 299.) The moderns are offering us a Bible the words of which are not underwritten and guaranteed by the divine Author, for He is responsible only for the thought; the expression of the thought is the work of man. The moderns actually say that. If they said that the form as well as the thought were given by the Holy Ghost, that would be verbal, mechanical inspiration! So we get a Bible whose statements of the saving truth are of human origin, and that is the end of all and any Christian assurance. Let us repeat that: "We emphasize the fact that without Verbal Inspiration we lack every guarantee that the divine content is expressed in Scripture correctly and without abbreviations." (Dr. Reu.) We repeat: "If God really did not guide these men in the choice of words but left this matter to the discretion of the writers, we could never feel free from the suspicion that these fallible human beings might have erred in the selection of their phraseology." (The Lutheran Teacher.) And remember, the moderns have introduced this monstrum incertitudinis into the holy of holies. Their half-and-half theory is applied to John 3:16 as well as to 1 Tim. 5:23. What results? "If the words godhead, election, redemption, imputation, regeneration, propitiation, sacrifice, atonement, faith, repentance, justification, sanctification, adoption, resurrection, heaven, hell, etc., were not inspired and infallible, then everything essential to Christian faith and life may be only old wives' fables. Without certainty and divine authority in the words of Scripture, it is patently impossible to believe in the things, or even to know the will of

God, for our salvation." (M'Intosh, *op. cit.*, p. 614.) "Ist wie Jacobs und Stump sagen, die Schrift wirklich unfehlbar (infallible, inerrant) in allen ihren theologischen Ausfuehrungen, so muessen auch alle Worte, die sich in diesen Ausfuehrungen finden, vom Heiligen Geiste (der allein unfehlbar das Richtige treffen kann) gesetzt sein. Finden sich in denselben Worte, die Menschen gesetzt haben, ohne dass der Heilige Geist dabei die Wahl geleitet hat, so kann von absoluter Unfehlbarkeit auch in den theologischen Ausfuehrungen nicht mehr die Rede sein. Auch die *loci classici* sind nicht mehr unfehlbar gewisse Wahrheiten, wenn die Wahl der Worte, aus welchen sie bestehen, fehlbaren Menschen ueberlassen war." (F. Bente, in *Lehre und Wehre*, 1904, p. 87.) We repeat: If the moderns are right, if the concept theory and the dynamic theory are the thing, the Christian is condemned to a life of uncertainty, doubt, and fear.

It is a frightful situation. The moderns tell the Christians that they must carefully sift the words of the fallible holy writers in order to find the truth of the divine thought hidden therein, and then tell them that there is no known process by which that can be accomplished. D. F. Forrester tells them: "All of them [the holy writers] struggled with evident limitations of temperament, environment, and vocation. In their case it is necessary not only to find out what they said, but also *what they were trying to say,* what the eternal Word of God was saying in them to all men everywhere. The wheat must be sifted from the chaff, the 'Word' taken from the worn-out wrappings. And then that Word' shall be made plain. All must be fitted to our modern thought. . . . What is warped and ill-balanced must be corrected; what was neglected must be added; what was soiled by the heat and dust of controversy must be polished until it is bright and clear again." (*The Living Church,* Feb. 11, 1933.) There is pure gold among all this dross — find it! But when we ask them for the Lydian stone which will infallibly show the gold, they tell us: There is no such thing. Dr. E. Lewis tells us: "What is of the *form* of revelation and what is of the *substance?* It may be that an infallibly exact criterion has not been given us." (*A Philosophy of the Christian Revelation,* p. 140.) Dr. L. Weigle just told us: "We do not know whether the words of the Bible given us are true or accurate, but there is a spirit in them that manifests an acceptable teaching." .The disturbed Christian asks Bishop D. Wilson to guide him in his search for the saving, divine truth and gets the answer: "Where nature ended and Inspiration began, it is not for man to say." (See W. Lee, *op. cit.*, p. 34.) The terrified Christian wants assurance as to whether every single word of John 3:16 is infallibly true — it is a matter of life and death to him — and Prof. R. F.

Grau advises him: "The boundaries between the divine and the human elements cannot be definitely fixed in a mechanical way. No one knows how much is divine, how much human." (See Pieper, *op. cit.*, I, p. 275.) We know the answer: every word is God's word. We need no Lydian stone where the Bible is concerned. It is all pure gold. All is well where Verbal Inspiration rules. But he is in a bad state whose spiritual advisers either tell him that there is no sure way of finding the priceless treasure of God's Word in this divine-human book or sell him divining rods — the Christian self-consciousness or "the spirit in the words" or "what is fitted to our modern thought" — which invariably lead him astray. "Of a truth," said Dr. Walther in the Lutherstunde, "it is not a small matter when a poor man is lying on his deathbed and seeks comfort in a passage of Scripture and the devil assaults him with the question: Yea, how do you know that God said that? May not the writer have misunderstood the Holy Spirit?" (See *Lehre und Wehre*, 1911, p. 155.)

Walther once more: "Dr. Luther writes in his *Large Confession* with reference to Zwingli's *alloeosis:* 'Beware, beware, I say, of the *alloeosis!* For it is the devil's mask.' . . . We must apply this to the so-called 'Gottmenschlichkeit der Schrift' (the divine-human nature of Scripture) as the term is used by modern-conservative theology: Beware, beware, I say, of this 'divine-human' Scripture! It is a devil's mask; for at last it manufactures such a Bible after which I certainly would not care to be a Bible Christian, namely, that the Bible should henceforth be no more than any other good book, a book which I would have to read with constant sharp discrimination in order not to be led into error. For if I believe this, that the Bible contains also errors, it is to me no longer a touchstone but itself stands in need of one. In a word, it is unspeakable what the devil seeks by this 'divine-human' Scripture. . . . Erbarme sich Gott seiner armen Christenheit in dieser letzten, betruebten und gefaehrlichen Zeit!" (*Lehre und Wehre*, 1886, p. 76.) The old evil Foe means deadly woe.

"Without a doubt," says Edwin Lewis, "our fathers came very close to Bibliolatry; they could make no distinction between the Word of God and the words of men by which that Word was given." (*The Faith We Declare*, p. 49.) We say: Blessed be our fathers, blessed be St. Paul, who taught us that every word of Scripture is the very word of God! That every word stands, now and forever, unbroken, unbreakable!

CHAPTER VI

Does Verbal Inspiration Imply an Atomistic Conception and Use of Scripture?

The moderns are bound to make the "sure Word" of Scripture (2 Pet. 1:19) unreliable. They have been telling the anxious Christian that the "mechanical, verbal theory" of inspiration is all wrong; that according to their dynamical canon the *words* in which the saving truth is revealed are purely human; that nobody knows whether the words of John 3:16 correctly express the divine thought. But they are not yet through with the dismayed Christian. Lest he still be disposed to base his trust on John 3:16 and similar passages of Holy Writ, they now tell him: Forget all about John 3:16; that is an individual statement and individual statements no longer count; it is foolishness to base doctrine and faith on particular passages.

DENOUNCING "ATOMISTIC VERBALISM"

That is the fifth objection of the moderns against Verbal Inspiration. They express their abhorrence of it in the word "atomistic." *The Luth. Church Quart.*, 1937, p. 195, declares: "It is, of course, no secret that Verbal Inspiration is not taught in some of the seminaries of the United Lutheran Church. . . . The purpose [of Professor Kretzmann's *The Foundations Must Stand*] of course is to prove that every word of the Scriptures was inspired directly and immediately. But by thus indiscriminately compiling all passages containing any reference to the word or the words of God and using them as proof texts for Verbal Inspiration, the real Lutheran meaning of the expression Word of God is obscured. What results is a legalistic and an atomistic conception of the Scriptures as the Word of God, far more congenial to Calvinism than to Lutheranism." *The Luth. Church Quart.*, 1939, p. 153, censures "the dogmatists and literalists" and commends those who "broke with the old atomistic method of proof texts." H. E. Fosdick: "Athanasius is typical of the general method of ancient interpretation. 'All parts of the Bible were equally good, in his judgment, as sources of proof texts.'. . . The new approach to the Bible gives us a comprehensive, inclusive view of the Scriptures and enables us to see them not piecemeal but as a whole. . . . It once more integrates the Scriptures, saves us from our piecemeal treatment of them, and restores to us the whole book seen in a unified development." (*The Modern Use of the Bible*, pp. 10, 27.) Atomistic — another one of these great swelling words which are designed to overawe the simple. It is the mark of scientific wisdom to take a comprehensive view of things, is it not? You would not want to study a writing in a piecemeal atomistic fashion, would you? [273]

Let us see, first, what exactly the moderns mean when they rail against the "atomistic method of proof texts" and, secondly, what this attitude towards the Bible involves.

Dr. J. Bodensieck: "May I mention another misuse of the Bible which the Church has often ignored and even condoned? I have in mind the indiscriminate use of Bible texts as proofs in the Catechism, or even in the science of dogmatics. Sometimes only a very superficial study of the text in its original setting in the Bible would have been sufficient to indicate that it was out of place in the Catechism or in the dogmatical discussion, where it was adduced as proof from Scripture. This use of the Bible has recently been branded as 'atomistic.' The Church should avoid every semblance of such abuse. . . . The 'atomistic' practice gives a distorted picture of the Bible and helps to destroy the proper understanding and appreciation of the Bible." (*The Modern Use of the Bible,* in *The Augsburg Sunday School Teacher,* July, 1938, p. 388 ff.)[274] Insisting that inspiration is not a piecemeal affair,

---

273) The following phrases will show the meaning of our term: "atomistic and fragmentary"; "life is not atomistic, it is corporate." *The Luth. Church. Quart.,* 1939, p. 153, says that the old atomistic method of proof texts is out of harmony with "the *organic* character of the Scriptures." H. F. Rall has the phrase "organicistic or corporate as against atomistic or individualistic." (*A Faith for Today,* p. 127.) The distinction between atomistic and corporate is, of course, good and necessary. Whether the moderns make the right use of this distinction in the matter before us remains to be seen.

274) The following excerpts from the article will show the writer's position with regard to Verbal Inspiration. "We may indeed find it very difficult to free ourselves from this misuse of the Bible as long as we cling to a very mechanical conception of inspiration. If the Bible, as we have it, is the dictation of the Holy Spirit down to the last letter, we will have to deny the existence in the Bible of various levels of religious understanding and spiritual depth. . . . Too often the Bible is reduced to the level of a well-stocked arsenal from which authoritative proof texts may be drawn almost at random. Instead of enlightening the mind and providing it with some understanding of the Bible, this practice actually obscures it by making it appear that every portion of the Book is authoritative doctrine — perhaps an extremist exegesis of 2 Tim. 3:16 f. contributed to this error. The Bible is no collection of doctrinal statements, but a book of life. . . . Those who followed them" [the Protestant fathers] "codified and systematized their thoughts and, in so doing, introduced the deplorable confusion of *contents* and *form* and ascribed to each the same divine authority. But if the same unfailing authority is ascribed to all the 'human' elements in the Bible (*e. g.,* categories of thought, the picture of the universe, even the fundamental ideas of ethical living) as to the unquestionably divine truths, then conflicts are inevitable and doubts must arise. . . . This, in my judgment, is the one valuable contribution in Fosdick's book *The Modern Use of the Bible, viz.,* his distinction between the Bible's central messages and their temporary expressions."

the Bible being inspired "as a whole," not in its statements on "details," J. M. Gibson has this to say to the "proof-texters": "A 'text' from one book was exactly the same as a 'text' from another. It could be cut out from its context and set alongside of a number of others cut out in the same way, to be used as 'proofs' of some controverted doctrine. For all the use men's names were, they might have been blotted out and the word 'God' put in instead. . . . The erroneous impression conveyed by the words is due to the old practice, so fruitful in error, of treating the Bible as a mere collection of texts, anyone of which may be taken by itself and treated as if it stood alone." (*The Inspiration and Authority of Holy Scripture,* pp. 74, 121, 222, 234.) V. Ferm, reading the requiem on Verbal Inspiration: "A literally infallible Bible, an assumption implied throughout the Lutheran symbols, verbally inspired, is a view that has passed by the board for good," declares: "Passages may no longer be wrested from their context and indiscriminately ascribed to 'the word of the Lord.' " (*What Is Lutheranism?* pp. 281 f.); and H. Wheeler Robinson makes the same indictment: "The Protestant appeal to the Scriptures as a text-book of doctrine did frequent violence to exegesis, and much of it reads strangely enough to us today." (*The Chr. Experience of the Holy Spirit,* p. 173.) The moderns take pleasure in reciting cases of such strange exegesis. Georgia Harkness: "As for the Bible, most people, at least most people sufficiently informed to be ministers of the Gospel, recognize the dangers inherent in the proof-text method. It is a truism that one can prove anything one likes from the Bible. In the last Presidential election, there was plastered in every New York subway train as a party slogan the affirmation, 'Ye shall know the truth, and the truth shall make you free.' " (*The Faith by Which the Church Lives,* p. 56.) O. L. Joseph: "Is not the practice of quoting texts at random, without regard to their context, largely responsible for many vagaries of the religious imagination, such as Christian Science, Theosophy, Spiritualism? It is worth recalling that the dogma of total depravity taught by St. Augustine was based upon five proof texts, three of which were mistranslations." (*Ringing Realities,* p. 218.) We read in the *Watchman-Examiner* of Dec. 28, 1941: "Communicants of the Apostolic Faith Church of Pittsburgh who were also members of the United Mine Workers were hard put to it, with their literalistic dependence upon the exact words of the English Bible, to determine their duty under the captive mines strike order. Surely enough, the strike was called by their 'higher-up' bosses, and they must be 'subject to the higher powers' (Rom. 13:1). . . . In like manner, the proof-text method of interpreting the Bible has caused great numbers of earnest, sincere people to do all sorts of absurd things." And Prof. J. C. W. Volck (Dorpat) went to the trouble of illustrating the absurdity of the atomistic proof-text method by quoting one half of Ps. 14:1: "There is no God." (See *Proc. Syn. Conf.*, 1886, p. 24.) — And that, say the moderns, is what we mean when we denounce the atomistic proof-text method: it is not permissible to quote texts at random and tear them out of their context.

There is something wrong here. There is nothing wrong about denouncing the *indiscriminate* use of proof texts. But a wrong is committed when this denunciation is coupled with the denunciation of Verbal Inspiration. The moderns have the habit of doing that. J. S. Whale fulminates thus: "The modern man is not impressed by the mere citation of texts; he rightly wants to understand them in their context. His very certainty that the Scriptures are the fount of divine wisdom . . . has set him free from the bondage of the letter, the prison house of verbal infallibility. . . . The Bible is abused when it is used merely as an armory of proof texts for defending some theological scheme (a game at which more than one can play, notoriously enough). We use the Bible rightly only when, to quote Luther, we see that it is the cradle wherein Christ is laid; that is, when we worship the Holy Child and not His crib." (*The Chr. Answer to the Problem of Evil*, p. 77.) The modern man is right in demanding that the text be quoted in its context. But why should Dr. Whale inveigh in this connection against the "prison house of verbal infallibility"? Note, too, that the *Luth. Church Quart.*, in denouncing the indiscriminate compiling of "proof texts," informs us that "Verbal Inspiration is not taught in some of the seminaries of the U. L. C." Note that the *Augsburg Sunday School Teacher* article, while castigating "the indiscriminate use of Bible texts as proofs," disavows "the mechanical conception of inspiration," "the dictation of the Holy Spirit *down to the last letter*," and speaks of the " 'human' elements in the Bible," mistaken notions, etc. Note that Gibson, who will not have "a text cut from its context," takes a fling at the verbal-inspirationists who declare that *God is the real author of these books*. There is something wrong here. Verbal Inspiration has nothing to do with the illicit quoting of proof texts. The verbal-inspirationists insist as strongly as the most liberal modern that when a text is quoted as a proof the literal sense of the text, the scope, and the context must be scrupulously observed. If Augustine based the dogma of total depravity on two proof texts, he won his case; if he based it in three instances on mistranslations, he did not do that because he believed in Verbal Inspiration. There is nothing in the doctrine of Verbal Inspiration that justifies, or even lends itself to, the misuse of the proof-text method. To be sure, verbal-inspirationists occasionally quote a text wrongly. But the same can be said of the anti-verbal-inspirationists. We can easily match every *lapsus* committed in this field by verbal-inspirationists with one committed by the dynamic-inspirationists and the non-inspirationists.[275] So you can hardly make Verbal Inspiration responsible for the use of misquotations. And when you produce your lists of misquotations for the purpose of discrediting Verbal Inspiration, you are aiming your blows at a straw man.

DENYING THE INSPIRATION OF THE WORDS OF SCRIPTURE

But in denouncing the "old atomistic method of proof texts" the moderns whom we have quoted and shall quote do not really mean the illicit use of proof texts. If they meant that, there would be no quarrel between us and them. Here we are one with them.[276] But what the moderns do not like and do not want is any and every use of proof texts for the establishment of doctrine. It will not be hard to establish that point. Let them tell us what they think, not of the illicit use of proof texts, but of their use in general.

---

275) Gibson proves his idea that the texts of Scripture are not binding with the proof text: "The letter killeth, but the spirit giveth life." (*Op. cit.*, p. 235.) N. R. Best proves that Scripture is subject to reason with the proof text Is. 1:18. (*Inspiration*, p. 118.) Dr. H. C. Alleman (*Luth. Church Quart.*, 1940, p. 356) proves that Christ "deliberately breaks Scripture" by quoting Matt. 5:38f., and H. F. Rall quotes the same text to prove that "you cannot accept the supremacy of Christ and hold to the infallibility of the Bible." (*Op. cit.*, p. 224.) Fosdick cites as proof text for his dogma that "at the beginning Hebrew religion had no hope of immortality" Eccl. 9:4-6 and 3:19. (*Op. cit.*, p. 25.) R. F. Horton proves that "the epistle of James disclaims infallibility "with the proof text: "In many things we offend all," Jas. 3:2. (*Revelation and the Bible*, p. 349.) H. W. Robinson proves that the prophets had "beneficent illusions" by quoting Jer. 20:7: "O Lord, Thou hast deceived me, and I was deceived." (*Op. cit.*, p. 174.) We have seen how the proof text 2 Tim. 3:16 fares at the hands of the moderns. (See again what has been said under No. 21, p. 211 ff.) Sherwood Eddy: "Can we claim that this (the Virgin Birth) is a foremost fundamental if, as we have seen, it has never been mentioned by Jesus or Paul, or in the first or last Gospel?" (See *The Presbyterian*, Dec. 22, 1927.) There are several queer things in this item. — Yes, to employ Whale's phraseology, the moderns, too, can play at the game of wrong proof-texting, and they are quite adept at it.

276) Cutting a text out of its context certainly may be called an atomistic use of Scripture. Verbal-inspirationists so use the term. Dr. Reu writes: "Even the formation of the word was taught by the Spirit. . . . So 1 Cor. 2:13, while not being the only proof passage for the *suggestio verbi*, is nevertheless an important statement concerning the question in hand. . . . We do not see any reason why we should eliminate 1 Cor. 2:13 from our discussion. Still less do we stoop to what some call an 'atomistic use of Scripture' when we refer to this passage, because the whole context speaks exactly of the same matter with which we are dealing here." (*Kirchl. Zeitschrift*, July, 1939, p. 421.) The trouble is, however, that with our moderns the "atomistic use of Scripture" means much more than this.

Schleiermacher, the Father of modern Protestant Theology, declared: "Quoting individual Bible passages in dogmatics is a most precarious business and cannot at all serve the purpose." (*Glaubenslehre*, I, § 30.) Notice that there is here no restriction. Not only the wresting of the passage out of its context is bad business; quoting individual passages is bad business. That has become an article of faith with the moderns. G. T. Ladd: "Especially was *suggestion of the words* held to be necessary to the inspiration of the Bible. . . . Especially strong and dominating was the tendency among those who held this dogma to regard the entire Bible as a kind of theological parade ground for proof texts. It was the *number* of such proof texts which was chiefly regarded." (*What Is the Bible?* P. 56 f.) *The Christian Century*, March 2, 1938: "No issue between the churches can now be settled by the quotation of a Biblical text, as our fathers used to assume. No issue will be settled by reference to an authoritarian standard, whether *doctrinal*" (our italics) "or ecclesiastical." They express their dissatisfaction with the fathers' way in the word "proof-texting." *The Chr. Century*, Feb. 22, 1939, praises "the inexhaustible resources of beauty and grandeur" in the Bible, but hastens to add: "This does not mean that we shall be saved by a return to proof-texting. Perish the thought!" The fathers are to be pitied, for, says H. F. Rall, "revelation meant to them so many doctrines or commandments handed down or so many words dictated to a writer. . . . When Paul wrote to his little churches here and there, he surely had not the faintest idea that centuries later theologians would be building up their theories on this phrase or that sentence in his letters." (*Op. cit.*, p. 228 f.) The poor fathers! "Luther's slavish dependence on proof texts" is the phrase used by G. Aulen; he adds the further statement: "Biblicism, the application of the theory of verbal inspiration, has laid a heavy hand on Christian theology." (*Das christliche Gottesbild*, p. 251.) No slavish dependence on proof texts for us, the children of the Reformation, declared the theologians gathered at Eisenach in 1917 to celebrate the four-hundredth anniversary of the Reformation. "Restricted, yet free! Restricted to the revelation within the Scriptures as a whole; restricted to the Christ of God whom the Scriptures urge. But free over against particular matters, free to form our opinion on the human garments in which the divine glory of the Scriptures is masked. . . . *One* service the Scriptures will, of course, no longer be able to render: they cannot by particular statements authenticate particular parts of the Confessions." And "this means," says the *Theol. Mthly.*, V, p. 7, "that under the operation of the slogan 'Restricted, yet free!' such things as proof texts cease to exist." And so it goes on and on. It seems impossible for a modern to write a book or an article on Inspiration without taking occasion to utter his disgust with the old atomistic proof-text method. M. Dods: "The Bible has so persistently been used as a textbook to prove dogma that this came to be considered its main use. . . . Each of its utterances, no matter in what department of truth, was supposed to be final and authoritative. . . . But the Bible must not be thought of as a collection of truths formulated in propositions which God from time to time whispered in the ear to be communicated to the world as the unchanging formulas of thought and life for all time." (*The Bible, Its Origin and Nature,* pp. 66, 97.) E. E. Flack: "No fundamental doctrine rests on a single isolated passage. Nor may several passages strung together in proof-text fashion fix faith. It requires the analogy of Scripture, the whole Scripture corroborating and authenticating its own testimony in the life of the true Church, to establish the truth as it is in Christ Jesus." (*The Lutheran,* Oct. 1, 1936.) W. A. Brown: "What we need in such a textbook is a compendium of simple principles capable of indefinite application and therefore needing continual reinterpretation in the light of expanding experience. We have seen that the Bible lends itself to such uses in a pre-eminent degree. But that is not the way those who are responsible for teaching the Bible have used it. Either (like the theologians) they have made it a dogmatic textbook, searching its pages for proof texts which could be made a test of orthodoxy or. . . ." (*A Creed for Free Men,* p. 230.) Sherwood Eddy expresses the idea of the moderns exactly when he rails at "a literal, orthodox Christianity based on an inerrant, verbally inspired, infallible Book" and declares: "The Bible is not intended as a storehouse of authoritative proof texts or pious mottoes, not as a shibboleth or a fetish or mystic book to be read for merit. It is not a mechanical, external authority to be blindly obeyed." (See *The Presbyterian,* Dec. 22, 1927.) The moderns will not own Luther in his slavish dependence on proof texts as their spiritual father. Let them, then, own themselves as children of the vulgar rationalists, one of whom, Heinrich Stephani, was not ashamed to lay down these principles in his *Winke zur Vervollkommnung des Konfirmandenunterrichts:* "Only that may be taught which Jesus and His apostles would teach if they lived today. . . . Bible passages must not be used as proof texts." (See *Kirchl. Zeitschr.,* 1939, p. 137.) [277]

---

277) We submit a few more pronouncements dictated by the proof-text-method phobia. We do not like to clutter up our pages with such material, but those who still think that, when the moderns reject the proof-text method, they have only the illicit use of proof texts in mind can use it. C. H. Dodd: "The method of reading the Pauline epistles as a set of documentary proofs for a fixed scheme of theology has resulted in giving a quite erroneous idea of Paul's real thought and,

The moderns frown upon and denounce the use of proof texts for the establishing of the Christian doctrine. To illustrate, what does the Bible teach on the Atonement? The proof texts will not help you to find that out, says E. Grubb; the teaching of the Bible on this point is hidden somewhere else. "An actual illustration of the appeal to the authority of the Bible may help in making clear what is meant. Suppose we are in doubt about the doctrine of Atonement and we wish to know, either for ourselves or for meeting the doubts of others, what the Bible teaches on the subject. The older method was to quote certain texts from the New Testament, such as those that refer to 'propitiation' and 'the blood of Christ,' and then to show that the doctrine of a blood sacrifice for sin, satisfying the wrath of God, ran through the whole of the Old Testament." That is all wrong. You must first establish

---

still more, in effectually concealing Paul the man behind a theological lay figure." (*The Authority of the Bible*, p. 12.) H. W. Robinson: "The revelation must be sought in that experience in its entirety rather than in particular 'texts' taken from it. . . . The Bible has often been degraded to the level of the *sortes Virgilianae*, a verbal oracle mechanically used." (*Op. cit.*, pp. 170, 175.) Gibson's statement on "treating the Bible as a mere collection of texts" goes on to say: "Some people, indeed, think that it is an end of all controversy to say, 'There it is in black and white.'" G. Wehrung: "Der evangelische Schriftgebrauch ist pneumatischer Art; er sucht nicht Lehrformeln oder Beweisstellen, sondern Leben weckende Zeugnisse; er sucht in und hinter diesen mannigfachen Christusbekenntnissen die innere Einheit, das eine Evangelium, das eine Gotteswort in den vielen Worten." (*Geschichte und Glaube*, p. 306.) The *Living Church*, March 9, 1938: "The Report of the Commission on Christian Doctrine states that 'stages of Biblical revelation are to be judged in relation to its historical climax,' the standard being 'the mind of Christ as unfolded in the experience of the Church.' The significance of this section of the report lies chiefly in its bearing upon homiletics. As 'the method of direct appeal to isolated texts' is so evidently liable to error, it is to be expected that preaching from isolated texts will gradually give place to genuine expository preaching in which the Word of God *contained*" (italics in original) "in the Scripture will be sought, studied in all the light that modern scholarship affords, and then applied to problems of the modern world." The sentence introducing this paragraph reads: "In the report of the Anglican Commission, so-called Fundamentalism receives its *coup de grace*. Explicitly and in forceful terms the Commission states its conviction that 'the tradition of the inerrancy of the Bible cannot be maintained in the light of the knowledge now at our disposal." The *Luth. Church Quart.*, 1939, p. 33 ff., has this to say on our subject: "There is a spirit of legalism that pervades many of the ranks of Midwestern Lutherans, a kind of approach to the truth of God which insists on 'book, chapter, and verse' for all the 'eye-blinks' of life and must be undergirded by the authority of print on paper for every conscious breath in order to be assured of full salvation. In its last analysis this resolves itself into a conception of the Holy Scriptures as a mechanical work of the Holy Spirit, inerrant in every word and detail in its original form." The *Lutheran* reprinted this Feb. 8, 1939. Prof. R. F. Grau: "Die Heilige Schrift ist uns nicht mehr ein grosser vom Himmel herab gesandter Gesetzeskodex mit seinen einzelnen Paragraphen, Beweisstellen" (proof texts) "genannt." (See Baier-Walther, *Compendium*, I, p. 102.)

"what are the different strains of teaching which the Bible contains" and then find out how much of this teaching "answers the deepest demands of our own reason and conscience. . . . The indiscriminate use of Scripture as a single source of equal value, as a quarry from every part of which stones may be indifferently collected to build up the temple of constructive dogmatics, will, it is hoped, soon pass away never to return." (*The Bible, Its Nature and Inspiration*, p. 240 ff.) May we use proof texts to prove the deity of Jesus? O. J. Baab tells us: "The Gospel of Matthew . . . made a liberal use of quotations from the Old Testament. These are *extracted from their context*" (our italics) "and made to fit the story of Jesus." Again: "Did Jesus believe that He was the Son of God? We have no uncontaminated first-hand reports of his utterances on the subject of God." "Current concepts as to deity and ideas of the supernatural definitely influenced the writers of the New Testament in their selection and interpretation of available material." So we cannot rely on these particular statements of the holy writers; their sense must be established by other considerations. Dr. Baab is right in concluding: "No wonder the literalistic interpreters of the Bible are stirred to indignant and vehement protest." (*Jesus Christ Our Lord*, pp. 11, 13, 38.) What about the doctrine of the Virgin Birth? E. Brunner: "In earlier days this discussion" (of the theory of the Virgin Birth) "used to be cut short by saying briefly, 'It is written'; that is, with the aid of the doctrine of Verbal Inspiration. Today we can no longer do this, even if we would. There are many indications that, even in this respect, even these early passages of Matthew and Luke once read very differently. Those arguments, however, are not adduced here in order to attack the doctrine itself, for this would be wholly out of keeping with the spirit of the rest of this book. All that is intended here is to show once more that the process of producing arguments and proofs based on Scripture, which is also untenable on general grounds, is here especially unfortunate." (*The Mediator*, p. 323 f.) Are there any *dicta probantia*, any *sedes doctrinae*, for the doctrine of the Church? No, indeed, says the *Luth. Church Quart.*, 1940, p. 20: "The doctrine of the Church does not rest on specific proof texts, but on the entire Biblical message, the center of which is God's forgiving grace. It rests on the Bible understood and interpreted as an organic unity having its center in the cross, or in justification by faith, or in grace." An introductory statement was: "An atomistic or legalistic attitude results in trying to make specific New Testament words and sayings binding as external forms on the Church." What do the moderns think of the theologian who bases his eschatological teaching on the pertinent Bible texts? F. Holmstroem calls him a slovenly, piddling theologian, calls his exegesis "schlendrianmaessige biblizistische Reproduktion." He reads the proof-text theologian 'this lesson: "Eine theologisch haltbare Eschatologie muss vielmehr ihre Aussagen organisch aus dem lebendigen Zentrum der biblischen Offenbarung, der 'Christustatsache,' herleiten." (*Das Eschatologische Denken der Gegenwart*, p. 312.) Should we base our teaching on the sin against the Holy Ghost on specific passages, such as Matt. 12:31, 32; Heb. 6:1-8 and 10:26? R. F. Horton examines these passages and ends up with the monstrous proposition: "Here, then, is a case in which, so far from believing that a doctrine must be a divine revelation because it occurs in the New Testament, we are forced to the opinion that, *if* it occurs in the New Testament, it is not a revelation, but merely a view of the author's, imperfect and limited as the judgments of even inspired men are apt on occasion to be. In other words, the revelation of God as a whole, the revelation in its crowned completeness, must be used as a criterion for determining the value of individual passages in the Scriptures; it can never be admitted that a single passage or even a small group of passages, teaching a special doctrine, may override the truth in its entirety when its full development is reached." (*Revelation and the Bible*, p. 337 f.)

We are at present particularly interested in the doctrine of inspiration. May we use proof texts for this all-important doctrine? *The Luth. Church Quart.* chides us for doing this: using proof texts to establish Verbal Inspiration results in a legalistic and an atomistic conception of the Scriptures, far more congenial to Calvinism than to Lutheranism. (See above.) "Luthardt simply ignores 2 Tim. 3:16, when he treats of the doctrine of inspiration and insists: 'Das Selbstzeugnis der Schrift beruht nicht sowohl *auf einzelnen Stellen der Schrift*, sondern auf der Schrift selbst, in dem Schriftganzen, und da ist es Aufgabe der Schriftwissenschaft, zu zeigen, in welchem Sinn man sie inspiriert nennen koenne.' It follows that the plowman or factory hand cannot know whether Scripture has been given by divine inspiration, and when he confronts Luthardt with the Scripture: 'All Scripture is given by inspiration of God' and says, 'Here it is written,' Luthardt answers: Brother, you cannot say that; it is the whole of Scripture that decides the matter; you must not operate with these individual passages." (Dr. Walther; see *Lehre und Wehre*, 1911, p. 151.)

The moderns abhor the proof-text method and stigmatize it as atomistic. It is *not* the illicit use of proof texts which they have in mind when they use this word. Sometimes they mention and stress the illicit method, but before long they reveal that it is the proof-text method in general which they abhor. The *Luth. Church*

Quart., 1940, p. 20, comes right into the open and declares that the use of specific proof texts to establish doctrines reveals an atomistic attitude. (See above.) The *Luth. Church Quart.,* 1937, p. 279, is equally clear on this point: "The Bible must never be thought of apart from the living, unitary Word and become a codex. Otherwise we have Bibliolatry and substitute a book for the creative Word. . . . The Fundamentalists make the Bible literalistic and legalistic in a Calvinistic manner, and forget that the letter killeth but the Spirit maketh alive. Out of the legalistic attitude toward the Word of God of the Bible has grown an atomistic conception of the Word, which substitutes words for the Word. The Word is not built up out of inspired words like atoms underlying the universe." [278] And the others of the moderns who do indeed specify the *"indiscriminate* use of Bible texts" in condemning the *"atomistic"* use of Scripture have more in mind than that. Else they would not go on to declare as the *Augsburg S. S. Teacher* article does, that not everything in the Bible is authoritative doctrine, that everything is not of the same divine authority, that there are "human" elements — errors — in the Bible,.that the Holy Ghost did not dictate everything *"down to the last letter."* Notice, too, how they couple "legalistic" with "atomistic." "The indiscriminate use of proof texts" implies "a legalistic and an atomistic conception of the Scriptures" — there is not much sense in calling the illicit use of proof texts legalistic. Legalistic, in the language of the moderns, means that the words are binding. Our *Luth. Church Quart.* article did not mean the *"indiscriminate"* but *all* use of proof texts. And so the phrase "the old atomistic method of proof texts" (see above) means that the method of using proof texts at all is atomistic. The word *atomistic* is there not used restrictively but descriptively. Or will the writer say that, when the fathers used proof texts, they regularly and habitually ignored the literal sense, the scope, and the context? [279] No, the fathers made habitual use of the *legitimate* proof-text method, based the doctrine on the *dicta probantia,* the *sedes doctrinae,* and that is what our moderns stigmatize as the old atomistic method. ´

278) Some more statements in this article by Dr. J. A. W. Haas will prove informative: "The older theory made men mere passive receivers of the Word. Their minds were pictured as blank slates on which the Spirit of the Word wrote his messages. . . . The atomistic verbalists err in not valuing the living logic of language. . . . The term 'words' (in 1 Cor. 2:13) is taken to mean every single word down to the minutest 'and.' . . . Out of the minute verbalistic conception grows the problem of the infallibility of the Word. Extreme verbalism demands the completeness of the text in every detail. It posits an original perfect text for all the books of. the Bible. . . . It is a mere fiction to uphold an infallibility in every statement and not merely in the essentials of faith."

279) Further on in this article (*Luth. Church Quart.,* 1939, p. 153 ff.) we read: "It must be maintained in the light of the recent history of

EMASCULATING THE WORDS OF SCRIPTURE BY MEANS OF THE "BROADER CONTEXT"

And they feel perfectly justified in calling that atomistic. We agreed with them that we would call that an atomistic use of Scripture when a text is quoted out of its context and in a sense not intended by the author. And that, say the moderns, precisely that, lies at the bottom of our argument against the proof-text method. You verbalists are content to quote isolated passages. You fail to take the wider context into consideration. You verbalists may have the literal sense on your side, but insisting on the literal sense, you become literalists. You fail to see the broader sense with which the "Word of God" contained in Scripture or the "whole of Scripture" or this or that or the other thing invests this text.

Let Professor Volck tell us something about this broader context. "Um die Sonderung des Gebietes des Untrueglichen von dem-jenigen, wo Irrtum moeglich ist, und weiter — die Scheidung vom Wesentlichen und Unwesentlichen in der Bibel vollziehen zu koennen, muss der Ausleger *alles einzelne* ihres Inhalts beurteilen nach seinem *Verhaeltnis zu dem Heil*, welches in der von ihr be-richteten Geschichte verwirklicht vorliegt. Er muss zusehen, *ob* und *in welchem* Zusammenhang es mit demselben steht." It is not sufficient to consider what common hermeneutics calls the context. You must study the relation of the individual passage to, and con-nection with, the whole history of salvation, before you can deter-mine whether the passage is true or erroneous. Dr. A. L. Graebner comments: "Volck need not tell us that you must not wrest a text out of its connection. We, too, know that you must always consider the context. But Volck says: Even if I perfectly understand the words of a passage in its connection and context, I know nothing at all about the matter; for I will still have to find out what the passage means in its relation to the whole of Scripture." (See *Proc. Syn. Conf.*, 1886, p. 23 f.) The hermeneutics of the moderns re-quires the consideration of the *broader context*. Neglect that, and your exegesis becomes atomistic.

What is this broader context? Some of the moderns make it extremely broad. They insist that the individual passages must be viewed in the light of present-day science. All human knowledge

---

theology that the day of compartmentalizing and isolating theology from the rest of human thinking and knowing has long since passed. . . . The business of theology has always been to define what is of faith and what is contrary to faith. But such definitions cannot come to rest in isolation from the total existing body of human knowledge. . . . The *Loci* of the Jena theologian [Gerhard] necessarily retained in many parts the serious limitations of a prescientific heritage both in method and conclusions." More on this anon.

forms an organic whole, and statements of the Bible must not be put in opposition to it. Condemning "the old atomistic method of proof texts," the *Luth. Church Quart.* (1939, p. 156) inveighs against "compartmentalizing and isolating theology from the rest of human thinking and knowing." The definitions of theology must not "come to rest in isolation from the total existing body of human knowledge." Would that mean that a specific text could no longer be used as a proof text since "science" has shown it to be in error? Most assuredly. The Anglican Commission has proclaimed that "the tradition of the inerrancy of the Bible cannot be maintained in the light of the knowledge now at our disposal." They tell the Bible-Christian: Do not be atomistic! Bring your Bible text into harmony with the whole of human knowledge by stripping it of its literal sense and finding the profounder, the prophetic sense intended. The story of the Creation and of the Fall are not to be taken literally; Jonah was not literally swallowed by the great fish; let the theologian find out for you what deeper truths are here hidden. "They are, says *Christendom*, I, p. 492, "poetic expressions of some profounder or larger truth than that which their formulators realized." And that applies to the teachings of the Bible in general. H. E. Fosdick: "It is impossible that a book written two or three thousand years ago should be used in the twentieth century A. D. without having some of its forms of thoughts and speech translated into modern categories." (*Op. cit.,* p. 885.) To retain the literal sense of the teaching concerning resurrection and the deity of Christ would be a piecemeal, atomistic treatment of these proof texts. Consider the wider context furnished by the growth of human knowledge that has set in since the Bible days.

One of the first rules inculcated by the anti-atomistic hermeneutics is: Give up your belief in the inerrancy of the Bible. C. H. Dodd, who condemns "the method of reading the Pauline epistles as a set of documentary proofs," goes on to say: "When the reader has discovered what the writer actually said and meant, he wants to ask further, Is this what I am to believe about God? Is it *true?* Probably no one who reads this book will think that this question has the self-evident answer, Of course it is true, *because* it is in the Bible." (*Op. cit.,* p. 297. — Italics in original.) The *Augsburg S. S. Teacher* article, which inveighs against the atomistic use of the Bible, speaks of the "human" elements, the erroneous statements, in the Bible and calls Fosdick's statement concerning the "temporary expressions" and "modern categories" a "valuable contribution." Dr. Haas, who does not like the "atomistic verbalists," insists that the theologians must no longer uphold the absolute infallibiliy of the Bible, its "infallibility in every statement." That is the reason why the Eisenach Convention rejected the *indiscriminate* use of proof texts: some of them may belong to "the human garments"; you cannot take them at their face value; you must use discrimination. And the Anglican Commission, convinced of the errancy of the Bible, tells the preachers that they must not use a proof text till science, etc., has proved that it is true.

That is rather crude, to let science and the ideology of modernism, etc., shed light on the individual passages. But the moderns have, in addition, something more spiritual to appeal to. That is the "spirit." Georgia Harkness, who recognizes "the dangers inherent in the proof-text method," finds her "authority not in the letter but in the Spirit." The text must not be taken literally. For that she is fighting, and she deplores the fact "that the battle is not yet won. Like the poor, literalism is always with us" (*op. cit.*, p. 57 f.). Dr. Haas complains that these "atomistic verbalists," these "Fundamentalists, make the Bible literalistic and legalistic in a Calvinistic manner and forget that the letter killeth but the Spirit maketh alive" (*loc. cit.*). V. Ferm, who will "no longer have passages wrested from their context," declares: "The authority of the Sacred Writings is no longer found in 'the letter' and sustained by some artificial theory of divine inspiration, but in the appeal of its spiritual content." (*Op. cit.*, p. 279.) That is pretty plain language. Passages must not be wrested from their context, the context in the old narrow sense; but neither must they be wrested from their true setting, taken out of their spiritual setting. It is exactly what the old Rationalists and their children, the Unitarians, contend for, exactly what the Unitarian W. E. Channing contends for: "We feel it our bounden duty to exercise our reason upon the Bible perpetually, to compare, to infer, to *look beyond the letter to the spirit . . .;* and, in general, to make use of what is known for explaining what is difficult, and for discovering new truths." (*Works of W. E. C.*, p. 368.) Ferm may have a different idea of what the "spirit" as opposed to the "letter" is than Channing has — none of them has ever told us exactly what this "spirit" is — but all of these men are agreed that you cannot use a proof text till its real meaning has been established, not from what the words in themselves say, but from what the "spirit" says they mean, or from what "the mind of Christ" reveals (Anglican Commission).

More definite information about this context in the wider sense. It is the "Word of God" that determines which parts of Scripture are true or what value they have. Scripture itself is not the Word of God. The Word of God is *contained* in Scripture, and everything else therein must be brought into harmony with this Word. The Anglican Commission warns against "preaching from isolated texts" and instructs the preachers first to seek and study "the

Word of God *contained* in the Scriptures," then study this Word of God *"in all the light that modern scholarship affords"* (our italics), and then see what they can do with a given text. The *Luth. Church Quart.*, 1935, pp. 258, 260, 264, tells us something about the nature of this Word of God and its relation to individual passages. "An individual brooding upon some condition of life, meditating upon some truth, communing with that beyond himself to which he gave the name God, and setting what he saw in life into the light of what he perceived through his spiritual insight, became convinced of a great truth. He felt that the truth thus communicated was the will of God for him for a people. 'The word of God came to him.' It was the word of God in the soul of a man. . . . Seekers for authority in Scripture cannot therefore find it in isolated portions and texts of the Bible, a procedure often followed in the effort to prove certain teachings and doctrines. The idea of verbal inspiration and the practice of literal interpretation may destroy the reality of the Bible's message. Its authority is not to be identified with the form of the language which announces the truth of God, but must be found in the light of the experience through which the word of God came to the soul of a man. . . . The teacher of religion speaks with confidence not because he quotes a Scripture but because the word of God has found him." The reality, the value, of a given text does not lie in the words of the text — a literal interpretation may destroy its value — but in its relation to the "Word of God." Dr. Haas, we heard, applies the same hermeneutics. "The Bible and its books are the depository and record of the Living Word. It must never be thought of apart from the living, unitary Word, and become a codex. Otherwise we have Bibliolatry and substitute a book for the creative Word. . . . The Word is not built up out of inspired words." Is John 3:16 inspired? That depends. First place it in the light of "the Word," and it may become a good proof text. Proof texts in themselves cannot prove a doctrine, said Dr. E. E. Flack. "No fundamental doctrine rests on a single isolated passage. Nor may several passages strung together in proof-text fashion fix faith." Then what proves the truth and value of a doctrine? Dr. Flack continues: "The standard by which all dogmas and teachers are to be judged is *not the Scriptures standing alone, but the Word of God* attested and authenticated in the Spirit-filled life of the early Church and projected through the centuries from faith to faith in the corporate mind of the true Church." (*Loc. cit.*) And Professor Wehrung told us that you must go back of the Biblical statements concerning Christ in order to find the "one Word of God in the many words"; standing alone, they are only words. — In a later section we shall further examine this hazy concept "Word of God" and the evil use to which the moderns put it.

OPERATING WITH THE MYSTERIOUS SCHRIFTGANZE

The method in greatest favor with the moderns, taking the place of the proof-text method that has been thrown to the moles and the bats, is to operate with the *Schriftganze*. The whole of Scripture, Scripture in its entirety, is the great regulative of the individual passages. It was Schleiermacher who got modern theology to substitute for the proof-text method ("quoting individual Bible passages in dogmatics is a most precarious business") the *Schriftganze* method; the doctrine must be based on "Scripture in its entirety," on "the organic whole of Scripture." "Practically all chief representatives of modern theology," says Pieper (*Chr. Dog., I,* p. 243), "from the extreme left to the extreme right wing, have adopted this method. Ihmels has it; Hofmann had it." Hofmann: "Nicht auf einzelne gottgewirkte Aussprueche oder Buecher in der Schrift beziehen sich Jesus und seine Apostel, sondern auf *die Schrift.* . . . Also die *Gesamtheit* der Schrift ist das einige Wort Gottes fuer seine Gemeinde. *Als Ganzes ist sie es,* und will nichts in ihr unterschieden sein, was nicht dafuer gaelte, und nichts dafuer gelten, was sich ausser ihr faende." (See *Lehre und Wehre,* 1875, p. 323.) We cannot quite understand the last sentence. It seems to make everything in Scripture God's Word, but that would be in contradiction to the general statement, which is very clear, that Scripture in its totality is God's Word, not in its individual statements, and that, like Jesus and His apostles, we must not operate with particular statements in Scripture.[280] Dr. J. Aberly makes the unassailable statement: "We need the whole Scriptures to give us the whole truth regarding God, man, and salvation," but he continues: "This attitude that we need the total view of Scriptural teaching rather than the fragmentary quotations of isolated passages, and that in this total view we must have the Spirit of Jesus to differentiate between what is temporary and what is permanent, this attitude will be found to be that of the New Testament writers and of Jesus Himself toward that unique revelation of God which we have in the Old Testament." (*The Luth. Church Quart.,* 1935, p. 118.) We need not point out that Jesus and the apostles actually did operate with "fragmentary quotations of isolated passages." What we

---

280) "*Gottgewirkte* Aussprueche" — that is a queer phrase. We could not use it. But Hofmann means exactly what the phrase states. He does not believe in verbal inspiration. He teaches that the prophets and apostles spoke and wrote only under a special influence of the Spirit. Kliefoth points that out and declares: "Von einer Eingebung des Inhalts der Heiligen Schrift durch den Geist Gottes ist keine Rede. . . . Hofmann kommt schliesslich doch zu einer Anschauung von der Heiligen Schrift, die sich im wesentlichen von der rationalistischen nicht unterscheidet." (See *Lehre und Wehre, loc. cit.*)

want to point out is that according to the theory of "Scripture as a whole" we need the Holy Spirit to tell us just how much of Scripture is reliable. The moderns are actually teaching that not individual texts but only the *Schriftganze* is reliable.[281] It amounts to the same thing when they appeal from the proof texts to "the Bible understood and interpreted as an *organic unity* having its center in the cross" (see above) or to "the *living center,* the 'Christustatsache' " (Holmstroem), to "the *inner content* of the revelation instead of its literary expression and record" (H. W. Robinson, *op. cit.,* p. 175), to "the *fundamental principles* of Scriptural teaching," etc. The moderns actually go so far as to proclaim it as their firm conviction that the whole of Scripture is inspired though individual passages are not inspired. J. M. Gibson: "Let it be noticed also that in this historical process of revelation we have not only relief from the most serious difficulties attaching to the view of verbal inspiration equally distributed through all the books, but also a strong and most striking confirmation of our faith in the divine inspiration of the Bible as a whole. . . . Remember, it is no question of details — of flies or lice or frogs. . . . The absolute inerrancy of every word of Scripture" is immaterial; what counts is "the substance or the spirit, the object and effect, of the whole." (*Op. cit.,* pp. 74, 77, 121.) Dr. M. Doerne finds that many portions of Scripture are purely human, erroneous; but nothing is lost as long as Scripture as a whole is recognized as "geistgewirkt": "Die kanonische Geltung der Schrift als dieses unzerreissbare geistgewirkte Ganze." (*Pastoralblaetter,* 1939, p. 233.) — The moderns certainly refuse to be known as atomistic verbalists; they are for the organic whole; they disdain the bondage of the letter.

There is a reason for that. They are convinced that the Bible teems with mistakes and ethical crudities and monstrosities. These blemishes must be taken care of, and the *Schriftganze* theory admirably serves that purpose. The blemishes are there, but since only the totality of Scripture counts, no one need bother about these little details. See Gibson's statement just quoted. See what use H. L. Willett makes of this theory: "No error has ever resulted in greater discredit to the Scriptures than that of

---

281) See also statements quoted above. H. E. Fosdick: No piecemeal treatment of the Scriptures, no Athanasian proof-texting, but "the whole book seen as a unified development." E. E. Flack: No stringing together of proof texts, but "the analogy of Scripture, the whole Scripture." The Eisenach Convention: Bound to Scripture as a whole, but free to reject particular statements! The *Luth. Church Quart.,* 1935, p. 260: "Seekers for authority in Scripture cannot find it in isolated portions and texts of the Bible. . . . The Bible, the whole Bible, not an isolated portion of it but its whole content revealing the will of God."

attributing to the Bible such a miraculous origin and nature as to make it an infallible standard of morals and religion. That it contains the Word of God in a sense in which that expression can be used of no other book is true. But its finality and authority do not reside *in all of its utterances,* but in those great characters and messages which are easily discerned as the mountain peaks of its contents. ·. . . So difficult are the narratives of the demons sent into the swine and the cursed fig tree that many who hold without hesitance to the inspiration and authority of the Book wonder if there has not been some error in the record at these points. This makes it evident that the authority which we recognize as truly present in the Biblical record does not inhere in the Book as such, nor in any particular portion of it. But rather it is found in the appeal which the *Scripture as a whole* makes to the moral sense within humanity. . . . One may apply to *the Scripture as a whole* the words of the Master: 'Heaven and earth shall pass away, but My Word shall not pass away.' " (*The Bible Through the Centuries,* p. 288 ff.) That was Hofmann's idea. As W. Rohnert puts it: "According to Hofmann the Bible contains, in individual portions, all kinds of erorrs, which are, however, rendered innocuous by the influence of the Bible itself. Hofmann declares: 'Die Verkuendigung keines einzelnen Apostels ist schlechthin' irrtumslos, da vielmehr die Schilderung des Bildes Christi hinter der ganzen vollen Herrlichkeit des Bildes zurueckbleibt; aber die *Gesamtverkuendigung* der Apostel enthaelt vollstaendig die Bedingungen eines schlechthin irrtumslosen Verstaendnisses Christi.' " (*Die Dogmatik der ev.-luth. Kirche,* p. 105.) [282] — Now we understand why the moderns have no use for the atomistic proof-text method of the fathers. The fathers did

---

282) A few more citations to show with what relief the moderns hail the Schleiermacher-Hofmann theory. F. Baumgaertel: "The letter *(Wortlaut)* of Scripture we consider of secondary importance. . . . The outstanding features, the *whole,* is what counts, not the details, which are in many instances erroneous and objectionable." (See Moeller, *Um die Inspiration der Bible,* p. 57.) Pfarrer Hoff: "Wir unterscheiden bei aller Ehrfurcht vor der Autoritaet der Heiligen Schrift als Ganzes das, was goettlich darinnen ist, von dem, was menschlich, allzu menschlich, was juedisch ist. . . . Das unterscheidet uns von der starren Orthodoxie, dass wir die sogenannte Verbalinspiration ablehnen. . . . Freilich, alles das fuehrt und muss fuehren auf Christus als vollkommene und hoechste Offenbarung Gottes." (See *Conc. Theol. Mthly,* V, p. 407.) Dr. G. Drach: "The human words of the Word of God are subject to . . . discrepancies of record, because the human authors were sinful human beings. . . . We repudiate the absolute infallibility of the Apostles. . . . The Bible, then, is the Word of God not because of any theoretical explanation of divine inspiration but because *as one connected, harmonious, authentic recorded whole,* from beginning to end, the Sacred Scriptures are 'they which testify of Christ.' " (*The Luth. Church Quart.,* 1936, p. 246 ff.)

not find any errors in the Bible. The moderns encounter errors on nearly every page and, naturally, fight shy of individual passages. But Scripture as a whole is God's inspired Word, and their conscience is at ease. Walther described the situation exactly when he said at a meeting of the Synodical Conference: "Sie sagen ausdruecklich: Man darf nicht sagen: 'Der Spruch ist Gottes Wort. Nein, das Ganze ist Gottes Wort, als Ganzes genommen ist es Gottes Wort!' Unter dem Schriftganzen aber verstehen sie das, was sie. aus der Schrift mit Weglassen dessen, was sie als irrig und fehlerhaft ansehen, herauskonstruiert haben." (See *Lehre und Wehre,* 1911, p. 151.) The Schriftganze has been invented for the purpose of emasculating and breaking all Scripture.

"Scripture as a whole" accomplishes great things for the moderns. It is the great corrective of the tainted portions of Scripture. It enables the moderns to give these inconvenient passages a proper form and makes it appear that such a treatment is proper and legitimate. Do you not see, said Professor Volck, that the words "There is no God" assume an altogether different meaning when the context is observed? Well, take every passage in its broader context, place it in the focus of the *Schriftganze,* and you will see whether it is true or how much of it, if anything, can retain its literal meaning. Under this treatment many a passage receives its *coup de grace.* We heard R. F. Horton: "The Revelation of God as a whole, the Revelation in its crowned completeness, must be used as a criterion for determining the value of individual passages in Scripture; it can never be admitted that a single passage, or even a small group of passages, teaching a special doctrine, *may override the truth* in its entirety when its full development is reached." (*Op. cit.,* p. 338.) If a particular passage is in conflict with the *Schriftganze,* it must go. Or it must be put in proper shape — which means the painless administering of the *coup de grace* — the literal meaning must be changed into a deeper meaning. That is how Fosdick and Willett want the proof texts treated which according to their literal meaning teach the old Christian doctrines; translate the old thought forms into modern categories. Hofmann got rid of the plaguing passages in the same way.[283] Why, any possible teaching may be constructed by means of this organic whole of Scripture. For instance, Scripture in itself contains not one word on "conversion in Hades." L. Dahle readily admits that. However, if we "go back to the fundamental

---

283) "In the case of Hofmann, too, the result [of operating with the "organic whole of Scripture"] was that he denied such fundamental doctrines as the inspiration of Scripture, the *satisfactio vicaria,* original sin, etc." (Pieper, *op. cit.,* I, p. 440.)

principles of Scriptural teaching," we are forced to come to such a conclusion. (See *Theol. Quart.*, 1908, p. 25.) — Proof texts *him*, proof texts *her* — what counts is Scripture as a whole.

Let Dr. H. Martensen conclude this section. "The use of the Scriptures in dogmatics must not consist in a mere appeal to single passages, or in a comparison of single passages; this mode of procedure too often betrays *the narrow-minded view that nothing is true which cannot be proved to be literally found in the Bible.* We agree rather on this point with Schleiermacher when he says that in our Biblical studies there should be constantly developed *a more comprehensive* use of the Scriptures, in which stress shall not be laid on single passages taken apart from the context, but in which attention is paid only to the longer and specially fruitful sections, in order thus to penetrate the course of thought of the sacred writers, and find there the same combinations as those on which the results of dogmatic study themselves rest." (*Christian Dogmatics*, p. 53.)

This, then, is the fifth objection: the doctrine of verbal inspiration is wrong because it results in an atomistic use of Scripture, permits and calls for the use of the proof-text method, and will not permit science or the *Schriftganze*, etc., to change the literal meaning of individual passages.[284] What is to be said of this objection? Three things are wrong with it.

---

284) Recall how *The Luth. Church Quart.* at the beginning of the present chapter (page 331) links the two statements that Verbal Inspiration is not taught in some of the U. L. C. seminaries and that the employment of the proof-text method indicates an atomistic conception of the Scriptures. Recall Gibson's statement that those who use proof texts do so because they hold that it is really God, not men, who wrote these words. Read the review of Dr. M. Graebner's *The Lord's Prayer and the Christian Life* in *The Luth. Church Quart.*, 1938, p. 224: "While the clarity and tone of writing are beyond criticism, one may question the adequacy of some of the demonstrations offered. The Bible is used as a source of proof in quite a literal sense. 'The Word of God came to prophets, evangelists, and apostles of old in the form of direct revelation from God on high. God spoke to them directly and gave them messages to transmit. . . .' '(The person who prays the Lord's Prayer sincerely, thoughtfully, and devoutly) will read the Bible with the determination of learning what God desires to teach him, and not with the idea of comparing God's Word with the so-called results of historical criticism or of scientific investigation.'" The latest pronouncement of *The Luth. Church Quart.* (April, 1942, p. 154) on this point: "The first of these two conceptions [of Inspiration defined at Omaha in the discussion of the Pittsburgh Agreement] has to do chiefly with the composition of Scripture. The process of inspiration is so far defined that it can be given a descriptive adjective; it is *verbal inspiration*. It means that the words of Scripture stand as they are because the Holy Spirit put them there just as they are. This conception of inspiration is set forth in the *Brief Statement of the Missouri Synod*. It appeals to certain proof texts and interprets them in the light of this conception."

PERFORMING AN INTELLECTUAL IMPOSSIBILITY

1) There is something wrong with the demand, basic to the whole present discussion, that the Christian doctrine must be derived not from the *sedes doctrinae,* the texts setting forth the doctrine, but from "Scripture as a whole." This demand asks us to perform an intellectual impossibility. We can understand what "the whole of Scripture" and "Scripture as a whole" means, but we cannot understand what "the whole of Scripture" as put into opposition to the component parts of Scripture means. Kliefoth's characterization of this concept has become classical. He calls it "eine unvollziehbare Phrase" — a phrase which cannot be used intelligently, an inconceivable concept.[285] Can the whole differ from the parts? Can you make the whole, which you get by adding the component parts, change these parts into something else? Common intelligence figures that when you have learned what all the single proof texts teach concerning doctrine — or any other subject of which they treat — you know what the whole Scripture teaches. But Schleiermacher and Hofmann and the *Luth. Church Quart.* tell us that the whole of Scripture cancels what the parts of Scripture declare. "The objections to the verbal inspiration of Holy Scripture do not manifest great ingenuity or mental acumen, but the very opposite. . . . The critics of His Word lose their common sense and become utterly unreasonable and illogical." In the course of this study we have dealt with a number of cases in point. The present case seems to be the prize fatuity. These men are asking us to believe that parts of Scripture are not inspired but the whole of Scripture is inspired. Hofmann tells us, keeping a sober face, that the message of not a single apostle is absolutely free of error, but their message as a whole, *die Gesamtverkuendigung,* produces an absolutely true and unerring knowledge of Christ. It passes comprehension. These men could not qualify as teachers of mathematics. They would not be permitted to teach their pupils that while the individual theorems are faulty and erroneous the science of mathematics as a whole is the absolute truth. They would not try to do that, of course, because they are convinced that the single theorems are true. But in theology, they think, a similar absurdity will pass. The whole of Scripture is trustworthy while the component parts of Scripture are faulty and untrustworthy! "There is nothing too

---

285) Pieper calls it a "senseless phrase. . . . Kliefoth is right, when, in his criticism of Hofmann's *Schriftbeweis,* he calls this placing of Scripture as a whole and its separate passages into opposition to one another an 'unachievable thought' ('unvollziehbare Phrase'). The fact of the matter is that we can obtain the whole of the Christian doctrine only in this way that we take the several doctrines from those passages — observing of course the context — which treat of the respective doctrines." (*Op. cit.,* I, p. 243 f.)

absurd," said H. M'Intosh, "to have been stated or imagined on this question." (*Is Christ Infallible and the Bible True?* p. 274.)[286]

And remember, the impossible *Schriftganze* is the big gun in this particular assault on Verbal Inspiration. Since we dare not be atomistic, the moderns declare, but must deal with Scripture as an organic whole, Verbal Inspiration must go. But viewed closely, this mighty, high-sounding *Schriftganze* turns out to be utter nonsense. Verily, the Lord taketh the wise in their own craftiness. Aiming to be wise, they became fools.[287]

---

286) Prof. A. Zich, in *The Northwestern Lutheran*, Nov. 10, 1935: "The editor of the *Presbyterian Tribune*, holding that the Bible contains 'inaccuracies, contradictions, outworn views, still says: 'Note also that this which we declare to be "the only infallible rule of faith and practice" is not any particular verse, sentence, or passage, nor all the verses in the Old and New Testaments, *taken each by itself*. It is "the Word of God" which is "the Scriptures." Clearly that means that our authority in matters of faith and practice is found in the Bible *as a whole*. Only as we take it all together, interpreting each particular statement in the light of its general purpose, spirit, and meaning, do we find that infallible guidance we need in order to believe and live rightly.' One might here object: How is any man to find out the 'general purpose, meaning, and spirit' of the whole if the particular 'verse, sentence, or passage' cannot be trusted because such verse, sentence, and passage may be inaccurate, self-contradictory, and outworn? If the component parts are unreliable, then how can the whole be 'infallible'? A chain is as weak as its weakest link; is it not? But we must not expect the detractors of Holy Writ to be reasonable. Very evidently the editor of the *Presbyterian Tribune* is trying hard to get away from some very clear teaching of the Bible in numerous single verses, sentences, and passages. . . ."

287) Some minor fatuities. J. Oman: "Doctrines are drawn from Holy Writ like legal decisions from the Statute Book. . . . As soon as it became 'Thus saith the Scriptures,' controversy entered the large field of differences in interpretation." (*Vision and Authority*, p. 182f.) *The Christian Century*, Feb. 10, 1937: "From Quakers to Roman Catholics, each claims to reflect the mind of Christ for his Church, and if anyone of them is right, Baptists must inevitably be wrong. Moreover, using the proof-text method, which Baptists themselves employ, each could draw a very respectable argument for its contentions from the New Testament." Distinguish between the illicit and the legitimate use of proof texts! It seems such a waste of time to call attention to this sophistry, committed also by other writers quoted above, that, because some abuse the proof-text method, the method itself is wrong. — Another sophistry is committed when these two statements are put in opposition: "The Bible is no collection of doctrinal statements" and "The Bible is a book of life." The Bible is both. — Another sophistry: Not all statements of the Bible are of the same importance, the genealogies are not so important as the Gospel. Nobody said that, and it has absolutely no bearing on the question whether every statement is authoritative. — Do not tell us that we need the whole of the Bible for the whole truth (we know that) when you propose to substitute in the next sentence for "all of the Bible" the fictitious "Scripture as a whole." — Luther helped to free us from the prison house of verbal infallibility? That is a case of ignorance. — The use of proof texts is not Lutheran but Calvinistic? Another case of ignorance. Calvin bowed to the authority of the letter, true. But so did Luther, only more so. — No; it is Catholic, says C. Stange. "Es ist eine Nachwirkung der katholischen Auffassung, wenn der Versuch gemacht wird, die einzelnen dogmatischen Aussagen aus der Schrift abzuleiten." (*Dogmatik*, I, p. 193.) We cannot go on any longer.

CATERING TO THE PRIDE OF THE FLESH

2) The refusal to bow to the authority of the letter and to accept every single chapter, section, verse, and sentence of the Bible as it stands — to rail at the proof-text method — is unworthy of the Christian. It does not spring from respect for Holy Scripture. Scripture asks us to treat all the words of Scripture as the very words of God (2 Tim. 3:16), precious beyond expression (Rom. 15:4). It springs from the pride of the carnal heart, which places the findings of human science above the assertions of Scripture and, in addition to that, does not like to have the theologian play the humble role of a catechumen, sitting at the foot of his teacher and simply listening to what he is told. Men do not like to take over what the apostles and prophets handed down to them and pass it on without any addition and elaboration and improvement of their own. It tickles the pride of the flesh to have something to do with constructing the saving doctrine. It makes so great an impression when the learned theologian tells his hearers that the fathers indeed knew no better than to take the doctrine from these simple proof texts, but that now men have arisen who are able to deal with the mysterious *Schriftganze* and shed new light on these old, misunderstood passages.[288] It is the pride of the flesh which is offended at Verbal Inspiration. If the doctrine of verbal inspiration be true, nothing is left for the theologian to do but to take over what he finds in Scripture and repeat it. What, cries out Sherwood Eddy, simply quote proof texts and blindly obey a mechanical, external authority! What, cries out H. W. Robinson, is the "mechanical use of a verbal oracle" our only business! J. M. Gibson knew a better way. "He began," says P. T. Forsyth, "in the old theory of inspiration, in which he would have remained had his been a metallic, inert, or mechanical mind." But he learned the secret of the *Schriftganze!* (Preface to Gibson's book, p. XIV.) This *"schlendrianmaessige Reproduktion"* of Biblical statements, says Holmstroem, does not suit the stature of the modern theologian. It is the pride of the flesh which is scandalized at the demand of Verbal Inspiration to let the text stand as it reads, and refuses to practice "atomistic verbalism." Scripture describes the man who is wise in his own conceit, who will "not consent to the *words* of our Lord Jesus Christ," as one who "is proud [puffed up], knowing nothing," 1 Tim. 6:3 f.

---

288) F. Buechsel: "Dies Gesamtzeugnis des Neuen Testaments zu erheben, erfordert ein betraechtliches Mass theologischer Arbeit." (*Die Offenbarung Gottes*, p. 112.) Professor Volck: "Das Befragen der Schrift ist keine so leichte Sache," particularly, of course, the investigation of "Scripture as a whole." (See Pieper, *op. cit.*, I, p. 398.)

May God give us grace to become and remain "atomistic verbalists." That is the genuine Lutheran attitude. In the controversy on the Lord's Supper Luther employed the proof-text method and said: "The text stands there too mightily." (XV:2050.) Zwingli scoffed at Luther for clinging to "fuenf arme und elende Worte," and the moderns would have told him to look beyond the proof text into the *Schriftganze,* but Luther answers: "They are revealing what kind of spirit is in them and how much they think of God's Word, ridiculing these precious words as five poor, miserable words; they do not believe that they are God's words. For if they believed that they are God's words, they would not call them miserable, poor words, but would prize one tittle and letter more highly than the whole world." (XX:1040.) Rall tells us that "Paul had not the faintest idea that centuries later theologians would be building up their theories on this phrase or that sentence in his letters" (*op. cit.,* p. 229), but Luther thought that that exactly was Paul's idea: "It is impossible, absolutely impossible, that there is a single letter in Paul which the entire Church should not follow and observe." (XIX:20.) Surely, Luther was an atomistic verbalist: "a single letter, yea, a single tittle, of Scripture counts for more than heaven and earth." (IX:650.) Luther was a humble Christian. He was not ashamed to be a catechumen of the apostles. We are not prophets, he says, but "what we can do and will do, if we, too, are sanctified and have the Holy Spirit, is to boast of being catechumens and pupils of the prophets, who simply *repeat* and preach what we have heard and learned from the prophets and apostles" (III:1890), and learned it not from the *Schriftganze* but from those poor, miserable words of the proof texts: "Zum andern sollst du . . . die muendliche Rede und *buchstabische Worte im Buch* immer treiben und treiben" (XIV:435), stick to the words lettered in the Book. Oh, what an atomistic verbalist! "O du demuetiger Luther!" was Walther's comment on this treatise of Luther. And Luther learned his theology from the apostles. The proof-text method is genuinely apostolic. Paul would base his argument on a single word! Gal. 3:16! Christ Himself used the proof-text method. "It is written"! (Matt. 4.) "Have ye not read?" (Matt. 19:4.) Our Lord bases His argument on one single word, John 10:35, and when He adds, "The Scripture cannot be broken," He condemns the *Schriftganze* method, which breaks one Scripture, one proof text, after the other.[289] And so

---

289) B. B. Warfield: "What is the particular thing in Scripture for the confirmation of which the indefectible authority of Scripture is thus (John 10:34f.) invoked? It is one of its most casual clauses — more than that, the very form of its expression in one of its most casual clauses. This means, of course, that in the Savior's view the indefectible authority of Scripture attaches to the very form of expression of its

we of the Missouri Synod and our brethren are going to retain the proof-text method. We shall keep on saying with Walther: "It is written — damit ist die Sache abgemacht." (*Walther and the Church*, p. 20.) And: "Wenn Paulus hier (2 Tim. 3:15) sagt: 'die heiligen Buchstaben', and darunter 'alles Geschriebene' im Alten Testament zusammenfasst, so soll damit recht hervorgehoben werden, dass jeder Teil, auch der geringste Teil, jeder Buchstabe so ist, wie man von dieser Schrift aussagt, heilig. Wir sollen glauben: Jeder Buchstabe ist vom Heiligen Geist." (*Lehre und Wehre*, 1911, p. 154.) "The *Brief Statment of the Missouri Synod* appeals to certain proof texts," says the *Luth. Church Quart.*, and we thank the *Quarterly* for spreading that far and wide. Ladd ridicules Calov for saying: "It is impious and profane audacity to change a single point in the Word of God and to substitute a smooth breathing for a rough one, or a rough for a smooth" (*op. cit.*, p. 58); but Calov can appeal to Christ, as Walther in connection with the words just quoted appeals to Christ, who insists on the authority of every jot and tittle (Matt. 5:18). — If it should happen that we misapply a proof text, we are grateful to him who censures us for that. We do not want to be guilty of an "atomistic use of Scripture" in the narrow sense. But when men censure us for using the "old atomistic method of proof texts" and call us "atomistic verbalists," we consider that high praise.

ROBBING US OF ALL OF THE BIBLE

3) The proposal to substitute the *Schriftganze* for the proof-text method is fraught with deadly peril. They offer us "Scripture as a whole" and take away from us the whole Scripture. First they told us that nothing is lost if only the Gospel truths in the Bible are retained. Then they said, when we began to study John 3:16: Take care — the *words* of John 3:16 are not inspired; you must not rely on the words, for that would be mechanical inspiration. And now they are telling us that it is futile to deal with single texts at all; that would be atomistic; John 3:16 in itself means nothing at all. There is nothing left of the Bible; doctrinal issues can no longer be settled by means of proof texts,

---

most casual clauses. It belongs to Scripture through and through, down to its *most minute particulars*, that it is of indefectible authority." (*Revelation and Inspiration*, p. 86). — J. L. Neve: "It is frequently said that the Bible is not first of all a book of proof texts (dicta probantia) for statements of dogmatics, because it is preeminently a means of grace. There is truth in this remark. of course; but because theology deals with things pertaining to salvation, a Church with a real appreciation of the Scriptures as a means of grace will always want to have her creed, her teaching, her dogmatics, in harmony with such Scripture. *Christ proved from Scripture;* the New Testament writers did it; the Church of all time has done it. The practice is inseparable from Lutheranism." (*Churches and Sects of Christendom*, p. 200.)

as the *Christian Century* informed us; and when the troubled
Christian takes up one of his cherished golden passages to comfort
his soul, he is told that individual passages no longer count.
As Volck in effect said: You must first find out what meaning this
passage gets from its relation to Scripture as a whole. "Das heisst
aber," says Dr. A. L. Graebner, "einem die Bibel ganz nehmen.
That is taking all of the Bible from me. . . . When in my dying
hour my senses weaken, the verse 'The blood of Jesus Christ, His
Son, cleanseth us from all sin' should be·sufficient to strengthen
and keep my faith. But now they tell me: No; only the organic
whole can do that." (*Proc. Syn. Conf.*, 1886 p. 24.) [290)]

No, no, say the moderns; we have taken from you only the
individual texts but have given you the Bible as a whole. — But
we cannot use your *Schriftganzes*. We do not know what it is.
And you do not know it. You have never told us by what exact
rules you came by it. You have nowhere published a syllabus of it.
The thing is too hazy for a man to deal with it. It has less substance than a dream. We try to grasp its message, and it constantly dissolves. There is no certainty of doctrine and of faith
where this nebulous thing serves as basis. Says the *Australian
Lutheran*: "The interpretation of Scripture operating with 'Scripture as one organic whole,' general scope of Scripture, entirety
of Scripture, '*das Schriftganze*,' allied with the subjective faith of
the theologian as a cojudge of doctrine, sets aside the *sedes doctrinae,* the clear Scripture passages which treat of the particular
doctrines, and *destroys all certainty* of doctrine." (See *Conc.
Theol. Mthly.*, X, p. 886.) Of course there is no certainty in the
new method. E. Grubb is frank to declare: "The indiscriminate
use of Scripture as a single source of equal value, as a quarry from
every part of which stones may be indifferently collected to build
up the temple of constructive dogmatics, will, it is hoped, soon
pass away never to return. The new view does not, it may be
urged, *give the same certainty as the old.*" He continues with the
cynical observation: "But if the old is becoming incredible, what

290) We read in *Modern Religious Liberalism*, by J. Horsch, p. 30:
"The real difficulty of our time, when we come to probe it, is the de-
thronement of the Bible from its position of unquestioned authority.
From the earliest period of Christianity, even in the writings of the
earliest Fathers, the Sacred Scriptures were held to be the standard
and the test of Christian truth: nothing was to be taught as essential
except what was contained in them or could be proved by them; and
up to the middle of the last century the imposing fortress of the Book
remained practically unquestioned and certainly unbreached. *A quotation from any part of it carried unquestioned weight,* and decisions
drawn from its decretals were the settlement of all strife. — [*Liberal*]
Protestants have lost their Bible and, in losing it, have lost their religion.
How can they shelter in a building which is demolished or which is ever
hidden by the scaffolding about it, necessary for perpetual repairs?"

then? May we not be meant to understand that the desire for infallibility is itself unhealthy?" (*Op. cit.*, p. 240.) There is no certainty about the *Schriftganze* because they have spun it out of their own heads and because they are not yet through with this spinning operation. The Anglican Commission has told us that Scripture alone does not furnish the standard of doctrine but that this standard is being unfolded "in the experience of the Church," and R. F. Horton told us that, when revelation has reached its crowned completeness, it will serve as a criterion. "Let the devil wait for that," said Luther, "I cannot wait so long." (VIII: 100.)

There is no certainty about this "Scripture as a whole." We ask the modern theologian how he knows that his *Schriftganze* — every theologian is at liberty to construct his own — is the right one, and the only answer he can give is that he feels it must be the right one. We cannot follow a leader who forsakes the well-established rules and simply follows his "intuition." We cannot follow a theological leader whose only guarantee for the truth of his teaching is his own word. Luther has warned us against these dreamers: "They speak such things only in order to lead us away from Scripture and make themselves masters over us that we should believe their *dream sermons* (Traumpredigten)" (V: 334.) And they refuse to tell us just how to construct the *Schriftganze* and just what it contains. "Boake Carter is writing a book in which he will tell of a 'secret Bible.' 'Research now going on bears out my contention that there are two Bibles,' Carter said. 'There is the "revealed Bible," which is being used today. Then there is a "secret Bible," which was written in code and carefully hidden. It has remained secret until this day.' Carter said the 'secret Bible' contains divinely inspired rules for all human conduct. . . ." (See *The Lutheran*, Nov. 4, 1941.) We are not going to base our hope of salvation on Boake Carter's "secret Bible." And we are not going to base our doctrine and faith on the mysterious *Schriftganze*.

Will you base your faith and hope of salvation on the conceit of some theologian? Just that is what they are offering you under the name of the *Schriftganze*. Luther's words, addressed to the *Schwaermer* of his day, fit the *Schwaermerei* under discussion exactly. "Grund und Ursache solches ihres Duenkels ist erstlich, dass man diese Worte 'Das ist mein Leib' [or any other proof text] muesse aus den Augen tun und zuvor durch den Geist die Sachen bedenken. . . . Da hast du eine gewisse Regel, die dich besser leitet in alle Wahrheit, denn der Heilige Geist selber tun kann, naemlich, wo die Heilige Schrift deinen Duenkel irret oder hindert, da tue sie aus den Augen und folge zuerst deinem Duenkel [conceit], so triffst du den rechten Weg gewiss allerdinge fein." (XX:

1022.) You may be sure that those who substitute "Scripture as a whole" for the individual statements of Scripture are not pleased with these individual statements, else they would not tell us to do away with them. And you may be sure that what they are offering us instead is not God's Word and revelation; else God would Himself have set it down in His Book. (The moderns surely are not going to tell us that they are receiving special revelations from heaven!) And since it is not God's Word, it is their own word, their own product, the product of their conceit. Dr. Pieper: "The 'whole of Scripture' or the 'whole of the Christian doctrine' which is constructed without considering the individual passages that treat of the doctrine is purely *man's own product."* (*Op. cit.,* I, p. 244.) Pieper continues: "This inconceivable concept — the whole of Scripture — as opposed to the individual statements is made use of to *put Scripture out of action* in the name of Scripture." Again: "This pretended 'Scripture as a whole' is made to serve as a check on the individual statements for the purpose of putting the quietus on Scripture itself. . . . He who obtains the 'whole' in any other way than through the parts, is fabricating his own Scripture; he is no longer a pupil but a critic of the word of Scripture." (II, p. 131.) The proposal to replace the individual statements of Scripture with "the whole of Scripture" is fraught with deadly peril. He who accepts the proposal is losing all of Scripture and getting in exchange fallible human opinions. True, this mysterious "whole of Scripture" as handled by some theologians leaves some Biblical doctrines intact. But in that case the "whole of Scripture" is guaranteed to give a greater assurance of the truth of the doctrine. And so the Christians are asked, in every case, to trust for their salvation in the vaporings of some poor little human being. The Christians are being solicited to trade in all of their good Bible for a counterfeit "whole." [291]

---

291) A similar imposition is practiced when the Christians are told to apply the spurious "analogy of faith" to individual passages of Scripture in order to get their "real" sense, a sense different from the literal sense. Recall the statement of Dr. E. E. Flack: "No fundamental doctrine rests on a single isolated passage. . . . It requires the analogy of Scripture, the whole Scripture, . . . to establish the truth as it is in Christ Jesus." The classical statement on this point is: "The Christian doctrines form for the believer, especially for the theologian, a recognizable, harmonious whole or system, which is constructed out of the perfectly clear passages of Holy Writ. This organic whole is the highest norm for the interpretation of Scripture, more important than parallelism, the comparison of the various passages which treat of a certain doctrine; in other words, it forms the analogy of faith." A full discussion of this analogy-of-faith canon is found in *Lehre und Wehre,* 1904, p. 406 ff. The same matter is treated in the article "Schriftauslegung und Analogie des Glaubens," *Lehre und Wehre,* 1907, p. 11 ff. It will be noticed that this "analogy of faith" is practically the same as the *Schriftganze,* and instead of "a similar imposition" we might have used the term "the

We shall not do it. We do not want the counterfeit "whole" because we have the real whole of Scripture. There is nothing atomistic about our treatment of Scripture. To us it is an un-

---

same imposition." It has the same disastrous effect: it cancels any clear passage of Scripture which is declared to be out of harmony with the "harmonious whole" which the theologian has constructed. There is an "analogy of faith." Luther and the fathers "understand by analogy of faith the clear Scripture passages that need no explanation but shine in their own light. These passages together are the 'analogy' or the 'rule of faith.' See Apology, *Trigl.*, 441, 60." (Pieper, I, p. 437.) "These clear passages are the *rule*, according to which every faithful teacher must explain dark passages as far as this is possible." (*Loc. cit.*) Operating, however, with the spurious "analogy of faith," theologians claim the right to divest a *clear* passage of its clear meaning in order to bring it into harmony with some other passage. That is not permissible. Christian theology does not engage in the business of harmonizing. Any teaching, clearly revealed, must stand, even though it seem out of harmony with another teaching, also clearly revealed. The harmonizers, however, feel justified to change any clear teaching, the meaning of any clear passage, in order to establish "a harmonious whole," to save their spurious "analogy of faith." To illustrate. At the time of the controversy on Conversion and Election these statements were made: "This universal comfort of the Gospel can only be preserved if the few texts of Holy Writ, in part not easily understood, which treat of the selection of a few persons, who will unfallibly be saved, are *not interpreted in such a way* that the many clear texts of the universal grace of God towards all men are darkened or suppressed, but if, on the contrary, the few *dark passages* are interpreted by means of the many clear passages." (Our italics.) Again: "The author [of a certain book] says it is vain and foolish to deny election because we cannot harmonize it with the teaching that God loves all men. Our reply is this: If a doctrine *cannot be harmonized* with John 3:16, it must be contrary to the Word of God and should therefore be dropped." There are many clear passages which teach particular election, the election of grace. But in order to harmonize them with other clear passages which teach universal grace, the analogy-of-faith theologians simply stamp the first group of passages "*dark* passages" and change their meaning. Walther certainly was right in saying: "To correct one doctrine of Scripture by another because reason insists that this passage is obscure and involves a contradiction, to correct it, yes, delete it entirely, on the plea that dark passages must receive their interpretation through the clear passages — dieses ist ein entsetzlicher Frevel." (See *Lehre und Wehre*, 1891, p. 68.) Luther: "To interpret *clear and certain* passages by means of other passages is making sport of the truth and hiding the light behind clouds. Do you say that all passages must be interpreted by means of other passages? That would be turning Scripture into an endless, rude chaos." (XX: 327.) Dr. Pieper's characterization of the spurious "analogy of faith: "Unter 'dem Ganzen der Schrift' versteht man nicht die Schrift *selbst*, sondern die *menschlich gereimte* Schrift, die Schrift, insofern sie von Menschen, insonderheit von den klugen Theologen, so *zurechtgeschnitten* ist, dass sie mit den *menschlichen* Gedanken von dem Zusammenhang der einzelnen Lehren sich reimt, ein dem Menschen '*erkennbares*' harmonisches Ganzes bildet. Das 'Ganze der Schrift,' das diese Leute im Sinne haben, ist ein *menschliches Machwerk.* Und wenn sie nun nach diesem *ihrem* 'Ganzen' die Schrift auslegen, so moegen sie noch so oft versichern, dass sie Schrift *durch Schrift* erklaeren: tatsaechlich wandeln sie genau in den Wegen der Papisten, Schwaermer und Rationalisten; sie legen die Schrift *nach ihren eigenen Gedanken* aus. Ihre 'Analogie des Glaubens' ist die Analogie *des menschlichen Ich.*" (*Lehre und Wehre*, 1907, p. 13.)

breakable, indivisible whole. "Not only are the various writings, when considered separately, worthy of God, but they together exhibit one complete and harmonious whole, unimpaired by excess or defect." (Bengel.) One whole, written by one Author, every word God's word. Ask Dr. C. C. Hein what the whole óf Scripture means, and he answers: "To the Lutheran Church the Bible as a whole as well as in all its parts is the pure infallible Word of God. . . . May Lutheranism preserve to the Christian world its own precious Reformation heritage: the Word of God, the whole Word of God and nothing but the Word of God." (*The Second Luth. World Convention,* p. 74 f.) Ask Luther, and he answers: "The entire Holy Scriptures are ascribed to the Holy Ghost." (III: 1889.) And the Holy Ghost in Scripture assures us: From Gen. 1:1 to Rev. 22:21 it is My Book, every word My word. We do not treat the Bible atomistically. We do not make of it a chaotic medley, parts contributed by the Holy Spirit, parts by this and that fallible human writer. We leave that to the moderns. Rudelbach tells them to reserve the term "atomistic" for themselves: "Auf Semler fussen wesentlich alle diejenigen unter den Neueren, die die Inspiration der Schrift als eine teilbare Groesse behandeln, nur dass sie, als Bemerkungs-Rhapsoden, noch atomistischer sind." (*Zeitschr. f. d. Gesamte Luth. Theol. u. Kirche,* 1842, zweites Quartalh., p. 10.) Not we but they tear Holy Scripture piecemeal. We treat it as a unity — and we treat it as an organic unity, one organic, harmonious whole. "Scripture," says Luther, and say we, "forms a harmonious whole and all examples and histories, yea, the entire Scripture in all its parts, aims at this, that one should learn Christ." (III:18.) We know that every book, every chapter, every verse, is integrated in this wonderful organism. We may not, in many cases, see the relation. We poor sinners know only in part. But we know that not a single member of this organism is useless or harmful. The poor, supercilious *Schriftganze*-theologians imagine that they know better than the Holy Ghost how to construct a harmonious whole, lay their unholy hands upon the sacred Book, and turn it over to the Church as a disfigured, mangled body. Blessed is he who receives Scripture as God gave it, and retains every verse and every statement in its literal sense. "We must have the whole Christ of the whole Bible if we want to have a whole salvation." (L. Keyser.) As you value your spiritual health, let Scripture stand as it is, with every part of it working towards that one end — the soul's salvation. "Darum heisst's: rund und rein, ganz und alles geglaubt oder nichts geglaubt. Der Heilige Geist laesst sich nicht trennen noch teilen, dass er ein Stueck sollte wahrhaftig und das andere falsch lehren oder glauben lassen." (Luther, XX:1781.)

CHAPTER VII

Does Verbal Inspiration Establish a "Legalistic Authority of the Letter"?

The indignation of the moderns reaches white heat when they are asked to receive every word of Scripture as inerrant and authoritative. If Verbal Inspiration means that every word of Scripture must be received as God's word, with unquestioning faith and obedience — and it means just that — they will have none of it. That is their strongest objection to Verbal Inspiration, and they express their abhorrence of it with the frightful word *legalistic*.

CALLING UPON THE CHRISTIANS TO BREAK WITH "THE LEGALISTIC EMPLOYMENT OF SCRIPTURE"

Let H. E. Fosdick tell us why he can no longer believe in Verbal Inspiration: "We used to think of Inspiration as a procedure which produced a book guaranteed in all its parts against error and containing from beginning to end a unanimous system of truth. . . . When Josiah swore the people to a solemn league and covenant, or when Ezra pledged the nation's loyalty to the keeping of the Levitical Law, the Bible which thus was coming into being, was primarily a book of divine requirements. It told the people what they ought to do. . . . One might have expected the Christians to break with this legalistic employment of Scripture," but "when the New Testament was added to the Old and the whole Book was bound up into unity by a theory of inerrant inspiration, Christians used the whole Book as the Jews had used part of it; it was a divine oracle to tell men how to live." (*The Modern Use of the Bible,* pp. 30, 236 ff.) R. Seeberg thanks God for the "fall of Verbal Inspiration." "The wall to which I refer was the *Verbal Inspiration of the Bible,* the conviction that every word of Holy Scripture was given by the inspiration of the Holy Spirit to the authors of the Old and New Testaments. . . . Every single word was regarded as of legal validity, and precisely on that account every single word was said to be given to man by the inspiration of God. It was not interests specifically Christian, but the theories and ideas of later Judaism which produced this 'old' theory of inspiration." (*Revelation and Inspiration,* pp. 1, 32.) *The Lutheran Church Quarterly* thus voices its protest: "It is of course no secret that Verbal Inspiration is not taught in some of the seminaries of the United Lutheran Church. . . . What results 'when the Word of God is identified with the words of the Scriptures' is 'a legalistic and an atomistic conception of the Scriptures, far more congenial to Calvinism than to Lutheranism. " (1937, p. 195.)

"Scriptural theology will not set up a deified Book in the place of the deified Church of Roman Catholicism nor hold to legalistic, unhistorical, and unpsychological theories of its inspiration. . . . It will not quibble over such questions as whether the Bible is the Word of God or contains the Word of God." (1934, p. 114. By Prof. T. A. Kantonen.) "Ockham regarded the Bible as an object of faith. In the Bible he found the positive expression of the will of God. Only Scripture could authoritatively establish what the content of faith was to be. The Bible was inspired, word for word! Ockham, it is true, surrendered his belief in canon law and in the legal authority of the Pope. But there was nothing particularly evangelical in this surrender; for he substituted an *authority which was just as legalistic — the Bible.*[1] (Our italics.) "The Bible became a legal (not evangelical) authority." (1940, p. 149.) "There is a spirit of legalism that pervades many of the ranks of Midwestern Lutherans, a kind of approach to the truth of God which insists on 'book, chapter, and verse' for all the 'eyeblinks' of life and must be undergirded by the authority of print on paper for every conscious breath in order to be assured of full salvation. In its last analysis this resolves itself into a conception of the Holy Scriptures as a mechanical work of the Holy Spirit, inerrant in every word and detail in their original form." (1939, p. 26.) "An atomistic or legalistic attitude results in trying to make specific New Testament words and sayings binding as external forms on the Church." (1940, p. 16.) J. P. Smyth is of the same mind: "Thus we find, in the first step of our investigation as to how God inspired the Bible, that He did not inspire it in the *rigid,* literal manner known as verbal inspiration. . . . Verbal inspiration is now fast being thrown to the moles and bats with the rest of the world's old, discarded mind-lumber." (*How God Inspired the Bible,* p. 118.) One more pronouncement to show how strongly the moderns feel on this matter. G. Wehrung: "Die Aufrichtung der Schrift als einer formal gueltigen Autoritaet genuegt also nicht. . . . Die gesetzliche Buchreligion. . . . Die Vorstellung einer mechanischen Inspiration ist auch schon auf juedischem Boden heimisch. Diesen intellektualistisch-gesetzlichen Schriftgebrauch duerfen wir heute als grundsaetzlich ueberwunden ansehen." (*Geschichte und Glaube,* pp. 301, 305.) The moderns feel that Verbal Inspiration implies "a legalistic authority of Scripture" and that "that is unworthy of [Christian] theology." (That is Dr. Pieper's diagnosis of the case. *Chr. Dog.,* I, p. 230.)

"Legalistic authority of Scripture" — could that mean that the moderns refuse to receive some of the Scripture statements or all of them as binding, authoritative? Hear G. Aulén: "Es ist nicht moeglich, alle einzelnen biblischen Aussagen als gleichwertige Gottesworte zu betrachten. . . . Es ist selbstverstaendlich, dass eine

Theorie, die jeder einzelnen Bibelaussage absolute goettliche Autoritaet zuerkennt, mit innerer Notwendigkeit den Blick fuer die
verschiedenen Richtungen in der Bibel truebt und zu einer Ver-
dunklung des eigentlich Christlichen fuehren muss. . . . . Der
Gedankengang des Legalismus draengt sich ueberall ein und praegt
die Theologie." (*Das Christliche Gottesbild,* pp. 251, 254.) The
conservative wing of the moderns denies that *every* statement of
the Bible is authoritative;[292] the larger group, the liberals, denies
that any statement is authoritative; "there are those," says *The
Living Church,* May 8, 1937, "who will say that they cannot see
how any New Testament passage can be taken in a doctrinaire
sense." Strahan is one of them. He declares that he and the
"Protestant scholars of the present day . . . do not open any book
of the Old or New Testament with the feeling that they are bound
to regard its teaching as sacred and authoritative. They yield to
nothing but what they regard as the irresistible logic of facts."
(Hastings, *Encyclopedia,* VII, p. 346.) Sherwood Eddy is another
one. "The Bible is not intended as a storehouse of authoritative
proof texts." G. L. Raymond "has found few, if at all intelligent,
who did not practically accept the text of Scripture as suggestive
rather than dictatorial." (*The Psychology of Inspiration,* p. 126.)
J. Aberly: "Let us in the first place notice that authority in religion
cannot be made to rest on a record in and by itself." (*The Luth.
Church Quart.,* 1932, p. 231.) E. E. Flack: "When we speak of the
authority of the Scriptures, we do not mean that they are independently authoritative. They have no authority either apart from
Christ, who is the primary authority, or apart from the Church,
in which Christ's power is operative." (*The Lutheran,* Oct. 1, 1936.)
On this point the conservatives among the moderns agree with the
liberals. Nitzsch-Stephan, as quoted by Pieper, *op. cit.,* I, p. 32, feels
justified in stating: "Nobody bases his dogmatics, in the Old
Protestant fashion, on the *norma normans,* the Bible." Everybody
feels like Th. Kaftan: "The modern theology, for which I stand,
refuses to submit to any purely external authority," this external
authority being Holy Scripture, the *written* word of the apostles
and prophets. (See Pieper, *op. cit.,* I, p. 273.) The moderns go so
far as to denounce Verbal Inspiration with its corollary that every
Bible statement calls for unquestioning faith and obedience as
unchristian. W. Herrmann declares: "The Reformation opposed

---

292) *Augsburg Sunday School Teacher:* "Too often the Bible is
reduced to the level of a well-stocked arsenal from which authoritative
proof texts may be drawn almost at random. . . . This practice makes
it appear that *every portion of the Book"* (our italics) "is authoritative
doctrine — perhaps an extremist exegesis of 2 Tim. 3:16, 17 contributed
to this error. The Bible is no collection of doctrinal statements but
a book of life. . . . If the same unfailing authority is ascribed to all the
'human' elements in the Bible, etc." (July, 1938, p. 388 f.)

to the Roman Church the fundamental principle that Christian doctrine is to be derived from the Scriptures alone. Everything depends, therefore, on a correct definition of this principle of the authority of Scripture adopted by the Evangelical Christianity that appeared in the Reformation. It would be unchristian if it meant the acknowledgment of any chance sentence of the Scriptures as God's word, by which a Christian ought to be guided in his life, and the community in its doctrine. Such a principle of the authority of Scripture would set a book above God's revelation." (*Systematic Theology*, p. 58.)[293]

NO LEGAL CODE! NO SLAVE MENTALITY! NO BIBLIOLATRY!

To express their abhorrence of the idea that every teaching of Scripture is binding upon us, the moderns make use of the opprobrious terms "manual of doctrine," "code of laws," etc. R. F. Grau: "Die Heilige Schrift ist uns nicht mehr ein grosser vom Himmel herabgesandter Gesetzeskodex mit seinen einzelnen Paragraphen, Beweisstellen genannt." (See Baier-Walther, I, p. 102.) Hofmann is the great authority for this. Obtaining doctrine out of Scripture, he says, "would imprint a legalistic feature on doctrine"; it would make of Scripture "a code of laws of faith [Sammlung von Glaubensgesetzen]." (*Schriftbeweis*, I, p.9. See Pieper, *op. cit.*, III, p. 510.) The liberals are in perfect agreement with this. H. E. Fosdick: The Christians, sad to say, refused "to break

---

293) Some more pronouncements. — Do these repetitions serve a good purpose? We want the moderns to bare their inmost thoughts to us. The more they say on this subject the less we will have to say in refutation. Their bare statements carry, for the Bible Christian, their own refutation. — *The Christian Century*, March 2, 1938: "No issue between the churches can now be settled by the quotation of a Biblical text, as our fathers used to assume. No issue will be settled by reference to an authoritarian standard, whether doctrinal or ecclesiastical." John Oman: "The teacher of divine truth . . . will not care to stop with authorities either of the Church or of the Scriptures." (*Vision and Authority*, p.188.) C. Stange: "The attempt to derive the individual dogmatical statements from Scripture, stems from the Romish view. Scripture is viewed as the dogmatical authority." (*Dogmatik*, p. 193.) Bishop Charles Gore: "It ought to be said frankly that Luther often clings to the older notion of a verbally inspired Bible. He actually speaks of the Holy Spirit as the *Author*" (italics in original) "of the books of Moses; he submitted his judgment undoubtingly to Scriptural statements on points of natural science; and in a famous controversy he appealed to a New Testament verse as an infallible oracle, to be accepted with the purest literalism. In some respects he fastened the letter of the Bible on those who followed him more bindingly than had been done before." (*The Doctrine of the Infallible Book*, p. 58.) F. Buechsel: "Die Offenbarung Gottes auf sein Wort zu beschraenken, ist falsch und ergibt leicht eine dogmatische Verknoecherung des Offenbarungsgedankens, *die das Wort Gottes schliesslich in eine Lehre verwandelt* und die Autoritaet des Wortes Gottes nicht ausreichend begruenden kann." (*Die Offenbarung Gottes*, p.3.) E. Brunner: "The doctrine of verbal inspiration materialized the authority of the Scriptures and ruled out the decision of faith." (*The Mediator*, p.343.)

with this legalistic employment of Scripture. . . . Ecclesiastical bodies have employed the Bible as though it·were a book of canon law to define the procedure and organization of Christian churches forever." (*Op. cit.*, p. 237.) H. L. Willett: "The Book does not claim to be a carefully prepared manual of conduct. It refuses to accept responsibility for the claim that all of its utterances are rules to be followed." (*The Bible through the Centuries*, p. 294.) J. Oman: "On the one hand, critical results are ignored, and doctrines are drawn from Holy Writ like legal decisions from the Statute Book." (*Op. cit.*, p. 182.) — H. C. Alleman: "Dr. Reu compares the Bible to a deed of sale. 'That the sale is reported in the newspapers does not add a single thing to the sale. . . . The sale is not closed until the deed is made out and handed to the new owner.' Thus Scripture is, as it were, the legal document of salvation. It sustains the same relation to our salvation that the deed of sale holds to the possession of property. . . . 'Is it,' says Dr. H. Offermann, 'because they do not yet — or no longer — understand the position of their own Church, but have been slipping, without knowing it, into an attitude toward the Bible which is essentially un-Lutheran because it is unevangelical, and are thinking of the Bible as a legal code, a law book with many paragraphs?' " (*Luth. Church Quart.*, 1940, pp. 353, 357.) H. Offermann's statement in *Luth. Church Quart.* of 1937, p. 407, is repeated in *What Is Lutheranism?* p. 67: "Lutherans do not regard the Scriptures as a legal code with many paragraphs. They accept the Scriptures, and they believe in them primarily because they believe in Christ." A. R. Wentz: "The spirit of essential Lutheranism does not rhyme with the literalism of the Fundamentalist, which makes the Bible a book of oracles, a textbook with explicit marching orders for the 'warfare between science and religion.' " (*What Is Lutheranism?* p. 91.) — It is clear that these men do not like Verbal Inspiration. As Dr. Pieper puts it: "In order to discredit Verbal Inspiration, it is further asserted that the verbal-inspirationists regard Holy Scripture as 'a law-codex which fell down from heaven,' as 'a paper pope,' etc." (*Op. cit.*, I, p. 365.)[294]

---

294) Do you care to hear additional statements? They will show how boldly and baldly the moderns express their aversion to Verbal Inspiration. E. Schaeder deplores that "people cultured in other respects are under the spell of monstrous ideas regarding the Bible and look upon it as a sacred codex which claims to be the product of the supernatural Spirit of God, who supplied to the Biblical authors all the words, not only the contents but also the required verbal form." (*Glaubenslehre fuer Gebildete*, p. 18 f.) Dr. Walther submits this specimen from Luthardt's *Theol. Literaturblatt*: "Es ist purer Missverstand; als ob der Verfasser die Zeit repristinieren wollte, welche die Bibel als ein unmittelbar vom Himmel herniedergekommenes Buch ansah und die Wahrheit ihres goettlichen Ursprungs so einseitig auffasste, dass sie

By now the indignation of the moderns has reached the boiling point. They give vent to their indignation in epithets such as "spiritual despotism," "slave mentality," etc. They denounce Verbal Inspiration as having built "a suffocating prison house" and stigmatize those who believe in the inviolability of every part of Scripture as "slaves of the letter," submitting to "the tyranny of words," the "tyranny of an infallible book." When we protest against giving the words of Scripture a new meanning in order to bring Scripture into harmony with "science" and "modern thought," they pity us and upbraid us for upholding "the enslaving legalism of the letter," "tyrannous literalism." And they have found a still more loathsome term of reproach. The verbal-inspirationists do homage to a "paper pope." The Pope exacts blind obedience of his slaves; and within Protestantism, where Verbal Inspiration

---

vergass, dass die Propheten und Apostel den Schatz goettlicher Weisheit in irdischen Gefaessen trugen." (*Lehre und Wehre*, 1886, p. 4.) R. Seeberg believes that the holy writers "did not think and write with the intention of producing fòrmulae for all times and circumstances," criticizes "the reformers of the Middle Ages, who questioned the legal authority of the Pope, but only in order that this legal authority might be the more definitely transferred to the Bible, which contained 'laws,' just as the findings of councils or the decrees of the Popes were laws legally binding for Christendom," and praises Luther, who brought it about that "Scripture ceases to be a code of laws." (*Op. cit.*, pp. 15, 20, 91. — But Luther was not consistent. On page 21 we read: "Yet Luther would at another time, without due previous reflection, make use of Scripture in all its parts, practically or polemically, as a divine law.") G. T. Ladd deplores that the pupils of Luther did not follow Luther — *that* Luther whom Seeberg praises. "The *post*-Reformation theory of the Bible considered the principal office of the Bible to be that of imparting a ready-made system of religious dogmas. . . . The theory proved itself a vicious one." (*What Is the Bible?* p. 413.) Those poor dogmaticians! Marcus Dods writes: "This was due to the pedantic and elaborate dogmatism of the seventeenth century. The Bible had so persistently been used as a textbook to prove dogma that this came to be considered its main use. . . . Each of its utterances, no matter in what department of truth, was supposed to be final and authoritative." "To think of the Bible as a convenient collection or summary of doctrine, a textbook of theological knowledge, is entirely to misconceive it. . . . The Bible must not be thought of as 'a collection of truths formulated in propositions which God from time to time whispered in the ear to be communicated to the world as the unchanging formulas of thought and life for all time.'" (*The Bible: Its Origin and Nature*, pp. 66, 96 f.) — Verbal Inspiration is a horrible thing in the eyes of the moderns. It asks us to regard the Bible as a lawbook and thus compels us, says W. Herrmann, to accept even the false teachings of the Bible! W. Herrmann actually states that the doctrine of predestination set forth Rom. 9—11 "has no basis in faith." That "brings us to face the question whether we are prepared to follow Scripture even in that which we cannot understand to be a notion rooted in our faith," which "faith" cannot accept. And "if we decide to do this," if we accept a teaching which we know to be false, but accept it because it is found in Scripture, "we are treating the Bible as a lawbook which requires from us external obedience" (*op. cit.*, p. 134). That ought to be sufficient to discredit Verbal Inspiration!

rules, Holy Scripture exercises the same tyranny![295] — Away with Verbal Inspiration, this dogmatic fetter (Lenski on 2 Thess. 2:4, 5, page 422: "Some of the newer commentators have found a new way to interpret this whole section — they have discarded the doctrine of inspiration, 'this dogmatic fetter'"), this cast-iron theory (M'Intosh, in *Is Christ Infallible and the Bible True?* p. 313:

---

295) R. F. Horton: "As a matter of fact, the Bible stood before that crude dogma of infallible inspiration was invented, and the Bible will stand when that dogma has passed away. . . . And if even one soul is led out of the comfortable but suffocating prison house of the received dogma into the open air of the true revelation, the author will not have toiled in vain." (*Revelation and the Bible*, pp. 25, 407.) J. S. Whale: "Loyalty to truth in the shape of literary and historical criticism . . . has set the modern man free from the bondage of the letter, the prison house of verbal infallibility." (*The Christian Answer to the Problem of Evil*, p. 77.) R. H. Strachan: "Very many today have rightly discarded the notion of accepting their religious beliefs on an external authority, such as they have been encouraged to believe are the Church or the Bible. . . . Such slave mentality is at the source of religious infallibilities: the infallible Book or the infallible Church." (*The Authority of Christian Experience*, pp. 16, 26.) G. A. Buttrick: "Craving external support, men raised an infallible book to the vacant throne. From that false move and its tyranny we now break free." (See *Conc. Theol. Mthly.*, XII, p. 223.) G. L. Raymond: Men who are "at all intelligent accept the text of Scripture as suggestive rather than *dictatorial*. . . . The apparent theory of Jesus was that if men came to take into their natures the inspiration derived from the suggestions that He gave them — from such a suggestion, for instance, as that they were sons of God — they could safely be left, in applying the suggestion, to exercise the 'liberty' with which He had made them 'free.'" (*Op. cit.*, pp. 126, 140.) E. H. Delk: "Higher criticism has set theology free from that tyrannous literalism and false idea of inspiration which made all attempts at the adjustment of theology with modern thought in history, science, and philosophy either impious or revolutionary. . . . No theory of verbal inspiration is any longer tenable." (*Luth. Church Quart.*, 1912, p. 568.) W. H. Greever in *The Lutheran World Almanac*, 1934—1937, p. 94: "This approach and view . . . guarantee the liberty of the evangelical spirit against the enslaving legalism of the letter," and in the *Luth. Church Quart.*, 1937, p. 221: "In Fundamentalism there is such rigid subservience to the legalistic authority of the letter in recorded revelation that the spirit, purpose, and content of revelation are subordinated and obscured, if not actually lost." G. Aulén, on Luther's attitude towards the Bible: "It is well known that at times he took an independent attitude, but often he slavishly depended on Bible texts. A classical example: his line of argumentation on the Lord's Supper." (*Op. cit.*, p. 251.) W. C. Berkemeyer: "There is a sense in which the very words of Scripture must be the standard, *not in any legal way* but because they provide the classic original expression of the ideas and experiences and facts which go to make up the Christian faith. . . . Such a theology will escape, as far as it is humanly possible, the 'tyranny of words.'" (*Luth. Church Quart.*, 1939, p. 345 f.) J. M. Gibson: "Our Lord said, 'Ye seek to kill Me, because My Word hath not free course in you.' 'Free course' observe, and that was said to those who believed in the most thorough way in the verbal and literal inspiration of the Scriptures. They were slaves of the letter and knew nothing of the freedom of the spirit. And so it often is in our own times." (*The Inspiration and Authority of Holy Scripture*, p. 108.) — "Alexander Schweizer sagt von der Heiligen Schrift: 'Sie ist kein papierner Papst, kein Stellvertreter Gottes und Christi, sondern sein Zeuge; nicht das schon fertige Gold, sondern das

"Akin to this is the misrepresentation that the upholders of the Bible claim adopt a slavish literalism; and rash writers like Dr. Horton, more apt at inept epithet than cogent argument, upbraid them as maintainers of a 'cast-iron theory'")! The moderns refuse to play such a humiliating role as to bow to every single statement made by the old prophets and apostles. Verbal Inspiration, the instrument of galling tyranny and dark superstition, must be thrown to the moles and bats.

The bitter invective against Verbal Inspiration reaches its climax in the use of the ugly word "bibliolatry." It is bad enough that the moderns use "biblicism" as a term of reproach. They make copious use of it. For instance — we need not multiply examples — G. Aulen has no use for "the old biblicism, which restricts the divine revelation to the Bible." "Biblicism, the application of the theory of verbal inspiration, laid its heavy hand on the theology of orthodoxy." "Everywhere the principle of legalism intrudes and molds the theology. That is the disastrous consequence of biblicism." (*Op. cit.*, pp. 251, 255, 386.)[296] But "biblicism" as a term of

---

reiches Gold in sich schliessende Erz; und dem christlichen Geiste in der Kirche kommt es zu, das Gold auszuscheiden.'" (See W. Rohnert, *Die Inspiration der Heiligen Schrift*, p. 233.) F. Gogarten: "Es ist in der Tat nicht so, dass fuer den protestantischen Glauben an Stelle des lebendigen roemischen Papstes der tote papierne Papst des Bibelbuchstabens getreten waere. Sondern der protestantische Glaube ist auf das lebendige Wort der Bibel gerichtet," etc. (See *Schrift und Bekenntnis*, 1928, p. 100.) G. P. Mains: "The Church arrogated to itself the claim of sole authority and infallible wisdom for the spiritual direction of mankind. . . .' It is still true that large sections of Christendom are under the nightmare spell of this spiritual despotism. Inheritances of this despotism are such gratuitous attributions as verbal and plenary inspiration, of inerrancy, assumption of the entire historic and scientific accuracy of Biblical statement. . . . The Reformers made the mistake, and most easily so, of assigning to the Bible alone the place of infallible and inerrant authority which the Church had so stoutly but falsely claimed for itself." (*Divine Inspiration*, pp. 79, 81.)

296) Let us get clear on the meaning of biblicism as the term is used by the moderns. It means, as Aulén tells us, the practice of sticking to the words of the Bible, treating them, all of them, as inspired and inviolable. They are biblicists, says P. Althaus, "who identify the Word of God and Scripture" and look upon the Bible as "the supernatural infallible manual of doctrine." "Biblicism has a legalistic conception of the Word of God, out of harmony with the Reformation." (*Die letzten Dinge*, pp. 67, 74.) In addition, biblicism restricts authority in religion to the Bible. *The Living Church*, Nov. 11, 1933: "It ought to be said at once that the New Testament is *one* of the sources of our faith, not the sole and exclusive source. . . . That is presupposed in the tradition of the Great Church everywhere outside the circle of sixteenth to twentieth century Protestant biblicism." The statement of the *Lutheran* of Oct. 7, 1936, quoted above: "The Scriptures are not independently authoritative. They have no authority either apart from Christ or apart from the Church," was made in connection with the discussion and repudiation of the "biblicism of the later dogmaticians." If that be biblicism, we want to be known as good, thoroughgoing biblicists.

reproach is not strong enough for them. "Bibliolatry" suits them better. H. E. Fosdick: "From naive acceptance of the Bible as of equal credibility in all its parts because mechanically inerrant, I passed years ago to the shocking conviction that such traditional bibliolatry is false in fact and perilous in result." (*Op. cit.*, p. 273.) E. Brunner repeats Fosdick's statement: "Orthodoxy has made the Bible an independent divine thing, which just as such, as a *corpus mortuum*, is stamped with divine authority. . . . This materialistic, or, to be more exact, this idolatrous acceptance of Bible authority has done great damage to Christian faith." (*The Word and the World*, p. 92.) J. A. W. Haas uses the same term: "We have been too much misled, even in the Lutheran Church, by the non-Lutheran conceptions of the Bible, which often tend to bibliolatry. . . . Let us return to the Biblical and Lutheran idea of the living Word." (*The Lutheran*, Dec. 8, 1932.) Again: "The Bible must never be thought of apart from the living, unitary Word and become a codex. Otherwise we have bibliolatry and substitute a book for the creative Word." (*Luth. Church Quart.*, 1937, p. 279.) And again: "There must be a clear distinction kept in mind between the Word of God and the Bible. . . . Luther and true Lutheranism do not worship the record. . . . Luther and true Lutheranism have never made a fetish of the Bible as a book." (*What Is Lutheranism?* p. 176.) M. G. G. Sherer: "Christian liberty knows how to distinguish between Scripture and Scripture, between the shell and the content, between the chaff and the wheat, between the letter and the spirit. . . . Christian liberty does not fall into the sin of bibliolatry." (*Chr. Liberty and Chr. Unity*, p. 81.) T. A. Kantonen: "A living theology . . . will not set up a deified book in the place of the deified Church of Roman Catholicism nor hold to legalistic, unhistorical, and unpsychological theories of its inspiration." (*Luth. Church Quart.*, 1934, p. 114.)

Is there not a stronger term than bibliolatry? Well, Haas used the term "fetish"; H. L. Willett uses it: "The higher criticism has forever disposed of the fetish of a level Bible; it has destroyed the doctrine of a verbal inspiration." (*Op. cit.*, p. 264.) And the Princeton professor Homrighausen warns all against listening to the verbal-inspirationists: "Be fearful of those who make the Bible a fetish." (See *Conc. Theol. Mthly.*, IX, p. 452.) "Relic-worship" also serves the purpose. Bishop H. Martensen (Denmark): "Here [in the orthodoxy of the seventeenth century] the Scriptures are

---

But you cannot insult a modernist more than by intimating that he has not freed himself from all traces of biblicism. When the moderns want to praise a book, they will say of it: "The volume is not marked (as so many are) by theological prejudice and Biblical bias." Thus the *Lutheran*, March 25, 1942.

regarded as a book of laws; and the individual Christian, not maintaining a relative independence over against the Scriptures, is unable to distinguish in the Scriptures between the essential and the incidental, and practices a genuine relic-worship towards the letter of the Bible." (*Christian Dogmatics*, p. 45.) The conservative moderns do not agree in many points with the liberal moderns, but do agree with them in denouncing the unquestioning acceptance of every Scripture teaching on the bare word of Scripture as a form of wicked idolatry. The liberal K. Thieme of Leipzig asks: "An welchen Universitaeten, so muss man neugierig fragen, gilt die Schrift als Wort goettlicher Offenbarung im Sinne von Laibles massiver *Bibelvergoetterung?*" And the conservative Freimund [Neuendettelsau] uses the stronger term *Vergoetzung.* "The Bible does not set itself up as an authority in questions of science, astronomy, history, ethnology; but it is the authority in questions concerning salvation. He that knows this will escape the danger *der Vergoetzung des einzelnen Worts* and of mistaking the hull for the kernel." (See *Ev.-Luth. Freikirche*, Aug. 2, 1931.) And some of the moderns think they have divine authority for this use of the term bibliolatry. G. T. Ladd thinks so. "Christ does not find fault with the Jews for diligent study of their Sacred Scriptures; He does accuse them of folly and sin in *idolizing the written word* while neglecting its ideal contents of truth." (*The Doctrine of Sacred Scripture*, I, p. 51.) C. A. Wendell thus sums up the case for the moderns: "Bibliolatry is perhaps the finest and most exalted form of *idolatry*" (our italics), "but idolatry it is nevertheless. It is not the Bible but God Himself who says, 'Thou shalt have no other gods before Me.' A stilted veneration for the Word betrays an inward weakness rather than a virile faith and out of it proceeds a nervous anxiety to prove the 'complete inerrancy' of the Bible 'from cover to cover.'" (*What Is Lutheranism?* p. 235.)[297] —

297) We submit a few more statements to show that the use of this term is not exceptional but very common with the moderns. Dr. Pieper quotes from *What do Unitarians Believe?*: "We do not regard the Bible as a fetish, a verbally inspired and infallible oracle of God." (*Op. cit.*, I, p. 329.) And many Trinitarians agree with the Unitarians on this point. E. Lewis: "Without a doubt our fathers came very close to bibliolatry, they could make no distinction between the Word of God and the words of men by which that Word was given." (*The Faith We Declare*, p. 49.) R. F. Horton: "It is from this dangerous, and in the last resort, idolatrous, perversion of Christianity that the line of argument pursued in the foregoing pages is intended to deliver us." (*Op. cit.*, p. 407.) J. P. Smyth (he who wants Verbal Inspiration thrown to the bats and moles): "This collection of living utterances given for our use we have almost treated as a fetish for our worship. . . . The intelligent veneration for a nobly inspired Book has degenerated into a foolish reverence for an idol; the faith that should have assimilated the *spirit* of the Bible has become a superstitious worship of letters and words." (*Op. cit.*, p. 54.) J. S. Whale (he who wants to be "free from the

The moderns, it is clear, hate Verbal Inspiration. We have established that out of their own mouths. They abominate a teaching which, as they feel, makes men worship a book, makes them slaves of the letter.

AWAY WITH THE BONDAGE OF VERBAL LITERALISM AND GIVE US THE FREEDOM OF THE SPIRIT!

They want to be free men. We heard the Eisenach Declaration of Independence: "Bound yet free! Bound to the revelation within the Scriptures taken as a whole. . . . But free with respect to particulars, free to form our opinion of the human garments in which the divine glory of the Scriptures is masked." (See *Theol. Mthly.,* V, p. 6.) We heard Bishop Martensen exhorting the Christians to "maintain a relative independence over against the Scriptures." And all of the moderns, the more or less conservatives, the liberals, and the ultraliberals, have taken up the cry. J. A. W. Haas: "What the theologians call the Word of God, namely, the spiritual content of the Bible, is an authority of freedom. It is not dependent upon a prior acceptance of an infallible record or any doctrine of inspiration. . . . With this approach to infallibility" ("the claims of a mechanically infallible Bible, verbally perfect, do not hold in the light of the facts") "in the authority of divine truth we do no injury to our moral freedom." (*What Ought I to Believe,* pp. 29, 30.) H. F. Rall: "Revelation meant to them [our fathers] so many doctrines or commandments handed down. . . . Free men know only one kind of authority — that of truth and right." (*A Faith for Today,* pp. 228, 232.) R. H. Strachan (he who speaks of "slave mentality"): "The authority of which we are in quest clearly must be an authority which does not destroy our personal freedom. It must compel a humble acceptance of the will of God and also clearly recognize the autonomy of the individual personality and our responsibility for our own beliefs." (*Op. cit.,* p. 19.) H. E.

---

bondage of the letter, the prison house of verbal infallibility") is "convinced that blind bibliolatry can be as pathetically wrong as what is called blind unbelief and that the way of obscurantism is the way of disaster" (*op. cit.,* p. 78). But why go on? Men who honestly believe that the Bible is not in all its parts God's very Word and then find other men who bow before these words and absolutely trust in them, cannot but say with S. Bulgakoff: "An exaggerated and one-sided bibliolatry treats the Word of God as a transcendent oracle. Such interpretation reminds us of the origin of bibliolatry, when a legalism of the letter of the Bible replaced, to a certain extent at least, that of the Church of Rome" (in *Revelation,* by J. Baillie and H. Martin, p. 155) and with Hans Rust (Koenigsberg): "We should like to have God's infallible Word placed in our hands directly, by means of Holy Scripture, in order to have all questions decided at once. But God willed otherwise. . . . God has kept His Church from making the Bible a revelation-idol, *sich aus der Schrift einen Offenbarungsgoetzen zu machen*" (*Vom Aergernis des Menschenworts in d. H. Schrift,* pp. 25, 30).

Fosdick: The Gospel must be "released from literal bondage to old categories and set free to do its work in modern terms of thought. . . . The new methods of study have given us His imperishable Gospel freed from its entanglements, to be preached with a liberty, a reasonableness, an immediate application to our own age, such as no generation of preachers in the Church's history ever had the privilege of knowing before." (*Op. cit.*, pp. 261, 273.) Col. R. G. Ingersoll, discussing the "mistakes of Moses" and related matters: "It is a question, first, of intellectual liberty, and after that, a question to be settled at the bar of human reason." (*Lectures*, p. 382.) Yes, and Luther, too, belongs in this class. G. Wehrung declares: "Wir muessen mit Luther und seinem Freiheitsgeist einig bleiben, indem wir alles Schriftwort danach schaetzen, ob es das Evangelium als Evangelium rein und ungetruebt zum Ausdruck bringt." (*Op. cit.*, p. 308.)

What kind of liberty are these men (excluding Luther) fighting for? They claim the right to criticize and correct Scripture. They claim the right to correct Scripture by stamping certain scientific and historical statements as false — that is the coarser method; or — and that is the finer, politer method — by investing certain stories, which are of course not literally true, with a deeper significance, as being poetic descriptions of some higher truth and as bearing some profound prophetic philosophy of history. The Biblical teachings, too, were good enough for those days, but must be translated into modern categories of thought.[298] The moderns

---

298) E. H. Delk: "Higher criticism has set theology free from that tyrannous literalism and false idea of inspiration which made all attempts at the adjustment of theology with modern thought in history, science, and philosophy either impious or revolutionary. . . . No theory of verbal inspiration is any longer tenable." (*Luth. Church Quart.*, 1912, p. 568.) O. L. Joseph: "If we are to escape the pitfalls of barren intellectualism, we must recognize that reason and faith are the twin guides to truth. When we imprison the reason within a Chinese wall of traditionalism, we imperil the prospects of liberty." The Bible is a book "containing errors." "Are we not doing injustice to the Book when we fail to discriminate between prose and poetry, between history and fiction, between biography and allegory, between folklore and faith?" (*Ringing Realities*, pp. 93, 217.) — T. A. Kantonen: "Relying upon the theory of the verbal inspiration of the Bible, the adherents of this approach have regarded the stories of the Temptation and the Fall as mere historical narratives rather than profound prophetic philosophy of history." (*Luth. Church Quart.*, 1935, p. 211.) Did Creation actually take place as the Bible tells it? O. F. Nolde: "Pupils ought forever to accept the story itself because of literary and religious merit. . . . They may later discard the scientific import of the story." (*Luth. Church Quart.*, 1939, p. 299.) Similarly, did the great fish swallow Jonah? The Bible does not really say so, says H. L. Willett. The romance is "perhaps intended as a symbol of Israel's engulfment and restoration" (*op. cit.*, p. 110). H. E. Fosdick: "When one has said all that needs to be said about the new views of the Bible, . . . in particular about the obvious changes in mental categories between Biblical times and our own, how empty is the issue of it all if it does not *liberate our mind from handicaps* and summon our

are thoroughly convinced that the Bible is full of mistakes and that many of its statements are unreliable and misleading. The mistaken views of the early Church, says Edwin Lewis, "have colored the Gospel records themselves" (*A New Heaven and a New Earth,* p. 175 f.). Why, Jesus Himself was not inerrant. That was either because He was a mere man or because of His self-limitation. (See what has been said on p. 71 ff.)[299] So the moderns claim it as their God-given right to subject the Bible to a careful scrutiny, to separate truth from error, to discriminate between the outworn forms of thought and the things of abiding value. Do not fail "to discriminate between prose and poetry," etc., says O. L. Joseph. "Christian liberty," says M. G. G. Sherer, "knows how to distinguish between Scripture and Scripture, between the chaff and the wheat." Did not A. Schweizer tell us long ago that the Bible is not a paper pope, that the gold it contains is mixed with dross, and that it is the business of the Christian spirit to smelt the ore and obtain the pure gold?

And when we protest that the statements, stories, and teachings of the Bible must be taken at their face value, they indignantly reply: Away with these old exegetical and dogmatical fetters! Our minds have been liberated from these handicaps. (Fosdick.) "Do not foreclose by an appeal to authority the whole line of detailed investigation!" (W. Sanday, *The Oracles of God,* p. 102.) "Let it be said in all seriousness that Lutheran exegesis will be seriously handicapped unless it abandons once and for all the unpsychological and mechanical theories of inspiration and unhistorical views of verbal inerrancy," etc. (T. A. Kantonen, "The Canned Goods of

souls the more clearly to the spiritual adventures for which the Scriptures stand! . . . To be a Bible Christian, must we think, as some seem to suppose, that a fish swallowed a man, or that the sun and moon stood still at Joshua's command, or that God sent she-bears to eat up children who were rude to a prophet? . . . To be a Bible Christian is a more significant affair than such bald literalism suggests." (*Op. cit.,* p. 181.) You must translate what the Bible literally teaches into modern categories of thought! "Decode the abiding meanings of Scripture from outgrown phraseology!" The Bible teaching on "the resurrection of the flesh" means nothing more than "the immortality of the soul" (*op. cit.,* pp. 123, 129). Yes, indeed, says Edwin Lewis, we may well regard the resurrection narratives "not as literal statements of fact but as a more or less pictorial effort on the part of the earlier Christian community to account for their experience of Christ." (See *Conc. Theol. Mthly.,* IV, p. 758.)

299) Fosdick's view, as presented in the *Christian Century,* Dec. 6, 1936: "There were theologians who justified the crusade, but tried not to lean too heavily upon Jesus for Scriptural support. Dr. Fosdick, for instance, frankly said: 'The Master never faced in His own experience . . . a national problem such as Belgium met when the Prussians crossed the border. . . . The fact is that Jesus did not directly face our modern question about war; they were not His problems, and to press a *legalistic* interpretation of special texts as though they were, is a misuse of the Gospel.'"

Past Theology," in the *Lutheran,* Dec. 12, 1935, to Jan. 2, 1936.)
Reviewing Dr. Lenski's "Interpretation of St. John's Gospel," the
Luth. Church Quart., Oct., 1932, says: "While the author would
count his verbal-inspiration theory the bulwark of his treatment,
as a matter of fact it is its strait jacket." (See the *Pastor's Monthly,*
1935, p. 262.) — It is no caricature when the mind of the moderns
is thus described in *Christian Dogmatics* (Dr. J. T. Mueller), p. 114:
"Chafing under the divine restraint, 1 Pet. 4:11, the exponents of
modern theology allege that belief in the divine inspiration of Holy
Scripture results in 'intellectualism,' 'biblicism,' 'letter service,'
'the constraint of the free spirit of investigation,' 'the failure to find
new religious truths,' 'the inability of the theologian to accommodate
himself to present-day religious thought,' and the like." J. M.
Haldeman: "The truth is (according to modernism) man of today
has altogether outgrown the Bible. It may have done for the infant state of the human mind, but to put the rising generation
under its *clamps and chains* would be to restrict the mental growth
of the human race." (*A King's Penknife,* p. 108.)

The Bible has lost its rights. One of these is the right to have
its statements understood and accepted *literally,* unless otherwise
indicated. The moderns recognize this right in the case of a
reputable human writing, but in the case of the Bible they have
*assumed the right to depart from the literal sense whenever it suits
them.* And they heap scorn and obloquy on those who insist on
abiding by the literal sense in spite of the protest of "science" and
modern thought. They call these men "dogmatists and literalists"
(*Luth. Church Quart.,* 1939, p. 153). N. R. Best thinks he has dealt
them a deathblow when he declares: "Their theory obliges them to
hold that every Bible verse in its simple literal sense is an explicitly exact statement of fact." (*Inspiration,* p. 118.) The reader
will understand the import of this statement when he reads the
preceding paragraph which unfolds the thesis: "Utterly vain is it
to talk of not employing human reason on the Bible." Georgia
Harkness speaks on the subject of literalism thus: "The revolt
against Fundamentalism has centered upon the other great pitfall
of reliance on the authority of the Bible, namely, the disregard of
historical and scientific fact that ensues from belief in its literal
inspiration. The battle is not yet won. Like the poor, literalism
is always with us." (*The Faith by Which the Church Lives,* p. 57.)
The moderns claim the right to nullify any statement or doctrine
of Scripture by simply pronouncing the magic word "literalism."
Do you believe that the bears ate the children? Fosdick tells you:
"That is bald literalism" and he glories in the fact of our "release
from literalism." (*Op. cit.,* p. 182.) Do you accept the Bible
teaching on the Fall and original sin? R. Niebuhr will tell you:

"Christian theology has found it difficult to refute the rationalistic rejection of the myth of the Fall without falling into the literalistic error of insisting upon the Fall as an historical event. One of the consequences of this literalism," etc. "The confusion revealed in the debate between Pelagians and Augustinians has been further aggravated by the literalism of the Augustinians." (*The Nature and Destiny of Man,* I, pp. 260, 267.) Do you believe in the Real Presence? Bishop Gore has told you: That is "purest literalism"; you have permitted Luther to put this bridle on you. Is Jesus Christ true God? O. J. Baab refuses to "ascribe deity to Jesus" and then looks with derision on us: "No wonder the literalistic interpreters of the Bible are stirred to indignant and vehement protest." (*Jesus Christ Our Lord,* pp. 11, 41.) Do you believe in Verbal Inspiration? Scripture plainly says that all the words of Scripture were inspired, 2 Tim. 3:16; 1 Cor. 2:13. Go to, say the moderns, that is a literalistic interpretation and cannot stand. *The Lutheran,* Feb. 30, 1936, reviewing Lenski's *Interpretation of First and Second Corinthians,* passes the verdict: "The verbal literalism of the author's view of inspiration is hardly congenial in the atmosphere of most present-day theological schools, even of our conservative Lutheran institutions." Lenski had written on 1 Cor. 2:13: "The very words which the apostles speak are taught them by the Spirit. He is their teacher even as to the 'words.' This is proof positive for Verbal Inspiration," etc. Yes, say the moderns, taken literally, this verse proves Verbal Inspiration; but we are not literalists. We refuse to be bound by the letter with respect to this teaching or any other teaching and statement of Scripture. Do not expect us to submit to any kind of legalistic constraint. — Note that the moderns use "legalistic" and "literalistic" as synonyms. *Luth. Church Quart.,* 1937, p. 279: "The Bible must never become a codex. Otherwise we have bibliolatry. . . . The Fundamentalists make it *literalistic and legalistic* in a Calvinistic manner and forget that the letter killeth but the Spirit maketh alive." The hue and cry is: "The enslaving legalism of the letter!" We will not have this "fetter," this "handicap," these "clamps and chains," this "strait jacket" of literalism put on us.

The moderns certainly do not like this thing "literalism." They make it responsible for all sorts of woes and evils. It destroys, for instance, belief in the Scriptures and keeps in spiritual death. G. L. Raymond: "This statement — 2 Cor. 3:6: 'The letter killeth, but the spirit giveth life' — the history of the world has proved to be true. As a fact, the letter has killed. It has done this both because the theory of literalism, so conscientiously advocated, has been the death of any form of belief in the Scriptures on the part of large numbers who could not fully ignore what to them have seemed to be discrepancies, and also because the truth, when considered only in itself, so far as it has been supposed to be identical with a form or a formula, has failed to stimulate to activity, and so to spiritual life." (*Op. cit.*, p. 193 f.)

The moderns do not want to be tied down to the letter. They want the freedom of the spirit. "Like the poor, literalism is always with us. . . . Literalize the Bible and you get weird nonsense. From Genesis to Revelation the Bible has been cheapened, perverted, flattened out to a dull dead level, by those who find their authority in the letter and not the spirit." (Harkness.) "The letter killeth, but the spirit giveth life!" And what is this "spirit" which gives the right understanding of Scripture or what is the "spiritual content" of Scripture which supersedes the literal form? The Unitarians identify this "spirit" with reason. Let the Unitarian W. E. Channing repeat his statement: "The Bible expects us to restrain and modify its language by the known truths which observation and experience furnish on these topics. . . . We feel it our bounden duty to exercise our reason upon it perpetually, *to look beyond the letter to the spirit*" (our italics), "to make use of what is known for explaining what is difficult and for discovering new truths." (*Works of W. E. Channing*, p. 368 ff.) [300] The more conservative moderns will not directly identify the "spirit" with reason. But they are rather hazy in defining this term of theirs. The best they can do is to tell us that it is "something in us," "the best in us," our "moral sense," our "spiritual understanding," etc. J. M. Gibson: "The letter killeth, but the spirit giveth life. . . . There must be *some soul in the person* reading it to put the color in from suggestions of it which it is possible to give." (*Op. cit.*, p. 235.) Hazy? C. H. Dodd: "The criterion lies within ourselves, in *the response of our own spirit* to the spirit that utters itself in the Scriptures." (*The Authority of the Bible*, p. 296.) Call it "spirit complex" and let it go at that. That is the term to which attention is called by Erik Floreen in his critique of Aulén's theology. "It would be legalistic [according to Aulén] to ground our faith on an outward authority, as on that of the Bible. . . . It is no vital

---

300) Similar statements. N. R. Best: "The contributions made to the Bible's contents by its prophets, its evangelists, its apostles, and above all by its immortal Messiah are literature of a quality shiningly beyond all categories of 'the letter,' which Paul complained of as 'killing' the spirituality of believers. They all are instead instinct with the spirit which 'giveth life.' Utterly vain then is it to talk of not employing human reason on the Bible." (*Op. cit.*, p. 117.) H. L. Willett: "It is inevitable that one who studies the Scriptures should bring every statement and precept to the bar of *his own sense of right* and judge it by that standard. . . . The Bible's overwhelming vindication, its right to the world's reverence, are found in its appeal to the *intelligent and sensitive spirit*." (*Op. cit.*, pp. 291, 299.)

matter to Dr. Aulén whether his teachings always agree with the Bible. He holds that faith owes its existence and growth to a 'spirit complex' controlled by the glorified Christ. This spirit complex he identifies with the Church." (See *The Luth. Companion,* Feb. 9, 1939.) And what is the "spiritual content" of the Bible which appeals to the "spirit complex" of the Church, the spiritual sense of the theologians? [301] Nobody has ever told us. We know that all the content of the Bible is spiritual. If that is not true, if only certain portions have spiritual value, we ought to know how to identify these portions. The moderns have never told us how to do that. They have never drawn up a precise list of the spiritual sections. Or rather, they have told us how to identify these portions: your "spirit" will pick them out. If your spirit responds to a certain section of the Bible, you can be sure that in that section the Spirit utters itself. (Dodd.) And that means that so much of the Bible is spiritual as the individual or the "Church" chooses to call spiritual. [302] And that means that the moderns are fighting for the freedom from Scripture. Their "spiritual liberty," the "liberty of the evangelical spirit against the enslaving legalism of the letter," is a revolt against the authority of Scripture in favor of the authority of man. They tell us very plainly that in fighting against this legalistic Verbal Inspiration, this legalism of the letter, their interest is to establish the authority of man over Scripture. What did C. H. Dodd say? "The criterion lies *within ourselves,* in the response of our spirit to the Spirit that utters itself in the Scriptures." Listen to what H. F. Rall says on this point: "Paul had not the faintest idea that centuries later theologians would be building up their theories on this phrase or that sentence of his letters. . . . There are two kinds of authority.

---

301) V. Ferm: "The authority of the Sacred writings is no longer found in 'the letter' and sustained by some artificial theory of divine inspiration but in the appeal of its *spiritual content.*" (*What Is Lutheranism?* p. 279.)

302) That is Rudelbach's diagnosis of the case. "Wie spaeter die Vernuenftler, so hatten zu jener Zeit die Paepstler vor allem den Spruch Pauli aufgegriffen, 'Der Buchstabe toetet, aber der Geist macht lebendig,' und mit der offenen Missdeutung, als ob der Apostel hier von zweierlei Schriftsinn, dem *buchstaebischen* und dem *geistlichen,* rede, verbanden sie die kecke Zumutung, dass die Schrift sich eben nach ihrem Geiste sollte wenden und drehen lassen. Trefflich fuehrt unser Luther wider Emser aus . . ., die Schrift leide ueberhaupt ein solches Spalten des Buchstabens und Geistes nicht" (*Zeitsch. f. d. ges. luth. Theologie,* 1840, zweites Quartalheft, p. 4). Nach *ihrem Geist* soll die Schrift sich wenden und drehen lassen! That in Scripture is spiritual which finds a response in your spirit, and when your spirit complex changes, that part of Scripture loses its spiritual content! — Here you have, by the way, the pedigree of the slogan "The letter kills, but the spirit gives life." The moderns got it from the Unitarians; the Unitarians got it from the rationalists (Vernuenftler); and the rationalists got it from the papists.

One is external, compulsive. It does not ask for understanding or conviction, but simply submission. The other is inner, moral, spiritual; it asks obedience, but the obedience must root in conviction and come as free choice. The former belongs to subjects, the latter to sons. Free men know only one kind of authority — that of truth and right." (*A Faith for Today*, pp. 229, 232.) And H. L. Willett uses very plain language: "The authority present in the Biblical record does not inhere in the Book as such nor in any particular portion of it. But rather it is found in the appeal which the Scripture as a whole makes to the moral sense within humanity, and in particular the urgency of the appeal made by certain parts of the record, notably the Gospels and the Pauline epistles. . . . The Book asks nothing for itself in the way of sovereignty over the minds of men. But it exercises that power by the sheer force of its appeal to all that is best within them. Its authority is not formal or arbitrary. It consists rather in the outreaching of the spirit of God in the men who wrote its various parts to the souls of those who study it." (*Op. cit.*, p. 292.) — Luther addressed the following to the spirituals of his day, but it describes the mind of the moderns exactly: "Their conceit sets up the rule that you must forget about these words 'This is My body' and study the matter spiritually. . . . Here you have a fine rule, which will guide you into all truth far better than the Holy Spirit can do it; *viz.*, wherever Holy Scripture stands in the way of your own opinion and conceit, forget about Scripture and follow your own conceit, and you will get along wonderfully. . . . Gott muss und soll sich gefangen geben, dass er seine Worte nicht setze, wann und wo er will, sondern wo und wie es ihm dieser Geist stimmt. . . . Der Geist hat abermal frei und schoen gewonnen." (XX: 1022 f.)

Another word on the conceit of these spirituals. They look with infinite contempt on us poor Bible-Christians, who stick to the words as written and simply repeat them. They despise our theological method as "mechanical," tell us that we have "a metallic, inert, or mechanical mind"; that our "viewpoint is wooden, rigid, and narrow"; that our dependence upon a book is "a dead and artificial thing." When we refuse to depart from the literal sense of the words "This is My body," E. S. Jones sneers: "How wooden and blocked off we've made Him!" Sticking to Verbal Inspiration, sticking to the text, involves "a loss of intellectual vitality." "Schlendrianmaessige Reproduktion!" "Mechanische und hoelzerne Vorstellung." "Die orthodoxe, versteinerte Verbalinspirationslehre." "Dogmatische Verknoecherung des Offenbarungsgedankens." "Es war der Fehler der Verbalinspiration, dass sie keine Aufgaben stellte, sondern die Hinnahme einer fertiggestellten Aufgabe verlangte." (B. Steffen.) Verbal Inspiration makes theology too easy. Hofmann told the verbal-inspirationist Philippi: "Mag immerhin fortschlafen, wer es gern bequem hat." (See Pieper, *op. cit.*, I, p. 147.) We need men, say the moderns, who are able to enrich the Bible with the results of their spiritual labors and experiences, who will soar on the pinions of the spirit through the regions of heaven and discover new and better truths, who "liberate their minds from handicaps and summon their souls the more clearly to the spiritual adventures for which the Scriptures stand" (Fosdick). — The moderns will not have the holy writers degraded to mere machines and therefore denounce the mechanical (verbal) theory of inspiration. And they will not have themselves degraded to mere machines and therefore denounce the legalistic (verbal) theory of inspiration.

GIVE US DOCTRINAL LIBERTY!

In the bill of rights set up by the moderns great stress is laid upon the freedom of doctrine. It would be legalistic to bind men to the doctrinal statements of the Bible, not to permit the Church to develop the doctrine according to the new light and understanding which the passing centuries gave her. You must not suppress the spirit, but let it go adventuring in the realm of doctrine. (Fosdick.) The doctrines set down in the Bible need revision and re-statement, for have not the apostles occasionally fallen into doctrinal error? Christ Himself is not altogether reliable. He did not know, said Fosdick, present conditions. And, more generally: "The demand even for an infallible Christ, in the sense that He reveals to us a special body of truth, beyond the reach of inquiry or intellectual reconstruction, . . . is simply to deny that the idea of evolution is applicable to the Christian faith." (R. H. Strachan, *op. cit.*, p. 199.) That means that Christ did not set down the doctrine in its final form. The Bible statements are merely "suggestive" (Raymond), or, as R. W. Nelson puts it: "The Bible is an inspired and inspiring source book, a gold mine of *initial data*, concerning God's plan of life for men" (*Christendom*, IV, p. 410). Develop these initial data; there are truths hidden there of which the apostles never dreamed. W. A. Brown: "Generation after generation has found the best of itself reflected in its pages and has discovered meanings in its teachings of which its authors never dreamed. . . . The Bible is a compendium of simple principles capable of indefinite application and therefore needing continual reinterpretation in the light of expanding experience." (*A Creed for Free Men*, pp. 227, 230.) In the light of expanding experience! "Much water has passed under the bridge since the sixteenth and seventeenth centuries," says V. Ferm (*op. cit.*, p. 279), and much more, say others, since the first century. Therefore we must "make readjustments with the findings of the best Biblical scholarship and interpretation, with the best recent scholarship" (Ferm). The doctrines cannot stand as they were "once delivered to the saints." They sorely need reinterpretation, rephrasing (and that is a polite way of saying that they need to be changed, abolished, turned into something else). Fosdick: "What is permanent in Christianity is not mental frameworks but abiding experiences that phrase and rephrase themselves in successive generations' ways of thinking." (*Op. cit.*, p. 103.) And, best of all, Scripture itself demands this progress, this freedom of doctrine. "The idea of a revelation confined to the writings cannot be said to be the idea of those Sacred Writings themselves." (Horton, *op. cit.*, p. 16.) Paul never intended to set down a final system of truth.[303]

There is no finality in doctrine — that is the Declaration of Independence proclaimed by the moderns. The truth is not "final and fixed." It would be a crime against intellectual and spiritual freedom to keep men from developing the saving doctrine. It would result in intellectual stagnation. Said Col. Ingersoll: "Whoever has quit growing, he is orthodox, whether in art, politics, *religion*, philosophy — no matter what. Whoever thinks he has found it all out, he is orthodox. Orthodoxy is that which rots, and heresy is that which grows forever. Orthodoxy is the night of the past, full of the darkness of superstition, and heresy is the eternal coming day, the light of which strikes the grand foreheads of the intellectual pioneers of the world." (*Op. cit.*, p. 314.)[304]

---

303) Fosdick says so. We read in the *Lutheran*, Jan. 15, 1931: " 'He Kept the Faith.' On Jan. 4 we 'listened in' to hear Dr. Fosdick's radio sermon. And when the text, 'He kept the faith,' issued from the transmitter, we were curious to know what the famous 'modernist' would make of it. What he did was to expound the theory that the great apostle's proudly cherished fidelity consisted in an ability to look forward and not chain himself to what was past. We were told that the faith he kept was not that of his youth nor of the part of his life when he was a Pharisee nor *of the period when he wrote to the Thessalonians.*"

304) Christian theologians say: "Die orthodoxe, versteinerte Verbalinspirationslehre." H. Kraemer speaks of "the clumsy form of the literal inerrancy of the document in which God's revelation is told" and of "the justified revolt of the human spirit against the intellectual bondage caused by the petrification of Christian truth" (*The Christian Message in a Non-Christian World*, pp. 10, 218). M. Maryosip: "The idea . . . that revelation is to be conceived in terms of words, texts, and even books, . . . the dogma of a verbal inspiration, . . . has paralyzed the intellect of those who have adopted it, as every mechanical conception of the truth must do." (*Why I Believe the Bible*, p. 112 f.) The *Luth. Church Quart.*, 1939, p. 348 ff., speaking of "the tyranny of words," declares that, "when we deal with these great New Testament terms and ideas, we deal not with pieces of a system of thought which can be put together to form some original divinely given theology. . . . In the past, theologians have been far too sensitive to orthodoxy and heresy." In a book review the *Lutheran*, May 26, 1927, complains that "to him [the author] every sentence of the Bible is absolutely true in every

And so the moderns have assumed the right to produce new doctrines, necessary for salvation. The conservatives insist upon this right as strenuously as the liberals. Hofmann contended that it is the business of the theologian "die alte Wahrheit auf neue Weise zu lehren und sie, gehorsam der Fuehrung des Geistes Gottes, zu *mehren*." P. Althaus, who quotes and approves this principle (see *Schrift und Bekenntnis*, July, 1930, p. 123), is busy applying it with all the rest of the moderns. He says: "Scripture is not an absolutely infallible manual of doctrine. . . . Our doctrine of justification is not simply a repetition of the New Testament doctrine and our eschatology is not simply a repetition of the Biblical doctrine but has its own form." (*Op. cit.*, pp. 61, 74.) And the liberals are certainly not going to be outdone by the conservatives. The Unitarian Channing told us that he is for "looking beyond the letter to the spirit and for discovering new truths." E. H. Delk gets violent on this subject: "To deny that modern thought has any new truths to offer is to deny the presence and leadership of God. It is a kind of atheism." (*Op. cit.*, p. 554.) — That is freedom with a vengeance! The real freedom of the spirit![305] Dr. Pieper says on our present subject: "Today we have to call particular attention to the fact that Paul insists on the perfection and completeness of the apostolic doctrine also over against such teachers as find it necessary to supplement and augment the doctrine of Christ on the pretense of a higher philosophical knowledge and a higher spirituality." (*Op.cit.*, p. 148.)

---

detail. The truth, historical, scientific, as well as religious, is final and fixed." And that is "so wooden and rigid and narrow." Fosdick: No unanimous system of truth in the Bible! (*Op. cit.*, p. 30.) C. S. Macfarland: "Christian revelation is not confined to a closed canon, to a stereotyped letter, or a strictly defined confession." (*Chr. Unity in Practice and Prophecy*, p. 27.) *The Living Church*, March 9, 1938, complains that "the Roman Church is doctrinally immobilized by its dogma of the inerrancy of Scripture." *The Christian Century*, Feb. 10, 1937, declares "that 'in the New Testament there is no unalterable doctrine which embraces the whole scheme of Christian thought. . . . The epistles are not contributions to a doctrinal system which shall be valid to all eternity.' . . . The Lutherans should be paged and told about it." The moderns do not want to be kept in a prison house, and they do not want God to be kept a prisoner. Says G. A. Buttrick: "How could God, so radiant and vital in His own life, be imprisoned in the past? And what is this doctrine of an inerrant Book but the assertion that God spoke then and cannot speak now, the avowal that the Everliving is the captive of antiquity?" (See *Conc. Theol. Mthly.*, XII, p. 223.)

305) Hofmann: "Following the promptings of the spirit," G. Aulén: "Ein Gott, von dessen Offenbarung nur als in der Vergangenheit geschehen gesprochen werden kann, ist kein lebendiger Gott. Man will Ernst machen mit dem Charakter des christlichen Gottesglaubens, dass er *Geistglaube* ist, und laesst den 'Geist' den immer gegenwaertigen Charakter der Gottesoffenbarung sein. Dieser Gedanke tritt . . . in Gegensatz zu dem alten Biblizismus und seiner Tendenz, die Gottesoffenbarung in und mit der Bibel 'abgeschlossen' sein zu lassen." (*Op. cit.*, p. 386.)

AWAY WITH THE LEGALISTIC CONCEPTION OF SCRIPTURE AS "THE WORD OF GOD"!

Finally, the moderns claim the right, in the interest of freedom to operate with the "Word of God." The Word of God, not the word of Scripture, is what counts. What is this "Word" of the moderns? Nobody knows exactly. The moderns know for sure what it is not. It is not Scripture. Dr. C. M. Jacobs: "With all the emphasis which we lay upon the Scriptures we do not identify them with the Word of God. . . . For this view of the Word of God and this view of the Scriptures the Philadelphia Seminary has stood, and for them it will continue, by God's help, to stand." "In Lutheran theology, the two are not equated." (*The Lutheran*, Jan. 12, 1933.) *Luth Church Quart.*, 1937, p. 195: "What results is a legalistic and an atomistic conception of the Scriptures as the Word of God, far more congenial to Calvinism than to Lutheranism. Calvinism identified the Word of God with the words of Scripture." E. Lewis agrees with that. We heard his statement: "Without a doubt our fathers came very close to Bibliolatry; they could make no distinction between the Word of God and the words of men by which that Word was given." H. L. Willett finds "portions in the Bible which are worthy to be called the Word of God to man." But "it is unfortunate that the Bible has been called the Word of God" (*op. cit.*, p. 289). Yes, and "it would be unchristian," says W. Herrmann, "if it meant the acknowledgment of any chance sentence of the Scriptures as God's Word" (*op. cit.*, p. 58). To be sure, "Scripture *contains* the Word of God," Willett goes on to say; and the *Luth. Church Quart.* and all the rest, the Unitarians, too, subscribe to that. But that is as far as they will go. They refuse to operate with the words of Scripture as such. They want to operate with the "Word of God."

Then tell us what this Word of God is. We get various answers. Some say it is God's revelation in history, what God did for man's salvation, "the succession of events in which and through which God made Himself known to men." — When God *tells* men what His actions mean, you can use the term "Word of God." But you cannot call the actions God's Word.[306] — Very well, others say, but God did explain these actions in Scripture: How-

---

306) *The Christian Century* is not liberal enough to identify actions with words. "The concept 'Word of God' was one of the most difficult upon which the conference (World Conference, Edinburgh) expended its effort. Happily there appeared to be no literalists in the conference. . . . The Word itself — what is it? 'It is ever living and dynamic and inseparable from God's activity. God reveals Himself to us by what He does.' I like this immensely; only I wish it had not been made obscure by the far-fetched necessity of connecting it up with the concept 'Word.' . . . It overstrains the meaning of 'Word' to make it bear the meaning of action." (Sept. 8, 1937, p. 1096.)

ever — they add at once — you cannot find this meaning, the Word of God, in all the words of Scripture. Only certain portions of Scripture are the Word of God. Which are these portions? Dr. Haas told us: "What the theologians call the Word of God, namely, the *spiritual content* of the Bible, is an authority of freedom." (In *What is Lutheranism?*, p. 176, he says: "There must be a clear distinction kept in mind between the Word of God and the Bible. . . . The Bible is the Word of God because it contains the Word of God," because of its "spiritual content.") Others, somewhat more specific, say the Word of God contained in the Bible is the Gospel; others, more indefinitely, the "Living Christ" (*Luth. Church Quart.*), the "Living Word" (E. Lewis). Now, we are willing, very willing, to call the Gospel the Word of God. But we also call the Law God's Word. And the moderns have never given us a reason why only the Gospel should be God's Word, not the Law. The Law was certainly spoken by God. The distinction the moderns make here is utterly arbitrary, not based in Scripture nor in common sense. Nor have the moderns ever told us just how much of the Bible is Gospel. Nor will they tell us which portions of the Bible have a spiritual content. We believe that everything in the Bible has a spiritual purpose. And we are waiting for the moderns to publish a list enumerating the spiritual portions.

And if we agree with the moderns that this and that section has a spiritual content, may we call these sections the Word of God? Oh, no, they tell us; these bare words, these words written by John or Paul, are not in themselves God's Word. You must separate the wheat from the chaff, distinguish between the form (the words) and the content of John 3:16 and Rom. 3:28 and find out, with the help of your Christian consciousness, etc., what the spiritual content is: that part of John 3:16 you have a right to call the "Word of God." "To us the 'Word of God' is the validly spiritual content which rises unmistakably in Scriptural utterances and in the pronouncements of Christlike Seers." (V. Ferm, in *What is Lutheranism?* p. 294.) But be sure you do not make a mistake. You would be mistaken if you relied on the bare words.

Perhaps K. Barth and his followers can clear up the matter. Barth teaches first, with the others, that not everything in the Bible is God's Word. "The Word of God is within the Bible." There is "a margin where the Bible ceases to be Bible" (*The Word of God and the Word of Man*, pp. 43, 65). There are places in the Bible "wo die Bibel aufhoert, Bibel zu sein" (*Das Wort Gottes und die Theologie*, p. 77). Then what about those portions which really are Bible? Barth and his followers tell us, secondly, that not even these portions are absolutely God's Word. They *become* God's

Word, and they *cease to be* God's Word, depending on something
else. Barth's classical phrase is: That is God's Word, "das mich
findet." Again: "We said of church proclamation that from time
to time it must become *God's Word.* And we said the same of
the Bible, that it must from time to time become *God's Word* . . .
in virtue of divine decision." (*The Doctrine of the Word of God*,
p. 131 f. See H. Sasse, *Here We Stand*, p. 161.)   Barth actually
teaches that these Gospel passages *are* not the Word of God but
only *become* the Word of God under certain circumstances.   One
of his followers, Adolf Keller, assures us that that is Barthianism's
definition of the Word of God in the Bible. "When we call the
Bible the Word of God, we are not referring to the human interpretation of God's Word, but only to that act of faith by which
we believe in the God who speaks in the Bible wherever, whenever,
and through whatever words He will." (*Religion and Revelation.*
See further *Conc. Theol. Mthly.*, VI, p. 715.) So, then, the Barthian
"Word of God" is not something on which you can lay your finger.
A lot of psychological operations are necessary in order to make
it assume some kind of form, and the form assumed ever remains
a hazy, evanescent phantasm.   In the words of Dr. D. S. Clark:
"Briefly stated, the new cult teaches that the Word of God is the
spiritual impression or influence made by the agency of the Holy
Spirit on the mind of the man as he reads the Scripture.   It is
a sort of invisible, intangible, indefinite, psychological something
which grips the mind while it uses the Scriptures as means or
medium of instruction and inspiration.   It is this that is put in
the place of the written Word." (See *Conc. Theol. Mthly.*, IX,
p. 779.)   And Barth has many mates and followers.   The leading
theologians of today are asking us to throw the idea that the
written word of Scripture is the Word of God to the moles and bats
and to operate with a "Word of God" which has no definite and
no lasting form.[307)]

---

307) A few examples: W. Herrmann: "At any moment of our inner
development, therefore, we can point to some parts of the Scriptures
which do not have for us the significance of the Word of God.   But this
does not rule out the possibility that these very parts of the Scriptures
may have possessed that significance for other people or may still
possess it, or that they may one day possess it for us as well." (*Op. cit.*,
p. 59.) G. Harkness: "Some parts of the Bible have more of the voice of
God than others. . . . Read in faith, the Bible is the Word of God."
(*Op. cit.*, p. 70 f.) The *Luth. Church Quart.*, 1935, p. 260 ff.: "Seekers for
authority in Scripture cannot find it in isolated portions and texts of
the Bible. . . . Finality is found in the final analysis, within the soul. . . .
Here the teacher of religion finds his authority. He speaks with confidence not because he quotes a scripture, but because the Word of
God has found him." C. Stange: "Der Buchstabe der Schrift ist erst
dann Gottes Wort, wenn er in der Wirkung auf uns lebendig geworden
ist." (*Op. cit.*, p. 193.) Cryptic phrases used by Professor Homrighausen:
"Far from being a mere mechanical phonograph record, the *Bible is*

And making the "Word of God" still more indefinite, they tell us that it is found and heard also outside of Scripture. In some crisis these men will say: "Wir bekamen ein Wort Gottes." "Das jetzt geschehende Wort Gottes in der Barmer Synode." "The claim has already been advanced that the Barmen Confession was inspired by the Holy Spirit and is consequently a Word of God." (H. Sasse, *Here We Stand*, p. 169.) Dr. Moffatt believes that "the revelation is communicated afresh to successive generations." (See *Conc. Theol. Mthly.*, XII, p. 304.) And God gives His Word not only by means of Scripture but also through the *viva vox* of the Church. — Now, what is the "Word of God?" Is it the *Schriftganze*? That would not help us much, since nobody has yet told us exactly what the "whole of Scripture" comprises. And the confusion grows when we find that while some moderns somehow identify the two concepts,[308] others tell us the "Word of God" also comprises the continuing revelation, and just what that is they will not tell us. If the *Schriftganze* is hazy, indefinite, and absolutely unreliable, the "Word of God" is doubly hazy, indefinite, and absolutely unreliable.

But the moderns claim the right to operate with, and ask men to base their faith on, this "Word of God." They will not operate with the literal word of Scripture. That would be legalistic.

---

rather a living interpretation" (italics in original). "We must remember that the Word of God is *God Himself*, disclosed, disclosed *first* in real historical events. . . . The Holy Spirit makes that Word real and contemporaneous to us through the Bible. *We* do not choose the Word of God. The Word of God *chooses* you and me. . . . The Word is its own criterion." (In the *Presbyterian*, March 24, 1938.) — And this is not a "new cult." Barth popularized it, but before him Coleridge and his school, which developed into the Broad Churchism of England, "held that to be the Word of God which finds a man or comes home to him with a feeling of light and warmth. Thus it exalted in a more or less capricious way what appealed to man as a detached unit by himself." (*The Presby. Guardian*, June, 1939.) And before that, Zwingli had the same idea. "Das Wort, das gehoert wird, ist keineswegs das Wort, durch welches wir glauben; denn wenn das gelesene oder gehoerte Wort glaeubig machen koennte, wuerden wir all' glaeubig sein. Das Glaubenswort haftet im Geiste der Glaeubigen, es selbst wird von niemand gerichtet, sondern von ihm wird das aeussere Wort gerichtet." Oekolampad: "Was die aeusserlichen Worte ueber das Getoen haben, das haben sie von dem innerlichen Gemuete und vom innerlichen Worte." (See Rudelbach, *Ref., Luthert. u. Union*, p. 118 f.)

308) E. Lewis: "The question is whether out of the New Testament in its entirety we can gather the Word of God. Precisely this is what the Church in its collective life has been able to do." (*Op. cit.*, p. 151.) C. H. Dodd tells us "something about the way in which the Bible as a whole may become the 'Word of God' to us" (*op. cit.*, p. 294). *Luth. Church Quart.*, 1936, p. 246: "The Bible is the Word of God not because of any theoretical explanation of the method of divine inspiration, but because as one connected, harmonious, authentic recorded whole the sacred Scriptures testify of Christ."

They want the right to pick and choose, to decide for themselves what in Scripture is really worth while. They demand that in the name of spiritual liberty. P. Althaus: "Wir sind in dem Hoeren auf das Wort *Gottes* in dem biblischen Wort von diesem letzteren als Menschenworte frei" — submitting to the Word of God in the Biblical word, we are not bound by the Biblical word as such, for that is the word of man. (*Op. cit.*, p. 61.) E. Schaeder: "The Spirit-wrought faith applies a sifting process to the Bible word. Through this sifting process it gets the Word of God." (*Theozentrische Theologie,* II, p. 69.) G. T. Ladd: "The Christian consciousness, the consciousness of the Church, discerns the Word of God" contained in the Bible. (*Op. cit.,* p. 453.) Recall Dr. Flack's statement: "The Word of God is greater than the Book. . . . The standard by which all dogmas and teachers are to be judged is not the Scriptures standing utterly alone, but the Word of God attested and authenticated in the Spirit-filled life of the early Church and projected through the centuries from faith to faith in the corporate mind of the true Church." (*The Lutheran,* Sept. 24 and Oct. 1, 1936.) "Faith refuses," says G. Wehrung, "to make a legalistic use of individual passages or of the entire Scripture. . . . We must be in accord with Luther and his spirit of freedom and apply this touchstone to every word of Scripture: does it give expression to the Gospel as Gospel, the pure and clear Gospel?" (*Op. cit.*, p. 306, 308.) Faith refuses to be bound by Scripture as it is written; faith knows how to break any Scripture and all Scripture!

This, then, is the charter of liberty proclaimed by the moderns: Having renounced the tyranny of the words of Scripture as such, we vow allegiance to the Word of God contained in them; and our Christian consciousness shall tell us how much of Scripture is the Word of God to which we can submit.

SHALL WE JOIN IN THE REVOLT AGAINST VERBAL INSPIRATION, "THE TYRANNY OF WORDS"?

We are asked to come in under the charter of liberty proclaimed by the moderns which calls for freedom from "the tyranny of words." We cannot do so, for three reasons.

A HOLY BONDAGE

First, we do not feel that Verbal Inspiration imposes a legalistic yoke on us. It does indeed require of us unquestioning acceptance of all the statements of Scripture. On that we and the moderns are agreed. We are bound by every word of Scripture. But we do not resent, nor rebel against, this bondage. It is a holy bondage.

We rejoice in it. Why? Verbal Inspiration has taught us that these words of Scripture are God's words. In every word of Scripture our glorious Lord, our gracious God, is speaking.

We can understand the attitude of the moderns. They conceive of the Bible as a more or less human product. "Die heilige Schrift," R. F. Grau and the rest say, "ist uns nicht mehr ein grosser vom Himmel herabgesandter Gesetzeskodex." But we know that it actually did come down from heaven. "Holy Scripture did not grow here on earth." (Luther, VII: 2095.) Therefore we give it honor and reverence and gladly obey every word of it.

The moderns are laboring under the delusion that ever so many of its statements are erroneous, that ever so many of its teachings need restatement and development. Verbal Inspiration has freed us from this delusion and superstition. We have learned that God's Book is perfect. We fear to lay unholy hands upon it. We tremble at God's Word. "As for me, every verse makes the world too small for me." (Luther, XX: 788.)

No, no; we do not feel that the command to "consent to the words of our Lord Jesus Christ" (1 Tim. 6: 3) puts us under a degrading bondage. When God addresses His servants, they say: "Speak; for Thy servant heareth," 1 Sam. 3: 10; "Thou hast the words of eternal life," John 6: 68. When we read and preach holy Scripture, we know that we are dealing with "the oracles of God," 1 Pet. 4: 11, and our hearts are filled with holy awe and humble obedience.[309]

That would make us slaves, blindly obeying their master. We like that word, bondservant, slave. Paul liked it: "Παῦλος δοῦλος Χριστοῦ Ἰησοῦ," Rom. 1: 1. He bestows that title of honor on the Christians: "δουλωθέντες τῷ θεῷ," Rom. 6: 22; "δουλεύουσιν, . . . ὑπακουή," Rom. 16: 18, 19. Lenski: "Acting the part of slaves who obey as slaves, obey without question every word of 'our Lord Jesus Christ,' to whom as *our* Lord all of us (you Romans and I) are slaves." Nor is the word "law" an evil word. It is high praise when it is said of a man: "The *law* of truth was in his

---

309) James Bannerman: "The modern theologian comes to the Bible and sits over its contents in the attitude of a judge who is to decide for himself what in it is true and worthy to be believed and what is false and deserving to be rejected, not in the attitude of the disciple who, within the limits of the inspired record, feels himself at Jesus' feet to receive every word that cometh out of His mouth. The assurance that the Bible is the Word of God, and not simply containing it in more or less of its human language, is one fitted to solemnize the soul with a holy fear and a devout submission to its declarations as the very utterances of God." (See B. Manly, *The Bible Doctrine of Inspiration*, p. 16.)

mouth," Mal. 2:6, and the child of God declares: "I will delight myself in Thy *statutes.*" Ps. 119:16. It does not jar us when Jesus bids us to "observe all things whatsoever I have *commanded* you," Matt. 28:20. The moderns declare that to observe all the commands laid down in Scripture or any of them, to follow scrupulously every or any teaching, and to stick to every word of the Bible is "legalistic." We say: No! That is yielding holy obedience to our Lord, who gave us all of Scripture by verbal inspiration. But that would make the Bible the "textbook of doctrine," a "manual," "a code of laws of faith" ("Sammlung von Glaubensgesetzen" (Hofmann, *Schriftbeweis*, I, p. 9)! That is what we want, definite teachings, inviolable teachings, set down by God Himself. We do not hesitate to say: Holy Scripture is "das *Lehrbuch* der christlichen Religion" (Pieper, *Chr. Dog.*, I, p. 79). We are not horrified when J. G. Machen declares: "The Bible is the supreme textbook on the subject of faith." (*What Is Faith*, p. 45.) "Auch unsere Vaeter sagen: 'Die Heiligen Schriften sind die unveraenderlichen Statuten der Kirche. Und nach diesen Statuten hat die Kirche ihr Handeln, ihr Tun und Lassen zu richten und alles in der Gemeinde zu beurteilen. In jedem Stueck soll sich die Gemeinde erkundigen nach dem Willen ihres Herren in der Schrift." (*Theol. Quartalschrift*, 1942, p. 31.) "When Tertullian speaks of the Scriptures as an 'Instrument,' a legal document, his terminology has an express warrant in the Scriptures' own usage of *tōrāh*, 'law,' to designate their entire content." (B. B. Warfield, *Revelation and Inspiration*, p. 33.) We do not at all feel degraded when we declare: "Ich bin gefangen; I am bound; I cannot escape it. The text stands there too mightily." (Luther, XV:2050.) Slaves of God, captives of His Word, bound by a text of Scripture — we are proud of this situation and condition. We do not want to break these holy bonds.

SLAVES OF GOD — GOD'S FREEDMEN

But *blind* obedience and *enforced* obedience and the like! The moderns are very emphatic on this point. "It is analogous to the Roman Church doctrine which requires from the individual believer the same axiomatic obedience to the teachings of the Church, a confidence in advance, an antecedent *sacrificium intellectus*, before one can come into contact with the contents of these teachings. This in both cases is what may be called blind authority and blind obedience." (E. Brunner, *The Word and the World*, p. 92.) *Blind* obedience — yes; we accept any *dictum* of Scripture unquestioningly, even when the matter is beyond our understanding. But not blind obedience if that means that the verbal inspirationists have no knowledge of the matter presented in

Scripture and give it little thought.[310] And *enforced* obedience? Absolutely no. The Christian gives willing obedience to the Word of God. The moderns seem to be entirely ignorant of the true state of affairs. As soon as Scripture (by what it says on Verbal Inspiration) has convinced a man that it is God's Word, the Christian no longer asks: Must I accept these statements? When he hears that God is assuring him that John 3:16 and all other Bible statements are His words, the sinner's heart leaps for joy and loves every single Scripture declaration. Have the moderns so little knowledge of the power of God's Word and particularly of the power of the Gospel? "The advocates of Verbal Inspiration do not set up Scripture as a 'paper Pope,' demanding external subjection without inner conviction, but Scripture is to them a book which — just *because* it is God's own Word — itself works faith and *eo ipso* willing and joyous acceptance through the operation of the Holy Spirit inherent in it." (Pieper, *op. cit.*, p. 365.) "Do these men not know that there is an obedience which is *produced by the Gospel,* an obedience which finds itself bound to the whole Word of its God?" (Dr. M. Reu, *Kirchl. Zeitschrift,* 1939, p. 190.)

And here is Christian liberty! Spiritual liberty springs from obedience to God. The knowledge and acceptance of the truth makes us free (John 8:31 f.). Liberated from the bondage of error and sin and endowed with the Spirit of God, we are free to follow His leading and enjoy something of God's liberty. For once we agree with *The Christian Century* (Feb. 11, 1942): "We are not morally free until we have surrendered our human will to the will of God. . . . 'Make me a captive, Lord,' sang George Matheson, 'and then I shall be free.'" Slaves we are of God, and God's freedmen. Let us change Haas's statement "What the theologian calls the Word of God, namely, the spiritual content of the Bible, is an authority of freedom" into: "The Word of God, Holy Scripture, is an authority of freedom. . . . It does no injury to our moral freedom." It gives us spiritual freedom. — Spiritual freedom is not license. Dr. Haas rejects "the claims of a mechanically infallible Bible, verbally perfect" and appeals to the "authority of freedom." The Christian is *not* free to subject Scripture to his criticism. It is not true that "Christian liberty knows how to

---

310) M'Intosh on "the misrepresentation that the upholders of the Bible claim adopt a slavish literalism, maintain a 'cast-iron theory'": "No intelligent defender of the truth of Scripture has ever advocated such a slavish literalism. There is a literalism which is not slavish but reverent, not forced but scientific: even that which leads to a scrupulous carefulness to ascertain, by correct exegesis, the precise meaning of the words of God," etc. This talk of "slavish literalism is nothing else than reckless and culpable misrepresentation, and a discreditable caricature of that position." (*Is Christ Infallible?* p. 315.)

distinguish between Scripture and Scripture, between the shell and the content," etc. (Sherer.) That is wicked license, abuse of freedom, anarchy, lawlessness. (The moderns have a horror of "legalism," "legalistic treatment of Scripture." Had they not better ask themselves whether their treatment of Scripture is "legal," right, and permissible? Let them talk less about "legalistic" and be more concerned about their illegal practices, their lawless treatment of Scripture.) But he enjoys true spiritual liberty who is able to give free assent to every word of Scripture.

What about the charge that Verbal Inspiration hampers the spirit and induces spiritual sluggishness, yea, the death of all theological aspirations? ("The letter killeth, but the spirit giveth life"!) The fact is that this doctrine — as every other Scripture doctrine — carries divine power. We need mention only one thing. It gives the believer the wonderful spiritual strength to suppress the strong carnal impulse to belittle God's Word and exercise mastery over it. It causes him to honor and magnify every word of Scripture.

And now for the charge of "bibliolatry" and related crimes. The moderns do not mean to say that we fall down before this Book and pray to it as though it were God. What they mean is that we receive every word of it as though it were God's own word and yield absolute obedience to it. We plead guilty to the charge. The verbal-inspirationist Luther thus dealt with Scripture. "Halte von dieser Schrift als von dem allerhoechsten, edelsten Heiligtum." For it is God's own word: "You are so to deal with it that you think that God Himself is saying this" (XIV: 4; III: 21). For the same reason the verbal-inspirationists Paul and Peter regarded Scripture as a holy thing, a sacrosanct volume, endued with all the majesty and authority of the eternal God. See 1 Cor. 2: 13; 1 Thess. 2: 13; 2 Pet. 1: 21. If you "identify Scripture and God's Word" as Pieper does (*op. cit.,* I, p. 256), as M. Loy does: "The Holy Scriptures are the very Word of God in matter and in form. 'All Scripture is given by inspiration of God.' In the Scriptures the Sovereign Lord of all has revealed His righteousness and His gracious will in *His own words*" (*Dist. Doctrines,* 1893, p. 6), as Luther and Paul and all the others do, how can you refrain from fearing, loving, and honoring these words as you fear, love, and honor God above all things? And we shall say something in addition. In a certain respect Scripture and God are identified. Scripture itself so identifies them. "Christus ehrte in allen Dingen seinen Vater. Darum kehrte er so angelegentlich die Schrift hervor. Denn er sah in der Schrift nichts anderes als das Wort und den Willen seines Vaters. . . . So tritt statt des Subjekts 'die Schrift' ohne weiteres das andere Subjekt 'Gott' in die Rede ein.

'Die Schrift sagt zu Pharao: Eben darum habe ich [das ist Gott] dich erwecket, dass ich an dir meine Macht erzeige." (G. Stoeckhardt; *Lehre und Wehre*, 1886, p. 212.)[311] Study also this statement of Dr. Pieper: "There is another series of Bible passages which must not be overlooked in connection with the question whether Scripture and the Word of God are identified or not. These are the passages which state that Scripture directs the course of all events in the world. All that has happened and will happen, from the beginning to the end of the world, must and will take place according to what is *written*. Thus Matt. 1:22; John 17:12; Matt. 26:54; Luke 24:44 ff.: 'that the Scriptures might be fulfilled.'" (*Op. cit.*, I, p. 258.) Scripture is clothed with all the majesty of God! — No, we do not worship the paper and the printer's ink, but we do give the words of Scripture, which are God's own words, the holy reverence which is due God. If bibliolatry be that, let there be more of it.

And what is this puerile talk about a "book-religion"? G. Wehrung talks about it: "Cornill has shown that with the solemn reception of Deuteronomy the book-religion was born. We add: the legalistic book-religion." (*Geschichte und Glaube*, p. 302.) Many others have taken up the cry.[312] The cry does not disconcert us. Our Christian religion *is* founded upon a Book. A. W. Pink declares in the opening sentence of his book *The Divine Inspiration of the Bible:* "Christianity is the religion of a Book. Christianity is based upon the impregnable rock of Holy Scripture." We are not ashamed to have our religion called a Book religion. Christianity derives its teachings from the Bible; and from the Bible it gets the power to translate these teachings into practice, into a living service. The Bible produces saving

---

311) M'Intosh: "Yea, so absolute is Paul on this — the trustworthiness, irrefragableness, and divine authority of Holy Writ — that, like Christ, the Scripture is by him personalized and identified with God. 'The Scripture saith unto Pharaoh' (Rom. 9:17), while in Genesis it is the Lord that actually utters the words. . . . And in Gal. 3:8 he says: 'The Scripture, foreseeing.' Thus personal powers and actions are ascribed to Scripture, because God and His Word are identified. Human language could not surpass this in expressing the fact that the Bible is the Word of God, true, trustworthy, and of divine authority." (*Op. cit.*, p. 403.) *Bibliotheca Sacra*, 1938, p. 16: "When contemplating the Bible's own claims to inspiration, of great significance indeed are those passages wherein God and His Word are treated as one and the same. Gal. 3:8; Rom. 9:17; Ex. 9:16. . . . God's Word, whether spoken or written, is the identification of Himself."

312) Harnack: "We do not believe in a book, but in Jesus Christ, our Lord and Savior." (See *Lehre und Wehre*, 1886, p. 345.) F. Buechsel deplores "dieses Buchwerden der Offenbarung" and speaks of the dangers that must follow "diesem Vorgang der Schriftwerdung" (*Die Offenbarung Gottes*, pp. 62, 67). *The Lutheran*, Nov. 22, 1928: "We are not founded upon any book nor even on the Scriptures. Christianity is founded upon the living Christ."

faith and a holy life. To be sure, the Christian religion does not consist in memorizing certain doctrines. And the Christian religion is not a mechanical affair. We know all that. But we also know that the only source of true spirituality is the Bible. A spirituality which flows from "the living Christ" apart from the Bible is false. "The words that I speak unto you," the words of My Book, "they are spirit and they are life," John 6: 63.[313]

We are going to remain God's bondsmen, bound to His Word, bound to every letter of it. To that Verbal Inspiration binds us. Is that legalism? Legalism is an evil thing. If we should ever become guilty of it; if we should, for instance, demand acceptance of this doctrine merely as a matter of legal requirement and not preach it as good news, as a saving doctrine, revealing the grace of God and winning the joyous assent of men, we want the moderns to call us to order for that. But when they call us legalists and literalists and bibliolaters because we are bound by every letter of Scripture, they are out of order. Rather, we shall let them do that and consider these nasty slurs high praise. Bishop C. Gore meant it as dispraise when he wrote: "Luther submitted his judgment undoubtingly to Scriptural statements on points of natural science; and in a famous controversy he appealed to a New Testament verse as an infallible oracle, to be accepted

---

313) The thoughts of this and the preceding paragraph are well expressed by B. B. Warfield: "What this church doctrine is, it is scarcely necessary minutely to describe. It will suffice to remind ourselves that it looks upon the Bible as an oracular book — as the Word of God in such a sense that whatever it says God says — not a book, then, in which one may by searching find some word of God but a book which may be frankly appealed to at any point with the assurance that whatever it may be found to say, that is the Word of God. . . . We know how, as Christian men, we approach this Holy Book — how unquestioningly we receive its statements of fact, bow before its enunciations of duty, tremble before its threatenings, and rest upon its promises. . . . As we sit in the midst of our pupils in the Sabbath school or in the center of our circle at home or perchance at some bedside of sickness or of death, or as we meet our fellow men amid the busy work of the world, hemmed in by temptation or weighed down with care, and would fain put beneath him some firm support and stay: in what spirit do we turn to the Bible then? With what confidence do we commend its every word to those whom we would make partakers of its comfort or of its strength? In such scenes as these is revealed the vital faith of the people of God in the surety and trustworthiness of the Word of God." (*Op. cit.*, p. 52 f.) And J. A. Cottam: "These advocates of such looseness charge us that we are worshiping a book. They charge us with being guilty of 'bibliolatry,' a nasty slur which is altogether beside the point. We worship no book, but we do worship the God who sent the Book, and be it ever remembered, that is no true worship of God that slights the Book He has given. If we honor God, we shall honor His Word, and we shall be jealous for that Word." . . . It produces "a holier life, a more pronounced separation from the world, a Christian integrity in business, political honesty, domestic fidelity, and a Christian devotion to the interests of others." (*Know the Truth*, p. 229 f.) That is our Book religion.

with the purest literalism. In some respects he fastened the letter of the Bible on those who followed him more bindingly than had been done before." (*The Doctrine of the Infallible Book*, p. 58.) May we ever receive this dispraise, this high praise, from the moderns! When they ask us to subscribe to their new charter of liberty, we shall tell them that we have a better one. In the words of Machen: "The Christian man finds in the Bible the very Word of God. Let it not be said that dependence upon a book is a dead or an artificial thing. The Reformation of the sixteenth century was founded upon the authority of the Bible; yet it set the world aflame. Dependence upon a word of man would be slavish, but dependence upon God's Word is life. Dark and gloomy would be the world if we were left to our own devices and had no blessed Word of God. The Bible to the Christian is not a burdensome law, but the very Magna Charta of Christian liberty." (*Christianity and Liberalism*, p. 78.)[314)]

---

314) In the preceding paragraphs the phrases "puerile talk," "nasty slurs," have been used. Rightly so. It seems that the moderns cannot write one chapter on Verbal Inspiration without "becoming utterly unreasonable and illogical" (Pieper's phrase). The present chapter — "legalistic" — is no exception. First and foremost, he is a poor theologian who is ignorant of, or ignores, the truth that there is an obedience to God's Word which proceeds from the Gospel, that it is the Gospel which wins men for Verbal Inspiration. — Then, there is sophistry back of the statements: The Bible is not a defining dictionary (Best), no collection of doctrinal statements, not a legal code. Half truths are untruths. — There is sophistry, the employment of false opposition, in the statements that Christianity is not founded on a book, but on the living Christ, that "the Christian's allegiance is not to a creed or a code or an organization; it is personal loyalty to the Lord" (T. A. Kantonen, *The Message of the Church to the World of Today*, pp. 70, 111). Both are true: Loyalty to Scripture is loyalty to Christ and vice versa. The same applies, in a measure, to the statement of the Pittsburgh Agreement: "The Bible is primarily not a code of doctrines, still less a code of morals, but the history of God's revelation for the salvation of mankind." And Prof. Grau's argumentation "Let us be on our guard lest we follow the footsteps of our orthodox fathers of the seventeenth century, who, after Luther had freed us from the law of works that ruled in the Middle Ages, established a law of doctrine (Lehrgesetz), made of Scripture a large manual of doctrine and in support of that invented their inspiration doctrine. . . . For faith has to do not with doctrine or dogma but with our God Himself and the Son of the Father, Jesus Christ" deserved Professor Stoeckhardt's reply: "Das ist wahrlich ein heilloses Raisonnement ueber Lehre, Dogma, Dogmatik." (*Lehre und Wehre*, 1893, p. 328.) — It is pettifoggery when E. Brunner says: "The doctrine of verbal inspiration . . . ruled out the decision of faith." (*The Mediator*, p. 343.) That misrepresents our teaching. H. F. Rall misrepresents our teaching when he describes our "theory as not asking for understanding or conviction but simply submission." (*A Faith for Today*, p. 232.) Dr. Haas writes: "The general attitude of Fundamentalists is to exalt the Bible in a legal way. It is often presented as a code to be followed mechanically." (*What Is Lutheranism?* p. 192.) When the Fundamentalists present the Bible as a code which must be followed, do they really say: to be followed *mechanically*? The "often" does not save the statement from being a misrepresentation. — In all

EITHER BONDMEN OF GOD'S WORD OR SLAVES OF MEN

The second reason why we refuse to come in under the charter of liberty proclaimed by the moderns is that it establishes spiritual slavery. The moderns have freed themselves from the authority of Scripture but have put on instead the shackles of human authority. They are not willing to submit to the absolute authority of God and His Word but are very willing to make poor man their authority. For one thing, they make "science" their authority in the question of the inerrancy of Scripture. Where Scripture is in conflict with "science," they unquestioningly accept the *dictum* of the scientist, the philosopher, and the higher critic. If you ask them why they charge Scripture with making these innumerable historical and scientific blunders, they tell us: Why, this scientist, that higher critic, says so. They seem to be unable to think that

---

fairness the moderns should not compel us to waste our time in dealing with the insinuation that we view the Bible "als einen vom Himmel gefallenen Gesetzkodex." We dealt with that insinuation by declaring that for a fact the Bible did not grow upon earth. Dr. Pieper takes it up from a different angle and has to waste six lines by pointing out: "Den Vertretern der Verbalinspiration ist so etwas nie eingefallen. Vielmehr lehren sie sehr klar, dass die Heilige Schrift nicht vom Himmel gefallen, sondern hier auf Erden durch Menschen und in menschlicher Sprache aus Eingebung des Heiligen Geistes geschrieben sei." (*Op. cit.,* I, p. 365.) And M'Intosh is right in calling this talk of "*slavish* literalism" "culpable misrepresentation," "a discreditable caricature." — Analyze the statement of Dr. Fosdick: "At times this endeavor to make the letter of the Bible a binding law has produced the deepest shames and tragedies that Christianity has known, ... 'Compel them to come in' (Luke 14:23) used as a commandment requiring religious persecution — such are a few samples of the cruel consequences of legalism." (*The Modern Use of the Bible,* p. 239.) It is true that Luke 14:23 has been misunderstood and misapplied in the way indicated. But if we remember that in the parlance of Dr. Fosdick "legalism," "making the letter of the Bible a binding law," is a description of Verbal Inspiration, we shall have to say that Dr. Fosdick is saying something which is not in accord with the facts. Verbal Inspiration does "make the letter of the Bible" a binding law. But Verbal Inspiration cannot be made responsible for the fact that men occasionally misinterpret the letter, the real meaning, of the Bible. — Analyze Dr. Ferm's statement. "The authority of the sacred writings is no longer found in 'the letter' and sustained by some artificial theory of divine inspiration but in the appeal of its spiritual content." (*What Is Lutheranism?* p. 279.) Surely, the "spiritual content" is what counts. But how can we get the "spiritual content" without the letter? Is the "spiritual content" floating in the air and not contained in the letter? — Analyze the concept "Word of God." It cannot be analyzed. It is too hazy and vague, void of definite meaning, indefinable. "Word of God," like the *Schriftganze,* is one of those *sine mente soni* with which modern theology likes to operate. The exact sciences refuse to deal with meaningless terms. Modern theology is not an exact science. — Finally, when the moderns have established what the *Schriftganze* or the "Word of God" teaches, do they tell their people that it does not matter whether these divine truths are accepted or rejected? We have never heard them say so. They demand acceptance of these teachings. But would that not be "legalistic"? In their own interest they ought to put a stop to this talk about "legalism."

the scientist may be wrong. They hold "science" in such high reverence that they consider it a *crimen laesae maiestatis* when the verbal-inspirationist declares: Scripture is right even though it goes against all "the established results of science" and "the best thought of the day." They are ever ready to uphold the claims of science over against the claim of Scripture. When we urge this claim of Scripture, they begin to rail about "slavish literalism," "legalistic subservience" to Scripture, while they themselves pay abject homage to the scientist and higher critic. What did Dr. Stoeckhardt tell them? "Will you say that secular history gives the lie to Scripture? . . . Are we to correct the Bible history on the authority of occasional scraps in the ancient tradition or the obscure language of the monuments, which are partly contradictory? . . . Das waere Wahnwitz." (*Lehre und Wehre*, 1886, p. 315.)

They are slaves, slaves of men, and they are proud of their slavery. In the expressive phrase of W. Moeller, modern theology is happy to act as the flunky and trainbearer of science. "Die heutige Theologie verbeugt sich vor jeder Wissenschaft oder auch oft Pseudowissenschaft und Naturphilosophie, die den Mund etwas voll nimmt, und erklaert sich bereit, Schleppentraegerdienste zu tun." (*Um die Inspiration der Bibel*, p. 36.)

The moderns like to raise the charge of biblicism, bibliolatry, against us. They charge us with having too much respect for the Bible. Recall G. Aulén's invective against "Luther's slavish dependence on Bible texts," against "the old biblicism, which restricts the divine revelation to the Bible"; "biblicism, the application of the theory of verbal inspiration, laid its heavy hand on the theology of orthodoxy." "Everywhere the principle of legalism intrudes and molds the theology. That is the disastrous consequence of biblicism." (*Das Chr. Gottesbild*, pp. 251, 255, 386.) These men need to be told what sort of latria they are committing. Erik Floreen tells them. In his critique of "The 'New Theology' in Sweden" he writes: "Dr. Aulén doesn't seem to regard the Bible as being inspired in any special sense at all. To him Scripture is the Word of God no more nor less than other Christian testimonies in the form of preaching, writing, and song, rendered throughout the history of the Church. Furthermore, it would be legalistic to ground our faith on an outward authority as on that of the Bible, he says. . . . What the liberal theologians fondly point out as a recent progress of revelation is, mainly, a renewed pursuit of that elusive phantom, a theological 'vetenskap,' or science, that would find favor with arrogant human reason. . . . Now and then one of our own writers uses the ridiculous expression, 'Bibliolatry.' Would not someone kindly coin two additional 'latries' to denote the worship of human reason and of 'vetenskapen'?" (See the *Luth. Companion,* Feb. 9, 1939.)

"Dependence upon God's Word is life, but dependence upon a word of man would be slavish." (Machen.) We would rather be bondmen of God and His Word than slaves of men.

Another point. The moderns, who condemn our acceptance of any statement of Scripture as final, stigmatizing that as "legalism" and "slavish literalism," ask us to bow before the authority of the Church and of the theologian. The Church, they say, is the final authority. Recall the statement of Dr. E. E. Flack (hundreds of others could be submitted): "The Word of God is greater than the Book. . . . The standard by which all dogmas and teachers are to be judged is not the Scriptures, standing utterly alone, but the Word of God attested and authenticated in the Spirit-filled life of the early Church and projected through the centuries from faith to faith in the corporate mind of the true Church. . . . The Scriptures have no authority either apart from Christ, who is the primary Authority, or apart from the Church, in which Christ's power is operative." (*The Lutheran,* Sept. 24, Oct. 1, 1936.) It is, then, the Church which gives Scripture its final, real authority. The real authority is the Church. But the Church is made up of men. The moderns are actually asking us to rely for the truth and certainty of our doctrine on the findings and pronouncements of — mere men!

They will even put it this way: the men to tell you what God really revealed in Scripture are the theologians; the common Christian is incapable of finding that out for himself; he must ask the guild of the theologians. — We can understand why the moderns take that position. According to them, what counts is not the words of Scripture but the "Word of God," "Scripture as a whole." And it takes uncommon skill to locate this elusive *Schriftganze,* to unravel this enigmatic "Word of God." F. Buechsel tells us, with a sober face, that it "calls for a great measure of theological ability to find this Word of God, this whole of Scripture." (*Die Offenbarung Gottes,* p. 112.) These men advertise themselves as "specialists." As Dr. Pieper puts it: "It has become the fashion among the experience theologians to talk as though it took specialists, men who are able to interpret 'the historical realities,' to discover the meaning of the individual Scripture statements. In reality, the situation is entirely different. The fact is that every bit of the 'historical reality' which is needed for the understanding of Scripture is provided *by Scripture* itself, in the context, and any reader or hearer of average intelligence can easily discern it. . . . The Pope declares that Scripture, lacking the interpretation of the 'Church,' is obscure. And modern Protestant theology, having discarded the Scripture principle, talks as though the meaning of the individual Scripture statements can be derived only from 'the full picture of the historical reality,' and that only specialists can give us this picture." (*Op. cit.*, II, p. 131 f.) [315] This situation is the natural product of the denial of Verbal Inspiration. If the bare statement of Scripture does not suffice to prove the statement, you will have to seek the proof elsewhere; you will have to appeal to other authorities. Dr. Bente puts it this way: "Reason tells these men: 'If the Bible blundered in astronomy, geology, physics, chronology, etc., you can believe the Bible also *in theologicis* only so far as you have established the correctness of its statements from other sources.' The only course of action left, then, to the General Council men is to follow blindly their authorities, Jacobs and Stump (provided that these authorities are not appealing to European authorities)" (*Lehre und Wehre,* 1904, p. 87).

But operating with human authorities in spiritual matters imposes spiritual slavery on the Christians. It is a popish abomination. The moderns like to characterize Verbal Inspiration as akin to Roman Catholicism. (E. Brunner, above: "This idolatrous acceptance of Bible authority . . . is analogous to the Roman Church doctrine which requires from the individual believer the same axiomatic obedience to the teachings of the Church," etc.) But it is the moderns who are putting the papistical yoke on the Church. In his essay on Inspiration Rudelbach calls attention to a passage in Luther describing the theological method of the papists and points out that that is a pretty fair description of

---

315) It seems incredible that men should be found within the Christian Church who could make the claim that they can tell better than Scripture itself what God really revealed and who tell the common Christian that he must consult them before he can be sure of the matter. But such men actually exist, even in the Protestant churches. Rudolf Hermann had dealings with that kind of theologians. He writes: "Wer wuerde bei einer Botschaft nicht grade im Wortlaut ihren Geist suchen? . . . Wenn nun ihr naeheres Verstaendnis die Theologie vermitteln muss — es genuegt ja schon, an das fremde Sprachgut zu erinnern, in das das Wort gefasst ist —, so tut sie das nicht als *Zwischeninstanz* zwischen dem Wort Gottes und uns Menschen. Vielmehr solche *Zwischeninstanzen wegraeumen* zu helfen, die Alleingueltigkeit von Gottes Selbstoffenbarung auch fuer die Kirche herausstellen zu helfen, ist sie da." (*Theol. Mil.*, XII, p. 10.) W. Vollrath had dealings with such men and writes: "Als ob der Allmaechtige nur durch Maenner, die Universitaeten besucht haben, seine Sache zu fuehren und in die Wahrheit zu leiten vermoechte! Als ob der Schoepfer eine besondere Vorliebe haette fuer Leute, die Grade erwarben und Lehrstuehle zieren! . . . Statt zu dienen, will er (der Standesduenkel) herrschen; statt zu verbinden, erneuert und befestigt er jene alte Kluft zwischen Laien, denen das Verstaendnis der Schrift unmoeglich sei, und *Sachkundigen*, die vorgeben, hier allein Bescheid zu wissen. . . . Diese Vorwaende fuehren unfehlbar in Schwaermerei. . . . Jenes Gebahren ueberlaesst unsere Kirche getrost den Papisten und Schwaermern alter und neuer Richtung." (*Vom Rittertum der Theologie,* p. 4.)

the doings of the moderns. The passage, using the incident of casting lots for the coat of Jesus as a parable, reads in part (IV:1307 ff.): "All admit what Jesus says, John 10:35: 'The Scripture cannot be broken,' and that its authority is absolutely inviolable, so that no man may contradict or deny it. This premise, or *maior*, that the perfect knowledge of God, theology, must be derived from Scripture all and everyone always admits. But where the *minor* is concerned, the soldiers at once make a farce out of Scripture through their arbitrary glosses and distinctions, so that the power and authority of all of Scripture goes by the board. For today, too, you cannot prove anything to the Pope or any Thomist by Scripture, even though they acknowledge the authority of Scripture. 'Let us not rend the coat,' they say, 'but cast lots for it', whose it shall be,' John 19:24. For is that not playing a game of chance with Scripture if one deals with it arbitrarily and twists it according to his whim? Do not the *magistri nostri* of the universities *take unto themselves the right to interpret Scripture*? And it has reached such a pass that they laugh at him who simply quotes Scripture, while they (as they say) operate with irrefutable arguments of reason. This is the game they play: They do not teach what Scripture demands, but each one tries his luck how he may square Scripture with his own ideas, how much of Scripture he can win. And in this game the Pope is (for that is his due) the chief of the soldiers, for he has passed a law, binding upon all, that it is his privilege, his alone, to interpret Scripture *definitive*. Others, too, may interpret Scripture, but only *magistraliter*, by way of disputation and investigation, not in such a way that their interpretation is final, *determinative*. For he plays with his partners in such a way that the die must fall in his favor, that he alone has the power to interpret Scripture." That fits the moderns fairly well. True, there is this difference that the moderns have gone beyond the Pope in that they do not acknowledge the supreme authority of Scripture even in theory. There is also this difference that they have not set up one among themselves as the chief. But this description fits absolutely: *nostri magistri* in the seats of learning have taken unto themselves the right to interpret Scripture, and they laugh at him who simply quotes Scripture.[316] Dealing with one of this ilk, Praelat Dr. Theodor Traub exclaims: "Das fehlte gerade noch,

---

316) We must quote one more sentence from our passage. "If you do not yet know who these four soldiers are, I will tell you: they are our honorable *magistri nostri*, who cheat with their *fourfold* sense of Scripture and, foisting their ridiculous interpretations on Scripture, make Scripture ridiculous." The papists played with the hidden sense back of the words. The moderns cheat by operating with the "Word of God" or the *Schriftganze* and making Scripture say what they please.

dass wir anstatt des *einen* unfehlbaren Papstes die vielen religions-
geschichtlichen Professoren mit ihren vielen sich widersprechenden
Behauptungen als Autoritaeten in Glaubenssachen annehmen
muessten!" (*Handreichung fuer Glauben und Leben,* p. 72.)
Luther: "Sie suchen ihre eigene Tyrannei, dass sie uns moegen
aus der Schrift fuehren, den Glauben verdunkeln, sich selbst ueber
die Eier setzen und *unser Abgott* werden." (V. 336.) "They speak
such things only in order to lead us away from Scripture and to
make themselves *masters over us* that we should believe their
dream-sermons" (Traumpredigten). (P. 335.)

We will have none of this! We will not make the Church
or any theologian our Pope. "Dependence upon God's Word is life,
but dependence upon a word of man would be slavish." We do
not feel degraded when we give unquestioning assent to the Bible,
to God and His Word; but we would feel debased if we had to
give one single point of our Christian faith into the keeping of
fallible men.

Once more: the moderns may say at this point that they
would not dream of dictating to the faith of the Christian — that
they are rather urging the Christian to fight for his rights and
be his own authority. — Yes, they are doing that. Recall R. H.
Strachan's statement: "Such slave mentality is at the source of
religious infallibilities: the infallible Book or the infallible Church.
. . . The authority of which we are in quest clearly must be an
authority which does not destroy our personal freedom. It must . . .
clearly recognize the *autonomy* of the individual personality," etc.
(*The Authority of Chr. Experience,* pp. 16, 19.) John Oman's
charter of liberty proclaims: "The teacher of divine truth will not
care to stop with authorities either of the Church or of the Scriptures." We must no longer "draw doctrines from Holy Writ like
legal decisions from the statute book." "Christ encourages His
disciples to rise above the rule of authorities and to investigate
till each is *his own authority.*" (*Vision and Authority,* p. 188.) The
moderns are actually calling upon the Christians to exercise
authority over Scripture, to decide for themselves how much of
Scripture may be accepted, how much must be rejected, to become
their own authorities. The gross rationalists ask the Christians
to set up their reason as the supreme authority. The subtle
rationalists ask them to set up their "Christian" judgment as the
supreme authority. (Ladd: "The Christian consciousness . . .
discerns the Word of God" in the Bible. [*What Is the Bible?* p. 453.]
The Living Church, Oct. 28, 1931, on "Authority in the Kingdom
of God": "Our *ultimate* appeal must be to religious experience
and the religious consciousness." A. Schweizer: "It is the business
of the Christian spirit to smelt the ore of the Bible and obtain
the pure gold." E. Schaeder: "The Spirit-wrought faith applies

a sifting process to the Bible word. Through this sifting process it gets·the Word of God." Zwingli: "Das Glaubenswort haftet im Geiste der Glaeubigen, es selbst wird von niemand gerichtet, sondern von ihm wird das aeussere Wort gerichtet." [See Rudelbach, *Ref., Luthert. u. Union,* p. 118.]) There can be no doubt about it, the moderns are asking the individual Christian to occupy the seat of supreme authority. It is a fact — a sorry fact indeed — that "modern theology has the same interest as Rome. According to its own declaration it wants to be freed from Scripture as the only source and standard of theology and instead of Scripture would make the decisive factor in the Church indeed not the ego of the *Pope,* but the 'experience' or — what is the same thing — 'the pious self-consciousness,' the ego of the theologizing subject" (Pieper, *op. cit.,* I, p. 273). This is the situation — the infamous situation: denouncing our reliance on the bare word of Scripture as slavish, the moderns are asking us to assert our own authority.

We cannot do it. It is the height of wickedness.[317] And it would lead us into slavery. Let no man think that he has achieved freedom when he asserts his autonomy over against Scripture and follows the dictates of his own will. He is a slave to his flesh. He is a willing slave indeed, but a slave he is nevertheless. He hears the call and invitation to put his spiritual affairs into the hands of the gracious Lord and follow His safe guidance, but his proud heart forbids him to do so. And he is unable to disobey his evil flesh. He cannot but submit to the tyrant. And he is proud of his servitude. He does not feel the shame of it. — Dependence upon God's Word is life and liberty; dependence upon a word of man — another's or your own — would be slavish.

THE RUIN WROUGHT BY THE REVOLT AGAINST VERBAL INSPIRATION

There is a third reason why we abhor and abominate the liberty proclaimed by the moderns. The emancipation from the "legalistic yoke" of Verbal Inspiration is fraught with frightful disaster. In the first place, it involves the loss of the Christian

---

317) It is a form of self-deification. Will not someone, as Erik Floreen would say, coin after the pattern of "Bibliolatry" an additional latria to denote the worship of human reason and of the "Christian consciousness"? — We shall set down again the statement of M'Intosh: "Thus through all the permutations and combinations and through all the multifarious phases of indefinite erroneousness, we are inevitably driven to the old and fatal issues of the common rationalistic principle, namely, that every varying man must become a judge and an authoritative standard himself. Having got rid of an infallible Bible and an infallible Christ, he must reach that supreme absurdity — an infallible self, 'Lord of himself, that heritage of woe,' as Byron says." (*Op. cit.,* pp. 32, 483.)   Prof. J. J. Reeve: "When one makes his philosophy his authority, it is not a long step until he makes himself his own God."

doctrine. How many of the Christian doctrines survive under the new order? The first doctrine marked for slaughter by the moderns is, of course, that of Verbal Inspiration itself. They have been filling the world with the cry that Verbal Inspiration is due to "a legalistic conception of Scripture" (*Luth. Church Quart.*); that "there is a spirit of legalism that pervades many of the ranks of Midwestern Lutherans, . . . which insist on 'book, chapter, and verse'" (*Luth. Church Quart.*); that "the older doctrine of inspiration led to the misconception of the Bible as a law code," which older doctrine of inspiration is not based on Scripture but on "an extremist exegesis of 2 Tim. 3:16, 17" (*The Augsburg Sunday School Teacher*); that "God did not inspire the Bible in the rigid, literal manner, known as verbal inspiration"; that, therefore, this doctrine must be "thrown to the moles and the bats with the rest of the world's old, discarded mind-lumber" (J. P. Smith, *How God Inspired the Bible*, p. 118); and that this "verbal literalism" called for by Verbal Inspiration "is hardly congenial in the atmosphere of our conservative Lutheran institutions" (*The Lutheran*). The moderns abhor Verbal Inspiration because their free spirit will not submit to be bound by the words of Scripture — that would be legalistic literalism; and there is great rejoicing in their camp that "it is fast being thrown to the moles and the bats."

The next doctrine to be thrown to the moles and bats is the teaching that Holy Scripture is the sole authority in religion, that the revelation of the divine truth given in Scripture is perfect and final. Bind men to what the fallible apostles wrote? That would be legalistic and bibliolatrous. Accept the teaching of Paul, Peter, and John as the final form of theology? That would make the men of the twentieth century mere catechumens of men of the first century and put the fetters of slavery on the free working of our Christian spirit. No, no, declares Aulen; the heavy hand of biblicism must be removed from theology; and: "A God, whose revelation is represented as having been given only in the past, is not a living God. . . . This thought militates against the old biblicism which holds that God's revelation is 'closed' in and with the Bible, and thus remains standing in the past." (*Op. cit.,* p. 386.) "Indeed, many would say that what we have in the New Testament is evidence that the faith may never be expected to assume a final form." Thus Edwin Lewis, in *The Faith We Declare*, p. 150. And: "A man may not want to say it in just the way in which Paul said it." (P. 104.) Naturally, for "the early Church" occasionally indulged in erroneous thinking, and "the New Testament naturally reflects this thinking" (*A New Heaven and a New Earth*, p. 175). Why, even Christ is not absolutely reliable, and we may have a better understanding of things than He

had. Thus R. Sockman (and a host of others): "In recovering
His authority, we can hardly believe that the Christ would wish His
followers to go barking at the heels of men, begging their attention. . . . Yet authoritative as the centuries have found Him to be,
what are nineteen hundred years in the life of the race? Can
we say that the Christ of Nazareth has given us the final wisdom?
May not the future outgrow Him?" (*Recoveries in Religion*,
p. 70.) The theology of the Bible is thus not final; the Christian
experience and the Christian consciousness must supplement it.
What did *A Creed for Free Men* (W. A. Brown) tell us? "The
Bible is a compendium of simple principles capable of indefinite
application and therefore needing continual reinterpretation in
the light of expanding experience." H. C. Sheldon has a chapter
in his *System of Christian Doctrine* on the "Question of the
Sufficiency of the Biblical Revelation, or of the Possibility of
Authoritative Supplements" (p. 149) and says: "A few words will
be appropriate on the question whether revelation needs, or admits
of, any authoritative supplements." The answer is that "it is the
vocation of the Christian consciousness" to serve as such a supplement.[318] The doctrine of the final and sole authority of Holy
Scripture has gone by the board. Scripture is broken indeed.

In fact, according to the consistent moderns, we really do
not need the Bible at all. We might be able to get along without it — just as at one time people did get along without it.
It would be another form of this wicked Bibliolatry to say the
contrary. Let R. F. Horton speak on this point: "Strange to
say, the Christians of whom we speak do not even notice that

---

318) It is about time that somebody give us a definition of this
Christian consciousness which tells us which parts of the Bible we may
accept and which truths we are to accept in place of those teachings of
the Bible which we must reject or which we find inadequate. This is
Sheldon's definition: "What is 'Christian consciousness' but a name for
the cardinal judgments and feelings of Christians, their religious modes
both in the line of thought and emotion? It may be defined in brief
as the educated reason and feeling of Christian believers." — We don't
think much of this "Christian consciousness" in its role of testing and
supplementing Scripture. Aside from the fact that the Christian commits a crime when he permits it to dictate to Scripture, he will never
know how to pin it down to a definite statement. As everybody knows,
our emotions and feelings are constantly changing. Besides, only the
cardinal feelings are authorized to speak. But the Christian will never
know whether his present feeling is a cardinal or a second-rate feeling.
"It is the *educated* reason and feeling of believers." How shall the
Christian know whether he is dealing with his educated or his old
carnal feeling? He may believe that his reason and feeling of the
moment is educated; how will he convince his brother, who reasons
and feels quite differently, that the latter needs more education?
Again, where shall we find an authoritative summary of the feeling
of the Christian believers? This "Christian consciousness" is just
about as hazy, indefinite, and cryptic as those two other favorite concepts
of the moderns: the *Schriftganze* and the "Word of God."

the New Testament is itself a record of the Christian faith being propagated at a wonderfully rapid rate without a New Testament at all. Peter had no writings to appeal to except the Old Testament Scriptures; Paul preached 'his Gospel' without any reference to a written Gospel, and never hinted that the further preaching of the faith should depend even on his own epistles. It may as well be frankly stated that the frantic and superstitious faith in the apostolic writings, a faith going far beyond what they claim or suggest themselves, may be simply the outcome of unbelief. People who are sunk in this kind of Bibliolatry, etc. . . . They really worship the Scriptures instead of the living God and make a slavish and unreasoning acceptance of all that is written take the place of an inward subjection to God, and a realized experience of His personal manifestation to the believing heart." (*Revelation and the Bible*, p. 218.) There is no *absolute* need of the Bible. Break it up!

Oh, yes, the Bible has its use. It should be studied; but bear in mind, what it says is *"suggestive* rather than dictatorial" (G. L. Raymond); it gives merely "the *initial* data" (R. W. Nelson); it contains good *"principles,* which, however, need continual reinterpretation" (W. A. Brown). It was never intended, say the moderns, as the sole source of doctrine.

Having gotten rid of Verbal Inspiration and the authority of Holy Scripture, the moderns are ready for the other Christian doctrines. Having set up the principle that it would be legalistic and slavish to bow to every word of Scripture, they feel free to change — discard — any Biblical teaching. Calling upon the Christians "to break with this legalistic employment of Scripture," H. E. Fosdick refuses to teach the deity, the real deity, of Jesus, the vicarious atonement, the resurrection of Jesus, and the resurrection of the flesh, eternal damnation, etc., etc. E. Brunner fulminates against "this idolatrous acceptance of Bible authority" and is thus in a position to rejoice over "the victory of biological evolutionism," etc., etc. (*op. cit.,* p. 92, 98). Bishop Aulén says it would be legalistic to ground our faith on an outward authority, as on that of the Bible, and so, as E. Floreen points out, "he finds himself justified in offering us a picture of Jesus quite different from that presented by the evangelists. The deity of the Savior is denied. . . . Dr. Aulén's teaching of the last things also departs considerably from Scripture. . . . It is supposed that an opportunity of conversion will be given after death." Must the real presence in the Lord's Supper be maintained? When Aulén declaims against "Luther's slavish dependence on Bible texts," he particularizes: "The classical example of this is Luther's argumentation in the controversy on the Lord's Supper." (*Op. cit.,*

p. 251.) Bishop Gore (and countless others) take the same position. Let us hear his statement again: "In a famous controversy Luther appealed to a New Testament verse as an infallible oracle." Applying the principle that it is the business of the theologian "to teach the old truth in a new way and, following the promptings of the Spirit of God, to augment and increase it," Hofmann gave the Church a doctrine of the Atonement which denies the *satisfactio vicaria,* etc. (See Pieper, *op. cit.,* p. 74.) And P. Althaus, working under Hofmann's charter of liberty, has told us that eschatology and the doctrine of justification must assume new forms. — How many Christian doctrines remain intact under the new charter of liberty? *Christendom,* as quoted on page 16, note 7, says: "The account of the creation in Genesis, the Christmas story of the Incarnation, the resurrection of the body of Christ, . . . the doctrine of the resurrection of the body, the doctrine of the virgin birth and the divinity of Christ — all these conceptions, intended at first quite literally, have for many devout Christians today only a symbolic function. . . . Hence they are still scrupulously retained, lovingly cherished, but considered as poetic expressions of some profounder or larger truth than that which their formulators realized." Dr. Muenkel, as quoted in Pieper (*op. cit.,* I, p. 157), reports thus: "There is hardly one doctrine left which has not, in a marked degree, been subjected to recastings, additions, and eliminations. Starting with the Trinity, proceeding to the doctrine of the person and the office of Christ, to the doctrines of faith and justification, of the Sacraments, and of the Church, down to eschatology, you will scarcely find anything in its old form and with its former value. Often it is changed to such a degree that only the old frame still reminds one of the old picture, and at times even the frame has been smashed as being too narrow and out of date. A small sample to illustrate this: While Christ according to the Church doctrine is true God also in His state of humiliation, they now have emptied Him of the divine attributes," [319] "without which no one can conceive of the deity, or they let Him gradually grow into His deity and achieve it in His resurrection. The death of Christ is no longer permitted to be

---

319) To illustrate, V. Ferm says: "We might well question whether or not the Christological doctrines of the ubiquity of Christ's body (a quasi-materialistic and pan-Christic doctrine borrowed from Duns Scotus), and *communicatio idiomatum* are satisfactory even from a Biblical point of view. Even the position which Luther himself took on the interpretation of the Eucharist may fairly be challenged as a necessarily true Biblical exegesis. The literalism applied to certain Biblical passages, etc. . . . The authority of the Sacred Writings is no longer found in 'the letter,' and sustained by some artificial theory of divine inspiration, but in the appeal to its spiritual content." (*What Is Lutheranism?* p. 279 f.)

taught as satisfying for our sins and reconciling us to God. The righteousness of faith, consisting in God's declaring us righteous, is said to be too wooden and external; in a covert manner the works are again brought in. Law and Gospel are again being churned together. . . . Would anyone dare to speak of development of the Lutheran doctrine when the most important parts of the Lutheran doctrine are swept out of doors like old rubbish? . . ." How much is left of the Christian doctrine where men operate with this new charter of liberty?

The liberals among the moderns have made a clean sweep of it. The conservative groups have retained some or many of the Christian doctrines. And still we maintain that the application of the principle of freedom from the letter of Scripture, of the right to develop the doctrine, involves the loss of the Christian doctrine. The only reason why the conservative moderns have not cast overboard all Biblical teachings is that, by the grace of God, they do not consistently apply their principle. "We ask," says L. Gaussen, "where do they mean to stop in the course they have begun? And by what reason would they stop those, in their turn, who would fain advance farther than they are willing to go? They make bold to correct one saying of God's Word; what right, then, have they to censure those who would rectify all the rest? . . . Where will you find the difference? It is in the species, not in the genus. It is in the quantity, and no longer in the quality, of imputations of error and tokens of irreverence. There is a difference in point of hardihood, none at all in point of profanation." (*Theopneustia*, p. 201.) Some of the moderns have not the hardihood to apply the principle under which they reconstruct — abolish — the doctrine of the vicarious atonement to the doctrine of the deity of Christ and of the Trinity. God has graciously kept them from going so far. But left to themselves, they would all land in the camp of modernism, liberalism. Hofmann's principle which permits him to teach the old truth in a new way, in such a way as to augment the old truth, is identical with Fosdick's principle: The Gospel must be "released from literal bondage to old categories and set free to do its work in modern terms of thought and speech" (*op. cit.*, p. 261), and nothing but the grace of God will keep the followers of Hofmann from becoming followers of Fosdick. Professor Bente solemnly warns the Church: "Men hate and assault the doctrine of verbal inspiration because it clamps the modern spirit which would be free of all authority. But when the dam of verbal inspiration is once broken, there is nothing to prevent the flood of modern rationalism from sweeping over the old orthodoxy." (*Lehre und Wehre*, 1910, p. 89.) The break-up is complete.

And we know what the chief concern, the fundamental doctrine, of rationalism is. It is salvation through works. The one important concern of rationalism is ethics. M. H. Krumbine tells us: "The one thing we know definitely about Jesus is His ethical teaching." (*Ways of Believing*, p. 71.) Shailer Mathews: "If Christians are to be interested in helping to make a better world, the Churches must make theology secondary to morality embodying the spirit of Jesus." (*The Church and the Christian*, p. 105.) And W. Herrmann, who insists that "such a principle of the authority of Scripture would set a book above God's revelation," proclaims his rationalism when he says: "The fundamental thought of Jesus' Gospel is that it is in God's rule in our hearts that our salvation consists." (*Syst. Theol.*, pp. 58, 115.) And the conservative moderns are headed towards this heathen heresy. Dr. Muenkel sees the development: "In a covert manner the works are drawn in again. Law and Gospel are again being churned together." [320] There can be no other development. Man is a born legalist, and if we permit our thoughts — call it reason outright or call it "Christian consciousness" — to correct or supplement the Scripture teaching, we shall inevitably gravitate toward the heathen doctrine of salvation through the Law. — What a tragic development! Here are men constantly mouthing the word "legalistic" and refusing to submit to "law" — and they end up by becoming slaves of the Law.

The loss of the Christian doctrine — that is the fatal consequence of the contention that Verbal Inspiration has a legalistic cast.

It has another evil consequence. It inflicts unspeakable harm on the Christian. (1) The Christian needs the Christian doctrine. His salvation is bound up with the *saving* doctrine, and we have just seen what happens to the Christian doctrine where the new charter operates, where men denounce adherence to the letter as legalistic and assume the right to manipulate and develop the Biblical teaching. Then what happens to the Christian who is under the spiritual care of the ultraliberal modern? Can faith survive where all the doctrines of the Church, the deity of Christ, the vicarious atonement, justification by faith alone, are denied? It cannot survive under the ministration of the liberal. And what happens to the Christian under the ministration of the conservative modern, who operates with a half or a fourth or a tenth of the Christian doctrine? The Christian needs the whole of the Christian doctrine. Oh, yes, God can save him, God is saving many who are

---

320) To illustrate, R. Jelke teaches that faith justifies because "that which Christ performed is reproduced in him (the believer) potentially, ethically," "dass sich in ihm das von Christo Geleistete potentiell, ethisch wiederholt." (*Die Grunddogmen des Christentums*, p. 64.)

being deprived by their teachers of much of the Christian doctrine. Their faith clings to, and is nourished by, the remnants of the saving truth left them. But they are in a sad state. Their faith is undernourished. God wants His Christians to live not by a fraction of the truth but by the whole truth. God wants a vigorous faith, and He has well provided for that. The moderns, however, withhold from God's children the wholesome food God has provided. The food which they provide is — if we may use a homely simile — lacking in necessary vitamins. The general situation obtaining in the Church today is well described by Dr. E. J. M. Nutter, dean of Nashotah House, in these words: "A horrid suspicion has been gaining ground here for some time, that in our threshing of the Word of God we have been throwing away the wheat, and drearily chewing on the chaff." [321] The moderns are committing a crime against God's children when they take away from their table much of the wheat of the saving doctrine and make them chew on chaff. They are raising an anemic, stunted generation. Oh, yes, there may be enough nourishment left to keep them alive, but this, too, may occur: some poor soul may not have strength enough to throw off the noxious effect of the false teaching set before him. And this may occur: in the hour of trial the poor soul may forget the saving truth, put its trust on a false teaching, and lose its salvation. The loss is on the head of him who tells people not to rely absolutely on the letter of Scripture.

---

321) Let us submit a few more statements by Dr. Nutter. They bear on the *general* subject of our writing. "We are sure that in pounding theology into our students we are not being stubbornly antiquated in a liberal and undogmatic world, but are heading the procession home. . . . Should the clergy and laity of this Church once realize that the Nicene Faith is in peril, the reaction is likely to be astonishing. It is for the preservation and promulgation of the Nicene Faith that Nashotah labors; and in our defense of such orthodox dogmas as the Virgin Birth, the Incarnation, and a Resurrection, neither metaphorical nor hallucinatory, we shall not budge. Our attitude to the Holy Scriptures is equally firm. Of course, we know all about J, E, D, P, and Q. We are acquainted with the Johannine problems. We even devote time to discussing such erudite subjects as form-criticism. This is what is called scholarship. But a horrid suspicion is gaining ground here for some years, that in our threshing of the Word of God we have been throwing away the wheat and drearily chewing on the chaff. . . . Untold harm has been done to Christianity in all its several sections by the uninspired ministry of men who only know what the Bible is not; and the saddest side of it is that the anticipated stampede of the intelligentsia into the Church, which was to follow the abandonment of miracle, has not taken place. A return to a Scripture that is really holy is imperative if our religion is to survive. . . ." (*The Living Church,* May 17, 1942.) — We have taken the liberty to generalize the statement concerning the chewing on the chaff and to apply it to what Hofmann and the rest offer the Church under the trademark "Die alte Wahrheit auf neue Weise zu lehren."

(2) Under the new charter of liberty the Christian can have no assurance of faith. We shall treat this more fully in the concluding chapter.

(3) The new-liberty men exert an evil influence on the Christian in this way, too, that they systematically train him in developing his pride of reason, the self-conceit of his flesh. They are instructing him to set his own judgment, his "Christian consciousness," or whatever you want to call it, over Scripture. The Christian faith is humble. That belongs to its very nature — believing is accepting and trusting the Word of God. The Christian faith submits to every word of Scripture and is outraged when Satan suggests that the Christian may know more about these things than the holy writers or may be able to express God's eternal thoughts better than they, than the Holy Ghost did. The Christian layman and the Christian theologian are content to sit at the feet of the prophets and take their wisdom from them. As Luther puts it: "Our pride is that we are catechumens and pupils of the prophets, that we repeat after them and preach what we heard from the prophets and apostles." (III: 1890.) "Und nichts Eigenes oder Neues setzen" (*loc. cit.*) — not attempt to "teach the old truth in a new way, add to it for the purpose of improving on it." But the moderns will not have the Christians take this attitude. When the moderns declaim that "they have attained *higher forms* than the prophets" (J. De Witt); when they virtually declare: "The truth is, man of today has altogether outgrown the Bible. It may have done for the infant state of the human mind, but to put the rising generation under its clamps and chains would be to restrict the mental growth of the human race" (see J. M. Haldeman, *A King's Penknife,* p. 108): they are causing the seed of wicked pride which is implanted in the heart of man to germinate and flourish. What thoughts must arise in the heart of the Christian when his teacher tells him: "Faith refuses to make a legalistic use of individual passages or of the entire Scripture. . . . We must be in accord with Luther and his spirit of freedom and apply this touchstone to every word of Scripture: Does it give expression to the Gospel as Gospel, the pure and clear Gospel?" (G. Wehrung, *Geschichte und Glaube,* pp. 306, 308.) The Old Adam in the Christian's heart will pride himself on being given the right to subject Scripture to his judgment. The Christian faith cannot do what Wehrung and the others are asking it to do. The rationalist, indeed, "comes to the Bible and sits over its contents in the attitude of a judge who is to decide for himself what in it is true and worthy to be believed, . . . not in the attitude of the disciple, who within the limits of the inspired record feels himself at Jesus' feet to receive every word that cometh out of His mouth"

(J. Bannerman). And the moderns are training their pupils in rationalistic pride and arrogance. This pride is an evil thing. "When we begin to be so proud and overweening as to judge according to our reason" on any doctrine of Scripture, . . . "then we are rude fellows, thinking more of our blind and poor reason than of the statements of Scripture. For Scripture is God's own witness concerning Himself, and our reason cannot know the divine nature; yet it wants to judge concerning that about which it knows nothing" (Luther, X:1018). Christian faith and pride, self-conceit, self-deification, do not go together. If this pride is not checked, it will destroy faith. And the moderns, asking the Christians to correct, improve on, reject Scripture, are cultivating this malignant thing.

This is St. Paul's judgment of the new charter of liberty: "If any man teach otherwise and consent not to wholesome words, even to the words of our Lord Jesus Christ, and to the doctrine which is according to godliness, he is proud, knowing nothing," 1 Tim. 6:3 f.[322] We shall remain under the charter given by our Lord: "If ye continue in My Word," in the word of Holy Scripture, "ye shall know the truth, and the truth shall make you free," John 8:31 f.

---

322) Moffatt's translation hits off some points very well: "Anyone who teaches novelties and refuses to fall in with the sound words of our Lord Jesus Christ and the doctrine that tallies with godliness, is a conceited, ignorant creature."

CHAPTER VIII

The Battle for Verbal Inspiration

(Final Résumé)

This is, and must be, the burden of our concluding remarks: Let us "earnestly contend for the faith which was once delivered unto the saints" (Jude 3); let us faithfully guard the precious doctrine of verbal inspiration.

THE BATTLE FOR THE BIBLE

We shall earnestly contend for it if we realize, in the first place, how much is at stake. We must realize what the Church would lose if she surrendered Verbal Inspiration. We would *lose our Bible*. The battle for Verbal Inspiration is not a mock battle played by children. It is not some unseemly brawl among squabbling theologians — *Theologengezaenk*. No; the Church is engaged in a life-or-death struggle. It is a battle for her most precious possession. The battle for Verbal Inspiration is a battle for the Bible.

Inspiration makes the Bible what it is — God's Word. If what the moderns have been telling us is true, namely, that half of the Bible contains human errors and that the other half, the good half, is brought to us in words of men's own choosing, then the Bible is nothing but a human book — the word of man, unreliable, at bottom useless. "As Walther pointed out in his first pronouncement in *Lehre und Wehre*, 1855, p. 248, the denial of the inspiration of Scripture is destructive of the very *ratio formalis Scripturae*; it takes away that which makes Scripture what it is; for Scripture is the Word of God because of its being inspired of God." (*Walther and the Church*, p. 12.) If we would retain our Bible, we cannot surrender Verbal Inspiration. "With the Biblical doctrine of the inspiration of Holy Scripture stand or fall the certainty, truth, and divine character of Scripture itself and of the entire Christian religion." (Walther, *Lutherstunde*.)

In very truth, the moderns are asking us to scrap our old Bible and let them give us a new Bible, one of their own making. The new Bible of the liberals is written in Fosdick's modern thought forms; the Jefferson Bible is already on the market. The new Bible of the "positive" group would eliminate the erroneous, unethical, and trivial sections which their first three objections specify. And their last three objections make short work of the rest of the Bible. The words in which the saving truth is revealed are not inspired; for that would imply a mechanical inspiration. And you

[410]

must not bind men to the words; for that would be atomistic and legalistic.

They have taken away the old Bible, and their new Bible contains nothing sure and definite. They tell us that only the concepts, not the words, of the old Bible are inspired. Who will be able to read their new Bible, which will contain not words, but concepts? — Their theologians have not yet been able to tell us exactly what the *Schriftganze* is. — They have not set down, in exact terms, what the "Word of God" says and in how far it agrees with the "Christian consciousness."

The moderns have scrapped the old Bible. It was not enough that they presented the Bible to the people as a tissue of truth and error, so that poor souls were filled with suspicion of the entire Bible and cried out: "We can no longer read it!" They had to go on and directly emasculate the true portions, causing the poor Christian to read the Gospel truths with doubt and lament: If John 3:16 is not in itself the Word of God, of what use is it to me?

The old Christian Bible, as the moderns offer it to the Church, presents a sorry appearance — mangled, mutilated, invalidated. Not a single passage and line is permitted to stand exactly as God wrote it. "Behold your Bible!" says the old evil Foe.

R. H. Malden, Dean of Wells, calls attention, in the opening paragraph of his book *The Inspiration of the Bible,* to William Chillingworth's statement "The Bible, and the Bible only, is the religion of Protestants" and declares: "Any form of religion which cuts itself loose from the Bible will very soon cease to be Christian, even if it should masquerade in Christian costume." Malden does not believe in Verbal Inspiration. He does not hesitate to cut out of the Bible the Imprecatory Psalms. He characterizes the story of Creation and of the Fall as fairy tales, etc. And this is his definition of Inspiration: "When we call the Bible inspired, we mean (or at least I mean) that it is of unique and permanent religious value." (P. 4.) Question: Does not a religious body which refuses to accept the Bible as the very Word of God, accepting it only as a valuable religious treatise, cut itself loose from the Bible, with all that this, according to Malden's own statement, involves?

Dr. H. C. Alleman wrote an article for *The Lutheran,* Dec. 4, 1940, on "Let There Be No Bible Blackout" and declared: "There is one subject on which Lutherans of all shades of confessional interpretation agree." But when Dr. Alleman insists that the Bible contains errors and contradictions (*Luth. Church Quart.,* 1940, p. 356), ridicules after the manner of D. F. Strauss the account of Jesus' riding on the ass, declares that "the pure Scriptures must be separated from their dregs and filth" (see *The Lutheran,* Jan. 14,

1937), and warns against making the Bible "a legal code," he is inducing a Bible blackout. He is creating distrust of the Bible.

John W. Haley's book *An Examination of the Alleged Discrepancies of the Bible* makes fine reading. It examines 571 doctrinal, ethical, and historical discrepancies, and disposes of them, generally in a very acceptable manner. It shows, for instance, that Strauss's ridicule about "Christ riding upon *both* animals, the ass and the colt," is not justified by the text.[323] And now mark the tragedy of this: Haley makes the fatal concession that the sacred writers were "not infallible in all respects," "were *not* supernaturally guarded against trifling inaccuracies in the detail of unimportant circumstances (Whately)," were not "supernaturally informed on matters of natural history, history, etc., but were left to the guidance of their natural faculties (Alford)." Worse than this, he distinctly disclaims *Verbal Inspiration*, even in the *religious* teaching of the Bible. "Inspiration deals primarily with *ideas* rather than with *words*. It suggests ideas to the mind of the writer, allowing him, generally, to clothe them in his own language." (Pp. 6, 157.) *Here* he takes common ground with Dr. Alleman and the rest of the concept-theory men. Recall statements like these: "Inspiration does not apply to the words, but only to the substance." (G. L. Raymond.) "We are thrown back on the inner content of the revelation instead of its literary expression." (H. W. Robinson.) "For every essential issue there is divine truth at hand; that its *verbal expression is of human origin* can be frankly recognized" (*The Lutheran*, June 21, 1928), or, as J. A. W. Haas puts it: "Men were never saved by a Bible that was mechanically perfect in its verbality." This teaching blacks out the Bible. Fallible men made the choice of the words dealing with the saving truth, and "we do not know," says L. A. Weigle, "whether the words of the Bible given us are true or accurate." And Seeberg assured us that "there can be no doubt that the Biblical authors could certainly draw conclusions intrinsically false from inspired truth." See how completely this theory of the moderns destroys the trustworthiness of our Bible even in its religious statements! Statements made by fallible men! And there is no way to tell "what is of the *form* of revelation and what is of the *substance*. It may be that an

---

323) Haley is not a discrepancy-hunter. On the contrary, he takes the discrepancy-hunters severely to task. "Moreover, I may be allowed to say that, the more thoroughly I have investigated the subject, the more clearly have I seen the flimsy and disingenuous character of the objections alleged by infidels. . . . One can scarcely read the pronouncements of these three (Strauss, Colenso, and Theodore Parker) and some others of their school without the conviction that the animus of these writers is often felicitously expressed by the old Latin motto, slightly modified: 'I will either find a discrepancy, or I will make one. *Aut inveniam discrepantiam, aut faciam.*'" (P. X, 25.)

infallibly exact criterion has not been given us." (E. Lewis.) "No one knows," declares Grau, "how much is divine, how much human." No one knows how much of John 3:16 is absolutely reliable; the *words* are not absolutely reliable. The Bible is completely blacked out! — What a disreputable thing our Bible has become! It is, according to the moderns, an indistinguishable compound of truth and error, as far as secular matters are concerned. And as far as religious truth is concerned, it is the same indistinguishable mixture of the divine and the human. "Those who reject the Church doctrine of inspiration in favor of some lowered form have never been able to agree among themselves as to which parts of the Bible are inspired and which are not or *to what extent any part is inspired.*" (L. Boettner, *The Inspiration of the Scriptures,* p. 82.) Such a Bible cannot serve us. "In short, if we should doubt the verbal inspiration of the Bible, namely, that the very words of Holy Scripture are God-breathed, the Bible would certainly be useless to us; for in that case we should certainly be assailed by doubts as to whether or not the human writers had really used the correct terms in setting forth the holy and sublime subject matter." (Pieper, *What Is Christianity?* P. 235.)

Put it this way: How much of the Bible is inspired? How much of it is worth keeping? The liberals say, Nothing is inspired. And the conservatives say, Nothing is inspired. These conservatives will tell us that, while they follow the liberals in rejecting many portions of the Bible as noninspired, they hold, in opposition to the liberals, that the religious portions are inspired. We must tell them that they do not in reality teach even that. "Nein, die Neueren leugnen im Grunde auch die Inspiration jener 'ewigen Heilsgedanken.'" (Stoeckhardt, *Lehre und Wehre,* 1886, p. 313.) Our Bible, as it happens, is made up of words. Take the words away, and no Bible is left; but our moderns stoutly maintain that these *words* — including the Gospel words — are not inspired. "The Word," says J. A. W. Haas, "is not built up out of inspired words." (*Luth. Church Quart.,* 1937, p. 279.) If you want to get the "Word," which is, they say, the real heart of Scripture, you must not look for words. The moderns ought in all fairness no longer confuse the Church by using the term "inspiration of the Bible." The Bible, which consists of words, is *not inspired* if the words are not inspired. James Orr, not at all a verbal-inspirationist, understands the matter perfectly and declares: "If there is inspiration at all, it must penetrate words as well as thought, must mold the expression." (*Revelation and Inspiration,* p. 209.) The verbal-inspirationist Dr. J. A. Dell, too, cannot understand why the moderns persist in keeping the term "inspiration" in their vocabulary. "The readers of this magazine (*Journal of Theol. of the A. L. Conf.*) will remember that I have shivered more than one lance in defense of the term 'verbal inspiration,' holding that, if the words are not inspired, the Bible is not inspired." He then goes on to show what meaning the moderns attach to their "inspiration" and that such an "inspired" Bible is useless.[324] The moderns ought to tell us openly what they are attacking. The attack on Verbal Inspiration, as Spurgeon once put it, is only the verbal form of the attack on inspiration itself.

The issue on which the battle for Verbal Inspiration is being fought is this: Shall we retain our old Bible or make us a new Bible? In those territories which the moderns have conquered men are practically writing new Bibles. "Every man is excogitating his own Bible." (Spurgeon.) [325] Moffat has just told us what process they apply.

They are asking us to give up our verbally inspired Bible and accept one which is to the half a human product. Do we realize what deadly woe the old evil Foe means? Walther realized it. "Beware, I say, of this 'divine-human Scripture.' It is a devil's mask; for at last it manufactures such a Bible after which I certainly would not care to be a Bible Christian, namely, that the Bible should henceforth be no more than any other good book, a book which I should have to read with constant sharp discrimi-

---

324) "What, then, does Dr. Moffatt, who calls the 'theory of verbal inspiration' a caricature, believe concerning this written record? He says: 'We may say that, as God's self-revelation enters into history and experience to carry out His purpose and to realize His will, preeminently through the life of Christ on earth, the Word cannot be confined to its immediate and original audience. These recipients attest it, but they do not exhaust its significance. In their testimony lies a historical guarantee of its characteristic qualities. But also through them the revelation is transmitted, it is communicated afresh to successive generations, and Scripture, or the written Word, is a vital factor in the process. The point with me is, Is it a *reliable* factor in the process of transmitting God's self-revelation to successive generations? Can I today rely on its statements (conveyed in words) as true? If it is a patchwork of the opinions of uninspired men, I could have little confidence in it." (See CONC. THEOL. MTHLY., XII, p. 304.)

325) Let us hear the whole passage from Spurgeon. It covers other sections, too, of this article. "To Luther Scripture was the last court of appeal. If any had convinced Luther of error out of that Book, he would gladly have retracted; but that was not their plan; they simply said, 'He is a heretic: condemn him or make him retract.' To this he never yielded for an instant. Alas, in this age numbers of men are setting up their own inspired writers. I have been told that every man who is his own lawyer has a fool for his client; and I am inclined to think that, when any man sets up to be his own Savior and his own revelation, much the same thing occurs. That conceited idea is in the air at present — every man is excogitating his own Bible. Not so Luther. He loved the sacred Book! He fought by its help. It was his battle-ax and his weapon of war. A text of Scripture fired his soul; but the words of tradition he rejected."

nation in order not to be led into error. . . . In a word, it is unspeakable what the devil seeks by this 'divine-human Scripture.'" (*Lehre und Wehre*, 1886, p. 76.)

Luther realized it. "If this be the attitude of Rome" [if this be the attitude of the moderns], "then blessed be the land of Greece, blessed be the land of Bohemia, blessed be all those who have separated themselves and gone out from this Babylon. . . . As matters now stand, faith has been extinguished in her midst, the Gospel proscribed, Christ banished, and the morals are worse than barbarian. Still there remained one hope: the inviolable authority of Holy Scripture remained; men had at least the right view of the Bible, though not the right understanding of its sense. But now Satan is capturing this, too, the stronghold of Zion and the tower of David, unconquered up till now." (XVIII: 425 f.) Breaking Verbal Inspiration, they are breaking the Bible.

THE BATTLE FOR CHRISTIAN THEOLOGY

The Church is in deadly peril. Let us repeat that in this form: she is facing the *loss of all Christian theology*. The Christian doctrine is based on the authority and trustworthiness of the Bible, and when the authority of the Bible is undermined, the Christian doctrine cannot stand.

Or put it this way: the principles on which the anti-inspirationists operate, the principle that science and the "Christian consciousness" have a voice in the interpretation of Scripture, that the *words* do not count because that would involve a "mechanical" inspiration and would lead to an atomistic and legalistic-literalistic use of Scripture, these principles lead, wherever they are consistently applied, to the nullification of all Christian doctrines. In the words of Dr. Pieper: "The result is that modern theology has lost the divine truth. It has renounced Holy Scripture as the infallible truth and the sole authority and has corrupted all the chief articles of the Christian doctrine, taking the very heart out of them." (*Proc., Del. Synod,* 1899, p. 34.) [326]

The termites are boring into the inside of the sills on which the house rests and devouring their structure. If they are not destroyed, the edifice of the Christian doctrine will fall.

We have already, more than once, dealt with this matter. Now we would emphasize one particular point: the denial of Verbal Inspiration does away with the *certainty of doctrine*. Where the

---

326) In the Introduction to Graebner's *The Problem of Lutheran Union* Dr. J. H. C. Fritz writes: "Recently, in one of its official publications, the *Lutheran Church Quarterly,* issue of January, 1935, the United Lutheran Church resented the very idea of doctrinal purity, and *by denying the verbal inspiration of the Scriptures* it removes on its part the *very foundation* for it."

moderns, have substituted doctrines of their own making for the Biblical doctrines, they cannot, of course, speak with assurance. But even where they have retained some or many of the Christian doctrines, the divine assurance of their absolute truth is lacking. In the words of Dr. Pieper: "All who refuse to 'identify' Scripture and the Word of God, that is, all who deny the inspiration of Scripture, practically make the entire Christian doctrine, the very center of it, too, uncertain." (*Lehre und Wehre*, 1928, p. 369.)

For these men do not believe that a doctrine is certain and absolutely true simply because Scripture teaches it. We believe that. Scripture, being the Word of God, given by inspiration, is the "sure Word," 2 Pet. 1:19. That guarantees the certitude of its teachings and gives us divine assurance. "*Homo est certus passive, sicut Verbum Dei est certum active.*" (Luther.) But the moderns, denying that the Scripture is the Word of God, cannot but deny, and do deny, that it is a sure word. They cannot, and do not want to, treat its statements as conclusive and infallible.

And will their substitute Bible supply the certitude of doctrine? The moderns base what they have retained of the Christian doctrine not on the words of Scripture but on the *Schriftganze,* on the "Word of God" hidden in Scripture. They base their doctrine on what their "Christian consciousness" has discovered to be this "Word of God." He who bases his teaching on "the infallibility of the letter of Scripture," says Ladd, finds himself "in the most insecure of all positions." It takes the "Christian consciousness, the spiritually illumined Christian reason and conscience, to discern the Word." (*What Is the Bible?* Pp. 453, 456, 468.) "Final authority," says the *Lutheran Church Quarterly,* 1935, p. 263 f., "is found in the final analysis within the soul. . . . Here the teacher of religion finds his authority. His message is an unceasing 'Thus saith the Lord,' and he speaks with confidence, not because he quotes a scripture, but because the word of God has found him." So, then, all that the moderns offer as the guarantee of the truth of their doctrine is the testimony of their reason, their experience, their feeling. Back of their "Thus saith the Lord" is the "Thus saith a fallible man."

The theology of the anti-inspirationists is from beginning to end a theology of uncertainty and doubt. It is throughout guesswork. They do not *know* how much of the Bible is of the substance of revelation and how much is the human forms. *Religion in Geschichte und Gegenwart* (rather liberal) states: "Als die Behauptung, dass alle Woerter der Heiligen Schrift eingegeben seien (Verbalinspiration) im 18. Jahrhundert zusammengebrochen war, war zwar der Glaube an die *Sach*inspiration geblieben, aber man wusste nicht sicher zu sagen, um welche Sache oder Sachen es sich handle." (P. 297.) The moderns have to guess at that. And when they have agreed that a certain passage must have a divine substance, Grau and Lewis tell us that there is no way of finding out how much of, say, John 3:16 belongs to the form (fallible human words) and what constitutes substance, the divine concept. You must guess at that.

More than that, the moderns cheerfully admit that their guess is probably wrong. What makes the guess is, according to their theology, the "Christian consciousness"; that finds the real Word of God in Scripture, tests the doctrinal statements of Scripture, formulates the Christian doctrine. But — this Christian consciousness changes with each generation. Their prophet Schleiermacher says so.[327] H. F. Rall speaks in the same strain: "Leaders tried to establish authoritative forms . . . of belief which should remain unchanged; but the Church itself never remained exactly the same in any two generations. . . . Christianity has been a religion of freedom and change and advance. . . . We do not stop with Christ, but He gives us the line of advance." (*A Faith for Today,* pp. 38, 50.) There are doctrines, too, we are told, concerning which the Christian consciousness has not yet come to a definite conclusion. "Die Kirche hat noch nicht gesprochen." "There are certain doctrines in which the Church has not made a final pronouncement" (*The Lutheran Companion,* March 30, 1939); and it will never make a final pronouncement on these doctrines or on any of the doctrines, for the Christian consciousness, the framer of the Christian doctrines, is forever changing its mind. Do not expect the moderns to give you a definite, fixed, stable system of doctrine. They cannot say: "This is the real Word of God," and: "Hoc *verbum Dei manet in aeternum.*" A man trained in the school of Schleiermacher, Hofmann, and Ladd speaks in this wise: What I tell you about sin and grace may be wrong; another generation may give us a better system of truth.[328]

---

327) "Dr. Patton, in his new book *Fundamental Christianity,* thus characterizes Schleiermacher's position: 'According to Schleiermacher, the New Testament is the record of the Christian consciousness of the apostolic age; but the Christian consciousness of a later age may be different, and in so far as it may differ, it has a right to supersede the record of the Christian consciousness of the early Church. The outcome of this principle would be that, the Christian consciousness being in a state of constant flux, no one can predict what the consciousness of the next age will affirm, and therefore no one can put much confidence in what the Christian consciousness of the present age affirms." (*Theol. Mthly.,* VI, p. 373.)

328) Let us add a note on the stupendous folly of this modern principle: the doctrine changes in line with the changing Christian consciousness. Its basic thought is that everything human is subject to change and that, since it is human to err, the change is desirable. — To be sure, anything of human contrivance is in need of improvement.

The theology of the moderns is uncertain, unstable, undecided, and they are proud of this fact. They tell us that this is the ideal situation. R. Sockman: " 'Man', says Middleton Murray, 'cannot accept certainties; he must discover them.' . . . When we start on the search for religious certainty and authority, we must realize that we travel in the realm of values and cannot, therefore, demonstrate absolute proof. . . . To be 'dead certain' would be deadly." (*Recoveries in Religion*, p. 36 f.) G. A. Buttrick: "Meanwhile we should frankly admit the bankruptcy of 'literal infallibility' and, under guidance of the facts, set out *on the long hard quest for truth*." (See *Conc. Theol. Mthly.*, XII, p. 223.) J. S. Whale repeats "Lessing's profound remark: 'If God held in His right hand all truth and in His left only the ever-active impulse to search for truth, even with the condition that I must always make mistakes, and said to me, "Choose!" I should humbly bow before His left hand and say, "Father, give me this. Pure truth belongs to Thee alone." ' " (*The Chr. Answer to Prayer*, p. 49.) Says the *Watchman-Examiner*: "We have come upon the blessed day of the 'open mind,' which means that we have no convictions any more, but opinions only, that is, that we hold our faith so lightly that we can easily let go of it and take hold of some other notion if the wind of popular favor changes; we are 'blown about by every wind of doctrine,' as the uncompromising apostle says." Do not ask the anti-inspirationists for a fixed system of truth.

What role would the Church play in the world if the moderns had their way? No longer "the pillar and ground of truth" (1 Tim. 3:15), proclaiming clearly and loudly the eternal truth committed to her, she would be turned into a debating society which discusses important questions but never reaches a conclusion. Listen to the wrangling, jangling voices! Should the deity of Christ be taught? Yes, says the affirmative side, Paul taught it. No, say the Anomoeans; Paul was there speaking only as a man. Is man justified by faith alone? Paul taught it, indeed, but the Christian consciousness of a later, the papistic, generation found that idea

---

We have no fault to find with Thomas Jefferson's principle that the constitution of a free people should provide within itself an opportunity for each generation to revise it completely. It is a fine thing when the civic and political consciousness of a people rises to higher levels. But we certainly find fault with Schleiermacher's application of this principle to the field of doctrine. Our doctrinal Constitution was not framed by fallible men but by the infallible Lord. Again, the school of Schleiermacher (the moderns) forget that there is something about man that does not change. His sinful nature and the great need resulting therefrom do not change. If in some future generation man's sinful nature should change for the better, we should need an improved system of doctrine. Again, the "Christian consciousness" that changes and then changes the Christian doctrine, is not a Christian consciousness. Finally, it is the Christian doctrine which forms the Christian consciousness, not *vice versa*.

intolerable, and it won by a majority vote. The moderns are pleased that the issue is not yet settled. Luther thought he had the right idea, but the Christian consciousness of the present generation wants the works drawn in again and is finding wide support. No issue can be settled in this debating society. It is no use to quote Scripture on any doctrine. The dissenter has the right, in this debating society, to veto it with the magic formula: Legalistic! Literalism!

The Church of the moderns plays a sorry role in the affairs of men. It has lost the voice of authority. It has lost its power. Its preachers are unable to say: *Haec dixit Dominus*. In the old Church no one was permitted to preach who was not sure of his doctrine, sure of its being God's doctrine. "Think of Luther's words in *Wider Hans Worst*" [St. L. ed., XVII: 1343] "in which he says that a preacher should 'declare boldly with St. Paul and all the apostles and prophets: *"Haec dixit Dominus*, God Himself hath said this."' And again: 'In this sermon I have been an apostle and prophet of Jesus Christ. Here it is not necessary, not even good, to ask for the forgiveness of sins. For it is God's Word, not mine, and so there can be no reason for His forgiving me; He can only confirm and praise what I have preached, saying: "Thou hast taught correctly, for I have spoken through thee, and the Word is mine." Anyone who cannot say this of his own preaching should stop, for he must surely be lying and blaspheming God when he preaches.'" (H. Sasse, *Here We Stand*, p. 161.) In the new Church such assurance is taboo. Men are horrified when a man ascends the pulpit of his church and cries out: "I place over against all sentences of the fathers, men, angels, devils . . . solely the Word of the eternal majesty, the Gospel. . . . That is God's Word, not ours. Here I stand, here I stay, here I make my boast, here I triumph, here I defy the papists, the Thomists, the Heinzists, Sophists, and all the gates of hell. God's Word is above all, the divine majesty is on my side." (Luther, XIX: 337.) Luther would not be permitted to teach in the seminary of the new Church. Luther who said: "A theologian and preacher must not say: 'Lord, forgive me if I have taught what is wrong'; but of everything that he teaches in public and writes he must be sure that it is God's Word." (XXII: 1507.) The seminary authorities would tell him: No man can be sure how much of Scripture is God's Word.

This new Church has lost the voice of authority, has lost its power. For "how is it possible for a preacher to be a power for God whose source of authority is his own reason and convictions" (*Fundamentals* III, p. 111), his Christian consciousness, his guess at what the Bible means? Dr. Clarence E. Macartney refuses to have any dealings with this debating society. "When Luther said:

'Here I stand, I cannot do otherwise. So help me God,' he was taking his stand upon the Scriptures. But *where does the Protestant Church today stand as to the Scriptures? Does it stand anywhere?* And when the authority of the Scriptures is gone, all that we have is a vague 'I think so.' Human wisdom and speculation is a poor substitute for a 'Thus saith the Lord.'" "Those who have departed from faith in an infallible Bible have made desperate, but utterly vain efforts to secure a suitable substitute and other standing ground. . . . No one can preach with the power and influence of him who draws a sword bathed in heaven and who goes into the pulpit with a 'Thus saith the Lord.'" (See *Conc. Theol. Mthly.*, V, p. 398; VIII, p. 395. L. Boettner, *op. cit.*, p. 81.)

Those who attend divine services in the new Church planned by the moderns are badly served. In his parable of the soldiers casting lots Luther quotes Eph. 4:14 and remarks: "Κυβεία [sleight] is originally dice-playing and here means just this, that they use the words of God like dice, find no certainty in them, but make them serve all manner of varying opinions. . . . For what other effect can these wavering opinions and uncertain teachings have than that they toss us who are children to and fro, carry us hither and yon, force and drive us whither they will?" (IV:1310.)

The poor people sing: *"Liebster Jesu, wir sind hier, Dich and dein Wort anzuhoeren";* we would hear the Word of Jesus! They are told by the preacher: The word of Jesus is hidden somewhere in Scripture, but the Christian consciousness of our theologians has not yet discovered the exact wording of it; wait till the Church has spoken.

The people ask: How much of what you are preaching is the absolute truth? The preachers tell them: Some of our preaching is not exactly the truth,[329] and the truths we do preach are more or less guesswork.

---

329) *Prophecy's Light on Today,* by C. G. Trumbull, p. 95: "A devoted Christian woman, who was a teacher in the Sunday school of a well-known church, went to her pastor one day to talk with him about doctrinal matters. She explained to him, inasmuch as she was very old-fashioned in her beliefs and was teaching the children in the Primary Department that the Bible was just what it claims to be, she wondered whether her pastor would really want to have her continue her work there or give it up. He assured her that he wished her to stay right on in her Sunday-school work there, saying: 'Most assuredly I do. I believe in teaching little children the Bible stories just as they are and, *when they are older, teach them the truth.'"* We heard the statement of a prominent Lutheran theologian: "Pupils may later discard the scientific import of the story." We heard the statement of *Christendom:* "The account of the Creation in Genesis, . . . the Christmas story of the Incarnation, . . . the doctrine of the divinity of Christ, . . . are still scrupulously retained, lovingly cherished, but considered as poetic expressions of some profounder or larger truth than that which their formulators realized." (I, p. 492.)

The Church would suffer a mortal hurt if Verbal Inspiration were lost. Why, there are men who deny Verbal Inspiration but still feel compelled to warn against accepting low views of inspiration. J. W. Haley advocates the concept theory and the partial-inspiration theory. "There is no need to ask whether everything contained in the writings of the apostles was immediately suggested by the Spirit or not. . . . For these things were not of a religious nature, and no inspiration was necessary concerning them." And now mark his words: "We will simply add that the view of inspiration exhibited in the foregoing extracts, while it very well meets certain exigencies of the case, seems nevertheless peculiarly liable to be misunderstood and abused. *There is ever far greater danger to be apprehended from a lax than from a strict theory of inspiration.*" (*Op. cit.*, p. 158. — Our italics.) And E. Grubb (extreme liberal) gives this cold-blooded diagnosis of the case: "Nor can we find in the Bible, any more than in the Church, a final and infallible standard of truth or duty. The Bible . . . is not infallible." And now: "The new view does not, it may be urged, give the same certainty as the old." And Grubb is pleased to have it so. He continues: "But, if the old is becoming incredible, what then? May we not be meant to understand that the desire for infallibility is itself unhealthy?" (*The Bible, Its Nature and Inspiration*, p. 239 f.)

Edwin Lewis wants certainty of doctrine. " 'Give us a sure word!' this is the cry which we daily hear. . . . Tell us, is there nowhere one word which stands above all other words, no truth of rocklike quality, which nothing can move? . . . Tell us, must we always flounder, must we always be experimenters, must we always build up only to tear down?" And he destroys all certainty of the Christian doctrine when he declares: "Without a doubt our fathers came very close to Bibliolatry; they could make no distinction between the Word of God and the words of men by which that Word was given." (*The Faith We Declare*, pp. 49, 188.)

Georgia Harkness declares: "There is nothing a Christian minister wants more than to be able to say the right things and to say them with authority." And how shall he find the truth? By applying the methods of liberal theology? No; for "liberal theology, by moving so far in the direction of capitulation to the scientific method, almost lost its soul." By relying on the statements of the Bible? No; for "the belief in the literal inspiration of the Bible" is "a great pitfall." How shall we, then, arrive at the truth and obtain certainty? Mark the tragedy of the answer given: "There is no neat formula." "There is nothing a Christian minister wants more than to be able to say the right things and to say them with authority. How shall we do it? There is no neat formula." (*The Faith by Which the Church Lives*, pp. 46, 57, 142.) — A theology which refuses to base its teachings on the word of Scripture has lost its soul, its power, its authority, its convictions.

Do we realize how much is at stake? At the Washington Debate the spokesman of the American Lutheran Church told the spokesman of the U. L. C.: "If behind Inspiration is placed a question mark, then all Christian doctrine is questionable." (See *Conc. Theol. Mthly.*, IX, p. 363.) Breaking down Verbal Inspiration, they are breaking down all Christian doctrine.

Do we realize how much Satan is interested in this matter? Dr. Bente writes in *Lehre und Wehre*, 1902, p. 130: "Today Satan is striking not so much at individual doctrines but rather at the foundation of all doctrines, at Scripture itself. . . . By yielding up the inspiration and infallibility of Scripture the Church would abandon every Christian doctrine to the whim and caprice of men. Nothing could give Satan and the enemies of the Church greater pleasure than to find that here in the Lutheran Church of America, too, as in that of Germany, this truth is being questioned or denied. It may at first sight seem an unwarranted statement, but it is actually so: the denial of the doctrine of inspiration overthrows the Christian theology. The Christian doctrines may indeed still stand for a time; but the entire theological edifice is undermined and hollowed out if it is no longer borne by the inspired, infallible word of Scripture. . . . If the theologian gives up the inspiration of Scripture, the old mighty γέγραπται has lost its force and value for him. If the Bible is no longer the infallible Word of God but a human fallible record of the things of which it treats, the *loci classici* and *dicta probantia* are no longer of any avail. A veritable deluge of all manner of skeptical questions concerning the origin and content of Scripture is unloosed, which cannot be checked and controlled."

THE BATTLE FOR THE FAITH

Have we the full sense of the grave peril confronting the Church? Here is the plain truth: the denial of Verbal Inspiration is *destructive of Christianity*. It involves the loss of the Bible; this carries with it the loss of the Christian doctrine; and all of that means the destruction of the Christian religion.

The Christian Church stands or falls with Verbal Inspiration. That was Dr. Walther's judgment. "Walther not only espoused, with sincere conviction, the doctrine of inspiration as the old Church maintained it, but also characterized the relinquishment of this doctrine as virtual apostasy from Christianity." (Pieper in *Lehre und Wehre*, 1888, p. 193. See also *L. u. W.*, 1911, p. 152.) We had his statement above: "With the Biblical doctrine of the inspiration of Holy Scripture stand or fall the certainty, truth, and divine character of Scripture itself *and of the entire Christian religion*."

The Church would commit suicide if she renounced Verbal Inspiration.

The Christian religion, objectively considered, the teachings of Christianity, cannot be maintained where Verbal Inspiration is abandoned. We have just finished discussing that point.

Nor can Christianity, subjectively considered, the Christian faith, the faith of the believer, stand where Verbal Inspiration falls. Let us now discuss this phase of it. We say that, when men deny that Scripture is verbally inspired, is the very Word of God, they are removing the foundation on which saving faith rests. "The denial of the inspiration of Scripture has these results: (1) We give up the knowledge of the Christian truth.... (2) *We relinquish faith in the Christian sense,* since the Christian faith can exist only *vis-à-vis* the Word of God. . . ." (Pieper, *Chr. Dog.,* I, p. 369.) That is one of the elementary truths of Christian theology. In the days of the old rationalism Woltersdorf gave expression to it in the lines:

> Wenn dein Wort nicht mehr soll gelten,
> Worauf soll der Glaube ruhn?
> Mir ist's nicht um tausend Welten,
> Sondern um dein Wort zu tun.

In the present day of the new rationalism *Signs of the Times* (March 26, 1940) gives expression to it in these words: "With the poet we say,

> O Lord and Master of us all,
> Whate'er our name or sign,
> We own Thy sway, we hear Thy call,
> We test our lives by Thine.

But *how can we hear His call* unless we believe in the inspiration of His message through the Bible? We must conclude that, if we discard the Bible, we deny Christianity." Faith rests on the inspired Scriptures.

On the verbally inspired Scriptures — that is another elementary truth of Christian theology. Rather, it is the same truth. Unless Scripture is verbally inspired, it is not inspired at all. And only because it is verbally inspired, is it the firm foundation of faith. The old rationalists presented the Bible as a purely human book. And Woltersdorf asked: Can faith rest on a human book? The moderns present the Bible as partly divine, partly human. And we ask, Can faith rest on declarations and doctrines which come to us in fallible human words? Ponder the words President C. C. Hein spoke at Copenhagen: "To the Lutheran Church the Bible as a whole as well as in all its parts is the pure and infallible Word of God, for the reason that the Holy Spirit has inspired it. The Lutheran Church does not distinguish between Scripture and the Word of God. . . . When we no longer hold fast the inspiration and inerrancy of Scripture, . . . the very foundation of our faith will have been undermined. Instead of being built upon something objectively certain, *viz.*, the eternal truth of God's Word, faith will be based upon something subjectively uncertain and liable to change, such as experience or ecclesiastical group consciousness. Yes, 'what shall be my faith's foundation when Thy Word no more avails?' (Woltersdorf.)" (*The Second Lutheran World Convention*, p. 75. — See also *Conc. Theol. Mthly.*, XIII, p. 609.)

Faith rests on the Word, *on the certain Word.* There can be no faith, *no assurance of faith,* if, as the moderns will have it, no man can know with certainty how much of John 3:16 and 1 John 2: 1, 2, etc., belongs to the substance, to God's truth, and how much belongs to the form, man's fallible record of it. But "faith" which remains in doubt is not the Christian faith. In his parable of the soldiers casting lots Luther calls attention to this fact. "Faith, if it be not real assurance, is not faith at all." IV: 1309.) [330]   Faith, indeed, always struggles with doubt; but if it be nothing but doubt, it is not faith at all. And the "faith" produced by the modern view of Scripture is, in its very essence, uncertainty and doubt. The modern view of Scripture is most certainly destructive of the Christian faith. In the words of B. B. Warfield: "The trustworthiness of the Scriptures lies at the foundation of trust in the Christian system of doctrine, and is therefore *fundamental to the Christian hope and life. The validity of the Christian's hope in the several promises of the Gospel rests on the trustworthiness of the Bible....* Such a Word of God Christ and His apostles offer us when they give us the Scriptures, not as man's report to us of what God says, but as the very Word of God itself, spoken by God Himself through human lips and pens." (*Revelation and Inspiration*, pp. 66, 71.)

President J. W. Behnken in the tract *Come, See!* p. 13: "If the Bible is not the dependable, inerrant Word of God, do you realize that we would have no solid foundation for our faith? Oh, what a blessed assurance to know that our Redeemer 'without if or and' taught that the Bible is God's Word. . . . He said to His Father: 'Thy Word is truth' (not Thy Word *contains* truth)."

Examine once again the statement of G. Wehrung and the many similar ones quoted above: "Faith refuses to make a legalistic use of individual passages or of the entire Scripture. . . . We must apply this touchstone to every word of Scripture: Does it give expression to the Gospel as Gospel, the pure and clear Gospel?" E. Schaeder: "The Spirit-wrought faith applies a sifting process to the Bible-word. Through this sifting process it gets the Word of

---

330) Luther is speaking of the Romish theology, but his words fit modern theology exactly. "What a dreadful picture! Not only is the voice of the Gospel silenced, but also the letter of it is made doubtful.... And these are the men whom all the world acclaims as the best teachers just because they teach that everything is uncertain, while we know that faith, if it be not real assurance, is not faith at all."

God, the Word of Christ." But if the words are not reliable as they stand, if the unreliable "religious self-consciousness" must find what is reliable, "faith" never reaches assurance. The faith grown by the moderns is not the Christian faith.

The faith grown by the moderns, relying upon an indefinite, unreliable Scripture, cannot stand in the day of spiritual affliction. Recall Walther's words: "When he is facing death and reaches out for some verse of Scripture to uphold him, Satan will whisper to him: Who knows whether' that particular passage is God's Word? It may belong in the erroneous section of the Bible. You cannot rely on it; you cannot die on it." Again: "It is not a small matter when a poor man is lying on his deathbed, seeks comfort in a passage of Scripture and Satan assaults him with the question: Yea, how do you know that God said that? May not the writer have misunderstood the Holy Spirit?" (*Proc. Iowa Dist.*, 1891, pp. 27, 61. *Lehre und Wehre*, 1911, p. 155.)

Is it, then, impossible for one who denies Verbal Inspiration to have the true Christian saving faith? God can bring such a one to faith and keep him in it. God performs miracles. By God's grace such a one clings to Scripture in spite of the *dictum* of his mind that Scripture is unreliable. Such a one, denying Verbal Inspiration, believes in it and practices it — he accepts Scripture as it stands as God's Word. But that is not the result of the teaching of the moderns. The denial of Verbal Inspiration can result, in and by itself, only in killing the assurance of faith, that is, killing faith itself. We repeat, in the solemn words of Stoeckhardt: "The teaching that the Bible is not the very Word of God robs the Christian of all comfort and all assurance. One who holds that the Bible is a book which has a divine and a human side, may easily, in the day of distress, in the hour of death, sink into despair. When he looks to, say, John 3:16, Satan may challenge him: Where is your guarantee that this word is not one of the human ingredients of Scripture, that God's love for the whole world of sinners is not merely a pious wish and self-delusion? But we believe that 'all Scripture is given by inspiration of God'; we can, by the grace of God, make the right use of the 'It is written'; with this weapon we can repel Satan, fell him with one little word." (*Proc. Central Dist.*, 1894, p. 21.)

Does the denial of Verbal Inspiration touch the heart of Christianity? Rudelbach declares: "Der Begriff der Eingebung der Heiligen Schrift gehoert mit zu den Wurzeln der Kirche und ist mit den Herznerven derselben verflochten." (*Zeitsch. f. die ges. luth. Theologie u. Kirche*, 1841, viertes Q. H., p. 1.) The moderns are uprooting the Christian doctrine and the Christian's faith.

The churches are today wandering about in the desert of uncertainty. J. H. Leckie declares in his *Authority in Religion:* "Religion without certainty is religion without strength." (P. 64.) Now, Leckie is doing all that he can do to destroy the Christian's trust in the reliability of the Bible. "It is certainly true that the doctrine of Biblical inerrancy and plenary inspiration, in the old sense, is among the things that have been and the powers that are dead." (P. 50.) In its place he and his confreres are offering the Church this substitute: "The ideal organ of authority in religion must be found in the soul of man, in that secret place of its life where the voice of God is heard, . . . in the 'religious consciousness.'" (Pp. 76, 81.) What is the result? Let Leckie himself tell us: "There is much confusion and a great unrest. Some are preaching the Gospel in exactly the old forms and assuring themselves that the old dogmatic foundations remain; . . . others are striving to make the general sense of the Scriptures the ultimate rule of faith; and others are still crying, 'Back to the historic Christ!' while many are going on in the way of their fathers, keeping to the ancient paths, but haunted by a constant doubt that the basis of belief is gone. Perhaps this state of uncertainty, of varied and doubtful answers, is a necessity of the time. It may be that the Church must even wander a while in the desert: it may be that the word of reconciliation cannot be spoken till the thought and research of this age have performed their perfect work, till the uses of its labors are done. . . ." (P. 54.) — And when that distant day arrives, if the Christians should agree to accept the "religious consciousness" as the organ of authority, all of them would verily be wandering in the desert, chasing after a will-o'-the-whisp.

J. W. Haley writes: "A celebrated infidel is said to have exclaimed in his last moments, 'I am about to take a leap in the dark.' Cast the Bible aside, and every man at death takes a leap in the dark." (*Op. cit.,* p. 52.) Haley takes the rationalists severely to task. But mark the tragedy! If his own theory is correct, if only the concepts, and not the words, are inspired, the Christian at death must take a 'leap in the dark.'"

Edwin Lewis writes: "If the Christian preacher has reached the conclusion that the Bible is nothing at all but a collection of ancient literature of varying degrees of excellence, of what use is it to talk of the Bible as the bearer to men of the Word of God; of what use is it to seek to find in its pages a truth which is authoritative for the whole of life; of what use is it for him to expound one of its great passages, he harboring in his own mind all the time the suspicion that the passage represents only one more human guess, and creating in the mind of his hearer a similar suspicion?" (*Op. cit.,* p. 191.) But when Dr. Lewis tells his hearers that they must distinguish between the Word of God and the words of men by which that Word was given (see above), and that "the claim of revelation has been released from the burden of much unnecessary baggage, the stranglehold of this verbalism has been broken" (*A Philosophy of the Chr. Rel.*, p. 35), he cannot but create in their minds the suspicion that John 3:16 is not altogether trustworthy; the words are mere human words, guesses at what the real Word of God might be.

In his book *Faith Under Fire*, which contains his talks to men in the various Civilian Defense services in England, Michael Coleman says: "People are asking questions about God. What do they want to know? 'Know' is the important word: men and women long to 'know,' not merely that belief in a God is probable and reasonable, but to 'know' God Himself." (P. 8.) And now mark what he tells these poor people on page 48: "So many people imagine that the Bible being the word of God means that God, as it were, wrote it Himself, or held the pen of the human writers. The real truth surely is that God continually revealed and man continually attempted to understand, and sometimes only half understood, the truth that was there. So in the Bible we shall expect to find not only God's truth, which is always eternally true, but also man's sometimes erring ways of expressing truth." Can "faith" which is based on such a book stand under fire?

Are they making sport of the anxious inquirer, of the distressed Christian? "Gute Gewissen schreien nach der Wahrheit, . . . und denselben ist der Tod nicht so bitter, als bitter ihnen ist, wo sie etwa in einem Stuecke zweifeln. There are many good men to whom this doubt is more bitter than death." (Apology, *Conc. Trigl.*, p. 290 f.) The Christian cries out: My faith will die unless it find assurance in a sure word; and these men tell him: It is your faith, your Christian consciousness, which must make the word of Scripture sure.

And what are they making of God? Is He, too, making sport of the distressed Christians? He gives them His Word for their stay and anchor and when they would cling to it, does He tell them that these words may have a different meaning from that which the holy writers put into them, that they must not make an atomistic and legalistic use of these passages?

"*O furor et amentia his saeculis digna!*" (Luther, XIX:620.) Luther was stirred to holy wrath and indignation by this fact: "Zuletzt, so sie gestossen sind mit der Schrift, dass sie nicht vorueber koennen, heben sie an und laestern Gott und sprechen: Sind doch St. Matthaeus, Paulus, Petrus auch Menschen gewesen, darum ihre Lehre auch Menschenlehre. . . . Der Apostel Rede ist ungewiss." (*Loc. cit.*) What would Luther have said of the present *saeculum*, in which the great majority of the Protestant theologians proclaim that half of the Bible is untrue and that what is true is couched in uncertain language? Let Stoeckhardt say it. "Of a truth, modern theology with its modern theory of inspiration is nothing but a deception of Satan, by means of which the Christians are led away from the sure, prophetic word, from the true Christ, from the true, living God, and cast into doubt, unbelief, damnation. May God protect us against such Satanic snares and keep us in the simplicity of faith." (*Lehre und Wehre*, 1893, p. 333.)

The Church is indeed engaged in a life-or-death struggle. "Let us not deceive ourselves," says Machen, "the Bible is at the foundation of the Church. Undermine that foundation, and the Church will fall. It will fall, and great will be the fall of it." (*Princeton Theol. Review*, 1915, p. 351.)

Mark the solemn words of Spurgeon: "The turning point of the battle between those who hold 'the faith once delivered to the saints' and their opponents, lies in the true and real inspiration of the Holy Scriptures. This is the Thermopylae of Christendom. If we have in the Word of God no infallible standard of truth, we are at sea without a compass, and no danger from rough weather without can be equal to this loss within. 'If the foundation be removed, what can the righteous do?' And this is a foundation loss of the worst kind." (See J. Horsch, *Modern Religious Liberalism*, p. 31.) The old evil Foe means deadly woe. He would break down Verbal Inspiration in order to break down the Christians' faith.

THE BATTLE-FIELD

The war is on. *Are we,* in the second place, *prepared for the conflict?* They are not prepared who fail to realize that the age-long battle of the Church for her life is today being fought on the question of inspiration. On this front the enemy is concentrating his forces. He is still attacking the deity of Christ and other fundamental doctrines, but at present he seems to be chiefly concerned about getting the Church to discard Verbal Inspiration. "Die gegenwaertig am meisten bekaempfte und gehasste Lehre ist ohne Zweifel die Lehre von der Verbalinspiration." (*Lehre und Wehre*, 1910, p. 89.) This doctrine has always been attacked. The Anomoeans did not like it. Paine and the old rationalists hated it. But at no time has such a concerted and determined effort been made to remove it as in our generation. Here is where the Church must marshal her forces.

Do we realize that the enemy hates and abominates Verbal Inspiration and is sparing no efforts to get the Church to renounce and discard it? The moderns are convinced that Verbal Inspiration is a wicked and a harmful doctrine, and they are determined to drive the "foul spook" out of the Church. They are very tolerant with regard to other doctrines. Their principle is that men must be permitted to teach what they please; but they will not tolerate the teaching of Verbal Inspiration. Here tolerance ceases to be a virtue. Against this doctrine they have declared war to the death. They feel that they are engaged in a holy crusade. "Now, like the knights at the lists of Ashby," shouts J. P. Smyth, "we have to ride openly at each of the tents and strike with ringing blows and with sharp end of the spear the shield of each foe with whom we mean to do battle, for the sake of the Bible and our disquieted brethren." They mean to do battle with the foe who teaches "that an inspired Bible must be absolutely infallible in every detail." (*How God Inspired the Bible*, p 56 f.) They are exulting over the great conquests they have already made in their holy war — "the claim of revelation has been released from the burden of much unnecessary baggage, the stranglehold of this verbalism has been broken" (E. Lewis) — and go forth to silence the few who still teach Verbal Inspiration. They are filled with indignation and horror that men would still retain "the old theory against the monitions of conscience. . . . The fall of the theory of verbal inspiration is an event of first rate importance. But in ecclesiastical practice men often involuntarily talk as if Verbal Inspiration still held its ground" (Seeberg, *op. cit.*, p. 2, 62). There are the Fundamentalists. They must be driven out. G. Harkness: "The battle against Fundamentalism, against the belief in the literal inspiration of the Bible, is not yet won. Like the poor, literalism is always with us." (*Op. cit.*, p. 57.) There are the Lutherans in America who must be won over. W. Gussmann: "The day of Verbal Inspiration has passed, and we shall have to tell our American brethren: We cannot turn the course of history backwards." (*Luth. Zeitblatt*, Jan., 1924.) There are the old-fashioned laymen. They must be rescued. B. Steffen: "While in point of fact Verbal Inspiration has long ago been overthrown by Biblical science, our laymen are tenaciously clinging to it. That is an intolerable situation, which cannot continue." (*Zentralinspiration*, p. 1.) The moderns are straining every effort to drive out the last defenders of Verbal Inspiration. They are getting ready to deal Verbal Inspiration its deathblow. In fact, "in the report of the Anglican Commission so-called Fundamentalism receives its *coup de grace*." (*The Living Church*, March 9, 1938.) The moderns have sworn not to rest till that has been accomplished. They are writing books and pamphlets on this subject, and it seems that they cannot write on any subject without coming back to this one subject. They are ridiculing Verbal Inspiration in the seminaries. They are denouncing it from the pulpits. They are attacking it not only in the *Christian Century* and the *Lutheran Church Quarterly*, but also in the *Ladies' Home Journal*, and laymen are joining them in that. — And shall we go on in our easy way, calmly ignoring the ceaseless activity of the foe? Do we feel that long articles on inspiration in our periodicals constitute useless baggage? Are we asking the preacher to discuss more important subjects in the pulpit?

Again, we must know — and be ready to defend — the exact point of attack. That is the inspiration *of the words*. The moderns are very willing to let us teach that the Bible is inspired and is a good book, a holy book. But they will not have us teach that the words of Scripture were chosen by the Holy Spirit and express the thought as perfectly and infallibly as only God can express it. They tell us plainly that we must not "make the words of Scripture coextensive and identical with the words of God." Thus Archdeacon Farrar.[331] They know exactly what we teach: "The theory of 'verbal inspiration' maintains that the entire corpus of Scripture consists of writings every word of which was directly 'dictated' by the Deity." Thus C. H. Dodd. (*The Authority of the Bible*, p. 35.) And that is exactly what they denounce. "Der Gedanke der Inspiration von Worten muss aufgegeben werden." Thus F. Buechsel. (*Die Offenbarung Gottes*, p. 115) — Let us not waste our time by defending what nobody attacks. The moderns are willing to let us retain any kind of vague inspiration, if it only be not *Verbal* Inspiration. The strategical point in the battle for the Bible lies here: Is Scripture absolutely infallible? Are the words of Scripture the identical words of God? And were Paul and Christ mistaken in teaching Verbal Inspiration?

We must know what the moderns are fighting for. They know exactly what they want. This is their ultimatum: Give up Verbal Inspiration and confess that the Bible is full of errors; there can be no peace between us until you let science in its various forms rule over the Bible. See *The Problem of Lutheran Union*, page 118: The *Magazin fuer Ev. Theologie und Kirche* of the former Evangelical Synod discusses Verbal Inspiration and quotes a sentence from Dr. Pfotenhauer's address delivered at the dedication of Concordia Seminary. Its comment is: "The Church will either have to say with President Pfotenhauer: 'We hold fast to the doctrine of verbal inspiration' or it will have to say: 'We acknowledge the need of the historical, critical method.' This

---

331) Farrar makes this demand even though he admits that Paul taught just that. "Paul shared, doubtless, in the views of the later Jewish schools — the Tanaim and Amoraim — on the nature of inspiration — . . . views which made the words of Scripture coextensive and identical with the words of God." But Paul was mistaken! (See Warfield, *op. cit.*, p. 175.) Hermann Schultz declared that Christ, too, was mistaken on this point. See footnote 265. We are here calling attention to this particular matter in order to show to what lengths the moderns will go in their warfare against Verbal Inspiration.

method is used in our seminary, and we rejoice in it, since that sponsored by Pfotenhauer today is absolutely untenable." Peace will be declared on the day that the Christians declare that the Bible is not absolutely trustworthy.

Furthermore, we need to know where the enemy is to be found. Singapore fell because its guns pointed only one way. The Church is fighting for its life, for Verbal Inspiration, against infidels like Ingersoll and Darrow and against the modernists. But there are also, as has been shown above, many among the "positive," the conservative theologians, who attack Verbal Inspiration just as vehemently as the modernists. They have gotten much of their ammunition from the pronounced foes of Christianity. Why, there are even Lutheran theologians who are out to storm this stronghold of Christianity, Verbal Inspiration. *The Theological Forum* (Norw. Luth. Church) wrote in 1934, p. 187: "One of the gravest dangers that are threatening the Christian Church today is that many who profess to be its members no longer accept the Bible as God's inspired Word. Even among Lutherans strange sounds are sometimes heard regarding this subject. There are some Lutheran theologians who find it rather difficult to declare unequivocally their exact position on the doctrine of the verbal inspiration of the Bible. To some of these it seems an unpleasant task to make their position clear.'" Yes, and some have unequivocally declared their exact position. Dr. H. A. Preuss knows who they are. He wrote in the *Lutheran Herald* of Feb. 20, 1935: "Let us awake from our peaceful, smug satisfaction as we tell the world that the Lutheran Church is free from the disease of modernism. . . . Here is a call to arms to the forces of truth against error, of Lutheran Bible Christians against Lutheran modernists. . . . Then, by the grace of God, the Lutheran brothers in Christ, of whatever nationality and whatever synod, will find themselves fighting shoulder to shoulder for truth against error, *for an infallible Bible against a human book,* for a divine Christ against a mere human Christ." There is a great host of Lutheran theologians who are asking the Church to substitute for an infallible Bible a human, or a partly human book. — We would be remiss in our duty as keepers of the stronghold if we permitted the fact that these conservatives, these Lutherans, do not make common cause with the modernists on every doctrine to blind our eyes to the fact that they are making common cause with these same modernists on the vital doctrine of inspiration. Their work is just as deadly, if not more so.

One more point: we of the Lutheran Church must take our place in the front ranks. There are parties in the Reformed Church, the Fundamentalists and others, who are fighting valiantly for Verbal Inspiration. They are doing this in spite of the fact that in many instances they have departed from the formal principle of the Reformation, the sole authority of Scripture. And shall we lag behind them? do less than they? God expects us to do more than they. The Lutheran Church has shaped its entire *corpus doctrinae* by the formal principle of the Reformation. Lutheranism lives and moves and has its being in God's Word and its sure message of salvation. It is instinctive in Lutheranism to give instant battle to him who infringes on the authority and trustworthiness of Holy Scripture. Understanding fully the *sola Scriptura,* the Lutheran Church is best equipped to lead in the holy war. God has placed a sacred responsibility upon Lutheranism today. Listen to these burning words: "Should Lutheranism ever relinquish the truth of the inspiration and inerrancy of the Scriptures, by that very act it would surrender the formal principle of the Reformation; for the very essence of that principle is the infallibility of the Scriptures. Then it would cease to be Lutheranism; and Luther's declaration 'The Word of God they shall let stand' would be mere mockery upon our lips, because we should have surrendered our heritage and *our divinely wrought distinctive character.* Oh, that we Lutheran Christians might be conscious not only of this, but also of the high and holy responsibility which God has placed upon Lutheranism today! In this age of unbelief, superstition, error, syncretism, and unionism, of sects and fanatics, may Lutheranism, standing as an immovable rock at the Christian world's very heart through faithful witness-bearing, preserve to the Christian world its own precious Reformation heritage, the Word of God, the whole Word of God, and nothing but the Word of God — the *infallible Word* of God as the only source of faith and the infallible standard for teachers and their teaching." (President Hein at Copenhagen; *loc. cit.*) Lutheranism must lead in the battle for Verbal Inspiration.

Many Lutherans have gone over to the enemy. Let those, then, that remain do *double duty.* Our glorious Lutheran Church must not be let down.

DEEP GUILE AND GREAT MIGHT ARE HIS DREAD ARMS IN FIGHT

We need to acquaint ourselves in the third place, *with the tactics of the enemy.* Wars are lost when the skill and power of the foe are underrated. "Deep guile and great might are his dread arms in fight." What tactics does he employ in his fight against Verbal Inspiration?

1. He insists that Scripture does not teach Verbal Inspiration. The first attack — the assertion that Scripture does not teach in-

spiration of any kind — fails in many cases. So a second maneuver is employed: Scripture certainly teaches inspiration, but not Verbal Inspiration. "The Bible itself does not make any claim to infallible authority for all its parts." (C. H. Dodd, *op. cit.*, p.14.) It is "an amazing statement that the Scriptures themselves teach that 'every word' contained in them is inspired by the Holy Ghost." (*The Lutheran World;* see *Lehre und Wehre,* 1904, p. 39.) "There is no assertion in Scripture that their writers were kept 'from error.'" (*Auburn Affirmation.*) How can Scripture teach Verbal Inspiration, they say, since the Bible contains thousands of errors? And this teaching would involve a mechanical inspiration and lead to atomistic and legalistic abuses of Scripture! The moderns would beguile the Christians with the thought that Verbal Inspiration is an unscriptural, an anti-Scriptural teaching and that, when they cast it to the moles and bats, they have Scriptural warrant for doing it.

This guileful attack on Verbal Inspiration is today usually put into this form: Verbal Inspiration is a mere human theory, without basis in Scripture, and must not be foisted on the Church; Scripture teaches the *fact* of inspiration, but does not define its extent; Verbal Inspiration is a theological or dogmatical deduction, not a dogma of Scripture but a theory invented by men. The moderns employ this maneuver on every possible occasion. They never tire of telling the Christians: you must accept the fact of inspiration but need not accept the theory of Verbal Inspiration.[332] The result

---

332) For instance, the commissioners of the U. L. C. declared at Baltimore: "The disagreement [on the doctrine of verbal inspiration] relates to a *matter of theological interpretation.*" (See *The Lutheran,* Oct. 5, 1938.) *The Augsburg Sunday School Teacher* finds that inspiration is taught in 2 Tim. 3:16, 17, but that the teaching of Verbal Inspiration is "perhaps" due "to an *extremist exegesis*" of this passage. Is Verbal Inspiration a fact or a theory? A. D. Mattson (Augustana Synod) writes in the *Journal of Theol.,* Am. Luth. Conf., 1941, p. 546 f.: "Theologians sometimes fail to make an adequate distinction between a fact and their theory about that fact. . . . The Christians must recognize that the Bible is inspired by the Spirit of God. That is a fact. However, many theories have been advanced as to how God inspired the Bible. . . . All theories of inspiration within the Lutheran Church are the theories of individuals, some more or less adequate. . . . Facts remain, but theories may be transitional." Referring to Verbal Inspiration ("the enslaving legalism of the letter"), W. H. Greever (U. L. C.) writes in *The Lutheran World Almanac* for 1937, p. 94: "The Scriptures declare the fact of inspiration, . . . but make no explanation concerning the issues involved in the 'theories' of form and degree which furnish the material for present-day controversies on the subject. The particular theories which men hold on this subject are, at the most, but deductions from the Scriptures, which, however rational and logical, cannot be demanded, legitimately, as articles of faith." H. W. Snyder (U. L. C.) declared at the Washington Debate, Nov. 1, 1937: "Some of our theologians, on the other hand, accuse the Synodical Conference of lending its weight to the verbal-inspiration theory. . . . There seems to be no question about there being an inspiration, but the manner and extent of it are a matter

of dispute." (See *Journal of the Am. Luth. Conf.*, 1938, March issue; *Conc. Theol. Mthly.*, 1938, p. 357 ff.) *The Lutheran*, Feb. 20, 1936: "The Lutheran Church has never formulated a theory of inspiration, it has merely stated its fact." *The Luth. Companion*, Dec. 16, 1933: "Does Dr. Lenski mean to imply that the fact of inspiration (which Lutherans accept) must be identified with the theory of verbal inspiration (a theory which is by no means unanimously accepted by consistent Lutherans)? The Lutheran Church has no official theory of inspiration." That applies, they further state, to the Church in general. C. Gore: "The Church never showed any disposition to define the scope of inspiration. There is no authoritative *dogma* about inspiration. There is to be found neither in the Bible nor in the words of the Church any authoritative definition of inspiration. If we are now unwilling to say that the Bible is the Word of God," etc. (*The Doctrine of the Infallible Book*, pp. 47, 62.) — The reader will notice that when the moderns speak of "the form and degree," of "the extent," they mean Verbal Inspiration. The reader will also notice that, when they throw these two terms: "*manner* and extent" together, they are practicing sophistry. Scripture does not reveal the "manner" of inspiration; it does not tell us "*how* God inspired the Bible." That was a miracle. Why do they couple these two terms, "manner" and "extent"? Note, finally, that Scripture teaches the fact of inspiration and the fact of Verbal Inspiration. Since Scripture says that *all Scripture* is given by inspiration, it teaches that all the words are inspired. Scripture does teach "*how* God inspired the Bible" — in this way that the Holy Spirit spoke the very words of Scripture. — The reader may have time to read and study the following declaration on this matter. J. O. Lang writes in the *Pastor's Monthly* of May, 1935: "We boldly assert that we accept no 'theory' of verbal inspiration, but rather the 'fact' of verbal inspiration. When we speak of a theory of verbal inspiration, we speak of something which may not be true, and we are endeavoring to explain just how it took place, and the 'how' the Church has never attempted to describe because the Bible does not describe it. Inspiration belongs to the sphere of the miraculous. However, when we state our doctrine of verbal inspiration, we are stating the fact which the Scriptures present, namely, that God so directed and controlled the holy writers that they wrote what He wanted them to write and the form in which He wanted it written. This is no 'theory.'" Samuel Miller's letter to Dr. J. A. Dell, published in the *Journal of the A. L. Conf.*, July, 1939, p. 10, states: "I want to thank you for your answer to an article entitled 'Some Thoughts on Inspiration' by Hjalmar W. Johnson. It seems strange that people cannot understand that the term 'verbal inspiration' designates the doctrine of the inspiration of the Bible and does not stand for a theory of the mode. I cannot help but wonder if they are ignorant of the meaning of the term or if they are willfully confusing the issue. Surely the Bible plainly states, and the Lutheran Confessions take it for granted, that the words by which God's revelation has been recorded were inspired by the Holy Spirit. It surely is a very subtle way of attack that those of us who hold to the doctrine of verbal inspiration shall now be called 'un-Lutheran.' . . ." Dr. J. A. Dell writes in the *Journal of the A. L. Conf.*, Sept., 1938, p. 2: "In the *Lutheran* of June 8 the subject 'Growing Unity' was discussed on the young people's page. There it was said: 'The differences that keep American Lutherans from complete unification are more on the surface than real. All agree that the Scriptures are inspired. But some insist that some certain method of inspiration should be accepted, while others, as in the United Lutheran Church, declare that the fact of inspiration must be accepted while the method may be a matter of opinion.' . . . Concerning the method none of us knows anything, and therefore concerning the method there can be no argument among us at all. . . . If there is so much agreement among us, what is all the argument about? All the argument is about the fact of inspiration, and there is none at all about the method. The difference among us is, that

of this insidious procedure is that men will say with J. P. Smyth: "The Bible itself nowhere directs us what we are to believe about inspiration. Indeed, the Bible says very little of its inspiration at all beyond merely asserting its fact. It leaves us entirely to our own judgment as to its nature and extent, and as to what is involved in the fact of a book being inspired." (*Op. cit.*, p. 59.) And the *Lutheran Herald,* Oct. 13, 1942, commends Edwin Lewis (the man who finds "much unnecessary baggage" in the Bible) for taking this position: "He accepts the *fact*" (italics in original) "of the inspiration of the Bible without much theorizing." People are made to believe that, while they are rejecting great portions of the Bible, they are still treating it as an inspired book.

2. The moderns minimize the importance of Verbal Inspiration. They suggest to the Christians that they can get along very well without it. The liberals tell them that there is no need of any inspiration at all. They say with the editor of *The Christian Century,* March 30, 1938: "The writers of the Bible were men like ourselves — like E. S. Jones and Kagawa, if you wish. . . . I cannot imagine what added authority the Bible would have if it were conceived as having been dictated by God to a stenographer." And those who want to be known as conservatives speak in the same way of Verbal Inspiration. They say with E. H. Delk: "It is an unnecessary point of view of what is essential to Christianity." (The *Luth Ch. Quart.*, 1936, p. 426.) They offer us substitutes, which are just as good as Verbal Inspiration, or rather, much better. All is well with you, they say, if only the concepts be inspired; all you need is the "Word of God" or the *Schriftganze;* be satisfied to have the Gospel truths inspired, and do not bother about the trivial matter of *plenary* inspiration; after all, it is not quantity but quality which counts: "the inspiration of the Holy Scriptures is qualitative but not quantitative." Bound to prove

---

while we all say 'The Scriptures are inspired,' we do not all seem to mean the same thing. For some seem to wish to reserve to themselves the right to reject some of the Scriptures or some portion of some of the Scriptures as uninspired and unreliable. You can see that this denies the *fact* of inspiration as concerns those rejected portions, and has nothing to do with method. . . ." *Conc. Theol. Mthly.*, 1939, p. 64 f., reprinted this and added the following: "The commissioners of the U. L. C. reported at Baltimore that 'the commissioners of the A. L. C. supported what is titled the 'Verbal Theory of Inspiration.' . . . The U. L. C. commissioners were 'unable to accept the statement of the Missouri Synod that the Scriptures are the infallible truth "also in those parts which treat of historical, geographical, and other secular matters." ' . . . Then the U. L. C. convention declared: 'We believe that the whole body of the Scriptures is inspired by God.' . . . And that means that the distinction between the *fact* of inspiration and the 'theory' of inspiration (verbal, plenary inspiration, absolute infallibility of Scripture being a mere theory) is a clumsy form of sophistry. It deals with an 'inspiration' which is not real inspiration."

that inspiration is relatively unimportant, the moderns point out that men were saved before an inspired Bible or an inspired New Testament existed. We heard R. F. Horton's statement "The New Testament is itself a record of the Christian faith being propagated at a wonderfully rapid rate without a New Testament at all. Peter had no writings to appeal to, except the Old Testament Scriptures; Paul preached his 'Gospel' without any reference to a written Gospel and never hinted that the further preaching of the faith should depend even on his own Epistles." (*Rev. and the Bible*, p. 218.) The inspired Scripture is of less importance than the *viva vox* of the Church — that is a commonplace of present-day theology. They will even say that it is of less importance, as the basis of faith, than "experience." In the words of Kahnis: "The true Christian bases his Christianity not on the inspiration and authenticity of Scripture but on the living fact of his real communion with God through Christ." — The moderns are urging the Christians to forsake the sure Word, the inspired Word, and to set out on the chase after an *ignis fatuus*.

A favorite device of the anti-inspiration propaganda is to denounce the verbal-inspirationists as quibblers and hairsplitters, ranting over theological *minutiae* and disturbing the peace of the Church with their unseemly brawls about "minute doctrinal differences." Let one example suffice. The *Luth. Church Quart.*, 1934, p. 114, declares: "Scriptural theology will not quibble over such questions as whether the Bible is the Word of God or contains the Word of God." The moderns tell their people — and our people — that it is unprofitable to discuss the question whether the Bible is inspired throughout or only in parts and that the verbal-inspirationists, neglecting the important matters of the Church, are wasting their time over trivialities. It is a clever piece of propaganda. Much would be gained for the cause of the moderns if the Christian people could be made to rate the defenders of Verbal Inspiration as trifling quibblers and unreasonable hairsplitters.

And as disturbers of the peace. The charge is made that those who insist on Verbal Inspiration are keeping the Christian churches apart, are keeping the Lutheran synods apart, are keeping them apart by holding out for trivialities. That is an intolerable state of affairs, says H. L. Willett: "The controversies over the inspiration of the Scriptures, . . . creation or evolution, etc., . . . are ceasing to be counted worthy of causing divisions among the friends of Jesus." (See the *Chr. Century*, Jan. 27, 1937.) There are Lutherans who speak in the same strain. Recall the statement by *Folkebladet*, Nov. 23, 1938: "The theory of verbal inspiration has brought more confusion among Christians than perhaps anything else. . . . When a subjective theory is elevated to the status of an objective primary truth, then *virvar* surely will ensue in the Church." Recall the statement by the *Lutheran* which Dr. Dell quoted above: "The differences that keep American Lutherans from complete unification are more on the surface than real" — one of the differences being that some insist on Verbal Inspiration; and that is such a trifling matter. It is quibbling, we heard the *Luth. Church Quart.* say. Again, it is said: "The achievement of closer unity among Lutherans will require, for one essential, a higher view of Scripture than is represented by the theory of inspiration by dictation." (1935, p. 417.) The *Lutheran Companion*, March 30, 1939, complains that "Lutheran unity is made contingent upon the acceptance of definite individualistic interpretations of certain doctrines in which the Church has not made a final pronouncement or has permitted considerable latitude of opinion." The *Lutheran Standard*, May 2, 1942, published the statement "that theological *minutiae* should never have become divisive in the Lutheran Church," and declared, March 22, 1941, that "to quibble over theories of inspiration is no less a disaster" and no less disgraceful than to quarrel over "the color of vestments." In the Washington Debate on Verbal Inspiration Dr. Snyder asked the representative of the A. L. C.: "Shall we quarrel over an adiaphoron while a sin-sick, needy world is hungering for the bread of life?" There are Lutherans who keep on saying: "Our petty divisions seem pitiful." "Our minor differences are not fundamental moral and religious differences." "When Lutherans forget their silly differences, then the Lutheran Church in America will grow as it never grew before." (See *Conc. Theol. Mthly.*, VIII, p. 546.) — It is a skillful maneuver, a crafty argument. Who does not desire to see all Christians united? Who does not realize the great importance of it? The moderns play upon this sentiment and, stressing the importance of union, aim to create in the Christians the idea of the relative unimportance of Verbal Inspiration and then proceed to characterize it as unimportant in itself.

3. The moderns distort, vilify, and damn Verbal Inspiration. The object of the lying campaign is to keep the Christians from having anything to do with such a disreputable thing. It is, they say, a crude dogma, a clumsy distortion of what Scripture teaches on this point. Few intelligent Protestants still hold it. How can they in view of the hundreds of errors in the Bible? There are, they say, very few theologians, and assuredly no eminently learned ones, who hold the old doctrine of verbal inspiration. It represents the unintelligent view of the fundamentalists, the incredible fatuity of the literalists. It is only the metallic, inert, wooden, and narrow mind of the obscurantists, reactionaries, pre-Kantians, antediluvians

that refuses to discard this dogma of the spiritually comatose seventeenth century, this worm-eaten dogmatism. This petrified inspiration dogma must be discarded with the rest of he world's old discarded mind lumber. Only an intellect childishly restricted will stand for it. No balanced mind will uphold it. It constitutes a mental aberration of the gravest type. Its avowal, one of them said, held to its last logic, would risk a trip to the insane asylum. There would be no purpose, said Dr. Kaftan, in discussing theological matters with people who believe in Verbal Inspiration.

Have nothing to do with it, the moderns exhort the Christian: for it is a new doctrine, *ein schlechthinniges Novum,* unheard of in the Church until the post-Reformation period. The Bible theologians invented it. The seventeenth-century theologians invented it. Luther got it from the Catholic theologians. The Lutherans took it over from the Reformed. To maintain it today *waere ein repristinierender Rueckgriff auf Luther oder gar auf das Bibeldogma des Altluthertums* (M. Doerne). And, worst of all, it would be Fundamentalism.[333]

Beware of Verbal Inspiration, say the moderns, for it is a hurtful dogma. It paralyzes the intellect. It restricts the mental growth of the human race. This cast-iron theory of the atomistic verbalists is a dogmatic fetter, a strait jacket, which handicaps the exegete. Worse than that, it is prolific of skepticism. The theory of literalism has been the death of any form of belief in Scripture; for there are the five hundred discrepancies and errors! *Seelenmordende Verbalinspiration!*

Beware of this evil thing! It is a wicked doctrine. It is not Christian. It is a heathen conception. It is a rabbinical superstition. Literal inerrancy is irreligious. It is immoral to hold that the doubtful ethics of the Bible were taught by God. — It cannot be upheld without the loss of intellectual integrity, of intellectual honesty, of the sense of truth. — It represents the Roman Catholic ideology. It is the product of rationalistic considerations. — It calls for, and creates, a slave mentality. This tyranny of an infallible book, this enslaving superstition, this bondage to old categories, must be broken, the prison house of verbal infallibility must be demolished. — This idolatrous acceptance of Bible authority, making the Bible a fetish, Bibliolatry, *sich aus der Schrift einen Offen-*

---

333) Are we Fundamentalists? Our Western District declared that *true fundamentalism* means: 1) Unqualified acceptance of every word of the Bible as divine, infallible, and eternal truth. . . . (See *Lehre und Wehre,* 1927, p. 247.) When the term of reproach "Fundamentalists" refers to this point, we are proud to be called that. — We are not in accord with the Fundamentalists on other important doctrines. The moderns who smear us as Fundamentalists surely know that. — It is a falsification of the historical facts to represent Fundamentalism in its fight for Verbal Inspiration as differing from Christianity.

barungsgoetzen machen, Vergoetzung des einzelnen Worts, is an idolatrous perversion of Christianity. — Verbal Inspiration is, in a word, a heresy. The foul spook must be cast out.

Will this lying propaganda have the desired effect? Is there *deep guile* and *great might* in it? The arguments advanced by the moderns are so puerile and fatuous that they should not beguile any Christian.[334] They do not appeal to the rational mind, and

334) R. F. Horton, for instance, proves that the written Word is not absolutely necessary with the fact that "the Christian faith was propagated [in the apostolic era] at a wonderfully rapid rate without a New Testament at all." The moderns make much of this argument. G. T. Ladd told us: "True Christian faith existed before the Bible." (*What Is the Bible,* p. 443.) *The Living Church,* Sept. 27, 1942: "The New Testament obviously cannot be the very foundation and basis of Christian truths which were taught to thousands by the early Church *before* the New Testament was produced." Here the Catholics come to the aid of the moderns. A leaflet sent in the other day by one of our readers has this: "Why do you Catholics consider the Church and not the Bible as your rule of faith? . . . The truth is that Christianity preceded the New Testament. The Gospels and Epistles were written for the benefit of a Church which had been in existence already for many years." Will such an argument beguile any Christian? To be sure, the inspired word of the Apostles created the Christian faith. Nothing else can create faith. But we have their inspired word in the inspired New Testament *and nowhere else.* We need the New Testament absolutely. The Catholic substitute (the pronouncements of the Church) and the Protestant substitute (the *viva vox* of the Church) cannot serve. Neither the Catholic nor the Protestant teachers and preachers speak by inspiration of God. — The denunciation of the "Fundamentalist literalism" operates with a transparent sophistry. The fact that Fundamentalists — and others — are often guilty of *literalistic* interpretations of Scripture does not prove that the statements of Scripture need not be taken *literally.* (See *Conc. Theol. Mthly.,* XII, p. 867, on the charge raised by C. L. Venable [U. L. C.] that "Missouri Lutherans" are guilty of "Bible literalism.") — Examine Kahnis' statement that "the true Christian bases his Christianity . . . on the living fact of his real communion with God through Christ." The *Proceedings of the Syn. Conference,* 1886, say on page 18: "What is 'the living fact of his real communion with God'? It means, if it means anything at all, 'his Christianity.' Das ist also das sauer erarbeitete Resultat, bei dem Kahnis ankommt, dass der wahre Christ sein Christentum stellt auf — sein Christentum." — Glance over the long list of absurdities examined in the preceding pages. There is the famous case of Luke dealing with a non-existent Lysanias — according to Bruno Bauer and D. F. Strauss. Errors have to be found in the Bible, if not by fair means, then by foul means. These same men, Strauss and Bauer, find a "contradiction" in the fact that the announcement made to Mary, Luke 1: 26 ff., and that made to Joseph, Matt. 1: 20, are not identical! How, then, can the Bible be verbally inspired? There is the famous case of Jonah's *dagah* — not a fish, but a skiff! And there is the crowning absurdity of the concept theory. "The extent of inspiration applies not to the words but to the sense." (G. L. Raymond.) The moderns are stupidly asking us to perform an intellectual impossibility. You cannot have the sense without the words. This favorite theory of the moderns is nonsense. And can you express this idea, this concept, in any other way than by using the *word* "nonsense"? Verily, "there is nothing too absurd to have been stated or imagined on this question" (M'Intosh). — The moderns are lacking in spiritual insight, too. Here they have been making concessions to the

they are repulsive to the Christian mind. But they must possess
a powerful influence. Else they could not have captivated this great
host of theologians. Their power lies in this, that they appeal to
the wicked flesh. There is "deep guile and great might" in the
tactics of the foe. His foolish and wicked arguments find instant
acceptance with the evil heart of man. Our evil heart is prejudiced
against God's Word. It delights in having God's Word besmirched.
Our proud flesh refuses to submit to Scripture, as Verbal Inspiration requires it to do, and hails the opportunity to sit in judgment
on Scripture, as the moderns ask it to do. It is thus that the foolish
objections against Verbal Inspiration carry great weight. And
the great danger of our losing the battle, of our giving up Verbal
Inspiration, lies in this, that our own flesh is the ally of the enemy.
When Satan rouses up the pride and wickedness of our flesh,
we have to contend with "deep guile and great might," against
superhuman forces. We cannot win the battle unless we use the
almighty resources which are at hand.

SCRIPTURE FIGHTING AND WINNING ITS OWN BATTLE

But the victory will be ours if, as we shall consider in the
fourth place, we employ against the tactics of the foe *the divine
strategy: bring the almighty Word into action.*

That was the strategy St. Paul employed. He knew that divine
power inheres in the Word, 1 Thess. 2:13; he did not enlist human
wisdom to fight its battle, but permitted the simple Word to
demonstrate its power, 1 Cor. 2:4, 5. That was Luther's strategy.
"Durch das Wort ist die Welt ueberwunden, ist die Kirche erhalten
worden; sie wird auch durch das Wort wiederhergestellt werden."
(XV: 2506.) All that Luther did was to put God's almighty Word
into action. "God's Word has been my sole study and concern,
the sole subject of my preaching and writing. Other than this
I have done nothing in the matter. This same Word has, while
I slept or made merry, accomplished this great thing." (XX: 21.)
The only method Luther employed to prove the truth of any
Scripture doctrine was to let Scripture speak for itself. "He loved
the Sacred Book! He fought by its help. It was his battle-ax
and his weapon of war." (Spurgeon.)

---

unbelievers, "shortened the lines of defense," but, as Dr. Nutter pointed
out in the *Living Church,* "the anticipated stampede of the intelligentsia
into the Church, which was to follow the abandonment of miracle, has
not taken place." The moderns do not know how to deal with unbelievers. And what advice are they giving the believer? They ask
him to rely on his "Christian consciousness" for finding and establishing
the truth. But we know, says Spurgeon, "that every man who is his
own lawyer has a fool for his client." What the moderns offer us on
Inspiration is devoid of common sense and of Christian sense.

How shall we prove the truth of Verbal Inspiration? Being a teaching of Scripture, it carries within itself divine power. It proves itself. All that we need to do is to proclaim: "All Scripture is given by inspiration of God," and let this Word do its work. It has the divine power to convince men of its truth and produce their joyful acceptance of it. Learn to apply this strategy, as Luther learned to do it. The *Princeton Theol. Review,* Vol. 15, pp. 513 and 555, thus describes Luther's strategy: "For Luther Scripture thus came to rest for its authority . . . on its own self-evidencing power. . . . The indefeasible certitude of the Christian as to the divinity of the Word comes from God Himself." Quoting Luther (Erl. Ed., 28: 298; St. L., XX: 74) to the effect that the Christian must be, and can be, "unshakably certain that it is God's Word, though all the world should fight against it," the *Review* points out: "Luther saw with hawklike clearness the main point in the solution of the problem of authority in the Christian religion: *the inspired Scriptures carry themselves;* they do not depend for their power on the testimony of the Church or any human authority, but only on the witnesss of the Holy Spirit who *creates in the believing heart the conviction of their divine origin and contents. . . .*"

We are asked to surrender (or modify) the doctrine of Verbal Inspiration. Our unbelieving, proud flesh asks it. We are sorely tempted to do it. But in this fearful conflict, which tries the soul and rends the heart, we shall gain the strength to overcome our flesh from this very doctrine itself. It speaks with divine power to our troubled soul. Let that power work in you! When we are tempted to delete 1 Tim. 5: 23 and 2 Tim. 4: 13, the Holy Spirit speaks out in our hearts: "All Scripture is given by inspiration of God!" When we are invited to strike out the account of Creation, of Jonah and the fish, and of the thousand other miracles, there comes the cry from heaven: "The Scripture cannot be broken!" When Satan asks us to split up John 3: 16 and 1 John 2: 2 into thoughts of God and words of men, the word: "which things we speak not in the words which man's wisdom teacheth, but which the Holy Ghost teacheth," reverberates in our hearts in "demonstration of the Spirit and of power." Verbal Inspiration teaches that the words of Scripture are God's words, and that teaching fills us with such holy awe of the majesty of Scripture that we trample the sacrilegious mutterings of our flesh underfoot as the evil spawn of Satan. Let this divine teaching do its work, and you will say: "God's Word counts for more than all angels and saints and creatures" (Luther, XVIII: 1322); you will say: This teaching of Scripture — Verbal Inspiration — has more weight than all the teachings of a pseudo-science and a pseudo-theology.

What shall we do when our proud flesh keeps on angrily protesting against Verbal Inspiration? Holy Scripture fights our
battles for us in this way, too, that in denouncing this awful wickedness it threatens those who persist in it with a terrible fate. Ponder
Matt. 11:25 and 1 Pet. 2:6-8! Woe unto him against whom God
finally pronounces the dread judgment of obduration, in consequence of which these things are now *hidden* from him, he is cut
off from understanding Scripture; that which is a savor of life unto
life has become a savor of death unto death unto him. If a man *will*
stumble at God's Word, it shall be to him a stumbling block and
a rock of offense. Hear again how Luther enforces this warning
of Scripture: "I beg and faithfully warn every pious Christian
not to take offense at the simple language and ordinary stories
which he frequently finds here. . . . For this is the Scripture which
makes fools of the wise and prudent and is open only to babes
and fools, as Christ says Matt. 11:25." (XIV:3.) Hear again how
Pieper enforces it: "One who criticizes Scripture — which, as God's
Word, will not be criticized but *believed* — comes under the fearful
judgment of God described Matt. 11:25." (*Op. cit.*, I, p. 280.) And
hear how J. W. Haley presents this Scripture truth: "Those who
are disposed to cavil find opportunities for caviling. *The disposition
does not miss the occasion*. . . . 'There is light enough for those
whose main wish is to see; and darkness enough for those of
an opposite disposition.' (Pascal.) . . . Those persons who cherish
a caviling spirit, who are bent upon misapprehending the truth
and urging captious and frivolous objections find in the sacred
volume difficulties and disagreements which would seem to have
been designed as stumbling stones for those 'which stumble at
the Word, being disobedient; whereunto also they were appointed'
(1 Pet. 2:8). Upon the willful votaries of error God sends 'strong
delusions, that they should believe a lie' (2 Thess. 2:11), that they
might work out their own condemnation and ruin. 'If we dis-
parage Scripture and treat it "as any other book," then Almighty
God, who is the Author of Scripture, will punish us by our own
devices. . . . Our presumption and our irreverence will be instruments of our punishment.' . . . When the difficulties of Scripture are
approached with a docile and reverent mind, they may tend to
our establishment in the faith; but when they are dealt with in
a querulous and disingenuous manner, they may become judicial
agencies in linking to caviling skepticism its appropriate penalty —
even to the loss of the soul." (*Op. cit.*, p. 39 f.) Haley addresses
this warning to skepticism. But it applies — Scripture applies it —
also to those who in more subtle ways deny the inspiration of
Scripture and deride the truth that the *words* of Scripture are the

very words of God. This warning of Holy Scripture is the power of God. It fills our hearts with fear and dismay over the frightful catastrophe which the machinations of Satan and the wickedness of our flesh are preparing for us. And the better we know our danger, and the more earnestly we call to God for His gracious help, the better prepared we are for receiving the full influence of the power of the teachings of Scripture.

And how shall we win others for the doctrine of Verbal Inspiration? Scripture wins its own battles. All that is required of us is to put the power of the Word into action — simply to proclaim the teaching of Scripture. That was Luther's strategy. When dealing with men who deny or doubt "that what Christ and the apostles spoke and wrote is the Word of God, . . . say only this: I shall give you sufficient ground from Scripture; if you believe, well; if not, just go your way" (IX:1238). As long as men will listen to us, we give them ground from Scripture. That has the power to convince them. And it is the only thing that can win them. They may for a time struggle against this doctrine of Verbal Inspiration as utter foolishness, but, as Dr. Walther says: "our only help lies in this, that the divine foolishness, the old unadulterated Gospel, be preached to it" (the present apostate world). (*Lehre und Wehre*, 1875, p. 41.) So we say: The only way to gain the victory in this battle is to preach the divine foolishness, the old unadulterated doctrine of Verbal Inspiration. That preaching, that testimony carries divine power.

When a man accepts Verbal Inspiration, a miracle is being wrought. Let us not attempt to argue men into accepting it. Our words of human wisdom cannot perform miracles. It takes almighty power to subdue the ratiocinations of the flesh. And this almighty power lies in the teaching of Scripture on Inspiration. Let us apply the power! — We can add nothing to it by our reasoning powers. But this great and glorious thing God permits us to do: we can proclaim His truth.

How many will be won through our testimony? That is not for us to say. That lies in the hands of the gracious Lord. But those that will be won will be won through the power of the Word, and we thank God for every opportunity given us to present the conquering doctrine of verbal inspiration to men.

We are fighting to win men for Verbal Inspiration, and we are fighting to preserve Verbal Inspiration for the Church. Are we fighting for a lost cause? We hear them shouting that our cause is doomed. They are getting ready to give Verbal Inspiration the *coup de grace*. But we know that it will never perish from the earth. The Bible has withstood all the assaults of the foe. It is an impregnable rock.[335]   And so has Verbal Inspiration stood, an impregnable rock, against all the assaults of the enemy, from the first century down to the present day. The clamor of Paine and Strauss, the clamor of the liberal and conservative moderns, could not silence its almighty voice. Many Christians, theologians and laymen, are broadcasting this powerful voice. In various church bodies this doctrine is being proclaimed with apostolic clarity and firmness. Will it endure unto the end? It will never perish. It will have its Thermopylaes, but it will never be utterly defeated. It will always remain to be the Christians' stay and comfort. Even if a time should come that it were no longer *publica doctrina* in any church body, it would be exercising its divine power secretly. If at some future time all the theologians of the world should meet in solemn conclave and promulgate the decree: *Si quis dixerit, Scripturam Sacram esse ipsum Verbum Dei, anathema sit,* the Christians would spurn that decree. In practice they would cling to, and apply, Verbal Inspiration. It is possible that a Christian theologian might *in disputationibus* argue against Verbal Inspiration, but in the hour of stress and trial he will, by the good grace of God, cling to John 3:16 as the verbally inspired, absolutely true and certain Word of God. All Christians will in the future as well as now believe, in their hearts, in Verbal Inspiration.

We do not know whether such a conclave will ever be held. We doubt it. But let that be as it may. We are concerned with the present. Verbal Inspiration is, thank God, the *publica doctrina* in large areas. And our sacred duty is to keep faithful watch and ward over it. And while the moderns are importuning us to join them in anathematizing it, we are glad of the opportunity God has given faithful witnesses to make its loud voice resound throughout the earth and bring assurance and comfort to many souls who, but for this testimony, would remain in uncertainty and doubt and might possibly despair.

---

335) J. R. Stratton, in his book *The Battle over the Bible,* says on page 16: "Intellectual pride has often rejected it (the Bible) because of the vanity of man's mind; and infidelity has battled against it with a ·relentlessness worthy of a better cause and a malignity unmatched elsewhere in the dark realm of prejudice, hatred, and spite. What has the result been? Always victory for the noble old Book! It has successfully resisted the sophistries of Hume, the misguided eloquence of Gibbon, the rationalism of Rousseau, the ignorant blasphemies of Thomas Paine, the satirical mockery of Voltaire, the idle quibbling of Strauss, the shallow witticism of Renan, the cheap buffoonery of Bob Ingersoll, the audacious assaults of the Communists of France, and the insidious duplicity of the rationalistic theologians of Prussianized Germany. As with Moses' bush, the Bible has burned, but it has not been consumed. Phoenixlike, it has risen from its ashes to new heights of usefulness and power."

LOYAL SOLDIERS

We shall certainly keep up the fight for Verbal Inspiration. That entails, as any other war, hardship and suffering. But the strength to bear that is supplied by the Word. There is the disturbing fact that the great majority of present-day theologians is against us. Those that fight for Verbal Inspiration are but few in number.[336] In this situation our flesh raises the disturbing question: If Verbal Inspiration be a doctrine of Holy Scripture, why would so many theologians refuse to accept it? May it not be an open question? Again, our flesh takes the defeatist attitude: What can your small number hope to accomplish against this vast host? And what have you to offer to offset the great learning and prestige on their side? — Verbal Inspiration will give us the strength to overcome these misgivings, doubts, and temptations. What Scripture says on Verbal Inspiration gives us divine assurance, and we shall maintain it though all the world should protest its truth. And as to those great resources which the foe can command, there are greater resources at our disposal. We have the almighty truth of Verbal Inspiration on our side. We can do miracles. "Das ist ein Wunder ueber alle Wunder," says Luther, "dass ein solch gering Wort, das kein Ansehen hat vor der Welt, soll so viel Leute gewinnen." (XII: 1568.) The Scripture truth that the Bible is verbally inspired is stronger than all the wisdom of the world and the might of the great number. The power of God's truth is fighting for us. This talk about the great majority being against us shall not disturb us. "I believe the Bible to be the inspired Word of God. . . . I can trust God, though I shall have to stand alone before the world in declaring Him to be true." (Dr. H. A. Kelly.) "Ob mir schon die ganze Welt anhinge und wiederum abfiele, das ist mir eben gleich, und denke: Ist sie mir doch zuvor auch nicht angehangen, da ich allein war." (Luther, XIX: 422.)

We need strength to bear the ridicule and the reproaches heaped upon us in this cause. No one can today uphold Verbal Inspiration without being made the butt of universal ridicule. Obscurantists! Backward theologians! Fundamentalists! Now, we can easily bear that; but it cuts deeper when we are re-

---

336) "It is, sad to say, true what Nitzsch-Stephan says of the 'present situation': 'In our day the orthodox doctrine of inspiration has hardly any significance in dogmatics. It is, true enough, being still upheld by a few, *e. g.*, Koelling and Noesgen, with some modifications. . . . The rest of the theologians, including the conservatives, reject the old doctrine.' Zoeckler mentions as lonely defenders of the old doctrine: Kohlbruegge, Gaussen, Kuyper, and 'among the Lutherans particularly Walther in St. Louis and with him the Missouri Synod.' Also most of the present-day Reformed theologians have given up the inspiration of Scripture." (Pieper, *op. cit.*, p. 327.)

proached — sometimes by well-meaning men — with sinning against God and men by taking such an uncompromising stand. When we refuse to be satisfied with the vague inspiration commonly taught and stand out for every jot and tittle of Verbal Inspiration, they say that that is due to sinful pride and carnal prejudice and wicked stubbornness. We could bear that, too; but then our own flesh raises the same clamor. Is Verbal Inspiration really so important? — In this fierce trial we fall back on our old strategy. We examine again all that Scripture says on Verbal Inspiration. Convinced of the truth of it, we know we would be sinning against God if we suppressed it. Convinced of its necessity, we know that we would be sinning against our fellow men if we yielded any part of it. And thus the Lord fulfills His Word "Thou, therefore, gird up thy loins, and arise and speak unto them all that I command thee. . . . For, behold, I have made thee this day . . . an iron pillar and brazen walls against the whole land. . . . They shall fight against thee; but they shall not prevail against thee" (Jer. 1:17 ff.). Scripture shall not be broken!

Will we stand firm when we are asked to sacrifice Verbal Inspiration in the interest of church union? Particularly at this point the foe displays "deep guile and great might." They say, at times, that the verbal-inspirationists lose nothing under this unionistic arrangement since they will be permitted to keep on teaching their peculiar doctrine to their heart's content; and our flesh is very willing to be beguiled by such suggestions. Or they tell us that we have no right to make Verbal Inspiration divisive of church fellowship since "the Scriptures declare the *fact* of inspiration but make no explanation concerning the issues involved in the '*theories*' *of form and degree*, which furnish the material for present-day controversies on the subject" (*The Luth. World Almanac*). Or: let the Scripture teaching be what it may, church union is of such supreme importance that all questions of inspiration are trivial in comparison. And our flesh fully agrees. We find it hard to stand firm. And when at this point the reproaches assume particular virulence — sinful pride, carnal prejudice, wicked stubbornness — and our own flesh begins to rage and rave, we begin to waver. In this crisis the Word of God comes to our aid. Let a man once be convinced of the truth and supreme importance of Verbal Inspiration, and he will be able to resist all temptations to compromise it. He will not only refuse to yield up one jot or tittle of it but will also refuse to give the hand of fellowship to those who deny all or any part of Verbal Inspiration; for that would make the denial of it a matter of little importance. Knowing that the Christians need the precious doctrine of verbal inspiration, he will not jeopardize their spiritual welfare by asking them to receive as their spiritual advisers those who deny either the truth or the importance of it. The truth of God's Word and the interest of his fellow Christians weigh so much for him that the reproach and shame he suffers in this cause weigh very little.

He maintains friendly relations with all who are searching for the truth, searching for it in God's Word, but he cannot make common cause with men who set out to ravage and despoil God's Word. He absolutely refuses to bid them Godspeed.

Stubbornness? May we be of those to whom the Lord says: "Behold, I have made Thy face strong against their faces, and thy forehead strong against their forehead. As an adamant harder than flint have I made thy forehead; fear them not, neither be dismayed at their looks," Ezek. 3:8, 9.[337]

Contend earnestly for the faith which was once delivered unto the saints! That is a call to arms which cannot be disregarded. We would not disregard it. Our flesh, indeed, would have us evade the service, and we need to be reminded, by the Law, of the punish-

---

337) J. A. Dell: "We desire unity among Lutherans but not unity at the expense of truth. If it comes to a choice between these two: (1) outward unity, with a hushing up and smoothing over of deep-going differences in our views regarding the reliability of the Bible, and (2) outward disunity, even controversy, with the result that this doctrine of inspiration is thrust into the foreground and thought about and debated — if it comes to a choice between these two, I say, the second alternative is much to be preferred. For the former can never lead to a real unity, but the latter may." (*Journal of the Am. Luth. Conf.*, March, 1938.) Th. Graebner, *The Problem of Lutheran Union:* "The United Lutheran Church is not at all minded to make *doctrine* an issue in an attempt at Lutheran union. . . . By denying the verbal inspiration of the Scriptures it removes on its part the very foundation for it (doctrinal purity)" (J. H. C. Fritz, page VII). "With the desire for union expressed in the resolutions (of the U. L. C. adopted at Savannah) we find ourselves in hearty agreement. . . . But it would be a fatal mistake to make a public declaration of unity if the reality of it is absent. . . . In the last decades there has arisen a new issue, indicated by the words 'higher criticism' and 'inspiration of the Bible,' on which, it seems, the various Lutheran bodies are not occupying common ground. Any attempt to bring about agreement between the synods will have to take this issue into consideration." (Wm. Arndt, p. 40.) — A church union between those who teach and those who deny, or tolerate the denial of, Verbal Inspiration will produce *virvar* with a vengeance. On Bible Sunday the first guest preacher will declare: "Is not the inspiration of Scripture too high and holy a reality to be defined in terms of stenography? . . . That avowal [of Verbal Inspiration], held to its last logic, would risk a trip to the insane asylum." And the second guest preacher will declare: "Beware, beware, I say, of this 'divine-human Scripture.' It is a devil's mask." Dr. Pieper thus describes the *virvar:* "In derselben Kirchengemeinschaft, so dass die Bekenner und die Bestreiter der goettlichen Autoritaet der Schrift eintraechtig und bruederlich beieinander wohnen, als ob nichts zwischen ihnen stuende? Das ist ein Unding, wiewohl es heutzutage sehr allgemein — auch in der amerikanisch-lutherischen Kirche — praktiziert wird." (*Lehre und Wehre*, 1928, p. 370.)

ment meted out to the traitor. But as far as we are spiritual, we enter the battle for Verbal Inspiration willingly and gladly. For we love this glorious doctrine. We owe so much to it. We owe to it the greatest blessing of Christianity: the assurance of God's grace. But for Verbal Inspiration the Gospel promises could not yield assurance and comfort. We fight for it not merely because it is one of the things which Christ has commanded us and must be observed but because it is tied up with the truth and reliability of the Gospel. We love this precious teaching.[338] It has comforted us and been our stay in the day of temptation and in the hour of affliction, and we want the future generations to be blessed by it. It is a stumbling block to the Jews and foolishness to the Greeks, but we have found it to be the power and wisdom of God and the foundation of our trust in the grace of God. "By pagan pride rejected, spurned," the Word, given by verbal inspiration, is our greatest treasure. We thank God that He has permitted us to enlist in its service.

" 'Hear, O heavens, and give ear, O earth; for the Lord hath spoken.' That is and must remain our battle cry. That is the device emblazoned on our banner. If ever our Synod should no longer hold this banner aloft, her fall would not be imminent but would already have set in, and she would be fit only to be cast away as insipid salt that no longer serves but only deserves to be trodden under foot." (Walther.) Taking up the battle cry Γέγραπται, as the Captain of our salvation sounded it against Satan, let us earnestly contend for the faith which was once delivered unto the saints and preserve unto the Church the precious doctrine of verbal inspiration. (See *Walther and the Church*, p. 24.)

---

338) "How thankful I am that in this evil world, where men are groping blindly and the blind are leading the blind, it is our privilege to have an infallible rule of faith and practice, even the Word of God! We cannot safely trust our own reason, for we do not know enough; nor our feelings, for they are unstable and biased by sin; nor science, because it cannot tell us what we most want to know; nor the teachings of the Church, for the Church is not infallible. But we can trust the Word of God, for it is God-given; it has been transmitted to us faithfully and it is being continually proved true. Therefore our duty is to lay aside all prejudices concerning it, to study it, to receive the Christ revealed therein, and to obey Him in all things." (J. H. McComb, *God's Purpose in This Age*, p. 73.) "The Bible abides as the faithful witness — the most faithful witness we have — concerning the character of God, the need of man, and the Gospel which alone can meet that need." (Dr. P. W. Evans, in the *Watchman-Examiner*, Aug. 14, 1941.)

CONTENTS

INDEX

By Professor Emeritus Wm. Schaller

(B. = Bible. V. I. = Verbal Inspiration)

to retain V. I. today, waere ein repristinierender Rueckgriff auf Luther 438.

Double bookkeeping: Inconsistency (*not* in disparaging sense) 75.

Doubt: "Doubt your doubts and believe your beliefs" (C. F. Deems) 39, 42; any Christian may be assailed by d. 75; its seed implanted in us by nature 30, 329.

Downs, F. S.: *The Heart of the Christian Faith* 209.

Drach, Dr. G. (in the *Luth. Ch. Quarterly*): "We repudiate absolute infallibility of apostles" 319; "dictation theory" traced to Zwingli and Gerhard 322; B. Word of God only when taken as connected whole 348.

Driver: Mentioned by *Bible Champion* (1923) 296.

Dunphy, Prof. W. H. (in *Living Church*): Runs close second to Paine 90; with Paine and Horine believes an almighty God, yet ridicules story of Jonah as absurd 91; employs caricature 180.

Dynamical theory of inspiration, nicely takes care of errors 319; does away with inspiration of words 323, 335.

Ebrard corrected Strauss 286.

Eddington, Prof., on changing science 142.

Eddy, Sherwood (in the *Presbyterian*): False reference from Scripture 335; B. no storehouse of authoritative proof texts 337, 353, 363.

Einstein: 59; does not believe in God; logically denies possibility of miracles 133; one who admits the supernatural has no right to deny the possibility of miracles, *ibid.*; says, "There are domains in which scientific knowledge has not yet been able to set foot" 139; Einstein's name has become the symbol for Science in Revolution against Itself 141f., 145; tells the conservative critics Josh. 10:12ff. may stay as originally written 146.

Eisenach Convention: proof texts 343; bound to Scripture as a whole, but free to reject particular statements (!) 347, 371.

Elert, W. (*Der christliche Glaube.* —*Morphologie des Luthertums*):

Gets things mixed criticizing Quenstedt 75; noch stand fuer Kopernikus und Kepler die Sonne fest (systems of science continually changing) 142; die Orthodoxie nahm die Schrift als Lehrbuch ueber alle darin vorkommenden heterogenen Inhalte 177; uses strong language beside the mark 310.

Ellis, W. T., tells Sunday school children about Cyrenius, confirming Luke 81.

"Elohist," "Jehovist" 143.

Encyclopaedia Biblica: Legend of Abraham 216.

Encyclopaedia Britannica: Molecules — atoms — electrons 141f.

Epiphanius († 407) reproved discrepancy-hunters 107; not a "mechanical inspirationist" 307.

Episcopius, S. († 1643, Arminian-Reformed), already had limited inspiration to so-called essentials 122.

Erasmus: No "interruption of inspiration" 255.

"Errorless" all-important word 284.

Errors: Moderns find in B. a) scientific errors (blunders in natural history, historical errors, etc., etc.), b) statements in conflict with the findings of higher criticism (inexact, false quotations, unfulfilled prophecies, and just plain mistakes) 8ff.; index errorum — Celsus, Porphyry, Voltaire, Paine, Ingersoll, Lessing worked on it, and now the moderns 19; no Christian can declare, in his sober mind, that God's Word contains them 30f.; we do not say that all who hold there are errors in B. are no longer Christians 75; teaching errancy of B. causes untold harm in Church 76; "myths" in B. (Harnack, Fosdick) 130.

Esther, Book of, "Fiction" 16, 163.

"Ethical blemishes" of B. 226ff.

Eusebius: "I deem it wicked presumption to say Scripture erred" 299.

Evangelical Synod: Its *Magazin* quotes Dr. Pfotenhauer 430.

Evans, Prof., advises to surrender parts of B. in order to save the rest 55.

Evjen, Prof. J. O. (*What Is Lutheranism?*): The B. not authority on geology, etc. 176; to Luther Scripture was binding as

Huxley into skepticism 26, 177, 194; would have continued to adhere to V. I. had his been a metallic, inert mind 35; finds contradiction in Eccl. 3:19 and Luke 12:7 101; few of Bible's books claim to be given by inspiration of God 113; full, real inspiration to be reserved for Gospel only 122; if all parts are inspired, one might preach on B. for 50 years and never once bring Gospel in 124, 167, 256; cannot call all B. organs or vehicles of inspiration perfect, but the result of the whole may be said to be perfect 128, 168; a man thoroughly inspired by God would be unmanned, dehumanized 136; what mortal could read a perfectly inspired B.? 137 f.; employs caricature 179; says moderns humbly sit at Christ's feet and accept what they find there 201; "proves" thesis that not all Scripture is inspired by quoting 2 Tim. 3:15 211; "impossible" sermon texts 261; only Gospel portions are inspired 292; against proof texts 333, 334, 335, 338, 347 (Schriftganze) 353; V. I. legalistic 367; will not directly identify the "spirit" 2 Cor. 3:6 with "reason" 376.

Girgensohn, K. (*Die Inspiration der H. Schrift*): Schrift *enthaelt Wort Gottes* 125; errors in the B. serve our salvation 128.

Gladstone, W. E. (*The Impregnable Rock of Holy Scripture*): 57, 58, 63, 132; science of one epoch abandoned by next (quoting Dr. Smith of Virginia U.) 141, 206, 231; extermination of Canaanites 238, 239, 240; swine into sea 246.

Glueck, Prof. Nelson: Solomon a scientist 209.

Goethe, J. W.: "Give us your convictions" 39; follies committed by him 97.

Gogarten, F.: "Der tote papierne Papst des Bibelbuchstabens" 368.

Goodspeed, Dr. Edgar J.: His book *How the Bible Came to Be* leaves guidance of Holy Ghost out of authorship of B. 69.

Gore, Charles, Bishop (*The Doctrine of the Infallible Book. — A New Commentary on Holy Scripture*): Admits Luther often clings to older notion of V. I. 48, 210; no reason to doubt existence of patriarchs as historic personages 80; Darius the Mede an entirely unknown person 83; his commentary rates Josephus higher than evangelists 84; believes that even inspiration did not safeguard apostles against stupid misinterpretation of Scripture 95, 96; fuller account of one evangelist over against others 97; Jesus conceivably cleanses Temple twice 99; slip of memory of Evangelist 104 f.; Lord probably not announced Trinitarian formula so explicitly as Matt. 28:19 106; second cock-crowing (Gore agrees with Stoeckhardt) 107; Second Epistle of Peter not by Peter 113; N. T. does not warrant identifying inspiration with infallibility on all subjects 114; does not think alike with Dr. Alleman as to Matt. 5:21 118; Jesus does not bind us by His allusion to Flood to suppose it occurred as described in Genesis; feels the same way about His allusion to Jonah's resurrection out of whale's belly — "if it were authentic" 120, 121; his phrase "criticism that is inspired by a dogmatic denial of the supernatural" 155; you dare not shackle science 175; light created before luminaries 205; Gore translates correctly "demand" in Ex. 11:2 245; grades of inspiration 269; Anglican form for ordination needs *addition,* bishops of today propose 293; faults Luther for his actually confessing Holy Ghost as *Author* of the books of Moses 364; Real Presence: purest literalism 375; unwittingly gives praise reprehending Luther for submitting his judgment undoubtingly to Scriptural statements on points of natural science 392; *satisfactio vicaria* denied 404; Church never showed any disposition to define scope of inspiration 434.

"Gottgewirkte Ausspprueche" — Hofmann's queer phrase 346.

Grace, Sergius P. (scientist, inventor, research specialist): Scientist . . . will never find ultimate meanings of energy, space, matter 149.

except arbitrary dogma of the Church 209; how sternly would Luther have rebuked baseless dogmatism: to question part of Scripture is to shake whole 210; serpent that speaks a fable 214; why, after 1 Sam. 16:18, does Saul not recognize David, chap. 17? 218; "pious fraud" 220; occasionally holy writers make false statements in good faith (!) 221; impossible apocryphal works like *Book of Enoch* worthy of credit 323; Samson should practice immoralities? 230; writer of Heb. 6:1-8 and 10:26,27 palpably fallible 232; crimes in book not emphatically enough condemned 243; imprecatory psalms 245; trivialities 249, 268; home-spun philosophy of Proverbs dictated by Holy Ghost? 259; distinguish divine truth from human imperfection 293; proof texts wrong way 335; sin against Holy Ghost merely view of writer 340; revelation of God *as a whole* is criterion 349, 357; V.I. legalistic 367; Horton more apt at inept epithet than at cogent argument 368; V.I. idolatrous 370; really do not need B. at all; Christianity throve without N.T. 402, 436, 439.

Horton, Walter M. (in *Revelation*): Revelation no substitute for reason 43.

Hovey, A. (*An American Commentary*): One blind man, two blind men; Hovey adduces possible explanation 104.

"Human side" of Scripture = the holy writers *causae efficientes* — "eigene produktive Geistestaetigkeit" (moderns) 325.

Hume, Sophistries of 444.

Humor, wit, not displeasing to God 258, 260.

Hutchins, Robert M. 205, 206.

Huxley, T.H.: Is forced into skepticism 26; designates evolution as hypothesis 157, 158; evangelist no inkling of legal and moral difficulties in the case of Gadarene pig-owners 231, 246.

Hypotheses are guesses, *e.g.*, Copernicanism, theories of higher criticism, doctrine of evolution 157.

Ignoratio elenchi 114.

Ihmels substitutes the Schrift-ganze method for proof-text method 346.

Imprecatory psalms 240, 241, 245.

Independent, The (liberal): Honest in pointing out Babylonian code contains no trace of Decalog 209.

Inerrancy, Infallibility of the B., cp. V.I.

Ingersoll, Col. R.J. (infidel) (*Lectures*): Openly professed agnosticism 70; gatherer of "contradictions" 19; "admit unreservedly mistakes in B., and Ingersoll's 'Mistakes of Moses' will collapse" (Prof. Evans) 55; I. drew on Paine and Voltaire, the latter two on Celsus 64; moderns plow with I.'s heifer 65 ff.; hare does not chew cud 87; mistakes in astronomy 89; had Joshua written "And the earth stood still," I. would have objected with equal vehemence 90; three million Jews at Exodus 92, 224; genealogies of Christ 106; reason given by God, He wants it to be used in judging Scripture 99; B. full of barbarism 227, 229; eternal punishment 232; polygamy 244; intellectual liberty 372; orthodoxy night of the past 380; Church fighting for its life, for V.I., against infidels like Ingersoll and against moderns 431; B. has successfully resisted cheap buffoonery of Ingersoll 444.

Inner content (das Schriftganze) 347.

Inscription on cross 97.

Inspiration "not same as infallibility (Dodel) 114; I. a miracle; we know blessed fact of it 140; men assailing V.I. are destroying foundation of faith 146 f.; learn distinction between revelation and inspiration 268; no "grades" of 269; no partial I. 292 ff.; if I. of words necessarily mechanical, then that of thoughts likewise (against "concept theory") 324; holy authors, to what extent active when writing the words of B. 325.

Intuition, literary and moral (Matthew Arnold), leads nowhere 280 f.

Is Christ Infallible and the Bible True? by Hugh M'Intosh 34.

Jacobs, H.E. (*A Summary of the Christian Faith.* — *The Lutheran*): Criticism of beginning

Lord's Supper: Difference in records 20.

Lorenz, Dr. A.: "The farther medical scientist advances in studies, the more he realizes how little he knows" 174.

Loy, M.: In Scriptures the Lord of all has revealed Himself in *His own words* 390.

Ludicrous assertions and arguments 214—224.

Luke criticized 11.

Lurton, D. E.: His foreword to Jefferson Bible 283.

Luthardt (*Theologisches Literaturblatt*): Partial inspiration 292; V. I. legalistic 365.

Luthardt-Jelke (*Kompendium der Dogmatik*): Erklaert Schrift fuer irrtumsfaehig 319; simply ignores 2 Tim. 3:16 when treating doctrine of inspiration 340.

Luther: Allzugenau die widerwaertigen Sprueche der Schrift klauben 19; die Schrift das hoechste Heiligtum 31; every single B.-text makes world too narrow 31; Scriptures *cannot* err 33; God does not lie, nor does His Word lie 37; "the Holy Spirit more learned than you" 49; we must become fools in Christ 50; die Schrift nicht als Gottes Wort annehmen ist verfluchter Unglaube 51; God does not lie 54; historians blunder 56; God's Word counts for more than all angels 58; one passage of Scripture has more authority than all books in world 59; confesses occasionally he was baffled 60; but his faith does not suffer thereby 62; variations in four records of institution of Lord's Supper purposely ordered by Holy Ghost 63; speaking of the Koran 77; wenn es nicht in der Bibel waere, wurde ich es (Historia des Jonas) verlachen 91; how N. T. quotes Old 93; zwei Tempelreinigungen 100; evangelists do not bind themselves to chronological order 101; Christus zeigt Kern des Gesetzes 117; "the entire B. is nothing but Christ" 126; Heilige Schrift nicht auf Erden gewachsen 139; earthen vessels 169; Gore: "L. clings to older notion of a verbally inspired B." 210; reason blusters and contends in attempting to defend God 238; so-called imprecatory psalms 239; Holy Ghost recorded what moderns are pleased to call "Schmutzgeschichten" 241; swine into lake 246; on trivialities 250, 252; Philemon 257; Jacob and Rachel 259 f.; Holy Ghost delights to describe these trivial things, *dass er also spielen und scherzen moege* 260; entire Scripture throughout nothing but Christ 261; der Heilige Geist kein Trunkenbold, der ein Wort sollte vergeblich reden 262; not a single letter in Paul which entire Church should not observe 263; "I beg and warn every pious Christian not to take offense at simple language and ordinary stories" 272; "sintemal kein Buchstabe in der Schrift vergeblich ist" 274; a myth lives on among moderns: Luther did not teach V. I. 290; truth about Luther and V. I. 291; Luther ist nicht nach kastrierten Spezialausgaben seiner Schriften zu beurteilen 291; "Scripture makes fools of all wise 297, 298, 440; Heilige Schrift nicht auf Erden gewachsen 312; Heilige Geist legte den Propheten das Wort in den Mund 315; beware of the *alloeosis!* 330; Luther clings to single words of Scripture 336, 354; Traumpredigten; Duenkel 357; the entire Scripture to be ascribed to Holy Ghost 360; Seeberg on Luther 366; Luther's words to the spirituals of his day 378; die Schrift das allerhoechste, edelste Heiligtum 390; Luther's description of theological method of papists and moderns 397, 424; "nichts Eigenes oder Neues setzen" 408; arrogance of reason 409; Rome [like the moderns] robs us of B. 414; Spurgeon's praise of Luther's attitude towards B. ibid; "*homo est certus passive, sicut Verbum Dei est certum active*" 416; "God Himself has said this," a preacher should boldly declare 419 f.; "here I stand—" ibid.; moderns use words of God like dice, find no certainty in them (Eph. 4:14) 420; faith real assurance 424; *O furor et amentia his saeculis digna!* 427; Word Luther's battle-ax (Spurgeon) 440; Luther saw that inspired Scriptures carry

violable 31; we refuse to say with the fallen angel: Yea, hath God really said this? 34; satanic pride 48; Jesus assures us of inerrancy of Scripture 71; Tholuck speaks *echt nestorianisch* 73; if B. fallible, Jesus deceiver 119, 121; manifesto of 617 scientists: What God has revealed in nature cannot contradict revelation in Scripture 206; voluminous quotations from Church Fathers prove they taught V. I. 210; Paul's parchment 254. — *Michigan District* (1895): No trivialities in B. (E. L. Arndt) 261. — *Minnesota and Dakota District:* Did Lord have right to demand from the Egyptians whatsoever He pleased? 245. — *Southeastern District* (1839): Inspiration a miracle 140. — *Texas District* (1939): Inspiration an article of faith (J. H. C. Fritz) 201. — *Western District* (1865): Christian not worried by "findings" of unbelieving scientists 62, 82; one blind man and two blind men 103, 135; of geographical statements of B. not one proved false 153; die Vernunft nach dem Fall nicht ein leuchtendes Licht 172; (1868) use of genealogies 256; thank God for the "trivialities" in the B.! 264. — *Synodical Conference:* On doubts aroused in Christians by "contradictions" 30, 75, 77; Grau: no certain rule for separating divine from human 125; presupposition that the gospels contain no error (Kahnis) 136; remarkable fact regarding variant readings 186; "Schmutzgeschichten" 230; Christ Himself distinguishes between the doctrine of apostles and their life 247; Thomasius: sacred writings produced by self-activity of their authors 325; Volck, Schriftganze 342, 356; Absurditaet Kahnis' 439. — *New South Wales District*, Australia: Imprecatory psalms 240, 243.
Prohibition, 1 Tim. 5: 23 against 255.
Prolepsis not uncommon in Scripture 103.
Proof texts: 331 ff.; right use of 334 f.; moderns, too, use proof texts, but illicitly 335; they abhor proof-text method 340; sophistries advanced to discredit proof-text method 352; want of

respect for Holy Scripture and self-pride cause opposition to proof-text method 353; Jesus, Paul, Luther used the method 354 f.
Prophecies "unfulfilled" 17.
Proverbs of Solomon criticized 258.
Psalms, Imprecatory 228 ff.
Psychology of B. Christian 196, 197; of skeptic 198; our knowledge of psychology very limited 312; Dr. Lewis' strange conception of psychology of Christian 288.
Ptolemaic theory: Reputable scientists agreed it might be true 145, 153.
Pulpit Commentary: Prof. Darwin on agricultural ant of Texas 85.
Pythagoras 59.

Quails, Story of, in Num. 11 involves no scientific impossibility 86.
Quenstedt, A.: No falsehood in canonical Scriptures 33; use of reason in B. study 199; taken to task by T. O. Summers for teaching mechanical inspiration 302; also by W. Lee, B. Manly, and others 305; how utterly untruthful the charge 306; assailed by Luthardt-Jelke 319.
Quoting, Free manner of, in N. T. strong proof for Inspiration 96.

Rabbi Sharfman replies to Rabbi Baron on miracles 133.
Rall, H. F. (*A Faith for Today*): Atomistic theory 332; uses proof text illicitly 335; pities fathers for "proof texts" 336; moderns want to be free men 371; two kinds of authority, one external, compulsive, other internal, moral, spiritual 377; misrepresents our teaching 393; like Grau admits uncertainty of his doctrine 417.
Rasmussen, C. C. (Gettysburg), ridicules gullibility of moderns 147.
Rationalism: Faith will not listen to 42; incipient rationalism 46 f.; unworthy of Christian to have dealings with wicked thing rationalism 47; engaged in a criminal business 47; corrections of Scripture spring from carnal pride 48; is unbelief 51; *rationalismus vulgaris* 215, 289.
Raumer, Carl von, himself a distinguished geologist but at the same time a Christian, counsels

teaching of Moses himself but the erroneous mode of interpreting his words 118.

Schaff, Ph.: Reality of miracles 41; in *Geschichte der Apostolischen Kirche:* "In cases where our knowledge not able to solve a B. difficulty," humbly bring every thought into captivity to obedience of Christ" 50.

Schallanalyse 143.

Schenkel (liberal): Error admitted at one point, admissible at all points 76, 77.

Scherer, P. E.: Genealogies [of Jesus] not to be regarded as inspired documents 11; warned students at Gettysburg against V. I. 29.

Schleiermacher: 59; father of modern Protestant theology 336; got modern theology to operate with *Schriftganze* 346; Schleiermacher-Hofmann theory hailed with relief by moderns 348; moderns' prophet; says Christian consciousness changes 417.

"Schlendrianmaessige Reproduktion" (Holmstroem) 353, 378.

Schleppentraegerdienste: Service of train-bearer, should theology perform it to science? 55, 395.

Schmidt, Nathanael, late professor of Cornell University, doubted that Jesus ever lived 85.

"Schmutzgeschichten": Moderns find in B. 241.

Scholz: N. T. variant readings 186.

Schreibfehler in Buechern Samuelis 102.

Schrift, Die Heilige; see Scripture, Bible

Schrift und Bekenntnis (Gogarten) 368; (Althaus) 381.

Schriftganze, Das: "Analogy of Scripture," "fundamental principles," "inner content," "living center," "organic unity," "Scripture as a whole" 340 ff.; Schleiermacher got modern theology to substitute it 'for proof-text method 346; moderns actually teach that not individual texts but only Schriftganze reliable 347; why moderns insist so strongly on Scriftganze: renders "errors" innocuous 347 f.; how it can be placed in opposition to *sedes doctrinae* (Schleiermacher, Hofmann, *Luth. Ch. Quarterly*) inconceivable, "eine unvollziehbare Phrase" (Kliefoth), a sense-

less phrase (Pieper), utterly illogical, prize fatuity (Engelder) 251; substituting Schriftganze for the proof-text method is 1) an intellectual impossibility, 2) unworthy of Christian, 3) fraught with deadly peril 251; no one knows what the Schriftganze is 356, 396, 411; Traumpredigten, Duenkel (Luther) 357, 399; is "Word of God" the "Schriftganze"? Both terms hazy, indefinite 385; vague, meaningless 394, 398, 402; on it moderns base theology 416; is all you need 435.

Schultz, Hermann: Fair example of "advanced" school 317; Christ, teaching words of Scripture are words of God, mistaken 430.

Schulverein, Der Deutsche Ev.-Luth.: "Wir halten fest an dem Wunder der Inspiration" 312.

Schulze, G., pastor of Walsleben, gives Christian answer to such as stress B. difficulties 63.

Schwaermerei, Luther's words on, fit Schriftganze agitation exactly 357.

Schweizer, Alexander: "Heilige Schrift papierner Papst" 367, 373; melt ore of B. and obtain pure gold 399.

Science: Moderns affirm it disproves V. I. 8; lower and higher science 11; ax-head sinks, fish swallowed a man, sun stands still, 121; trusting it more than B. madness (Stoeckhardt) 57; of the eighty geological theories counted by the French Institution in 1806 as hostile to the B. not one now stands 57; unscholarly habits of *ibid.;* its statements sometimes counterfeit 58; almost every science "sows its wild oats" (Dr. Gore) 76; *true* science does not rule out miracles 131, 139, 143, 145, 154; pretensions of 139; science of today correction of science of yesterday 141; is — and always will be — in flux" (Prof. T. V. Smith, U. of Chicago) 143, 145; essence of science theory and hypothesis *ibid.;* one hypothesis tears down other (Dr. L. Fuerbringer) 143; "B. out of harmony with science" is bandied about as an axiom 171; "science" not equivalent to "scientists" 171, 172; strictly, there is no modern science but

LIST OF BIBLE PASSAGES